# THE WAYS THAT OFTEN PARTED

# EARLY CHRISTIANITY AND ITS LITERATURE

David G. Horrell, General Editor

Number 24

SBL PRESS

# THE WAYS THAT OFTEN PARTED

## Essays in Honor of Joel Marcus

*Edited by*

Lori Baron, Jill Hicks-Keeton, and Matthew Thiessen

**SBL PRESS**

**Atlanta**

Copyright © 2018 by Society of Biblical Literature

Library of Congress Cataloging-in-Publication Data

Names: Baron, Lori, editor. | Hicks-Keeton, Jill, 1983– editor. | Thiessen, Matthew, 1977– editor. | Marcus, Joel, 1951– honoree.
Title: The ways that often parted : essays in honor of Joel Marcus / edited by Lori Baron, Jill Hicks-Keeton, and Matthew Thiessen.
Description: Atlanta : SBL Press, [2018] | Series: Early Christianity and its literature ; number 24 | Includes bibliographical references and indexes.
Identifiers: LCCN 2018033060 (print) | LCCN 2018043496 (ebook) | ISBN 9780884143161 (ebk.) | ISBN 9780884143154 | ISBN 9780884143154 (hbk. : alk. paper) | ISBN 9781628372168 (pbk. : alk. paper)
Subjects: LCSH: Christianity and other religions—Judaism. | Judaism—Relations—Christianity. | Church history—Primitive and early church, ca. 30-600. | Judaism—History—Post-exilic period, 586 B.C.-210 A.D.
Classification: LCC BM535 (ebook) | LCC BM535 .W2933 2018 (print) | DDC 261.2/609015—dc23
LC record available at https://lccn.loc.gov/2018033060

Printed on acid-free paper.

# Contents

# Cursus Vitae of Joel Marcus

| | |
|---|---|
| 1951 | Born in Harvey, Illinois |
| 1979 | Graduated with a BA in Jewish History and Civilization from New York University |
| 1981 | Graduated with an MA in New Testament from Columbia University/Union Theological Seminary |
| 1983 | Graduated with an MPhil in New Testament from Columbia University/Union Theological Seminary |
| 1985 | Graduated with a PhD in New Testament from Columbia University/Union Theological Seminary |
| 1985–1992 | Assistant Professor of New Testament, Princeton Theological Seminary |
| 1988–1989 | Visiting Scholar, Hebrew University, Jerusalem |
| 1992–1999 | Lecturer in Biblical Studies, University of Glasgow |
| 1992–1999 | Coeditor, Studies in the New Testament and Its World (T&T Clark) |
| 1996 | Visiting Professor, University of Oslo |
| 1998–2001 | Editorial board member, *Journal for the Study of the New Testament* |
| 1999–2001 | Professor of New Testament and Christian Origins, Boston University School of Theology |
| 1999–2003 | Cochair, Biblical Theology Consultation, Society of Biblical Literature |
| 2000–present | Member, The Biblical Theologians |
| 2001–present | Professor of New Testament and Christian Origins, Duke Divinity School |
| 2001–2004 | Editorial board member, *Interpretation* |
| 2001–2005 | Editorial board member, *New Testament Studies* |
| 2003–2006 | Member, Working Group on the Identity of Jesus, Center for Theological Inquiry, Princeton |
| 2004–2005 | Fellow, National Humanities Center |

2011–present   Member, Duodecim Theological Society

## Publications

### 1982

- "The Evil Inclination in the Epistle of James." *CBQ* 44 (1982): 606–21.

### 1984

- "Mark 4:10–12 and Markan Epistemology." *JBL* 103 (1984): 557–74.

### 1986

- "The Evil Inclination in the Letters of Paul." *IBS* 8 (1986): 8–21.
- *The Mystery of the Kingdom of God.* SBLDS Series 90. Atlanta: Scholars Press, 1986.
- Review of *The Writings of the New Testament: An Interpretation*, by Luke Timothy Johnson. *PSB* 7 (1986): 296–98.

### 1987

- Review of *Mark: A New Translation with Introduction and Commentary*, by C. S. Mann. *ThTo* 44 (1987): 301.

### 1988

- "Entering into the Kingly Power of God." *JBL* 107 (1988): 663–75.
- "The Gates of Hades and the Keys of the Kingdom (Matt 16:18–19)." *CBQ* 50 (1988): 443–55.
- "'Let God Arise and End the Reign of Sin!' A Contribution to the Study of Pauline Parenesis." *Bib* 69 (1988): 386–95.
- "Paul at the Areopagus: Window on the Hellenistic World." *BTB* 18 (1988): 143–48.
- Review of *Messianic Exegesis: Christological Interpretation of the Old Testament in Early Christianity*, by Donald Juel. *ThTo* 45 (1988): 263.

## 1989

◆ *Apocalyptic and the New Testament: Essays in Honor of J. Louis Martyn*. Edited by Joel Marcus and Marion L. Soards. JSNTSup 24. Sheffield: JSOT, 1989.

◆ "The Circumcision and the Uncircumcision in Rome." *NTS* 35 (1989): 67–81.

◆ "The Epistle of James." Pages 339–43 in vol. 2 of *The Books of the Bible*. Edited by Bernhard W. Anderson. New York: Scribners, 1989.

◆ "In the World but Not of It." *Katallagete* 11 (1989): 22–28.

◆ "Jane Austen's *Pride and Prejudice*: A Theological Reflection." *ThTo* 46 (1989): 288–98.

◆ "Mark 9:11–13: 'As It Has Been Written.'" *ZNW* 80 (1989): 42–63.

◆ "Mark 14:61: 'Are You the Messiah-Son-of-God?'" *NovT* 31 (1989): 125–41.

◆ "'The Time Has Been Fulfilled!' (Mark 1:15)." Pages 49–68 in *Apocalyptic and the New Testament: Essays in Honor of J. Louis Martyn*. Edited by Joel Marcus and Marion L. Soards. JSNTSup 24. Sheffield: JSOT, 1989.

◆ Review of *The End of Christendom*, by Malcolm Muggeridge, and *The First Coming: How the Kingdom of God Became Christianity*, by Thomas Sheehan. *Katallagete* 11 (1989): 22–28.

◆ Review of *Messianic Exegesis: Christological Interpretation of the Old Testament in Early Christianity*, by Donald Juel. *CBQ* 51 (1989): 373–75.

## 1990

◆ "The Pharisee and the Tax Collector." *PSB* 11 (1990): 138–42.

◆ Review of *The Demise of the Devil: Magic and the Demonic in Luke's Writings*, by Susan R. Garrett. *PSB* 1 (1990): 295–96.

◆ Review of *Das Markusevangelium*, by Dieter Lührmann. *CBQ* 52 (1990): 351–53.

## 1991

◆ Review of *Mark 1—8:26*, by Robert A. Guelich. *CBQ* 53 (1991): 703–5.

## 1992

- "The Jewish War and the *Sitz im Leben* of Mark." *JBL* 111 (1992): 441–62.
- *The Way of the Lord: Christological Exegesis in the Gospel of Mark.* Louisville: Westminster John Knox; Edinburgh: T&T Clark, 1992.
- Review of *Mark*, by Donald H. Juel. *PSB* 13 (1992): 243–44.
- Review of *A Marginal Jew: Rethinking the Historical Jesus, Volume 1: The Roots of the Problem and the Person*, by John P. Meier. *PSB* 13 (1992): 244–46.

## 1993

- "Epilogue." Pages 291–96 in *Faith and Polemic: Studies in Anti-Semitism and Early Christianity.* Edited by Craig A. Evans and Donald R. Hagner. Philadelphia: Fortress, 1993.
- Review of *The Beginning of Jesus' Ministry according to Mark's Gospel, 1:14—3:6: A Redaction Critical Study*, by Scaria Kuthirakkattel. *CBQ* 55 (1993): 162–63.
- Review of *Judaism: Between Yesterday and Tomorrow*, by Hans Küng. *PSB* 14 (1993): 89–90.
- Review of *Studies in the Jewish Background of Christianity*, by Daniel R. Schwartz. *CBQ* 55 (1993): 844–45.

## 1994

- "Authority to Forgive Sins Upon the Earth: The *Shema* in the Gospel of Mark." Pages 196–211 in *The Gospels and the Scriptures of Israel.* Edited by Craig A. Evans and W. Richard Stegner. JSNTSup 104. Sheffield: Sheffield Academic, 1994.
- Review of *Toward a Theological Encounter: Jewish Understandings of Christianity*, by Leon Klenicki. *PSB* 15 (1994): 77–78.
- Review of *Teaching with Authority: Miracles and Christology in the Gospel of Mark*, by Edwin Keith Broadhead. *JTS* 45 (1994): 219–22.
- Review of *Mark: A Commentary on His Apology for the Cross*, by Robert H. Gundry. *JTS* 45 (1994): 648–54.

## 1995

- "Jesus' Baptismal Vision." *NTS* 41 (1995): 512–21.
- "Mark and Isaiah." Pages 449–66 in *Fortunate the Eyes That See: Essays in Honor of David Noel Freedman in Celebration of His Seventieth Birthday*. Edited by Astrid B. Beck et al. Grand Rapids: Eerdmans, 1995.
- "The Old Testament and the Death of Jesus: The Role of Scripture in the Gospel Passion Narratives." Pages 205–34 in *The Death of Jesus in Early Christianity*. Edited by John T. Carroll and Joel B. Green. Peabody, MA: Hendrickson, 1995.
- Review of *Isaiah in the Gospel of Mark 1–8*, by Richard Schneck. *CRBR* 8 (1995): 294–96.
- Review of *Die Passionsgeschichte des Markusevangeliums: Überlegungen zur Bedeutung der Geschichte für den Glauben*, by Urs Sommer. *CRBR* 8 (1995): 299–301.
- Review of *Israel's Scripture Traditions and the Synoptic Gospels: Story Shaping Story*, by Willard M. Swartley. *PSB* 16 (1995): 87–88.
- Review of *The Rise and Fall of Jewish Nationalism: The History of Jewish and Christian Ethnicity in Palestine within the Graeco-Roman Period, 200 BCE to 135 CE*, by Doron Mendels. *JQR* 86 (1995): 237–38.

## 1996

- "Modern and Ancient Jewish Apocalypticism." *JR* 76 (1996): 1–27.

## 1997

- "Blanks and Gaps in the Parable of the Sower." *BibInt* 5 (1997): 1–16.
- *Jesus and the Holocaust: Reflections on Suffering and Hope*. New York: Doubleday, 1997. Dutch translation: *Jezus en de holocaust: Beschouwingen over lijden en hoop*. Baarn: Ten Have, 1998. Repr., Grand Rapids: Eerdmans, 2017.
- "Scripture and Tradition in Mark 7." Pages 177–96 in *The Scriptures in the Gospels*. Edited by Christopher Tuckett. BETL 131. Leuven: Peeters, 1997.
- Review of *Die anderen Winzer: Eine exegetische Studie zur Vollmacht Jesu Christi nach Markus 11:27—12:34*, by Ulrich Mell. *JBL* 116 (1997): 744–46.

- Review of *Related Strangers: Jews and Christians, 70–170 CE*, by Stephen G. Wilson. *JR* 77 (1997): 614–15.

## 1998

- "The Intertextual Polemic of the Markan Vineyard Parable." Pages 211–27 in *Tolerance and Intolerance in Early Judaism and Christianity*. Edited by Graham Stanton and Guy Stroumsa. Cambridge: Cambridge University Press, 1998.
- "Rivers of Water from Jesus' Belly (John 7:38)." *JBL* 117 (1998): 328–30.
- Review of *Follow Me: Disciples in Markan Rhetoric*, by Whitney Shiner. *JBL* 117 (1998): 536–38.

## 1999

- "The Beelzebul Controversy and the Eschatologies of Jesus." Pages 247–78 in *Authenticating the Activities of Jesus*. Edited by Craig A. Evans and Bruce D. Chilton. NTTS 28.2. Leiden: Brill, 1999.
- "A Note on Markan Optics." *NTS* 45 (1999): 250–56.
- Review of *Évangile de Marc: Commentaire*, by Paul Lamarche. *CBQ* 61 (1999): 160–61.
- Review of *The God of Israel and Christian Theology*, by R. Kendall Soulen. *PSB* 20 (1999): 330–31.
- Review of *Isaiah's New Exodus and Mark*, by Rikki E. Watts. *JTS* 50 (1999): 222–25.
- Review of *The Temptations of Jesus in Mark's Gospel*, by Susan R. Garrett. *ThTo* 56 (1999): 272.

## 2000

- *Mark 1–8: A New Translation with Introduction and Commentary*. AB 27. New York: Doubleday, 2000.
- "Mark—Interpreter of Paul." *NTS* 46 (2000): 473–87. Repr., pages 29–49 in *Mark and Paul: Comparative Essays Part II; For and Against Pauline Influence on Mark*. Edited by Eve-Marie Becker, Troels Engberg-Pedersen, and Mogens Müller. BZNW 199. Berlin: de Gruyter, 2013.
- "The Millstone." *Christian Century*. September 13–20, 2000.

- "Uncommon Sense" and "Counting Diamonds." *Christian Century.* August 30–September 6, 2000.
- Review of *The Theology of the Gospel of Mark*, by William R. Telford. *ExpTim* 111 (2000): 235–36.

## 2001

- "The Once and Future Messiah in Early Christianity and Chabad." *NTS* 47 (2001): 381–401.
- "Under the Law: The Background of a Pauline Expression." *CBQ* 63 (2001): 72–83.

## 2002

- Review of *Mark and Mission: Mk 7.1–23 in Its Narrative and Historical Contexts*, by Jesper M. Svartvik. *BibInt* 10 (2002): 452–55.
- Review of *Mark: Images of an Apostolic Interpreter*, by C. Clifton Black. *PSB* 23 (2002): 100–101.
- Review of *Logos and Law in the Letter of James: The Law of Nature, the Law of Moses, and the Law of Freedom*, by Matt A. Jackson-McCabe. *CBQ* 64 (2002): 577–79.

## 2003

- "Son of Man as Son of Adam." *RB* 110 (2003): 38–61, 370–86.

## 2004

- "John the Baptist and Jesus." Pages 179–97 in vol. 1 of *When Judaism and Christianity Began: Essays in Memory of Anthony J. Saldarini.* Edited by Alan J. Avery-Peck, Daniel Harrington, and Jacob Neusner. 2 vols. JSJSup 85. Leiden: Brill, 2004.

## 2006

- "*Border Lines: The Partition of Judaeo-Christianity*: A Conversation with Daniel Boyarin." *Henoch* 28 (2006): 24–30.
- "Crucifixion as Parodic Exaltation." *JBL* 125 (2006): 73–87.
- "Idolatry in the New Testament." *Int* 60 (2006): 152–64.

- "Jewish Christianity." Pages 87–102 in *Origins to Constantine*. Edited by Margaret M. Mitchell and Frances M. Young. CHC 1. Cambridge: Cambridge University Press, 2006.

## 2007

- "The Last Enemy." *ExpTim* 118 (2007): 287–88.
- "Meggitt on the Madness and Kingship of Jesus." *JSNT* 29 (2007): 421–24.

## 2008

- "Identity and Ambiguity in Markan Christology." Pages 133–47 in *Seeking the Identity of Jesus: A Pilgrimage*. Edited by Beverly Roberts Gaventa and Richard B. Hays. Grand Rapids: Eerdmans, 2008.
- "Idolatry in the New Testament." Pages 107–31 in *The Word Leaps the Gap: Essays on Scripture and Theology in Honor of Richard B. Hays*. Edited by J. Ross Wagner, C. Kavin Rowe, and A. Katherine Grieb. Grand Rapids: Eerdmans, 2008.
- Review of *Not by Paul Alone: The Formation of the Catholic Epistle Collection and the Christian Canon*, by David R. Nienhuis. *CBQ* 70 (2008): 384–85.

## 2009

- *Mark 8–16: A New Translation with Introduction and Commentary*. AB 27A. New York: Doubleday, 2009.
- "*Birkat Ha-Minim* Revisited." *NTS* 55 (2009): 523–51.
- "'I Believe; Help My Unbelief!' Human Faith and Divine Faithfulness in Mark 9.14–29." Pages 39–49 in *Paul, Grace and Freedom: Essays in Honour of John K. Riches*. Edited by Paul Middleton, Angus Paddison, and Karen Wenell. London: T&T Clark, 2009.

## 2010

- "The *Testaments of the Twelve Patriarchs* and the *Didascalia Apostolorum*: A Common Jewish Christian Milieu?" *JTS* 61 (2010): 596–626.

## 2012

- "A Jewish-Christian 'Amidah?" *Early Christianity* 3 (2012): 215–25.
- "Jesus the Jew in Recent Western Scholarship." Pages 235–50 in *Gospel Images of Jesus Christ in Church Tradition and in Biblical Scholarship: Fifth International East-West Symposium of New Testament Scholars, Minsk, September 2 to 9, 2010.* Edited by Christos Karakolis, Karl-Wilhelm Niebuhr, and Sviatoslav Rogalsky. WUNT 288. Tübingen: Mohr Siebeck, 2012.
- "Israel and the Church in the Exegetical Writings of Hippolytus." *JBL* 131 (2012): 385–406.

## 2013

- "No More Zealots in the House of the Lord: A Note on the History of Interpretation of Zechariah 14:21." *NovT* 55 (2013): 22–30.
- "Passover and Last Supper Revisited." *NTS* 59 (2013): 303–24.

## 2014

- "'The Twelve Tribes in the Diaspora' (James 1.1)." *NTS* 60 (2014): 433–47.

## 2016

- "The Spirit and the Church in the Gospel of Mark." Pages 395–403 in *The Holy Spirit and the Church according to the New Testament: Sixth International East-West Symposium of New Testament Scholars, Belgrade, August 25 to 31, 2013.* Edited by Predrag Dragutinović, Karl-Wilhelm Niebuhr, and James Buchanan Wallace. WUNT 354. Tübingen: Mohr Siebeck, 2016.

## 2017

- "Barclay's Gift." *JSNT* 39 (2017): 324–30.
- "Johannine Christians and Baptist Sectarians within Late First-Century Judaism." Pages 155–63 in *John and Judaism: A Contested Relationship in Context.* Edited by R. Alan Culpepper and Paul N. Anderson. RBS 87. Atlanta: SBL Press, 2017.

2018

- "Lou Martyn, Paul, and Judaism." *Journal for the Study of Paul and His Letters* 7 (2018): forthcoming.
- *John the Baptist in History and Theology*. Studies in Personalities of the New Testament. Columbia, SC: University of South Carolina Press, 2018.

Doctoral Students

- Warren Carter. "Discipleship, Liminality, and Households: A Literary-Historical Study of Matthew's Gospel with Particular Reference to Matthew 19–20." PhD diss., Princeton Theological Seminary, 1991.
- Jung Hoon Kim. "The Significance of Clothing Imagery in the Pauline Corpus." PhD diss., University of Glasgow, 1998.
- Suzanne Watts Henderson. "And He Gave Them Authority: Christological Discipleship in Mark 1–6." PhD diss., Duke University, 2004.
- Love L. Sechrest. "A Former Jew: Paul and the Dialectics of Race." PhD diss., Duke University, 2006.
- Timothy Wardle. "Continuity and Discontinuity: The Temple and Early Christian Identity." PhD diss., Duke University, 2008.
- Matthew Thiessen. "Genealogy, Circumcision, and Conversion in Early Judaism and Christianity." PhD diss., Duke University, 2010.
- Jill Hicks-Keeton. "Rewritten Gentiles: Conversion to Israel's 'Living God' and Jewish Identity in Antiquity." PhD diss., Duke University, 2014.
- Lori Baron. "The Shema in John's Gospel against Its Backgrounds in Second Temple Judaism." PhD diss., Duke University, 2015.
- Doron Wilfand. "Mark, Matthew, and the Tanakh: A Comparison of Tanakh References in Mark and Matthew." PhD diss., Duke University, 2016.
- David Smith. "Luke, the Jews, and the Politics of Early Christian Identity." PhD diss., Duke University, 2018.

# Abbreviations

## Primary Sources

| | |
|---|---|
| *1 Apol.* | Justin Martyn, *First Apology* |
| 1 Clem. | 1 Clement |
| 1 En. | 1 Enoch |
| 2 Bar | 2 Baruch |
| 4 Bar | 4 Baruch |
| Acts Phil. | Acts of Philip |
| *Adv. Jud.* | Tertullian, *Adversus Judaeos* |
| *Ages.* | Plutarch, *Agesilaus* |
| *Agr.* | Philo, *De agricultura* |
| *A.J.* | Josephus, *Antiquitates judaicae* |
| *Anc.* | Epiphanius, *Ancoratus* |
| *Ann.* | Tacitus, *Annales* |
| *Annun.* | Pseudo-Gregory of Nyssa, *On the Annunciation* |
| Apoc. Pet. | Apocalypse of Peter |
| *Apol.* | Tertullian, *Apologeticus* |
| Apophth. Patr. | Apophthegmata Patrum |
| Apos. Con. | Apostolic Constitutions and Canons |
| *Ascet.* | Maximus the Confessor, *Liber Asceticus* |
| *Autol.* | Theophilus, *Ad Autolycum* |
| b. | Babylonian Talmud |
| Barn. | Epistle of Barnabas |
| Ber. | Berakhot |
| *B.J.* | Josephus, *Bellum judaicum* |
| *C. Ap.* | Josephus, *Contra Apionem* |
| *C. Ar.* | Athanasius, *Orationes contra Arianos* |
| *Cels.* | Origen, *Against Celsus* |
| *Civ.* | Augustine, *De civitate Dei* |
| *Claud.* | Suetonius, *Divus Claudius* |

| | |
|---|---|
| *Comm. Isa.* | Eusebius, *Commentary on Isaiah* |
| *Comm. Matt.* | Jerome, *Commentariorum in Mattaeum libri IV* |
| *Comm. Ps.* | Eusebius, *Commentary on the Psalms*; Theodoret of Cyrrhus, *Commentary on the Psalms* |
| *Contempl.* | Philo, *De vita contemplativa* |
| *Dem.* | Aphraates, *Demonstrations* |
| *Demosth.* | Plutarch, *Demosthenes* |
| Deut. Rab. | Deuteronomy Rabbah |
| *Dial.* | Justin Martyr, *Dialogue with Trypho* |
| Did. | Didache |
| Did. apost. | Didascalia apostolorum |
| Diogn. | Epistle to Diognetus |
| *Ecl.* | Clement of Alexandria, *Eclogae Propheticae* |
| *Ep.* | *Epistulae* |
| Ep. Pet. | Epistula Petri |
| *Eph.* | Ignatius, *To the Ephesians* |
| *Fr. Matt.* | Origen, *Fragmenta ex commentariis in evangelium Matthaei* |
| *Fr. Ps.* | Didymus of Alexandria, *Fragmenta in Psalmos* |
| *Haer.* | Hippolytus, *Refutatio omnium haeresium*; Irenaeus, *Adversus haereses* |
| *Hist. Armen.* | Agathangelos, *History of the Armenians* |
| *Hist. eccl.* | Eusebius, *Historia ecclesiastica*; Socrates Scholasticus, *Historia ecclesiastica* |
| *Hist. rom.* | Dio Cassius, *Historiae romanae* |
| Hom. | Pseudo-Clementine, Homilies |
| *Hom.* | Hesychius of Jerusalem, *Homilies* |
| *Hom. Gen.* | John Chrysostom, *Homiliae in Genesim* |
| *Hom. Lev.* | Origen, *Homiliae in Leviticum* |
| *Hom. Matt.* | John Chrysostom, *Homiliae in Matthaeum* |
| *Inst.* | Quintilian, *Institutio oratoria* |
| Jub. | Jubilees |
| *Jud. gent.* | John Chrysostom, *Contra Judaeos et gentiles quod Christus sit deus* |
| Kil. | Kil'ayim |
| KP | Kerygmata Petrou |
| *Leg.* | Philo, *Legum allegoriae* |
| LXX | Septuagint |
| m. | Mishnah |

| | |
|---|---|
| *Magn.* | Ignatius, *To the Magnesians* |
| *Magn. Cat.* | Theodore the Studite, *Magna catechesis* |
| *Marc.* | Seneca, *Ad Marciam de consolation* |
| Mart. Pol. | Martyrdom of Polycarp |
| Menah. | Menahot |
| *Mos.* | Philo, *De vita Mosis* |
| *Mut.* | Philo, *De mutatione nominum* |
| MT | Masoretic Text |
| *Or.* | Basil of Selucia, *Orations*; Tertullian, *De oratione* (*Prayer*) |
| *Or. Graec.* | Tatian, *Oratio ad Graecos* (*Pros Hellēnas*) |
| *Orat.* | Michael Choniates, *Orationes* |
| *Pan.* | Epiphanius, *Panarion* (*Adversus haereses*) |
| *Phaed.* | Plato, *Phaedo* |
| *Phld.* | Ignatius, *To the Philadelphians* |
| *Post.* | Philo, *De posteritate Caini* |
| Pr. Man. | Prayer of Manassah |
| Ps.-Clem. Rec. | Pseudo-Clementine Recognition |
| Pss. Sol. | Psalms of Solomon |
| *P.W.* | Thucydides, *Peloponnesian War* |
| Sanh. | Sanhedrin |
| *Sat.* | Juvenal, *Satires* |
| Shabb. | Shabbat |
| Sib. Or. | Sibylline Oracles |
| Sifre Deut. | Sifre Deuteronomy |
| *Smyrn.* | Ignatius, *To the Smyrnaeans* |
| SP | Samaritan Pentateuch |
| *Spir.* | Basil of Caesarea, *De Spiritu Sancto* |
| *Strom.* | Clement of Alexandria, *Stromateis* |
| t. | Tosefta |
| T. Ab. | Testament of Abraham |
| T. Iss. | Testament of Issachar |
| T. Levi | Testament of Levi |
| T. Mos. | Testament of Moses |
| T. Reu. | Testament of Reuben |
| T. Sol. | Testament of Solomon |
| Ta'an. | Ta'anit |
| Tg. Isa. | Targum Isaiah |
| Tg. Neof. | Targum Neofiti |
| Tg. Ps.-J. | Targum Pseudo-Jonathan |

| *Top.* | Cosmas Indicopleustes, *Topographia* |
|---|---|
| *Trall.* | Ignatius, *To the Trallians* |
| Tri. Trac. | Tripartite Tractate |
| *Trin.* | Cyril of Alexandria, *Trinity*; Hilary of Poitiers, *On the Trinity*; Pseudo-Athanasius, *On the Most Holy Trinity* |
| Vit. Pach. | Life of Pachomius |
| *Vit. Thecl.* | Pseudo-Basil of Selucia, *The Life and Miracles of Thecla* |
| y. | Jerusalem Talmud |
| Yevam. | Yevamot |

## Secondary Sources

| AB | Anchor Bible |
|---|---|
| ABRL | Anchor Bible Reference Library |
| ACNT | Augsburg Commentaries on the New Testament |
| AJEC | Ancient Judaism and Early Christianity |
| AnBib | Analecta Biblica |
| *ANF* | Roberts, Alexander, and James Donaldson. *The Ante-Nicene Fathers: Translations of the Writings of the Fathers Down to A.D. 325.* 10 vols. 1885–1887. Repr., Peabody, MA: Hendrickson, 1994. |
| ANTC | Abingdon New Testament Commentaries |
| ANTZ | Arbeiten zur neutestamentlichen Theologie und Zeitgeschichte |
| ArBib | The Aramaic Bible |
| *AS* | *Aramaic Studies* |
| ASV | Anmerican Standard Version |
| *ASTI* | *Annual of the Swedish Theological Institute* |
| AV | Authorized Version |
| BAGD | Bauer, Walter, William F. Arndt, F. Wilbur Gingrich, and Frederick W. Danker. *Greek-English Lexicon of the New Testament and Other Early Christian Literature.* 2nd ed. Chicago: University of Chicago Press, 1979. |
| BBB | Bonner biblische Beiträge |
| BDAG | Danker, Frederick W., Walter Bauer, William F. Arndt, and F. Wilbur Gingrich. *Greek-English Lexicon of the New Testament and Other Early Christian Literature.* 3rd ed. Chicago: University of Chicago Press, 2000. (Danker-Bauer-Arndt-Gingrich) |

| BEATAJ | Beiträge zur Erforschung des Alten Testaments und des antiken Judentum |
| BECNT | Baker Exegetical Commentary on the New Testament |
| BETL | Bibliotheca Ephemeridum Theologicarum Lovaniensium |
| *BibInt* | *Biblical Interpretation* |
| BibInt | Biblical Interpretation Series |
| BJRL | *Bulletin of the John Rylands University Library of Manchester* |
| BZNW | Beihefte zur Zeitschrift für die neutestamentliche Wissenschaft |
| CBET | Contributions to Biblical Exegesis and Theology |
| CBM | Chester Beatty Monographs |
| *CBQ* | *Catholic Biblical Quarterly* |
| CEJL | Commentaries on Early Jewish Literature |
| CHANE | Culture and History of the Ancient Near East |
| CHC | Cambridge History of Christianity |
| CHJ | Cambridge History of Judaism |
| CIJ | Frey, Jean-Baptiste. *Corpus Inscriptionum Judaicarum*. 2 vols. Rome: Pontifical Biblical Institute, 1936–1952. |
| CJA | Christianity and Judaism in Antiquity |
| ConC | Concordia Commentary |
| CRINT | Compendia Rerum Iudaicarum ad Novum Testamentum |
| CSCO | Corpus Scriptorum Christianorum Orientalium. Edited by Jean Baptiste Chabot et al. Paris, 1903. |
| CSHJ | Chicago Studies in the History of Judaism |
| *CurTM* | *Currents in Theology and Mission* |
| DJD | Discoveries in the Judaean Desert |
| *DSD* | *Dead Sea Discoveries* |
| EJL | Early Judaism and Its Literature |
| EKKNT | Evangelisch-katholischer Kommentar zum Neuen Testament |
| *ETL* | *Ephemerides Theologicae Lovanienses* |
| *ExpTim* | *Expository Times* |
| FARG | Forschungen zur Anthropologie und Religionsgeschichte |
| FAT | Forschungen zum Alten Testament |
| FC | Fathers of the Church |
| FJTC | Flavius Josephus: Translation and Commentary |

| FRLANT | Forschungen zur Religion und Literatur des Alten und Neuen Testaments |
| GCS | Die griechischen christlichen Schriftsteller der ersten [drei] Jahrhunderte |
| *HBT* | *Horizons in Biblical Theology* |
| HSS | Harvard Semitic Studies |
| *HTR* | *Harvard Theological Review* |
| HUT | Hermeneutische Untersuchungen zur Theologie |
| IBC | Interpretation: A Bible Commentary for Teaching and Preaching |
| ICC | International Critical Commentary |
| *Int* | *Interpretation* |
| *JAC* | *Jahrbuch für Antike und Christentum* |
| JAJSup | Journal of Ancient Judaism Supplement |
| *JBL* | *Journal of Biblical Literature* |
| *JECS* | *Journal of Early Christian Studies* |
| *JEH* | *Journal of Ecclesiastical History* |
| *JJS* | *Journal of Jewish Studies* |
| *JMEMS* | *Journal of Medieval and Early Modern Studies* |
| *JNES* | *Journal of Near Eastern Studies* |
| *JQR* | *Jewish Quarterly Review* |
| *JRS* | *Journal of Roman Studies* |
| JSHRZ | Jüdische Schriften aus hellenistisch-römischer Zeit |
| *JSJ* | *Journal for the Study of Judaism in the Persian, Hellenistic, and Roman Periods* |
| JSJSup | Supplements to Journal for the Study of Judaism in the Persian, Hellenistic, and Roman Periods |
| *JSNT* | *Journal for the Study of the New Testament* |
| JSNTSup | Journal for the Study of the New Testament Supplement Series |
| JSOTSup | Journal for the Study of the Old Testament Supplement Series |
| *JSP* | *Journal for the Study of the Pseudepigrapha* |
| JSPSup | Journal for the Study of the Pseudepigrapha Supplement Series |
| *JTS* | *Journal of Theological Studies* |
| KEK | Kritisch-exegetischer Kommentar über das Neue Testament (Meyer-Kommentar) |

| | |
|---|---|
| Lampe | Lampe, Geoffrey W. H., ed. *Patristic Greek Lexicon.* Oxford: Clarendon, 1961. |
| LCL | Loeb Classical Library |
| LD | Lectio Divina |
| LNTS | Library of New Testament Studies |
| LSJ | Liddell, Henry George, Robert Scott, Henry Stuart Jones. *A Greek-English Lexicon.* 9th ed. with revised supplement. Oxford: Clarendon, 1996. |
| LSTS | The Library of Second Temple Studies |
| *MdB* | *Le Monde de la Bible* |
| MS(S) | manuscript |
| *Mus* | *Muséon: Revue d'études orientales* |
| NAB | New American Bible |
| NCB | New Century Bible |
| *NedTT* | *Nederlands theologisch tijdschrift* |
| NET | Neutestamentliche Entwürfe zur Theologie |
| NHS | Nag Hammadi Studies |
| NIGTC | New International Greek Testament Commentary |
| NJB | New Jerusalem Bible |
| *NovT* | *Novum Testamentum* |
| NovTSup | Supplements to Novum Testamentum |
| *NPNF* | Schaff, Philip, and Henry Wace, eds. *A Select Library of Nicene and Post-Nicene Fathers of the Christian Church.* 28 vols. in 2 series. 1886–1889. Repr., Peabody, MA: Hendrickson, 1994. |
| NRSV | New Revised Standard Version |
| NTAbh | Neutestamentliche Abhandlungen |
| NTL | New Testament Library |
| *NTS* | *New Testament Studies* |
| NTTSD | New Testament Tools, Studies, and Documents |
| OG | Old Greek |
| OLA | Orientalia Lovaniensia Analecta |
| *OTP* | Charlesworth, James H. *Old Testament Pseudepigrapha.* 2 vols. New York: Doubleday, 1983, 1985. |
| *ParOr* | *Parole de l'orient* |
| P. | papyrus |
| par(r). | parallel(s) |

| | |
|---|---|
| PG | Patrologia Graeca. = Migne, Jacques-Paul, ed. *Patrologiae Cursus Completus*: Series Graeca. 162 vols. Paris, 1857–1886. |
| *PGM* | Preisendanz, Karl, ed. *Papyri Graecae Magicae: Die griechischen Zauberpapyri.* 2nd ed. Stuttgart: Teubner, 1973–1974. |
| PL | Patrologia Latina. = Migne, Jacques-Paul. *Patrologiae Cursus Completus:* Series Latina. 217 vols. Paris, 1844–1864. |
| pl. | plural |
| PTS | Patristische Texte und Studien |
| RBS | Resources for Biblical Study |
| Rec. | Pseudo-Clementine, Recognitions |
| REB | Revised English Bible |
| *REJ* | *Revue des études juives* |
| *RelArts* | *Religion and the Arts* |
| *RHPR* | *Revue d'histoire et de philosophie religieuses* |
| RSV | Revised Standard Version |
| RV | Revised Version |
| SBAB | Stuttgarter biblische Aufsatzbände |
| SBLDS | Society of Biblical Literature Dissertation Series |
| SBLMS | Society of Biblical Literature Monograph Series |
| SBLTT | Society of Biblical Literature Texts and Translations |
| SC | Sources chrétiennes. Paris: Cerf, 1943– |
| *SecCent* | *Second Century* |
| SJ | Studia Judaica |
| SJC | Studies in Judaism and Christianity |
| SJLA | Studies in Judaism in Late Antiquity |
| *SLJT* | *St. Luke's Journal of Theology* |
| SNTSMS | Society for New Testament Studies Monograph Series |
| *SNTU* | *Studien zum Neuen Testament und seiner Umwelt* |
| SP | Sacra Pagina |
| *ST* | *Studia Theologica* |
| StBibLit | Studies in Biblical Literature (Lang) |
| STDJ | Studies on the Texts of the Desert of Judah |
| StPB | Studia Post-biblica |
| Str-B | Strack, H. L., and P. Billerbeck. *Kommentar zum Neuen Testament aus Talmud und Midrasch.* 6 vols. Munich: Beck, 1922–1961. |

| StT | Studi e Testi, Biblioteca apostolica vaticana |
| SVTG | Septuaginta: Vetus Testamentum Graecum |
| SVTP | Studia in Veteris Testamenti Pseudepigraphica |
| TANZ | Texte und Arbeiten zum Neutestamentlichen Zeitalter |
| TBN | Themes in Biblical Narrative |
| TCS | Text-Critical Studies |
| *TLZ* | *Theologische Literaturzeitung* |
| *TS* | *Theological Studies* |
| TSAJ | Texte und Studien zum antiken Judentum |
| TUGAL | Texte und Untersuchungen zur Geschichte der altchristlichen Literatur |
| *TynBul* | *Tyndale Bulletin* |
| *VC* | *Vigiliae Christianae* |
| v.l. | varia lectio |
| *VT* | *Vetus Testamentum* |
| VTSup | Supplements to Vetus Testamentum |
| WBC | Word Biblical Commentary |
| WGRWSup | Writings from the Greco-Roman World Supplement Series |
| WUNT | Wissenschaftliche Untersuchungen zum Neuen Testament |
| *ZAW* | *Zeitschrift für die alttestamentliche Wissenschaft* |
| *ZKG* | *Zeitschrift für Kirchengeschichte* |
| *ZNW* | *Zeitschrift für die neutestamentliche Wissenschaft und die Kunde der älteren Kirche* |
| *ZTK* | *Zeitschrift für Theologie und Kirche* |

# Introduction

Lori Baron, Jill Hicks-Keeton, and Matthew Thiessen

> That's what history is: the story of everything that needn't have been like
> that.
> —Clive James, *Cultural Amnesia: Necessary Memories from History and*
> *the Arts*

The earliest Jesus followers were Jews. Christian triumphalist theology was
not inevitable. Ancient documents resist modern distinctions. Literary
evidence of Christian origins exhibits diverse engagement with the traditions of ancient Israel, variously understood by the ancient authors, who
furthermore disparately understood themselves in relationship to the Jesus
movement and (other) iterations of Jewish thinking and practice. Con-
textualizing New Testament and cognate literature in antiquity challenges
how modern Christians frequently use the Bible to make supersessionist
claims about Judaism. Such are the intellectual and methodological commitments that Duke students have encountered for a decade and a half in
divinity school classes and doctoral seminars taught by Joel Marcus, Professor of New Testament and Christian Origins at Duke Divinity School.

Focused around historical interactions and formations of Judaism and
Christianity in antiquity, this volume is dedicated in Joel's honor. While
accurate, Joel's institutional title does not exhaust his interests. Neither
his scholarship nor his teaching is done in isolation of critical reflection on ancient Judaism and on the historical relationship of Judaism
to Christianity.[1] We three editors each encountered Joel as our doctoral
advisor and mentor, and in this collection we have gathered some of his

---

1. See Joel Marcus, "Jewish Christianity," in *Origins to Constantine*, ed. Margaret M. Mitchell and Frances M. Young, CHC 1 (Cambridge: Cambridge University
Press, 2006), 87–102.

colleagues, students, and friends to reflect on this topic about which he cares deeply, both professionally as a New Testament scholar interested in ancient Judaism and personally as a Jewish Christian for whom both parts of that moniker are self-defining.[2] Recognizing the complex interactions of these formative traditions in Joel himself and in the variety of settings in which we contributors have encountered Joel and his work, we seek in this volume not to offer one coherent narrative of how Judaism and Christianity became recognizably separate entities. Rather, contributors offer a series of snapshots of how Jews and Christians (variously defined) engaged in interaction, conflict, and collaboration in the first four centuries CE, with the bulk of the essays treating first- and second-century literature. The unifying thesis of this volume is that Christianity's eventual distinction from Judaism was messy and multiform, occurring at different paces in diverse geographies with varied literary resources, theological commitments, historical happenstance, and political maneuvering.

Many scholars who address the question of the parting of the ways have sought to pinpoint a precise historical moment or period as the time at which Christianity and Judaism became distinct. Influential scholars such as James D. G. Dunn and Shaye J. D. Cohen have argued for a second-century CE date for such a parting.[3] Others seek a parting in the third

---

2. See Joel Marcus, *Jesus and the Holocaust: Reflections on Suffering and Hope* (New York: Doubleday, 1997; repr., Grand Rapids: Eerdmans, 2017).

3. Among others, see James D. G. Dunn, *The Partings of the Ways: Between Christianity and Judaism and Their Significance for the Character of Christianity* (London: SCM, 1991); Dunn, ed., *Jews and Christians: The Parting of the Ways, A.D. 70 to 135*, WUNT 66 (Tübingen: Mohr Siebeck, 1992); and Shaye J. D. Cohen, "The Ways That Parted: Jews, Christians, and Jewish-Christians, ca. 100–150 CE," in *Jews and Christians in the First and Second Centuries: The Interbellum 70–132 CE*, ed. Joshua Schwartz and Peter J. Tomson, CRINT 13 (Leiden: Brill, 2014), 307–39. Prior to Dunn and Cohen, see Marcel Simon, *Verus Israel: Étude sur les relations entre Chrétiens et Juifs dans l'Empire Romain (135–42)* (Paris: Editions de Boccard, 1948). Interestingly, in the preface to the second edition of his *Partings of the Ways* (2006), Dunn concedes that he was wrong to date the parting to the second century CE. In answer to the question of when the ways finally parted, he states: "Over a lengthy period, at different times and places, and as judged by different people differently, depending on what was regarded as a non-negotiable boundary marker and by whom. So, early for some, or demanded by a leadership seeking clarity of self-definition, but for many ordinary believers and practitioners there was a long lingering embrace which was broken finally only after the Constantinian settlement" (xxiv).

and fourth centuries CE.[4] This volume resists the temptation to identify a particular point in time, a junction that creates a Y, when such a definitive parting occurs.[5] The title of this volume points in this direction: Jews who did not believe in or follow Jesus and Jews and gentiles who did believe in Jesus forged numerous partings, some minor and some major, some temporary and some irrevocable, some local and some, eventually, more widespread. How does one describe this history apart from providing admittedly incomplete snapshots of various moments in this history?[6] The essays in this volume are properly understood as examinations of certain points of convergence and divergence. We seek to mediate between the double error of, on the one hand, imposing the expectation of an inevitable eventual parting on our early materials and, on the other, resisting any notion of distinction and polemic. In other words, we eschew both *telos* and chaos.

To that end, this series of case studies cumulatively illustrates how a variety of ways not only parted but also intermingled—early and late, intentionally and accidentally, over and over again. By inserting the word *often* into our title, we intend to unsettle the implicit assumption within some scholarship that envisages, in the words of Anders Klostergaard Petersen, "a common road that at a certain junction divides not into parallel roads, but into a Y without any mutual connection—apart from their common point of origin—and without any possibility for later intertwinements."[7]

---

4. Most famously, Daniel Boyarin, *Border Lines: The Partition of Judaeo-Christianity*, Divinations (Philadelphia: University of Pennsylvania Press, 2006), but James Parkes (*The Conflict of the Church and the Synagogue: A Study in the Origins of Anti-Semitism* [London: Soncino, 1934], 153) makes overtures toward this position at times.

5. For a similar criticism of the effort to locate a particular point in history as the definitive moment of a parting, see the astute comments of Annette Yoshiko Reed and Adam H. Becker, "Introduction: Traditional Models and New Distinctions," in *The Ways That Never Parted: Jews and Christians in Late Antiquity and the Early Middle Ages*, ed. Adam H. Becker and Annette Yoshiko Reed (Minneapolis: Fortress, 2007), 22–23.

6. For this helpful metaphor, see Wayne A. Meeks, "Breaking Away: Three New Testament Pictures of Christianity's Separation from the Jewish Communities," in *"To See Ourselves as Others See Us": Christians, Jews, "Others" in Late Antiquity*, ed. Jacob Neusner and Ernest S. Frerichs (Chico, CA: Scholars Press, 1985), 93–116.

7. Anders Klostergaard Petersen, "At the End of the Road: Reflections on a Popular Scholarly Metaphor," in *The Formation of the Church*, ed. Jostein Ådna, WUNT 183 (Tübingen: Mohr Siebeck, 2005), 54. See also Bernd Wander, *Trennungsprozesse zwischen frühem Christentum und Judentum im 1. Jahrhundert nach Christus: Datier-*

As Annette Yoshiko Reed and Adam Becker write in the preface to the second edition of *The Ways That Never Parted*, "one can no longer assert that 'Judaism' and 'Christianity' were separated without also asking where and when, by whom and for whom. No longer can scholars assume that there was a single historical moment after which the texts, beliefs, and practices of Jews became irrelevant to those of their Christian contemporaries—nor the converse."[8] So, while the title of this current volume might be read as a polemical response to Reed's and Becker's *The Ways That Never Parted*, the cumulative findings of the following essays in fact provide additional evidence for the argument their volume makes. After all, ways that eventually did part can only be understood to have parted often, if indeed there was no one single, definitive, early parting of the ways between Judaism and Christianity.

Joel's interest in and scholarship on Judaism and early Christianity had their academic birth at Union Theological Seminary in New York under the direction of Raymond E. Brown and J. Louis Martyn. Readers will no doubt detect within this volume some arguments that are deeply indebted to the apocalyptic interpretation of the Jesus movement that Martyn, following Ernst Käsemann, championed. As such, some essays stress what appears to be distinctive and unique to the various Christ-following writers under consideration. In keeping with Käsemann and Martyn, some of the essays see the Christ event as something that cuts like a scalpel through Jewish salvation history and apocalyptic time.[9] Other essays, particularly those authored by former students of Joel, strive to find what early Christ followers, as first-century Jews, shared in common with some, if not all, of

---

bare Abfolgen zwischen der Hinrichtung Jesu und der Zerstörung des Jerusalemer Tempels, TANZ 16 (Tübingen: Francke, 1994).

8. Adam H. Becker and Annette Yoshiko Reed, "Preface to the Fortress Paperback Edition," in *The Ways That Never Parted: Jews and Christians in Late Antiquity and the Early Middle Ages*, ed. Adam H. Becker and Annette Yoshiko Reed (Minneapolis: Fortress, 2007), xi.

9. J. Louis Martyn, *Theological Issues in the Letters of Paul* (Nashville: Abingdon, 1997). One could also point to Douglas A. Campbell, *The Deliverance of God: An Apocalyptic Rereading of Justification in Paul* (Grand Rapids: Eerdmans, 2009). For a quite different account of Paul's apocalypticism, one that does not posit such a sharp distinction between Paul's apocalypticism and Jewish apocalypticism more broadly, see J. P. Davies, *Paul among the Apocalypses: An Evaluation of the "Apocalyptic Paul" in the Context of Jewish and Christian Apocalyptic Literature*, LNTS 562 (London: T&T Clark, 2016).

their fellow Jewish compatriots. The diversity found within this volume, we think, points to tensions within Joel's own formation and scholarship, tensions that continue to exist due to his tenacious intellectual honesty, which keeps him from arriving at facile or convenient conclusions. We offer these essays to Joel out of our inestimable esteem for his lifetime of work on this topic.

## Snapshots of the Ways That Often Parted

Timothy Wardle explores the parting of the ways between Jews and Samaritans with an eye toward seeing what light this earlier parting might shed on the later parting between Jews and Christians. The essay proceeds by discussing four specific aspects germane to current discussions of the relationship between Jews and Samaritans—terminological decisions pertaining to the titles *Jews* and *Samaritans*, competition between the Samaritan and Jewish temples, development of distinct and competing Pentateuchal traditions, and polemical rhetoric that served to deepen the fissures that had developed between these two peoples. Wardle concludes that each of these topics points to a late second- or early first-century BCE date as decisive for the widening schism between Jews and Samaritans. Following this discussion of Jews and Samaritans, these same four areas—terminology, temple, text, and rhetoric—are then briefly compared to similar issues that can be seen in the parting of the way between Jews and Christians. Though the parallels between Samaritans and Jews, on the one hand, and Jews and Christians, on the other, are certainly not exact, there is enough overlap to draw some intriguing conclusions illustrating the schisms that sometimes developed between groups that jointly revered the God of Israel.

Albert Baumgarten investigates Josephus's portrayals of Jesus and John the Baptist in relation to the parting of the ways. He argues that, while Josephus did not believe that Jesus was the Messiah, he nonetheless characterizes John in a positive manner. Although Josephus depicts other contemporary prophetic figures in a negative light, he affirms John's piety. Baumgarten contrasts Matthew and Mark, who emphasize John's eschatological message in light of the marriage of Antipas and Herodias, with Josephus, who ignores this aspect. He suggests that, while Josephus and the gospel writers likely drew from a common pool of oral tradition, Josephus omits John's critique of the royal marriage, because to acknowledge it would be to give authority to John's message that the eschaton was imminent. Josephus, while admiring John's piety, was at odds with John's eschatology. Baumgarten notes that in Josephus's view, John—and possibly even Jesus—fit within the limits of Jewish diversity. Over time, these limits became more restricted, as seen in the case of Celsus's Jew.

Matthew Thiessen revisits one of the most startling claims the apostle Paul makes, that uncircumcised gentiles can be both sons and seed and therefore heirs of Abraham. Many interpreters have seen here a radical difference between Paul and other second-temple Jews, a difference that presages the parting of the ways where two distinct social groups, one that became predominantly gentile and one that remained genealogically Jewish, made competing claims about who were the rightful heirs of Abraham. Thiessen argues that Paul's vision of uncircumcised gentile seed of Abraham fits within a stream of eschatological thought already attested in the second-century BCE work known as the Animal Apocalypse. The author of the Animal Apocalypse depicts gentiles at the end of the age being turned from nonkosher animals into Abraham-like cows. This eschatological transformation indicates that God has made the gentiles into cows like Abraham's inheriting son, Isaac, and not into Jews, who are depicted as sheep. Consequently, at least one other early Jewish author believes gentiles, as gentiles, can become Abrahamic seed and that they do so through God's eschatological transformation.

Michael Winger examines Gal 2, analyzing the sharp changes in tone and mode of discourse used by Paul to demonstrate that, in the new world brought by Christ, the distinction between Jews and gentiles has disappeared. Consequently, Winger sees an early parting between Paul and contemporary Jews. With a carefully crafted story of his relations with Cephas, Paul draws his audience into increasing tension, resolved finally in a dramatic confrontation showing that attempts to maintain the division between Jews and gentiles amount to destructive "role-playing." Paul's denunciation of Cephas ends the story; the rest of Gal 2 reexamines the Jew-gentile distinction from two additional perspectives: first, by abstract logical analysis, and then through an imaginative invocation of the actual experience that both Paul and his audience, Jew and gentile alike, have had of Christ.

In 2 Cor 3, Paul contrasts Moses's veil and his own παρρησία, a contrast that has implications for the question of the parting of the ways between Judaism and Christianity. Susan Grove Eastman explores the cultural implications of male veiling in the first century, asking how they contribute to Paul's explication of Moses's veil in the larger context of 2 Cor 1–7. She concludes that in Paul's exegesis the veil hides not the glory of the

Mosaic covenant but its transitional status and lethal endpoint. Paul's own ministry also is suffused with death as a medium of revelation, however, complicating the contrast between Paul and Moses.

John M. G. Barclay examines the tension in some early Christian writings between the perceived newness of the Christ event and the Jewish scriptures. Barclay argues that an emphasis on the uniqueness of the "epiphany" of Christ requires some writers to appropriate and reinterpret the Jewish scriptures, which they do in various ways, using diverse methods. Barclay focuses on Deutero-Pauline literature, the Letter to Diognetus, and 2 Clement as illustrative of the array of strategies that some early Christians deployed: some Christianize the Jewish scriptures, rendering their authors as followers of Jesus; some ignore them; and some remove them from their Jewish context and apply their message directly to gentile Christian communities. Barclay's study thus highlights the role that Christian appropriation of Jewish scriptures plays in the parting of the ways. He concludes by considering the implications for contemporary Jewish-Christian relations.

Suzanne Watts Henderson addresses the question of whether Mark was a supersessionist. This earliest gospel includes traditions long cited to support the view that Christians have replaced Jews as God's chosen people. Chief among those traditions are Jesus's sayings about garments and wineskins (Mark 2:21–22) and the parable of the wicked tenants (12:1–12). This chapter reconsiders these passages in light of their literary and historical context in ways that complicate the standard supersessionist reading. Rather than supplanting Jewish tradition per se, these teachings cast a vision for messianic community defined not by religious or ethnic categories but by trust in God's sovereign power.

Claudia Setzer argues that the damaging effect of the "blood cry" of Matt 27:25 has distracted us from seeing its function in the Gospel. She argues that the verse represents the end point of Matthew's systematic search for the culprit in Jesus's death. Two strands of tradition come together in this verse: the Sinai/covenant tradition and the anti-Pharisaic tradition of killing the prophets. Matthew employs associations of Sinai, covenant, and "all the people" to weave the scene into a larger narrative of God's relation to Israel. At the same time, the verse echoes anti-Pharisaic material in Matt 23, possibly representing actual polemic between Matthew and his contemporaries over Jesus's death and resurrection. Building on the argument of Anders Runesson that Matthew's Gospel presents intra-Pharisaic conflict, Setzer suggests that Matthew is confronting local antagonists who maintain a continuing identity as Pharisees. Matthew casts blame for the death of Jesus on his proximate opponents, situating it as an event within the greater history of the covenant people Israel. He leaves open the question of their future reconciliation.

Jesus does not cite the Shema (Deut 6:4–5) in John's Gospel as he does in the Synoptic Gospels; nevertheless, Lori Baron argues, John emphasizes the unity of Jesus and God in a way that evokes the Shema. Building upon Joel's work on the Shema in Mark, Baron contends that John's Christological interpretation of the Shema reflects a *Sitz im Leben* in the late first century, when the conflict between some Jews who believe in Jesus and some who do not has escalated. By deploying the Shema in order to include Jesus within the divine unity, John answers the charge that Jesus has made himself equal to God. Baron also maintains that John draws upon an eschatological interpretation of the Shema found in Israel's prophets in order to portray the community of believers in terms of the restoration of Israel. Jeremiah, Ezekiel, and Zechariah look to a time when there would be one God and one people; so, too, John portrays believers in Jesus as the fulfillment of that unity. The Johannine Shema has implications for the parting of the ways, as it depicts believers in Jesus as Israel restored, effectively excluding Jews who do not believe in Jesus from the covenant community.

In part due to critical reflection on the question of the parting of the ways, the hypothesis of a Johannine community behind the Gospel and Epistles of John as posited and developed by J. Louis Martyn and Raymond E. Brown has come under increasing attack in the last twenty years. Martinus C. de Boer critically examines the work of two prominent critics of the Martyn-Brown hypothesis: Richard Bauckham and Adele Reinhartz. De Boer argues that the original proposals of Martyn and Brown, for all their shortcomings, uncertainties, gaps, and questionable claims, provide a much more convincing explanation of the Johannine evidence than the counter-proposals of Bauckham and Reinhartz.

While the Messianic Secret motif is usually associated with Mark's Gospel, Susan Miller demonstrates that Jesus's messianic identity remains hidden to many in John's Gospel as well. In this essay, Miller argues that John's Gospel draws upon an extant tradition of a hidden Messiah. Miller notes that Jewish apocalyptic literature evinces a theme of a preexistent Messiah who would be revealed at the end of the age. She links this motif to John's Gospel, where Jesus speaks publicly about his identity and yet humans are not able to recognize Jesus apart from divine revelation. Miller traces this theme throughout John, highlighting the failure of Jewish leaders to recognize Jesus as Messiah. The leaders' blindness, which John attributes to God's purposes, is depicted as the cause of a growing rift between Jews who follow Jesus and those who do not.

Foregrounding literary analysis as a way into historical questions about the parting of the ways, Jill Hicks-Keeton offers a narrative-critical reading of the temple incident in John 2. She demonstrates through this analysis how the Gospel of John participated in the struggle over who could claim to be the rightful inheritors of the traditions, and specifically the scriptures, of ancient Israel. Arguing that the pedagogy of the Johannine text compels the Gospel's readers to anticipate Jesus's resurrection as the focal point of this narrative unit and, further, that the disciples' puzzling quotation of Ps 69 in connection to Jesus's outburst should be understood as a proleptic reference to Jesus's resurrection, Hicks-Keeton suggests that the resurrected Jesus was understood by John's community as the restored temple, a symbol of God's presence and favor specifically for Jesus followers. The Gospel thereby (accidentally) provided theological resources for subsequent, bigger partings as John's methods and conclusions were later extracted from a Jewish context and leveraged by gentile Christians against Jews.

Rather than examining Jewish or Christian texts, Bart D. Ehrman approaches the question of the parting of the ways by examining Roman administrative actions against Christ followers from the time of Claudius to Diocletian. Ehrman argues that, through this entire period (41–305 CE), the emperors believed they could distinguish Christians from Jews. Based on this argument, Ehrman extrapolates to conclude that it is therefore likely that other pagans also thought they could make a clear distinction between Christians and Jews. Importantly, Ehrman does not conclude from this that Judaism and Christianity were *actually* two distinct religions throughout this period; instead, he argues that this imperial distinction provoked Christian thinkers to appropriate Jewish sacred scriptures in order to insulate themselves from accusations of belonging to a new religion.

Whereas Paul uses the term *Ioudaismos* to refer to observance of the torah and the Jewish way of life in general, Daniel Boyarin argues that Ignatius deploys it in an unprecedented manner, to specify a type of Christianity that finds its basis in the interpretation of the Jewish scriptures. Ignatius contrasts *Ioudaismos*—this way of valuing claims about Christ in light of scripture—with *Christianismos*. For Ignatius, *Christianismos* is not primarily an exegetical enterprise but is rather a commitment to speaking about the revelation of Jesus Christ, the good news of Jesus's life, death, and resurrection. Ignatius thus produces Judaism as a way of inscribing the tension between these two approaches to Jewish scriptures and in so doing, he creates an Other against which followers of Jesus—newly-called *Christianoi*—are able to define themselves.

Dale C. Allison Jr. argues that the Paraleipomena Jeremiou, also known as 4 Baruch, is a Christian revision of a Jewish original. Against a number of other scholars, he presents evidence to demonstrate that, while the original version was Jewish, the revised version of this book no longer offers hope to Jews in the aftermath of the destruction of Jerusalem. Instead, it has become a triumphalist account of Christian supersessionism. He also highlights a number of Christian additions to the text that other scholars have neglected to notice. Allison concludes that in 4 Baruch the parting of the ways is complete. There is no future for Jews or Judaism; Jeremiah has become Christian and the Church has taken Israel's place.

Lucas Van Rompay examines a work preserved in Armenian under the title "An Exposition of the Gospel" and attributed to the fourth-century Syriac author Ephrem. Van Rompay discusses several passages in which Israel and Judaism are presented in positive ways. Even though the author claims that his community has a gentile past, he sees the return to, and the embrace of, "the blessed land and the inheritance of Israel" as the ultimate vocation of Christians that have wandered outside the land. With its insistence on the continued interdependence between Judaism and Christianity, this text attests to the existence in fourth-century Syria or Armenia of a less exclusive, and more dynamic, view of the relationship between the two religious communities.

Finally, Philip S. Alexander views the parting of the ways through the lens of the *Toledot Yeshu*, a complex, dynamic tradition of stories about Jesus that circulated among Jews, beginning early in the common era and continuing until the present time. Alexander traces the literary development of these stories and catalogues the various Hebrew and Aramaic extant manuscripts. He describes the *Toledot Yeshu* as antigospel literature, stories that served as counter-narratives to gospel infancy narratives, passion narratives, and Acts. These stories had an apologetic thrust, providing an oppressed Jewish minority with a way to discredit Christian claims about Jesus. Alexander raises the question of whether the *Toledot Yeshu* are, in fact, a counter-narrative to the gospels, or whether the gospels themselves are a counter-narrative to prior stories about Jesus's life, death, and resurrection. He suggests that the *Toledot Yeshu* play a larger role in studies of the development of the gospel tradition and the parting of the ways.

From these brief summaries, it is clear that the essays in this volume approach the question of the parting of the ways from multiple starting points using a variety of methods. Some investigate documents heretofore unexamined for their relevance to the separation of Judaism and Christianity (Alexander, Allison, Thiessen, Van Rompay). Others reevaluate well-known gospel texts (Baron, de Boer, Henderson, Hicks-Keeton, Miller, Setzer), Pauline texts (Eastman, Winger), and other early Christian writings (Baumgarten, Boyarin, Barclay) in light of novel literary, historical, and theological considerations. Still others engage in comparative studies within Second Temple Judaism (Wardle) and the Roman political sphere (Ehrman). There are doubtless other texts and traditions yet to be mined for their pertinence to the topic at hand, and our efforts to honor Joel would be incomplete if we did not invite the reader to enter the fray and build upon the research begun here.

In addition to fresh studies of ancient texts and investigations into unexamined texts, are there new methodologies that might be applied to our topic? How might Wardle's comparative work or Ehrman's use of Roman legal material mark a new way forward? Is it possible, or even desirable, to seek broader patterns among the diverse and divergent viewpoints represented by the work contained in this volume and in other monographs and articles on the parting of the ways? A completely satisfying answer to all of our questions, to quote one of Joel's favorite poets, may be "blowin' in the wind," but as this volume hopefully demonstrates, new insights are possible.

## Bibliography

Boyarin, Daniel. *Border Lines: The Partition of Judaeo-Christianity*. Divinations. Philadelphia: University of Pennsylvania Press, 2006.

Campbell, Douglas A. *The Deliverance of God: An Apocalyptic Rereading of Justification in Paul*. Grand Rapids: Eerdmans, 2009.

Cohen, Shaye J. D. "The Ways That Parted: Jews, Christians, and Jewish-Christians, ca. 100–150 CE." Pages 307–39 in *Jews and Christians in the First and Second Centuries: The Interbellum 70–132 CE*. Edited by Joshua Schwartz and Peter J. Tomson. CRINT 13. Leiden: Brill, 2014.

Davies, J. P. *Paul among the Apocalypses: An Evaluation of the "Apocalyptic Paul" in the Context of Jewish and Christian Apocalyptic Literature.* LNTS 562. London: T&T Clark, 2016.

Dunn, James D. G., ed. *Jews and Christians: The Parting of the Ways, A.D. 70 to 135.* WUNT 66. Tübingen: Mohr Siebeck, 1992.

———. *The Partings of the Ways: Between Christianity and Judaism and Their Significance for the Character of Christianity.* London: SCM, 1991.

———. Preface to *The Partings of the Ways: Between Christianity and Judaism and Their Significance for the Character of Christianity.* 2nd ed. London: SCM, 2006.

James, Clive. *Cultural Amnesia: Necessary Memories from History and the Arts.* New York: Norton, 2008.

Marcus, Joel. *Jesus and the Holocaust: Reflections on Suffering and Hope.* New York: Doubleday, 1997. Repr., Grand Rapids: Eerdmans, 2017.

———. "Jewish Christianity." Pages 87–102 in *Origins to Constantine.* Edited by Frances Young and Margaret Mitchell. CHC 1. Cambridge: Cambridge University Press, 2006.

Martyn, J. Louis. *Theological Issues in the Letters of Paul.* Nashville: Abingdon, 1997.

Meeks, Wayne A. "Breaking Away: Three New Testament Pictures of Christianity's Separation from the Jewish Communities." Pages 93–116 in *"To See Ourselves as Others See Us": Christians, Jews, "Others" in Late Antiquity.* Edited by Jacob Neusner and Ernest S. Frerichs. Chico, CA: Scholars Press, 1985.

Parkes, James. *The Conflict of the Church and the Synagogue: A Study in the Origins of Anti-Semitism.* London: Soncino, 1934.

Petersen, Anders Klostergaard. "At the End of the Road: Reflections on a Popular Scholarly Metaphor." Pages 45–72 in *The Formation of the Church.* Edited by Jostein Ådna. WUNT 183. Tübingen: Mohr Siebeck, 2005.

Reed, Annette Yoshiko, and Adam H. Becker. "Introduction: Traditional Models and New Distinctions." Pages 1–33 in *The Ways That Never Parted: Jews and Christians in Late Antiquity and the Early Middle Ages.* Edited by Adam H. Becker and Annette Yoshiko Reed. Minneapolis: Fortress, 2007.

Simon, Marcel. *Verus Israel: Étude sur les relations entre Chrétiens et Juifs dans l'Empire Romain (135–42).* Paris: Editions de Boccard, 1948.

Wander, Bernd. *Trennungsprozesse zwischen frühem Christentum und Judentum im 1. Jahrhundert nach Christus: Datierbare Abfolgen zwischen der Hinrichtung Jesu und der Zerstörung des Jerusalemer Tempels.* TANZ 16. Tübingen: Francke, 1994.

# Samaritans, Jews, and Christians:
## Multiple Partings and Multiple Ways

### Timothy Wardle

It is a privilege for me to contribute to this volume honoring Joel Marcus. It was during the early stages of my dissertation research under Joel's direction that I first stumbled upon several articles about the Samaritans and the complex history that they shared with their Judean neighbors to the south. I believe Ferdinand Dexinger's "Limits of Tolerance in Judaism: The Samaritan Example" was the first, and from there I encountered Yitzak Magen's archaeological work atop Mount Gerizim and a whole host of other scholars interested in different aspects of Samaritan existence, both ancient and modern.[1] At the same time, and partly due to Joel's influence, I began reading everything I could find on the parting of the ways between Jews and Christians. Both of these interests found their way into my dissertation on Christian appropriation of temple terminology in the first century, and each has been of continuing interest ever since. For this reason, these two topics—the Samaritans and the parting of the ways— will be the subject of this essay.

In the lexicon of scholarly discourse on late Second Temple Judaism and the origins of Christianity, the term *parting of the ways* has become synonymous with discussions of the emergence of the early Christian movement as an entity distinct from, and often defined against, the Judaism of the first few centuries CE. One of the first figures to utilize the term parting of the ways was James D. G. Dunn, in *The Partings of the Ways between Christianity and Judaism and Their Significance for the Character*

---

1. Ferdinand Dexinger, "Limits of Tolerance in Judaism: The Samaritan Example," in *Jewish and Christian Self-Definition*, ed. E. P. Sanders, Albert I. Baumgarten, and Alan Mendelson, 3 vols. (London: SCM, 1981), 2:88–114. Several of Yitzhak Magen's works will be cited below.

*of Christianity* in 1991.[2] In 2003, Adam H. Becker and Annette Yoshiko Reed published a rejoinder of sorts in their volume entitled *The Ways That Never Parted: Jews and Christians in Late Antiquity and the Early Middle Ages*.[3] Since then, numerous other descriptions have been offered, but no consensus has been reached as to which metaphor best encapsulates the process by which Christianity became its own "thing" alongside but distinct from Judaism.[4] In this essay I have chosen to retain the terminology of the parting of the ways, not because it is the best term, but because it is a convenient and well-known shorthand for the process by which Christianity emerged out of Judaism. I have also chosen, though, to describe the division between Jews and Samaritans as an earlier parting of the ways, and to see what fruitful avenues of exploration might be found in placing the parting between Samaritans and Jews alongside a discussion of the parting between Jews and Christians. My aim is not to produce an exhaustive study on the subject but rather to highlight a few suggestive points of contact common to these two partings. In what follows I explore several issues germane to current discussions of the fraying of relationships between Jews and Samaritans: terminology, temple, texts, and polemical rhetoric. Following this discussion, I will reflect on the significance of the overlaps that emerge between these two partings.

Terminological Distinctions

The tale of early Judaism involves several partings. Centuries prior to the emergence of Christianity, an earlier division was taking shape between two peoples living in the ancient heartland of Israel and Judah: Judeans

2. James D. G. Dunn, *The Partings of the Ways between Christianity and Judaism and Their Significance for the Character of Christianity* (London: SCM, 1991).

3. Adam H. Becker and Annette Yoshiko Reed, eds., *The Ways That Never Parted: Jews and Christians in Late Antiquity and the Early Middle Ages* (Minneapolis: Fortress, 2007).

4. See, e.g., Daniel Boyarin, *Border Lines: The Partition of Judaeo-Christianity*, Divinations (Philadelphia: University of Pennsylvania Press, 2004); Adele Reinhartz, "A Fork in the Road or a Multi-lane Highway? New Perspectives on the 'Parting of the Ways' between Judaism and Christianity," in *The Changing Face of Judaism, Christianity, and Other Greco-Roman Religions in Antiquity*, ed. Ian H. Henderson and Gerbern S. Oegema (Gütersloh: Gütersloher Verlagshaus, 2006), 280–95; Tobias Nicklas, *Jews and Christians? Second Century "Christian" Perspectives on the "Parting of the Ways" (Annual Deichmann Lectures 2013)* (Tübingen: Mohr Siebeck, 2014), 223–24.

and Samarians, or Yahwistic Judeans and Yahwistic Samarians, or Jews and Samaritans.[5] Choosing the correct terminology to describe people groups and their evolving identities is never easy, as identity is a fluid thing. What should we call the people who are the subject of this chapter?

Discussions of the meaning of the terms יהודי and Ἰουδαῖος in the ancient world are fairly well known, and so they will be summarized here briefly. Originally, the terms יהודי and/or Ἰουδαῖος were used in a geographic or ethnic sense to refer to someone who lived in, or was from, the territory of Judea. Thus, to be a Ἰουδαῖος meant that one was a Judean. But beginning in Hasmonean times in the mid- to late second century BCE, and continuing into the first centuries BCE and CE, the term Ἰουδαῖος became more expansive, emphasizing to a greater extent the religious and cultural practices of those in Judea.[6] Thus, a non-Judean who worshiped the God of Israel and adopted a Judean way of life could now be called a Ἰουδαῖος, or Jew. These two meanings—Judean and Jew—were not mutually exclusive. Second Maccabees, for example, uses the term Ἰουδαῖος on several occasions, with the usual meaning of Judeans. But it also uses the term Ἰουδαῖος in the more religious sense when noting that "people could neither keep the Sabbath, nor observe the festivals, nor so much as confess themselves to be Ἰουδαῖον" in light of Antiochus's oppressive decrees (6:6). Whatever is meant by Ἰουδαῖος, it clearly cannot mean Judean, because the action is occurring in Judea. Rather, in 2 Maccabees we see the term Ἰουδαῖος used to describe people who espoused a particular way of life: Jews. Thus, from at least the second century BCE, the terms יהודי and Ἰουδαῖος can refer to both a Judean and a Jew, with the latter slowly becoming the more prevalent term.

Similar ambiguity exists in discussions of Samaritans.[7] While the term *Samaritan* has sometimes been used to refer to anyone living in the tra-

---

5. Gary Knoppers, *Jews and Samaritans: The Origins and History of Their Early Relations* (New York: Oxford University Press, 2013), 12–17.

6. Shaye J. D. Cohen, "*Ioudaios, Iudaeus,* Judaean, Jew," in *The Beginnings of Jewishness: Boundaries, Varieties, Uncertainties* (Berkeley: University of California Press, 1999), 137; Daniel R. Schwartz, *Judeans and Jews: Four Faces of Dichotomy in Ancient Jewish History* (Toronto: University of Toronto Press, 2014), passim. In contrast, see Steve Mason, "Jews, Judaeans, Judaizing, Judaism: Problems of Categorization in Ancient History," *JSJ* 38 (2007): 457–512.

7. Jan Dušek, *Aramaic and Hebrew Inscriptions from Mt. Gerizim and Samaria between Antiochus III and Antiochus IV Epiphanes,* CHANE 54 (Leiden: Brill, 2012), 80–81; Reinhard Pummer, *The Samaritans in Flavius Josephus,* TSAJ 129 (Tübingen:

ditional area of the Northern Kingdom of Israel following the Assyrian invasion, nearly all agree that the term most appropriate for these people is *Samarians*. The construction of a Persian-period temple on Mount Gerizim, however, and loyalty to this temple on the part of some of the inhabitants of Samaria seem to have brought about a new Samaritan identity in ensuing centuries. Exactly when this distinct Samaritan identity emerged is a matter of some debate, but most scholars agree that the second century BCE, a century that witnessed the destruction of the Samaritan temple on Mount Gerizim and the beginnings of the Samaritan Pentateuch, was particularly important for the emergence of Samaritan identity.[8] As with the term Jew, the term Samaritan developed from an originally geographic term that was broadened to incorporate religious and cultural elements. These two new nomenclatures—Jew and Samaritan—surface at approximately the same time, as both begin to be recognizable and distinct terms in the second century BCE. Later Samaritan sources, however, prefer the terms *keepers* or *guardians* (שמרים) to that of Samarians or Samaritans, indicating an understanding of themselves as the true Israelites in possession of the Mosaic law.[9]

Terminological discussions are important, for they seek to do justice to the complexities of emerging communal identity in the ancient world. But while much can (and has) been made of the differences between Jews and Samaritans, it remains that the two groups shared a common heritage and strong familial tie. Both groups—Judeans/Jews and Samarians/Samaritans—shared a common ancestry as descendants of the nation of Israel. Both lived in the ancestral homeland of ancient Israel and claimed descent from the tribes of Israel. Both were Yahwist, worshiped God in temples dedicated to the God of Israel, and had high priests with impeccable pedigrees.[10]

---

Mohr Siebeck, 2009), 4–7; R. J. Coggins, *Samaritans and Jews: The Origins of Samaritanism Reconsidered* (Oxford: Blackwell, 1975), 8–9.

8. See, e.g., Dušek, *Aramaic and Hebrew Inscriptions*, 71–72; Knoppers, *Jews and Samaritans*, 172; Reinhard Pummer, *The Samaritans: A Profile* (Grand Rapids: Eerdmans, 2016), 5, 24–25; Stefan Schorch, "The Construction of Samari(t)an Identity from the Inside and from the Outside," in *Between Cooperation and Hostility: Multiple Identities in Ancient Judaism*, ed. Rainer Albertz and Jakob Wöhrle, JAJSup 11 (Göttingen: Vandenhoeck & Ruprecht, 2013), 136.

9. See Coggins, *Samaritans and Jews*, 8–12; V. J. Samkutty, *The Samaritan Mission in Acts*, LNTS 328 (London: T&T Clark, 2006), 59; Pummer, *Samaritans in Flavius Josephus*, 4–7.

10. Knoppers, *Jews and Samaritans*, 190–92.

Both understood the Pentateuch to be their sacred text. Both practiced circumcision, observed the Sabbath, and the like.[11] While tensions certainly existed between Judeans and Samarians in the Persian and Hellenistic periods, cordial interactions between the two communities seem to have been more the norm. The Elephantine correspondence, for example, reveals positive relations between Samaria and Judea, as their joint reply to the Jews in Egypt attests.[12] Similarly, the author of 2 Maccabees includes the Samaritans in his description of "our people/race" (τὸ γένος; 5:22–23) and notes that when Antiochus Epiphanes initiated his persecution of the Judeans (τοὺς Ιουδαίους), he sent repressive decrees against both the Jerusalem and Mount Gerizim temple cults (6:1–6).[13] In the second century BCE, the term *Israelites* is used for both Jews and Samaritans (see the Delos inscriptions; 1 Macc 3:15, 41; 7:9, 13, 23), and both Jews and Samaritans experienced diasporas that were oriented toward the traditional homeland.[14] Even more, in the final centuries BCE and the early centuries CE, both groups worshiped in synagogues and used the menorah as a central symbol.[15]

These two groups clearly held much in common. But events in the second century BCE were to alter the power dynamics, and thus the relationship, between these two peoples; the emergence of the Maccabean dynasty led directly to the waning of Samarian political influence. As relations became more strained, the tendency seems to have moved away from tolerance and toward intolerance and antagonism. Since I am primarily interested in the second century BCE and onwards, in what follows I will use the terms Jews and Samaritans unless the situation clearly calls

---

11. Coggins, *Samaritans and Jews*, 8–9.

12. See papyri 30–34 in A. E. Cowley, *Aramaic Papyri of the Fifth Century B.C.* (Oxford: Clarendon, 1923), 108–29.

13. Jonathan Goldstein, *2 Maccabees: A New Translation with Introduction and Commentary*, AB 41A (Garden City: Doubleday, 1983), 261; Daniel R. Schwartz, *2 Maccabees*, CEJL (Berlin: de Gruyter, 2008), 270–78; József Zsengellér, "Maccabees and Temple Propaganda," in *The Books of the Maccabees: History, Theology, Ideology; Papers of the Second International Conference on the Deuterocanonical Books, Pápa, Hungary, 9–11 June, 2005*, ed. Géza G. Xeravits and József Zsengellér, JSJSup 118 (Leiden: Brill, 2007), 186–87.

14. See, e.g., Dušek, *Aramaic and Hebrew Inscriptions*, 73–81; Pummer, *Samaritans*, 72–76; Knoppers, *Jews and Samaritans*, 171; Magnar Kartveit, *The Origins of the Samaritans*, VTSup 128 (Leiden: Brill, 2009), 218–19.

15. Steven Fine, *The Menorah: From the Bible to Modern Israel* (Cambridge: Harvard University Press, 2016), 67–71.

for more precise terminology. We now move toward a discussion of that which separated these two peoples.

## Jerusalem, Mount Gerizim, and Cultic Tensions

In 538 BCE, Cyrus allowed the Judeans to return to Jerusalem and rebuild their temple. Though not as grand as Solomon's temple, within a few decades the city was once again home to a temple dedicated to the worship of the God of Israel. For half a century, this temple represented the sole Yahwistic temple in the ancestral lands of the nation of Israel. But the construction of a temple on Mount Gerizim in the early Second Temple period was to have a profound effect both on relations between Jews and Samarians and on the rise of the Samaritans as a distinct people.[16] Josephus places the construction of this temple in the time of Alexander the Great (*A.J.* 11.324), but excavations carried out on Mount Gerizim between 1984 and 2006 by Yitzhak Magen revealed the remains of an earlier Persian-period temple dating to the mid-fifth century BCE.[17] Situated at the place where Joshua is said to have proclaimed the blessings of the covenant (Deut 27:11–12; Josh 8:33), and directly above the patriarchal city of Shechem where Abraham and Jacob built altars and Joseph was buried (Gen 12:6–7, 33:18–19; Josh 24:32), the location of the Gerizim temple was solidly anchored in seminal events in Israel's past. Moreover, a proper Israelite priesthood, equal in legitimacy to the priesthood ensconced in the Jerusalem temple, presided over the worship of the God of Israel at Gerizim.[18] The presence of a fifth-century BCE temple on Mount Gerizim meant that two temples dedicated to the God of Israel—one at Jerusalem and the other at Gerizim—were constructed around the same time and coexisted for hundreds of years. While it is unclear exactly how the cultic personnel associated with one site viewed the other site and its cultic personnel, the existence of two Yah-

---

16. For a recent view that the origins of the Samaritans should be dated to the time of the construction of the Samaritan temple, see Kartveit, *Origins*, 531.

17. Yitzhak Magen, "The Dating of the First Phase of the Samaritan Temple on Mount Gerizim in Light of the Archaeological Evidence," in *Judah and the Judeans in the Fourth Century B.C.E.*, ed. Oded Lipschits, Gary N. Knoppers, and Rainer Albertz (Winona Lake, IN: Eisenbrauns, 2007), 163–64; Magen, *Mount Gerizim Excavations*, 2 vols. (Jerusalem: Israel Antiquities Authority, 2008), 2:167–69.

18. Knoppers, *Jews and Samaritans*, 190–92; Magen, "Dating of the First Phase of the Samaritan Temple," 188; Timothy Wardle, *The Jerusalem Temple and Early Christian Identity*, WUNT 2/291 (Tübingen: Mohr Siebeck, 2010), 116–17.

wistic temples was to have significant consequences. Since both temples were almost certainly overseen by members of the same priestly clan, many of the continuing beliefs, practices, and traditions shared by Judeans and Samarians likely stemmed from ongoing communication between the two.[19] But the existence of two temples dedicated to the one God of Israel also meant that, in time, they were to become rivals.

For the first few centuries of the existence of both temples the Samarians held considerable political clout, much more than did their neighbors to the south in Jerusalem.[20] At the dawn of the second century BCE this situation seemed destined to continue, as Samaria and the regions surrounding Mount Gerizim increased in population and material wealth and as the Samaritan temple was enlarged and extensively renovated.[21] As one example of the political ascendancy and influence of the Samarians during this time, Samaria was named as one of the four Seleucid eparchies in Palestine, with Judea seemingly subsumed underneath Samaria.[22]

The political fortunes of both Samaria and Judea changed, however, with the rise of the Hasmoneans in the mid-second century. Following their consolidation of power, the Hasmoneans began a campaign of territorial acquisition, winning battles against the neighboring peoples of Samaria, Idumea, Galilee, Gilead, Perea, and Moab.[23] Simultaneously, they were able to gain a number of important diplomatic concessions from the Seleucids, including the title of high priest (1 Macc 10:17–21; Josephus, *A.J.* 13.45); three tracts of Samarian land: Aphairema, Lydda, and

---

19. Knoppers, *Jews and Samaritans*, 190–91.

20. This political situation was a continuation of the earlier situation in Israelite history prior to the Assyrian invasion in the late eighth century, when the kingdom of Israel politically and economically dwarfed the kingdom of Judah in the south.

21. Knoppers, *Jews and Samaritans*, 169–73; Magen, "Dating of the First Phase of the Samaritan Temple," 187.

22. Dušek, *Aramaic and Hebrew Inscriptions*, 70–73; Magen, *Mount Gerizim Excavations*, 176; see Josephus, *A.J.* 12.154–224. Antiochus III does not seem to have distinguished between Samaritans and Jews. The same rights given to the Jews in Jerusalem were also granted to the Samaritans and Mt. Gerizim.

23. Knoppers, *Jews and Samaritans*, 172; Menachem Mor, "The Samaritans in Transition from the Persian to the Greek Period," in *Judah between East and West: The Transition from Persian to Greek Rule (ca. 400–200 B.C.E.); A Conference Held at Tel Aviv University, 17–19 April 2007 Sponsored by the ASG (the Academic Study Group for Israel and the Middle East) and Tel Aviv University*, ed. Lester L. Grabbe and Oded Lipschits, LSTS 75 (London: T&T Clark, 2011), 191–98.

Ramathaim (1 Macc 11:34–36; compare with 10:30, 38); and tax exemptions that were not granted to those who sacrificed at the Gerizim temple (1 Macc 11:34).[24] In short, by the second half of the second century BCE, the political winds of fortune had clearly turned toward Judea and the Hasmoneans. In 111–110 BCE, John Hyrcanus destroyed the Samaritan temple (*A.J.* 13.254–256, 275–279; *B.J.* 1.63) and a few years later took control of the entire region (*A.J.* 13.275–281; *B.J.* 1.64–65).[25]

Why Hyrcanus decided to destroy the Samaritan temple is not entirely clear. It may be that he wished to integrate those living in Samaria into the Hasmonean state and to force their allegiance to the Jerusalem temple and its priesthood.[26] Alternatively, he may have felt threatened by the Samaritan priesthood, which had a much older and more prestigious priestly heritage than did the upstart Hasmonean family, and so decided to rid the region of any sacerdotal rivals.[27] In any case, it is clear that the destruction of the Samaritan temple on Mount Gerizim drove a sharp wedge between Jews and Samaritans, exacerbating tensions that had likely been simmering for quite some time. While the destruction of the temple on Mount Gerizim did not completely sever the relationship between Jews and Samaritans, it did sharpen the animosity and mistrust between the two.[28] The lingering effects of the destruction of the Samaritan temple continued to divide Jews and Samaritans for centuries to come.

### The Pentateuch, Textual Emendations, and Sectarian Changes

A second point of discussion among scholars interested in Samaritanism and early Judaism has to do with texts. In the centuries leading up

---

24. Knoppers, *Jews and Samaritans*, 172; Seth Schwartz, "The 'Judaism' of Samaria and Galilee in Josephus's Version of the Letter of Demetrius I to Jonathan (*Antiquities* 13:48–57)," *HTR* 82 (1989): 377–91; Goldstein, *2 Maccabees*, 433.

25. Knoppers, *Jews and Samaritans*, 173; Magen, *Mount Gerizim Excavations*, 170–71.

26. For a recent discussion of Hyrcanus's actions, see Jonathan Bourgel, "The Destruction of the Samaritan Temple by John Hyrcanus: A Reconsideration," *JBL* 135 (2016): 505–23.

27. Timothy Wardle, "The Power of Polemics: Jewish Slander Against Samaritans in the Late Second Temple Period," in *Biblical Themes and Traditions in the Pseudepigrapha*, ed. Craig A. Evans and Paul Sloan (London: T&T Clark, forthcoming).

28. See, e.g., John 4:9, 20; *A.J.* 18.29–30; 20.118; Lawrence H. Schiffman, "The Samaritans in Tannaitic Halakhah," *JQR* 75 (1985): 323–50.

to the Common Era, Jews and Samaritans both viewed the Pentateuch as their foundational text. For Samaritans, the Pentateuch was the only text granted this status, whereas Jews held the Pentateuch as the most important of several literary collections (that is, the Torah, Prophets, and Writings).[29] The authority each community granted the Pentateuch meant that both communities shared the Pentateuch's origin stories and narratives of group identity (for example, the accounts of the creation of the world, the formation of people of Israel, bondage in and deliverance from Egypt, the making of a covenant between God and the people, and the time of desert wanderings). Moreover, as Gary Knoppers has pointed out, the hundreds of commandments found in the Pentateuch regulating civil, political, communal, and religious life also connected these two communities, for the daily practices and rituals that each respective community found normative derived from texts that were very nearly identical.[30] As is well known, however, more than one Pentateuch emerged in the final centuries BCE, with two of the most important being the Masoretic Text (MT) and Samaritan Pentateuch (SP).[31]

When speaking about the major sectarian differences between the MT and SP, three particular readings are often cited.[32] The first is the Samaritan Tenth Commandment found in Exod 20:17 and Deut 5:18. This commandment, which combines Exod 13:11a, Deut 11:29b, 27:2b–3a, 4a, 5–7, and 11:30, differs from the MT in its instructions to build an altar to the God of Israel on Mount Gerizim. Second, the well-known Deuteron-

---

29. Knoppers, *Jews and Samaritans*, 178. It is, of course, easy to slip into anachronism here, as the Pentateuch, Prophets, and Writings were still evolving as collections and did not yet hold the status that they later would. But of the three, the Pentateuch seems to have been given pride of place, with many early Jewish texts prominently featuring pentateuchal stories (e.g., Jubilees, Book of the Watchers, and the Genesis Apocryphon).

30. Knoppers, *Jews and Samaritans*, 178.

31. For the purposes of this paper, I leave the LXX aside.

32. Edmond L. Gallagher, "Is the Samaritan Pentateuch a Sectarian Text?," *ZAW* 127 (2015): 96–107; Pummer, *Samaritans*, 202–7; Knoppers, *Jews and Samaritans*, 184–88; Stefan Schorch, "Der Pentateuch der Samaritaner: Seine Erforschung und seine Bedeutung für das Verständnis des alttestamentlichen Bibeltextes," in *Die Samaritaner und die Bibel: Historische und literarische Wechselwirkungen zwischen biblischen und samaritanischen Traditionen/The Samaritans and the Bible: Historical and Literary Interactions between Biblical and Samaritan Traditions*, ed. Jörg Frey, Ursula Schattner-Rieser, and Konrad Schmid, SJ 70 (Berlin: de Gruyter, 2012), 5–29.

omistic exhortation in the MT that the people are to worship the God of Israel in "the place that YHWH your God will choose [יבחר]" is expressed in the SP as "the place that YHWH your God has chosen [בחר]." Thus, in the cult-centralization formulas throughout Deuteronomy (Deut 12:5 and other places), the MT and SP differ in the form of the verb, with the MT preferring the imperfect form (יבחר) to allow for Jerusalem to be the chosen location and the SP adopting the perfect form (בחר) in order to emphasize Mount Gerizim as the cultic site. Third, in Deut 27:4, the MT states that, when the people of Israel cross the Jordan and enter into the land, they are to set up stones and build an altar on Mount Ebal. The SP, on the other hand, commands the Israelites to set up the altar at Mount Gerizim, not Ebal.

What should we make of these differences? For a long time, scholars assumed that the differences between the MT and SP were due to Samaritan sectarian changes and that the MT tradition was the original from which the Samaritan text had deviated. This assumption has been called into question in recent years, with a growing number of scholars asserting that the Samaritan version may be older.[33] Adrian Schenker has led the charge here, arguing that some of the Old Latin, Bohairic, and Coptic versions of the LXX agree with the SP. On the basis of this evidence, he asserts that the SP readings retain earlier readings and that the MT and SP should both be understood as emended texts, and not just the SP.[34] As a result, the MT reading of יבחר in Deuteronomy, along with the placement of Ebal in Deut 27:4, are, according to Schenker, late Judean alterations, with the only real sectarian change in the SP being the Samaritan tenth commandment.[35] In short, while there is much that we do not and cannot know about how the MT and SP came into being, Samaritans and Jews

---

33. See, e.g., Pummer, *Samaritans*, 198–207; Knoppers, *Jews and Samaritans*, 179–84.

34. Adrian Schenker, "Le Seigneur choisira-t-il le lieu de son nom ou l'a-t-il choisi? L'apport de la Bible Grecque ancienne á l'histoire du texte Samaritain et Massorétique," in *Scripture in Transition: Essays on Septuagint, Hebrew Bible, and Dead Sea Scrolls in Honour of Raija Sollamo*, ed. Anssi Voitila and Jutta Jokiranta, JSJSup 126 (Leiden: Brill, 2008), 339–51; Stefan Schorch, "The Samaritan Version of Deuteronomy and the Origin of Deuteronomy," in *Samaria, Samarians, Samaritans: Studies on Bible, History, and Linguistics*, ed. Jozsef Zsellengér, SJ 66 (Berlin: de Gruyter, 2011), 23–37.

35. Dušek, *Aramaic and Hebrew Inscriptions*, 115–16, and Schorch, "Samaritan Version of Deuteronomy," 23–36, agree with Schenker, while Knoppers, *Jews and Samaritans*, 186–87, disagrees, preferring to see the SP as the sectarian text.

both seem to have emended the texts to fit their theological and political aims, with the importance of Mount Gerizim of principal concern.

Textual modifications in the MT and SP regarding Mount Gerizim are not the only issues being rethought. One of the primary ways the SP differs from the MT is through the presence of harmonizations or textual expansions. These harmonizations, which made the pentateuchal texts align more closely with each other, were often explained as the result of Samaritan scribal sensitivity to points of tension between the various pentateuchal books.[36] However, several of the harmonizations once thought to be distinctively Samaritan are also evidenced in various Dead Sea Scrolls and witnesses to the LXX. For example, 4QpaleoExod[m] contains excerpts of Deuteronomy that have been inserted into Exodus in order to more closely align each book with the other, a modification of the sort often associated with sectarian readings in the SP (see also 4QDeut[n]; 4Q158; 4Q175; 4QNum[b]; and 4QExod–Lev[f]).[37] These agreements between the SP, select Dead Sea Scrolls, and several witnesses to the LXX are significant, because the scrolls and LXX texts do not contain the sectarian additions seen in the SP. Consequently, the presence of harmonizations in a text can no longer be understood as a distinctly Samaritan phenomenon, as a variety of Jewish texts contain the same or similar textual expansions. Moreover, the very existence of these non-Samaritan harmonizing texts strongly suggests that any Jewish or Samaritan sectarian emendations occurred at a much later date than previously thought.

This observation on textual harmonization, taken together with our earlier discussion on the emphasis on Mount Gerizim in the SP, suggests that the Pentateuch was still in the process of achieving its final form in the second century BCE. Who was responsible for preserving, shaping, and transmitting these texts? Since both Jews and Samaritans held the Pentateuch in such high regard, the most plausible scenario for continued

---

36. See Knoppers, *Jews and Samaritans*, 181; Kartveit, *Origin of the Samaritans*, 265–88; Molly M. Zahn, *Rethinking Rewritten Scripture: Composition and Exegesis in the 4QReworked Pentateuch Manuscripts*, STDJ 95 (Leiden: Brill, 2011), 135–77.

37. For example, in SP Deut 9:20 Moses declares that Yahweh was so angry with Aaron following the episode of the golden calf that Yahweh would have killed Aaron if Moses had not interceded. 4Qpaleo–Exod[m] also contains this reading, as do several witnesses to the LXX; while this same gloss appears in SP Exod 32:10, it is absent from MT Exod 32:10. See Knoppers, *Jews and Samaritans*, 182; Pummer, *Samaritans*, 201; Judith E. Sanderson, *An Exodus Scroll from Qumran: 4QpaleoExod[m] and the Samaritan Tradition*, HSS 30 (Atlanta: Scholars Press, 1986).

transmission of the text in Judea and Samaria would be the priestly elite at both temples.[38] If so, this suggests centuries of cooperation between the upper echelons of Samarian and Judean society in preserving and maintaining the Pentateuch, with the distinctive elements that mark the MT and SP only entering the text at a fairly late stage in the process. What historical circumstances might have led to these textual emendations at the hands of both Jewish and Samaritan scribes? Very likely it was Hyrcanus's destruction of the temple on Mount Gerizim and Jewish (or Hasmonean) attempts to delegitimize Samaritan claims to the sacredness of Mount Gerizim, with a resulting emphasis in Samaritan sources on the "rightness" of Mount Gerizim's location.[39] If this is correct, then these modifications would have entered the textual traditions that became the MT and SP in the late second or first century BCE.

## Polemic, Rhetoric, and Power Dynamics

Above and beyond the pentateuchal textual emendations that sought to delegitimize the other, a handful of late Second Temple Jewish texts began to distance themselves from Samaritans and delegitimize Mount Gerizim. Several derogatory terms for Samaritans begin to appear in the literature, such as Cutheans and Sidonians, which effectively label the Samaritans as foreigners. But the terms I will focus on here, and which first appear at the outset of the second century BCE, are those of *Shechemites* and *fools*. The earliest example of this latter term being equated with the Samaritans is found in Ben Sira (Sir 50:25–26 [MS B]), which states:

> Two nations my soul detests, and the third is not even a people [איננו עם]: Those who live in Seir, and the Philistines, and the foolish people that live in Shechem [וגוי נבל הדר בשכם]. (my trans.)

According to Ben Sira, those living in Shechem—the Samaritans—are described as foolish (נבל) and as not even a people (לא עם). Intriguingly, the Greek translation of Ben Sira, dating to the late second century BCE, reads slightly differently:

---

38. Knoppers, *Jews and Samaritans*, 190.
39. Pummer, *Samaritans*, 207; Knoppers, *Jews and Samaritans*, 213–16.

Two nations my soul detests, and the third is not even a people: Those
who live in Samaria, and the Philistines, and the foolish people that live
in Shechem. (my trans.)

Two observations will here suffice. First, in the Hebrew version of Ben
Sira, the description of the Samaritans as "fools" or the "foolish people in
Shechem" is likely dependent on a particular understanding of Deut 32:21,
which reads: "I will make them (Israel) jealous with what is no people
[לא עם], and provoke them with a foolish nation [גוי נבל]." Ben Sira and
others after him appear to have used this Deuteronomic language to refer
to those living in Shechem and Samaria, as these inhabitants were commonly understood to have a mixed lineage due to their mingling with
other races.[40] Second, the Greek replacement of Seir with Samaria may
indicate a furthering deterioration in the relationship between Judea and
Samaria, with those living in the ancient heartland of Israel now perceived
as more distant from Judea than the descendants of those living around
Mount Seir, the ancient Edomite enemies of Israel.[41]

This description of those living at Gerizim as "foolish" (נבל) is a
charge that begins to show up in other Jewish texts dated to the second
century BCE and later.[42] 4Q372, for example, disparages the Samaritans
in similar fashion:[43]

---

40. James L. Kugel, *Traditions of The Bible* (Cambridge: Harvard University Press,
1998), 423–35; Magnar Kartveit, "Who Are the Fools in 4QNarrative and Poetic
Composition[a-c]," in *Northern Lights on the Dead Sea Scrolls: Proceedings of the Nordic
Qumran Network 2003–2006*, ed. Anders Klostergaard Petersen, STDJ 80 (Leiden:
Brill, 2009), 132.

41. Schorch, "The Construction of Samari(t)an Identity," 137.

42. James Kugel, "Testament of the Twelve Patriarchs" in *Outside the Bible: Ancient
Jewish Writings Related to Scripture*, 3 vols., ed. Louis H. Feldman, James L. Kugel, and
Lawrence H. Schiffman (Philadelphia: Jewish Publication Society, 2013), 2:1733; Mat-
thew Goff, "The Foolish Nation That Dwells in Shechem: Ben Sira on Shechem and the
Other Peoples in Palestine," in *The "Other" in Second Temple Judaism: Essays in Honor
of John J. Collins*, ed. Daniel C. Harlow et al. (Grand Rapids: Eerdmans, 2011), 173–88;
Kartveit, "Who Are the Fools," 119–33.

43. Proposals for the date of 4Q372 range widely. On paleographic grounds, it
likely dates to the late Hasmonean or early Herodian periods. But its reference to the
Samaritan temple, with no mention of its destruction by Hyrcanus, strongly suggests
that it was composed prior to 110 BCE, and thus very likely in the second century
BCE. See Douglas Marvin Gropp, *Wadi Daliyeh II: The Samaria Papyri from Wadi
Daliyeh*, DJD 28 (Oxford: Clarendon, 2001); Hanan Eshel, "The Prayer of Joseph, a

[and fools were dwelling in the land (ונבלים ישבים)]⁴⁴ and making for
themselves a high place upon a high mountain [that is, the Samaritan
temple on Mount Gerizim] to provoke Israel to jealousy … and they
acted terribly with the words of their mouth to revile against the tent of
Zion. (lines 11–14)⁴⁵

Here we see the characterization of a certain people as "fools" in the same
breath as a reference to a "high place on a high mountain," which many
take to mean the Samaritan temple on Mount Gerizim. Moreover, the
construction of this high place is described as a provocative act directed
toward those living in Jerusalem and its temple—the "tent of Zion." The
Testament of Levi makes a similar claim, asserting that the city of Shechem
will be called the "city of fools" because they committed a great outrage, or
folly, in Israel by defiling Dinah (7.2–3). From a slightly later time, Philo
echoes this same sentiment, arguing that Shechem is the "son of folly" and
those in Shechem are the "fools who attempt to seduce her" (*Mut.* 193–
195, 199–200).

This equation of Samaritans with Shechemites and fools is a serious
allegation, and one that is likely dependent upon the account in Gen 34
of Shechem's rape of Dinah and the subsequent description of this action
as a נבלה, often translated as an "outrage" or "folly."⁴⁶ The two words נבל
(fool) and נבלה (outrage or folly) have clear semantic links, and it is this
connection that T. Levi 7 and Philo demonstrate: having committed this

Papyrus from Masada and the Samaritan Temple on ΑΡΓΑΡΙΖΙΝ" [Hebrew], *Zion*
56 (1991): 125–36; Esther Chazon with Yonatan Miller, "'At the Crossroads': Anti-
Samaritan Polemic in a Qumran Text about Joseph," in Harlow et al., *"Other" in Second
Temple Judaism*, 381–87. For an argument against seeing this text as anti-Samaritan,
see Robert A. Kugler, "Joseph at Qumran," in *Studies in the Hebrew Bible, Qumran, and
the Septuagint Presented to Eugene Ulrich*, ed. Peter W. Flint, Emanuel Tov, and James
C. VanderKam, VTSup 101 (Boston: Brill, 2006), 261–78; Matthew Thiessen, "4Q372
1 and the Continuation of Joseph's Exile," *DSD* 15 (2008): 380–95.

44. The phrase "fools were dwelling in the land" is taken from 4Q371 and fills a
lacuna in 4Q372.

45. Translation from Eileen Schuller and Moshe Bernstein, "4QNarrative and
Poetic Composition^a–c," in *Qumran Cave 4.XXVIII, Miscellanea, Part 2*, by Moshe
Bernstein et al., DJD 28 (Oxford: Clarendon, 2001).

46. The term נבלה often functions as a technical term, referring to a particular
type of egregious sin, which often involves sexual violence or misconduct (Gen 34:7;
Deut 22:21; Josh 7:15; Judg 20:6; 2 Sam 13:12; Jer 29:23). See Kartveit, "Who Are the
Fools," 132.

נבלה (outrage), the city of Shechem will henceforth be known as the city of נבלים (fools). In making this connection between the words "fool" (נבל) and "outrage" (נבלה), the Testament of Levi makes explicit what is only implicit in Ben Sira and 4Q372: that the "fools" in Shechem (that is, the Samaritans) are both descendants of the Shechem responsible for the "outrage" against Dinah and outsiders to the nation of Israel. As such, they are deserving not only of scorn and revulsion, but also of any violence that may come their way.

Violence is exactly what happened. In two successive campaigns at the close of the second century BCE, John Hyrcanus destroyed the Samaritan temple on Mount Gerizim, along with the cities of Shechem and Samaria, and incorporated the region of Samaria into the burgeoning Hasmonean kingdom. What is intriguing is the role that rhetoric may have played in creating this atmosphere of violence.[47] The first explicitly anti-Samaritan rhetoric in Jewish literature starts to emerge in the early second century BCE when the Samari(t)ans were much stronger politically. At the time, this rhetoric could not be acted upon. But the rise of the Hasmoneans in the middle of the second century BCE shifted the power dynamics, and the politically ascendant Jews/Judeans were now in a position to act upon a century of denigration and foreignization of the Samaritans. And act they did, destroying the Samaritan temple and forcing the Samaritans to bend the knee to the emerging Jewish power.

## Summary Comments on the Parting between Jews and Samaritans

The second century BCE was an important one for Jewish-Samaritan relations. At the close of the third century BCE, the relationship seems to have been relatively cordial, albeit with the Samaritans holding most of the cards politically and economically. The textual emendations that would come to characterize the MT and SP had not yet come into being, and it is likely that the high-priestly families ensconced in Jerusalem and Mount Gerizim jointly continued to be responsible for preserving and passing down the texts. Some tensions between Judeans and Samarians undoubtedly existed, but the extant Jewish literature from the time contains no evidence of the polemical language that would soon emerge.

---

47. Wardle, "Jewish Slander."

By the end of the second century, however, the landscape had changed significantly. The Samaritan temple on Mount Gerizim, and the surrounding cities in the region, had been destroyed. Subtle alterations to the Pentateuch began to enter the manuscript traditions in the late second and early first century, a process that led to the texts we today call the SP and MT. Even more, Jewish rhetoric directed towards their Samaritan neighbors intensified and likely played a role in the Hasmonean decision to see the Samaritans as outsiders and destroy the temple on Mount Gerizim. As a result, by the end of the second century BCE, the relationship between Jews and Samaritans had been substantially altered, with animosity now more the rule than the exception. Continuing contacts between Jews and Samaritans indicate that the polarization that led to a rift between the two was not complete or decisive.[48] But the boundary markers had definitely shifted.

The Parting(s) of the Way(s): Samaritans, Jews, and Christians

What light might this discussion of the parting of the ways between Samaritans and Jews shed on the eventual parting of the ways between Jews and Christians several centuries later? Below I make only a few, necessarily brief, observations.

Some of the same besetting terminological issues scholars have with discussions of Jews and Samaritans also appear in discussions of Jews and Christians, though in different forms. In the case of Jews and Samaritans, originally geographical terms eventually broadened to include issues of religious and cultural practice. But even with this semantic expansion, there are no examples of people who were both Judean and Samarian, or Jewish and Samaritan, at the same time. The geographic overtones still seem important. The situation between Jews and Christians, however, is different, as a person could simultaneously be both Jew and Christian. Not all Christians fell into both categories. But from the very beginning, a number of Jewish followers of Jesus could and did simultaneously claim both Jewish and Christian identity. That it was possible to hold together these two identities suggests that this second parting of ways was a bit different than the first, as the term Christian was not ethnically bound in the same way as the term Samaritan. If the identity options had been Jew or

---

48. Knoppers, *Jews and Samaritans*, 218–39.

gentile, I think the answer would be that a person could not be both. But when issues of belief come to the fore, and conversion to a particular way of life in the world is elevated beyond ethnic lines, then this scenario of dual identity, someone being both Jew and Christian, becomes possible. Several terms have been proposed to account for this situation—Jewish Christians, Christian Jews, and Apostolic Jews, among others—but none has yet carried the day. Since this volume is dedicated to Joel, I point the reader toward his fine article on this subject and move on to a discussion of temples, texts, and polemics.[49]

For Jews and Samaritans, the destruction of the Samaritan temple played a pivotal role. Jews were responsible for the destruction of the Gerizim temple, which meant that continuing animosity on the part of Samaritans toward Jews was heavily based on something that the Jews had done to them. There is nothing analogous to this situation in the parting of ways between Jews and Christians. The Romans, not the Christians, were responsible for the Jerusalem temple's downfall. Yet, for both partings, the temple does seem to have played a role. While their respective temples were still standing, Samaritans and Jews likely saw their temple as the one true place where the God of Israel could and should be worshiped. After the destruction of the Gerizim temple was a fait accompli, adherents to the Jerusalem temple could claim it as the one temple where the God of Israel was rightfully and properly worshiped. Similarly, before the destruction of the Jerusalem temple, early Jewish-Christians began to appropriate temple and priestly language and apply it to their own community, meaning that there were once again two temples (one physical, one metaphorical) in existence at the same time. In the aftermath of the year 70 CE, some Christian authors saw in the Jerusalem temple's destruction confirmation that God's presence now resided in their community

---

49. Joel Marcus, "Jewish Christianity," in *Origins to Constantine*, ed. Francis Young and Margaret Mitchell, CHC 1 (Cambridge, Cambridge University Press, 2006), 87–102. Cf. Anders Runesson, "Inventing Christian Identity: Paul, Ignatius, and Theodosius I," in *Exploring Christian Identity*, ed. Bengt Holmberg, WUNT 226 (Tübingen: Mohr Siebeck, 2008), 72–74; Matt Jackson-McCabe, ed., *Jewish Christianity Reconsidered: Rethinking Ancient Groups and Texts* (Minneapolis: Fortress, 2007); Oskar Skarsaune and Reidar Hvalvik, eds., *Jewish Believers in Jesus: The Early Centuries* (Peabody: Hendrickson, 2007); James Carleton Paget, "Jewish Christianity," in *The Early Roman Period*, ed. William Horbury, W. D. Davies, and John Sturdy, CHJ 3 (Cambridge: Cambridge University Press, 1999), 731–75.

alone.[50] For each community, then, the temple mattered, with each (Jews, Samaritans, and Christians) claiming their temple—metaphorical or not, destroyed or not—as the rightful temple.

Texts also played an important role in each parting of the ways. For the parting between Jews and Samaritans, the emphasis is squarely on the emergence of different textual traditions that later became the SP and MT. Whereas earlier scholars labeled textual differences as sectarian and attributed them to the Samaritans, current scholars now speak of textual emendation as something in which both sides were likely complicit.[51] In short, the focus is on how shared texts were altered to produce discrete manuscript traditions. By contrast, Jews and Christians in the first century CE shared the same scriptures and did not alter them in competing ways—a couple hundred years seem to have made the text less open to change. Nevertheless, different texts were read. Jews in the land of Israel, along with many early Jewish-Christians, read the Jewish scriptures in Hebrew, whereas many diaspora Jews, diaspora Jewish-Christians, and gentile Christians claimed the LXX as their sacred text. Who read what text was complicated, with the Jewish tradition ultimately gravitating toward the MT and the Christian tradition claiming the LXX. In addition, in the early centuries of the Common Era, Jews and Christians penned new texts—the Mishnah and New Testament, respectively—that began to be seen as authoritative in their own right. These two collections of literature, which originated from very different hermeneutical starting points, were the lens through which each group viewed the Jewish scriptures and which largely determined their respective interpretative outcomes. As a result of these divergent versions, texts, and presuppositions, Jews and

---

50. For a recent discussion of the relevant second-century texts, see Nicklas, *Jews and Christians*, passim. For a discussion of temple language being applied to the Christian community, see Timothy Wardle, "Pillars, Foundations, and Stones: Individual Believers as Constituent Parts of the Early Christian Communal Temple," in *Sacrifice, Cult, and Atonement in Early Judaism and Christianity: Constituents and Critiques*, ed. Henrietta L. Wiley and Christian A. Eberhart, RBS 85 (Atlanta: SBL Press, 2017), 289–310.

51. For a recent discussion of scribal involvement in textual variations, see David Andrew Teeter, *Scribal Laws: Exegetical Variation in the Textual Transmission of Biblical Law in the Late Second Temple Period*, FAT 92 (Tübingen: Mohr Siebeck, 2014), 7–33, 161–64.

Christians often held very different and distinctive understandings of the Jewish scriptures.[52]

So a battle over sacred texts seems to have emerged in both partings, both over *what* should be read as well as *how* one should read. Jews, Samaritans, and Christians all made specific claims based on particular readings of sacred texts, with these claims helping to shape the distinct communities that eventually emerged from these partings. All three communities appear to have operated on the assumption that their reading and interpretation of the text was the only proper and faithful one.

When we turn to the influence of rhetoric and polemics in creating and sustaining divisions between Jews/Samaritans and Jews/Christians, some interesting parallels also emerge. In both partings, power dynamics underwent a profound upheaval in the course of a century or two. At the beginning of the second century BCE, the Samarians/Samaritans were more politically ascendant than the Judeans/Jews, and in the middle of the first century CE, non-Christian Jews were in a politically and numerically advantageous position over against the emerging Jewish-Christian movement. In the ensuing years, the less politically ascendant group (Jews in the second century BCE and Christians in the first century CE) began to use polemical language to castigate the more powerful group and assert their own identity claims.[53] A century (or three) later (the late second century BCE for Jews and several centuries later for Christians), the tables had turned, with the formerly disadvantaged group in a different political or numerical situation. On the Jewish side, John Hyrcanus marched north, destroyed Mount Gerizim, and forced the Samaritans to bend to his will (at least politically). A century of othering had made the Samaritans outsiders to the covenant, at least according to some Jews. Active persecution of Jews by Christians took many more centuries to become reality, but the conditions that made this marginalization possible were laid already in the early centuries CE. In both situations, decades (and centuries) of polemics led to intolerance and persecution.

---

52. For example, see James D. G. Dunn, ed., *Jews and Christians: The Parting of the Ways* (Grand Rapids: Eerdmans, 1992).

53. Polemic almost certainly went both ways, but our textual evidence is, unfortunately, very uneven. The extant Samaritan literature from the second century BCE and Jewish literature from the first century CE are devoid of the same level of rhetorical vitriol as that found in Jewish and Christian sources from the same period.

## A Final Observation

It is an interesting exercise to compare the parting of the ways between Samaritans and Jews with the parting of the ways between Jews and Christians. Much more could be said in each of the above comparisons, but time and space do not allow for a more precise analysis. Here, though, I offer a final observation. The significance that each group placed on a temple, the emphasis on correct texts and interpretations of them, and the animosity displayed against the Other all seem to point in the direction of a single/ primary claim: that "we" are the only ones who can properly worship the God of Israel. Implicit in this claim is another claim: that "we" are the rightful descendants of the nation of Israel and thus the people that God has chosen. This claim is not always spelled out, but hints of it are evident in both partings. Tensions over the location of the real temple between Jews and Samaritans move in this direction, as do the development of two different pentateuchal traditions containing important claims and the later Samaritan preference for the title of guardians or keepers when referring to their own community. Early Christian works such as the Epistle of Barnabas and Justin's *Dialogue with Trypho* make similar claims, asserting that Christians are the true inheritors of the Jewish scriptures, covenants, and promises made to Israel.[54] For all three communities, battles over rightness may really have been battles over who could legitimately claim to be the chosen people of the God of Israel. Or, to put the matter somewhat differently, disagreements between Samaritans, Jews, and Christians over the right to assume the mantle of Israel led to at least two partings and multiple possibilities of ways forward.

---

54. These presuppositions undergird the entirety of works like the Epistle of Barnabas and Justin's *Dialogue with Trypho*. See also Shaye J. D. Cohen, "The Ways That Parted: Jews, Christians, and Jewish-Christians ca. 100–150 CE," in *Jews and Christians in the First and Second Centuries: The Interbellum 70–132 CE*, ed. Joshua J. Schwartz and Peter J. Tomson, CRINT 15 (Leiden: Brill, 2017), 307–39; Peter Richardson, *Israel in the Apostolic Church*, SNTSMS 10 (Cambridge: Cambridge University Press, 1969), 1–32.

# Bibliography

Becker, Adam H., and Annette Yoshiko Reed, eds. *The Ways That Never Parted: Jews and Christians in Late Antiquity and the Early Middle Ages*. Minneapolis: Fortress, 2007.

Bourgel, Jonathan. "The Destruction of the Samaritan Temple by John Hyrcanus: A Reconsideration." *JBL* 135 (2016): 505–23.

Boyarin, Daniel. *Border Lines: The Partition of Judaeo-Christianity*. Divinations. Philadelphia: University of Pennsylvania Press, 2004.

Chazon, Esther, with Yonatan Miller. "'At the Crossroads': Anti-Samaritan Polemic in a Qumran Text about Joseph." Pages 381–87 in *The "Other" in Second Temple Judaism: Essays in Honor of John J. Collins*. Edited by Daniel C. Harlow, Matthew Goff, Karina Martin Hogan, and Joel S. Kaminsky. Grand Rapids: Eerdmans, 2011.

Coggins, R. J. *Samaritans and Jews: The Origins of Samaritanism Reconsidered*. Oxford: Blackwell, 1975.

Cohen, Shaye J. D. "*Ioudaios, Iudaeus*, Judaean, Jew." Pages 69–106 in *The Beginnings of Jewishness: Boundaries, Varieties, Uncertainties*. Berkeley: University of California Press, 1999.

———. "The Ways That Parted: Jews, Christians, and Jewish-Christians ca. 100–150 CE." Pages 307–39 in *Jews and Christians in the First and Second Centuries: The Interbellum 70-132 CE*. Edited by Joshua J. Schwartz and Peter J. Tomson. CRINT 15. Leiden: Brill, 2017.

Cowley, A. E. *Aramaic Papyri of the Fifth Century B.C.* Oxford: Clarendon, 1923.

Dexinger, Ferdinand. "Limits of Tolerance in Judaism: The Samaritan Example." Pages 88–114 in vol. 2 of *Jewish and Christian Self-Definition*. Edited by E. P. Sanders, Albert I. Baumgarten, and Alan Mendelson. 3 vols. London: SCM, 1981.

Dunn, James D. G., ed. *Jews and Christians: The Parting of the Ways*. Grand Rapids: Eerdmans, 1992.

———. *The Partings of the Ways between Christianity and Judaism and Their Significance for the Character of Christianity*. London: SCM, 1991.

Dušek, Jan. *Aramaic and Hebrew Inscriptions from Mt. Gerizim and Samaria between Antiochus III and Antiochus IV Epiphanes*. CHANE 54. Leiden: Brill, 2012.

Eshel, Hanan. "The Prayer of Joseph, a Papyrus from Masada and the Samaritan Temple on ΑΡΓΑΡΙΖΙΝ" [Hebrew]. *Zion* 56 (1991): 125–36.

Fine, Steven. *The Menorah: From the Bible to Modern Israel*. Cambridge: Harvard University Press, 2016.

Gallagher, Edmond L. "Is the Samaritan Pentateuch a Sectarian Text?" *ZAW* 127 (2015): 96–107.

Goff, Matthew. "The Foolish Nation That Dwells in Shechem: Ben Sira on Shechem and the Other Peoples in Palestine." Pages 173–88 in *The "Other" in Second Temple Judaism: Essays in Honor of John J. Collins*. Edited by Daniel C. Harlow, Matthew Goff, Karina Martin Hogan, and Joel S. Kaminsky. Grand Rapids: Eerdmans, 2011.

Goldstein, Jonathan. *2 Maccabees: A New Translation with Introduction and Commentary*. AB 41A. Garden City: Doubleday, 1983.

Gropp, Douglas Marvin. *Wadi Daliyeh II: The Samaria Papyri from Wadi Daliyeh*. DJD 28. Oxford: Clarendon, 2001.

Jackson-McCabe, Matt, ed. *Jewish Christianity Reconsidered: Rethinking Ancient Groups and Texts*. Minneapolis: Fortress, 2007.

Kartveit, Magnar. *The Origins of the Samaritans*. VTSup 128. Leiden: Brill, 2009.

———. "Who Are the Fools in 4QNarrative and Poetic Composition[a-c]." Pages 119–34 in *Northern Lights on the Dead Sea Scrolls: Proceedings of the Nordic Qumran Network 2003–2006*. Edited by Anders Klostergaard Petersen. STDJ 80. Leiden: Brill, 2009.

Knoppers, Gary. *Jews and Samaritans: The Origins and History of Their Early Relations*. New York: Oxford University Press, 2013.

Kugel, James L. "Testament of the Twelve Patriarchs." Pages 1697–1855 in vol. 2 of *Outside the Bible: Ancient Jewish Writings Related to Scripture*. Edited by Louis H. Feldman, James L. Kugel, and Lawrence H. Schiffman. 3 vols. Philadelphia: Jewish Publication Society, 2013.

———. *Traditions of The Bible*. Cambridge: Harvard University Press, 1998.

Kugler, Robert A. "Joseph at Qumran." Pages 261–78 in *Studies in the Hebrew Bible, Qumran, and the Septuagint Presented to Eugene Ulrich*. Edited by Peter W. Flint, Emanuel Tov, and James C. VanderKam. VTSup 101. Boston: Brill, 2006.

Magen, Yitzhak. "The Dating of the First Phase of the Samaritan Temple on Mount Gerizim in Light of the Archaeological Evidence." Pages 157–212 in *Judah and the Judeans in the Fourth Century B.C.E.* Edited by Oded Lipschits, Gary N. Knoppers, and Rainer Albertz. Winona Lake, IN: Eisenbrauns, 2007.

———. *Mount Gerizim Excavations*. 2 vols. Jerusalem: Israel Antiquities Authority, 2008.

Marcus, Joel. "Jewish Christianity." Pages 87–102 in *Origins to Constantine*. Edited by Francis Young and Margaret Mitchell. CHC 1. Cambridge: Cambridge University Press, 2006.

Mason, Steve. "Jews, Judaeans, Judaizing, Judaism: Problems of Categorization in Ancient History." *JSJ* 38 (2007): 457–512.

Mor, Menachem. "The Samaritans in Transition from the Persian to the Greek Period." Pages 191–98 in *Judah between East and West: The Transition from Persian to Greek Rule (ca. 400–200 B.C.E.); A Conference Held at Tel Aviv University, 17–19 April 2007 Sponsored by the ASG (the Academic Study Group for Israel and the Middle East) and Tel Aviv University*. Edited by Lester L. Grabbe and Oded Lipschits. LSTS 75. London: T&T Clark, 2011.

Nicklas, Tobias. *Jews and Christians? Second Century "Christian" Perspectives on the "Parting of the Ways" (Annual Deichmann Lectures 2013)*. Tübingen: Mohr Siebeck, 2014.

Paget, James Carleton. "Jewish Christianity." Pages 731–75 in *The Early Roman Period*. Edited by William Horbury, W. D. Davies, and John Sturdy. CHJ 3. Cambridge: Cambridge University Press, 1999.

Pummer, Reinhard. *The Samaritans: A Profile*. Grand Rapids: Eerdmans, 2016.

———. *The Samaritans in Flavius Josephus*. TSAJ 129. Tübingen: Mohr Siebeck, 2009.

Reinhartz, Adele. "A Fork in the Road or a Multi-Lane Highway? New Perspectives on the 'Parting of the Ways' between Judaism and Christianity." Pages 280–95 in *The Changing Face of Judaism, Christianity, and Other Greco-Roman Religions in Antiquity*. Edited by Ian H. Henderson and Gerbern S. Oegema. Gütersloh: Gütersloher Verlagshaus, 2006.

Richardson, Peter. *Israel in the Apostolic Church*. SNTSMS 10. Cambridge: Cambridge University Press, 1969.

Runesson, Anders. "Inventing Christian Identity: Paul, Ignatius, and Theodosius I." Pages 59–92 in *Exploring Christian Identity*. Edited by Bengt Holmberg. WUNT 226. Tübingen: Mohr Siebeck, 2008.

Samkutty, V. J. *The Samaritan Mission in Acts*. LNTS 328. London: T&T Clark, 2006.

Sanderson, Judith E. *An Exodus Scroll from Qumran: 4QpaleoExod^m and the Samaritan Tradition*. HSS 30. Atlanta: Scholars Press, 1986.

Schenker, Adrian. "Le Seigneur choisira-t-il le lieu de son nom ou l'a-t-il choisi? L'apport de la Bible Grecque ancienne á l'histoire du texte

Samaritain et Massorétique." Pages 339–51 in *Scripture in Transition: Essays on Septuagint, Hebrew Bible, and Dead Sea Scrolls in Honour of Raija Sollamo*. Edited by Anssi Voitila and Jutta Jokiranta. JSJSup 126. Leiden: Brill, 2008.

Schiffman, Lawrence H. "The Samaritans in Tannaitic Halakhah." *JQR* 75 (1985): 323–50.

Schorch, Stefan. "The Construction of Samari(t)an Identity from the Inside and from the Outside." Pages 135–50 in *Between Cooperation and Hostility: Multiple Identities in Ancient Judaism*. Edited by Rainer Albertz and Jakob Wöhrle. JAJSup 11. Göttingen: Vandenhoeck & Ruprecht, 2013.

———. "Der Pentateuch der Samaritaner: Seine Erforschung und seine Bedeutung für das Verständnis des alttestamentlichen Bibeltextes." Pages 5–29 in *Die Samaritaner und die Bibel: Historische und literarische Wechselwirkungen zwischen biblischen und samaritanischen Traditionen/The Samaritans and the Bible: Historical and Literary Interactions between Biblical and Samaritan Traditions*. Edited by Jörg Frey, Ursula Schattner-Rieser, and Konrad Schmid. SJ 70. Berlin: de Gruyter, 2012.

———. "The Samaritan Version of Deuteronomy and the Origin of Deuteronomy." Pages 23–37 in *Samaria, Samarians, Samaritans: Studies on Bible, History, and Linguistics*. Edited by Jozsef Zsellengér. SJ 66. Berlin: de Gruyter, 2011.

Schwartz, Daniel R. *2 Maccabees*. CEJL. Berlin: de Gruyter, 2008.

———. *Judeans and Jews: Four Faces of Dichotomy in Ancient Jewish History*. Toronto: University of Toronto Press, 2014.

Schwartz, Seth. "The 'Judaism' of Samaria and Galilee in Josephus's Version of the Letter of Demetrius I to Jonathan (*Antiquities* 13:48–57)." *HTR* 82 (1989): 377–91.

Skarsaune, Oskar, and Reidar Hvalvik, eds. *Jewish Believers in Jesus: The Early Centuries*. Peabody: Hendrickson, 2007.

Teeter, David Andrew. *Scribal Laws: Exegetical Variation in the Textual Transmission of Biblical Law in the Late Second Temple Period*. FAT 92. Tübingen: Mohr Siebeck, 2014.

Thiessen, Matthew. "4Q372 1 and the Continuation of Joseph's Exile." *DSD* 15 (2008): 380–95.

Wardle, Timothy. *The Jerusalem Temple and Early Christian Identity*. WUNT 2/291. Tübingen: Mohr Siebeck, 2010.

———. "Pillars, Foundations, and Stones: Individual Believers as Constituent Parts of the Early Christian Communal Temple." Pages 280–310 in *Sacrifice, Cult, and Atonement in Early Judaism and Christianity: Constituents and Critiques*. Edited by Henrietta L. Wiley and Christian A. Eberhart. RBS 85. Atlanta: SBL Press, 2017.

———. "The Power of Polemics: Jewish Slander against Samaritans in the Late Second Temple Period," in *Biblical Themes and Traditions in the Pseudepigrapha*. Edited by Craig A. Evans and Paul Sloan. London: T&T Clark, forthcoming.

Zahn, Molly M. *Rethinking Rewritten Scripture: Composition and Exegesis in the 4QReworked Pentateuch Manuscripts*. STDJ 95. Leiden: Brill, 2011.

Zsengellér, József. "Maccabees and Temple Propaganda." Pages 181–95 in *The Books of the Maccabees: History, Theology, Ideology; Papers of the Second International Conference on the Deuterocanonical Books, Pápa, Hungary, 9–11 June, 2005*. Edited by Géza G. Xeravits and József Zsengellér. JSJSup 118. Leiden: Brill, 2007.

# John and Jesus in Josephus:
# A Prelude to the Parting of the Ways

Albert I. Baumgarten

> Consider the distinctive appearance of prophets. They tend to arise in peripheral areas of society, and prophets tend to be shaggy, unkempt individuals. They express in their bodies the independence of social norms which their peripheral origins inspire in them. It is no accident that St John the Baptist lived in the desert and wore skins.
>
> —Mary Douglas, *Natural Symbols*, 97

## Preludes

John the Baptist and Jesus occupy leading and interconnected roles in the narrative of the gospels, with the center of attention focused on Jesus and with John regularly portrayed as subordinate to Jesus.[1] John and Jesus also

---

1. This article is written in grateful acknowledgment of all that I have learned from Joel Marcus over the years and with special appreciation for all that he has taught me about John the Baptist. At the same time, I cannot follow Marcus's arguments that John was pointing to Jesus as the greater one to come. In my view, any passage that asserts that John diminished himself in respect to Jesus, was subordinate to him in any way, is suspect. This is my principal disagreement with Marcus's forthcoming book on the Baptist, of which he was kind enough to send me a draft prior to its publication. Marcus adopts the competition hypothesis between the disciples of John and Jesus, each set proclaiming the superior status of the figure they revered, but he does not carry that conclusion to its logical end in every single possible case, as I see it.

For a specific example in published material in which I disagree with Marcus, see Joel Marcus, "John the Baptist and Jesus," in *When Judaism and Christianity Began: Essays in Memory of Anthony J. Saldarini*, ed. Alan Avery Peck, Daniel Harrington, and Jacob Neusner, JSJSup 85 (Leiden: Brill, 2004), 179–84. Marcus discussed John's charging of his disciples in Q, Matt 11:2–6 // Luke 7:18–23, to ask Jesus "Are you the coming one?" (184–87). This passage has posed a difficulty to generations of com-

attracted the attention of Josephus, but they were discussed independently, without indication that they might be linked in any way. What is notable about Josephus's comments on the two figures is that he presented John as "a good man" (*agathon andron*), who "exhorted the Jews to lead righteous lives, to practice justice towards their fellows and piety towards God" (*A.J.* 18.117 [Feldman]).

By contrast, Josephus recounted the stoning of James the brother of Jesus and others for "transgressing the law" by the rash and daring high priest Ananus, who followed Sadducean traditions, which Josephus categorized as heartless or savage (we might say "stringent"). This event took place in 62 CE, in the interlude between the death of Festus and the appointment and arrival of Albinus as procurator. Josephus did not specify just how these men "transgressed the law" and committed a capital crime (at least according to Ananus and the members of the Sanhedrin he convened who judged James).[2] But Josephus noted that these actions offended those inhabitants of Jerusalem who were considered the "most fair minded and strict in observance of the law" (*A.J.* 20.201), by which perhaps Jose-

---

mentators. Marcus solved the dilemma by proposing that John's support for Jesus was of the "intermediate kind"; John knew that Jesus was his superior, even if John did not yet acknowledge Jesus as the Messiah (187–97). Nevertheless, as Elijah, John wondered who would be his successor, the ultimate redeemer, someone not a mere minor figure like Elisha, but someone Davidic. This concern was especially pressing for John towards the end of his life, and it motivated the charge to his disciples attested in Q, Matt 11:2–6 // Luke 7:18–23, to ask Jesus "Are you the coming one?" I prefer taking the competition hypothesis to its logical conclusion and understanding the inquiry concerning "the coming one" as yet another neat rhetorical attempt to have John downgrade himself. He wanted his disciples to ask Jesus "Are you the coming one?" because John knew that *he, John himself, was not* "the coming one," the supreme figure in the scenario of the end of days! See further the appendix to this paper.

For my application of the competition hypothesis to another specific case, see Albert I. Baumgarten, "An Ancient Debate of Disciples," in *Perceiving the Other in Ancient Judaism and Early Christianity*, ed. Michal Bar-Asher Siegal, Wolfgang Grünstäudl, and Matthew Thiessen, WUNT 394 (Tübingen: Mohr Siebeck, 2017), 1–18.

2. In Eusebius's account of the trial and execution of James (*Hist. eccl.* 2.23), the villains were the scribes and Pharisees, reprising their part in the trial and execution of Jesus. James's offense was also specified in this version: the scribes and Pharisees feared that too many people were accepting Jesus as Messiah, and when James refused to deny the status of Jesus he was lynched. My analysis of the death of James in this essay is limited to the information in Josephus.

phus meant to include himself.[3] Again, Josephus did not indicate just what the "most fair-minded and strict in observance of the law" found offensive in the actions of Ananus and his collaborators. Were they convinced that whatever the convicted men had done was not a capital offense, not an offense at all, or perhaps their disagreement was merely procedural? However, in narrating this episode, Josephus characterized Jesus as the "so-called messiah" (*tou legomenou Christou*; *A.J.* 20.200), which Origen correctly understood as signifying that Josephus "did not believe in Jesus as Christ" (*Cels.* 1.47).[4]

How did Josephus know about John and Jesus? He witnessed the events in 62 CE directly, so even if he was young at the time[5] he should have had direct knowledge about Jesus, who he was, what his followers believed, and how they lived. However, John was executed sometime before Josephus was born. Whatever he knew about John may have come from his followers (about whom we learn elsewhere) or from the pool of oral traditions about the Jewish past on which Josephus (and the rabbis) drew, for which Vered Noam has argued persuasively.[6]

Josephus is one of the best witnesses to the Jewish world in the land of Israel and the diaspora in the first century CE. The difference between his favorable evaluation of John and denunciation of Jesus as the so-called messiah is therefore worthy of notice.[7] This article is intended to explore that difference and to view it in the framework of the parting of the ways that eventually divided between Jews and Christians. The argument is that

---

3. Even if Josephus, having been born in 37 CE, was only fifteen years old at the time. But Josephus was proud to insist that he was a precocious and learned youth, even a year earlier, at the age of fourteen, helping the chief priests and principal men of the city understand legal matters more precisely (*Vita* 8–9).

4. As John P. Meier noted, after an extended discussion of this passage and citing Louis Feldman, "few have doubted the genuineness of this passage on James." John P. Meier, "Jesus in Josephus: A Modest Proposal," *CBQ* 52 (1990): 81.

5. See n. 3 above.

6. Vered Noam, "Did the Rabbis Cause the Hasmoneans to be Forgotten? A Reconsideration" [Hebrew], *Zion* 81 (2016): 295–333.

7. For the purposes of this article, I focus on Josephus and do not take up at least one other first-century Jew who rejected faith in Jesus, Saul of Tarsus (Paul), at least in the early part of his career. In any case, Saul (Paul) never fully elaborated why he reached that conclusion earlier in his life, and thus the question is clouded in speculation.

Josephus's divergent estimates of John and Jesus were preludes to the parting of the ways.[8]

To be more specific, at the outset, at least in the case of Jesus, if those who were "most fair minded and strict in observance of the law," perhaps including Josephus himself, disapproved of the execution of James as having somehow transgressed some law, being a follower of Jesus was not a severe offense in their eyes. One is very far from the rabbinic traditions, attested centuries later, that saw Jesus as a deceiver and inciter to idolatry, מסית ומדיח, who was convicted as a result of entrapment (permitted only for these most serious of crimes) and executed by stoning, having been convicted by a Jewish court (t. Sanh. 10.11 parr.).[9] This contrast indicates that the parting of the ways, which would later take place, was in its bare infancy at the time of Josephus, and it is in this sense that I propose to view Josephus's description of John as a different sort of prelude to the parting of the ways.

Gaps in the Evidence

Some of the gaps in the evidence provided by Josephus have already been noted, but they deserve further attention concerning both John and Jesus. For John the matter is less acute: Josephus explicitly explained the meaning and purpose of John's baptism as he understood it, as will be discussed further below, but Josephus never elaborated John's message, why it attracted the multitudes, and why it made Herod Antipas fear John's influence, with the result that Herod had John executed as a preemptive measure. We can only surmise just what these missing pieces might have been.

For Jesus the deficiency is grave. While virtually all scholars agree that Josephus did not write the text of the Testimonium Flavianum as we now have it in *A.J.* 18.63–64, just what he wrote there remains uncertain despite numerous scholarly efforts.[10] Perhaps the simplest and most obvious solution is that the original description of Jesus there was unfavorable, in line with the characterization of Jesus as the so-called messiah in *A.J.* 20.200,

---

8. This topic has achieved important renewed interest since the publication of Adam H. Becker and Annette Yoshiko Reed, eds., *The Ways That Never Parted: Jews and Christians in Late Antiquity and the Early Middle Ages*, TSAJ 95 (Tübingen: Mohr Siebeck, 2003).

9. For Ben Stada as a derogatory name for Jesus, see n. 15 below.

10. See, e.g., Meier, "Jesus in Josephus." It seems superfluous to cite the extensive literature on the topic, which I see as inconclusive.

discussed above. In sum, therefore, the only safe conclusion is that Josephus did not believe that Jesus was the Messiah, but, unfortunately, his specific reasons for this disbelief remain unknown.

However, all is not lost. Ancient sources concerning other Jews more or less contemporary with Josephus suggest at least two plausible possibilities for the reason(s) Josephus did not believe in Jesus as Christ.[11] The most likely possibility, in my opinion, and the one with the longest life in the history of the polemics between Jews and Christians, is that Josephus was one of those Jews for whom a messiah who died on the cross was a stumbling block (and for Greeks a folly), as Paul noted in 1 Cor 1:23.[12] This was not the way most ancient Jews expected the finale of the messianic scenario to unfold. The dilemma posed by the cross was echoed a century after Paul by Justin's Trypho who commented: "whether Christ should be so shamefully crucified, this we are in doubt about" (*Dial.* 89 [Roberts-Donaldson]). The issue did not fade from Jewish consciousness.[13] Even later in the second century CE, a generation or so after Justin, this objection to the messianic status of Jesus was repeated by Celsus's Jew, who stated clearly that the expected redeemer to come, as predicted by the prophets, would be "one who will be a great prince, lord of the whole earth, and of all nations and armies" (*Cels.* 2.29 [Chadwick]).[14] This did not fit Jesus, whom Celsus's Jew viewed as a "man who was arrested most

---

11. I limit the suggestions in this section to arguments attested in authors as close as possible chronologically to Josephus, more or less up to the second half of the second century CE, in order to avoid the possible anachronism of attributing to him objections to the messianic status of Jesus that may have only entered later, as the discussion/debate between the communities progressed. See also n. 7 above.

12. Usually dated to 53–54 CE.

13. The best commentary on the stumbling block of the cross, an instrument of capital punishment of the most excruciating sort, was restated in modern terms by the American Jewish comedian Lenny Bruce (1925–1966), who noted that it was a good thing that Jesus was executed two thousand years ago because if he had been executed today Catholic school children would be wearing little electric chairs around their necks instead of crosses.

14. For my arguments that Celsus's Jew was a real figure, not the creation of Origen's derogatory imagination, see Albert I. Baumgarten, "The 'Rule of the Martian' in the Ancient Diaspora: Celsus and His Jew," in *Jews and Christians in the First and Second Centuries: How to Write Their History*, ed. Peter J. Tomson and Joshua J. Schwartz, CRINT 13 (Leiden: Brill, 2014), 398–430. See also Maren Niehoff, "A Jewish Critique of Christianity from Second Century Alexandria: Revisiting the Jew Mentioned in *Contra Celsum*," *JECS* 21 (2013): 151–75.

disgracefully and crucified" (*Cels.* 2.31). His death was "shameful" (*Cels.* 2.39). Furthermore, Celsus's Jew asked Jesus: "How can a dead man be immortal?" (*Cels.* 2.17).[15] If I may put words into Josephus's mouth, I imagine him saying that Jesus could not have been the Messiah because of his ignominious death on the cross. The ultimate redeemer of the world should not end his career on earth that way. At the same time, if Josephus disapproved of the punishment of James and his associates by Ananus, as argued above, perhaps Josephus was convinced that belief in Jesus as the Messiah might be shameful, foolish, and absurd, but it was not a capital offense, perhaps not one at all, just pure inanity.

Alternately, perhaps Josephus believed that the disciples faked the resurrection by stealing the body, a claim "widely known and current in Jewish circles to this day," which Matthew[16] tried to deflect (Matt 28:15), and which Justin also knew (*Dial.* 108). Justin charged that the Jews

> have sent chosen and ordained men throughout all the world to proclaim that a godless and lawless heresy had sprung from one Jesus, a Galilean deceiver, whom we crucified, but his disciples stole him by night from the tomb, where he was laid when unfastened from the cross, and now

---

15. The shame of the cross also coheres well with the rabbinic tradition in b. Shabb. 104b, as analyzed by David Rokeach, who based one key conclusion on t. Shabb. 11:15, the earliest source to mention the figure then taken up in b. Shabb. 104b. Rokeach noted that, according to all the manuscripts of t. Shabb. 11:15 except for the Erfurt manuscript, the correct reading of the name of the evil magician who brought spells from Egypt and also identified as *ben Pandira* (the Roman soldier identified as Jesus's biological father, according to rabbinic sources and Celsus's Jew; Origen, *Cels.* 1.32), was *ben Satra*. Rokeach suggested understanding *ben Satra* as "*ben stauros*," *stauros* being Greek for cross, so that *ben stauros* meant that Jesus was dubbed "the crucified one," a derogatory epithet connecting this rabbinic tradition back to Paul's observation that Jesus's death on the cross was a stumbling block for Jews. See David Rokeach, "Ben Stada Is Ben Pandira" [Hebrew], *Tarbiz* 39 (1969–1970): 15–17. Compare Peter Schäfer, *Jesus in the Talmud* (Princeton: Princeton University Press, 2007), 17, who discussed b. Shabb. 104b and understood the passage to refer to Jesus. Schäfer did not note Rokeach's suggestion. Instead, Schäfer took his cue from the identification by Rav Hisda of *Ben Stada* with *Ben Pandira* and explained *ben Stada* as meaning the son of a woman who went astray (i.e., was unfaithful to her husband), who was a *sotah* (Num 5:5–31). Schäfer was aware of the reading *ben stara* in some manuscripts of b. Shabb. 104b. He suggested that *stara* may refer to the scratches/tattoos on his body by means of which *ben stara* brought witchcraft from Egypt (*biseritah*) (*Jesus in the Talmud*, 149 n. 8).

16. Usually dated after 70 CE, perhaps 80–90 CE.

deceive men by asserting that he has risen from the dead and ascended to heaven. (*Dial.* 107 [*ANF* 1:253])

This was another matter that had a long life and resonated among Jews.

In general, however, perhaps these attempts to fill in missing pieces in the account in *A.J.* 20.200 are superfluous and also far too speculative: the gaps are far too wide. It may be better to conclude that Josephus was dubious of the merits of any number of different "prophetic figures," such as the "impostor" (*goēs*) Theudas (*A.J.* 20.97–98), or the "Egyptian, who declared that he was a prophet" (*prophētēs einai legōn*; *A.J.* 20.169–173).[17] His respect for traditional practice was as one might expect from a Jerusalem priest. Commenting on Judah the Galilean and Saddok the Pharisee who founded an "intrusive fourth school of philosophy," of which Josephus disapproved in extreme terms, he noted that "innovation and reform in ancestral traditions weigh heavily in the scale in leading to the destruction of the congregation of the people" (*A.J.* 18.9 [Feldman]). His reluctance to explain in detail the meaning of the vision of the stone in Daniel (*A.J.* 10.207) has usually been taken as his determination to distance himself from any messianic speculation that might offend his Roman patrons.[18] Jesus the so-called messiah would have been no exception.

## Why John?

To summarize the analysis thus far, the primary question that emerges concerns John. Josephus's denial of the messianic status of Jesus has echoes down through the centuries and fits well with his prejudices as attested elsewhere in his works. However, given Josephus's disdain for prophetic figures, why did he portray John so favorably, as a good man, who "exhorted Jews to lead righteous lives and to practice justice towards their fellows and piety towards God?" At least, according to Mark 11:27–33 //

---

17. For this topic and discussion of these individuals, see Rebecca Gray, *Prophetic Figures in Late Second Temple Jewish Palestine: The Evidence from Josephus* (Oxford: Oxford University Press, 1993), 112–45.

18. Arnaldo Momigliano, "What Flavius Josephus Did Not See," in *Essays on Ancient and Modern Judaism*, ed. Silvia Berti, trans. Maura Masella-Gayley (Chicago: University of Chicago Press, 1994), 71–75. But see also Steve Mason, "Josephus, Daniel and the Flavian House," in *Josephus and the History of the Greco-Roman Period: Essays in Memory of Morton Smith*, ed. Fausto Parente and Joseph Sievers, StPB 41 (Leiden: Brill, 1994), 172–75.

Matt 21:23–27 // Luke 20:1–8, the chief priests and lawyers in the temple court reacted to John's mission as we might have expected Josephus to react. They were unwilling to acknowledge that John was a prophet, yet they feared "the people," who believed that he was a prophet (see also Matt 14:5). This contrast strengthens the question of how and why John was exempt from Josephus's usual bias against prophetic figures.[19]

The answer suggested in this paper is that Josephus's approving evaluation of John was a result of the circumstances of John's death. My goal is to develop a suggestion made by Joel Marcus (see further below) with the assistance of James Scott's analysis in *Domination and the Arts of Resistance*, in particular the prestige and charisma acquired by someone who dares to give voice to the "hidden transcript."[20] Furthermore, if Josephus's denial of Jesus may offer one relatively easy and accessible window of insight into the eventual parting of the ways, what insight can be gained into that process from his endorsement of the piety of John?[21]

## Josephus's John in Comparative Perspective

But first, in order to place Josephus's account of John's death in its proper context, two comparisons between Josephus's John and the John of the gospels require attention. They show that these are two separate and parallel accounts, which we should be careful to keep apart and not combine recklessly with each other, especially since they diverge so explicitly in explaining the circumstances of John's death, the focus of the discussion below.

For example, the gospels described John's dress and diet in some detail. He was a "shaggy, unkempt" man who expressed in his body his independence of the usual social norms (to refer back to the epigraph of this article). These aspects of John's demeanor earned widespread disdain,

---

19. I note the similarities between John and figures such as Theudas and the Egyptian despite Gray's decision not to include the Baptist in her study. See Gray, *Prophetic Figures*, 5–6.

20. James Scott, *Domination and the Arts of Resistance: Hidden Transcripts* (New Haven: Yale University Press, 1990), 202–27. See below.

21. I leave aside for separate extended discussion elsewhere the likelihood that John and Jesus may have been exemplars of two different modes of piety or holiness: one (John's) which emphasized holiness as being exemplified by strict restrictions (note John's diet and dress), and the other with holiness expressed in freedom from restriction (Jesus: e.g., Mark 2:28 parr., "the Son of Man is sovereign even over the Sabbath"). Josephus might have well approved of the former and disapproved of the latter.

as reflected in the comment in Matt 11:18 // Luke 7:33 that John's refusal to eat bread and drink wine, like any normal person, showed that he was possessed, that is, stark raving mad. Yet, is it an accident that Josephus did not note these details, which reflected criticism of John, while focusing on his esteem in the eyes of the Jews?[22]

John's baptism, according to Josephus, did not promise pardon for sins committed; that would have been blasphemous usurpation of a divine privilege, as only God can pardon sins (Mark 2:7). Instead, Josephus insisted that John's baptism was a consecration of the body. Scholars have long surmised that Josephus formulated this understanding of John's baptism in opposition to the complex and somewhat obscure formula known from the gospels that John's baptism was one of "repentance that resulted in forgiveness of sins" (Mark 1:4 parr.).[23] However, even if Josephus was unaware of how Jesus and his followers understood John's baptism—that is, even if Josephus's understanding was not formulated in opposition to that found in the gospels—it was definitely different.[24] This explicit difference underlines the point asserted above: great care must be shown to avoid conflating Josephus's testimony on John with that of the gospels. The

---

22. Josephus may have also had a personal reason for omitting these details about John, as Josephus had spent three years in the desert with Bannus (*Vita* 11), another marginal figure whose lifestyle was a protest against other Jews, until Josephus had enough and "returned to the city," choosing to live as a Pharisee. If John's way of life were stressed with its critique of the larger society and the disparaging response it evoked, that rejoinder might have also been directed against Bannus and against Josephus, his former disciple.

23. See the extended discussion in my forthcoming article, "The Baptism of John in a Second Temple Jewish Context," forthcoming.

24. Scholars have struggled at length, but with little success, to understand John's baptism in terms of other immersions practiced by Jews of the Second Temple era. See, e.g., Joan E. Taylor, *The Immerser: John the Baptist within Second Temple Judaism* (Grand Rapids: Eerdmans, 1997), 49–101. It was an innovation associated directly with John: it was John's baptism, unlike all other immersions, as already signaled by the fact that it was dubbed by the name of an individual. As I have argued in the article cited in the previous note, I understand John's baptism as a consecration modeled on the consecration familiar to Second Temple Jews on visiting the Jerusalem temple, as a special preparation for encounter with the divine, by someone who was already ritually pure; in John's case, the person he baptized was getting ready to meet God at the end of time. John may have innovated and introduced a new ritual of his own, but this fit well in the limits of what was familiar and acceptable to Josephus, with his "conservative" Jerusalem-based priestly outlook.

integrity of each source deserves respect. At the same time, the common pool of knowledge about the Jewish past to which I referred above allows for some bridges to be built between the information in each independent set of sources.[25]

## John's Death

From the context and manner in which Josephus first introduced John to his readers, it is clear that John was viewed favorably by the Jews of his time and that this favorable opinion was the source of Josephus's treatment of John. This was due to the circumstances of his death: Herod Antipas's defeat at the hands of Aretas "seemed to be divine vengeance, and certainly a just vengeance for his treatment of John, surnamed the Baptist" (*A.J.* 18.116 [Feldman]). Josephus concluded his remarks on John in the same vein: "the verdict of the Jews was that the destruction visited on Herod's army was a vindication of John, since God saw fit to inflict such a blow on Herod" (*A.J.* 18.119). But what had John done to make himself so venerated and his execution by Herod Antipas such a terrible transgression that Jews explained it as a provocation of divine wrath, which then resulted in the defeat of Herod's army? Here the accounts in Josephus and the gospels diverge.

I begin with the gospels. Mark's version notes John's critique of Herod Antipas's marriage to Herodias as forbidden. John told Herod: "You have no right to your brother's wife" (6:18 NEB). Despite the fact that John's criticism was directed against Herod Antipas, the principal role of the villain in this version was played by Herodias, who "nursed a grudge against John and would willingly have killed him," for his criticism of her marriage to Antipas. She, however, was restrained by her husband's admiration for John (6:19), because Herod considered John just and holy and liked

---

25. John P. Meier recognized the need to keep the parallel sources, Josephus and the gospels on John, independent. "John the Baptist in Josephus: Philology and Exegesis," *JBL* 111 (1992): 225–37. He translated Josephus somewhat differently than I would. However, for current purposes, Meier also appreciated the need to build bridges between these sources in order to obtain a more complete picture. Meier suggested that the problem with John's teaching that dismayed Herod was that it appealed to tax collectors and soldiers, borrowing that point from the gospels. These officials served Herod and were among the pillars of his regime. If John came to control them, this was a danger to Herod's rule that he could not tolerate and that needed to be eliminated (237).

to listen to John, even if Herod found John perplexing (6:20). Herodias later found her opportunity when her daughter pleased Herod, who then offered her any request she might make; at her mother's suggestion, the daughter asked for the head of John (6:21–25). Having made the promise in public, Herod had no choice but to comply (6:26). Presumably, not to keep his word to fulfill any request Herodias's daughter made would have made Antipas look foolish and incompetent in the eyes of his guests.[26]

Mark presented John's criticism of the marriage as an individual reaction, of no wider resonance, perhaps that of a religious crank or eccentric *nudnik*, which angered Herodias directly and personally, and her only, but did not otherwise have a resounding effect in extended Jewish circles. Even Herod himself, to whom John's criticism was directed as the male partner in the forbidden marriage, did not share Herodias's hatred of John. Herod considered John just and holy. Indeed, Herod's fear of John's influence with the masses, which is so important in Josephus's account, is missing in Mark.

A different version of the material available in the pool of information on John's death is narrated in Matt 14. John again told Herod: "You have no right to your brother's wife" (14:4 NEB), but this time Herod himself was the villain of the piece. He was angered by John and would have liked to put John to death. The restraint in executing John, in this version, was Herod's fear of the people, who considered John a prophet (14:5). Again, we learn of the banquet at which Herodias's daughter danced and of the oath to grant any request she might make. The daughter then asked for John's head (note, not at the suggestion of her mother, as above, in Mark), and Herod had no choice but to grant the request as the oath had been made in public.

The similarities and differences between Mark and Matthew are easily tabulated. Both share John's rebuke of Herod: "You have no right to your brother's wife," and both stories culminate in the party and dance, with Herod's oath obligating him to overcome any reluctance to execute John.

---

26. As we have been reminded to our dismay in recent years, public executions, beheadings in particular, attract a gruesome curiosity. For John the Baptist, see the painting by Caravaggio in Saint John's Cathedral in Malta, "The Beheading of Saint John the Baptist," at https://tinyurl.com/sbl4525a. Caravaggio may well have known from personal experience just how these deeds were done. His painting depicts the moment when the sword has already done its job and the executioner is using a knife to cut the last connections between the head and the body.

However, the differences are also apparent: Herodias as villain in Mark, while Herod is the villain in Matthew, with Herodias's role missing entirely there. She is mentioned only as the mother of the dancing girl (14:6). Mark's Herod considered John just and holy, while in Matthew it was the people who considered John a prophet. The delay in executing John in Mark was due to Herod's personal admiration for John, while the fear of the people was the reason for the delay in Matthew.

With Josephus we enter a seemingly different tableau. He related that John was "a good man, who exhorted Jews to lead righteous lives." The villain of his piece was Herod, but not for any reason connected with the marriage between Herod and Herodias. Herod feared John's influence with the crowds, which might lead to an upheaval, which Herod preempted by executing John. The illegal marriage, the party, and the dance did not feature at all in Josephus's explanation of how John came to be executed.

Nevertheless, Josephus was aware of criticism of the Herod Antipas-Herodias marriage as contrary to Jewish law. He told how the tetrarch Herod Antipas had fallen in love with his sister-in-law before starting out for Rome and how he "brazenly broached to her the subject of marriage" (Feldman). She accepted, with the marriage to take place when Antipas returned from Rome, and on the condition that Antipas dismissed his current wife, the daughter of Aretas, King of Petra (*A.J.* 18.109–110). Later in the same book of *Antiquitates*, Josephus related a different version of events. Now Herodias was the one who "flouted the way of our fathers" and took it into her head to marry Herod, her husband's brother. To do this, she parted from a living husband (*A.J.* 18.136).

## Bridges

Despite the differences between these testimonies, the existence of a pool of oral information about the Jewish past to which I referred above allows building bridges between them.[27] These bridges confirm the conclusion that our information about John comes from some common pool, on which each of the different authors drew in order to shape their portrait of John.

The first of these possible bridges is between the information in Mark and Josephus. According to Mark, Herod Antipas considered John just

---

27. See above, n. 25.

and holy and liked to listen to John, even if Herod found John perplexing (6:20). This agrees with Josephus's assessment of John as a "good man" who "exhorted the Jews to lead righteous lives, to practice justice towards their fellows and piety towards God" (*A.J.* 18.117). Furthermore, if Herod actually listened to John, even if he found him perplexing, he might have well personally and directly appreciated the danger John might pose to his rule, which would make the decision to eliminate John as a preemptive move motivated by John's popularity with the people, according to Josephus, comprehensible in context.

Another possible bridge is between the information in Matthew and Josephus. According to this source, Herod would have liked to eliminate John, who angered him (presumably, in context, for criticism of his marriage) but was restrained from doing this because he feared the populace who considered John a prophet. Here too, John's popularity with the people according to Matthew coheres with the information in Josephus about Herod's fears of John's status that might undermine his regime.

## Hidden Transcripts and Charisma

The most important bridge concerns John's critique of Herod's marriage. I have already noted that, even though he did not connect this critique with Herod's decision to execute John as in the gospels, Josephus was aware of popular criticism of Herod for this action.

What if we take a hint from the gospels and put together their pieces of information with that in Josephus and conclude that John's criticism of Herod's marriage was not motivated by his being a religious crank or eccentric *nudnik,* as Mark might suggest? As Marcus notes, John's criticisms of the Antipas-Herodias union was an example of *parrēsia*, free, bold, and subversive speech, a much-revered virtue in the hierarchical and often repressive Hellenistic world, but it was subject to swift and effective revenge as well.[28] This opens the possibility to concluding that John achieved stature in the eyes of the wider population, as reported by Josephus, because he was brave and articulated the "hidden transcript" cir-

---

28. Joel Marcus, *Mark 1–8: A New Translation with Introduction and Commentary,* AB 27 (New York: Doubleday, 2000), 395. See also W. D. Davies and Dale C. Allison Jr., *A Critical and Exegetical Commentary on the Gospel according to Saint Matthew,* 3 vols., ICC (Edinburgh: T&T Clark, 1991), 2:470: "Indeed, given the political situation, a denunciation of Herod's marriage may have been politically explosive."

culating among Herod's subjects, which disapproved of this marriage as
forbidden to a Jew, which made Herod into an illegitimate ruler in the eyes
of contemporary Jews in his dominion.

The fate of those daring souls who defy the public transcript and
reveal the hidden one suppressed by regime has been analyzed in detail by
Scott, and the case of Herod Antipas and the Baptist fits the pattern Scott
set out perfectly. No effort is spared to ensure the total dominance of the
public transcript.[29] However, according to Scott, there were (and continue
to be) moments when unusual individuals of exceptional bravery dared
to say out loud and in public, for the first time, what others usually only
whispered in secret. Scott had a particular interest in the sort of authority or charisma attained by those who made the hidden transcript public.
Otherwise ordinary people, of no previous special distinction, were transformed. They attained a stature far greater than they had known before;
they became political stars intoxicated with their new status and ener-
gized by their daring to say things previously suppressed. Once someone
risked breaking the wall of public silence imposed by fear, others might
follow the lead, and an epidemic of political courage might ensue as more
and more people recognized that the person who first took the chance
to attack the public transcript was speaking for them as well. As events
then unfolded, if the perceived dangers in speaking out were reduced, the
consequences might be far-reaching. These new public stars could lever-
age the status achieved in one context into other areas, beyond the topic
on which they first dared to speak out. They might achieve wide-ranging
authority, endangering the survival of the existing regime: its impotence
might be revealed—a "paper tiger"—and its downfall hastened.[30] For these
reasons, governments are sensitive in the extreme in identifying verbal
and symbolic acts of defiance. One cannot be too careful in noting these
threats and dealing with them appropriately.[31]

However, these acts of defiance are irrevocable—someone who gives
voice to the hidden transcript cannot usually simply say "sorry" and

---

29. Scott, *Domination and the Arts of Resistance*.

30. Scott, *Domination and the Arts of Resistance*, 202–27, esp. 221–27.

31. The thoroughgoing intensive attempt to promote the public transcript and
make it invincible, while suppressing any possible expression of dissent, whether
verbal or symbolic, during the reigns of Nero and Domitian has been well documented by Shadi Bartsch, *Actors in the Audience: Theatricality and Doublespeak from
Nero to Hadrian*, Revealing Antiquity 6 (Cambridge: Harvard University Press, 1994).

return to the old order. If the regime is still strong enough, those who dare to criticize it in public are burning their bridges behind them. If they calculate incorrectly, the price for their courage might be high; the cost of outright confrontation might be one's life. This is what happened to John.

## Closing the Circle

If this explanation of the circumstances of John's death is valid, closing the circle in which it is set requires setting forth the reasons why each of the sources that drew on the common pool of information about John told the story as they did, with the emphases they stressed and the items they chose not to include.

First the gospels, Mark in particular. If John's criticism of Herod Antipas's marriage to Herodias was presented as the work of a religious crank or an eccentric *nudnik* rather than as the actions of someone who touched a live issue of wide resonance in the Jewish world in the land of Israel of his time, this made it easier to subordinate John to Jesus. John was not such a major figure and had no central place in the perception of Jews of his day. As such, he had no central role in the scenario of the end of days and could well point to a "greater one to come" who would occupy that place. This fit well with the consistent effort in the gospels to have John exalt Jesus and demean himself: "As he grows greater I must grow less" (John 3:30).

For Josephus, the issues and objectives were different. He noted the widespread criticism of the marriage of Antipas and Herodias but did not link it with John's esteem in the eyes of the populace. Speculation is inevitable in suggesting why Josephus did not make this connection. Perhaps he simply did not know of this correlation. More likely, in my opinion, is that Josephus did not want to relate that John leveraged the status achieved by this criticism in order to promote his eschatological message. In general, while the gospels stressed the eschatological aspect of John's work—it was preparation for the imminent end of days—Josephus did not mention it at all. This was in line with Josephus's consistent attitude toward imminent expectation of redemption at the end of days as displayed in his works (noted above). If Josephus had noted that John's prestige in the eyes of the people was earned by his criticism of the marriage, it might have obliged him to tell that this action also lent greater authority to John's preaching concerning the eschaton. It would be completely plausible for John to take advantage of the authority he achieved in order to bolster his message concerning the end times. Indeed, in trying to convince people that the end times are imminent, any sort of evidence or argument is valuable in overcoming doubt.[32] But any link between status achieved by one set of deeds and employing that status to support millennial hopes would have contradicted Josephus's objectives. I propose that Josephus did not mention the actions that earned John authority, such as the critique of the royal marriage, in order to avoid discussing the way this authority was leveraged to back up the message of imminent redemption and the preaching of the need to prepare for that consequence.

## Acceptable and Legitimate Variety

In the course of this essay I have indicated several reasons why Josephus could have considered John unfavorably: he innovated by introducing a new ritual, baptism of his own outside the usual framework of sorts of immersions—and Josephus decried innovations.[33] John could easily have been classified among the problematic independent religious leaders such as Theudas and the Egyptian, whom Josephus denounced. Yet, this was not the path Josephus chose. John's baptism, according to Josephus, did not usurp the divine privilege of forgiving sins. John encouraged Jews to live a life of piety, and if the gospel accounts are to be believed, John himself lived by extremely stringent standards. This fit well with Josephus's sympathies for groups or individuals that raised the level of holiness in their lives by scrupulous (hypernomic?) observance.[34] This sympathy is demonstrated elsewhere in his works, such as in the description of the Essenes in *B.J.* 2.119–161, where he explicitly noted that their beliefs and way of life made them attractive (*B.J.* 2.158), or the three years he himself spent with Bannus (*Vita* 11).[35] If one accepts the account in the first chapters of

---

32. See Albert I. Baumgarten, "Four Stages in the Life of a Millennial Movement," in *War in Heaven/Heaven on Earth: Theories of the Apocalyptic*, ed. Stephen D. O'Leary and Glen S. McGhee (London: Equinox, 2005), 62.

33. See above, n. 24.

34. See above, n. 21.

35. As the reader will note, I omit discussion of the Pharisees. This is because their status in Josephus's eyes is not clear. His programmatic statements about them do not cohere. They were the "first school" in *B.J.* 2.162. They excelled in *akribeia*, exactness in interpreting the law, in *B.J.* 2.162 and *Vita* 191, all this apparently favorable, but this quality was noted in explicitly derogatory terms in *A.J.* 17.41. These circumstances convinced Steve Mason that Josephus was consistently unfavorably inclined towards the Pharisees in all his works. Steve Mason, *Flavius Josephus on the Pharisees: A Com-*

Luke, according to which John was of priestly descent, perhaps Josephus, a Jerusalem priest himself, was inclined to be sympathetic to a fellow priest, even if that priest might otherwise fall into a category of which Josephus usually disapproved.

In short, however Josephus understood the limits of acceptable and legitimate variety in the Jewish world of his day—one should remember that he considered three very different philosophies equally valid expressions of Judaism—John did not exceed these parameters. Even Jesus, whom Josephus did not believe to be the Messiah, may not have broken the bounds of legitimate variety for Josephus as catastrophically as Jesus and his followers did for Ananus and his followers or as they later would for Celsus's Jew, who addressed his fellow Jews who now believed in Jesus: "what was wrong with you, citizens [*politai*, that is, nominal members of the same group], that you left the law of our fathers ... and have deserted us for another name and another life?" (Origen, *Cels.* 2.1).[36] In these senses,

position-*Critical Study*, StPB 39 (Leiden: Brill, 1991), 372–75. I find this suggestion hard to accept. It runs afoul of the highly favorable things Josephus said about Simon son of Gamaliel in *Vita* 192 (cf. Steve Mason, *Flavius Josephus: Life of Josephus, Translation and Commentary*, FJTC 9 [Leiden: Brill, 2003], 98–99), despite the fact that Josephus was narrating events that took place in the Galilee, during the revolt, decades earlier than when he wrote *Vita*, and about a time, "then," when Simon was allied with John of Gischala and involved in treacherous dealings to depose Josephus. Simon was a Pharisee, from Jerusalem, of brilliant ancestry, and a man "full of insight and reason, able to rectify matters that were sitting badly by virtue of his own practical wisdom." This praise reminds me of Thucydides on Themistocles (*P.W.* 1.138.3), as a man of outstanding natural judgment and great discernment, able to find the best solution to difficult matters with quick and exceptional insight. Perhaps the best conclusion is to view Josephus's inconsistency concerning the Pharisees as one more example of his lack of consistency in many other matters. See Shaye J. D. Cohen, *Josephus in Galilee and Rome: His* Vita *and Development as a Historian* (Leiden: Brill, 1979), 47.

36. Just what might this "other name" have been? Was it already *Christians*, the name the group took for itself in Antioch, according to Acts 11:26? It is difficult to know, but for what it is worth, Celsus's Jew refers to his "citizen" opponents simply as "believers in Christ" (Origen, *Cels.* 2.8). What were the practices followed in this "other life" that involved leaving "the law of our fathers," as Celsus's Jew charged? Would these opponents have agreed that they were living "another life" or had left "the law of our fathers"? How would they have understood their status? Unfortunately, Celsus's Jew as summarized for us by Origen did not specify. One can be fairly certain that Celsus's Jew, writing polemically, would not have presented these opponents as they would have understood themselves or as they wanted their way of life characterized. Furthermore, whatever Celsus's Jew might have written would have been

Josephus's comments on John were a prelude to the sorts of diversity many ancient Jews could accept as authoritative, while Jesus's teachings as elaborated over time came to be seen as breaking those limits. By the end of the process of the "parting of the ways," ancient Jews came to agree with Celsus's Jew and recognize that those who followed Jesus were perceived as having "another name" and living "another life, leaving the law of our fathers." They had crossed an invisible line into a different but unacceptable way of serving the God of the Hebrew Bible.[37]

## Appendix
## Matt 11:2–6 // Luke 7:18–23

These verses, virtually universally acknowledged as coming from Q, have posed a difficulty to generations of commentators, from antiquity through the early modern period and up to our times. As Ulrich Luz recognized, they were problematic and obscure and therefore generated many explanations.[38] In light of all the gospel reader knew of the Baptist and of his supposedly absolute loyalty to Jesus, why would John need to ask his dis-

---

further refracted through the lens of Origen's reply. It is therefore not surprising that the passages in which Origen quoted and discussed the comments made by Celsus's Jew (Origen, *Cels.* 2.238–254), in which he presented and contested the reasons these former Jews decided to become "believers in Christ," are hard to understand and abound in obscurities. See further the summary and analysis of these passages in Baumgarten, "Rule of the Martian," 415–18.

If this paper began with noting the gaps in the evidence this footnote concludes on the same point. The gaps in drawing a comprehensive picture of the Jewish "believers in Christ" opposed by Celsus's Jew are no less evident. It requires effort and ingenuity to close these gaps, to the extent possible. For another example of the analysis needed to close a different case of gaps in the evidence, see the essay by Daniel Boyarin, "Why Ignatius Invented Judaism," in this volume.

37. I have learned much from my honorary membership in 2017–2018 in the research group "Contours and Expressions of the Self in Ancient Mediterranean Cultures," at the Israel Institute for Advanced Studies of the Hebrew University, a group headed by Professors Maren Niehoff and Ishay Rosen-Zvi. I have derived particular benefit, for which I am most grateful, from extended conversation with Professor Eve-Marie Becker of Aarhus University. Nevertheless, as always, there should be no suspicion of guilt by association. The sole responsibility for the content and argument of this article is mine.

38. Ulrich Luz, *Matthew 1–7: A Commentary*, trans. J. E. Crouch, Hermeneia (Minneapolis: Fortress, 2007), 131.

ciples to query Jesus whether he was the "coming one"? Indeed, not surprisingly, as Luz noted, this very question angered Luther as unnecessary and of no great consequence.[39]

One of the oldest solutions to this dilemma goes back to Origen (*Fr. Matt.* 220) and was adopted by other Fathers of the Church, such as Jerome (*Comm. Matt.* 11.1–2). This was a pedagogical exercise: John asked his disciples to determine the status of Jesus so that those disciples would be certain of what John already knew, that Jesus was the coming one. However, this explanation clashes with the context. Jesus responds: "Go tell John" (Matt 11:4 // Luke 7:22). The answer, whatever it meant, was intended directly for John and not for his disciples.[40]

If the disciples were not the intended audience, then suggestions such as that of Walter Wink are also undermined.[41] Wink noted that John is presented in these verses as unconvinced by Jesus's reply as reported by his disciples. For Wink, this "open-ended" characteristic of the story shows that it was intended for the remaining disciples of John who were still loyal to him, in hopes that it would help convince them to switch their allegiance to Jesus. However, if this is the correct interpretation, would not the story have been more effective in convincing John's disciples to back "the right horse" if John had been presented as having been convinced?

Another possibility that has been raised was that John asked not because (God forbid!) he doubted that Jesus was the Messiah, but because he was disappointed that Jesus had not made more progress in advancing the divine kingdom, in particular in cleansing the Jews of evils such as Herod Antipas and Herodias. Perhaps John had an intense personal interest in the imminent end and its judgment, as this would mean the liberty of captives (see Isa 61:1 and 42:7), especially of his own libera-

---

39. Luz, *Matthew 1–7*, 133.

40. For this reason, despite its ancient and distinguished pedigree, this explanation has been rejected by modern commentators including Marcus, "John the Baptist and Jesus," 186. See also Alfred Plummer, *A Critical and Exegetical Commentary according to the Gospel of St. Luke*, ICC (Edinburgh: T&T Clark, 1914), 202; Davies and Allison, *Critical and Exegetical Commentary*, 2:241.

41. Walter Wink, *John the Baptist in the Gospel Tradition*, SNTSMS 7 (Cambridge: Cambridge University Press, 1968), 24–25. See also François Bovon, *Luke 1: A Commentary on the Gospel of Luke 1:1—9:50*, trans. J. Crouch, Hermeneia (Minneapolis: Fortress, 2012), 281.

tion from prison and evading a death sentence.[42] However, if these were John's concerns they were not answered in the encounter of his disciples with Jesus. Furthermore, despite whatever answer John received about the status of Jesus, he remained in prison and was executed.

Other scholars have focused their attention on the question of whether this account of John's disciples and Jesus is historical.[43] The complex questions of the historical Jesus are not my concern here, but as suggested to me by Eve-Marie Becker (see note 37, above), if there was anything historical about John's inquiry to Jesus it was that, knowing that his death was imminent, John was concerned for the future of his disciples in these new circumstances. Who would take care of them and guide them after his death? Indeed, if one wanted to push this possibility to the extreme, in its original hypothetical context, John's request to his disciples to inquire of Jesus might have been an expression of John's superiority to Jesus. That is, as leader/founder of the movement, John was asking his disciple Jesus, whom he had baptized, and who perhaps had special stature among John's followers: what will be your role in *my* group after I am gone? In any case, as the incident was narrated in the gospels, it created the difficulty discussed above, because John was supposed to know that he was a mere forerunner, subordinate to Jesus.

Marcus's solution to the difficulty was summarized above, and it does not need full repetition here.[44] Marcus suggested that John affirmed Jesus's ministry and recognized Jesus as greater than himself, even if at the beginning John did not yet acknowledge Jesus as the Messiah. Marcus then explained the passages in Q, Matt 11:2–6 // Luke 7:18–23, in light of this interpretation of the sources. What I find problematic in this solution, again as indicated in greater detail above, is that even if Marcus's explanation does not have John acknowledge Jesus as Messiah at the outset, it has John recognize himself as inferior to Jesus, who was his superior. As such, it does not take adequate account of the consistent, prevalent, tendentious, and self-serving tendency of the gospels to have John accept Jesus as the greater figure in the scenario of end time.

---

42. Luz, *Matthew 1–7*, 303; Donald A. Hagner, *Matthew 1–13*, WBC 33A (Dallas: Word, 1993), 300.

43. E.g., Joseph A. Fitzmyer, *The Gospel according to Luke I–IX: Introduction, Translation and Notes*, AB 28A (New York: Doubleday, 1982), 663; Davies and Allison, *Critical and Exegetical Commentary*, 2:245.

44. See note 1.

Despite his pious perspective, I find Jean Daniélou more perceptive. He understood these passages as John placing himself in the hands
of Jesus.[45] While Daniélou took this as historical fact as now told in Q, I
prefer to see this account through the lens of the hermeneutic of suspicion.
John was presented as asking who was "the one to come" in order to eliminate himself from consideration for that role and thus clear the field for
Jesus to be the supreme individual of the end of days. As Alfred Plummer
put it, "John's sending to Jesus is strong evidence that he was not seriously
in doubt as to His Messiahship."[46]

## Bibliography

Bartsch, Shadi. *Actors in the Audience: Theatricality and Doublespeak from
Nero to Hadrian*. Revealing Antiquity 6. Cambridge: Harvard University Press, 1994.

Baumgarten, Albert I. "An Ancient Debate of Disciples." Pages 1–18 in *Perceiving the Other in Ancient Judaism and Early Christianity*. Edited by
Michal Bar-Asher Siegal, Wolfgang Grünstäudl, and Matthew Thiessen. WUNT 394. Tübingen: Mohr Siebeck, 2017.

———. "The Baptism of John in a Second Temple Jewish Context." Forthcoming.

———. "Four Stages in the Life of a Millennial Movement." Pages 61–75 in
*War in Heaven/Heaven on Earth: Theories of the Apocalyptic*. Edited
by Stephen D. O'Leary and Glen S. McGhee. London: Equinox, 2005.

———. "The 'Rule of the Martian' in the Ancient Diaspora: Celsus and
His Jew." Pages 398–430 in *Jews and Christians in the First and Second
Centuries: How to Write Their History*. Edited by Peter J. Tomson and
Joshua J. Schwartz. CRINT 13. Leiden: Brill, 2014.

Becker, Adam H., and Annette Yoshiko Reed, eds. *The Ways That Never
Parted: Jews and Christians in Late Antiquity and the Early Middle
Ages*. TSAJ 95. Tübingen: Mohr Siebeck, 2003.

Bovon, François. *Luke 1: A Commentary on the Gospel of Luke 1:1—9:50*.
Translated by J. Crouch. Hermeneia. Minneapolis: Fortress, 2012.

Cohen, Shaye J. D. *Josephus in Galilee and Rome: His* Vita *and Development
as a Historian*. Leiden: Brill, 1979.

---

45. Jean Daniélou, *The Work of John the Baptist*, trans. J. A. Horn (Baltimore:
Helicon, 1966), 118–19.
46. Plummer, *Gospel of St. Luke*, 202.

Daniélou, Jean. *The Work of John the Baptist*. Translated by J. A. Horn. Baltimore: Helicon, 1966.

Davies, W. D., and Dale C. Allison Jr. *A Critical and Exegetical Commentary on the Gospel according to Saint Matthew*. 3 vols. ICC. Edinburgh: T&T Clark, 1991.

Feldman, Louis H., trans. *Josephus, Jewish Antiquities: Books XVIII–XX*. LCL. Cambridge: Harvard University Press, 1965.

Fitzmyer, Joseph A. *The Gospel according to Luke I–IX: Introduction, Translation and Notes*, AB 28A. New York: Doubleday, 1982.

Gray, Rebecca. *Prophetic Figures in Late Second Temple Jewish Palestine: The Evidence from Josephus*. Oxford: Oxford University Press, 1993.

Hagner, Donald A. *Matthew 1–13*. WBC 33A. Dallas: Word, 1993.

Luz, Ulrich. *Matthew 1–7: A Commentary*. Translated by J. E. Crouch. Hermeneia. Minneapolis: Fortress, 2007.

Marcus, Joel. "John the Baptist and Jesus." Pages 179–97 in *When Judaism and Christianity Began: Essays in Memory of Anthony J. Saldarini*. Edited by Alan Avery Peck, Daniel Harrington, and Jacob Neusner. JSJSup 85. Leiden: Brill, 2004.

———. *Mark 1–8: A New Translation with Introduction and Commentary*. AB 27. New York: Doubleday, 2000.

Mason, Steve. *Flavius Josephus: Life of Josephus, Translation and Commentary*. FJTC 9. Leiden: Brill, 2003.

———. *Flavius Josephus on the Pharisees: A Composition-Critical Study*. StPB 39. Leiden: Brill, 1991.

———. "Josephus, Daniel and the Flavian House." Pages 161–91 in *Josephus and the History of the Greco-Roman Period: Essays in Memory of Morton Smith*. Edited by Fausto Parente and Joseph Sievers. StPB 41. Leiden: Brill, 1994.

Meier, John P. "Jesus in Josephus: A Modest Proposal." *CBQ* 52 (1990): 76–103.

———. "John the Baptist in Josephus: Philology and Exegesis." *JBL* 111 (1992): 225–37.

Momigliano, Arnaldo. "What Flavius Josephus Did Not See." Pages 67–78 in *Essays on Ancient and Modern Judaism*. Edited by Silvia Berti. Translated by Maura Masella-Gayley. Chicago: University of Chicago Press, 1994.

Niehoff, Maren. "A Jewish Critique of Christianity from Second Century Alexandria: Revisiting the Jew Mentioned in *Contra Celsum*." *JECS* 21 (2013): 151–75.

Noam, Vered. "Did the Rabbis Cause the Hasmoneans to Be Forgotten? A Reconsideration" [Hebrew]. *Zion* 81 (2016): 295–333.

Plummer, Alfred. *A Critical and Exegetical Commentary according to the Gospel of St. Luke.* ICC. Edinburgh: T&T Clark, 1914.

Rokeach, David. "Ben Stada Is Ben Pandira" [Hebrew]. *Tarbiz* 39 (1969–1970): 9–18.

Schäfer, Peter. *Jesus in the Talmud.* Princeton: Princeton University Press, 2007.

Scott, James. *Domination and the Arts of Resistance: Hidden Transcripts.* New Haven: Yale University Press, 1990.

Taylor, Joan E. *The Immerser: John the Baptist within Second Temple Judaism.* Grand Rapids: Eerdmans, 1997.

Wink, Walter. *John the Baptist in the Gospel Tradition.* SNTSMS 7. Cambridge: Cambridge University Press, 1968.

# Paul, the Animal Apocalypse,
# and Abraham's Gentile Seed

## Matthew Thiessen

One of the most striking claims that the apostle Paul made—and he made quite a few—is that gentiles, *as* gentiles, were not merely included in God's eschatological salvation in Christ but had also become sons and seed of Abraham.[1] To be sure, Jews frequently acknowledged that certain non-Jewish kinship groups were genealogically related to Abraham. After all, the ancestral narrative of Genesis explicitly links the Ammonites and Moabites to Lot, Abraham's nephew. Further, Genesis connects various kinship groups to Ishmael, Abraham's son through Hagar (Gen 25:12–18; compare with 1 Chr 1:28–31).[2] It also connects the Midianites and other kinship groups to the sons Abraham had through Keturah (Gen 25:1–6). Finally, it connects the Edomites to Esau, Abraham's grandson (Gen 36).

---

1. The former claim, as Paula Fredriksen and Terence Donaldson make clear, was fairly common among early Jews. Paula Fredriksen "Judaism, the Circumcision of Gentiles, and Apocalyptic Hope: Another Look at Galatians 1 and 2," *JTS* 42 (1991): 532–64; Terence Donaldson, *Judaism and the Gentiles: Jewish Patterns of Universalism (to 135 CE)* (Waco, TX: Baylor University Press, 2007).

2. For a discussion of the identity of the peoples associated with these figures, see Ralph W. Klein, *1 Chronicles: A Commentary*, Hermeneia (Minneapolis: Fortress, 2006), 72–73. The LXX of Gen 25 has ostensibly the same list of persons but with two slight modifications: first, Dumah (דומה) is rendered as Ἰδουμα; second, Jetur (יטור) is rendered as Ἰετουρ, although see the slight variations in a number of LXX manuscripts in John William Wevers, *Genesis*, SVTG 1 (Göttingen: Vandenhoeck & Ruprecht, 1974), 243. In Chronicles, the LXX translator renders יטור as Ἰεττουρ. It is possible, therefore, that the LXX translator of Genesis believed, on etymological grounds, that two of Ishmael's sons were the fathers of the Idumaeans and the Ituraeans, something the LXX translator of 1 Chronicles also believed.

As Israel Eph'al has noted, despite the fact that biblical texts make no link between Ishmael and the Arabs,[3] Second Temple Jews felt comfortable making just this connection as early as the second century BCE. For instance, Jub. 20.12–13 states, "Ishmael, his sons, Keturah's sons, and their sons went together and settled from Paran as far as the entrance of Babylon—in all the land toward the east opposite the desert. They mixed with one another and were called Arabs and Ishmaelites."[4] In the first century CE, Josephus too links Ishmael to the Arabs, stating that since Ishmael was circumcised at the age of thirteen, his descendants, the Arabians, circumcise their sons at the age of thirteen (*A.J.* 1.214; compare with *A.J.* 2.32, 213).

Even where Jewish writers were not constrained or tempted by the genealogical claims of Genesis or Chronicles, though, they at times forged genealogical bonds with non-Jewish groups. First Maccabees 12:20–21 purports to preserve the letter of the Spartan Areus, who claimed that the Spartans and Jews were brothers and that the Spartans were of the *genos* of Abraham. While this letter is surely fictional, it does show that at least one Second Temple Jew could make such a claim.[5]

None of this evidence, though, compares to Paul's claims that uncircumcised gentiles can be Abrahamic seed—a title that our extant Jewish literature reserves only for Isaac and those descended from him (and ultimately from Jacob, Gen 21:9). For ancient Jews, only Israelites (and then, later, Jews) are Abrahamic seed who have inherited or stand to inherit God's various promises to Abraham. As Terence L. Donaldson concludes, "The truly anomalous aspect is Paul's insistence that uncircumcised *ethnē-*

---

3. Israel Eph'al, "'Ishmael' and 'Arab(s)': A Transformation of Ethnological Terms," *JNES* 35 (1976): 225–35. See also Birgit van der Lans, "Belonging to Abraham's Kin: Genealogical Appeals to Abraham as a Possible Background for Paul's Abrahamic Argument," in *Abraham, the Nations, and the Hagarites: Jewish, Christian, and Islamic Perspectives on Kinship with Abraham*, ed. Martin Goodman, George H. van Kooten, and J. T. A. G. M. van Ruiten, TBN 13 (Leiden: Brill, 2010), 307–18.

4. Translations of Jubilees are taken from James C. VanderKam, *The Book of Jubilees*, CSCO 511 (Leuven: Peeters, 1989).

5. So Burkhart Cardauns, "Juden und Spartaner: Zur hellenistisch-judischen Literatur," *Hermes* 95 (1967): 317–24, and Erich S. Gruen, "The Purported Jewish-Spartan Affiliation," in *Transitions to Empire: Essays in Greco-Roman History, 360–146 B.C., in Honor of E. Badian*, ed. R. W. Wallace and E. M. Harris, Oklahoma Series in Classical Culture 21 (Norman: University of Oklahoma Press, 1996), 254–69.

in-Christ are at the same time full members of Abraham's 'seed' (*sperma*)."[6] I have made a similar claim that "Paul's belief that uncircumcised gentiles can be Abraham's heirs is without parallel" in early Judaism.[7]

## The Messianic Descendant of Abraham in the Animal Apocalypse

In this essay I would like to call into question this claim. Simply put, Paul's assertion that uncircumcised gentiles can become Abrahamic seed is not quite as anomalous as Donaldson and I have each suggested. Rather, a similar thought is preserved in the Animal Apocalypse, a Jewish work that was composed about two hundred years prior to Paul's letter to the Galatians. In this essay, then, I seek to show that what at first glance appears to be Paul doing something distinctive in relation to his fellow Jews was in fact anticipated about two hundred years before Paul in the Animal Apocalypse.

The Animal Apocalypse is remarkable for the way in which it consistently deploys kosher imagery throughout the book. This imagery suggests that there is an ontological gap between gentiles and Jews.[8] Originally humanity was bovid, yet after the sexual mating with angelic beings, humanity became a variety of different, predominantly nonkosher species. Only the line of Seth and Shem retained its original bovid nature.[9] Even Ishmael, Abraham's son, being a wild ass, is not kosher. While one might attribute this lack of kosherness to his mother, Hagar, who is an Egyptian, and thus a wolf (1 En. 89.13),[10] Esau shares the same mother and father

---

6. Terence Donaldson, "Paul within Judaism: A Critical Evaluation from a 'New Perspective' Perspective," in *Paul within Judaism: Restoring the First-Century Context to the Apostle*, ed. Mark D. Nanos and Magnus Zetterholm (Minneapolis: Fortress, 2015), 296.

7. Matthew Thiessen, *Paul and the Gentile Problem* (New York: Oxford University Press, 2016), 129.

8. David Bryan nicely stresses the irreducible significance of this imagery for the author's ideology. David Bryan, *Cosmos, Chaos and the Kosher Mentality*, JSPSup 12 (Sheffield: Sheffield Academic, 1995).

9. On the numerous words used to refer to cattle, see Patrick A. Tiller, *A Commentary on the Animal Apocalypse of 1 Enoch*, EJL 4 (Atlanta: Scholars Press, 1993), 226–27.

10. Of the gentiles, Kathy Ehrensperger states: "Almost all of them are wild animals, or, more precisely, predators, and no *domesticated* animals are included in this zoological park, with the exception of sheep, bulls, and cows…. Distinct from domes-

as Jacob, and yet he, too, is ontologically distinct—a black wild boar, not a
snow-white sheep like Jacob. Even more surprising, Jacob differs from his
father Isaac and his grandfather Abraham. Whereas Abraham and Isaac
are snow-white cows, Jacob becomes the first snow-white sheep. Thus,
he is pure like the Shemite line to which Abraham and Isaac belong, but
he is not himself a Shemite. Jacob's birth marks the beginning of a new
species—sheep. Contrary to August Dillmann, the introduction of sheep
at this point does not indicate a loss of power among the righteous line
of humanity. Rather, the shift from cattle to sheep signals the end of the
Sethite/Shemite line and the birth of the new nation of Israel.[11] The author
intends no criticism here of the birth of Israel.[12] After all, unlike the earlier
Shemites, the introduction of sheep signals the end of the possibility of
new species coming out of the pure line of humanity: from now on, sheep
give birth *only* to sheep. This distinction between Jacob and his father
and grandfather likely arises out of the author's reading of Gen 25:23,
which speaks of Jacob and Esau as two nations (גיים/ἔθνη) in Rebekah's
womb. This development, then, is a good thing. No further speciation
into impure animals occurs within Jacob's line. Significantly, even as the
author promotes this ideology, he is aware of and acknowledges Israel's
past sins. These sins, though, do not change the essential character of the
sheep. Sheep may become blinded and go astray (1 En. 89.33, 54; 90.26),
but sheep they remain. The work exhibits an essentializing understanding of what makes a Jew a Jew or an Israelite an Israelite or an Ishmaelite
an Ishmaelite.[13] From Jacob's generation onward, one's ethnic identity is

---

ticated animals, these wild animals are not guarded or guided by a fence or shepherd, but they are roaming wild. They exert destructive power when in contact with
domesticated animals. Thus, the core aspect they represent is conflict, most violent
conflict against the domesticated sheep and cattle." Kathy Ehrensperger, "The Pauline
Ἐκκλησίαι and Images of Community in Enoch Traditions," in *Paul the Jew: Rereading
the Apostle as a Figure of Second Temple Judaism*, ed. Gabriele Boccaccini and Carlos
Segovia (Minneapolis: Fortress, 2016), 204.

    11. Dillmann, *Das Buch Henoch* (Leipzig: Vogel, 1853), 255.

    12. Contrary to the claims of Tiller, *Commentary on the Animal Apocalypse*, 20,
and Daniel C. Olson, *A New Reading of the Animal Apocalypse of 1 Enoch: "All Nations
Shall be Blessed,"* SVTP 24 (Leiden: Brill, 2013), 54.

    13. Olson (*New Reading*, 76) rightly notes this same aspect to the color coding
of the work: "no animal in the allegory changes its color.... One's color seems as fixed
from birth as one's species. There is no indication that an animal has any choice about
its color, or any power to change it. Color coding in the allegory affirms that there is

something inherited and immutable. It runs in the blood and cannot be overcome. Once a gentile, always a gentile. Once a Jew, always a Jew.

The work, consequently, belongs within a stream of Jewish ideology of exclusion that conceived of ethnic identity as something immutable and irrevocable. It is no more likely that a gentile could turn himself or herself into a Jew than it is that a wolf or an ass or a camel could turn itself into a kosher animal such as a cow or sheep.[14] Yet within a text that promotes genealogical exclusion, there is also a profound confidence that Israel's God had not abandoned gentiles to their state of genealogical impurity. Long after all cows had disappeared from the earth, a snow-white cow will suddenly be born:

> Then I saw that a snow-white cow was born, with huge horns; all the beasts of the field and all the birds of the sky feared him and made petition to him all the time. I went on seeing until all their kindred were transformed, and became snow-white cows; and the first among them became something, and that something became a great beast with huge black horns on its head. The Lord of the sheep rejoiced over it and over all the cows. (1 En. 90.37–38 [trans. Isaac; *OTP* 1:71])[15]

Although the author does not delve into the manner in which the birth of this snow-white cow relates to the surprising transformation of the gentiles, it is clear that there is some connection between the two events. It

---

an element of strict determinism operating within the plane of history. The white are elect and the black are not."

14. On this exclusionary ideology, see Matthew Thiessen, *Contesting Conversion: Genealogy, Circumcision, and Identity in Ancient Judaism and Christianity* (New York: Oxford University Press, 2011).

15. I find no reason to agree with Günter Reese, Karlheinz Müller, and Andreas Bedenbender that these two verses are a later interpolation, since there is no textual support to their claims. Further, central to their arguments is the dubious assumption that one cannot be Israel-centric in one's thought and simultaneously hope for God's eschatological deliverance of the gentiles. Günter Reese, *Die Geschichte Israels in der Auffassung des frühen Judentums: Eine Untersuchung der Tiervision und der Zehnwochenapokalypse des äthiopischen Henochbuches, der Geschichtsdarstellung der Assumptio Mosis und der des 4Esrabuches*, BBB 123 (Berlin: Philo, 1999), 42–43, Karlheinz Müller, *Studien zur frühjüdischen Apokalyptik*, SBAB 11 (Stuttgart: Katholisches Bibelwerk, 1991), 164–66, and Andreas Bedenbender, *Der Gott der Welt tritt auf den Sinai: Entstehung, Entwicklung und Funktionsweise der frühjüdischen Apokalyptik*, ANTZ 8 (Berlin: Institut Kirche und Judentum, 2000), 208–11.

may not be accurate to call this newly born cow a messianic figure, but he is obviously a figure of considerable eschatological significance. Other interpreters have suggested that this eschatological bull is "the new Adam" or an allusion to Seth or to Noah,[16] but I wonder if it is not more accurate to refer to this bull as the seed of Abraham and Isaac, who were, after all, the last white cows to be born on earth. Further, unlike Adam, Seth, or Noah, this eschatological cow was born in the midst of a variety of unclean animals, just as Abraham and Isaac were (1 En. 89.10–11).[17] I do not intend to claim that these are mutually exclusive designations: ultimately, there is a line of white bulls that runs from Adam to Isaac that disappears and then miraculously reappears at the end of human history.

What is perhaps surprising to our minds, though, is that these various non-Jewish groups do not become Jews—God does not turn them into sheep, but cows after all.[18] These cows, then, are gentiles who once again belong to a righteous and pure line descended from Abraham. They are Abrahamic seed who inherit God's eschatological salvation as uncircumcised gentiles. One might even say, as does Paul, that, when the eschaton comes and this vision is fulfilled, these gentiles, "like Isaac, are children of the promise" (κατὰ Ἰσαὰκ ἐπαγγελίας τέκνα ἐστέ, Gal 4:28). Incidentally, I should stress, in contrast to scholars such as Patrick Tiller, who argues that "in the restored race of humanity there will be neither Jew nor Gentile, but one Adamic race,"[19] that even as the author envisages gentiles being

---

16. For Adam, see Johannes Pedersen, "Zur Erklärung der Eschatologischen Visionen Henochs," *Islamica* 2 (1926): 419, and J. T. Milik with Matthew Black, *The Books of Enoch: Aramaic Fragments of Qumrân Cave 4* (Oxford: Clarendon, 1976), 45. For Seth, see A. F. J. Klijn, "From Creation to Noah in the Second Dream-Vision of the Ethiopic Enoch," in *Miscellanea Neotestamentica*, ed. T. Baarda, A. F. J. Klijn, and W. C. Van Unnik, NovTSup 47 (Leiden: Brill, 1978), 158. For Noah, see George W. E. Nickelsburg, *1 Enoch 1: A Commentary on the Book of 1 Enoch, Chapters 1–36; 81–108*, Hermeneia (Minneapolis: Fortress, 2001), and Tiller, *Commentary on the Animal Apocalypse*, 384. For the "true" Jacob, see Olson, *New Reading*, 31.

17. Olson notes the parallel to Abraham, but fails to note the parallel to Isaac (*New Reading*, 28 n. 39). Nonetheless, Olson overinterprets the data that this white bull is the "true" Jacob (31).

18. Consequently, Christopher Rowland's claim that these gentiles are proselytes who accept torah and undergo circumcision is false. Christopher Rowland, *Christian Origins: An Account of the Setting and Character of the Most Important Messianic Sect of Judaism* (London: SPCK, 2002), 216.

19. Tiller, *Commentary on the Animal Apocalypse*, 385. Similarly, Nickelsburg, *1 Enoch 1*, 403, and Olson, *New Reading* 19–21. Tiller goes so far as to conclude that the

transformed into Abraham-like seed (that is, cows), he does not appear to
envisage Jews turning into cows. This passage, after all, explicitly has to do
with the beasts of the field and birds of the air, not the sheep. Further, the
author continues to call God the "Lord of the sheep," a designation that the
work uses of God only *after* Israel comes into existence. If God can only
be called the "Lord of the Sheep" after sheep are born, presumably he can
go by this title only as long as sheep continue to exist. Jews, for this author,
remain Jews.[20] Only gentiles transform into Sethite or Abrahamic (one
might even call it "Isaacic") humanity.[21]

### Christ, the Seed of Abraham

All of this thinking parallels quite closely Paul's claims in his Letter to the
Galatians, where he argues that his gentile readers in Galatia must not
undergo circumcision and adoption of the Jewish law (Gal 5:2–4). They
must not, in other words, judaize (2:14). Instead, they must place their
confidence in the fact that Israel's God has, in Christ Jesus, addressed the
gentile predicament. Paul, too, after all, thinks of Jewish and gentile identity in essentialist terms: he and Peter, he says, are Jews by nature (φύσει
Ἰουδαῖοι), and not (by nature) gentile sinners (2:15). As Pheme Perkins
notes, "By using the expression 'born Jews,' he makes it clear that there
is a boundary that [gentiles] can never cross, not even by being circumcised…. Paul resists any possibility that the differences would be erased
by Gentiles assimilating to Jewish practices."[22] Pauline scholars, especially those within the so-called New Perspective on Paul, often attempt

---

author thinks that the nation of Israel itself was one of the negative developments of
human history, a development that God obliterates at the eschaton (*Commentary on
the Animal Apocalypse*, 20). So too Olson: "In the end, the history of Israel the nation
serves no other purpose [than to illustrate moral responsibility], and it disappears
when the 'true Israel' appears" (*New Reading*, 14–15).

20. So, too, Donaldson, *Judaism and the Gentiles*, 88–89.

21. Genevieve Dibley makes a similar point in an unpublished paper entitled
"Abraham's Uncircumcised Children: The Enochic Precedent for Paul's Program of
Gentile Reclamation *qua* Gentiles," paper presented at the Annual Meeting of the
Society of Biblical Literature, San Diego, CA, 25 November 2014. See also Ehrens-
perger, "The Pauline Ἐκκλησίαι."

22. Pheme Perkins, *Abraham's Divided Children: Galatians and the Politics of
Faith*, The New Testament in Context (Harrisburg, PA: Trinity Press International,
2001), 58.

to distance Paul from this ethnic stereotyping and essentializing ideology. For instance, James D. G. Dunn claims that Paul is here merely "echoing the language of more traditional Jews." In fact, Dunn avers, "It is this very distinction that [Paul] will be going on to question."[23] But this essentializing understanding of Jewishness and gentileness is, well, essential to Paul's gospel.

This genealogical gap between Jews and gentiles creates quite a problem for Paul, since he is convinced that God has made a series of promises to Abraham that can only be enjoyed by those who are his seed. Paul claims that Abraham's seed is Christ (Gal 3:16). Because gentile followers of Christ have received Christ's *pneuma*—Christ's stuff—they have now been infused with an essence genealogically descended from Abraham himself.[24] They have become Abrahamic seed, as Paul says in Gal 3:29: "If you [gentiles] are of Christ [or, perhaps better, a body member of Christ], then you are the seed of Abraham, and heirs according to the promise." This genealogical descent that gentiles receive in Christ is no mere metaphor;[25] it represents Paul's conviction that in the reception of Christ's *pneuma* gentiles have undergone something akin to pneumatic gene therapy.

What does all of this mean for the study of Paul? Simply put, we cannot distance Paul from the supposedly ethnocentric and particularistic thinking of his fellow contemporary Jews. As Jon D. Levenson has

---

23. Quotations come from James D. G. Dunn, *The New Perspective on Paul*, rev. ed. (Grand Rapids: Eerdmans, 2008), 232 and 187.

24. On this claim, see Caroline Johnson Hodge, *If Sons, Then Heirs: A Study of Kinship and Ethnicity in the Letters of Paul* (Oxford: Oxford University Press, 2007), Stanley K. Stowers, "What Is 'Pauline Participation in Christ'?," in *Redefining First-Century Jewish and Christian Identities: Essays in Honor of Ed Parish Sanders*, ed. Fabian E. Udoh et al., CJA 16 (Notre Dame: University of Notre Dame Press, 2008), 352–71, and Thiessen, *Paul and the Gentile Problem*, 105–28.

25. For instance, note the hesitancy of C. K. Barrett, *From First Adam to Last: A Study in Pauline Theology* (New York: Scribners, 1962), 78: "'Descent,' if you may call it that, from Abraham is a matter of election, and it passes through Christ as through a channel, in whom all that the person of Abraham adumbrated was fulfilled. The old collectivity of race had to be destroyed in order that the new collectivity might be established in Christ." This verse also undermines the claims of J. Louis Martyn (*Galatians: A New Translation with Introduction and Commentary*, AB 33A [New York: Doubleday, 1997], 374–75), who suggests that Paul's concern with divine sonship in Galatians 3–4 minimizes the significance of Abrahamic sonship.

nicely put it, "For Paul, the Church is not just a particularistic community; *it is made up exclusively of descendants of Abraham.*"[26] Paul is deeply concerned about questions of descent, genealogy, and ethnicity. His gospel requires that gentiles become genealogically connected to Abraham in order to inherit God's promises to Abraham's seed. For Paul, this is no mere fictive kinship, but a kinship forged on the basis of the best type of matter—*pneuma*, not *sarx*.

### The Difference between Paul and the Animal Apocalypse

To this point I have tried to demonstrate that Paul's claims about uncircumcised gentiles becoming sons and seed of Abraham are not as unparalleled as previously thought. Both Paul and the author of the Animal Apocalypse believe that at the eschaton God will rewrite gentile DNA in order to genealogically connect them to Abraham. At the same time, the shape of this eschatological incorporation of the gentiles continues to distinguish them from Jews.

But there is one significant difference between Paul's claims and those of the Animal Apocalypse. According to the Animal Apocalypse, gentile sons and seed of Abraham are yet to appear. Their eschatological re-creation has not yet happened. While the author's views on what precisely the eschaton looks like are unclear, presumably he thought there would be a massive cosmological transformation accompanying this genealogical transformation of gentiles. In other words, the signs of the times would indicate clearly to all that the eschaton was indeed happening.

---

26. Jon D. Levenson, *Inheriting Abraham: The Legacy of the Patriarch in Judaism, Christianity, and Islam*, Library of Jewish Ideas (Princeton: Princeton University Press, 2012), 28. Levenson concludes that "one cannot adequately grasp Paul's theology without reckoning with this simple but momentous fact: for Paul, *the Gentile Christian has abandoned the Adamic identity for the Abrahamic*" (*Inheriting Abraham*, 157). Here I would note that there is a difference with the Animal Apocalypse, which sees Adam, Abraham, and gentiles at the eschaton belonging to the same genealogical trajectory. Martha Himmelfarb makes a similar point: "Paul does not simply claim that the difference between Jews and gentiles is no longer relevant; he insists that gentiles too have become children of Abraham, and he supports this radical claim by means of exegesis of the Jews' own authoritative scriptures." Martha Himmelfarb, *A Kingdom of Priests: Ancestry and Merit in Ancient Judaism* (Philadelphia: University of Pennsylvania Press, 2006), 177.

Paul, on the other hand, was convinced that the eschaton had arrived. As he tells his readers in Corinth, he and they belong amongst those "upon whom the ends of the ages has come" (εἰς οὓς τὰ τέλη τῶν αἰώνων κατήντηκεν, 1 Cor 10:11). Paul's claims are predicated upon his assumption that God's eschatological salvation has *now* come in Christ. Paul may well believe that God's Messiah has come in order to address the gentile problem. But what evidence do others have to confirm these facts? Where is the cosmological transformation evident? How can people who do not believe that Jesus is Israel's Messiah confirm Paul's assertions about a new genealogical connection between Abraham and gentiles forged by Christ's *pneuma*? Since there is simply no empirical evidence for Paul's claim, who can blame others, be they Jews or non-Jews, for concluding that Paul is guilty of brazenly destroying barriers and boundaries that Israel's God had set up between the seed of Jacob and the rest of the nations? To anyone unconvinced by Paul's claims that the eschaton has arrived, it looks like Paul's gentile communities are willfully appropriating Jewish identity for themselves in a way that would undermine and possibly undo Jewish identity. If uncircumcised gentiles are now reckoned among Abraham's inheriting seed, is there any room left for Jewish identity? Paul thinks so, as he makes clear in Rom 3:1–2 and 9:1–5, but the long history of interpretation of Paul's letters shows that most of his readers concluded otherwise.

Even if one believes Paul that gentile followers of Christ and Jewish followers of Christ are now equally Abrahamic seed, what are the social implications? Can a Jewish follower of Christ marry his daughter off to an uncircumcised gentile follower of Christ? They are, after all, both Abrahamic seed! But they are not precisely the same Abrahamic seed. The gentile follower is akin to the white cattle of the Animal Apocalypse. He may now be purified, but he is not the same species as the Jewish follower of Christ, who is akin to the white sheep of the Animal Apocalypse. Surely, their shared purity does not suggest that a cow and a sheep should breed. It is precisely these sorts of lived social issues that likely plagued the early Christ-following movement. No wonder some followers of Jesus, both Jews and gentiles, wanted to simplify things by trying to turn cows into sheep, so to speak. How much easier things would have been were all followers of Jesus turned into sheep. Or, to draw from Paul's own language, how much easier it would be if all the branches growing out of the cultivated olive tree consisted of cultivated olive wood, not a mixture of wild and cultivated. Paul's gospel, though, insists upon the absolute necessity of difference, while at the same time making claims about Jews and gentiles being Abraham's seed, and about Greekness and Jewishness—circumcision and uncircumcision—meaning nothing for those in Christ. Internally, how do Pauline communities build and sustain unity when Paul's letters emphatically reassert ethnic difference—or at least the distinction between Jews and non-Jews? On an olive tree this might be easy, but what about human relations? If Jewish believers are to continue in their Jewishness, and gentile believers in their gentileness (but righteously!), then over and over again gentile believers might feel like they were missing out on things like Sabbath, dietary laws, circumcision, and so on. In fact, Paul's *refusal* to permit gentiles to do these things would almost inevitably result in a sense of inferiority.

## Conclusion

In his depiction of Israel's history and the inclusion of gentiles at the eschaton, the author of the Animal Apocalypse anticipated Paul's claims that uncircumcised gentiles could become Abrahamic descendants by almost two centuries. For both authors, the gentiles are made Abrahamic seed not through anything they have done, such as law observance, but through an act of God that is in some way connected to an eschatological figure who precipitates this genealogical transformation. It is not so much the structure, or even the content, of Paul's thinking that differs from a work like the Animal Apocalypse, but the timing. But this is no small difference. The timing of his claim opens Paul's gospel up to much misunderstanding, both by those outside Paul's communities, who have very good reasons to worry about what looks like an inexcusable erasure of the boundary between Jew and gentile, and by those inside Paul's communities, who were trying to figure out how Jewish seed of Abraham and gentile seed of Abraham were meant to live together now that the end of the ages has come and yet not quite come.

## Bibliography

Barrett, C. K. *From First Adam to Last: A Study in Pauline Theology.* New York: Scribner's Sons, 1962.

Bedenbender, Andreas. *Der Gott der Welt tritt auf den Sinai: Entstehung, Entwicklung und Funktionsweise der frühjüdischen Apokalyptik.* ANTZ 8. Berlin: Institut Kirche und Judentum, 2000.

Bryan, David. *Cosmos, Chaos and the Kosher Mentality*. JSPSup 12. Sheffield: Sheffield Academic, 1995.

Cardauns, Burkhart. "Juden und Spartaner: Zur hellenistisch-judischen Literatur." *Hermes* 95 (1967): 317–24.

Dibley, Genevieve. "Abraham's Uncircumcised Children: The Enochic Precedent for Paul's Program of Gentile Reclamation *qua* Gentiles." Paper presented at the Annual Meeting of the Society of Biblical Literature. San Diego, CA. 25 November 2014.

Dillmann, August. *Das Buch Henoch*. Leipzig: Vogel, 1853.

Donaldson, Terence. *Judaism and the Gentiles: Jewish Patterns of Universalism [to 135 CE]*. Waco, TX: Baylor University Press, 2007.

——. "Paul within Judaism: A Critical Evaluation from a 'New Perspective' Perspective." Pages 277–301 in *Paul within Judaism: Restoring the First-Century Context to the Apostle*. Edited by Mark D. Nanos and Magnus Zetterholm. Minneapolis: Fortress, 2015.

Dunn, James D. G. *The New Perspective on Paul*. Rev. ed. Grand Rapids: Eerdmans, 2008.

Ehrensperger, Kathy. "The Pauline Ἐκκλησίαι and Images of Community in Enoch Traditions." Pages 183–216 in *Paul the Jew: Rereading the Apostle as a Figure of Second Temple Judaism*. Edited by Gabriele Boccaccini and Carlos Segovia. Minneapolis: Fortress, 2016.

Eph'al, Israel. "'Ishmael' and 'Arab(s)': A Transformation of Ethnological Terms." *JNES* 35 (1976): 225–35.

Fredriksen, Paula. "Judaism, the Circumcision of Gentiles, and Apocalyptic Hope: Another Look at Galatians 1 and 2." *JTS* 42 (1991): 532–64.

Gruen, Erich S. "The Purported Jewish-Spartan Affiliation." Pages 254–69 in *Transitions to Empire: Essays in Greco-Roman History, 360–146 B.C., in Honor of E. Badian*. Edited by R. W. Wallace and E. M. Harris. Oklahoma Series in Classical Culture 21. Norman: University of Oklahoma Press, 1996.

Himmelfarb, Martha. *A Kingdom of Priests: Ancestry and Merit in Ancient Judaism*. Philadelphia: University of Pennsylvania Press, 2006.

Hodge, Caroline Johnson. *If Sons, Then Heirs: A Study of Kinship and Ethnicity in the Letters of Paul*. Oxford: Oxford University Press, 2007.

Klein, Ralph W. *1 Chronicles: A Commentary*. Hermeneia. Minneapolis: Fortress, 2006.

Klijn, A. F. J. "From Creation to Noah in the Second Dream-Vision of the Ethiopic Enoch." Pages 147–60 in *Miscellanea Neotestamentica*. Edited by T. Baarda, A. F. J. Klijn, and W. C. Van Unnik. NovTSup 47. Leiden: Brill, 1978.

Lans, Birgit van der. "Belonging to Abraham's Kin: Genealogical Appeals to Abraham as a Possible Background for Paul's Abrahamic Argument." Pages 307–18 in *Abraham, the Nations, and the Hagarites: Jewish, Christian, and Islamic Perspectives on Kinship with Abraham.* Edited by Martin Goodman, George H. van Kooten, and J. T. A. G. M. van Ruiten. TBN 13. Leiden: Brill, 2010.

Levenson, Jon D. *Inheriting Abraham: The Legacy of the Patriarch in Judaism, Christianity, and Islam.* Library of Jewish Ideas. Princeton: Princeton University Press, 2012.

Martyn, J. Louis. *Galatians: A New Translation with Introduction and Commentary.* AB 33A. New York: Doubleday, 1997.

Milik, J. T., with Matthew Black. *The Books of Enoch: Aramaic Fragments of Qumrân Cave 4.* Oxford: Clarendon, 1976.

Müller, Karlheinz. *Studien zur frühjüdischen Apokalyptik.* SBAB 11. Stuttgart: Katholisches Bibelwerk, 1991.

Nickelsburg, George W. E. *1 Enoch 1: A Commentary on the Book of 1 Enoch, Chapters 1–36; 81–108.* Hermeneia. Minneapolis: Fortress, 2001.

Olson, Daniel C. *A New Reading of the Animal Apocalypse of 1 Enoch: "All Nations Shall be Blessed."* SVTP 24. Leiden: Brill, 2013.

Pedersen, Johannes. "Zur Erklärung der Eschatologischen Visionen Henochs." *Islamica* 2 (1926): 416–29.

Perkins, Pheme. *Abraham's Divided Children: Galatians and the Politics of Faith.* The New Testament in Context. Harrisburg, PA: Trinity Press International, 2001.

Reese, Günter. *Die Geschichte Israels in der Auffassung des frühen Judentums: Eine Untersuchung der Tiervision und der Zehnwochenapokalypse des äthiopischen Henochbuches, der Geschichtsdarstellung der Assumptio Mosis und der des 4Esrabuches.* BBB 123. Berlin: Philo, 1999.

Rowland, Christopher. *Christian Origins: An Account of the Setting and Character of the Most Important Messianic Sect of Judaism.* London: SPCK, 2002.

Stowers, Stanley K. "What Is 'Pauline Participation in Christ'?" Pages 352–71 in *Redefining First-Century Jewish and Christian Identities: Essays in Honor of Ed Parish Sanders.* Edited by Fabian E. Udoh et al. CJA 16. Notre Dame: University of Notre Dame Press, 2008.

Thiessen, Matthew. *Contesting Conversion: Genealogy, Circumcision, and Identity in Ancient Judaism and Christianity*. New York: Oxford University Press, 2011.

———. *Paul and the Gentile Problem*. New York: Oxford University Press, 2016.

Tiller, Patrick A. *A Commentary on the Animal Apocalypse of 1 Enoch*. EJL 4. Atlanta: Scholars Press, 1993.

VanderKam, James C. *The Book of Jubilees*. CSCO 511. Leuven: Peeters, 1989.

Wevers, John William. *Genesis*. SVTG 1. Göttingen: Vandenhoeck & Ruprecht, 1974.

# Unveiling Death in 2 Corinthians

Susan Grove Eastman

As an astonishing sequence from Saint Paul shows: "We all, with face unveiled and revealed (*anakekalummenō prosōpō*), serving as an optical mirror to reflect (*katoptrizomenoi*) the glory of the Lord, we are transformed in and according to his icon (*eikona*), passing from glory to glory, according to the spirit of the Lord" (2 Cor 3:18). It seems practically useless (and impossible as well) even to outline a commentary.[1]

Jean-Luc Marion's words, "it seems practically useless (and impossible as well) even to outline a commentary," could well warn off any further commentary on Paul's notoriously difficult evocation of veiling and unveiling in 2 Cor 3–4. But that difficulty has not stopped many interpreters from trying. Indeed, ignoring his own advice, Marion adds:

In the vision, no visible is discovered, if not our face itself, which, renouncing all grasping (*aesthesis*) submits to an apocalyptic exposure ... here our gaze becomes the optical mirror of that at which it looks only by finding itself more radically looked at: we become a visible mirror of an invisible gaze that subverts us in the measure of its glory. The invisible summons us, "face to face, person to person" (1 Cor 13:12).[2]

Here Marion deploys Paul's puzzling phrase in 2 Cor 3:18, "beholding as in a mirror" (κατοπτριζόμενοι),[3] to articulate the role of icons: rather than

---

I dedicate this contrarian essay to my old comrade Joel, in celebration of his frank speaking and enduring friendship.

1. Jean-Luc Marion, *God without Being* (Chicago: University of Chicago Press, 2012), 21–22.

2. Marion, *God without Being*, 22.

3. Unless otherwise indicated, all biblical translations are my own.

becoming a final resting place for the human gaze, such that the invisible and transcendent is reduced to a visible object, icons invite the viewer into a reciprocal exchange in which she discovers herself as "the mirror of an invisible gaze." The gaze subverts because it reframes self-knowledge in light of God's glory, and it welcomes the viewer into a face-to-face encounter that transforms, such that unveiled human faces become mirrors of God.

Marion's comments highlight the *visual* aspects of Paul's language in 2 Cor 3–4.[4] This visuality plays out in both negative and positive depictions: positively, vision and transformation are closely linked (3:18), and they are accompanied by openness and frankness of speech. Negatively, the obstruction of vision signals a lack of communication and understanding. Both vision and its absence are communicated through the image of the veil: Moses's veiled face (3:13), and the unveiled faces of "all of us" who behold the glory of the Lord as in a mirror (3:18). It is this image that forms the focus of this study, through attention to three interpretive probes: First, in the cultural context of Paul's Corinthian auditors, what are the connotations of veiling and unveiling faces, particularly male faces? Second, what themes are highlighted by the conjunction of such connotations with Paul's interpretation of the Sinai story? Third, how are these themes amplified in the larger context of 2 Cor 1–7?

## The Problem of Moses's Veil

In his advice to orators, Quintilian discusses figures of speech that conceal rather than disclose the realities at issue. He uses examples from visual art to get across his meaning:

> In a picture, the full face is most attractive. But Apelles painted Antigonus in profile, to conceal the blemish caused by the loss of one eye. So too, in speaking, there are certain things which have to be concealed, either because they ought not to be disclosed or because they cannot be expressed as they deserve. Timanthes, who was, I think, a native of Cynthus, provides an example of this in the picture with which he won the victory over Colotes of Teos. It represented the sacrifice of Iphigenia,

---

4. For extensive discussion of the visual aspects of 2 Cor 2:14–3:17, see Jane Heath, *Paul's Visual Piety: The Metamorphosis of the Beholder* (Oxford: Oxford University Press, 2013), 197–225.

and the artist had depicted an expression of grief on the face of Calchas and of still greater grief on that of Ulysses, while he had given Menelaus an agony of sorrow beyond which his art could not go. Having exhausted his powers of emotional expression he was at a loss to portray the father's face as it deserved, and solved the problem by veiling his head (*velavit eius caput*) and leaving his sorrow to the imagination of the spectator. (*Inst.* 2.13 [Butler])

The grief of Iphigenia's father exceeded representation, says Quintilian, so the painter Timanthes veiled the father's face, inviting the viewers to supply the hidden emotion. As material objects covering human faces, veils invite and indeed require the spectators to supply what is obscured, by using their culturally shaped imaginations. So also, the accomplished orator will leave narrative gaps in his speech, not saying too much but rather allowing his audience to fill in the lacunae, guided by verbal cues.

The veil covering Moses's face is just such a narrative gap, both in Paul's retelling of the Sinai story and in Exod 34 itself. Exodus implies that Moses covers his face because it shines so intensely from the divine presence that the sons of Israel cannot bear to look at it (Exod 34:30). Paul evokes this implication in 2 Cor 3:7, when he says, "the sons of Israel were unable to gaze intently at Moses's face because of its glory." But, in fact, the Israelites do look at Moses's shining face, not once but repeatedly; every time Moses goes in before the Lord he removes the veil, and he does not replace it until after he delivers God's words to Israel (Exod 34:33–35). In a suggestive exploration of the reception history of Moses's veil, Brian Britt discusses this odd discrepancy, observing that Moses puts on the veil when he is not speaking, whether to the Lord or the people. He puts on the veil, that is, when he is incommunicado: "The covered prophet is a silent prophet."[5] Francis Watson also notes this pattern and the question it leaves unanswered—why the veil? As Watson observes, "At the heart of Paul's reading is an attempt to provide a solution to a problem posed by the text itself."[6]

The problem for modern readers of Paul's solution is that he compounds the mystery behind Moses's veil rather than illuminating it. Paul says, "Having such a hope, we have great boldness [παρρησία], not like

---

5. Brian M. Britt, *Rewriting Moses: The Narrative Eclipse of the Text*, JSOTSup 402 (London: T&T Clark, 2004), 86.

6. Francis Watson, *Paul and the Hermeneutics of Faith* (New York: T&T Clark, 2004), 292.

Moses, who put a veil over his face so that the sons of Israel could not gaze intently at τὸ τέλος τοῦ καταργουμένου" (2 Cor 3:12–13). Every aspect of this enigmatic phrase is debated. As Richard Hays quips, "It is hard to escape the impression that, to this day, when 2 Corinthians 3 is read a veil lies over our minds."[7] If we take a cue from Quintilian, however, we might ask how Paul's first-century auditors would fill in the meaning of the veil covering Moses's face. Doing so shines a spotlight on certain themes in Paul's dense and convoluted argument in 2 Cor 3–4: liminal status, death, and separation that impedes understanding. These themes in turn receive fuller, paradoxical development in the larger context of 2 Cor 1–7.

### Cultural Valences of the Veil

I begin by imaginatively taking a seat among the Corinthians as they listen to Paul's words depicting Moses putting a veil over his face. What might be the valence of such a covering? In a wide-ranging study of the multivalent meanings of the veil, focusing on its occurrence in ancient Greek culture but also extending into the time of the empire, Douglas Cairns identifies two recurring motifs in both women's and men's veiling: concealment of strong negative emotions, particularly grief, and concealment of a liminal state or change in status, often although not always associated with death. In both ways, the veil marks a separation from one's social relationships.[8]

Veils were used by women, and occasionally by men, to hide strong expressions of emotion, particularly grief.[9] Timanthes's depiction of a veil over the face of Iphigenia's father is a case in point. The Old Greek

---

7. Richard B. Hays, *Echoes of Scripture in the Letters of Paul* (New Haven: Yale University Press, 1989), 123.

8. Douglas Cairns, "The Meaning of the Veil in Ancient Greek Culture," in *Women's Dress in the Ancient Greek World*, ed. L. Lewellyn-Jones (London: Duckworth, 2002), 73–93. In a discussion of male veiling and its significance in the use of icons in the Byzantine era, Glenn Peers makes a similar point; see Glenn Peers, "Icons' Spirited Love," *RelArts* 13 (2009): 218–47. After noting Odysseus's assumption of a veil at transitional points in his journey, Peers adds, "Other heroes of the ancient world, like Achilles, Ajax, Oedipus, and Hippolytus for example, also veiled themselves at critical junctures. Covering and uncovering the face were always potent acts in the Greek world that connoted uncertainty, transition, and ambivalence, among other meanings" (227–28).

9. See Cairns, "Meaning of the Veil," 74–76. For an example from the late first century BCE, see Chariton's romance, *De Charea et Callirhoe*. Callirhoe frequently

also provides a striking example of such veiling, in the account of David's response to the news of Absalom's treachery:

> And David went up the ascent of the [Mount of] Olives, ascending and weeping and veiling his head [ἀναβαίνων καὶ κλαίων καὶ τὴν κεφαλὴν ἐπικεκαλυμμένος], and he went up barefoot, and all the people went up with him, [every] man veiling his head, ascending and weeping [ἀναβαίνων καὶ κλαίων καὶ τὴν κεφαλὴν ἐπικεκαλυμμένος]. (2 Sam 15:30)

Here veiling masks grief, and nothing impugns either David's masculine stature or that of each man (ἀνήρ) who emulates him. If anything, the text's emphasis on the masculinity of those who follow David enhances his stature in what otherwise might be considered questionable behavior. Yet, at the same time, the veil also covers David's liminal status as his kingship is brought into question by Absalom's actions.

In many instances, male veiling of the face carries a whiff or a full-blown stench of shameful behavior. Suetonius and Tacitus record Nero's mock marriage in which, veiled as a bride, he insisted on a public wedding ceremony with a castrated boy.[10] The sense of shame carries over into metaphorical uses of the term; men veil depraved appetites and shameful actions.[11] Sometimes the veil is simply a metaphor for shame itself, as in a striking example from Jeremiah:

> From our youth shame [αἰσχύνη] has devoured our fathers' labors.... We fell asleep in our shame, and our dishonor veiled us [ἐκοιμήθημεν ἐν τῇ αἰσχύνῃ ἡμῶν καὶ ἐπεκάλυψεν ἡμᾶς ἡ ἀτιμία ἡμῶν], because we and our fathers sinned against the Lord our God from our youth even to this day; and we did not obey the voice of the Lord our God. (Jer 3:25)[12]

The shame here is not due to a transgression of cultural norms but to disobedience to God's commandments.

---

veils herself when she weeps; sometimes she covers her face (1.2.6) and sometimes her head (1.11.2; 3.3.14).

10. Suetonius, *Nero* 6.28.1; Tacitus, *Ann.* 15.37. See also Juvenal, *Sat.* 2.19–27, where he lampoons similar "weddings."

11. Tacitus, *Ann.* 6.51; 6.20; 11.21; Seneca, *Ep.* 1.16.57; Plutarch, *Ages.* 37.6.

12. Again, in Jeremiah's lament over the drought that devastates Judah, the farmers are put to shame; they express their shame by veiling their heads: ᾐσχύνθησαν γεωργοί ἐπεκάλυψαν τὴν κεφαλὴν αὐτῶν (Jer 14:4).

In 2 Cor 3:13, does Moses's veil cover such shame? Does it, perhaps, cover the judgment that issues in such shame? I am not arguing for a scriptural echo here but rather exploring the complex valences of veiling as covering something that is hidden from public view, whether strong emotion or shame, or both. But veiling also covers liminal states and in particular the state of death or impending death.[13] A particularly telling example comes from Plutarch's account of the suicide of Demosthenes. Cornered by his enemies, Demosthenes asks for time to write a letter before being taken captive:

> "Wait a little, then, that I may write a message to my family." With these words, he retired into the temple, and taking a scroll, as if about to write, he put his pen to his mouth and bit it, as he was wont to do when thinking what he should write, and kept it there some time, then covered and bent his head [εἶτα συγκαλυψάμενος ἀπέκλινε τὴν κεφαλήν]. The spearmen, then, who stood at the door, laughed at him for playing the coward, and called him weak and unmanly [μαλακὸν ἀπεκάλουν καὶ ἄνανδρον], but Archias came up and urged him to rise, and reiterating the same speeches as before, promised him a reconciliation with Antipater. But Demosthenes, now conscious that the poison was affecting and overpowering him, uncovered his head [ἐξεκαλύψατο], and fixing his eyes upon Archias [καὶ διαβλέψας πρὸς τὸν Ἀρχίαν]. (*Demosth.* 29.3 [Perrin])

Demosthenes gets up, stumbles outside, and dies. But he has the last word, a manly word accompanied by a direct gaze, vindicated through his self-chosen death.

In the story his veil functions in at least three ways: it hides Demosthenes's action and perhaps his emotion; it hides his transition from life to death; and it is misread by the soldiers, who naturally interpret it as unmanly, soft behavior—behavior, that is, like that of feminine Callirhoe hiding grief. Only when Demosthenes unveils his face and looks Archias in the eye is his masculine status restored. Cairns comments,

> The concealment which his enemies took to imply disgrace was a foil for the greater glory of a self-chosen death, a moral victory which lives forever in Plutarch's anecdote. So the ἀρετή of the successful male … must

---

13. Sometimes, although not always, a veil was placed over the face of a corpse. See, e.g., Seneca, *Marc.* 15.3.

be allowed to shine; it requires revelation, not concealment, proclamation, not silence. Silence, on the other hand, is a woman's ornament.[14]

Plutarch's account of Demosthenes thus illustrates not only the use of a veil to cover and simultaneously convey a transition from life to death, but also the questionable status associated with masculine veiling, precisely because it may connote effeminacy.[15] The veil conceals a liminal state on the way to death; it obstructs communication as well as vision; and it certainly impedes a proper understanding on the part of Demosthenes's captors. These themes are summed up in Cairns's concluding observations:

> Veiling occurs when one's social self, the public identity to which one was previously committed, is challenged or threatened, whether in reality or in ritual—when one's honour is impugned or at stake (and when one's veiling will express embarrassment, shame, or anger), when one's status as a participant in a relationship is undone by death.[16]

Thus, male veiling of the face conveys a variety of social messages. It may indicate extreme grief and loss; it may hide shameful behaviors or convey a sense of shame; it may hide death or a transition from life to death. Surely the Corinthians' cultural imagination would not be immune to these complex practices and the valences of veiling for both men and women, not only in Corinthian culture, but also in their common life and worship.[17] The image of Moses wearing a veil comes within the ambit of such valences, such that it seems unlikely that they would picture the veil as hiding a static, consistent and positive emotion or status—for example,

---

14. Cairns, "Meaning of the Veil," 80. See also Peers, "Icons," 227.

15. A woman covers herself as a sign of modesty (αἰδώς); an honorable man needs no such cover but rather acts with openness and frankness (παρρησία). For a New Testament text associating modesty (αἰδώς) with women's dress and silence, see 1 Tim 2:9–11.

16. Cairns, "Meaning of the Veil," 81–82.

17. In fact, we know that questions about women's and men's head coverings already have arisen in their worship together and that Paul addresses these issues in terms of honor and shame (1 Cor 11:4–6, 14–15). See the extensive discussion in Anthony Thiselton, *The First Epistle to the Corinthians*, NIGTC (Grand Rapids: Eerdmans, 2000), 823–33. For discussion of male veiling in the context of prayer and worship, see Richard Oster, "When Men Wore Veils to Worship: The Historical Context of 1 Corinthians II.4," *NTS* 34 (1988): 481–505. The key point here is that veiling is seen culturally as a matter of honor and shame along gender lines.

an enduring state of glory. Rather, they might wonder whether Moses's veil covered a change in status, even a transition from life to death.

Just as the story of Iphigenia and visual clues in Timanthes's painting hint at the grief hidden behind the veil covering Iphigenia's father's face, so the story of Sinai and the clues in Paul's interpretation hint at the enigma behind Moses's veil. With the emotive valences of male veiling in mind, therefore, I turn to Paul's treatment of Moses's veil in 2 Cor 3:1–4:6, and to links between that puzzling argument and the larger context of 2 Cor 1–7. As we shall see, attentiveness to the connotations of male veiling highlights two aspects of that treatment: first, the contrast between open proclamation and manifestation, on the one hand, and "the hidden things of shame" (ἀπειπάμεθα τὰ κρυπτὰ τῆς αἰσχύνης), on the other; second, the juxtaposition of life and death, sometimes sharply distinguished from each other, sometimes so compressed as to denote a single reality.

## Paul and Moses in 2 Corinthians 3

Paul's first explicit reference to Moses's veil starkly contrasts the ministry of Moses and that of Paul and his fellow missionaries:

> Ἔχοντες οὖν τοιαύτην ἐλπίδα πολλῇ παρρησίᾳ χρώμεθα καὶ οὐ καθάπερ Μωϋσῆς ἐτίθει κάλυμμα ἐπὶ τὸ πρόσωπον αὐτοῦ πρὸς τὸ μὴ ἀτενίσαι τοὺς υἱοὺς Ἰσραὴλ εἰς τὸ τέλος τοῦ καταργουμένου.

> Having such a hope, we are very bold, not like Moses, who used to put a veil over his face, so that the sons of Israel might not gaze upon the τέλος of what was being annulled. (2 Cor 3:12–13)

Several characteristics of this packed statement stand out for further investigation: the contrast between Moses's veiled face and the παρρησία of Paul and his coworkers; the function of hope as the basis for Paul's παρρησία; the translation of τέλος; the translation of τοῦ καταργουμένου and its referent. Pondering the significance of Moses covering his face, we particularly notice the emphatic contrast between Paul's παρρησία and Moses's veil and the transient sense of the phrase, τοῦ καταργουμένου, over against "what abides" (τὸ μένον) in 3:11.

By this point in the letter, Paul has established two patterns of opposing statements that set the stage for his depiction of the veiled Moses. First, in a chiastic series of parallel clauses, Paul employs a grammatical pattern of "not this, but that" (οὐ … ἀλλά):

A. You show [φανερούμενοι] that you are a letter of Christ ministered by us, written *not* with ink *but* with the Spirit of the living God, *not* on tablets of stone *but* on tablets of fleshly hearts (3:3)

B. Such is the confidence [Πεποίθησιν] that we have through Christ toward God, *not* that we are competent [ἱκανοί] of ourselves to consider anything as coming from ourselves, *but* our competence is from God, who has made us competent as ministers of a new covenant (3:4–6a)

A. *not* of the writing *but* of the Spirit, for [γάρ] the writing kills, but the Spirit makes alive (3:6b).

The contrast in 3:3 between different *kinds* of writing—not in ink but with the Spirit of the living God—and different *locations* for the writing—not on stone but on fleshly hearts—is amplified in 3:6 by the contrast between an implied written covenant and the new covenant, which is of the Spirit. These oppositions bracket the claim that Paul's ministry is not based on a self-generated competence (ἱκανός) but on competence that originates in God and thereby generates confidence in God.

This juxtaposition of human incompetence with confidence in God picks up on the question of 2:16b–17, which also uses the contrastive pattern, οὐ … ἀλλά:

> Who is competent [ἱκανός] for these things? For *we are not*, like so many, peddlers of the word of God, *but* as from sincerity, *but* as from God, in the sight of God we speak in Christ [κατέναντι θεοῦ ἐν Χριστῷ λαλοῦμεν].

"These things" refer back to Paul's immediately preceding depiction of his mission as a divinely led triumphal procession in Christ, giving out an aroma "from death to death" for the perishing and "from life to life" for those being saved (2:14–16a). This theme of death and life is the first motif highlighted by the image of a veiled face; it resurfaces in 3:6–7: "the writing kills, but the Spirit makes alive."

## From Life to Death

The Spirit gives life because it is the Spirit of the living God (v. 3), who alone can make alive. But why and in what way does the writing kill? In 3:7–11, Paul proceeds to answer that implicit question, through a new set of contrasts between his ministry and that of Moses, set forth in a repeated *qal wahomer* rhetorical pattern: "If ... then how much more ..." (εἰ ... πολλῷ μᾶλλον ...):

> Now *if* the ministry of death [Εἰ δὲ ἡ διακονία τοῦ θανάτου], carved in letters on stone, came in glory so that the sons of Israel could not gaze upon the face of Moses because of the glory of his face, a glory that is being annulled [τὴν καταργουμένην], *how much more* will the ministry of the Spirit be glorious? (3:7–8)

> For *if* there was glory in the ministry of condemnation, *how much more* does the ministry of righteousness abound in glory? (3:9)

> For *if* what is being annulled [τὸ καταργούμενον] [came] through glory, *how much more* glorious is what abides? (3:11)

Interpreters who want to argue for Paul's continuity with Moses and a positive assessment of the Mosaic covenant, emphasize the way the *qal wahomer* argument depends on a positive view of the original glory of the Mosaic covenant, as indeed it does. The glory of Moses's ministry is divine glory; the glory on Moses's face is divine glory. Paul is not denigrating the giving of the Mosaic covenant but rather deploying that original glory to communicate the much greater glory of the new covenant. He makes this purpose clear in his explanatory sentence, "for what once had glory has come to have no glory, because of the surpassing glory" (3:10).

Along the way, however, Paul also characterizes the giving of the commandments on Sinai in three important ways: it was a "ministry of death" (3:7); it was a "ministry of condemnation" (3:9); and it is "being done away with" or "annulled" (3:11, 13).[18] Over against this three-fold depiction is the contrasting depiction of the ministry of the new covenant (3:6) as "the ministry of the Spirit" (3:7), "the ministry of righteousness" (3:9),

---

18. In 3:7, Paul uses the feminine singular participle καταργουμένην to modify the glory of Moses's face as being brought to an end; in 3:11 and 3:13, he uses the neuter singular participle in a general sense to refer to the preceding depiction (3:7–10) of the giving of the commandments in 3:7–10. See the discussion in Linda Belleville, *Reflections of Glory: Paul's Polemical Use of the Moses-Doxa Tradition in 2 Corinthians 3.1–18*, JSNTSup 52 (Sheffield: Sheffield Academic, 1991), 202–3; Victor Paul Furnish, *II Corinthians*, AB 32A (New York: Doubleday, 1984), 203; Scott Hafemann, *Paul, Moses, and the History of Israel: The Letter/Spirit Contrast and the Argument from Scripture in 2 Corinthians 3*, WUNT 81 (Tübingen: Mohr Siebeck, 1995), 355.

and "what abides" or is permanent (3:11). Thus, by the time Paul's listeners hear the contrast in 3:12–13 between Moses and "we" who have great boldness (παρρησία), they have been primed by a series of oppositions contrasting life with death and what abides with what is being annulled. On the one hand, there is a ministry of open speech "in the sight of God," in which the Spirit of God writes on tablets of fleshly human hearts. This is a ministry whose competence is sourced in God, through which the Spirit makes alive, a ministry of righteousness with an abiding future. On the other hand, Paul speaks of a ministry written on tablets of stone, issuing in death and condemnation, and itself having no lasting existence; it is not simply "fading"; it is being "done away with," "abolished," "nullified," "made ineffective," "brought to an end."[19] The contrast with permanence in 3:11 is explicit and unavoidable: there is no permanence, no lasting hope, associated with the covenant of Moses. The language of life, the Spirit, righteousness, and permanence grounds the hope of which Paul speaks in 3:12, and its accompanying boldness (παρρησία), in contrast with Moses's veil. All attempts to interpret the meaning of Moses's veil must wrestle with this opposition between Pauline παρρησία and Moses's veil, between what is being done away with and what abides, and between that which gives life and that which kills.

## The τέλος of What Is Being Annulled

I noted earlier that Paul's exegesis of the Sinai accounts in Exodus exploits a narrative gap: the question of why Moses wore a veil and the enigma behind the veil. Is it Moses's continually shining face?[20] Is it the fading of his face, in between his meetings with God in the tent?[21] I have suggested two strands of conceptual overlap between the cultural valences of

---

19. See BAGD, s.v. "καταργέω." This translation accords with Paul's extensive use of καταργέω elsewhere in his letters, such as in Rom 3:3, 31; 6:6; 7:2, 6; 1 Cor 2:6; Gal 5:4. See Furnish, *II Corinthians*, 203–5; Hays, *Echoes*, 133–34; Hafemann, *Paul, Moses*, 301–9. Pace Belleville, *Reflections of Glory*, 204–6; Watson, *Hermeneutics*, 293–94 n. 42.

20. So Hafemann, *Paul, Moses, and the History of Israel*, 286–99. Hafemann argues precisely that the veil hides Moses's persistently shining face, whose glory is the divine glory. The veil, that is, protects Israel from looking continuously at God's glory, which would be lethal to them in light of their sin. Hafemann notes that the Israelites did look at Moses's shining face but argues that they did so only briefly.

21. So Watson, *Hermeneutics*, 293. Despite this difference with Hafemann,

the (male) veil and Paul's thematic emphases: the contrast between open proclamation and obstructed vision and the liminal state of a transition from life to death. Mutually amplified by cultural context and textual clues, these themes help decode the enigma concealed behind the veil. If veils obstruct vision and hide transitions from life to death, Paul's depiction of the giving of the commandments as the "ministry of death" and the "ministry of condemnation" (3:7, 9) fits the description.

What, then, is the τέλος of this covenant? Rightly observing that Moses is transfigured "from man into text" in 3:15, Richard Hays argues that the passage as a whole concerns the correct interpretation of the Mosaic text, an interpretation possible only through the lens of a conviction that Christ is the fulfillment of the covenant.[22] He contends such an interpretation yields a christological conclusion: the τέλος hidden behind Moses's veil is not the termination of Moses's ministry but its goal and fulfillment in Christ. The covenant and ministry of Moses, melded with the text of Moses, points to "the glory of God made visible in Christ"; in its location over the hearts of those who read Moses in the synagogue (3:15) as well as over the gospel itself for those who are perishing (4:3), the veil obstructs the "true significance of Moses/Torah."[23] Only through ongoing transformation into the image of the crucified Christ may interpreters gain the "new covenant reader competence" that makes such interpretation possible and the "hermeneutical freedom" that comes with such competence. Such transformed competence, in turn, means that "the community of the church becomes the place where the meaning of Israel's Scripture is enfleshed."[24]

A great deal could be said about this interpretation, but here I simply note the fusion of hermeneutical concerns with the interpretation of τέλος as goal or fulfillment rather than end or termination. The true significance of Moses's covenant is Christ and the embodied community that belongs to Christ, and Moses has an ongoing role in pointing to that significance. In Hays's view, therefore, the Mosaic covenant is not annulled, but it is carried forward by being resignified through Paul's ecclesiocentric reading strategy. Such a hermeneutical focus is the central point of

---

Watson agrees that Paul is reading Exod 32–34 as a unit, including the deadly consequences of Israel's worship of the golden calf.

22. Hays, *Echoes*, 145.
23. Hays, *Echoes*, 146.
24. Hays, *Echoes*, 148–49.

Paul's exegesis in 2 Cor 3–4, yielding a nonallegorical, nonsupersessionist Pauline hermeneutic.

Understandably, Daniel Boyarin pushes back. Although he accepts Hays's interpretation of τέλος as signifying the fulfillment, rather than the termination, of the Mosaic covenant and as pointing to Christ and the glory of the community in Christ, for Boyarin the problem is that this *is* an allegorical reading of Moses as text, and as such, in effect it is supersessionist: "Thus, the move of the modern readers of Paul, such as Hays, who deny the allegorical and supersessionist movement of Paul's text is ultimately not convincing. The supersessionism cannot be denied, because an enfleshed community was already and still living out the 'Old' Covenant."[25] Boyarin has a point; to read Moses as Hays does, or rather as Hays argues that Paul does, would be to deny the on-going reality of Jewish life and community or at least a place for that ongoing reality in Paul's conception of history. The price of continuity for the Mosaic covenant, interpreted as pointing to the glory of Christ, is the denial of continuity for the Jewish community that lives out that covenant. The life of the community and the interpretation of its sacred texts cannot be disentangled. For this reason, perhaps the question of supersessionism that Boyarin poses cannot be answered from within the text itself; its answer will be rendered differently by the experience and judgment of different living, interpretive communities of practice.[26] Non-Jews are not in a position to deny Boyarin's comment on 2 Corinthians, particularly if Hays is correct in his claim that Paul sees the Mosaic covenant as pointing to the glory of God enfleshed in the Christian community.

What if, however, τὸ τέλος τοῦ καταργουμένου does not point forward to Christ or the Christian community, and does not signify fulfillment but termination? What if Paul is continuing to comment on the Sinai story? This is the argument of Francis Watson, who sees Paul as a careful exegete of the Exodus narrative. Paul's charge, "the writing kills," states in a nutshell the lethal outcome of the golden calf incident at the base of Sinai:

---

25. Daniel Boyarin, "The Subversion of the Jews: Moses's Veil and the Hermeneutics of Supersession," *Diacritics* 23 (1993): 20.

26. In my judgment, in Romans Paul clearly sees an ongoing role for the Jewish people in the divine plan, and he never replaces "Israel" with the church or designates the church by the name "Israel." See my "Israel and the Mercy of God: A Re-reading of Galatians 6:16 and Romans 9–11," *NTS* 56 (2010): 367–95. Such an argument is not in view, however, in 2 Cor 3–4.

"The reference can only be to the story of Moses's first descent from the mountain: for Moses's advent with the first pair of stone tablets issues in the death of three thousand of the people of Israel (Exod 32.6)."[27] Watson further argues that Paul conflates Moses's first descent with his second, after which Moses puts the veil over his shining face. These are "two sides of the single event of the giving of the law," such that "the glory and the killing belong together.... The divine writing that once killed is still a writing that kills."[28]

For this reason, Watson interprets τὸ τέλος τοῦ καταργουμένου as "the end of that which was passing."[29] That is, what is hidden behind Moses's veil is not a covert witness to Christ as the goal or fulfillment of the Mosaic covenant; what is hidden is the lethal effect of that covenant, and its transitory status. As Paul states explicitly in 3:7–9, when Moses came down the mountain he brought with him a ministry of death and condemnation, glorious but also fatal. So the veil conceals the double reality of the old covenant: it ends in death, and it is coming to an end. For Watson, this also is a matter of hermeneutics, but it finds within Moses as text both a sly cover-up and an admission of limitation:

> We have here a self-referential parable or allegory of the Torah. In the allegorical figure of the veiled Moses, the Law of Moses secretly acknowledges that it does not speak with complete openness, that it conceals the fact of its own transitoriness, and that its glory is destined to be eclipsed by a surpassing glory that endures forever.[30]

In Watson's view, then, Paul interprets the stories of Sinai as communicating "two unpalatable truths": "that the text kills, and that it conceals the fading of its own glory." Paul comes to this reading of Exodus through the conjunction of the gospel and the scriptural narrative; his hermeneutic is "guided by the claims of the gospel," but it also relies on a rigorous engagement with the text.[31]

---

27. Watson, *Hermeneutics*, 288. See also Hafemann, *Paul, Moses, and the History of Israel*, 189–231, 278–86.

28. Watson, *Hermeneutics*, 289. Watson adds in a footnote, "This 'killing' is therefore actual rather than hypothetical" (289 n. 35).

29. Watson, *Hermeneutics*, 293. See also 293–94 n. 42.

30. Watson, *Hermeneutics*, 299.

31. Watson, *Hermeneutics*, 310.

Building on Watson's analysis, but also diverging from it, I suggest reading τέλος as "endpoint": the endpoint or final outcome of the commandments is death, not life. This is a reading that stays within the ambit of the Exodus narrative without an explicit christological τέλος, but it nonetheless derives from Paul's convictions about Christ.[32] In this sense, then, for Paul the recognition of the covenant's abrogation as well as its deadly endpoint also derives from his new standpoint in Christ. Such a reading coheres with Paul's comments elsewhere about the lethal effect of the commandments, notably Rom 7:9–11: "the very commandment that promised life proved to be death to me" (Rom 7:10). From that standpoint, Paul looks back at the Sinai account and spotlights the death that accompanied Moses's first descent from the mountain.

According to such a reading, then, a peek behind Moses's veil would not reveal a vision of glory, nor the Christian community as a glorious embodiment of the meaning of the Mosaic covenant; it would reveal death, and through that an indirect witness to the limitation of the commandments and the necessity for a new covenant.[33]

## Paradoxical παρρησία

But, of course, the veil impedes vision; it does not facilitate it. No peeks allowed! This brings us to the second theme highlighted by the cultural connotations of male veiling: separation and impaired communication in contrast with open, frank speech. As we have seen, Paul describes his manner of speaking as "from God, in the sight of God" (2:17), and the Corinthians themselves as "manifesting" that they are letters of Christ (3:3). This theme of open proclamation is deeply intertwined with a contrast between incompetence and divinely sourced confidence. Just as Paul's competence is "from God," so also the Corinthians' own identity as a "letter of Christ" is from the Spirit, and the "new covenant" is also from the Spirit. Thus, the character of both the Corinthians themselves and the "new covenant" as originating in the Spirit is linked to the character of

---

32. See *Hermeneutics*, 294, 298. Note also that Watson sees Paul's reading as frankly allegorical but, again, not in an explicitly christological way. Rather, any "witness" to Christ on the part of the old covenant is "indirect," as a witness to its own inability to give life and, therefore, its own transitory status.

33. See Gal 3:21: "If a law had been given which could make alive, then righteousness would be by the law." But in Paul's eyes, such a law was not given.

Paul's ministry as sourced by God and not of human origin. Such a divine origin also points to hope, grounded in the permanence of the ministry thus gifted by God; the resulting παρρησία contrasts sharply with Moses's veil, which obstructs understanding (3:14–15; 4:3–4). Paul's παρρησία (3:12–13) is demonstrated by his rejection of "the hidden things of shame" (ἀπειπάμεθα τὰ κρυπτὰ τῆς αἰσχύνης) in favor of "the open manifestation of the truth, commending ourselves to every person's conscience in the sight of God" (τῆς ἀληθείας συνιστάνοντες ἑαυτοὺς πρὸς πᾶσαν συνείδησιν ἀνθρώπων ἐνώπιον τοῦ θεοῦ) in 4:2.

This contrast between manly παρρησία and shameful secrets may evoke cultural associations of frank speech with an absence of shame, and hiddenness and silence with the modesty proper to women.[34] Indeed, when Britt traces the reception history of Moses's veil in both literature and art, he finds suggestive implications of the gendered associations of the veil. Neither Josephus nor Philo alludes to Moses's veil; whether this is because of the gendered connotation of veiling or for other reasons is difficult to say. What is clear is that there are very few depictions of Moses wearing a veil in either Jewish or Christian art. Rather, in Christian art frequently the veiled Moses is transposed into the female figure of blindfolded Synagogue.[35] In Britt's view, "The frequency of the female Synagogue and the scarcity of the veiled Moses reflect the Christian feminization (and denigration) of Judaism." He adds, "The act of unveiling itself, as imagined in 2 Corinthians 3, is particularly damaging to Moses's masculinity and integrity."[36] For Britt, however, the lasting significance of the veil is that it encodes silence—the silence of Moses when veiled—into the event of revelation itself. "To accept a version of Moses who is disempowered, and hence feminized, by a veil, was almost always too costly a bargain for Jewish and Christian interpreters. But to encounter the veil episode of Exodus is to accept ambiguity, silence, and an endlessly paradoxical idea of revelation."[37]

I do not think Paul emasculates Moses, or if he does, he emasculates himself at the same time. For as a look at 2 Cor 1–7 shows, Paul's own idea of proclamation is not so far off from Britt's interpretation of Moses's

---

34. For παρρησία as connoting an absence of shame, see Furnish, *II Corinthians*, 231.

35. Britt, *Rewriting Moses*, 110–11.

36. Britt, *Rewriting Moses*, 111.

37. Britt, *Rewriting Moses*, 111.

veil. It is not silent—quite the opposite—but it is ambiguous and endlessly paradoxical, holding in tension the incommensurable binaries of despair and hope, death and glory. For if Moses's ministry is one of death, Paul's ministry is saturated with death, even mediated by death—yet this death is not concealed but rather publicly proclaimed and embodied as a paradoxical manifestation of life.

## Death and Life in 2 Cor 1–7

After his initial greeting to the Corinthians, Paul immediately launches into a thanksgiving to God, the "father of mercies and the God of all comfort" (ὁ πατὴρ τῶν οἰκτιρμῶν καὶ θεὸς πάσης παρακλήσεως), for receiving and thus being able to share divinely given comfort in the midst of affliction (1:3–7).[38] Indeed, in the midst of overwhelming affliction, "we despaired of life itself":

> ἀλλὰ αὐτοὶ ἐν ἑαυτοῖς τὸ ἀπόκριμα τοῦ θανάτου ἐσχήκαμεν, ἵνα μὴ πεποιθότες ὦμεν ἐφ᾽ ἑαυτοῖς ἀλλ᾽ ἐπὶ τῷ θεῷ τῷ ἐγείροντι τοὺς νεκρούς

> We had received the sentence of death in ourselves, but that was to make us rely not on ourselves but on God who raises the dead. (2 Cor 1:9)[39]

With Paul's description of the tablets Moses brought down from the mountain as a ministry of condemnation and death fresh in our minds, the phrase "sentence of death" is particularly striking. Apparently, death also describes Paul's ministry, although that experience is mitigated by reliance on God who raises the dead. Paul's ministry is not characterized by the absence of death but by hope in the face of death.

---

38. Paul's depiction of God as the "Father of mercies" may well anticipate his exposition of Exodus in chapter 3. The vocabulary of παράκλησις reverberates through these verses, in counterpoint to overflowing afflictions; both the suffering and the comfort are shared with Christ (1:5) and with the Corinthians (1:6–7).

39. Furnish treats these verses as a "rounding off" of Paul's litany of affliction and comfort and v. 12 as the beginning of the body of the letter, which introduces the theme of godly communication (*II Corinthians*, 129). But this is to miss the themes of death and resurrection that also thread through chapters 1–7. The themes of living together and dying together, in shared affliction and shared consolation, recur in 7:3–4, forming an *inclusio* with 1:3–7.

Immediately following this confession of despair and hope, in which the threat of death and the promise of resurrection are tightly compressed, Paul launches into a boast about the "godly sincerity" (εἰλικρινείᾳ τοῦ θεοῦ) of his behavior in the world and with the Corinthians (1:12), such that his letters to the Corinthians are transparent and comprehensible. As Paul puts it, "For we do not write anything to you except what you can read and understand. And I hope that you will understand completely [οὐ γὰρ ἄλλα γράφομεν ὑμῖν ἀλλ' ἢ ἃ ἀναγινώσκετε ἢ καὶ ἐπιγινώσκετε· ἐλπίζω δὲ ὅτι ἕως τέλους ἐπιγνώσεσθε], as you have understood in part, so that you will have a boast in us, as do we in you, on the day of the Lord Jesus" (1:13–14).[40] This juxtaposition of affliction and effective communication would not be particularly notable, except that the pattern repeats. The next occurrence is 2:14–17, where Paul describes his ministry as an odor "from death to death" for the perishing, and "from life to life" for those being saved. His proclamation is ambiguous in its effects, scattering death and life abroad. But this ambiguity is not due to any lack of clarity in Paul's speech; rather his speech is sincere and open before God and human beings.

In 4:7–12, Paul again juxtaposes death, hope, and confident proclamation. Here he depicts the apostolic ministry as a counter-intuitive embodied proclamation of Christ; it is counter-intuitive because death communicates life. The climax and summary explanation of his catalogue of afflictions is this:

πάντοτε τὴν νέκρωσιν τοῦ Ἰησοῦ ἐν τῷ σώματι περιφέροντες, ἵνα καὶ ἡ ζωὴ τοῦ Ἰησοῦ ἐν τῷ σώματι ἡμῶν φανερωθῇ. ἀεὶ γὰρ ἡμεῖς οἱ ζῶντες εἰς θάνατον παραδιδόμεθα διὰ Ἰησοῦν, ἵνα καὶ ἡ ζωὴ τοῦ Ἰησοῦ φανερωθῇ ἐν τῇ θνητῇ σαρκὶ ἡμῶν.

always carrying in the body the death of Jesus, so that the life of Jesus may also be manifested in our bodies. For while we live we are being delivered over to death for Jesus's sake, so that the life of Jesus may be manifested in our mortal flesh. (2 Cor 4:10–11)

---

40. Paul's reference to writing anticipates 3:1–16; the assertion that the Corinthians can read and understand what he writes sets up a contrast with his assertion that a veil lies over the reading of the old covenant, obscuring understanding (3:14–15). Belleville (*Reflections*, 136–37) thus treats 1:12–3:3 as a unit of thought concerning "reading," "understanding," and "letters," but she misses the theme of death introduced earlier in the letter.

Paul could be reflecting on his own experience in Asia, on the near-despair of life itself and the "sentence of death," which he interpreted as a call to rely on the God who raises the dead (1:8–9). But now he narrates the experience of affliction as a sharing in the death of Jesus, and through that, a proclamation of Christ's death and resurrection. Contrary to cultural expectations, the unveiled apostle is a vulnerable apostle, in human terms a completely disempowered prophet. Yet here, as in 1:8–14, Paul instead proclaims his bold public pattern of speech, and as in 1:9, his confidence is based on God who raises the dead:

> Having the same spirit of faith according to what is written, "I believed, therefore I spoke," we also believe, and so we speak, knowing that the one who raised the lord Jesus also will raise us with Jesus and establish us together with you. (2 Cor 4:13–14)

In both bodily experience and speech, Paul seems to see a link between the extreme afflictions he and his colleagues suffer and the manifestation of Christ. This link is the amplification and experiential expression of his claim in 4:2: Paul's "manifestation of the truth" happens through being delivered up to death "so the life of Jesus may be manifested in our bodies" (4:10). Furthermore, in 6:4 Paul expands on the theme of self-commendation in 4:2: "We commend ourselves as God's servants in every way [ἐν παντὶ συνιστάντες ἑαυτοὺς ὡς θεοῦ διάκονοι]: in great endurance, in afflictions," and the catalogue of afflictions goes on. But suddenly Paul shifts from the hardships he endures to the presence of God: "in purity, knowledge, forbearance, kindness, the Holy Spirit, genuine love, truthful speech, and the power of God" (6:6). Compressed together, extreme affliction and the power of God culminate in a series of existential paradoxes— "as dying, and behold we live; as punished, and yet not killed; as sorrowful, yet always rejoicing; as poor, yet making many rich; as having nothing, and yet possessing everything" (6:4–10). What is the outcome of this paradoxical embodied expression of hope in affliction? Once again, it is transparent and effective communication: "Our mouth is open to you, Corinthians; our heart is wide" (6:11).

These three passages (1:8–14, 4:7–14, 6:4–10) combine references to affliction and death with references to Paul's apostolic proclamation. They express the anguish and hope of the apostle and his fellow missionaries— anguish almost to the point of death, hope in the God who raises the dead. Such suffering teaches reliance on God rather than human power (1:9,

4:7). In 6:4–10, the catalogue of afflictions moves into an affirmation of the power of God in the midst of affliction, climaxing in a paradoxical union between death and life in the experience of the apostles. In each case, Paul moves from that experience to an assertion of confident proclamation; the suffering and the hope are themselves modes of manifesting Christ, amplified by bold public speaking. In each case, that boldness arises out of the experience of hope in extremis.

## "We All, with Unveiled Faces, Beholding as in a Mirror the Glory of the Lord, Are Being Transformed into the Same Image, from Glory to Glory"

I have argued that Paul exploits a narrative gap in the Exodus narrative and, in so doing, evokes some of the emotional valences associated with the image of a veiled man. Chief among these associations are a transitional status moving from life to death and separation that obstructs understanding. According to this interpretation, Moses is not covering permanent and abiding glory, but rather the end of the glory and the lethal endpoint of the covenant: death, and the transition from life to death, hides behind the veil. But the veil also obstructs vision and thereby understanding. Both of these themes come to the fore in Paul's treatment of the veil in 3:13–16 and 4:3. By way of contrast, in both his representation of Moses's veil and the larger context of the letter, Paul repeatedly emphasizes the openness and boldness of his proclamation, combined with a public manifestation of the truth. The rallying cry of this unveiled speech and manifestation is 3:18: "And we all, with *unveiled faces*, beholding as in a mirror the glory of the Lord, are being transformed into the same image, from glory to glory."

What we have seen, however, is that the theme of open proclamation is inseparable from the themes of affliction and death in Paul's own ministry. If Moses's ministry is a ministry of death, Paul's ministry seems drenched in death, almost overtaken by death, quintessentially mediated by death. For Paul, as much as for Moses, "the glory and the killing belong together."[41] Nonetheless, in sharp distinction from the ministry of Moses, the endpoint of Paul's ministry is life. It is characterized by incommensurable binaries of hope and despair, life in the midst of death. What are we to make of this?

---

41. Watson, *Hermeneutics*, 288. See Martin Luther's words: when "God quickens, he does so by killing" (*The Bondage of the Will*, trans. J. I. Packer and O. R. Johnston [Westwood, NJ: Revell, 1959], 101).

It seems to me that death itself is transformed. As Paul puts it in 5:14, Christ "died for all, therefore all died." Christ's death therefore encompasses human death, such that death becomes a union with Christ; in 4:8–10, Paul narrates his own experiences of extreme affliction as inhabited by Christ's death:

> We are afflicted in every way, but not crushed; perplexed, but not driven to despair; persecuted, but not forsaken; struck down, but not destroyed; always carrying in the body the death of Jesus, so that the life of Jesus may also be manifest in our bodies [πάντοτε τὴν νέκρωσιν τοῦ Ἰησοῦ ἐν τῷ σώματι περιφέροντες, ἵνα καὶ ἡ ζωὴ τοῦ Ἰησοῦ ἐν τῷ σώματι ἡμῶν φανερωθῇ].

This union with Christ in death leads to hope that comes from relying on the God who raises the dead (4:13–14). Having such a hope, then, Paul's gospel is unveiled, in an unveiling that includes frank speech, not only about hope, but also about affliction, despair, suffering, and death. The section 2 Cor 1–7 abounds in such speech, in service to Paul's appeal to the Corinthians: "Our mouth is open to you, Corinthians; our heart is wide" (6:11). But such speech is also part and parcel of proclaiming the extreme paradox of a crucified Lord, and that gets to the heart of the transformation envisioned in 3:18. The transforming vision is one in which glory and death go together, precisely because the target image is that of the crucified Lord mirrored in human faces.

When Paul and his comrades look in the mirror with unveiled faces, what do they see? They see their own disfigurement, their mental distress and physical hardships, their debased and liminal social status, their mortal flesh. This is the "apocalyptic exposure" of which Marion speaks:

> Here our gaze becomes the optical mirror of that at which it looks only by finding itself more radically looked at: we become a visible mirror of an invisible gaze that subverts us in the measure of its glory. The invisible summons us, "face to face, person to person" (1 Cor. 13:12).[42]

Indeed, as Marion's comments illuminate, the apocalyptic exposure is also a double exposure, because superimposed on their reflected mortal flesh is the death of Jesus; shining through their reflected image is the divine image.

---

42. Marion, *God without Being*, 22.

Held by the divine gaze so intimately inhabiting their flesh, Paul and his colleagues find life in the midst of death, and boldness in the midst of dishonor.

On the one hand, this discovery is commensurate with Israel's experience of God: "The Lord kills and makes alive; the Lord brings down to the grave and raises up" (1 Sam 2:6). God's sovereignty over both death and life is the source of Israel's hope no less than Paul's. But even in speaking thus, it is important to acknowledge the rift already opened up between Paul's proclamation of a crucified Christ and the faith of his kinsfolk according to the flesh (Rom 9:3). The divine gaze subverts at least in part by removing every other basis for confidence, competence, or hope—including the Mosaic commandments. In this sense, Paul's reading of Moses may be seen as radically destabilizing of Jewish allegiance to torah, in a subversion radiating out from his own experience and embracing all human experience, pagan or Jewish. As such, it bears the seeds of the parting of the ways, not because Paul sought such a separation—he emphatically did not—but because the church subsequently developed his interpretation of the Sinai narrative in supersessionist ways. As we have seen, later Christian art took up the image of Moses wearing a veil and transposed it into the image of the Synagogue as a blindfolded female slave, over against the victorious figure of Ekklesia. In such artistic representations, Paul's interpretation of Moses's veil becomes a violent caricature of his message, while the weakness and death intrinsic to his own ministry are silenced.[43] Paul's paradoxical, afflicted proclamation in 2 Corinthians has no room for such triumphalism, but ironically, as is often the case in Pauline interpretation, his own voice has been drowned out by his later interpreters.

## Bibliography

Belleville, Linda. *Reflections of Glory: Paul's Polemical Use of the Moses-Doxa Tradition in 2 Corinthians 3.1–18*. JSNTSup 52. Sheffield: Sheffield Academic, 1991.

---

43. See the perceptive comments by J. Louis Martyn on the statues flanking the south portal of Strasbourg Cathedral: they "portray a proud and triumphant church, and a humbled and blindfolded synagogue. Consciously those statues were thought to present Paul's theology as it emerges in 2 Corinthians 3. Unconsciously they reflect the forms of anti-Semitism that were widespread among Christians in medieval Europe" (J. Louis Martyn, *Theological Issues in the Letters of Paul* [Nashville: Abingdon, 1997], 193).

Boyarin, Daniel. "The Subversion of the Jews: Moses's Veil and the Hermeneutics of Supersession." *Diacritics* 23 (1993): 16–35.

Britt, Brian M. *Rewriting Moses: The Narrative Eclipse of the Text.* JSOTSup 402. London: T&T Clark, 2004.

Butler, H. E., trans. *The Institutio Oratoria of Quintilian.* 4 vols. LCL. Cambridge: Harvard University Press, 1920.

Cairns, Douglas. "The Meaning of the Veil in Ancient Greek Culture." Pages 73–93 in *Women's Dress in the Ancient Greek World.* Edited by L. Lewellyn-Jones. London: Duckworth, 2002.

Eastman, Susan. "Israel and the Mercy of God: A Re-reading of Galatians 6:16 and Romans 9–11." *NTS* 56 (2010): 367–95.

Furnish, Victor Paul. *II Corinthians.* AB 32A. New York: Doubleday, 1984.

Hafemann, Scott. *Paul, Moses, and the History of Israel: The Letter/Spirit Contrast and the Argument from Scripture in 2 Corinthians 3.* WUNT 81. Tübingen: Mohr Siebeck, 1995.

Hays, Richard. *Echoes of Scripture in the Letters of Paul.* New Haven: Yale University Press, 1989.

Heath, Jane. *Paul's Visual Piety: The Metamorphosis of the Beholder.* Oxford: Oxford University Press, 2013.

Luther, Martin. *The Bondage of the Will.* Translated by J. I. Packer and O. R. Johnston. Westwood, NJ: Revell, 1959.

Marion, Jean-Luc. *God without Being.* Chicago: University of Chicago Press, 2012.

Martyn, J. Louis. *Theological Issues in the Letters of Paul.* Nashville: Abingdon, 1997.

Oster, Richard. "When Men Wore Veils to Worship: The Historical Context of 1 Corinthians II.4." *NTS* 34 (1988): 481–505.

Peers, Glenn. "'Icons' Spirited Love." *RelArts* 13 (2009): 218–47.

Perrin, Bernadotte, trans. *Plutarch's Lives.* LCL. Cambridge. Harvard University Press, 1919.

Thiselton, Anthony. *The First Epistle to the Corinthians.* NIGTC. Grand Rapids: Eerdmans, 2000.

Watson, Francis. *Paul and the Hermeneutics of Faith.* New York: T&T Clark, 2004.

# "Being a Jew and Living as a Gentile": Paul's Storytelling and the Relationship of Jews and Gentiles according to Galatians 2

## Michael Winger

In his letter to the young church he had founded in Galatia, the apostle Paul offers a series of propositions about following Jesus Christ—or perhaps, since the subject matter is not merely abstract, we might say that here Paul presents reflections about the life of one, such as himself, who follows Jesus Christ:

> 15 We who are Jews by birth, and not gentile sinners, 16 knowing, however, that one is not justified by works of law, but through the faith of Jesus Christ, we too trusted in Jesus Christ, in order to be justified by the faith of Christ and not by works of law, because by works of law no flesh is justified.[1] 17 If, then, seeking to be justified in Christ, we ourselves are found to be sinners, is Christ therefore a servant of sin? Nonsense! 18 Rather, if I build up again what I destroyed, that shows me a transgressor. 19 For I, through law, died to law, that I might live to God. I have been crucified with Christ; 20 it is no longer I that live; rather, Christ lives in me. What I now live in the flesh I live in the faith of the Son of God who loved me and gave himself for me. 21 Thus, I do not nullify the gift of God; rather, if justification is through the law, then Christ died for nothing. (Gal 2:15–21)[2]

Martin Luther found in this passage "the true meaning of Christianity"; Hans Dieter Betz calls the passage as a whole the *propositio* of the letter

---

1. "Faith of Christ" (πίστις Χριστοῦ) may alternatively be rendered "faith in Christ"; there is an apparently interminable debate over which is preferable. The difference is not material to this paper.

2. Unless otherwise stated, all translation of the New Testament are my own.

to the Galatians, "setting forth … briefly and completely" the points to be discussed in the balance of the letter.[3]

But almost perversely, it would seem, Paul has introduced these theological reflections with a personal attack on Peter (under his Aramaic name Cephas), by most accounts the first among Jesus's lifetime companions and apostles, and also on both Paul's own long-time associate Barnabas and other unnamed Jewish Christians whom Paul groups with Cephas and Barnabas.[4] This attack could hardly be sharper, charging both falsehood and betrayal of the gospel:

> 11 But when Cephas came to Antioch I opposed him to his face, because he stood condemned. 12 For before certain emissaries came from James, he ate with the gentiles; but when they came he withdrew, 13 and set himself apart, fearing those of the circumcision, and the rest of the Jews took up the same role, so that even Barnabas was carried away in this role-playing.[5] 14 But when I saw that they were not following the truth of the gospel, I said to Cephas, in the presence of everyone, "If you, a Jew, live like a gentile and not like a Jew, how can you make gentiles act like Jews?" (Gal 2:11–14)

But this attack is as brief as it is sharp. In verse 15, Paul's tone changes abruptly from acerbic to contemplative, and he actually invokes Cephas and Barnabas, whom he has just condemned, in his own support. In verses 15–17, Paul's repeated references to "we who are Jews by birth," and yet

---

3. Martin Luther, *Lectures on Galatians*, vol. 26 of *Luther's Works*, ed. Jaroslav Pelikan (Saint Louis: Concordia, 1963), 136; Hans Dieter Betz, *Galatians*, Hermeneia (Philadelphia: Fortress, 1979), 114. Cf. Richard N. Longenecker, *Galatians*, WBC 41 (Grand Rapids: Zondervan, 1990), 80–81; Martinus C. de Boer, *Galatians*, NTL (Louisville: Westminster John Knox, 2011), 139 (Paul's "second textually relevant summary of the gospel"). A. Andrew Das states: "This paragraph is the *nexus* of almost every major debate in Pauline theology." Andrew Das, *Galatians*, ConcC (Saint Louis: Concordia, 2014), 239.

4. Paul generally uses the name "Cephas" (besides Galatians, see 1 Cor 1:12, 3:22, 9:5, and 15:5), except in one place which we shall examine as we proceed. Here I will follow Paul's usual practice.

5. Paul's term for role-playing is ὑπόκρισία, which in ancient Greek did not have the necessary negative connotation of its descendant "hypocrisy" (see LSJ, s.v. "ὑπόκρισία"). In this context, role-playing is clearly condemned, but it is misleading to build the condemnation into Paul's choice of words. As will become apparent, I consider the concept of role-playing important to Paul's meaning.

"justified by faith," evidently includes Cephas, Barnabas, and "the other Jews" along with himself.[6] Cephas and Barnabas are no longer the equivocating "you" of verse 14; they are joined to Paul, in "we."

What enables Paul to draw on Cephas for support in verse 15, in spite of Cephas's apparent repudiation described in verses 12b–13 of the freedom from law urged by Paul, is simply that before Cephas withdrew from this freedom, he had accepted it: Cephas, like Barnabas and the other Jewish Christians in Antioch, had "eaten with the gentiles" (v. 12a), thus acknowledging that Christians, whether gentile or Jewish, need not observe Jewish food laws.[7] Didn't Cephas then abandon this position? Not in Paul's view; the subject here is law, and once it is established that observance is optional, as Cephas, Paul, Barnabas, and the rest of the Jewish Christians in Antioch had already demonstrated by eating with gentiles, then it is no longer law, even if one follows it sometimes.[8] This underlies Paul's charge of role-playing: Cephas and Barnabas and the other Jewish Christians pretend to be law observant, but they are not; their observance is merely a matter of convenience, and it shows no respect for the law as law; as Paul says, they are simply playing a role.

Although I think this must be Paul's line of thought, he does not express it as directly as one might expect. His account of what happened in Antioch hampers him; its ringing conclusion puts the emphasis on Cephas's disagreement with Paul, not his agreement. Paul's argument would be clearer if he first recounted how Cephas "lived like a gentile" and then added that this fundamental point was not disturbed by occasions when Cephas did follow Jewish practice. That approach would also be more polite, smoother; it would largely remove the occasion for Paul's anger, so clearly expressed in verse 14. But Paul's anger is part of his story, and we shall see that in this letter his anger serves a purpose.

---

6. See Martinus C. de Boer, "Paul's Use and Interpretation of a Justification Tradition in Galatians 2.15–21," *JSNT* 28 (2005): 189–216.

7. On the relation of eating "with gentiles" to Jewish law, see further n. 13 below.

8. Apparently, not everyone shared this view. The vehemence with which Paul tells the Galatians in 5:2–3 that the law must be observed as a whole—"Look, I, Paul, tell you … I testify …" (Ἰδε ἐγὼ Παῦλος λέγω ὑμῖν … μαρτύρομαι …)—indicates that the Galatians have not realized this. (What the Jewish Christian missionaries among them may have said on the subject is uncertain.) Nevertheless, Paul considers his own view on the subject to be so obviously right that he can proclaim it without citing any authority. See also Jas 2:10: "Whoever keeps the whole law but fails in one point is guilty of all of it."

Paul had multiple objectives in discussing Cephas, and to understand the apparent break in Paul's thought between 2:14 and 2:15, we need to sort these objectives out. I would like to put it this way: Paul is presenting the gospel, but he is also presenting a story—in fact, several stories. These objectives are not distinct, for the gospel, the good news, is itself a story. But storytelling has certain dynamics, which it will be useful to explore, and it will also be useful to separate out certain strands of Paul's stories.

The gospel story is fundamental, and it is alluded to throughout this letter, for instance, in 1:1 ("God the father ... raised [Jesus] from the dead"), 2:20 ("the son of God ... loved me and gave himself for me"), 3:13 ("Christ ... became a curse for you"), including what one might call the background story of Israel (for instance, 3:15–20, 4:21–31), in which lies the distinction between Jews and gentiles that is so prominent in this letter. Another story is the story of the Galatian community to which Paul writes; parts of this story are referred to in 4:13–15 (concerning Paul's initial reception in Galatia), 3:1–5 (concerning the Galatians' reception of the spirit), and 1:6; 5:2–4, 7–8, 12; Gal 6:12–13 (all alluding to developments in Galatia after Paul's departure).

But these are scattered fragments; they allude to stories, without being stories themselves. Paul's own story, told in 1:11–2:14, is different; beginning with Paul's life in Judaism, it proceeds through God's revelation of his son to Paul and the history of Paul's apostolate to the gentiles, reaching its dramatic climax in the episode in Antioch. The outline of this story is simple; it is introduced by Paul's declaration that he received the gospel by a revelation of Jesus Christ and not from any human (1:11–12), and the story can be viewed as a demonstration of that claim. But this claim is not entirely clear. Since Paul had persecuted the church, he must have known something about it, leading to his persecution; presumably he learned this in an ordinary, human way. In 1 Cor 15:3–7, Paul says that he received traditions of the crucifixion and resurrection; these appear to be human. What then did Paul receive "through a revelation of Jesus Christ" (1:12)?

Some guidance is provided by 1 Cor 1:18: "The word of the cross [ὁ λόγος ... ὁ τοῦ σταυροῦ] is foolishness to those who are perishing, but to us who are being saved it is the power of God." Evidently the same word— the same doctrine—can be perceived differently. Connecting this to Paul's own history as he recounts it to the Galatians, it seems evident that Paul knows about these two contrary perceptions because he himself has experienced the word of the cross in both of these ways; once, he heard this word as foolishness, and he persecuted those who proclaimed it; then, he perceived the word's divine power, and proclaimed it himself.[9] *Power* is key here; Gal 1:15–16 tells how God empowered Paul to proclaim the good news of the son of God to gentiles; this entailed the revelation that the crucified one is indeed the son of God, but it does not necessarily entail the delivery of additional propositions concerning him.

The issue Paul addresses here is not how he first learned doctrine, but how he came to believe it, and how he was commissioned to proclaim it. Of doctrine, Paul has to this point in his letter mentioned only the general propositions that God raised Jesus Christ from the dead (1:1) and that Jesus "gave himself for our sins, to rescue us from the present evil age" (1:4); the first of these propositions was surely known (although not accepted) by Paul before his call, and he may have known the second too—at least, there is nothing to indicate that Paul was introduced to this proposition only by revelation. The central issue seems to be Paul's commission, and the key to this, becoming clear as Paul proceeds, is that this was a commission to preach *to the gentiles*. As Paul's story develops, a new story line appears on the subject of Jews and gentiles, and it is this line, culminating in the dramatic confrontation of 2:14, that introduces the main theme of Paul's letter.

Paul is not naturally given to storytelling; nowhere else in his letters do we find anything like this long, detailed personal narrative—thirty-three verses occupying a quarter of this letter, the only indubitable first-hand account of events anywhere in the New Testament.[10] To our great good fortune, this narrative concerns not only Paul but also the other apostle generally considered a preeminent leader of the early church, Peter (or Cephas). It is our good fortune, but it is not chance, that Paul has chosen to tell just this detailed story with just these two principal characters.

For Paul's theme of independence from human authority, Cephas is an ideal character, who from his position among the apostles could be taken as a symbol of human authority within the Christian community.

---

9. Paul's zeal to persecute the word hints that he already perceived its power, only not that the power was divine; it was a threat because of its power.

10. John M. G. Barclay argues that the story presented by Paul in Gal 1–2 should be read not as Paul's personal story, but as that of the gospel. John M. G. Barclay, "Paul's Story: Theology as Testimony," in *Narrative Dynamics in Paul: A Critical Assessment*, ed. Bruce W. Longenecker (Louisville: Westminster John Knox, 2002), 133–56. This is an important reading of Paul's story, but there are separate levels of reading, and the personal level as I outline it contributes to Paul's argument.

Likewise, it appears in the course of Paul's story (as we shall see) that Cephas is central to proclaiming the gospel to Jews, again making him an ideal contrast for Paul's purposes. But Paul does not treat Cephas as an ideal, symbolic character; his story is concrete, with encounters between Paul and Cephas in three separate episodes, following a brief prologue. Let us look at each of these.

The prologue talks of Paul's "life in Judaism," with Paul's "persecuting the church of God" apparently based on Paul's "zeal for [his] ancestral traditions" (1:13–14), and then the sharp reversal brought when God "revealed his son to [Paul] in order that [Paul] might proclaim the gospel among the gentiles" (1:15–16). Thus, Paul introduces the Jewish-gentile divide in passing; it is in the background, but it will not stay there.

The three episodes follow: (1) Paul explains that after God "revealed his son in me" (1:15–16), thus turning Paul from "his former life in Judaism" (1:13), he did not confer with any other apostles until three years later when he went to Jerusalem and spent fifteen days with Cephas (1:17–18). This is a concession subordinate to Paul's point: he did consult with Cephas, but only once, long ago (as Paul will go on to say), and only after his own mission was well underway. He adds that he saw no other apostles during this visit except James the brother of the Lord, and he closes his account of this visit declaring, "Before God, I do not lie!"[11] Evidently, someone has told the Galatians a different story about Paul's relations with other apostles, probably to imply some kind of subordination; it seems likely that those who tell this story claim authority from these other apostles, which entitles them to correct Paul. But we note that, by Paul's account, his work among gentiles is not questioned in this visit to Jerusalem.

(2) Paul then jumps fourteen years to another visit to Jerusalem.[12] The basic story of this second trip to Jerusalem seems simple, but Paul complicates it in ways that I will discuss shortly. Prompted "by revelation," Paul went with his colleagues Barnabas and Titus to present the gospel Paul preached among gentiles "privately to those of repute." Paul says that these

---

11. This account gives a revealing glimpse of early Christians. From Acts, one gets the impression that the apostles were continually absorbed in apostolic business, but here a visiting Christian missionary spends two weeks with Cephas, and in all of this time, only one of the other apostles drops by.

12. Perhaps eleven years; it is not clear whether the fourteen years are measured from the previous episode (1:17–18) or from the revelation (1:15–16). See de Boer, *Galatians*, 107.

leaders of the Jerusalem community "saw that I was entrusted with the gospel for the uncircumcised, just as Peter for the circumcised"; that is, Paul clarifies, "the one working through Peter for a mission for the circumcised worked also through me for the gentiles." Therefore, "knowing the grace given to me, James and Cephas and John, the ones considered pillars, gave the right hand of fellowship to me and Barnabas, that we should go to the gentiles and they to the circumcised."

Thus Gal 2:1–2 and 7–9 (omitting vv. 3–6, to which we shall turn back shortly). These five verses seem to present a complete story, confirming Paul's gospel and its independence from human authority—the issue identified in 1:6–12—along with the project of a separate gentile mission, which in chapter 1 is merely mentioned (1:16), and apparently taken for granted. Now the validity of this mission is taken up, but it is not decided by the authority of the apostles; rather, "those of repute" recognize that a higher authority is involved, "working through" both Cephas and Paul, evidently in harmony. This does not answer every question that Paul addresses in writing to the Galatians. While acceptance of separate missions to Jews and gentiles by "the pillars" generally supports the position that Paul expresses in 2:15–21 and subsequently in this letter, that "works of [Jewish] law" are not for gentiles, the mere term "gospel for the uncircumcised" is ambiguous. Evidently a "gospel for the uncircumcised" does not require circumcision, but it does not necessarily follow that gentiles are free from all law-observance.[13] According to Acts, what appears to be the same meeting ended with a decree that allowed gentiles to remain uncircumcised, but it directed them to observe some laws, including some food laws: "They should abstain from meat sacrificed to idols and from blood and from what is strangled and from unchastity" (Acts 15:28–29). But while the Acts formula does not require full compliance with Jewish food laws, it is inconsistent with Paul's belligerent claim that "to me the highly

---

13. For some issues, see Paula Fredriksen, "Judaizing the Nations: The Ritual Demands of Paul's Gospel," *NTS* 56 (2010): 232–52. On these laws more generally, see Richard Bauckham, "James and the Gentiles (Acts 15.13–21)," in *History, Literature, and Society in the Book of Acts*, ed. Ben Witherington (Cambridge: Cambridge University Press, 1996), 154–84; Peter J. Tomson, *Paul and the Jewish Law: Halakha in the Letters of the Apostle to the Gentiles*, CRINT 1 (Assen: Van Gorcum, 1990), 177–80; Klaus Müller, *Tora für die Völker: Die noachidischen Gebote und Ansätze zu ihrer Rezeption im Christentum*, 2nd ed., Studien zu jüdischem Volk und christlicher Gemeinde 15 (Berlin: Institut Kirche und Judentum, 1998), 137–99.

regarded ones added nothing." In Gal 5:2, Paul gathers his full authority
("Look, I myself, Paul, declare ...") to establish that accepting circumcision entails full submission to Jewish law. While it is possible that Paul
would have regarded submission to commands other than circumcision as
a matter of indifference, the weight of the evidence is against his treating
any part of the law as indifferent. We know from 1 Cor 8 that Paul rejected
any command to abstain from meat sacrificed to idols; he merely coun-
seled abstention when partaking might confuse "the weak." Thus, Acts is
evidently mistaken, since, as Paul goes on to say, not only did gentiles in
Antioch ignore Jewish food laws in the aftermath of the Jerusalem conference, but Cephas himself initially joined these gentile meals.[14] Moreover,
if there were such a specific directive out of Jerusalem, Paul could gain
no advantage by omitting it, for he would surely know that the men who
are troubling the Galatians must be aware of this directive and that they
would bring it forward against him. Paul's account is probably accurate as
far as it goes, and the account in Acts, written later and based on unknown
sources of information, is mistaken in the details of what happened on
that occasion in Jerusalem; but it could reflect a subsequent interpretation
of what is ambiguous in Paul's first-hand account.[15] Paul's account is also
supported by his unusual use of the Greek name Peter, rather than Cephas,
in describing the outcome of the Jerusalem meeting, for which the most
plausible explanation is that, as many have proposed, Paul is quoting from

---

14. Unless "eating with gentiles" means merely eating in their company, without
sharing their food. But how would that be "living like a gentile"? Both Paul's attack on
Cephas in v. 14 and his argument in vv. 15–18 make sense only if Cephas had actually
violated Jewish law.

15. It has been suggested that Luke knew and used Paul's letters and that he might
have interpreted Paul's statements in Galatia to support his narrative. William O.
Walker Jr., "Acts and the Pauline Corpus Reconsidered," *JSNT* 24 (1985): 3–23; Lars
Aejmelaeus, *Die Rezeption der Paulusbriefe in der Miletrede (Apg 20:18–35)*, AASF
B/232 (Helsinki: Suomalainen Tiedeakatemia, 1987); Richard I. Pervo, *Dating Acts:
Between the Evangelists and the Apologists* (Santa Rosa, CA: Polebridge, 2006), 51–147;
Joseph B. Tyson, *Marcion and Luke-Acts: A Defining Struggle* (Columbia: Univer-
sity of South Carolina Press, 2006). In the absence of evidence establishing literary
dependence, this is speculative at best. In any case, it seems clear that Luke did not
know Galatians, for Gal 1:22 ("I was not known by sight to the assemblies in Christ in
Judea") contradicts the claim in Acts 26:9–10 that Paul persecuted followers of Jesus
in Jerusalem.

some actual document emanating from the conference which says "Peter" rather than "Cephas."[16]

As Paul describes this meeting in Jerusalem, it supports his argument to the Galatians about authority in a delicately balanced way; it shows that Paul's circumcision-free mission was accepted by the Jerusalem leaders, without, however, being dependent on their authority; they recognize Paul, they do not rule him. Both points are important to Paul. (Note how he says that he was not summoned to Jerusalem; he went "by revelation.")[17] As for the place of gentiles, the issue has now been noted, but it seems resolved.

This brings us to verses 3–6, which, on their face, do not seem to affect Paul's account of the outcome of this conference, though they sit in the middle of it. Other features also distinguish these verses: their acerbic tone and their apparently disordered syntax.

> 3 But not even my companion Titus, a Greek, was compelled to be circumcised. 4 But because of some false brothers who were brought in, who came in to spy out the freedom which we have in Christ Jesus, in order that they might enslave us—5 to them for even an hour we did not yield obedience, so that the truth of the gospel could remain for you—6 but from those considered to be something—what they once were[18] is nothing to me, God has no favorites—to me the highly regarded ones added nothing. (Gal 2:3–6)

After verse 3, which is straightforward, Paul's thought seems to start and stop several times, and some thoughts are left hanging.[19] In the long,

---

16. Betz, *Galatians*, 97; Longenecker, *Galatians*, 55–56.

17. The importance to Paul of this delicate balance clarifies his statement that "I put before them the gospel which I preach among gentiles, but privately to those highly regarded, *lest I run or have run in vain*" (2:2; emphasis added). Paul wanted the Jerusalem leaders to accept his gospel, without acknowledging that they had authority to reject it. Probably it was rhetorical excess to suggest that either their rejection of his gospel, or their claiming authority to approve it, would have made Paul's own work vain; but he saw obstacles to his work in either direction. This probably lay behind his desire for a private meeting. (Note that the "lest" clause may modify either "I put before them" or "but privately.")

18. Probably, companions of Jesus.

19. Different translations make different attempts to straighten out Paul's syntax. I put a full stop at the end of v. 3 and then not until the end of v. 6; AV and RV, in contrast, run v. 3 together with vv. 4 and 5, with a full stop before v. 6; RSV and NRSV

run-on sentence which makes up verses 4–6, there appear to be two main clauses, similar in import: *we did not yield obedience to them* and *the highly regarded ones added nothing to me*. The introductory "because of" is never completed; Paul never says what happened "because of" the "false brothers," except that it was not the circumcision of Titus.[20]

In spite of the confused syntax, the gist of Paul's account is clear. False brothers were "brought in" to Paul's session with "those of repute," which Paul had thought would be private; probably it was "those of repute" who brought them in—no one else is identified who might have done this. It is also clear that Paul is angry at all of them. The confused syntax displays Paul's anger; he does not finish saying what happened "because of" the false brothers because he rushes on to declare, with palpable contempt, that nothing significant did: "Even for an hour we did not yield obedience."

The text here is agitated because Paul is agitated; that is, here Paul relives the agitation of the conflict he describes. Is he still agitated over events that, by his own account, were so inconsequential? I think that misses the point; Paul re-creates his agitation as a way of involving the Galatians in the scene he describes; *involving them* is key to Paul's purpose in telling this story.

The agitation itself suggests that what Paul describes was not actually inconsequential. The point here is not what happened but what failed to happen. If Paul wanted "the highly regarded ones" in Jerusalem to acknowledge that "the gospel for the uncircumcised" was a gospel free of all Jewish law, and perhaps also that even Jews "are not justified by works of law," then he did not get what he wanted; and this was a failure of "the highly regarded ones," urged on by "the false brothers." Moreover, the result of this failure is now apparent in Galatia, where—as the balance of Paul's letter makes clear—the false brothers' program is again being urged.

At this point in his story, Paul has presented a first scene in which Cephas is central; although much must have been said between the two

---

have full stops at the end of vv. 3 and 5; REB at the end of vv. 3, 4a and 5; NAB only at the end of 5; and NJB has no full stop until the end of v. 6. All of these renderings may help a reader to understand the text, but I think the text's disorder is itself a significant point.

20. Some have claimed ambiguity over whether Titus was *actually* circumcised, just not *required* to be circumcised, but the text does not support so skeptical a reading. See the discussion in Longenecker, *Galatians*, 50; de Boer, *Galatians*, 111 n. 164.

men in two weeks, Paul recounts none of it.[21] In the second scene, Cephas is at the periphery; although he is one of the "highly regarded ones" mentioned in 2:2, we do not learn this until 2:9, where Cephas is listed (in second place) among James and John. Nevertheless, Paul's disappointment with "the pillars" is likely to have focused on Cephas, the one among them with whom Paul acknowledges extensive previous contact and who has probably known about Paul's gentile mission for at least eleven years. In any event, it is not James or John but Cephas who is central to Paul's story.

(3) Now comes the third episode, in which disappointment is explicit and is declared abruptly at the outset, even before it is explained. The emphasis is on what Paul did: "I opposed [Cephas] to his face" (2:11). The confrontation that appears at the beginning of this letter in Paul's relations with the Galatians now enters Paul's story; the hints of 2:4–6, which seemed to have been buried in the agreement described in 2:7–10, now prove to have been prescient, and the neat division between "the circumcised" and "the uncircumcised" laid out in 2:7–8 is revealed as illusory.[22] This is the point of 2:11–14 and Paul's dramatic, unanswered challenge to Cephas in 2:14. Some of the details of what preceded this confrontation are hazy, but the confrontation is clear and deliberate; instead of discussing the matter privately with Cephas, as one might expect among colleagues, Paul confronts Cephas "before everyone."

In brief, apparently Jewish and gentile Christians in Antioch shared common meals, ignoring Jewish dietary laws, and when Cephas came to Antioch, he joined these common meals.[23] Then, representatives of James

---

21. Did the succeeding years see no other contacts (perhaps correspondence) between the two men? It is impossible to say, but letters are a pale substitute for speech or action; it would be natural for a storyteller to neglect letters.

22. Or perhaps insignificant. The two terms retain different meanings; in a different context, to a different audience, probably largely Jewish, Paul does attach a kind of significance to the distinction (see Rom 9–10). But even there, Paul does not draw back from his proclamation that "there is neither Jew nor Greek in Christ Jesus" (Gal 3:28).

23. Evidently, everyone in Antioch recognized the importance of a common meal, shared by all members of the community. (I think it implausible that such importance would be attached merely to sitting in the same place, while eating different food.) In a community with both Jews and gentiles, this could happen in two ways: if everyone followed Jewish practice or if no one did. In Antioch, the second practice was followed until Cephas broke it, and it was left to the gentiles to save the situation by switching to the first practice.

arrived who kept kosher, and Cephas began to eat with them instead of the gentiles—Paul says out of fear, but Cephas, who probably knew these men, might have seen it as a comradely gesture—and first other Jews followed Cephas, and then, finally, the gentile Christians. The upshot was that the community again shared a common meal, only now it was a kosher meal.

Now comes the climactic scene. Declaring to the Galatians that Cephas was not following the gospel and that both Cephas and the other Jewish Christians were "playing a role," Paul recounts his public rebuke: "If you, a Jew, live like a gentile and not like a Jew, how can you make gentiles act like Jews?"

This is tendentious and deliberately provocative. Would Cephas agree that he has "lived like a gentile"? Paul's evidence is that, in a particular situation, Cephas ate meals not prepared according to Jewish food rules; there is no claim of any other departure from torah. From a strict torah-observance standpoint, Cephas has failed, but if he observes the law otherwise, he is not acting like any actual gentile.

Do the gentiles in Antioch come to "act like Jews" (ἰουδαΐζειν)? They, reciprocally, have eaten kosher meals in a particular situation; but do the gentiles eat all of their meals with Jews? Do they follow Jewish food rules when no Jews are present? Do they themselves even know the relevant rules? Do they observe any other Jewish practices? What does Cephas have to do with all of this? Also, do the gentiles believe—has anyone told them—that they are required to observe Jewish food rules—as, apparently, the Galatian gentiles have been told that they are required to be circumcised? Paul does not say; he prefers not to burden his story with details which would blunt the drama of the scene. But if the gentile Christians in Antioch do not keep kosher consistently and are not trying "to be justified by works of law," what exactly is wrong?[24]

Perhaps with this question we have gone astray. It is natural to expect a parallel between the situation in Galatia and the situation in Antioch, which Paul describes to the Galatians, but, after all, it is not the gentiles in Antioch whom Paul criticizes; it is the Jews. But if Paul's rebuke of the Jews is not about misleading the gentiles, what is it about?

---

24. Why does Paul not have more to say about "the ones from James"? They seem partly to blame for Cephas's actions (he "fear[ed] those of the circumcision"), and their strict law observance put them farther from the gentiles than Cephas or Barnabas. But a focus on them would complicate an account which Cephas's inconsistency makes simple. They add nothing to Paul's story.

I think that it is about the Jews' own confusion; the Jews, in Paul's view, have misled themselves. They are maintaining a division that no longer exists. Listen to Paul's rebuke of Cephas: "Jew … gentile … Jew … gentile … Jew …" like a drumbeat. We are just a page from Paul's explicit dissolution of this division in 3:28: "There is no Jew or Greek … for we are all one in Christ Jesus." This is foreshadowed in a paradox displayed in 2:14. Jews and gentiles in Antioch have been eating the same meals, first according to gentile practice and then according to Jewish practice; now Paul says that this series of meals—the same meals for everyone—has, on the one hand, made the Jews into gentiles but, on the other hand, the gentiles into Jews. How could that be true? If it is, how can one tell which is which? The distinction between Jew and gentile has been dissolved. Neither term marks an identifiable group, and to claim to be either is merely to assume a role—precisely Paul's charge against Cephas and the other Jewish Christians in Antioch.[25]

What about James's emissaries—and, for that matter, James himself (supposing that these emissaries fairly represent James)? So far as Paul's account discloses, they have kept the law faithfully; it is not a "role" for them. True. But they must see that it is a role for Cephas and the Jewish Christians of Antioch, and they accept this role-playing. "We" in verses 15–17 does not include James's representatives, but "we" are accepted by those representatives. Here lies the importance of Paul's declaration that he condemned Cephas "before everyone." The men from James might have kept aloof from Cephas and the others as betrayers of the law, and therefore false followers of Jesus, but they do not. The law may not be a role for them, but accepting that it is merely a role for their Jewish colleagues, they accept that it is not essential, even for Jews.

Let us now look back over this story and recall key points. The development of Paul's narrative can be plotted on two scales. One scale we might call dramatic; this is the degree to which Paul brings his audience into a scene, allowing them to imagine that they are present at the events

---

25. In a different context, Paul acknowledges the propriety of taking such a role but for a reason not available to Cephas in Antioch. Paul tells the Corinthians that "to those under the law I became as one under the law" but his purpose then was *that I might gain those under the law* (1 Cor 9:20). In Antioch, Cephas is not trying to gain the ones from James; dining with them does not spread the gospel, and it risks dividing the community. Thanks to the gentiles, that did not happen in Antioch, but it could happen elsewhere.

Paul describes. The second scale is conflict, as a part of the scenes in Paul's story; this conflict might be described abstractly, in terms of the issues at stake, but Paul's story makes the conflict concrete and personal: Paul against Cephas. The story moves along these two scales together. Of the first episode, we are told only that it lasted two weeks; dramatically, it is less than a scene, and there is no suggestion of conflict. The second episode, which follows immediately although the passage of time is noted, includes a little detail—almost enough for a scene, although the disjointed way in which the story is told makes it difficult to visualize. Key points of discussion are paraphrased, if not quoted exactly. Conflict is presented, although it seems to have crept into Paul's account almost against his intention and to have been resolved. Is this clumsiness, or is Paul ratcheting up the tension in preparation for his climactic scene?

In the third episode, everything is tightly woven; the course of events is clear, leading to the one direct statement reported in Paul's narrative—indeed, anywhere in Paul's letters—and here the conflict hinted in Paul's account of the second episode is explicit. As Paul becomes more explicit, conflict moves to the center; it dominates this scene, which ends abruptly, with the conflict unresolved.

So abrupt is the ending, in fact, that many readers do not recognize it as an ending; wanting to know what happened after Paul delivered his dramatic rebuke of Cephas, they infer that verses 15–21 tell what happened: Paul continued to speak, enlarging on his view of the relationship between law and righteousness (verses 15–18), then turning to his personal experience of the law, life, death, Christ and God (verses 19–21).[26] I think this interpretation misses Paul's tone and his storytelling. The story has posed a problem, and while the problem can be posed in other ways—in Romans Paul does pose it in other ways—this story dramatizes the problem; it draws in the reader or hearer as eyewitness to events that make the problem real, concrete, and disturbing. But the solution to the problem posed by the story is not to be found in the story. Galatians 2:14 has left us in a

---

26. See, for example, Ernest de Witt Burton, *A Critical and Exegetical Commentary on the Epistle to the Galatians*, ICC (Edinburgh: T&T Clark, 1921), 117; Heinrich Schlier, *Der Brief an die Galater: Übersetzt und erklärt*, KEK 7 (Göttingen: Vandenhoeck & Ruprecht, 1965), 87; J. Loius Martyn, *Galatians: A New Translation with Introduction and Commentary*, AB 33A (New York: Doubleday, 1997), 246. Contra Betz, *Galatians*, 58; de Boer, *Galatians*, 129; Longenecker, *Galatians*, 63. Das, *Galatians*, 238, is undecided (but on p. 196 he places a closing quotation mark at the end of 2:14).

paradoxical, impossible position, and getting out of this position requires a different approach. This is what Paul undertakes in 2:15–21—actually, two different but related approaches.

The change in tone and mode of discourse from verse 14 to verses 15–21 is too marked for the one to continue the other. Not only is verse 14 acerbic and confrontational, while verses 15–16 are calm and reflective; the complex syntax of the latter two verses (four subordinate clauses appended to the main clause, ἡμεῖς ... ἐπιστεύσαμεν) is literary through and through, impossible in speech. That Paul continues after verse 16 with another eighty-three words in fifteen clauses, without interruption or reply, confirms that we have no conversation here.[27] (Are we to suppose that Cephas and Barnabas crept away, accepting Paul's rebuke in silence? If so, why doesn't Paul say so?)

In 2:14, Paul's story arrives at the deconstruction of the Jew-gentile division that is taken for granted everywhere. The conflict is not resolved but rejected. Paul does not wish to diminish the impact of this step; his dramatization and personalization rather emphasize it. That is the point of Paul's story, and especially its dramatic concluding scene. Now Paul steps back to consider the basis and effect of what his story has shown. In verses 15–21 Paul shifts, rhetorically, twice. First, he restates as an issue of principle what he has just described as a personal conflict between Cephas and himself. Next, he again restates this issue in personal terms but now as a personal experience which he evidently expects all to share: himself, the Galatians, presumably Cephas.

Thus in verse 15 Paul leaves his story behind, and he turns to "abstract, argumentative writing," to borrow Bernard Williams's description of the philosophical approach to issues of conduct.[28] He steps back for a moment from his rejection of the distinction between gentiles and Jews, assuming for the purpose of his argument that Jews are, as they may think, opposed to "gentile sinners," and then he proceeds to show in a fresh way that this cannot be true. The personal remarks and references to specific actions in verse 14 are replaced by general propositions applying to all persons in a defined category. *Knowing that we are justified by the faith of Christ and not by works, we trusted in Christ and not in works*—a general proposition

---

27. The change in mode of discourse is also marked by asyndeton, the absence of any particle connecting v. 15 with what precedes it.

28. Bernard Williams, *Ethics and the Limits of Philosophy* (Cambridge: Harvard University Press, 1985), 1.

is put forth and an inference is drawn; the logic is clear. Then another inference is suggested, and rejected: *If, seeking justification in Christ, we are seen to be sinners, has Christ brought about sin? Nonsense!* Why nonsense? Because the inference here is drawn from an invalid premise. Omitting works of law is not a sin; the error to be avoided is, rather, self-contradiction: if I contradict myself, I myself show that I am wrong. The abstract logical mode continues; the logic of self-contradiction is clear. (We shall consider in a moment where the self-contradiction lies.)

Paul's argument in verses 15–17 is grounded in the experience alluded to in verses 11–14 ("knowing … we are … we trusted"), but the mode of discourse is different, suited to the practical question which confronts the Galatians and exercises Paul: must the Galatians, who are gentile, observe Jewish law—and especially, must they be circumcised? How might this question be resolved, except through general and abstract argument? In verses 15–18, Paul has taken a natural path. But there is another approach to a question of what to do, which is through one's own experience; and in verse 19 Paul slides away from abstract argument into what appears to be a personal account of his experience, an account which is not precise or logical, nor is it a story like that in 1:11–2:14; it is a third way, sugges-tive and imaginative. *I through law died to law* (v. 19). Paul's language is elliptical; we cannot tell whether he is describing a scene or summarizing a course of events or sliding into some flight of fancy. This seems to be something that has happened to Paul, something that grew out of the law and yet, paradoxically, severed his connection to the law. It is difficult to say more than this with confidence. Paul has chosen language that cannot be taken literally; there is no physical death here. (Was this the moment of God's revelation of his son to Paul? But how did that grow out of the law?) *To live to God* suggests submission and dedication to God, but if Paul had meant only (or exactly) that, he could have said it that way; call-ing this Paul's *life* suggests that what has happened to Paul is, somehow, the fundamental basis of what he now is.[29] At the same time, Paul's para-doxical assertion that he is no longer himself but a vessel for Christ (v. 20) challenges logic in its attempt to convey Paul's experience. But then, in closing this meditation, Paul's "if … then" formulation in verse 21 again invokes logic: *if the law suffices for justification, then* Christ's death was

---

29. The ambiguity of Paul's claim is heightened by the breadth of meaning of the dative θεῷ, which I have rendered "to God," but it could be translated in various other ways, such as "for God," "in God," or "by God."

pointless. Significantly, here Paul presents an unreal condition as though real: not "if the law *did* suffice" (secondary tense, with ἄν), but "if it *does*"; this is Paul's normal method in responding to an unreal condition which others claim is fulfilled.[30] With a rhetorical flourish, Paul turns back this charge of nullifying the gift of the law onto those (presumably the Jewish Christian missionaries in Galatia) who make it: *God's inviolable gift is not the law but Christ.*

We can now review the reference to self-contradiction in verse 18. The preceding verses (verses 15–17) invite us to think that verse 18 refers back to law: taking up law again after abandoning it would be a contradiction.[31] But verses 19–20 suggest a reference forward, to Paul himself; it would be a contradiction—surely it would be impossible!—for him to take up the old self which no longer lives.[32] We do not have to choose between these options, which are both consistent with Paul's thought; the old self and the law are bound together. In verse 18, Paul suggests a double point, relying on both logical thought and personal experience, two points that do not conflict but reinforce one another.[33]

Paul's emphasis in verses 19–20 on his experience raises a question: Will his experience matter to the Galatians? Granting that they first heard the good news from Paul, his authority is now under attack; in this situation, would not using his experience to support his authority amount to pulling himself up by his own bootstraps? No. The key here is that Paul offers his experience as illustrative and suggestive, not authoritative. He assumes that the Galatians have had a similar experience (how could they understand him otherwise?), and it is to that experience, not his own, that Paul now appeals. Just after this, Paul invokes the Galatians' experience directly, reminding them that they received the spirit "from faithful hearing" (ἐξ ἀκοῆς πίστεως, 3:2, 5)—surely Paul's own experience as well, alluded to in 2:15–17: the same experience for Jew and gentile. We can

---

30. See Michael Winger, "Unreal Conditions in the Letters of Paul," *JBL* 105 (1986): 110–12.

31. So most commentaries—for example, Burton, *Galatians*, 130: Betz, *Galatians*, 120–21; Martyn, *Galatians*, 255–56. The term "transgressor" (παραβάτης) makes a reference to law seem natural; but since (as we have seen) Paul is moving into highly metaphorical language, a common literal meaning is not decisive.

32. Verse 18 introduces the first-person singular, which dominates vv. 19–20 (eleven verbs or pronouns), in contrast to the first-person plural of vv. 15–17b (five verbs or pronouns).

33. Note that Paul uses a plural form (ταῦτα) to mark what he has destroyed.

also see this connection in 4:6, "God sent the spirit of his son into our hearts, crying 'Abba! Father!'" (note "our"), and in 4:9, "You have come to be known by God"—like Paul himself. Finally, we can see this in the close of Galatians, where Paul declares that through the cross of Christ "the cosmos has been crucified to me, and I to the cosmos," and "neither is circumcision anything, nor uncircumcision, but new creation" (6:14–15).[34] The experience here is universal, not Paul's alone; otherwise, how could it bring "new creation," the end of both circumcision and uncircumcision? The themes of 2:19–20 are repeated: death (death to law, crucifixion with Christ, crucifixion to the cosmos) but also life (life to God, Christ within, new creation). In this passage, crucifixion is inverted, as though the crucified one is the crucifier; it is "the Lord Jesus Christ" who breaks the connection with the old cosmic order of circumcision and uncircumcision, Jew and gentile (6:15). Whose connection? Not Paul's alone; Paul stands for everyone whose life is newly created in Christ.

What Paul does with these experiences of Christ, or of the spirit, is quite different from what he does with his account of his experiences with Cephas. That is a story intended to draw Paul's audience into events in which they had no part—to make them feel as though they were present, to involve them in a developing and dramatic conflict, first as remote observers, then more intimately, and finally as virtual witnesses of an explosive encounter between Paul and Cephas, in the presence of all the affected parties, both gentiles and Jews, even representatives of James the brother of the Lord (perhaps the colleagues of the Jewish Christian missionaries in Galatia?). In this way, the Galatians are invested in the outcome.[35] That is the narrative's function in leading Paul's audience to the dissolution of the barrier between gentiles and Jews that Paul first depicts through this narrative. In 2:15–21, proceeding to explain why this dissolution is necessary, Paul judges that now he can invoke the Galatians'

---

34. Some later manuscripts have "your" rather than "our" in 4:6, but "our" is "strongly supported by early and diversified witnesses." Bruce M. Metzger, *A Textual Commentary on the Greek New Testament*, 2nd ed. (Stuttgart: Deutsche Bibelgesellschaft, 1994), 526.

35. "For the effect of genius is not to persuade the audience but rather to transport them out of themselves. Invariably what inspires wonder, with its power of amazing us, always prevails over what is merely convincing and pleasing. For our persuasions are usually under our own control, while these things exercise an irresistible power and mastery and get the better of every listener" (Longinus, *De sublimitate* 1.4 [Halliwell and Fyfe]).

own experience, which Paul takes to be similar to his own. He cannot do this by telling a story, however, because stories require details, and Paul does not know the details of the individual Galatians' stories. Of necessity, Paul's method changes.

What does not change is the underlying theme that what one knows is what has happened. The division between Jew and gentile disappears because it has—not as a matter of theory, but as a matter of fact—in Galatia just as in Antioch: a lesson of Paul's story.

## Bibliography

Aejmelaeus, Lars. *Die Rezeption der Paulusbriefe in der Miletrede (Apg 20:18–35)*. AASF B/232. Helsinki: Suomalainen Tiedeakatemia, 1987.

Barclay, John M. G. "Paul's Story: Theology as Testimony." Pages 133–56 in *Narrative Dynamics in Paul: A Critical Assessment*. Edited by Bruce W. Longenecker. Louisville: Westminster John Knox, 2002.

Bauckham, Richard. "James and the Gentiles (Acts 15.13–21)." Pages 154–84 in *History, Literature, and Society in the Book of Acts*. Edited by Ben Witherington. Cambridge: Cambridge University Press, 1996.

Betz, Hans Dieter. *Galatians*. Hermeneia. Philadelphia: Fortress, 1979.

de Boer, Martinus C. *Galatians*. NTL. Louisville: Westminster John Knox, 2011.

———. "Paul's Use and Interpretation of a Justification Tradition in Galatians 2.15–21." *JSNT* 28 (2005): 189–216.

Burton, Ernest de Witt. *A Critical and Exegetical Commentary on the Epistle to the Galatians*. ICC. Edinburgh: T&T Clark, 1921.

Das, A. Andrew. *Galatians*. ConC. Saint Louis: Concordia, 2014.

Fredriksen, Paula. "Judaizing the Nations: The Ritual Demands of Paul's Gospel." *NTS* 56 (2010): 232–52.

Halliwell, Stephen, and W. H. Fyfe, trans. *Poetics. On the Sublime*. LCL. Cambridge: Harvard University Press, 1995.

Longenecker, Richard N. *Galatians*. WBC 41. Grand Rapids: Zondervan, 1990.

Luther, Martin. *Lectures on Galatians*. Vol. 26 of *Luther's Works*. Edited by Jaroslav Pelikan. Saint Louis: Concordia, 1963.

Martyn, J. Louis. *Galatians: A New Translation with Introduction and Commentary*. AB 33A. New York: Doubleday, 1997.

Metzger, Bruce M. *A Textual Commentary on the Greek New Testament*. 2nd ed. Stuttgart: Deutsche Bibelgesellschaft, 1994.

Müller, Klaus. *Tora für die Völker: Die noachidischen Gebote und Ansätze zu ihrer Rezeption im Christentum.* 2nd ed. Studien zu jüdischem Volk und christlicher Gemeinde 15. Berlin: Institut Kirche und Judentum, 1998.

Pervo, Richard I. *Dating Acts: Between the Evangelists and the Apologists.* Santa Rosa, CA: Polebridge, 2006.

Schlier, Heinrich. *Der Brief an die Galater: Übersetzt und erklärt.* KEK 7. Göttingen: Vandenhoeck & Ruprecht, 1965.

Tomson, Peter J. *Paul and the Jewish Law: Halakha in the Letters of the Apostle to the Gentiles.* CRINT 1. Assen: Van Gorcum, 1990.

Tyson, Joseph B. *Marcion and Luke-Acts: A Defining Struggle.* Columbia: University of South Carolina Press, 2006.

Walker, William O., Jr. "Acts and the Pauline Corpus Reconsidered." *JSNT* 24 (1985): 3–23.

Williams, Bernard. *Ethics and the Limits of Philosophy.* Cambridge: Harvard University Press, 1985.

Winger, Michael. "Unreal Conditions in the Letters of Paul." *JBL* 105 (1986): 110–12.

# The Epiphany of Christ and the Identity of Scripture

John M. G. Barclay

The hallmark of Joel Marcus's outstanding scholarship is his special combination of historical precision and theological sensitivity. Throughout his work, careful attention is paid to a vast range of primary sources, with an unflinching commitment to treat them honestly, however inconvenient the results. But with this is combined an acute consciousness of the theological issues at stake in the interpretation of both Jewish and Christian texts. Whatever Joel discusses, one knows that it *matters,* and nowhere more so than in the subject matter of this volume. As a long-time friend of Joel's, and erstwhile colleague (at Glasgow University in the 1990s), I can attest that his personal and academic concerns have had a profound influence on me. I am still recovering from the effects of his brilliant and existentially shattering 1995 Good Friday sermons at Glasgow's Episcopal Cathedral, which have now been republished for the good of us all.[1]

Among the central themes of Joel's scholarship, not least in his seminal work on Mark, are the christological exegesis of the Old Testament and the apocalyptic character of early Christian theology.[2] *Apocalyptic* conveys a fairly precise cluster of features in Joel's work, as in the scholarship of J. Louis Martyn and Martinus de Boer with which he dialogues. The approaching end of the world, the expected arrival of God's dominion in

---

1. Joel Marcus, *Jesus and the Holocaust: Reflections on Suffering and Hope* (New York: Doubleday, 1997; repr., Grand Rapids: Eerdmans, 2017).

2. From his voluminous scholarship, I mention here only his *The Way of the Lord: Christological Exegesis of the Old Testament in the Gospel of Mark* (Louisville: Westminster John Knox; Edinburgh: T&T Clark, 1992) and his universally acclaimed Anchor Bible commentary on Mark: *Mark 1–8: A New Translation with Introduction and Commentary,* AB 27 (New York: Doubleday, 2000); *Mark 8–16: A New Translation with Introduction and Commentary,* AB 27A (New York: Doubleday, 2009).

power, the cosmic battle to free humanity from its slavery to suprahuman powers—these are all features central to Joel's reading of Mark.[3] But there is also an epistemological element to this phenomenon, because what happens in Christ constitutes a revelation, a making manifest of something that was previously hidden and heretofore unknown: at the turn of the ages something *new* happens both in knowledge and in salvation, something neither present nor possible before.[4] There is here a possible tension between the claim of novelty in revelation and the christological exegesis of the ancient scriptures: was what was now known already somehow "in" the scriptural text (in which case, why was it not known before?), or was it a new knowledge genuinely unheard of before, never before available to human articulation or understanding? This tension goes right to the heart of the subject matter of this book. It is clear that as early Christian groups developed a sense of identity self-consciously different from that of Jews—and that process was patchy, with multiple variations in location, time, and social level—questions regarding the significance, identity, and interpretation of the scriptures were bound to arise. Numerous early Christian sources indicate how fraught these questions became both within Christian communities and in debate, real or imagined, with non-Christian Jews who disputed Christian readings of their scriptural heritage. In general, the earlier that Christian groups were dominated socially and intellectually by their gentile members, the more one might expect them to downplay the Jewish identity and interpretation of the scriptures, if they had access to these texts, or paid attention to them, at all; where Jewish counter-claims about the meaning of scripture are heard, as in the Epistle of Barnabas and Justin's *Dialogue with Trypho*, the extent and the vehemence of the gentile Christian response testifies to their intellectual discomfort on this matter. Correlatively, the more the gentile Christian church regarded itself as something wholly new on the world stage (even if known by God from all eternity), and the more it therefore emphasized the novelty of salvation and revelation in Christ, the more freedom one

---

3. See Marcus, *Mark 1–8*, 71–73, with recurrent emphasis throughout his commentary.

4. See Mark 4:11–12 on the "mystery of the dominion of God" revealed only to Jesus's disciples and 4:22 on the making manifest of something "hidden," with Joel's commentary ad loc. See also the seminal essay by J. Louis Martyn, "Epistemology at the Turn of the Ages," in *Theological Issues in the Letters of Paul* (Edinburgh: T&T Clark, 1997), 89–110.

might expect it to have in the ways it classified and used (or disregarded) the scriptures. In this essay, I want to tease out a particular strand in early Christian discourse on the epiphany of Christ and the church and to trace some of its effects on the ways scripture is described and deployed. For the sake of breadth, I sacrifice depth, but I hope that the questions at least will be stimulating to a scholar who unfailingly poses the most penetrating questions, both to the sources and to students and peers.

## Novelty and Revelation: Exploring a Question

Despite the cultural disadvantage of doing so, the early Christians made a habit of claiming for themselves the status of novelty.[5] Jesus's message was hailed as "new teaching" (Mark 1:27), a form of "new wine" (Mark 2:22); at the Last Supper he was remembered as inaugurating a "new covenant" (Mark 14:24; compare with 1 Cor 11:25). Paul considers himself a minister of this "new covenant" (2 Cor 3:6; compare with Heb 8:8, 12:24), but he also speaks more expansively of a "new creation" (Gal 6:15; 2 Cor 5:17), in which, he proclaims with excitement, "the old has passed away; behold, the new has arrived" (τὰ ἀρχαῖα παρῆλθεν, ἰδοὺ γέγονεν καινά, 2 Cor 5:17). With the appearing of Christ, a "new humanity" has been established (Eph 2:15), in which the believer is "dressed" at baptism (Col 3:10; Eph 4:24).[6] The Epistle of Barnabas celebrates the formation of Christ's "new people" (7.5), with a "new law" (2.6), while the Epistle to Diognetus, to which we will return, raises as one of its lead questions "why this new people or way of life [καινὸν τοῦτο γένος ἢ ἐπιτήδευμα] came into being now and not before" (1). Such an emphasis on novelty could also be applied to the realm of knowledge, not least in conjunction with the notion of a mystery that is now revealed in Christ but was previously hidden or unknown.[7]

---

5. See Suetonius's sneer concerning their *nova superstitio* (*Nero* 16); for nuance on Greek perceptions on this matter, see Armand D'Angour, *The Greeks and the New: Novelty in Ancient Greek Imagination and Experience* (Cambridge: Cambridge University Press, 2011).

6. On the clothing imagery, see Jung Hoon Kim, *The Significance of Clothing Imagery in the Pauline Corpus*, JSNTSup 268 (London: T&T Clark, 2004).

7. For identification and discussion of a "revelation schema" of hidden wisdom now revealed, see Nils Dahl, "Formgeschichtliche Beobachtungen zur Christusverkündigung in der Gemeindepredigt," in *Neutestamentliche Studien für Rudolf Bultmann: Zu seinem siebzigsten Geburtstag am 20. August 1954*, ed. Walther Eltester, BZNW 21 (Berlin: Töpelmann, 1957), 3–9; Michael Wolter, "Verborgene Weisheit und Heil für

Thus, famously and influentially, Paul declares in 1 Cor 2:7–10 that the wisdom of the cross was unknown and unknowable for the "rulers of this age," since it is a

> wisdom of God hidden in a mystery [θεοῦ σοφίαν ἐν μυστηρίῳ τὴν ἀποκεκρυμμένην], which God fixed beforehand [προώρισεν] for our glory … as it is written, "what eye has not seen and ear has not heard, and has not entered into a human heart, what God has prepared for those who love him," this God has revealed to us through the Spirit; for the Spirit searches all things, even the depths of God.[8]

Communicated by the Spirit, this truth is only available to "spiritual people" who have "the mind of Christ" (1 Cor 2:12–16); it apparently was not, and could not have been, available to anyone else, at any other time.[9] Nonetheless, Paul speaks of this matter by reference to "what is (that is, has been) written [καθὼς γέγραπται]," even if here what was previously written says only *that* the unimaginable has been prepared, not *of what* it consists. Elsewhere, of course, following already established tradition, Paul speaks of the Christ event as taking place "in accordance with the scriptures" (1 Cor 15:3–4). In his unusual but apparently well-considered expression, the scripture "seeing in advance [προϊδοῦσα] that God would justify the nations by faith, preached the good news in advance [προευηγγελίσατο] to Abraham: 'in you all the nations will be blessed'" (Gal 3:8; citing Gen 12:3, 18:18). This predictive work of scripture is elsewhere attributed specifically to the prophets, since the good news of God was "pre-promised [προεπηγγείλατο] through the prophets in the holy scriptures" (Rom 1:1–2).

Paul's letters thus contain *both* discourse about a prehidden mystery, revealed only now, for the first time, in the event of Christ and by the gift of the Spirit, *and* discourse about scriptural announcements and promises which anticipated what took place in Christ and in the effects of his

---

die Heiden: Zur Traditionsgeschichte und Intention des 'Revelationsschemas,'" *ZTK* 84 (1987): 297–319. See now the full and illuminating discussion in T. J. Lang, *Mystery and the Making of a Christian Historical Consciousness: From Paul to the Second Century*, BZNW 219 (Berlin: de Gruyter, 2015), to which I am indebted in what follows.

8. Translations here and elsewhere are my own.

9. Cf. 2 Cor 4:3–6, where the light that shines in the darkness (which corresponds to the blindness over the minds of unbelievers)—the light of the knowledge of the glory of God—is available only in "our hearts," "in the face of Jesus Christ."

coming. This latter conviction—that scripture must somehow speak of Christ and of what God has done through his life, death, and resurrection—is clearly present from the very beginning of the Jesus movement (1 Cor 15:3–5) and accords with the Jewish origins of the movement; however different the members of this movement felt themselves to be, the scriptures were the natural reservoir for their speech about themselves and about the action of God in Christ. Thus begins a long and increasingly comprehensive rereading of the scriptures which, like that conducted by the Dead Sea sect, is conscious of its own hermeneutical endeavours and its retrospective discovery of the deeper meanings of the text (see Luke 24:27, 44–45). Demonstrating the "fulfilment" of the scriptures—their integration with Christian convictions in a schema whereby what was said in advance has now become true—becomes a key ideological task in the early Christian movement and, where it engaged with contradictory Jewish readings of the same scriptures, one fraught with difficulty and inclined to polemics. But it was also possible to draw out the other dimension of Pauline discourse, highlighting the unprecedented and previously inconceivable novelty of what had "appeared" or "been made manifest" in Christ; and on this line of thought, what one should expect of the scriptures, and what status or meaning they should have, might be very unclear.

The letters of Ignatius of Antioch indicate the intellectual and practical difficulties of those inclined to pursue what we might call the epiphanic interpretation of the Christ-event. In *Eph.* 19, Ignatius emphasizes the cosmic novelty of the Christ-event—the human "manifestation" of God in the birth, life, death, and resurrection of Christ. The brightness of the star was unprecedented: "its light was indescribable and its novelty [ἡ καινότης αὐτοῦ] occasioned astonishment" (19.2). Not only did it surpass all other stars, but the appearance of "this novelty without parallel" (ἡ καινότης ἡ ἀνόμοιος αὐτοῖς) created confusion concerning its origin. This was not a new stage in the unfolding history of salvation but an unprecedented change in the condition of the cosmos: "all magic was destroyed and every kind of evil disappeared" when "God became manifest in a human way for the sake of the newness of eternal life" (θεοῦ ἀνθρωπίνως φανερουμένου εἰς καινότητα ἀδίου ζωῆς, 19.3). This newness, which is also called "the dissolution of death," surely refers to the resurrection, an event that is utterly new in the history of the cosmos (19.3). What began here had been "prepared by God" (τὸ παρὰ θεῷ ἀπηρτισμένον, 19.3), but to judge from the opening of this letter, this event, together with the church, had

been "foreordained before the ages" (τῇ προωρισμένη πρὸ αἰώνων, proem).[10]
It was integral to God's pretemporal plans for the world but not part of a
historical process rolling out across time.[11]

This emphasis on *ex nihilo* newness seems to be matched by Ignatius's comments in *Magn.* 8, where he speaks of God "manifesting himself"
through his Son, and of this Son, God's word, coming forth from silence
(ἀπὸ σιγῆς). However, in this context, Ignatius speaks also of "divine
prophets" who "lived according to Jesus Christ" (Ignatius, *Magn.* 8.2).
The context indicates that here, as in *Philadelphians*, Ignatius was strug-
gling to clarify what to say about those (probably fellow Christians) who
had greater familiarity with the scriptures, and were pressing its authority (including, perhaps, some of its commandments) as the interpretative
grid within which to understand the Christ-event.[12] Ignatius's reaction is
to interpret their views as "false opinions," based on "old fables" (*Magn.*
8.1) and following "old ways" (9.1), "bad yeast" which has grown "old and
sour" as opposed to the "new yeast" which is Jesus Christ (10.2; compare
with 1 Cor 5:7). He also, significantly, interprets their proposed scriptural
framework as "living according to Judaism," and he declares that to do
that "now" is to admit that one has not received God's grace (*Magn.* 8.1;
compare with 10.1: "it is absurd to proclaim Jesus Christ and to judaize").
Ignatius will not jettison the scriptures altogether, but he redescribes what
he takes from them as "the prophets," a time-free group of people who
cannot be classed as "old" because "they lived according to Jesus Christ"
and "were inspired by his grace" (*Magn.* 8.2). It appears that Ignatius's
epiphanic scheme, with its emphasis on the novelty of the Christ-message
that was manifested "from silence," requires him to reclassify the scriptures as "the prophets" and to present them as far as possible in terms
contemporaneous with Christ, not as figures from a pre-Christian era but

---

10. Cf. Ign. *Magn.* 6.1, where Jesus is described as being "with the Father before
the ages [πρὸ αἰώνων] and manifested at the end."

11. See further the discussion of mystery and revelation in Ignatius in Lang,
*Mystery*, 131–47. If there is an οἰκονομία for Ignatius, it concerns "the new man Jesus
Christ" (Ignatius, *Eph.* 20.1).

12. The reconstruction of Ignatius's problematic is notoriously difficult. See, for
instance, C. K. Barrett, "Jews and Judaizers in the Epistles of Ignatius," in *Jews, Greeks
and Christians: Religious Cultures in Late Antiquity; Essays in Honor of William David
Davies*, ed. Robert Hamerton-Kelly and Robin Scroggs (Leiden: Brill, 1976), 220–44;
Judith M. Lieu, *Image and Reality: The Jews in the World of the Christians in the Second
Century* (Edinburgh: T&T Clark, 1996), 23–56.

as people already living "according to Christ" and beneficiaries of his (in fact, newly appeared) grace. Since Jesus is, for Ignatius, "our only teacher" (9.1), the prophets also were "his disciples in the Spirit," who awaited him as their teacher (9.2). Since they rightly expected him, they were, in fact (Ignatius says), raised by Christ when he arrived (9.2), so that they became his disciples not only from the past but actually in his own time.[13] Here, in other words, the prophets are made as contemporary with Christ and with the church as it is possible for them to be.

The same problematic in the handling of scripture seems to under-lie the contorted discussions of Ignatius, *Phld.* 6–9. There Ignatius warns against those who would "interpret Judaism to you" (ἐὰν δέ τις Ἰουδαϊσμὸν ἑρμενεύῃ ὑμῖν, 6.1), and the word "interpret" (followed by "hear") suggests that what is at stake here is the interpretation of texts, whether by Jewish or gentile Christians.[14] Ignatius once again makes "speaking about Christ" the only criterion of value; anything else is just a relic of the past, "monu-ments and tombs of the dead" (6.1). The status and authority of the scrip-tures have clearly come to a head when Ignatius was confronted by people (probably Christians) who said "if I do not find it in the archives, I do not believe (it to be) in the gospel" (8.2).[15] The "archives" here almost certainly refer to the scriptures, depicted as an ancient and authoritative text, and Ignatius here faced those whose interpretation of the gospel was framed (and limited) by these scriptures. His initial reaction was to claim the same ground ("I said, 'It is written' "), but they clearly challenged him robustly ("They said, 'that is just the question,' " 8.2), and he was not only out of his depth intellectually but also on uncomfortable ground theologically. His immediate fall-back is revealing: "For me, Jesus Christ is the ancient records; the untouchable records are his cross and death, and his resurrec-tion, and the faith that comes through him" (8.2). Once again, the pressure of the claim to "newness" makes Ignatius disinclined to appeal to anything

---

13. Ignatius presumably has Matt 27:52–53 in mind, the raising of "the saints" who came out of their tombs, entered Jerusalem, and "appeared to many." The con-nection is dismissed by Schoedel, who appeals to a more general "descent of Christ into Hades," but the specific mention of their resurrection is too striking a parallel to ignore; see W. R. Schoedel, *Ignatius of Antioch: A Commentary on the Letters of Igna-tius of Antioch*, Hermeneia (Philadelphia: Fortress, 1985), 124.

14. See Schoedel, *Ignatius*, 203 ("perhaps it was the 'expounding' [exegetical expertise] that was the problem, and not the 'Judaism' [observance])." See also the essay in this volume by Daniel Boyarin.

15. I follow here the well-reasoned translation of Schoedel, *Ignatius*, ad loc.

from the pre-Christian past: the "archives" can and should stretch no further back than the death and resurrection of Christ.

One might understand how someone with such views on the new epiphany in Christ and the Jewishness of the scriptures might end up, in due course, in the Marcionite church. But Ignatius himself does not go that far, not only because he maintains a positive view of creation but also because he can retain the scriptures provided they remain within a unified field whose center and focus is Christ. As the "high priest," Christ alone is entrusted with "the hidden things of God" (Ignatius, *Phld.* 9.1).[16] He is "the door of the Father" through whom Abraham, Isaac, Jacob, the prophets, the apostles, and the church all enter, as a united phenomenon (9.2). Without entering into scriptural exegesis, Ignatius sweeps up the biblical patriarchs and the scriptural texts (relabeled "the prophets") into the company of the apostles and the church, provided that all find their focal point in Christ. But even in this unity, he wants to keep clear the absolute priority of "the gospel" (the message about Jesus, not, it appears, a written text): "But there is something special [ἐξαίρετον] about the gospel—that is, the coming of the Savior, our Lord Jesus Christ, his suffering and resurrection. For the beloved prophets issued their proclamation with a view to him; but the gospel is the completion of immortality" (9.2). One may indeed "love the prophets" inasmuch as they hoped in Christ, were saved by Christ, stood in unity with Christ, were worthy of his love and admiration, and were testified to by Christ and "co-numbered in the gospel of our mutual hope" (5.2). But all this heavy labor to "Christianize" the prophets, together with anxiety about their Jewishness and their location in history before the event of Christ, indicates clearly the tension Ignatius is working within. At the end of the day, there is a clear order of priority: "pay attention to the prophets, but especially [ἐξαιρέτως] to the gospel" (Ignatius, *Smyrn.* 7.2), because there the new, salvific, and revelatory events are recounted: "the passion is clearly shown to us, and the resurrection is perfected" (7.2).

Ignatius therefore indicates what might happen when one emphasizes the newness of salvation and of revelation in Christ. Such an emphasis can raise questions about the status and authority of the scriptures known to

---

16. Schoedel, *Ignatius*, ad loc. references Josephus's parallel and contemporary claims for the priests' role in guarding the "records" of the Jews (*C. Ap.* 1.29–30). That *Christ* is here entrusted with the hidden things of God may echo, but correct, Paul's comment that the Jews have been entrusted with "the oracles of God" (Rom 3:2, a text to which we shall return at the end).

precede Christ and anxiety about their Jewishness in a movement becoming self-consciously different, proud of its "Christian" label and capable of constructing a novel antithesis between "Christianism" and "Judaism" (Ignatius, *Magn.* 10.2; *Phld.* 6.1). This does not necessarily require the repudiation of those scriptures, but it is telling that Ignatius works hard to wrestle them away from what he calls "Judaism" and that his preferred label for these texts is "the prophets," a label that helps to bring them into the closest possible relation to Christ.[17] Ignatius might have attempted to claim, as did some other early Christians, that the truth about Christ was somehow known, even previously revealed, but latent in the persons, objects, events, or predictions of the scriptural texts. Instead, he emphasized the novel, epiphanic character of the Christ-event, and thus the former *hiddenness* of the truth, and this made it difficult to name the role of the scriptures or to clarify their relation to Christ. Alerted to this difficulty from the example of Ignatius, we may now trace the strategies of some other early Christian texts where the revelation of a previously hidden Christ is a particularly significant theme.

### Epiphany and Scripture in Some Early Christian Texts

There are a number of early Christian texts that make a point of identifying the Christ-event as an epiphany or revelation and that accompany that motif with the statement or implication that what became known in Christ was not, and could not have been, known beforehand. In many cases, this is expressed in terms of a "hidden mystery," planned or prepared before all time but not previously revealed or known within human time.[18] In other cases, a connection is drawn between a pretemporal reality and the present church, while the whole pre-ecclesial span of human history is left as an empty space. In all such cases, a question may arise about the status and identity of scripture—what it is, where it comes from, and what it is about. That question is not always directly addressed, but it will be worth teasing

---

17. Ignatius once also refers to "the law of Moses" (*Smyrn.* 5.1), but "prophets" is clearly his preferred term. Josephus also speaks of the authors of scriptural history as "prophets" but for very different reasons (*C. Ap.* 1.37, 40); see my *Against Apion*, FJTC 10 (Leiden: Brill, 2007), ad loc.

18. For exploration of this motif, see especially Lang, *Mystery*, who brings out the importance of this schema for the development of an early Christian consciousness of time.

out what may be deduced from what is said, and what is left unsaid, in this regard. We will confine our attention here to three bodies of evidence: the deutero-Pauline material in the New Testament, the Epistle to Diognetus, and the homily known as 2 Clement.

## Deutero-Pauline Materials

The letter to the Colossians is the first to develop the mystery-language (derived from 1 Cor 2) into the outline of a temporal scheme. According to this letter, Paul was commissioned to preach "the mystery that was hidden from the ages and from the generations [τὸ μυστήριον τὸ ἀποκεκρυμμένον ἀπὸ τῶν αἰώνων καὶ ἀπὸ τῶν γενεῶν], but has now been revealed [νῦν δὲ ἐφανερώθη] to his saints, to whom God wished to make known the riches of the glory of this mystery among the nations, which is Christ among you, the hope of glory" (Col 1:26–27). Notable here (and in Eph 3:3–6) is the stress on the realization of this mystery in the sphere of "the nations," as if what really could not have been guessed before was the establishment and growth of the *gentile* church. No reference is made in Colossians to the Abrahamic promises or Isaianic prophecies, which were so important to Paul in this regard (there are no references to scripture at all in this letter), as if the gentile church has, for this author, come out of nowhere and is quite independent of the scriptural and Jewish basis that some were claiming for it. If there are some Jewish dimensions to what the author of Colossians is combatting,[19] it is significant that these are dismissed as "human tradition" (2:8) or "human commands and teaching" (2:22), no more than a "shadow" of what was to come (2:17). There is nothing here to encourage the expectation that scripture might be a helpful frame or reference point for understanding Christ; his mystery was, after all, only "now" made manifest to his saints.

In Ephesians, the gentile church is linked with the "polity" of Israel (2:11–22), but the "revealed mystery" language is retained, and expanded, in a way that stands in some tension with this link. According to Ephesians, believers have been chosen and foreordained in Christ *before* the foundation of the world (1:4–5, 11; 3:10–11), outside and before any covenant history with Israel. God's plan for the fullness of time (1:9)

---

19. For discussion of the target of Colossians, and the difficulty in reconstructing it, see my *Colossians and Philemon* (Sheffield: Sheffield Academic, 1997), 37–55.

constitutes a mystery made known to Paul "by revelation" (3:3), which was "not made known in other generations to the children of men" (ὃ ἑτέραις γενεαῖς οὐκ ἐγνωρίσθη τοῖς υἱοῖς τῶν ἀνθρώπων), as it has "now been revealed to his holy apostles and prophets in the Spirit" (3:5).[20] Alongside this claim, there is reference within 2:11–22 to the "covenants of promise" (2:12), but it is not clear how this can be correlated with the unknowable mystery. Certainly, where scripture is cited in this letter (4:8–9), it is introduced in the same way (διὸ λέγει) as is an early Christian saying (5:14), and both are taken to refer in an unmediated way to Christ. The same is true, famously, in the interpretation of Gen 2:24 in Eph 5:31–32. There is no indication here that this verse comes from the past (or refers to the past) and is only now, secondarily, referred to Christ: a gentile reader, unfamiliar with the origin of this text (which is not introduced as scripture or contextualized in the past) could be forgiven for thinking that in some mysterious way the text was only ever about Christ coming to join himself to his "wife," the church, just as he descended and then ascended to give her gifts (4:8–9).[21]

The same schema of mystery once concealed and now revealed is present in the deutero-Pauline doxology in Rom 16:25–27.[22] Here Paul's gospel is said to be "in accordance with a revelation which was kept in silence for long ages" (κατὰ ἀποκάλυψιν μυστηρίου χρόνοις αἰωνίοις σεσιγημένου, 16:25).[23] This mystery, in accord with now familiar language, "has now been revealed" (φανερωθέντος δὲ νῦν)—and then, rather surprisingly, there is added "and was made known through the prophetical scriptures" (διά τε γραφῶν προφητικῶν ... γνωρισθέντος, 16:26). It is unclear at first how something "kept in silence" could *also* be said to have been made known

20. The "as now" (ὡς νῦν) is to be taken not in a relative ("to the extent that it has now") but in an absolute sense, as Lang rightly insists (*Mystery*, 95). This differentiates "in unconditional terms the previous generations of concealment and the current era of revelation ... that which was not known in earlier generations was not in any way accessible to the human mind." The "prophets," named here after "the apostles," in connection with the Spirit, and after reference to what has "now" been revealed, appear to be Christian prophets, as in 2:20. If reference is made here to the scriptures (as "prophets"; see the discussion of Ignatius above and of Rom 16:26 below), the assertion of a previously unknowable mystery seems to be contradicted.

21. The "commandment" in 6:2 is also timeless, extracted from its original frame in the law of Moses (which is now abolished, 2:15).

22. On its inauthenticity and interpretation, see Lang, *Mystery*, 110–17.

23. Cf. the word spoken "out of silence" in Ignatius, *Magn.* 8.2 (discussed above).

through the prophetical scriptures, and the phrase might be an adden-
dum intended to correct the mystery-schema, and perhaps to align it with
Rom 1:2. In any case, what is clear here is that, if the scriptures are to be
accorded any place, it is under the rubric of "prophet" (as in Ignatius),
which might be taken in the sense either of "foretelling" or of "speaking
forth" on behalf of God. If taken in this latter sense, the scriptures might be
appropriated in this deutero-Pauline milieu not as a *past* document looking forward to Christ but as a timeless speech from God, which is heard to
make known the truth not before Christ but at the same time as, or even
after, the coming of Christ.

The Pastoral Epistles continue the same tradition about a "revelation," "appearance," or "epiphany" of Christ, decreed before all time, but
"now" manifested.[24] The letters celebrate "the grace given us in Christ
before long ages [πρὸ χρόνων αἰωνίων; compare with Rom 16:25], but
now revealed [φανερωθεῖσαν δὲ νῦν] through the epiphany [ἐπιφανεία] of
our Savior Christ Jesus" (2 Tim 1:9–10; compare with 1 Tim 3:16). As in
Ignatius (*Eph.* 19.3), what is revealed here *could not* have been revealed
before, because it concerns the destruction of death, "bringing to light
life and immortality" (2 Tim 1:10). Much the same language is used in
Titus (1:2, 2:11, 3:4), suggesting a cluster of epiphany phrases, which had
now become creedal statements in these Pauline churches. This does not
mean that the scriptures are ignored or repudiated, but neither are they
regarded as past, forward-looking documents in which were provided
advance glimpses of the Christian truth. Persons from scripture are cited
as tales of warning (Adam and Eve, 1 Tim 2:13–14; Jannes and Jambres,
2 Tim 3:8–9) and, more positively, "all scripture" is taken to be God-
breathed and "useful for teaching, reproof, correction, and education
in righteousness" (2 Tim 3:15–16). All this is for the sake of "the man
of God" who is "equipped for every good work" (2 Tim 3:17)—in other
words, it has contemporary Christian meaning and purpose—but nothing is indicated regarding its past origins or its address to Israel. Where
what is labeled "scripture" is (very rarely) cited, it "speaks" in the present tense (1 Tim 5:18), and here a saying from the gospel tradition ("the
laborer is worthy of his wage") is cited under the same rubric as a text
from Deut 25:4. No reader could have guessed from this that the scrip-

24. See Andrew Y. Lau, *Manifest in Flesh: The Epiphany Christology of the Pastoral Epistles*, WUNT 2/86 (Tübingen: Mohr Siebeck, 1996).

tures were *written before* Christ, or that they spoke to and about Israel. The Pastor is strongly opposed to "myths" and "genealogies" (1 Tim 1:4; 4:7; 2 Tim 4:4; Titus 1:14; 3:9), and he is wary of "the law," which is not really relevant to Christian believers (1 Tim 1:7–11), constitutes only "human commands" (Titus 1:14) and only causes disputes (Titus 3:9). As in Ignatius, the source of this confusion is labeled as "Jewish" ("Jewish myths," Titus 1:14; "those from circumcision," Titus 1:10) and probably concerns Christian believers who framed the Christ-event and its demands on believers by reference to scriptural stories and laws. Scripture used as the historical and legal frame of the gospel is labeled as "myth" and "genealogy," and it is associated with Jews; scripture as the moral guide for believers in the wake of the epiphany of Christ can be used as scripture, but its historical origins and its cultural associations with the Jewish people are carefully washed out.

The Epistle to Diognetus

The second-century Epistle to Diognetus makes a special point of the "newness" of the Christian faith, and its attitude to the scriptures is simpler still: it ignores them.[25] A heavy emphasis is placed here on the claim that the Christian truth, revealed by and in Christ, was simply inconceivable and unimaginable before God himself revealed it in the person of his Son. "Do not expect to learn from any *human* the mystery of their [the Christians'] religion" (4.6). Christians have not discovered this teaching through reflection or through the thinking of "inquisitive" people (5.3), since this is not an "earthly discovery" that has been handed down (παρεδόθη) to them or a mortal idea (7.1). What Christians believe, then, is no cultural heritage, the product of human history, or cogitation. Far from it! For what person had any idea what God was like before God himself came on the scene (8.1)? The sending of the Son is here taken to be not only a unique salvific event (about which chapter 9 is eloquent in praise of God's mercy to the unrighteous); it is also an epistemic event not only unimaginable

---

25. With most scholars, I take chapters 11–12 as from a different document and by a different author, *pace* L. W. Barnard, "The Epistle Ad Diognetum: Two Units from One Author," *ZNW* 56 (1965): 130–37. For a critical edition and commentary, see Clayton N. Jefford, *The Epistle to Diognetus (with the Fragment of Quadratus): Introduction, Text, and Commentary*, Oxford Apostolic Fathers (Oxford: Oxford University Press, 2013).

but by definition impossible before God himself stepped onto the human scene. "For no-one either saw God or made him known [ἐγνώρισεν], but he revealed himself [αὐτὸς δὲ ἑαυτὸν ἐπέδειξεν]" (8.5). God, of course, had great and inexpressible thoughts before this time, but he shared them not with human beings, only with his Son (8.9).

> And so, as long as he confined this in a mystery and kept his wise plan to himself, it appeared that he did not care about us, or give us any attention. But when he revealed [ἀπεκάλυψε] it through his beloved Son and manifested [ἐφανέρωσε] the things prepared from the beginning, he shared all things with us at once, that we might participate in his benefits, and see and understand. Which of us could ever have expected such things? (Diogn. 8.10–11)

It appears there is no space here for even a provisional, partial, or anticipatory expectation in the form of scriptural texts.

This emphasis on the unique, unanticipated, and unprecedented divine self-revelation in Christ is clearly connected both to the unique status of Christ and to his unique salvific achievement. It was only when the sum of human sin was so great, and that it was patently clear that humans deserved nothing but punishment and death, that God determined to intervene in grace: "When the time arrived that God had planned to manifest at last [λοιπὸν φανερῶσαι] his own kindness and power," he did not destroy us but, unbelievably, took our sins upon himself (9.2). This great salvific paradox, so far beyond human comprehension, is a good part of why the author of this text insists on the human inability to anticipate this event. But he is also concerned to insist throughout that the Christian phenomenon, paradoxical in so many other ways as well, is not another cultural product or human tradition, but a divine reality injected into, but at odds with, human history and culture. The third phenomenon he charts—different from both Greek and Jewish religion—is not just another inherited tradition. No reference is made in this text (Diogn. 1–10) to the scriptures, either as a part of the Jewish tradition (although many other Jewish phenomena are named in chapters 3–4) or among the resources of the Christian community. The scriptures are simply passed over in silence. It is hard to see how they could be integrated into the schema of revelation, and neither as human nor as divine speech could they compare with the unique revelation of God's nature and kindness in Christ. The christological epiphany has squeezed other media of revelation off the theological map.

## 2 Clement

The second-century homily known as 2 Clement has been unjustly over-looked in most accounts of early Christianity.[26] It speaks from within a gentile Christianity that is busy reminding itself of its ultimate allegiance and its moral obligations. Striking here is the assertion that the church is a form of "creation from nothing," a phenomenon planned from eternity but newly appeared on the world stage by a miracle of divine creation. Presuming that the addressees were gentiles and former idolaters (1.6–7), the author is highly conscious that a gentile church, worshiping the true God by abandoning idolatry, is a wholly novel phenomenon in human history, and celebrates the fact that God "called us when we were nothing [οὐκ ὄντας] and willed us into being from non-existence" (1.7). This, he insists, is exactly what Isa 54 is about (compare with Gal 4:27): the "barren woman" who had no children but now has many is the church, because it once had nothing and suddenly has many children (gentile believers). In fact, the text says that "the deserted woman" has *more* children than the one who had a husband, and this means that "our people" (ὁ λαὸς ἡμῶν) appeared to have been deserted by God, "but now we who have believed have become more than those who seem to have God" (2.3). This latter category appears to refer to the Jewish people,[27] and it bespeaks a gentile Christian communal consciousness as being both separate from the Jewish community and (in its local environment) larger than it.

This new and impressive historical phenomenon appears to have no historical origin or precursor, but it does have another kind of origin, one that is spiritual and from before all time. What the author calls "the first church, the spiritual one" (ἡ ἐκκλησία ἡ πρώτη ἡ πνευματική) was created "before the sun and moon" (14.1): it is not just of the present, but it has existed from the beginning (or from above, ἄνωθεν, 14.2). As the body of Christ, the church is what was referred to as "the female" in relation to

---

26. See now Christopher Tuckett's excellent edition and commentary: *2 Clement: Introduction, Text, and Commentary*, Oxford Apostolic Fathers (Oxford: Oxford University Press, 2012).

27. So, rightly, J. B. Lightfoot, *The Apostolic Fathers: Part I, S. Clement of Rome*, 2 vols. (London: Macmillan, 1890), 2:215. Tuckett doubts this interpretation on the grounds that "there is no clear instance elsewhere in *2 Clement* of an attempt to differentiate the Christian community from Jews" (*2 Clement*, 143), but it is hard to know who else might be said to "seem" to have God.

Christ (as the male), when the scripture says "God made male and female" (14.2); and like Christ, it is spiritual. The historical phenomenon of the church is thus, like the coming of Christ, a manifestation of an eternally existent phenomenon: the church "was made manifest in the last days [ἐφανερώθη ἐπ᾽ ἐσχάτων τῶν ἡμερῶν], in order to save us" (14.2), just as Christ "made manifest to us [ἐφανέρωσεν] the truth and the heavenly life" (20.5).[28] Both Christ and church (an inseparable unity) constitute an epiphany that has recently appeared on the world stage, much as in the deutero-Pauline traditions we have traced above.

What does this mean regarding the status and identity of what we call the Old Testament or the Jewish scriptures? Second Clement is replete with citations and allusions to a range of sources: some gospel traditions known from elsewhere (including a saying known otherwise only in the Gospel of Thomas), some Jesus-tradition otherwise unknown, some allusions to noncanonical Jewish sources (Tobit, whose language is echoed in 16.4), and some texts we would identify as scriptural.[29] It is significant that the word *scripture* is used in 2 Clement both for Jesus/gospel sayings (now known in a written form; see, for example, 2.4) and for what we call Old Testament texts (for example, in 6.8), as if the whole pool of textual material from which this author can draw is undifferentiated, without demarcation regarding date, source, or cultural identity. Just as "the Lord" both spoke (εἶπεν) and speaks (λέγει) in the gospel tradition (9.11, 8.5), so "the Lord" both spoke (εἶπεν) and speaks (λέγει) in texts that we would demarcate as from an earlier, scriptural source (17.4, 13.2), suggesting a kind of timeless contemporaneity between all these textual materials. It is striking that on several occasions texts that were originally addressed to Israel, and which distinguished Israel from "the nations," are now taken to be addressed immediately, and without any hermeneutical effort, to the gentile church: "This people honors me with their lips, but their heart is far from me" (Isa 29:13, cited by Jesus against his Jewish contemporaries in Mark 7:6) is taken to be addressed directly to the church in 2 Clem 3.5, while the danger that God's name might be "slandered among the nations" (Isa 52:5, cited by Paul in criticism of his Jewish contemporaries in Rom

---

28. The subject that was made manifest in 14.2 could be either Christ or the church (see Tuckett, *2 Clement*, 254–55), but since the church is the "body of Christ" there is no real difference between them. As the next verse indicates, the church was "made manifest" in the flesh of Christ (14.3).

29. See the helpful table of citations in Tuckett, *2 Clement*, 35–36.

2:24) is addressed directly to a gentile church which takes "the nations" (τὰ ἔθνη) to refer to non-Christian outsiders (13.1–2). In other words, this gentile church sees itself uncomplicatedly as the addressee of this scripture, without recognizing that it once or first had reference to others and can apply to the church only by a hermeneutical transference. "The books" and "the apostles" speak together and directly about the church (14.2);[30] the Jewish origin of these texts and their historical reference to the Jewish people are blanched out. Where the textual origin of a saying within "the books" is named, it is striking that the text is introduced not with "Isaiah said" or "Ezekiel wrote" but "it says in Isaiah" (2.3) or "the scripture says in Ezekiel" (6.8). In other words, Isaiah and Ezekiel refer here not to a *person* but to a *text*, and although *we* might inquire into their historical origin and setting, 2 Clement offers no encouragement to show interest in such matters. For a spiritual church that has newly arrived "from above" onto the historical scene, this makes perfect sense: it has no interest in pre-Christian roots or historical precursors or even anticipatory predictions. Isaiah could hardly speak to the church at a time when it had not yet appeared. Where the Epistle to Diognetus simply ignores the scriptures, 2 Clement makes much use of them, but it considers itself free to take the whole scriptural resource as timelessly addressed to the church.

## Conclusions

It is clear that the epiphany schema we have traced fits well with the expansion of gentile Christianity, as it became increasingly independent of its Jewish roots: gentile churches, abandoning pagan worship and devoting themselves to Christ, were indeed a novel phenomenon on the historical scene. The label "Christian" by which they were increasingly known, was not only different from "Jew," but under this label they were treated by outsiders as a different kind of social phenomenon.[31] Ignoring or repudiating

---

30. Manuscript C has only "the books" (τὰ βιβλία), while manuscript S has "the books of the prophets" (τὰ βιβλία τῶν προφητῶν); see above for the labeling of scripture as "the prophets," and on the textual difference, Tuckett, *2 Clement*, 253. Elsewhere there is reference to "the prophetic word" (ὁ προφητικὸς λόγος, 11.2), but this seems to be an early Christian saying.

31. For the distinction between "Jews" and "Christians" in Roman authors of the first century, see John M. G. Barclay, "'Jews' and 'Christians' in the Eyes of Roman Authors c. 100 CE," in *Jews and Christians in the First and Second Centuries: How to*

the classic practices that distinguished Jews as Jews (food laws, circumcision, Sabbath, and Jewish festival observance), and endowed with their own Christian rituals (baptism and the Eucharist meal) that could be practiced in a way that looked back in history no further than the Christ-event itself, the gentile churches were inclined to see Christ and themselves as a newly arrived phenomenon, planned and known by God from all eternity, but a mystery previously concealed and only now made plain and active on the human stage. Where they had access to the scriptures, it was easy to hear these not as ancient documents that were spoken to and for the Jewish people but as a timeless textual resource by which they were both described and addressed as gentile Christians. If the mystery was previously hidden, it can hardly have been previously revealed. Where the scriptures were taken in their historical sense to be the cultural and legal frame for the gospel, they could appear to gentile Christians all too Jewish. Some might therefore repudiate them altogether (Marcion), some might ignore them (Epistle to Diognetus), some might meld them with the emerging gospel traditions (2 Clement), and some might label them as "prophets," reframed and rendered disciples of Christ (Ignatius). Simply as "scripture" or "the books," it was not clear that this resource was either old or Jewish; what mattered was how it spoke directly to the needs of the gentile church.

Other options were, of course, possible. Where the scriptures were recognized as written from a time before Christ and spoken originally to or about Jews, early Christians entered into competition with Jewish interpretations of these scriptures, making strong claims that the texts *really*, at a deeper or more significant level, spoke about Christ and the church. The Epistle of Barnabas enters this competition with energy and aggression, effectively claiming the Jews' inheritance for the church. Justin's *Dialogue with Trypho* and Melito's *Peri Pascha* are the most sophisticated second-century examples of this competition, which requires the claim that Christians—uniquely enlightened by the grace of God—can understand the Jewish scriptures better than Jews themselves, seeing latent, fuller meanings that can only be seen by those who believe in Christ. Notoriously, Justin thus claims that the scriptures are "not yours, but ours" (*Dial.* 29.2).

For Jewish-Christian relations today, neither removing the Jewish identity of the scriptures nor competing with Jews for their right interpretation

*Write Their History*, ed. Peter J. Tomson and Joshua Schwartz, CRINT 13 (Leiden: Brill, 2014), 313–26.

and proper ownership are satisfactory options. Is it possible now for the scriptures to be *shared* by Christians and Jews on noncompetitive terms? Perhaps "identity" and "ownership" are precisely what hampers us here. In Pauline terms, the scriptures are "the oracles of *God*" entrusted to Jews (Rom 3:2, ἐπιστεύθησαν τὰ λόγια τοῦ θεοῦ). They belong to Israelites (9:4) but only as "gifts" (11:29), possessed but not owned. In Christian theology, they are entrusted *also*, secondarily, to Christians but not with exclusive or superior rights. Each community seeks to attend to these texts for what they are—first and foremost, oracles *of God*, not cultural or historical products of any one community. The Christian reading of these texts will be necessarily christological—it can hardly be otherwise without denying the lordship of Christ over all history and time—but a Jewish reading will find its own fuller Jewish meaning in texts that are hardly bound to their historical origins. Both sets of readings can be relativized by the recognition that what is being heard here is not the property of any one community or tradition but a divine speech that makes the text neither "ours" nor "yours." Because they recognize the scriptures as entrusted to Jews, Christians should not and need not deny their original and continuing Jewish habitat; they do not have to be dehistoricized and decoupled from Judaism in the ways we have traced in the texts discussed above. The gifts of God are, as Paul says, irrevocable (11:29). But because they fundamentally belong to *God*, and not to any one historical or human community, they also demand attention from all people, including Christians. To speak of this God as "Israel's God" might be to suggest that God is a human product or possession, who belongs to Israel but is now competed for by an alien upstart. But if the God who elects Israel in mercy is not a human construct or product, Israel belongs to God, not God to Israel. In other words, what is needed most, and most urgently, is not that we deconstruct the historical processes by which Jews and Christians began to compete but that we deconstruct the very notion of competition, in the *theological* recognition that it is God who owns us, not we who own God. Thus the scriptures become a continuing resource for both communities, who are committed to hear afresh how their own all-too-human traditions can be enriched and corrected by "the oracles of God" and who recognize that in this endeavor, to which each tradition is separately committed, they will each have much to learn from the other.

## Bibliography

Barclay, John M. G. *Against Apion*. FJTC 10. Leiden: Brill, 2007.

———. *Colossians and Philemon*. Sheffield: Sheffield Academic, 1997.

———. "'Jews' and 'Christians' in the Eyes of Roman Authors c. 100 CE." Pages 313–26 in *Jews and Christians in the First and Second Centuries: How to Write Their History*. Edited by Peter J. Tomson and Joshua Schwartz. CRINT 13. Leiden: Brill, 2014.

Barnard, L. W. "The Epistle Ad Diognetum: Two Units from One Author." *ZNW* 56 (1965): 130–37.

Barrett, C. K. "Jews and Judaizers in the Epistles of Ignatius." Pages 220–44 in *Jews, Greeks and Christians: Religious Cultures in Late Antiquity; Essays in Honor of William David Davies*. Edited by Robert Hamerton-Kelly and Robin Scroggs. Leiden: Brill, 1976.

D'Angour, Armand. *The Greeks and the New: Novelty in Ancient Greek Imagination and Experience*. Cambridge: Cambridge University Press, 2011.

Dahl, Nils. "Formgeschichtliche Beobachtungen zur Christusverkündigung in der Gemeindepredigt." Pages 3–9 in *Neutestamentliche Studien für Rudolf Bultmann: Zu seinem siebzigsten Geburtstag am 20. August 1954*. Edited by Walther Eltester. BZNW 21. Berlin: Töpelmann, 1957.

Jefford, Clayton N. *The Epistle to Diognetus (with the Fragment of Quadratus): Introduction, Text, and Commentary*. Oxford Apostolic Fathers. Oxford: Oxford University Press, 2013.

Kim, Jung Hoon. *The Significance of Clothing Imagery in the Pauline Corpus*. JSNTSup 268. London: T&T Clark, 2004.

Lang, T. J. *Mystery and the Making of a Christian Historical Consciousness: From Paul to the Second Century*. BZNW 219. Berlin: de Gruyter, 2015.

Lau, Andrew Y. *Manifest in Flesh: The Epiphany Christology of the Pastoral Epistles*. WUNT 2/86. Tübingen: Mohr Siebeck, 1996.

Lieu, Judith M. *Image and Reality: The Jews in the World of the Christians in the Second Century*. Edinburgh: T&T Clark, 1996.

Lightfoot, J. B. *The Apostolic Fathers: Part I, S. Clement of Rome*. 2 vols. London: Macmillan, 1890.

Marcus, Joel. *Jesus and the Holocaust: Reflections on Suffering and Hope*. New York: Doubleday, 1997. Repr., Grand Rapids: Eerdmans, 2017.

———. *Mark 1–8: A New Translation with Introduction and Commentary*. AB 27. New York: Doubleday, 2000.

———. *Mark 8–16: A New Translation with Introduction and Commentary*. AB 27A. New York: Doubleday, 2009.

————. *The Way of the Lord: Christological Exegesis of the Old Testament in the Gospel of Mark*. Louisville: Westminster John Knox; Edinburgh: T&T Clark, 1992.

Martyn, J. Louis. "Epistemology at the Turn of the Ages." Pages 89–110 in *Theological Issues in the Letters of Paul*. Edinburgh: T&T Clark, 1997.

Schoedel, W. R. *Ignatius of Antioch: A Commentary on the Letters of Ignatius of Antioch*. Hermeneia. Philadelphia: Fortress, 1985.

Tuckett, Christopher. *2 Clement: Introduction, Text, and Commentary*. Oxford Apostolic Fathers. Oxford: Oxford University Press, 2012.

Wolter, Michael. "Verborgene Weisheit und Heil für die Heiden: Zur Traditionsgeschichte und Intention des 'Revelationsschemas.'" *ZTK* 84 (1987): 297–319.

# Was Mark a Supersessionist?
## Two Test Cases from the Earliest Gospel

Suzanne Watts Henderson

Any parting(s) of the ways postdates the Gospel of Mark. Yet the under-lying premise—that Jewish and Christian identities grew gradually more distinct over time—draws attention to fault lines that appear already in the first century CE. While other contributors evaluate evidence of an emerg-ing binary divide, this chapter examines two Markan passages that hint at a Christian separation from Judaism long before we can speak of an insti-tutional parting. Both the sayings about garments and wineskins (Mark 2:21–22) and the parable of the violent tenants (Mark 12:1–12) suggest to many that Mark's message is at least consistent with later supersessionist claims found in the Epistle of Barnabas, Justin's *Dialogue with Trypho*, and the writings of Tertullian.[1]

But was Mark a supersessionist? Do these sayings cast Mark's Jesus as an advocate for the replacement of the Jewish people by the church? This essay explores the passage's claims, as well as their literary and historical settings, in ways that complicate such widely held views. As we shall see, both the sayings about the garment and wineskins and the parable of the

Almost three decades ago, Joel Marcus allowed me to participate as a seminary student in a doctoral seminar on the Gospel of Mark, an experience that stoked an interest in the earliest gospel that has only grown over time. Almost two decades ago, he joined Duke's faculty just in time to direct my doctoral dissertation on discipleship in Mark, published as *Christology and Discipleship in the Gospel of Mark*, SNTSMS 135 (Cambridge: Cambridge University Press, 2006). Through it all, and to this day, Joel has continued to challenge, support, and strengthen my work. I count him as friend and mentor extraordinaire—God's grace in human form, really. It is with deep grati-tude that I offer this essay in his honor.

1. See, e.g., Barn. 13.1; Justin, *Dial.* 25–27; Tertullian, *Adv. Jud.* 6.3.

violent tenants promote fidelity to God's imperial power, manifest through Jesus's messianic mission, more than they posit the replacement of Jews by Jesus's gentile followers as distinct ethnoreligious groups. Even more, these passages retain reverence for the pillars of Second Temple Judaism—torah and temple—even as they issue prophetic critique of their guardians in both narrative and historical contexts. Ultimately, our findings will elucidate Mark's message to his own community, which found itself in the crosshairs of ethnoreligious and imperial conflict.

## What Is Old? What Is New? Rethinking Mark 2:21–22[2]

Scholars widely assert that the sayings found in Mark 2:21–22 depict the incompatibility of the "new" age Jesus inaugurates with the "old" structures of Judaism, which Mark closely associates with the law.[3] What is more, many find that they convey the superiority of Jesus over his torah-observant detractors, suggesting supersessionist leanings on Mark's part. But two aspects of this traditional view warrant careful reconsideration.

First, interpreters generally assume that the sayings pit what is new against what is old, with a clear preference for the new. Early on, Tertullian interpreted the saying this way: "Everything has been changed from carnal to spiritual by the new grace of God which, with the coming of the gospel, wiped out the old era completely" (*Or.* 1.2).[4] Recent commentators

---

2. This section distills the findings of my article, "What Is Old? What Is New? A Reconsideration of Garments and Wineskins," *HBT* 34 (2012): 118–38.

3. Interpreters who use language of "incompatibility" include John R. Donahue and Daniel J. Harrington, *The Gospel of Mark*, SP 2 (Collegeville, MN: Liturgical Press, 2002), 109; Adela Yarbro Collins, *Mark: A Commentary*, Hermeneia (Minneapolis: Fortress, 2007); R. T. France, *The Gospel of Mark: A Commentary on the Greek Text*, NIGTC (Grand Rapids: Eerdmans, 2002), 141; Robert A. Guelich, *Mark 1–8:26*, WBC 34A (Dallas: Word, 1989), 115; Bas M. F. van Iersel, *Mark: A Reader-Response Commentary*, trans. W. H. Bisscheroux, JSNTSup 164 (Sheffield: Sheffield Academic, 1998), 156; Joel Marcus, *Mark 1–8: A New Translation with Introduction and Commentary*, AB 27 (New York: Doubleday, 2000), 235; Robert H. Stein, *Mark*, BECNT (Grand Rapids: Baker Academic, 2008), 140. See also M. Eugene Boring, *Mark: A Commentary*, NTL (Louisville: Westminster John Knox, 2006), 86–87, who notes the "impossibility of mixing old and new," and Ben Witherington, III, *The Gospel of Mark: A Socio-rhetorical Commentary* (Grand Rapids: Eerdmans, 2001), 126, "the incongruity of juxtaposing two things which do not fit."

4. Tertullian, *Disciplinary, Moral, and Ascetical Works*, trans. Roy Joseph Deferari, FC 40 (Washington, DC: Catholic University of America Press, 1959), 158.

have continued the trend. Thus, Joanna Dewey says that Jesus's illustrative examples here "justify the new against the old."[5] R. T. France goes even further, maintaining that the disciples "represent a vital new perspective which supersedes the traditional patterns of religion."[6] Joel Marcus himself notes that the passage's closing slogan—"New wine into new wineskins!" (Mark 2:22)—at least raises the possibility that Mark's Jesus subverts not just Pharisaic practices but the law of Moses itself.[7] In any case, interpreters typically read the sayings as tantamount to Jesus's endorsement of the new *at the expense of the old*.[8]

A second assumption that undergirds this reading concerns the images' allegorical denotations. Interpreters commonly associate the new patch and the new wine with either Jesus himself or his gospel message. Joachim Jeremias, for instance, takes the new wine to symbolize the era of salvation inaugurated by Jesus, a view found throughout commentaries today.[9] In a similar vein, Adela Yarbro Collins maintains that for Mark's audience, the "new" hearkens back to Mark 1:27: "His teaching is 'new,'" she explains, "because he announces that the 'time' is fulfilled and the kingdom of God has drawn near."[10] Marcus shares this apocalyptic lens and emphasizes the "eschatological newness of Jesus' ministry."[11]

This correlation of the new with Jesus's apocalyptic and eschatological mission leads naturally to the identification of the old with the "closed religious system of Israel," which implicitly derives its structure from torah.[12] Though commentators tread lightly on such a reading, often assigning the perspective to Mark's *Sitz im Leben* rather than to Jesus himself, the link between the old in these sayings and the torah-based teachings of the scribes and Pharisees within the Markan literary setting is widely taken

---

5. Joanna Dewey, "The Literary Structure of the Controversy Stories in Mark 2:1–3:6," *JBL* 92 (1973): 398.

6. France, *Mark*, 137.

7. Marcus, *Mark 1–8*, 239. He does not, however, conclude that it does.

8. See Guelich, *Mark*, 114, who notes that "the mention of the wine as well as the wineskins may again indicate the absence of any value judgments favoring either the new or the old, since both have their value which is lost."

9. Joachim Jeremias, *The Parables of Jesus*, trans. S. H. Hooke (London: SCM, 1963), 118–19.

10. Collins, *Mark*, 200.

11. Marcus, *Mark 1–8*, 235.

12. Francis J. Moloney, *The Gospel of Mark: A Commentary* (Peabody, MA: Hendrickson, 2002), 67.

as a given. Few exegetes, it seems, have heeded Calvin's admonition that those who think Jesus "compares worn-out garments and decayed bottles to the Pharisees, and new wine and fresh cloth to the doctrine of the gospel have no probability on their side."[13]

Working in tandem, then, these two interpretive moves detect in the sayings a partiality for the new age of God's gospel, promoted by Jesus, over the old era of Judaism, dominated by meticulous adherence to torah. Yet, close attention to the sayings in their narrative setting highlights several weaknesses in such a supersessionist reading of Mark's Jesus. Not only do the sayings themselves reveal more interest in preserving the old than many have recognized, but they also signal a concern with socioreligious adherence to Jesus's christological mission as agent of God's in-breaking reign.

## A Close Reading of Mark 2:21–22

Our study sets aside the question of the sayings' origin to focus on their setting in Mark, where they lie at the heart of Mark's controversy stories— and more specifically, between two stories about Jesus's disciples.[14] The sayings themselves offer, in parallel form, two illustrative examples drawn from the imagery of everyday life:[15]

A   οὐδεὶς ἐπίβλημα ῥάκους ἀγνάφου ἐπιράπτει ἐπὶ ἱμάτιον παλαιόν:

B   εἰ δὲ μή, αἴρει τὸ πλήρωμα ἀπ᾽ αὐτοῦ τὸ καινὸν τοῦ παλαιοῦ

B′   καὶ χεῖρον σχίσμα γίνεται.

A   καὶ οὐδεὶς βάλλει οἶνον νέον εἰς ἀσκοὺς παλαιούς:

B   εἰ δὲ μή, ῥήξει ὁ οἶνος τοὺς ἀσκοὺς

---

13. John Calvin, *A Commentary on a Harmony of the Evangelists, Matthew, Mark, and Luke*, trans. William Pringle, 3 vols. (Grand Rapids: Baker Books, 1845–1846), 1:407.

14. Those who believe the verses include previously independent sayings that have been situated in their present literary context either by Mark or by a pre-Markan editor include Joachim Gnilka, *Das Evangelium nach Markus*, 5th ed., 2 vols., EKKNT 1.1–2 (Neukirchen-Vluyn: Neukirchener Verlag, 1998), 1:111–13; Dewey, "Literary Structure," 398; Collins, *Mark*, 197.

15. The diagram that follows resembles, almost identically, the findings of Joanna Dewey, *Markan Public Debate: Literary Technique, Concentric Structure, and Theology in Mark 2:1–3:6*, SBLDS 148 (Atlanta: Scholars Press, 1980), 92, with one rather significant difference: what I label B′, she identifies as a separate unit (C). In my reading, the additional καί clause in each case further elaborates the εἰ δὲ μή scenario.

B′  καὶ ὁ οἶνος ἀπόλλυται καὶ οἱ ἀσκοί:

C  ἀλλὰ οἶνον νέον εἰς ἀσκοὺς καινούς.

The pattern of repetition is evident, if not precise: the verses begin with a negative assertion about what "no one" does (A); they then consider the consequences about the action mentioned (B), with an elaboration of the outcome (B′). The parallel breaks down, though, with the introduction of a concluding positive statement about "new wine" (C) in verse 22; verse 21 lacks such an affirmation.[16] Thus, the concluding affirmation stands out rhetorically as the sayings' punch line, stressing the fitting alignment between new wine and new wineskins. But does that emphasis on newness suggest that the old has entirely lost its value? Let us consider the sayings in turn.

In the first maxim, Mark's Jesus invokes the example of an uncured piece of cloth affixed to an old garment, presumably for the purpose of mending it. An "unfulled" (ἀγνάφου) patch was unbleached and unprocessed, meaning that naturally occurring oils that prevent shrinkage had not yet been extracted by either the passing of time or a curing process. To affix a fresh, uncured patch upon a well-worn garment would be a shoddy piece of tailoring indeed. Rather than restoring the worn fabric, it would exacerbate the problem: the new patch would "take up the fullness" (αἴρει τὸ πλήρωμα) from the old garment and in turn leave "a greater tear" (χεῖρον σχίσμα; Mark 2:21).[17]

The language here is notably apocalyptic. The πληρ- word group identifies "fullness" and "fulfillment" with God's impinging reign. In Mark, Jesus proclaims the gospel this way: the "time has been *fulfilled*, and the reign of God has drawn near" (Mark 1:15); more subtly, the fullness of the baskets collected after both feeding stories (Mark 6:43; 8:20) points to eschatological abundance. Likewise, Paul writes of the fullness that the inclusion of gentiles within God's sweeping plan of salvation entails (Rom 11:12, 25), and he points to the fulfillment of torah within the age of the spirit (Gal 5:14; Rom 8:4; 13:10). Against this backdrop, Mark 2:21 at least leaves open the possibility that the well-worn garment already contains a certain fullness.[18] The saying's warning against adhering to that garment, in turn, emphasizes the *loss it suffers as a result.*

---

16. Though present in most manuscripts, the phrase does not appear in D.

17. Unless otherwise stated, all biblical translations are my own.

18. Wisdom 1:7 maintains that the "spirit of the Lord has filled the world"; cf. Sir 24:26, which claims it is the law of Moses that "overflows" with wisdom.

Similarly, the use of "schism" in this saying connotes apocalyptic and sociological concerns. On the one hand, Mark employs the verb σχίζω in two pivotal instances to convey the revelatory rupture of the heavens: at Jesus's baptism (Mark 1:10) and of the temple curtain at his death (Mark 15:38). In each case, the rift yields access to the divine realm and in turn sanctions Jesus's divine sonship in a manner that echoes the Isaianic plea: "Oh that you would tear open the heavens and come down" (Isa 64:1). Mark's admonition in 2:21 about a "greater schism" seems to situate Mark's community in relation to "those outside" (compare with Mark 4:10–12). As Marcus puts it, this saying may thus refer to "the futility of trying to mend the schism between Jewish Christians [namely, some among Mark's audience] and other Jews."[19] Given that the old garment stands in need of repair, then, it is not the application of a patch that is problematic but rather the application of a patch *that has not accommodated to the condition of the garment.*

The saying about new wine and old wineskins deploys another common-sense example to illustrate what "no one" does. Again, the maxim itself complicates the view that Mark's Jesus assigns a categorically positive value to what is new and a corresponding negative value to what is old. To be sure, New Testament writers consistently associate the dawn of the messianic age with what is new. Not only do onlookers in Mark marvel at Jesus's "new teaching" (Mark 1:27), but Jesus also foretells his drinking "the new" in the kingdom of God (Mark 14:25). In a similar vein, the Fourth Gospel heralds a "new commandment" imparted by Jesus (John 13:34)—"that you love one another" (compare with Lev 19:18)—while Paul affirms both a "new covenant" (1 Cor 11:25; 2 Cor 3:6) and the "new creation" (Gal 6:15; 2 Cor 5:17) instituted through the gospel. In each case, though, what is new is not entirely new. Just as Jesus's teaching is rooted in the Jewish prophetic tradition, both the new commandment and the new creation entail an essential renewal of esteemed tradition.[20] If, in Paul's view, the "old has passed away" (2 Cor 5:17), the new creation also carries a sense of God's reestablishment of the original plan for the created order, this time through a "new" or "last" Adam (1 Cor 15:45–49; Rom 5:12–21).

Another assumption associated with the traditional, supersessionist reading warrants rethinking: the superiority of new wine over old. Though

19. Marcus, *Mark 1–8*, 238.
20. See Collins, *Mark*, 200: "all these traditions had to be reevaluated and reformed."

interpreters have been mostly silent on the point, wine connoisseurs everywhere would affirm that fresh or young wine is generally considered inferior to wine that has been aged with time. Sirach 9:10 expresses a clear preference for aged wine, likening new friends to new wine in that they are unproven. In a later setting, the rabbis will contrast the one who learns from a child—"who eats sour grapes and drinks fresh wine"—with the one who learns from the older, wiser sages—"who eats ripe grapes and drinks vintage wine" (m. Avot 4:20).

Note, too, that the language used here is rather aggressive: βάλλει adds force to the action of pouring the wine into the skins; ῥήξει describes what the wine does to those skins; and ἀπόλλυται denotes the destructive outcome for both wine and skins. The sweeping devastation conveyed in the saying surely signals no preference for new over old; to the contrary, it seems to lament the loss of both old and new wine, as well as the container.[21] Taken together, the sayings about the garment and the skins work in tandem to convey the deleterious effects of superimposing new on the old in the first instance and containing new within the old in the second. In both cases, the sayings preserve inherent value in the old; its loss comes at great cost. Taken at face value, the sayings together suggest that the new threatens the viability of the old, not vice versa; moreover, the sayings manifest at least equal, if not greater, interest in the preservation of the old (compare with Luke 5:39).[22] Already, the widely assumed interpretive partiality toward the new, over and against the old, seems to stand on shaky textual ground.

---

21. The sayings may promote a principle of consistency that echoes biblical teachings against diverse kinds. Torah itself forbids the mixing of crops, animals behind a plow, and fibers in a garment (Lev 19:19; Deut 22:9–11), and exilic and postexilic writings frequently advocate strict separation, in social relationships, from those outside the community—a practice evident among Qumran covenanters to the extreme. For a discussion of the biblical view of diverse kinds, see Jacob Milgrom, *Leviticus 17–22: A New Translation with Introduction and Commentary*, AB 3A (New York: Doubleday, 2000), 1660, who maintains that "mixtures belong to the sacred sphere, namely, the sanctuary." Evidence that the laws of diverse kinds applied to the priests as well appears, e.g., in m. Kil. 9:1.

22. Moloney notes the shift from the first to the second saying, which he says "focuses on the need to preserve new wine" (*Mark*, 67). Dewey's view is less compelling: "the new is an active threat to the continued existence of the old.... Given the danger of the new to the old, the new is to be established, not the old preserved" (*Debate*, 93).

## Mark 2:21–22 in Literary Context

If careful attention to the sayings themselves undermines the notion that they promote the superiority of what is new over what is old, their rhetorical function within Mark's controversy stories challenges the view that the new designates Jesus's radical eschatological message, while the old represents the Pharisees' stodgy torah-based traditions. Typically, commentators interpret these originally independent sayings in light of what comes before: the dispute about Jesus's nonfasting disciples (Mark 2:18–20). But important thematic links with the grain field episode that follows (Mark 2:23–28) situate Mark 2:21–22 as a narrative hinge between the two disputes that share an interest in the correlation between Jesus's mission and the conduct of his disciples.[23] The sayings thus emphasize *allegiance to* Jesus's messianic mission more than *rejection of* torah.

Joanna Dewey's rhetorical analysis of the Markan controversy stories assigns central position to Mark 2:18–22, yet she sees the sayings in question here as mostly unrelated to their surroundings.[24] Rather than addressing the fasting issue per se, Mark 2:21–22 broadly signals, she thinks, the "fundamental change" introduced by the dawn of God's kingdom.[25] Yet several features link the surrounding disputes about fasting and feasting with one another as well as with the sayings about the garment and wineskins.

First, both concern not the conduct of Jesus himself but *that of his disciples.* The controversy that precedes our sayings queries Jesus about his disciples' failure to fast (Mark 2:18), while the one that follows finds that their grain-plucking violates Sabbath law (Mark 2:23). While interpreters generally note the role of the disciples in both stories, they tend to emphasize Jesus's role as authoritative leader of the group.[26] Yet the controversies'

---

23. See Guelich, who forges a connection between all of 2:18–22 and its surrounding stories about feasting, noting the "common theme[s] of Jewish praxis" and the "presence of Jesus with his disciples" (*Mark*, 108).

24. Dewey, *Debate*, 89.

25. Dewey, *Debate*, 94, against Rudolf Bultmann, *The History of the Synoptic Tradition*, trans. John Marsh, rev. ed. (New York: Harper & Row, 1968), 19.

26. Rather promisingly, Guelich notes, "The contrast between the old and the new [in Mark 2:21–22] certainly corresponds to the contrast between the conduct of John's and Jesus' disciples." Yet, he concludes more broadly that "the point of correspondence between the parables and the import of 2:18–19a is this incompatibility of the old and the new orders" (*Mark*, 115). However, David Daube establishes the pattern

narrative attention to the *followers'* behavior, not *Jesus's*, comports well with the sayings' interest in likeness of patch to garment and wine to wine-skins.

Second, the surrounding disputes revolve around the disciples' con-duct *with respect to Jewish practice*. When Jesus's detractors ask why his followers are not fasting, the underlying premise is that they belong to a Jewish apocalyptic movement like that of John the Baptist; indeed, at least some Pharisees understood fasting as a way of participating in the dawn-ing messianic age (b. Sanh. 97–98).[27] In any case, the challenge about fast-ing identifies Jesus's disciples, not inappropriately, with a torah-centered eschatological movement.

The second challenge goes further, accusing Jesus's disciples of vio-lating Sabbath laws that lie at the heart of torah. As many have noted, the disciples' activity did not necessarily constitute an infraction. Though Philo and some later rabbinical traditions assign plucking grain to the category of "work" (see, e.g., Philo, *Mos.* 2.22; y. Shabb. 7.9b; t. Shabb. 9:17), the issue is notably absent from the Mishnah's list of forbidden Sab-bath activities (m. Shabb. 7:2), perhaps because it entails harvesting for immediate rather than future consumption.[28] As Collins rightly notes, "Jesus and some of his fellow Jews may have disagreed about how to apply the principle."[29]

---

of mutual responsibility between master and disciple for their respective behavior, a pattern evident in Seneca: "He who forbids not sin when in control commands it" (Seneca, *Troades* 290; cited by Daube, "Responsibilities of Master and Disciple in the Gospels," *NTS* 19 [1972]: 5).

27. A wide range of groups in Second Temple Judaism fasted, to varying degrees. Leviticus promotes self-denial on the Day of Atonement (Lev 16:29; 23:29), and fast-ing often accompanies repentance (cf. Dan 9:3; 10:3). Over time, fasting came to be associated with preparation for holy war (1 Sam 7:6; 1 Macc 3:47) and, in turn, for the ultimate apocalyptic battle. Josephus mentions a fast called by Ananias, a lay Pharisee, during the Jewish War (*Vita* 290). As a sectarian group in Egypt, the Therapeutae fasted during the night, leaving the day for the more venerable work of contemplation (Philo, *Contempl.* 34). The Pharisees practiced fasts of repentance (m. Ta'an. 1:4–5; b. Ta'an. 10a), and the Didache promotes fasting on Wednesday and Friday, as opposed to the "hypocrites," who fasted, as a group, on Monday and Thursday (Did. 8.1–2).

28. The Mishnah's list of thirty-nine activities that constitute "work" (Exod 20:8–11; Deut 5:12–16) includes the "generative" categories from sowing to preparation of food for consumption (see also Deut 34:21). Deuteronomy 23:25, though, distin-guishes between plucking by hand and harvesting by sickle.

29. Collins, *Mark*, 204.

Besides the torah-observance that the challenges themselves presume, Jesus's responses on fasting and feasting unfold within the framework of Jewish thought, not apart from it. On the question of fasting, Mark's Jesus neither denies his eschatological leanings nor distances himself from other Jewish movements to which his interlocutors have likened his. To the question at hand, he offers this response: "The sons of the bridegroom cannot fast while the bridegroom is with them, can they? As long as they have the bridegroom with them, they cannot fast" (Mark 2:19). Thus, he appropriates the biblical motif of a wedding (for example, Isa 54:4–8; 62:4–5; Ezek 16:1–63), casting himself in the role of bridegroom (see Isa 62:5).[30] Like his Jewish interlocutors, Jesus associates eating and drinking with the vindication of Israel (Isa 62:9), but he implies that in his ministry, the end has already begun. His disciples' eating and drinking is consistent with its arrival; they will fast, in turn, when he has been "taken away" (Mark 2:20).

In a similar manner, Mark's Jesus invokes biblical tradition to offer a two-fold response to the more serious charge of Sabbath violation. First, he cites the scriptural story of David and the bread of the presence as warrant for plucking grain, even on the Sabbath, to satisfy human hunger (Mark 2:25–26; compare with 1 Sam 21). Jesus casts the behavior of his companions against the backdrop of biblical precedent, likening his own authority to that of Israel's vaunted sovereign.[31]

The second element of Jesus's response to the grain field challenge similarly mines scripture—this time torah itself—to defend his disciples' practice (Mark 2:27–28). Note the verses' parallel structure:

Τὸ σάββατον διὰ ἄνθρωπον ἐγένετο
    καὶ οὐχ ὁ ἄνθρωπος διὰ τὸ σάββατον·
ὥστε κύριός ἐστιν ὁ υἱὸς τοῦ ἀνθρώπου καὶ τοῦ σαββάτου.

Invoking the divinely ordained pattern of creation portrayed in Gen 1, Jesus implies that, as the crowning work that bears the very imprint of the Creator's image, humanity both participates in God's rest (Gen 1:27, 2:3)

---

30. Witherington suggests that "There may then be an implicit claim that Jesus now fulfills for Israel, or at least for his own disciples, the role previously predicated of God" (*Mark*, 124–25).

31. Jesus's association with David in this gospel is a strained one. On the positive side, Mark 10:47–48 and 11:9–10 join this passage in casting Jesus in Davidic hues. Yet, a more negative view can be found in Mark 12:35–37. The backdrop of the Jewish War—fueled by militaristic expectations for a Davidic Messiah—likely explains this narrative tension.

and exercises God-given dominion (Gen 1:26–31). Such an interpretation is not, of course, unique. As Ben Witherington notes, Jewish writers often maintained that "the world and its institutions were to be managed by human beings, not the other way around."[32] Josephus notes that a similar practice governed conduct during the Maccabean Revolt (*A.J.* 12.6.2; compare with 1 Macc 2:39–41), and the Babylonian Talmud later will claim that the Sabbath "is committed to your hands, not you to the Sabbath" (b. Yoma 85b). If Mark's Jesus asserts human authority over the Sabbath, he does so while affirming the principle of Sabbath as part of the (re)new(ed) creation, which by design promotes human welfare.

Finally, and perhaps most notably, Jesus's response to both objections *casts his disciples as vital participants* in his own mission. Though some take the phrase "sons of the bridegroom" (Mark 2:19) to mean either wedding guests or attendants,[33] Mark likely forges an intimate connection between Jesus as "bridegroom" (νυμφίος) and the disciples as his "sons." The familial intimacy implied here resembles, for instance, T. Levi 18.12–13, where "sons" of the new priest wield authority to trample wicked spirits. In this response, Jesus emphasizes the correlation between his own redemptive presence and the disciples' participation in it.[34]

Jesus's response to the Sabbath objection only amplifies this interest in the disciples' alignment with his mission. Besides Jesus's misidentification of Abiathar as high priest and the fact that in 1 Samuel it was David who ate what was not lawful (Mark 2:26), simply put, Mark's account elevates both *Jesus's authority* and the *disciples' role* in the story, as they become participants in his authoritative action: "He gave [the bread] also to those who were with him" (Mark 2:26).[35]

---

32. Witherington, *Mark*, 131. He cites 2 Esd 6:54 and 2 Bar 14.18 as representative examples.

33. Guelich (*Mark*, 110) supports the latter, due to the "repeated reference to the 'bridegroom.'"

34. Most scholars take Mark 2:20 to address the shift from the absence of fasting during Jesus's earthly ministry and its practice among early Christian communities like Mark's (see, e.g., Did. 8.1). When Jesus adds, "The days will come when the bridegroom is taken away from them, and then they will fast on that day" (Mark 2:20), he essentially legitimates that development, suggesting that the proper time for fasting "will come"—and indeed, in Mark's setting, already has.

35. See Maurice Casey, who suggests an Aramaic backdrop for the use of the Greek preposition ἐπί that identifies Abiathar with the general setting. Maurice Casey, *Aramaic Sources of Mark's Gospel*, SNTSMS 102 (Cambridge: Cambridge University

The surrounding passages promote a close correlation between the disciples' conduct and their master's mission. In this respect, they supply interpretive handles for our reading of Mark 2:21–22, highlighting the sayings' *alignment of his disciples' behavior with Jesus's messianic agenda*. Rather than juxtaposing the old era of Jewish tradition with the new era of the gospel, the passage presupposes the validity of torah even as it subsumes religious tradition under the expansive, inclusive vision of a new world order established in Jesus's christological career. As new patch and new garment, Mark's Jesus implies, the disciples must attach themselves to the one who launches a renewal of all things. In their context in Mark, these sayings frame discipleship as a matter not just of following after Jesus but of actively manifesting the messianic age he establishes.[36]

## The Parable of the Violent Tenants:
## Replacement Theology Writ Large? (Mark 12:1–12)

We turn, more briefly, to the parable of the violent tenants, a story that many take as a blueprint for outright "replacement theology." Scholars agree that Jesus's interlocutors in the parable's present context are Jewish authorities named as "the chief priests, the scribes, and the elders" (Mark 11:27).[37] For some, it is temple officials, rather than the people as a whole,

---

Press, 1998), 151. Str-B 1:618–19 notes that the rabbis sometimes link the event of 1 Samuel to Sabbath observance, but that view is not in play in the biblical texts in question—either 1 Samuel or Mark. Casey seems to force the evidence when he cites b. Menah. 95b, which stipulates that the bread was baked just prior to the Sabbath (*Aramaic Sources*, 155). For disciples as authoritative participants in Jesus's actions, see Neil R. Parker, *The Marcan Portrayal of the "Jewish" Unbeliever: A Function of the Marcan References to Jewish Scripture*, StBibLit 79 (New York: Lang, 2008), 175: "The priest assumes a role equally important [to David's] in 1 Sam, but in Mark he merely serves to provide a temporal context, and that the companions of David who receive no mention in 1 Sam are co-actors with him in Mark."

36. Cf. Martin Hengel, who maintains that Jesus's relationship with his disciples "does not reproduce the tendency, observable in the rabbinical teacher-pupil relationship, for the pupil to learn the *halakah* from the everyday behavior of the teacher … following after him did not mean imitating individual actions of his." Martin Hengel, *The Charismatic Leader and His Followers*, trans. James C. G. Grieg (Edinburgh: T&T Clark, 1981), 53. This passage seems to undermine such a distinction, if not in the ministry of the historical Jesus, then at least in Mark's Gospel.

37. Indeed, as starting point, this link is almost universally accepted (see Mark 12:12). See Aaron A. Milavec, "A Fresh Analysis of the Parable of the Wicked Hus-

whom Jesus links with the tenants who deploy violent means as they lay illegitimate claim to the vineyard and its produce.[38]

Others think Mark expands the identity of the tenants to include the entire *ethnos* called Israel. Often taking interpretive bearings from Mark's *Sitz im Leben*, these interpreters read the promise that the owner "will come and destroy the tenants and give the vineyard to others" (Mark 12:9) as a transfer of God's favor from the Jewish people to the (largely) gentile church. Marcus thinks it is possible that, for Mark's audience,

> Israel has lost its status as the people of God—as symbolized by its catastrophic defeat in war—and has been replaced by the church. Our parable thus moves in the direction of supersessionism.[39]

In a similar vein, Craig Evans describes the story as "an allegory of God's dealing with stubborn Israel, Israel's persecution and murder of the prophets, the final killing of God's Son Jesus, and judgment on Israel and vindication of Jesus."[40] Kelly Iverson finds that the "narrative requires a more expansive view of the tenants" that "envisions a broader constituency of religious leaders and the people of Israel."[41] These and other interpreters read the parable as a dislocation of God's favor from the Jewish people to members of the gentile church, who have become "participants in the blessings of the kingdom that have previously centered on Israel."[42]

But is this reading warranted, both in the gospel story and in Mark's context? Attention to the parable itself and its literary setting will attune us

---

bandmen in the Light of Jewish-Catholic Dialogue," in *Parable and Story in Judaism and Christianity*, ed. Clemens Thoma and M. Wyschogrod, Studies in Judaism and Christianity (New York: Paulist, 1989), 106: "on this identification, I have not yet found a single scholar who would disagree."

38. Many interpreters expand the cast of characters named in Mark 11:27 to encompass other officials, including the Pharisees and Herodians mentioned in Mark 12:13. See, e.g., Collins, *Mark*, 547; Witherington, *Mark*, 321–22; Boring, *Mark*, 331.

39. Joel Marcus, *Mark 8–16: A New Translation with Introduction and Commentary*, AB 27A (New Haven: Yale University Press, 2009), 814. See also Marcus, "The Intertextual Polemic of the Markan Vineyard Parable," in *Tolerance and Intolerance in Early Judaism and Christianity*, ed. Graham N. Stanton and Guy G. Strousma (Cambridge: Cambridge University Press, 1998), 211–27.

40. Craig A. Evans, *Mark 8:27–16:20*, WBC 34B (Dallas: Word, 2001), 216.

41. Kelly R. Iverson, "Jews, Gentiles, and the Kingdom of God: The Parable of the Wicked Tenants in Narrative Perspective (Mark 12:1–12)," *BibInt* 20 (2012): 319.

42. Iverson, "Jews, Gentiles," 329.

to neglected features that challenge a supersessionist reading. As we shall see, the apocalyptic divide the parable forges between tenants and "others" concerns neither ethnicity nor religious tradition and its guardians, narrowly understood. Instead, our study detects a dividing line between two kinds of power: *conventional power* expressed through grasping and violence, and *divine power* associated with God's coming kingdom. Our parable is no narrative rejection of an *ethnos*, no early sounding of way parting. It is rather a prophetic story that lays bare the notion that pretentious power wielded by violence ultimately crumbles under its own weight.

A Close Reading of Mark 12:1–12

Despite Adolf Jülicher's admonitions against reading parables allegorically, interpreters freely adopt this approach with the story of the violent tenants. Consistently, they view God as landowner, the prophets as the servants, and Jesus as rejected son (compare with Mark 1:11, 9:7). Consensus breaks down, though, when it comes to identifying the vineyard, its tenants, and the "others" to whom the land is ultimately entrusted. Careful attention to the parable complicates the traditional reading that divides Israel from the church and Jews from Christians.

The parable begins by describing in detail the care the owner takes to enhance his vineyard's security and profitability: Ἀμπελῶνα ἄνθρωπος ἐφύτευσεν, καὶ περιέθηκεν φραγμὸν καὶ ὤρυξεν ὑπολήνιον καὶ ᾠκοδόμησεν πύργον (Mark 12:1). Those attuned to Jewish scripture readily detect echoes of Isa 5:1–7, where the prophet uses the image of vineyard to represent God's people: "The vineyard of the Lord of hosts is the house of Israel, and the people of Judah are his pleasant planting" (Isa 5:7; see also Jer 2:21; Ezek 19:10–14; Hos 10:1). Since a wide range of Jewish texts invoke this image to describe God's faithful people (see, for example, 1QS VIII, 5; XI, 7–9; 2 Bar 57.2; 4 Ezra 5.23), it is likely that both Jesus's and Mark's audiences would connect vineyard with the house of Israel.

Yet the details in the parable also suggest a more precise connection with Jerusalem and its temple. For one thing, Jewish tradition sometimes identifies Isaiah's watchtower, wine vat, and fence with the temple structure and its altar.[43] These careful and costly improvements to the

---

43. E.g., 4Q500; 1 En. 89.56, 66–67; Tg. Isa. 5:1–2. See Johannes C. de Moor, "The Targumic Background of Mark 12:1–12: The Parable of the Wicked Tenants," *JSJ* 29 (1998): 69–71. See also Marcus, *Mark 8–16*, 802.

vineyard, then, signal the owner's investment in its flourishing and pro-
tection. Implicitly, the Jerusalem temple belongs squarely within the
owner's plan for the vineyard's well-being.

Another feature worth noting is the parable's succinct reference to the
owner's departure. Mark writes, καὶ ἐξέδετο αὐτὸν γεωργοῖς, καὶ ἀπεδήμησεν
(Mark 12:1). Notably, the story remains silent on the cause of his leaving,
though absentee landlords were commonplace in first-century Palestine
and thus in Jesus's stories (see, for example, Mark 13:34; Matt 24:45–46;
25:14–15).[44] Yet the (divine) owner's absence likely needed no explanation
for an audience acquainted with Jewish tradition. As Johannes C. de Moor
puts it, "Already in the Old Testament itself the Babylonian Exile was seen
as a period of divine absence from Israel (Isa 54:7–8) and the removal of
God's presence at that time became a classic theme in rabbinic Judaism."[45]
Notably, Ezekiel links the departure of God's glory to the violence and
bloodshed rampant in Jerusalem (see Ezek 10–11). Later texts such as the
Isaiah Targum preserve what was likely a view current in the first century:
God had departed from the temple because of Israel's sins (Tg. Isa. 5:2, 5).

Whatever its cause, the owner's departure means he engages tenants
(γεωργοῖς) to cultivate the vineyard, to their benefit as well as the owner's.
To equate these tenants with the people of Israel proves problematic on
several points. For one thing, the relationship between tenants and vineyard owner is *transactional and economic* from the outset. The tenants are
workers-for-hire under a commercial contract with the owner. It is the
vineyard that is prized by the owner; the tenants simply do the owner's
bidding. The interpretive shift that identifies the tenants with either the
people of Israel or their religious leaders, broadly speaking, fails to account
for Judaism's core claims about God's intimate, even familial, ties with
God's people.[46]

The tenants' violent response toward the servant sent "in season" (τῷ
καιρῷ) to collect the owner's due "from the fruits of the vineyard" (Mark

---

44. See Martin Hengel, "Das Gleichnis von den Weingärtnern Mc 12,1–12 im
Lichte der Zenon-papyri und der rabbinischen Gleichnisse," *ZNW* 59 (1968): 21–23.

45. De Moor, "Targumic Background," 67.

46. Marcus (*Mark 8–16*, 814) thinks Mark does pivot in this direction and calls
the parable "almost a parody of Isaiah 5; the people of Israel are no longer symbolized
by the vineyard, which in Isaiah remains God's treasured possession despite his anger
at its misuse" and are "represented, rather, by workers who have contracted to tend the
vineyard and who can easily be replaced if they prove unsuitable for the job."

12:2) further complicates the view that they broadly represent the Jewish people or even their leaders. To be sure, the tenants' treatment of the owner's emissaries fits well within the biblical traditions about rejected prophets, who often face persecution for their loyalty to God (Jer 26:20–23; 1 Kgs 18:4, 13; 19:10, 14; 2 Chr 24:21). Typically, though, prophets meet violent ends not through the will of the *people as a whole* but because *those in power* name them as imminent threats to personal, economic, or national security.

Of course, it is the murder of the last agent, the owner's beloved son, that draws the question of inheritance into view and propels the parable toward the tenants' destruction and replacement by "others" (Mark 12:6–9). Clearly, the son is a cipher for Jesus, who in Mark has already pointed to his own death three times (Mark 8:31, 9:31, 10:33–34); for all the secrecy in this gospel, Jesus's destiny is already out in the open.[47] In the parable, the tenants' motives are at least twofold. Like the servants who precede him, the son's very presence reminds the tenants that they are guardians, not owners, of the vineyard; their property rights are ceded rights, constrained by the terms of their tenancy. Thus, the son disrupts their inflated sense of authorized entitlement. But the son's arrival compounds this disruption since he *is* the vineyard's legitimate heir to the vineyard. Because the tenants have read themselves into that role, thinking "the inheritance will be ours" (Mark 12:7), the son becomes an outright obstacle to their presumptive possession.

It is thus in the tenants' treatment of both servants and son that their identity comes to clearer light. Rather than designating a people or even their leaders as a discrete group, the tenants seem to represent those in Jesus's or Mark's world who *wield religious or political power in ways that grasp for both resources and authority that are not, rightly speaking, their own*. In Jesus's and Mark's apocalyptic view, that power befits the present evil age, which will soon give way to God's sovereign, inclusive sway. Their destruction will come as the scales of divine justice prevail, and they find themselves crushed under their own violent ways.

Indeed, the promise that the owner will "destroy the tenants and give the vineyard to others" (Mark 12:9) announces that coming destruction. True, the parable's language suggests that the outcome entails an act of

---

47. On the possibility that the parable, as originally told, could refer to other faithful figures, even faithful Israel, see de Moor, "Targumic Background," 75–76.

retributive justice on the owner's part. But Jewish apocalyptic thought looks toward God's arrival within the human sphere to set things right (see Isa 64:1). In any case, the tenants suffer the same destiny they have inflicted on the owner's servants and son.

But who are the "others" to whom the vineyard will be given? Though some think the term designates the gentile church and thus "moves in the direction of supersessionism,"[48] the parable itself suggests a more nuanced interpretation. If the owner forcibly removes the tenants for their greedy violence and usurpation of power, the others may simply be understood as those whose care for the vineyard arises from allegiance to (faith in?) the owner. They take their place as its guardians and beneficiaries, not its presumed proprietors.

Jesus uses a citation of Ps 118:22 (LXX 117:22) to confirm the reversal of fortune announced in Mark 12:9: "The stone that the builders rejected has become the cornerstone" (Mark 12:10). Though the verse's original setting hails the psalmist's salvation from "the nations" (Ps 118:10), Mark's Jesus invokes it to herald the son's vindication. Mark is in line with Jewish texts that read the rejected stone as Davidic Messiah,[49] but with a twist: Jesus's vindication comes not by his *exercise* of conventional power but as one who *suffers under it*.

## Mark 12:1–12 in Literary Context

The passage concludes with an editorial gloss noting that "they" (read: the chief priests, scribes and elders named in Mark 11:27) understand that "he had told this parable against them" (Mark 12:12). As we shall see, the wider literary context offers interpretive guidance about the grounds on which these leaders are culpable. The parable's self-contained critique against violent power wielded for economic gain fits well thematic concerns found in the passage's literary setting. Rather than wholesale condemnation of Jewish tradition, Jewish leaders, or the Jewish people, Mark's story contrasts those aligned with the values of the present evil age (the tenants) with those loyal to God's reign ("others").

---

48. Marcus, *Mark 8–16*, 814.

49. Marcus thinks that the insurgents whose actions led to the Jewish War found inspiration in the verse as evidence that God was on their side. Joel Marcus, *The Way of the Lord: Christological Exegesis of the Old Testament in the Gospel of Mark* (Louisville: Westminster John Knox, 1992; Edinburgh: T&T Clark, 1992), 115–18.

Selected examples from the parable's surrounding passages draw that contrast into sharper relief. For instance, Jesus enters Jerusalem in a prophetic act that identifies him with Zechariah's humble king, whose triumph entails an end to military power and the dawn of "peace to the nations" (Zech 9:9–10; see Mark 11:1–11). Once inside the temple precinct, Jesus channels prophetic polemic against both economic injustice (Mark 11:15; compare with Jer 7:5–7) and insists that the temple be a "house of prayer for all the nations" (Mark 11:17; Isa 56:7). In this pairing of episodes, Mark's Jesus casts a vision derived from Jewish tradition that positions Jerusalem and its temple as emblems of God's ways of peace and justice for all people.

A dispute with Pharisees and Herodians that follows our parable sets up a similar contrast of allegiances. Intending to trap Jesus, these interlocutors ask about the legality of paying Roman taxes. Jesus sees their "hypocrisy" (Mark 12:15): their own authority, perhaps even livelihood, depended on Roman taxation. After pointing out the image of Caesar marking the coin's face, he responds somewhat enigmatically: "Give to the emperor the things that are the emperor's and to God the things that are God's" (Mark 12:17). Most interpreters find in this answer an anachronistic separation of religious from political power (see Justin, *1 Apol.* 17.2) and tacit acceptance of imperial commerce (see Rom 13:1–7). Yet the passage's literary link to the vineyard parable at least raises the possibility that the conversation underscores its critique. Like the tenants who would enrich themselves with the land's bounty, refusing to render the owner's "share of the produce" (Mark 12:2), Jesus's response may subtly signal the conflicting loyalties embedded in the question (compare with Matt 6:24 and Luke 16:13 on the impossibility of serving "two masters").[50]

Finally, the end of Mark 12 combines two passages that drive home competing economic values: the condemnation of the scribes (Mark 12:38–40) and the story of the widow's offering (Mark 12:41–44). They share an interest in widows—a quintessentially vulnerable social group (see, for example, Isa 10:1–2, Zech 7:10)—even as they contrast the scribes' avarice with a widow's generosity. On the one hand, the scribes "devour widows' houses" (Mark 12:40), while well-resourced worshipers

---

50. We need not adopt a classist reading of the passage to entertain the notion that Mark's Jesus thinks everything belongs to God. See Richard A. Horsley, *Hearing the Whole Story: The Politics of Plot in Mark's Gospel* (Louisville: Westminster John Knox, 2001), 43.

give "large sums ... out of their abundance" (Mark 12:41, 44). On the other hand, an unnamed widow offers "out of her poverty ... everything she had" (Mark 12:44). Like the woman who later anoints Jesus with precious alabaster oil (Mark 14:3–9), the widow casts her loyalty, her lot, and her very livelihood with God and God's economy.

Both the parable itself and its literary setting in Mark's Gospel point toward a vision of God's coming kingdom that rejects violent, usurping power. As Mark's Jesus makes his way around Jerusalem and its temple, he consistently signals loyalty to God and God's just ways, even when they collide with systems designed to devour. The parable thus stands as a narrative alert that such collision is inevitable for those who cast their allegiance with the new world order. It also offers a narrative promise that the seizing, destructive ways of the present evil age will soon lose their sway.

### Was Mark a Supersessionist? Some Tentative Suggestions

Was Mark a supersessionist? More specifically, did Mark tell Jesus's story in a way that suggested that the church had taken the place of Israel as God's chosen people? We have considered two passages often cited to support such a view. Taken together, the saying about garments and wineskins and the parable of the violent tenants concern two main pillars of Jewish tradition: torah and temple. If these passages subvert such central elements of Israel's religious practice, replacement theology may well find an early precedent in Mark's Gospel.

Our study, though, has highlighted the more complex and nuanced views of torah and temple portrayed in these gospel episodes. Rather than subverting torah, the sayings in Mark 2:21–22 mainly concern allegiance to Jesus's messianic vision of a new world order, rooted in torah if sometimes at odds with its interpreters. Rather than undermining the role of the Jerusalem temple or even its leaders broadly speaking, Mark 12:1–12 issues a prophetic indictment against a particular kind of guardianship marked by grasping and violence. To interpret either passage as veering toward supersessionism is to overlook the complex claims of the text itself, as well as each passage's relationship to the wider gospel story.

Those who do see Mark as an incipient supersessionist base this reading mostly on the evangelist's own audience. On the consensus view that Mark addressed a (mostly) gentile church somehow affected by the fallout from the Jewish War (66–73 CE), this interpretive lens posits a Jew-gentile distinction in sweeping, binary terms. Our reading, though, detects a different dividing line, one that cuts along the question of allegiance and distinguishes those who *trust in God's coming reign* as manifest in Jesus as its anointed agent, and *those who remain aligned with the present world order*. Indeed, if there is a contrast that appears in both cases, it is a contrast between systems that stymie human flourishing and those that promote it. Neither Jesus nor Mark expressly denies the value of torah or temple per se (but see also Mark 7:19); neither Jesus nor Mark denies the place of the Jewish people as a whole in God's sweeping renovation of the earth.

This reading of both passages in their Markan literary context fits well the contours of power in play in both Jesus's historical ministry and Mark's *Sitz im Leben*. As many have noted, Jesus's apocalyptic vision of God's coming reign ultimately led to his own death at the hands of those invested in maintaining the "peace and security" of Jerusalem. Though some think he died because of a misunderstanding—he meant to usher in a spiritual kingdom, not one that would compete on political terms—it is also possible that officials detected in his "soft power" a dire and ominous peril. If these passages promote loyalty to an alternative kind of power, they help make just this case.[51]

But what about Mark's own setting? Did the gentile church find in this gospel a reassurance that they, not the Jewish people, were the true Israel? Several observations complicate such a view of ethnoreligious separation and help to make sense of the dialectic relationship between old and new that both passages promote, a dialectic that played out in the reality on the ground—if not on the written page—for centuries.[52]

First, evidence from Mark's Gospel suggests that its audience was persecuted on *both religious and political grounds*. As *ex eventu* prophecy, Mark 13:9 signals just this reality: "As for yourselves, beware; for they will hand you over to councils; and you will be beaten in synagogues; and

---

51. History is full of those whose "soft power" has rendered them vulnerable to persecution and death. In recent history, those associated with movements led by Martin Luther King Jr., Nelson Mandela, and Omar Barghouti have been targeted by political officials not because they took up arms but because their nonviolent tactics have posed a more momentous threat.

52. See, e.g., Paula Fredriksen, "What 'Parting of the Ways'?: Jews, Gentiles, and the Mediterranean City," in *The Ways That Never Parted: Jews and Christians in Late Antiquity and the Early Middle Ages*, ed. Adam H. Becker and Annette Yoshiko Reed (Tübingen: Mohr Siebeck, 2003), 35–63, and Judith Lieu, " 'The Parting of the Ways': Theological Construct or Historical Reality?" *JSNT* 56 (1994): 101–19.

you will stand before governors and kings because of me, as a testimony to them." [53] This statement echoes Jesus's own story, which features both religious (Mark 14:53–65) and political interrogation (Mark 15:1–4), but it likely also telegraphs the experience of Mark's community as common enemy to both Roman and Jewish officials.

At least in part, their persecution seems to stem from their *ambiguous relationship to Judaism*. On the one hand, they followed a Jewish Messiah; on the other hand, Jesus's apocalyptic vision rejected the kind of nationalist, ethnic vision found in the anti-gentile rhetoric of Jewish Zealots.[54] Thus, Mark addresses a community whose socioreligious identity lies in a state of flux and is vulnerable for being either not Jewish enough[55] or religious radicals aligned with an anti-imperial message and figure.

Indeed, scholars agree on this point: Mark insists that the audience's *persecution derives from their identity as a messianic community*. The Gospel's central section, with its repeated "cost of discipleship" instructions, refer to the loss of life (Mark 8:35) as a pattern that marks anyone who would "come after" Jesus (Mark 8:34; compare with Mark 1:17). Mark 13 identifies social and cosmic turmoil as the "birth pangs" of the new creation (Mark 13:8). Like the book of Revelation, this earliest gospel promotes a kind of meantime endurance that entails loyalty to God and God's kingdom even as the empire and its minions seem to hold sway (Mark 13:13).

Against this backdrop, both passages in question promote *adhesion to* Jesus's own messianic purposes and thus allegiance to God's sovereign power. In turn, they also engender *cohesion within* a socioreligious group just beginning to forge its identity. Put another way, the Gospel of Mark itself constitutes insider discourse designed to shore up the legitimacy of a nascent socioreligious worldview that is under threat. Rather than apologetic material crafted for outsiders, these episodes invoke putative events from Jesus's ministry as authoritative basis for that allegiance. Joining new to new introduces a process that Collins calls "a kind of 'fermentation' ...

---

53. Though direct evidence is lacking of such interrogation, Josephus notes that Zealot leaders convened sham courts to "try" those who opposed the revolt and had ample influence with the masses to sway public opinion (Josephus, *B.J.* 4.335–344).

54. On the sociopolitical backdrop of the Jewish War, see esp. Joel Marcus, "The Jewish War and the *Sitz im Leben* of Mark's Gospel," *JBL* 111 (1992): 441–62.

55. For evidence of tension between the Jewish revolutionaries and Jews who advocated peace with Rome, see Josephus, *B.J.* 2.411–430; 4.128, 143, 193–196, 334.

[which is] unsettling, even dangerous."[56] To acknowledge the vineyard's rightful owner (Mark 12:17) is to belie the power associated with the present evil age—power expressed through grasping and violence.

## Bibliography

Boring, M. Eugene. *Mark: A Commentary*. NTL. Louisville: Westminster John Knox, 2006.

Bultmann, Rudolf. *The History of the Synoptic Tradition*. Translated by John Marsh. Rev. ed. New York: Harper & Row, 1968.

Calvin, John. *A Commentary on a Harmony of the Evangelists, Matthew, Mark, and Luke*. Translated by William Pringle. 3 vols. Grand Rapids: Baker Books, 1845–1846.

Casey, Maurice. *Aramaic Sources of Mark's Gospel*. SNTMS 102. Cambridge: Cambridge University Press, 1998.

Collins, Adela Yarbro. *Mark: A Commentary*. Hermeneia. Minneapolis: Fortress, 2007.

Daube, David. "Responsibilities of Master and Disciple in the Gospels." *NTS* 19 (1972): 1–15.

De Moor, Johannes C. "The Targumic Background of Mark 12:1–12: The Parable of the Wicked Tenants." *JSJ* 29 (1998): 63–80.

Dewey, Joanna. "The Literary Structure of the Controversy Stories in Mark 2:1–3:6." *JBL* 92 (1973): 394–401.

———. *Markan Public Debate: Literary Technique, Concentric Structure, and Theology in Mark 2:1–3:6*. SBLDS 148. Atlanta: Scholars Press, 1980.

Donahue, John R., and Daniel J. Harrington, *The Gospel of Mark*. SP 2. Collegeville, MN: Liturgical Press, 2002.

Evans, Craig A. *Mark 8:27–16:20*. WBC 34B. Dallas: Word, 2001.

France, R. T. *The Gospel of Mark: A Commentary on the Greek Text*. NIGTC. Grand Rapids: Eerdmans, 2002.

Fredriksen, Paula. "What 'Parting of the Ways'?: Jews, Gentiles, and the Mediterranean City." Pages 35–63 in *The Ways That Never Parted: Jews and Christians in Late Antiquity and the Early Middle Ages*. Edited by Adam H. Becker and Annette Yoshiko Reed. Tübingen: Mohr Siebeck, 2003.

---

56. Collins, *Mark*, 200.

Gnilka, Joachim. *Das Evangelium nach Markus*. 5th ed. 2 vols. EKKNT 1.1–2. Neukirchen-Vluyn: Neukirchener Verlag, 1998.

Guelich, Robert A. *Mark 1–8:26*. WBC 34A. Dallas: Word, 1989.

Henderson, Suzanne Watts. *Christology and Discipleship in the Gospel of Mark*. SNTSMS 135. Cambridge: Cambridge University Press, 2006.

———. "What Is Old? What Is New? A Reconsideration of Garments and Wineskins." *HBT* 34 (2012): 118–38.

Hengel, Martin. *The Charismatic Leader and His Followers*. Translated by James C. G. Grieg. Edinburgh: T&T Clark, 1981.

———. "Das Gleichnis von den Weingärtnern Mc 12,1–12 im Lichte der Zenon-papyri und der rabbinischen Gleichnisse." *ZNW* 59 (1968): 1–39.

Horsley, Richard A. *Hearing the Whole Story: The Politics of Plot in Mark's Gospel*. Louisville: Westminster John Knox, 2001.

Icrsel, Bas M. F van. *Mark: A Reader-Response Commentary*. Translated by W. H. Bisscheroux. JSNTSup 164. Sheffield: Sheffield Academic, 1998.

Iverson, Kelly R. "Jews, Gentiles, and the Kingdom of God: The Parable of the Wicked Tenants in Narrative Perspective (Mark 12:1–12)." *BibInt* 20 (2012): 305–35.

Jeremias, Joachim. *The Parables of Jesus*. Translated by S. H. Hooke. London: SCM, 1963.

Lieu, Judith. "'The Parting of the Ways': Theological Construct or Historical Reality?" *JSNT* 56 (1994): 101–19.

Marcus, Joel. "The Intertextual Polemic of the Markan Vineyard Parable." Pages 211–27 in *Tolerance and Intolerance in Early Judaism and Christianity*. Edited by Graham N. Stanton and Guy G. Strousma. Cambridge: Cambridge University Press, 1998.

———. "The Jewish War and the *Sitz im Leben* of Mark's Gospel." *JBL* 111 (1992): 441–62.

———. *Mark 1–8: A New Translation with Introduction and Commentary*. AB 27. New York: Doubleday, 2000.

———. *Mark 8–16: A New Translation with Introduction and Commentary*. AB 27A. New Haven: Yale University Press, 2009.

———. *The Way of the Lord: Christological Exegesis of the Old Testament in the Gospel of Mark*. Louisville: Westminster John Knox, 1992; Edinburgh: T&T Clark, 1992.

Milavec, Aaron A. "A Fresh Analysis of the Parable of the Wicked Husbandmen in the Light of Jewish-Catholic Dialogue." Pages 81–115 in *Parable and Story in Judaism and Christianity*. Edited by Clemens

Thoma and M. Wyschogrod. Studies in Judaism and Christianity. New York: Paulist, 1989.

Milgom, Jacob. *Leviticus 17–22: A New Translation with Introduction and Commentary*. AB 3A. New York: Doubleday, 2000.

Moloney, Francis J. *The Gospel of Mark: A Commentary*. Peabody, MA: Hendrickson, 2002.

Parker, Neil R. *The Marcan Portrayal of the "Jewish" Unbeliever: A Function of the Marcan References to Jewish Scripture*. StBibLit 79. New York: Lang, 2008.

Stein, Robert H. *Mark*. BECNT. Grand Rapids: Baker Academic, 2008.

Tertullian. *Disciplinary, Moral, and Ascetical Works*. Translated by Roy Joseph Deferari. FC 40. Washington, DC: Catholic University of America Press, 1959.

Witherington, Ben, III. *The Gospel of Mark: A Socio-rhetorical Commentary*. Grand Rapids: Eerdmans, 2001.

# Sinai, Covenant, and Innocent Blood Traditions in Matthew's Blood Cry (Matt 27:25)

Claudia Setzer

I am delighted to offer this work in honor of my friend and colleague, Joel Marcus. Ever since our lives intersected as graduate students, Joel has been a model to me of a keen and thoughtful scholar whose learning informs his loving humanity. He has always kept in mind the implications of New Testament scholarship for the understanding of Jews and Judaism in the world. I offer this essay on one of the most difficult verses in the New Testament in the hope that it will enhance that understanding.

While the Gospel of Mark mentions the word *blood* only three times, twice in reference to the woman with a hemorrhage (5:25, 29) and once in the eucharistic formula at the Last Supper (14:24), Matthew is preoccupied with it, his ferocious creativity at work on issues of blood, guilt, and the fulfillment of prophecy. His eleven references to blood are concentrated in two places, Matthew's diatribe against the Pharisees (Matt 23) and in the lead-up to the passion (Matt 27), two bodies of material that seem connected. The most arresting image is in 27:25, where Pilate attempts to dissuade the people calling for Jesus's death, "And in answer all the people said, 'His blood be on us and on our children.'"

Matthew introduces two strands of thought in his Gospel that involve innocent blood, what I have named the Sinai/covenant strand and the culpable Pharisees strand. Blood itself has two dimensions: the blood of purification and salvation is sprinkled on Israel at Sinai, ratifying the covenant, then later poured out for many in the eucharistic formula (26:28), and the blood of guilt and culpability is expressed by Judas's "blood money" (27:4, 6, 8) and Pilate's statement, "I am innocent of this man's blood" (27:24).

Matthew's startling addition to the already dramatic scene of the two outcries for crucifixion and Pilate's evasion of responsibility is explained almost universally by scholars as Matthew's reference to the destruction of the Jerusalem temple in 70 CE, explained retrospectively as punishment of the Jewish people (or of the Jews of Jerusalem) for the death of Jesus.[1] Certainly such an explanation fits with a Deuteronomistic worldview that sees suffering as God's punishment for faithlessness and wrongdoing. A host of early Christian interpreters follow this line of reasoning.[2] Even the pagan Celsus knows that Christians blamed Jews for Jesus's death and suffered God's anger, although it is Origen who links it most clearly to Jerusalem's demise (*Cels.* 4.22).

Yet we may have it backwards. Rather than looking for an explanation for the destruction of Jerusalem and the temple, Matthew is looking for the culprit in Jesus's death, and animated by anger at fellow Jews who have not accepted Jesus, he finds the destruction of 70 CE as proof of their sin.

---

1. A complete bibliography on the passion narrative is beyond the scope of this article. The reader would do well to consult general commentaries by W. D. Davies and Dale C. Allison Jr., *A Critical and Exegetical Commentary on the Gospel according to St. Matthew*, 3 vols., ICC (London: Bloomsbury, 1988–1997); Ulrich Luz, *Matthew 21–28: A Commentary*, Hermeneia (Minneapolis: Fortress, 2005); and Craig Evans, *Matthew*, New Cambridge Bible Commentary (Cambridge: Cambridge University Press, 2012). Works on the passion include Raymond E. Brown, *The Death of the Messiah*, 2 vols., ABRL (New Haven: Yale University Press, 1994); John T. Carroll and Joel B. Green, *The Death of Jesus in Early Christianity* (Peabody, MA: Hendrickson, 1995); Frank Matera, *Passion Narratives and Gospel Theology* (Mahwah, NJ: Paulist, 1986). Some frequently-cited older works on Matt 27:25 include Vincent Mora, *Le Refus d'Israël: Matthieu 27,25*, LD 124 (Paris: Cerf, 1986); Hans Kosmala, "His Blood Be Upon Us and Upon Our Children (the Background of Matthew 27:24–25), *ASTI* 7 (1970): 94–126; J. Dominic Crossan, "Anti-Semitism and the Gospel," *TS* 26 (1965): 189–214; Joseph P. Fitzmyer, "Anti-Semitism and the Cry of 'All the People,'" *TS* 26 (1965): 667–71; Timothy B. Cargal, "'His Blood Be Upon Us and Upon Our Children': A Matthean Double Entendre," *NTS* 37 (1991): 101–12. Amy-Jill Levine considers the verse's lack of historicity, as well as its use by theologians and others in later history to demonize Jews in *The Misunderstood Jew: The Church and the Scandal of the Jewish Jesus* (San Francisco: HarperCollins, 2006), 99–102, 168. John Connolly notes this verse surfaced in justifications of anti-Semitism during the Nazi era, *From Enemy to Brother: The Revolution in Catholic Teaching on the Jews* (Cambridge: Harvard University Press, 2012), 3, 25.

2. Justin Martyr is the first of the ancient writers outside the New Testament who saw the destruction of Jerusalem in 70 as punishment for the death of Jesus; see *1 Apol.* 32.4–6; 47–49; 53.2–3; *Dial.* 25.5; 26.1; 108.2–3. Origen reiterates the charge (see *Cels.* 4.22). Eusebius confirms it as part of the Pella legend, where Jews who accepted Jesus escaped Jerusalem unharmed, *Hist. eccl.* 3.5.3–6.

Moreover, as W. D. Davies and Dale C. Allison Jr. suggest, Matt 24 shows that 70 CE was not an isolated event but one of a number of tribulations that would continue until the end.[3]

## Innocent Blood and the Sinai/Covenant Motif

In composing his passion narrative, Matthew relies heavily on Mark,[4] crafting a careful whodunit. He presents in turn the usual suspects who share in the guilt for handing over Jesus—Judas, the chief priests often with elders/scribes (with Matthew's add-on "of the people"), and then Pilate. Following the Markan narrative, he brings the next group on stage, ὁ ὄχλος ("the crowd") who calls for Barabbas's release and twice calls out for Jesus's crucifixion. While Matthew hardly means to exonerate any of these players, he continues his hunt for the ones responsible for Jesus's death. Matthew suddenly changes ὁ ὄχλος to πᾶς ὁ λαός ("all the people") who cry "his blood be on us and on our children" (v. 25).[5] With this cry, the search comes to an end. No one else comes forward to talk about guilt, innocence, or blood, and the story drops back into following the Markan narrative. Pilate, the crowds, and even "all the people" melt away. The shift in narrative suggests Matthew has presented the final answer as to who is guilty of shedding Jesus's blood. It is πᾶς ὁ λαός, all the people.

But has the Gospel prepared the reader for this? In following Mark's passion narrative, Matthew's earlier predictions of Jesus's being "handed over" or betrayed are remarkable for their variety and ambiguity, including: "into the hands of men" (17:22), "to the chief priests and scribes" and "to the gentiles" (20:18–19), an anonymous group (26:2, specifically Matthean), and "into the hands of sinners" (26:45). The prediction in 16:21 says Jesus will suffer from the "elders, chief priests, and scribes," and 17:12 says that, like Elijah, he will suffer from the scribes. Judas is "the betrayer" or "the one who hands him over" in four places (26:15–16, 25, 48; 27:3). In 27:1–2, the chief priests and elders of the people hand him over to Pilate. In 27:18, Pilate knows it was out of envy that "they" had delivered him

---

3. Davies and Allison, *Matthew*, 3:330–31.

4. For a discussion of Matthew's special material and redactional activity in the passion narrative, see Davies and Allison, *Matthew*, 3:578–79; Donald Senior, "Matthew's Special Material in the Passion Story," *ETL* 63 (1987): 272–94; and Brown, *Death of the Messiah*, 1:754–56, 831–39.

5. Unless otherwise noted, all biblical translations are my own.

up, probably referring to the chief priests and elders mentioned six verses earlier. In 27:20, immediately before our verse, the chief priests and elders persuade *the crowd* "to ask for Barabbas and destroy Jesus." At least at the level of the unfolding drama, we have not been prepared by Matthew's use of Markan material to expect "all the people" or even "the people" to be the betrayers of Jesus. Even Matthew's own prediction in 26:2 simply says that the Son of Man will be delivered up, but it does not say to whom.

Yet, if we look more closely, Matthew *has* prepared the readers for the participation of all the people. Jesus is, from the moment of his naming, the prophet who will save the people from their sins (1:21). A certain "people" language intrudes at crisis points, when Matthew adds "of the people" to designated parties. The chief priests and scribes *of the people* cite Mic 5:2 to Herod about the one to come "to govern my people Israel" (2:5). When Jesus enters the temple, "the chief priests and elders *of the people*" question his authority to teach (21:23). "The chief priests and elders *of the people*" gather before Caiaphas to conspire against Jesus (26:3). Judas arrives at Gethsemane to betray Jesus with a big crowd and "the chief priests and elders *of the people*" (26:47). Again, in 27:1 "the chief priests and elders *of the people* conferred together against Jesus in order to bring about his death" before they hand him over to Pilate.

The additional phrase "of the people" never appears in Mark or Luke. So anyone who wants to argue that Matthew wants to implicate only the Jewish leaders must reckon with his apparent blurring of the distinction between the leaders and the people.[6] Furthermore, the term *lead-*

---

6. Many interpreters argue that Matthew's complaint is solely or primarily with Jewish *leaders*; see Matthias Konradt, *Israel, Church, and the Gentiles in the Gospel of Matthew*, trans. Kathleen Ess, Baylor-Mohr Siebeck Studies in Early Christianity (Waco, TX: Baylor University Press, 2014), 89–90, 101–7, 135–39; J. R. C. Cousland argues that the crowds represent the people of Israel as distinguished from the authorities, while ὁ λαός varies with context. J. R. C. Cousland, *The Crowds in the Gospel of Matthew*, NovTSup 102 (Leiden: Brill, 2002), 86. In our verse, he suggests it signifies the leaders and the people. Davies and Allison argue that the Jewish leaders, the Jerusalem crowds, and the Roman governor are all guilty, but not equally so, "the chief culprits are the Jewish leaders" (*Matthew*, 3:593). Carroll and Green say "not just the religious authorities but all the people" (*Death*, 47). Brown thinks that Matthew means that God has visited or will visit his blood on all involved and that most surely includes "all the people" (*Death of the Messiah*, 1:839). Warren Carter understands the narrative as a pitting of Roman power against God's power. Pilate is responsible for Jesus's death, and he manipulates the people into accepting the guilt: "Jesus is crucified not because

*ers* is vague, useful for eliminating the problem of Matthew's seeming to assign guilt to all of Israel, but it does not do justice to the different groups mentioned in the Gospel who enjoyed relatively different relations with Rome. Matthew also expands the crowd language at the entry to Jerusalem, emphasizing Jesus's acclaim as the people's prophet (21:8–11; compare with Mark 11:8–10). Our verse (27:25), however, is the only place in the Gospel where the designation πᾶς ὁ λαός ("all the people") appears. Exegetes from Anthony Saldarini to Pope Benedict XVI have pointed out the literal impossibility of this verse, since all the people of Israel could not be in Jerusalem, much less gather before Pilate.[7]

We have also been prepared for the participation of the people by the narrative of Israel's history. Our verse, "His blood be upon us and upon our children," bears an extraordinarily heavy freight of associations from the Septuagint and Jewish interpretation. As Matthew reflected on the meaning of Jesus's death, he employed earlier biblical themes of the persecution of the prophets and the spilling of innocent or righteous blood. He is deeply invested in the story of Jeremiah, whose persecution is linked to the first destruction of Jerusalem.[8] Raymond Brown cites Jer 26 (LXX 33) as the most immediate backdrop to Matthew's passion narrative in its featuring of priests and prophets against Jeremiah, the participation of the whole people, the mention of innocent blood, the prophecy of destruction of the city, and the attempt to kill the prophet.[9] Michael Knowles shows

---

the people call for it. Jesus is crucified because the elite engineer it." Carter, though more focused on Roman imperialism, also implicates the "religious leaders" as allied with Pilate. Warren Carter, *Matthew and Empire: Initial Explorations* (Harrisburg, PA: Trinity Press International, 2001), 167. Anthony Saldarini emphasizes that it is only the group before Pilate, "a subgroup led away from Jesus by the institutional leaders of Israel." Anthony Saldarini, *Matthew's Christian-Jewish Community*, CSHJ (Chicago: University of Chicago Press, 1994), 32.

7. Saldarini, *Matthew's Christian-Jewish Community*, 32–33; Kosmala, "Blood Upon Us," 96–99; Joseph Ratzinger (Pope Benedict XVI), *Jesus of Nazareth: From the Baptism in the Jordan to the Transfiguration*, trans. Adrian J. Walker (San Francisco: Ignatius Press, 2011), 186.

8. See Michael Knowles, *Jeremiah in Matthew's Gospel: The Rejected Prophet Motif in Matthaean Redaction*, JSOTSup 68 (Sheffield: JSOT, 1993); David Moffitt, "Righteous Bloodshed, Matthew's Passion Narrative, and the Temple's Destruction: Lamentations as a Matthean Intertext," *JBL* 125 (2006): 299–320; and Catherine Sider Hamilton, *The Death of Jesus in Matthew: Innocent Blood and the End of Exile*, SNTSMS 167 (Cambridge: Cambridge University Press, 2017).

9. Brown, *Death of the Messiah*, 2:1450.

how Matthew has superimposed Jeremiah onto Jesus's story. He suggests an overall redactional strategy by Matthew to present Jesus as one of a line of prophets whom Israel rejected, persecuted, and killed.[10] Knowles argues that Matthew uses the theme in service of a Deuteronomistic message that explains the fall of Jerusalem and the rise of the Matthean community as a "new Israel."[11] David Moffitt has stressed three verses in Lamentations (2:15; 3:15; 4:13) as a structuring device for Matthew's Gospel, or "intertext," that links shedding of the blood of the righteous to the destruction of Jerusalem.[12] But I would point out that a major difference between Jeremiah and Jesus is that Jeremiah escapes death.

Although prophets tend to die natural deaths, the persecution theme mutated into the theme of killing the prophets in Jewish interpretation.[13] A recent dissertation by Catherine Sider Hamilton explains Matt 27:25 relative to "innocent blood" traditions of Cain's murder of Abel in Second Temple literature and in rabbinic interpretations of the death of Zechariah.[14] Both murders demand subsequent judgment and destruction but also imply restoration. So Knowles, Moffitt, and Sider Hamilton, stressing different texts, say that Matthew's use of blood language sounds the twin notes of punishment and redemption, and this tendency puts them in the context of the destruction of Jerusalem.

To explain Matthew's use of πᾶς ὁ λαός, I add another piece of septuagintal luggage to the already heavily laden verse, namely, associations with covenant and Sinai.[15] As I have suggested, the reader is struck by Matthew's idiosyncratic and seemingly extraneous use of "all the people," and the assigning to them of ultimate responsibility after others had already sealed Jesus's fate. Yet, while πᾶς ὁ λαός is unique in the gospels, it is quite

---

10. Knowles, *Jeremiah in Matthew's Gospel*, 284–89.

11. Knowles identifies twenty-two passages that contain twenty-six allusions to the figure Jeremiah, twenty from the book of Jeremiah itself, four from Lamentations, which is traditionally ascribed to Jeremiah, and two from Baruch, Jeremiah's secretary. In addition to these textual allusions, he says the prophet Jeremiah himself is a type for Matthew's Jesus.

12. Moffitt, "Righteous Bloodshed."

13. In *The Lives of the Prophets*, for example, Isaiah is sawn in two, and Jeremiah is stoned to death.

14. Sider Hamilton, *Death of Jesus in Matthew*. See also, Sider Hamilotn, "'His Blood Be upon Us': Innocent Blood and the Death of Jesus in Matthew," *CBQ* 70 (2008): 82–100.

15. Davies and Allison also note this (*Matthew*, 591–92).

common in the Septuagint. Several have noted the formula in the list of curses in Deut 27:15–26, "and all the people shall say 'Amen.'"[16] In the Torah, its most frequent use is in Exod 18–34, where it appears twenty times. Its appearance clusters around passages relating to Moses as judge and representative of the people (18:13–23; 33:8–10; 34:10) and around the covenant and Sinai revelation, including God's calling upon them to be his covenant people in 19:4–6, the people witnessing Sinai (19:11, 16, 18 [not in RSV]), and the people agreeing to "do" and "hear" all the things that the Lord has spoken (19:8; 24:3). In Exod 32:3, the same words describe the people who took off their gold earrings and gave them to Aaron to fashion the Golden Calf. "All the people" also appears frequently in 1–4 Kingdoms, expressing unity between king and the people in battle, in covenant (4 Kgdms 23:2), in grief (2 Kgdms 3:32; 15:30), in rejoicing (3 Kgdms 1:39–40), and in king-making (1 Kgdms 10:24).

It is the trope of covenant in particular that informs Matt 27:25, I suggest, because of several elements also evident in the Gospel, namely, the appearance of Moses, the prophet *par excellence* in Jewish tradition, who declares God's words to the people, the juxtaposition of πάντα τὰ ἔθνη and πᾶς ὁ λαός, the unified cry of πᾶς ὁ λαός in response, and the sprinkling of blood on the people. Exodus 19:4–6 contains the words of God's choosing of Israel as covenant partners. He chooses them as his special possession from out of πάντα τὰ ἔθνη, if they keep the covenant (v. 5). All the people, πᾶς ὁ λαός, answer in unison, saying "all the things that the Lord has said, we will do and we will hear." In Exod 24:3, the same language appears: "Moses came and told the people all the words of God and the ordinances. All the people answered in one voice, 'All the words which the Lord has spoken, we will do and we will hear.'" Several rituals follow, including Moses's writing the words of the Lord and offering burnt offerings and peace offerings. Moses reads the book of the covenant before the people, they repeat their promise to uphold the covenant, and then Moses takes half the blood of the offerings and dashes it over the people, saying "See the blood of the covenant that the Lord made with you concerning these words" (24:8).

In Exodus, πᾶς ὁ λαός refers to Israel as covenant partner, chosen and separated out as a holy people from πάντα τὰ ἔθνη, affirmed by their

---

16. Brown, *Death of the Messiah*, 1:837; Davies and Allison, *Matthew*, 3:591. Pilate's hand washing echoes Deut 21:7 and Pss 26:6; 73:13.

answering in one voice that they will do and hear all that God has commanded, and fixed by the receiving of blood upon themselves. In Matthew's Gospel, πᾶς ὁ λαός answer Pilate in one voice, taking Jesus's blood upon themselves. By Matt 28:19, Jesus's message is to go to πάντα τὰ ἔθνη, teaching them to observe Jesus's commandments. While Exodus begins with all the nations, out of whom God picked one holy nation in covenant, Matthew starts with the one nation in covenant but ends with all the nations.

Given Matthew's literary care, these echoes of covenant and Sinai cannot be coincidental, but we do not know *why* Matthew introduces these parallels at the point when Jesus's death is sealed. Are these reminders of Sinai polemical or hopeful? If all the nations are now to receive the commandments, do they replace or include Israel? Is Matthew putting in a reminder of Israel's status as covenant people, with a hint of reconciliation? Is this group in Jerusalem like Israel in the desert who failed to heed Moses and suffered a period of exclusion but who were ultimately brought to the Promised Land? Or does Matthew denounce Israel, as if to say "This is the covenant people, and see how they have reversed their status and betrayed the covenant in an ugly parody of Sinai?" In other words, is it both Israel *and* the nations, or the nations instead of Israel?[17] Matthew has not, in my opinion, given us a definitive answer. Furthermore, he has muddied the waters by introducing another strand of argument.

## Innocent Blood and Culpable Pharisees

In addition to the Sinai language, the other "backdrop" to Matt 27:25 is the anti-Pharisaic polemic of chapter 23, where Matthew incorporates Q-material and organizes woes against the Pharisees[18] into a single sharp public critique. Both theme and language link Matt 27:25 to chapter 23, since both focus on shedding of the blood of the righteous (δίκαιοι) and innocent prophets. The Pharisees appear righteous (23:28), build tombs to prophets, and decorate monuments of the righteous (23:29), but they kill and persecute prophets. In the final woe (vv. 29–36), Matthew writes that

---

17. Saldarini suggests that the whole world means the empire and includes gentiles and Jews, especially those outside Judea (*Matthew's Christian-Jewish Community*, 81).

18. In Luke, the woes are scattered throughout the Gospel and appear in private and public settings.

they can expect all the righteous blood ever shed on earth, beginning with the righteous Abel, to come upon them (appearing twice in v. 35) *in this generation* (v. 36). This charge answers the putative claim of their innocence. The language of righteous innocence precedes our verse in chapter 27 in the words of Pilate's wife about Jesus, "have nothing to do with that righteous one." Other references to innocence and blood surround Jesus's arrest and condemnation, as Judas says, "I have sinned in betraying innocent [ἀθῷον, which some manuscripts change to δίκαιον] blood," or as Pilate claims, "I am innocent of his man's blood" (which some manuscripts change to "this righteous blood," or "this righteous man's blood").[19] Both Matt 23 and Matt 27 echo refrains of innocent or righteous blood and culpability.

Our verse, 27:25, is also linked to Matt 23 by the parent/children metaphor, the notion of punishment coming upon the subsequent generation for ancestral crimes. Particularly if, as many argue, chapter 23 addresses Matthew's Jewish contemporaries fifty years after Jesus's death, these contemporaries qualify as the "children" of the people of Israel of Jesus's time depicted in 27:25 as saying "his blood be on us and our children." Matthew indicts the Pharisees in the deaths of the prophets and the righteous from the first murder, with little worry about anachronism. In the midst of the diatribe of chapter 23, he puts the opponents' claim into direct speech: "If we had lived in the days of our fathers, we would not have taken part with them in shedding the blood of the prophets" (v. 30). Matthew's Jesus seizes on this, saying "You witness against yourselves, that you are the sons of those who murdered the prophets." They admit the ancestral guilt, and our verse in 27:25 completes the idea that the guilt transfers to a subsequent generation.

The natural claim of these opponents, like any later Jews, would be that they take seriously the prophetic critique, saying "We do not kill prophets, as might have occurred in the past. We understand this is a warning. We had nothing to do with Jesus's death, nor do we accept the idea that it caused the loss of the Temple."[20] Matthew's response is: "You're all saying it, but I can show you the proof: first, you admit you descend from the prophet-murderers. Second, you continue this persecution (v. 34), killing and crucifying prophets that God sends and scourging them

---

19. Some form of the word *righteous* appears twenty times in Matthew.

20. Later rabbinic tradition, too, will suggest that the temple was destroyed because of sectarian hatred (b. Yoma 9b).

in your synagogues." Matthew puts into direct speech both this Pharisaic claim of innocence and the later Pharisaic claim that the resurrection is a fraud in 27:63–64. These two statements, put in the mouths of the Pharisees, are exclusively Matthean and unusual for their content. All other direct discourse from Pharisees in Matthew's Gospel is Markan in origin and usually constitutes questions about practice put to Jesus.[21] Both the Pharisaic claim of innocence and the imposter argument represent positions with which Matthew obviously disagrees, suggesting he is refuting claims of others.

The melding of parental and filial guilt and finger-pointing at his contemporaries is reinforced by predicting imminent punishment, "Fill up then, the measure of your ancestors. You snakes, you brood of vipers! How can you escape being sentenced to hell?" (v. 32). Matthew 23:35–36 predicts that the Pharisees will now receive recompense for the blood of the righteous and the blood of the innocent, from Abel to Zechariah up to "this generation," presenting a broad sweep of history.[22] The blood of the innocent prophets will come upon this last generation. Chapter 23 ends with Q material lamenting Jerusalem as a city that kills the prophets and whose "house," the temple, is now forsaken. These themes reverberate with Matt 27 as a whole, where Jesus's death is interpreted in line with the persecutions of Zechariah and Jeremiah, and with verse 25 in particular, where the children will receive recompense for Jesus's execution because of their ancestors' guilt. I suggest that 27:25 is part of a web of polemic against the Pharisees that appears throughout the Gospel. Implicated in the persecution of Jesus during his lifetime, they are implicated by extension in his death, via numerous thematic reminders in Matt 23 and then in 27:62–66 as they also try to suppress reports of his resurrection.

We have, then, these two traditions around blood: Sinai/covenant and culpable Pharisees. Echoes of Sinai and covenant appear in our verse (27:25) via the language of all the people responding together and the act of blood coming upon the people via sprinkling. At the same time, echoes of culpable Pharisees appear via the metaphor of ancestral/filial guilt and the killing of the innocent Abel and the righteous prophets. I suggest that our verse is the place where these two trajectories cross or come together. They are different narratives that do not neatly fit together, which makes room

---

21. A few exceptions are Matt 9:11; 12:24; 22:42.
22. See Edmon L. Gallagher, "The Blood from Abel to Zechariah in the History of Interpretation," *NTS* 60 (2014): 121–38.

for a multiplicity of interpretations. Is it Israel as a whole or the Pharisees in particular who are responsible for Jesus's death? Matthew would have it both ways if he could. Note, for example, how he links leaders, especially Pharisees, to the whole people throughout the Gospel.

Our verse represents the culmination of the innocent blood narrative, where the people's prophet meets his inevitable death at the hands of the people. The Pharisees, not mentioned in this verse, were particularly linked to the people and implicated in these innocent blood traditions in chapter 23. At the same time, our verse is part of the grand narrative of Israel's history, a crisis point like Sinai or the golden calf incident, where the covenant people are distinguished from all the nations.

To return to our earlier question, whether in Matthew's view Israel is rejected or Israel will be redeemed, the Gospel author has not given us a clear answer. That there is culpability is clear, since 27:25 is the point at which the search for the guilty comes to a stop. But could the echoes of Sinai serve as a reminder that this is the covenant people, sprinkled with blood again, on track for redemption? Matthew, we know, can hold opposing ideas in tension with one another.[23]

Moreover, does the movement to πάντα τὰ ἔθνη in 28:19 include the *ethnos* of Israel or not? One's view will be driven by how one understands the question of Matthew's relation to the Jewish community and the question of whether the Gospel's polemic is *extra muros* or *intra muros*. This question and the search for an overarching message about Israel's fate in Matthew's Gospel has produced reams of intelligent scholarship that surveys the same evidence to come to different conclusions.[24] Some agnosticism on these questions seems appropriate.

---

23. Several scholars argue that the two uses of blood imply Israel will ultimately be redeemed by Jesus's salvific act. Cargal suggests that our verse is a double entendre, both placing judgment on the Jewish people and implying their forgiveness via Jesus's blood sacrifice ("'His Blood Be Upon Us and Upon Our Children,'" 111–12). John Paul Heil voiced a similar view in *The Death and Resurrection of Jesus: A Critical Reading of Matthew 26–28* (Minneapolis: Fortress, 1991), 76. Carroll and Green allow that this is a possible understanding of the verses around blood, raising the possibility that even Judas might be forgiven (*Death of Jesus*, 45–48, 59).

24. Konradt considers the characterization of conflict with the authorities and Jesus's popularity with the people to mean Israel *qua* Israel maintains its unique position as God's people, but now Gentiles have access to salvation on an equal footing (*Israel, Church, and Gentiles*, 159–60). John P. Meier, in an early work, says Jesus's death and resurrection means Israel is no longer the people of God and the church is the new

We know neither Matthew's frame of reference nor all the shared assumptions of Matthew and his readers. They may simply take for granted their status as part of Israel and find his evocations of Sinai to be ironic. His frames of reference are mostly local and inaccessible to us. Consider writing a text or email today and how easily nuance or intention can be misunderstood. How much more so is this true for an ancient document from an unknown community. For example, we do not know the precise identity of the Pharisees he complains about.

While several scholars have floated proposals as to the identity of Matthew's opponents, one from Anders Runesson has the benefit of simplicity. Runesson suggests that they *were* Pharisees, one of multiple voluntary associations within a larger common Judaism.[25] As Seth Schwartz, E. P. Sanders, and others argue, a mainstream, public Judaism reverenced God, temple, and torah in a form of civil religion, which continued after 70. Within that rubric, Runesson notes, many smaller synagogues functioned as private, voluntary associations with particular identities, as for example, "the synagogue of the freedmen" (Acts 6:9). This model presumes a city of relative size that accommodated multiple Jewish groups. Some have proposed Tiberias or Sepphoris for Matthew's setting.[26] The example of Paul shows that Pharisees also functioned outside the land of Israel, but we know little more than that. Runesson's model allows us to jettison once and for all the pedagogic model of Venn diagrams of the larger circle rep-

---

people of God. John P. Meier, *Matthew* (Wilmington, DE: Glazier, 1980), 343. Graham Stanton concludes that Matthew had left the larger Jewish community at the time of the writing of the Gospel and that he saw his community as a new people. Graham Stanton, *A Gospel for a New People* (Louisville: Westminster John Knox, 1992). In marked contrast, David Sim, Anthony Saldarini, and Andrew Overman argue that Matthew's community was made up of Jewish believers in Jesus who still saw themselves as part of Israel. David Sim, *The Gospel of Matthew and Christian Judaism* (Edinburgh: T&T Clark, 1998); Anthony Saldarini, *Matthew's Christian-Jewish Community*; Andrew Overman, *Matthew's Gospel and Formative Judaism* (Minneapolis: Fortress, 1990). The debate is well-summarized in Anders Runesson, "Rethinking Early Jewish-Christian Relations: Matthean Community History as Pharisaic Intragroup Conflict," *JBL* 127 (2008): 96–97 nn. 3–4; and in Davies and Allison, *Matthew*, 1:7–58.

25. Anders Runesson, "Rethinking Early Jewish-Christian Relations." An abridged version of this article appears as "Behind the Gospel of Matthew: Radical Pharisees in Post-war Galilee?," *CurTM* 37 (2010): 460–71.

26. See Aaron M. Gale, "The Gospel according to Matthew," in *The Jewish Annotated New Testament*, ed. Amy-Jill Levine and Mark Z. Brettler (New York: Oxford University Press, 2011), 41–42.

resenting the Jewish community and the smaller circle representing Matthew's *ekklesia* and attendant discussion of where to put Matthew.

Runesson further argues that the Mattheans had been part of this Pharisaic association, but it is in the midst of a schism at the time of the Gospel's redaction. This intriguing idea has the benefit of explaining Matthew's continuing use of the term *Pharisee*, as well as his very pointed anger and attack. Certainly it sounds as if Matthew knows these people personally, seeing the size of their phylacteries and length of their fringes, seeing them give alms, and finding them personally irritating, perhaps, suggests Runesson, because they are perverting these shared customs. He suggests these Pharisees may have still held power over the Matthean Christians (10:17; 23:35). As we have shown, Matthew blames them for everything—Jesus's death, the destruction of Jerusalem, even the death of the righteous like Abel and Zechariah, who lived long before any Pharisees existed.

Although it became standard to suggest that the Pharisees ceased to exist after 70, we know virtually nothing about what was happening in the immediate aftermath of 70, the time when the Gospel takes its final shape.[27] The vague terms for this period include *formative Judaism, mainstream Judaism*, and *early rabbinic Judaism*. Martin Goodman has noted that the assumption that sectarianism ceased is only an assumption.[28] In a later article, he notes that Josephus, writing in the nineties of the first century, speaks about Pharisees, Sadducees, and Essenes as groups still in existence.[29] Jodi Magness cites evidence of some continued purity practices, including straining out gnats and flies in Jerusalem, sectarian laws relating to slaughter of locusts and fish at Qumran, as well as artifacts associated

---

27. Peter Schäfer has been instrumental in increasing skepticism around the idea of a synod at Yavneh accompanied by the coalescing of power around the rabbis. Annette Yoshiko Reed charts the scholarly dismantling of this myth of rabbinic hegemony and discipline in "When Did the Rabbis Become Pharisees? Reflections on Christian Evidence for Post-70 Judaism," in *Envisioning Judaism: Studies in Honor of Peter Schäfer on the Occasion of His Seventieth Birthday*, 2 vols., ed. Ra'anan S. Boustan et al. (Tübingen: Mohr Siebeck, 2013), 2:859–96. See also, Seth Schwartz, *Imperialism and Jewish Society: 200 B.C.E to 640 C.E.* (Princeton: Princeton University Press, 2001), 91–93, 96–99.

28. Martin Goodman, "Sadducees and Essenes after 70 CE," in *Crossing the Boundaries: Essays in Biblical Interpretation in Honour of Michael D. Goulder*, ed. Stanley E. Porter, Paul Joyce, and David E. Orten, BibInt 8 (Leiden: Brill, 1994), 347–56.

29. Martin Goodman, "Religious Variety and the Temple in the Late Second Temple Period and Its Aftermath," *JJS* 60 (2009): 202–13.

with purity observance in areas associated with priestly and elite families, all of which she links to Sadducees.[30] If Sadducees and Essenes might have continued their practices, how much more so might Pharisees, who had a more portable piety? James F. Strange notes the archaeological evidence for material that mirrors the six concerns of the Pharisees, including serving at table, ritual immersion, and belief in resurrection. The fact that similar artifacts appear over a geographic spread suggests that some group may have standardized practice outside the temple in these matters. After 70 in particular, he suggests the Pharisees as the most likely candidates.[31] Moreover, if Pharisees *qua* Pharisees are still recognizable in Matthew's time, we do not need to assume they are ciphers for an emerging rabbinic movement that is flexing its muscles. Reed shows that such a scenario is without evidentiary support for Matthew's time. Intriguingly, Matthew's Pharisees as latter-day rabbis do seem to appear in the early fourth-century Christian Pseudo-Clementine Homilies, but they are pictured positively and embodied by Peter. Since these materials mesh with rabbinic and epigraphic material from the same period, she suggests that groups of Jews and Christians are reimagining their origins, sometimes in relation to one another.[32]

The assumption that the destruction of the temple was a watershed in Jewish history and the end of sectarianism has been questioned in a series of essays in the book of that name (*Was 70 CE a Watershed in Jewish History?*).[33] If we may downplay the effect of 70 for the land of Israel, how much more so can we downplay it for the diaspora? Even allowing for the older model of the gradual replacement and refashioning of the Pharisees by the rabbis, neither the Pharisaic practices nor sense of identity would evaporate overnight. In our own time, we see that practices associated

---

30. Jodi Magness, "Sectarianism before and after 70 CE," in *Was 70 CE a Watershed in Jewish History? On Jews and Judaism before and after the Destruction of the Second Temple*, ed. Daniel Schwartz and Zeev Weiss, with Ruth A. Clements, AJEC 78 (Leiden: Brill, 2012), 69–89.

31. James F. Strange, "Archaeology and the Pharisees," in *In Quest of the Historical Pharisees*, ed. Jacob Neusner and Bruce Chilton (Waco, TX: Baylor University Press, 2007), 237–51.

32. Reed, "When Did the Rabbis Become Pharisees?," 885–93.

33. Schwartz contends that the momentous change came with the Roman takeover in 63 BCE (*Was 70 CE a Watershed?*, 7, 13). He also notes that the idea of rabbinic influence has been undermined in recent years by the work by Catherine Hezser and Hannah Cotton.

with identity are hardy. Some Catholics today still avoid meat on Fridays and some Jews who do not keep kosher nevertheless avoid pork. The end of the Civil War in the United States did not mean states in the former Confederacy lost a sense of themselves as unique, nor did Tibetan identity cease with Chinese incorporation. Furthermore, being a Pharisee continued to confer legitimacy and status in the late first century and perhaps later. Josephus stresses his own Pharisaic credentials (*Vita* 12), while Luke underscores Paul's legitimacy by stressing his identity as a Pharisee (Acts 5:34; 22:3; 23:6). Justin refers to Pharisees in his list of Jewish sects (*Dial.* 80.4–5), which perplexes everyone.

Finally, if we accept Runesson's model, any question of Matthew's remarks being about Judaism or Israel must be set aside. Matthew's group of Christ-believers are members or ex-members of a Pharisaic association, one of several synagogues within a Greco-Roman city that includes public synagogues and private associations. Matthew does not talk about Jews or Judaism in the abstract. Rather, Matthew casts blame for the death of Jesus on his proximate opponents, situating it as an event within the grand history of Israel. Whether there will be reconciliation or a future for them, Matthew, like the prophets, leaves as an open question.

## Bibliography

Brown, Raymond E. *The Death of the Messiah*. 2 vols. ABRL. New Haven: Yale University Press, 1994.

Cargal, Timothy B. "'His Blood Be Upon Us and Upon Our Children': A Matthean Double Entendre." *NTS* 37 (1991): 101–12.

Carroll, John T., and Joel B. Green. *The Death of Jesus in Early Christianity*. Peabody, MA: Hendrickson, 1995.

Carter, Warren. *Matthew and Empire: Initial Explorations*. Harrisburg, PA: Trinity Press International, 2001.

Connolly, John. *From Enemy to Brother: The Revolution in Catholic Teaching on the Jews*. Cambridge: Harvard University Press, 2012.

Cousland. J. R. C. *The Crowds in the Gospel of Matthew*. NovTSup 102. Leiden: Brill, 2002.

Crossan, J. Dominic. "Anti-Semitism and the Gospel." *TS* 26 (1965): 189–214.

Davies W. D., and Dale C. Allison Jr. *A Critical and Exegetical Commentary on the Gospel according to St. Matthew*. 3 vols. ICC. London: Bloomsbury, 1988–1997.

Evans, Craig. *Matthew*. New Cambridge Bible Commentary. Cambridge: Cambridge University Press, 2012.

Fitzmyer, Joseph A. "Anti-Semitism and the Cry of 'All the People.'" *TS* 26 (1965): 667–71.

Gale, Aaron M. "The Gospel according to Matthew." Pages 41–42 in *The Jewish Annotated New Testament*. Edited by Amy-Jill Levine and Mark Z. Brettler. New York: Oxford University Press, 2011.

Gallagher, Edmon L. "The Blood from Abel to Zechariah in the History of Interpretation." *NTS* 60 (2014): 121–38.

Goodman, Martin. "Religious Variety and the Temple in the Late Second Temple Period and Its Aftermath." *JJS* 60 (2009): 202–13.

———. "Sadducees and Essenes after 70 CE." Pages 347–56 in *Crossing the Boundaries: Essays in Biblical Interpretation in Honour of Michael D. Goulder*. Edited by Stanley E. Porter, Paul Joyce, and David E. Orten. BibInt 8. Leiden: Brill, 1994.

Hamilton, Catherine Sider. *The Death of Jesus in Matthew: Innocent Blood and the End of Exile*. SNTSMS 167. Cambridge: Cambridge University Press, 2017.

———. "'His Blood Be upon Us': Innocent Blood and the Death of Jesus in Matthew." *CBQ* 70 (2008): 82–100.

Heil, John Paul. *The Death and Resurrection of Jesus: A Critical Reading of Matthew 26–28*. Minneapolis: Fortress, 1991.

Knowles, Michael. *Jeremiah in Matthew's Gospel: The Rejected Prophet Motif in Matthaean Redaction*. JSOTSup 68. Sheffield: JSOT Press, 1993.

Konradt, Matthias. *Israel, Church, and the Gentiles in the Gospel of Matthew*. Translated by Kathleen Ess. Baylor-Mohr Siebeck Studies in Early Christianity. Waco, TX: Baylor University Press, 2014.

Kosmala, Hans. "His Blood Be Upon Us and Upon Our Children (the Background of Matthew 27:24–25)." *ASTI* 7 (1970): 94–126.

Levine, Amy-Jill. *The Misunderstood Jew: The Church and the Scandal of the Jewish Jesus*. San Francisco: HarperCollins, 2006.

Luz, Ulrich. *Matthew 21–28: A Commentary*. Hermeneia. Minneapolis: Fortress, 2005.

Magness, Jodi. "Sectarianism before and after 70 CE." Pages 69–89 in *Was 70 CE a Watershed in Jewish History? On Jews and Judaism before and after the Destruction of the Second Temple*. Edited by Daniel Schwartz and Zeev Weiss, with Ruth A. Clements. AJEC 78. Leiden: Brill, 2012.

Matera, Frank. *Passion Narratives and Gospel Theology*. Mahwah, NJ: Paulist, 1986.

Meier, John P. *Matthew*. Wilmington, DE: Glazier, 1980.

Moffitt, David. "Righteous Bloodshed, Matthew's Passion Narrative, and the Temple's Destruction: Lamentations as a Matthean Intertext." *JBL* 125 (2006): 299–320.

Mora, Vincent. *Le Refus d'Israël: Matthieu 27,25*. LD 124. Paris: Cerf, 1986.

Overman, Andrew. *Matthew's Gospel and Formative Judaism*. Minneapolis: Fortress, 1990.

Ratzinger, Joseph (Pope Benedict XVI). *Jesus of Nazareth: From the Baptism in the Jordan to the Transfiguration*. Translated by Adrian J. Walker. San Francisco: Ignatius Press, 2011.

Reed, Annette Yoshiko. "When Did the Rabbis Become Pharisees? Reflections on Christian Evidence for Post-70 Judaism." Pages 859–96 in vol. 2 of *Envisioning Judaism: Studies in Honor of Peter Schäfer on the Occasion of His Seventieth Birthday*. 2 vols. Edited by Ra'anan S. Boustan et al. Tübingen: Mohr Siebeck, 2013.

Runesson, Anders. "Behind the Gospel of Matthew: Radical Pharisees in Post-war Galilee?" *CurTM* 37 (2010): 460–71.

———. "Rethinking Early Jewish-Christian Relations: Matthean Community History as Pharisaic Intragroup Conflict." *JBL* 127 (2008): 95–132.

Saldarini, Anthony. *Matthew's Christian-Jewish Community*. CSHJ. Chicago: University of Chicago Press, 1994.

Schwartz, Seth. *Imperialism and Jewish Society: 200 B.C.E to 640 C.E.* Princeton: Princeton University Press, 2001.

Senior, Donald. "Matthew's Special Material in the Passion Story." *ETL* 63 (1987): 272–94.

Sim, David. *The Gospel of Matthew and Christian Judaism*. Edinburgh: T&T Clark, 1998.

Stanton, Graham. *A Gospel for a New People*. Louisville: Westminster John Knox, 1992.

Strange, James F. "Archaeology and the Pharisees." Pages 237–51 in *In Quest of the Historical Pharisees*. Edited by Jacob Neusner and Bruce Chilton. Waco, TX: Baylor University Press, 2007.

# The Shema in Mark and John and the Parting of the Ways

Lori Baron

## Introduction

In Mark 12:28–34, Jesus responds to a question about the most important commandment with the opening lines of the Shema, Israel's central confession of faith (Deut 6:4–5). The first verse, the declaration of the unity of God, has special significance for Mark: ἄκουε, Ἰσραήλ, κύριος ὁ θεὸς ἡμῶν κύριος εἷς ἐστιν (Mark 12:29). In "Authority to Forgive Sins Upon the Earth: The *Shema* in the Gospel of Mark," Joel Marcus argues that the Markan Jesus alludes to the Shema in two other passages, where the adjective εἷς and the noun θεός are joined (Mark 2:17; 10:18).[1] These passages are all fundamental to Mark's Christology; in these three instances, Jesus subtly applies the word εἷς to himself in a way that links him with God. Each time Jesus uses εἷς of himself, he challenges his interlocutors, along with the reader, to grasp his identity more fully.

Building on Marcus's work on the Shema in Mark, this essay argues that the Fourth Evangelist makes a similar move for similar reasons: although the Johannine Jesus does not cite the Shema, the evangelist, too, links the word εἷς with Jesus in order to highlight Jesus's unique relationship with God.[2] In both Mark and John, this christological use of the Shema reflects

---

1. Joel Marcus, "Authority to Forgive Sins upon the Earth: The *Shema* in the Gospel of Mark," in *The Gospels and the Scriptures of Israel*, ed. Craig Evans and W. Richard Stegner, JSNTSup 104 (Sheffield: Sheffield Academic, 1994), 196–207.

2. I treat the use of the Shema in Matthew (22:34–40) and Luke (10:25–29) in my forthcoming book, *The Shema in the Gospel of John*, WUNT 2 (Tübingen: Mohr Siebeck, forthcoming). Matthew and Luke both omit the citation of Deut 6:4 and their wording of Deut 6:5 varies from Mark and from one another. In general, Matthew and Luke weaken the christological import of the Markan Shema as they rearrange Mark for their own literary and theological purposes.

a common *Sitz im Leben* in the late first century, when some Jewish religious authorities alleged that messianic claims about Jesus infringed upon the unity of God.[3] This conflict is more pronounced in John than in Mark. So, too, John's use of the Shema is much more thoroughgoing than Mark's: whereas the Markan Jesus uses the Shema to hint at Jesus's true identity, John boldly proclaims Jesus's divinity. Moreover, the Johannine Shema does not focus strictly on Christology; it also attends to ecclesiology. In this essay, I will show that in John, believers in Jesus form a unity with Father and Son, an eschatological Shema foreshadowed by the Hebrew prophets and noted in Second Temple Jewish literature as well. For John, this unity has begun to take shape among believers in Jesus; they are the eschatological people of God, united with God and with one another in fulfillment of the promised restoration of Israel. Jews who do not believe in Jesus, however, are excluded from this unity and, in effect, from the covenant of Israel.

The use of the Shema in both Mark and John has implications for the parting of the ways between Judaism and Christianity. This essay will show that what is intimated in Mark is explicit and more developed in John. This raises the question of whether or not the author(s) responsible for the final shape of John's Gospel drew from Mark's Gospel or had access to Markan tradition, a question worthy of consideration but that is beyond the scope of this study.[4] I am suggesting that what we do see in a comparative study of Mark and John is a revolutionary and perhaps an evolutionary use of the Shema, one that provides us with a glimpse into the way some early followers of Jesus described who they thought Jesus was.[5] Although there

---

3. Marcus, "Authority," 198–200.

4. Perhaps the ideas presented here provide one bit of evidence toward an affirmative answer. For a historical survey of John's relationship to the Synoptic Gospels, see D. Moody Smith, *John Among the Gospels*, 2nd ed. (Columbia: University of South Carolina Press, 2001).

5. The christological use of the Shema may not have originated with Mark, as we see it already developing in Paul, e.g., 1 Cor 8:4–6; Gal 3:20; Rom 3:30. Interpreters who recognize the presence of the Shema in 1 Cor 8 include Hans Conzelmann, *1 Corinthians: A Commentary on the First Epistle to the Corinthians*, trans. J. W. Leitch, Hermeneia (Philadelphia: Fortress, 1975), 142–46; Richard B. Hays, *First Corinthians*, IBC (Louisville: John Knox Press, 1997), 140; Joseph A. Fitzmyer, *First Corinthians: A New Translation with Introduction and Commentary*, AB 32 (New Haven: Yale University Press, 2008), 336, 341–43; Craig S. Keener, *1–2 Corinthians* (Cambridge: Cambridge University Press, 2005), 73–74; Ben Witherington, III, *Conflict and Community in Corinth: A Socio-rhetorical Commentary on 1 and 2 Corinthians* (Grand Rapids: Eerdmans, 1995),

was no complete parting of ways between Jews and Christians by the time of the composition of the Fourth Gospel,[6] Mark's christological use of the Shema—taken even further by John—evinces a widening gap between those Jews who believed in Jesus and those who did not.

## The Shema in the Gospel of Mark

Jesus cites the Shema in Mark 12:28–34. Up to this point in the narrative, various Jewish leaders have questioned Jesus on an array of topics: the baptism of John, paying taxes to Caesar, and the resurrection of the dead (11:27–12:27). Their intent is to trap him into saying something that would discredit him as a true interpreter of the torah (12:13). The scene of the Markan Shema is slightly different. Jesus is approached by a scribe who approves of how Jesus has responded thus far. His question is sincere, "Which commandment is the first, the most important of all?"[7] Jesus responds:

> The first is, "Hear, O Israel, the Lord our God, the Lord is one [κύριος εἷς ἐστιν]. And you shall love the Lord your God from your whole heart and from your whole soul and from your whole mind and from your whole strength." And the second is this, "And you shall love your neighbor as yourself. There is no other commandment greater than these."
> And the scribe said to him, "Well spoken, teacher; you have truthfully said that he is one [εἷς ἐστιν] and there is no other beside him; and to

---

197–98; N. T. Wright, *The Climax of the Covenant: Christ and Law in Pauline Theology* (Minneapolis: Fortress, 1993), 120–36. Note also the possibility of Mark as a Pauline Gospel in Joel Marcus, "Mark—Interpreter of Paul," *NTS* 46 (2000): 473–87.

6. On the parting of the ways as a process that was not complete until the middle of the fourth century, see for example, Daniel Boyarin, *Dying for God: Martyrdom and the Making of Christianity and Judaism* (Stanford, CA: Stanford University Press, 1999); cf. Adam H. Becker and Annette Yoshiko Reed, eds., *The Ways That Never Parted: Jews and Christians in Late Antiquity and the Early Middle Ages* (Minneapolis: Fortress, 2007).

7. For the idea that the *Shema* is both the most important commandment and equivalent to the first commandment of the Decalogue, see Joel Marcus, *Mark 8–16: A New Translation with Introduction and Commentary*, AB 27A (New Haven: Yale University Press, 2009), 836–37; cf. Reuven Kimelman, "The Shema Liturgy: From Covenant Ceremony to Coronation," in *Kenishta: Studies of the Synagogue World*, ed. Joseph Tabory (Ramat-Gan: Bar-Ilan University Press, 2001), 68–80; Patrick D. Miller, "The Most Important Word: The Yoke of the Kingdom," *Iliff Review* 41 (1984): 17–29.

love him from the whole heart, and from the whole understanding, and from the whole strength, and to love the neighbor as oneself is greater than all burnt offerings and sacrifices." (Mark 12:29–33)[8]

The scribe affirms the unity of God, along with Jesus's pairing of love of God and love of neighbor, ideas commonly linked in Second Temple literature.[9] Jesus responds to the scribe positively, "You are not far from the kingdom of God" (Mark 12:34). While Jesus approves of the scribe's rejoinder, he also insinuates that the scribe is still at a distance from the kingdom. Jesus, however, does not explain the nature of this gap or how the scribe might bridge it.[10]

The passage that immediately follows contains a clue to the obstacle that seems to be, in Jesus's view, keeping the scribe at a distance from the kingdom. In 12:35–37, Jesus teaches about the identity of the Son of David, citing Ps 110:1: "How is it that the scribes say that the Messiah is the son of David? David himself said in the Holy Spirit, 'The Lord said to my lord, "Sit on my right until I put your enemies under your feet."' David himself calls him 'Lord,' so how is he his son?"[11] Marcus interprets this passage as a challenge to Jesus's Davidic lineage and to the adequacy of the title "Son of David" for Jesus, and he may be right.[12] The Markan Jesus tends to refute scribal opinions so that agreement here would be exceptional.[13] Even more significant is Mark's tendency to redefine Jesus's

---

8. All translations are mine.

9. On this pairing in Second Temple literature, see Dale C. Allison Jr., *Resurrecting Jesus: The Earliest Christian Tradition and Its Interpreters* (London: T&T Clark, 2005), 149–65.

10. Note that early rabbinic literature associates the *Shema* with the kingdom of God; see Stefan C. Reif, *Problems with Prayers: Studies in the Textual History of Early Rabbinic Liturgy*, SJ 37 (Berlin: de Gruyter, 2006); Marcus, *Mark 8–16*, 837, 845; Marcus, "Authority," 197.

11. On the significance of Ps 110 for early Christians, see David Hay, *Glory at the Right Hand: Psalm 110 in Early Christianity*, SBLMS 18 (Chico, CA: Scholars Press, 1973), 162; cf. Donald Juel, *Messianic Exegesis: Christological Interpretation of the Old Testament in Early Christianity* (Philadelphia: Fortress, 1988), 135–50. For a discussion of Ps 110 and the theme of Jesus's eschatological kingship, see Joel Marcus, *The Way of the Lord: Christological Exegesis of the Old Testament in the Gospel of Mark* (Edinburgh: T&T Clark, 1992), 132–37.

12. On the inadequacy of the title "Son of David" for Jesus in Mark, see Marcus, *Mark 8–16*, 847–48; Marcus, *Way of the Lord*, 130–52.

13. Marcus, *Mark 8–16*, 847.

kingship in a way that deemphasizes Jesus as a triumphant, Davidic Messiah who is victorious over Israel's earthly foes; rather, in Mark, Jesus's kingship is revealed in his suffering and death.[14]

On the other hand, Marcus acknowledges that there are counterarguments to his assertion that Jesus refutes any claim to Davidic descent. Elsewhere in the narrative, for example, Bartimaeus calls Jesus "Son of David" (10:47–48), as does the crowd at the triumphal entry (11:9–10). Jesus does not reject the title in either instance. In addition, I suggest that in Mark 12:35–37, the main focus is not Davidic descent, but the use of the word κύριος for the Messiah in Ps 110, a word which Mark links to Jesus here and which resonates with the previous passage.

The juxtaposition of the Markan Shema (12:28–34) with the question about David's Son (12:35–37) is central to the paradox of Markan Christology.[15] In 12:28–34, Jesus upholds the unity of God, along with the commands to love God and neighbor. In 12:35–37, however, Jesus speaks of one who will be glorified at God's right hand, who is rightly called κύριος. The placement of these passages side by side reconciles two conflicting scriptural expectations: κύριος εἷς ἐστιν ("the Lord is one," Deut 6:4) and εἶπεν κύριος τῷ κυρίῳ μου ("the Lord said to my lord," Ps 110:1)— the monotheistic confession that there is only one Lord and a belief in a quasi-divine "lord" exalted to God's right hand who participates in God's kingly rule. When interpreted together with the previous passage, Mark 12:35–37 moves the scribe, along with the reader, toward a deeper understanding of Jesus's identity. In Mark 12, Deut 6:4 and Ps 110:1, linked by the word κύριος (MT: יהוה), mutually illumine one another, striking a balance between the affirmation of God's oneness and the exaltation of God's anointed ruler.[16] A complete understanding of Jesus's identity is what the

---

14. Marcus, *Way of the Lord*, 150; cf. Marcus, "Crucifixion as Parodic Exaltation," *JBL* 125 (2006): 73–87.

15. So Marcus, *Way of the Lord*, 146.

16. George Keerankeri also notes that κύριος is a *Stichwort* connecting Mark 12:29–35 and 12:35–37. The joining of Deut 6:5 and Lev 19:18 on the basis of the phrase "and you shall love" is matched here by the linkage of Deut 6:4 and Ps 110:1 based on the word κύριος. George Keerankeri, *The Love Commandment in Mark: An Exegetico-Theological Study of Mk 12,28-34*, AnBib 150 (Rome: Editrice Pontificio Instituto Biblico, 2003), 175–79. John P. Meier opines that the former constitutes an example of the exegetical technique *gezerah shavah*, by which two passages of scripture are used to interpret one another based on a common word or phrase. John P. Meier, *A Marginal Jew: Rethinking the Historical Jesus*, 5 vols., ABRL (New Haven: Yale

scribe of Mark 12:28 still lacks: Jesus is God's exalted κύριος who participates in the sovereign rule of the one God.

Mark concludes the Son of David passage by pointing out that "the
great crowd heard him [ἤκουεν αὐτοῦ] with delight" (12:37). Like the noun
κύριος, the verb ἀκούω also links the two Markan passages. The crowd of
common people *hears*, just as Israel was commanded to hear (Deut 6:4).
They understand what the Jewish leaders and even the friendly scribe do
not. They respond positively to the Shema's imperative and to the teaching of Jesus, the κύριος. The Markan Shema, along with the citation of Ps
110:1, is thus freighted with christological implications and demonstrates
for Mark's readers that belief in Jesus is compatible with the unity of God.

Mark's interpretation of the Shema may have served to deflect accusations that his Christology infringed upon Jewish monotheism: Jesus's
inclusion in the kingly rule of God does not violate monotheism; rather,
it redefines monotheism to include Jesus, crucified, risen, and exalted to
God's right hand.[17] For Mark, to fulfill the Shema's command to hear, and
to love God with all one's heart, soul, mind, and strength, is to recognize
Jesus as κύριος.

### The Shema in Mark 2:7

Aside from Ps 110, the only other passage in the Hebrew Bible that
describes an exalted figure alongside God is Daniel's Son of Man, who is
brought to the Ancient of Days and given an everlasting dominion (Dan
7:13–14).[18] Marcus argues that it is precisely in Jesus's role as Son of Man
that Mark is able to maintain the paradox of his Christology.[19] As was the
case with the quasi-divine figure of Ps 110, the power and authority of the
Son of Man is not his own, but it is derived from the one God.

---

University Press, 1991–2016), 4:495. So also Birger Gerhardsson, who points out the
equivalence of ὅμοιος in the Matthean version with the Hebrew שוה (*The Shema in the
New Testament: Deut 6:4–5 in Significant Passages* [Lund: Novapress, 1996], 211). If
Meier is correct (see his caveats in that regard), then the Markan joining of Deut 6:4
and Ps 110:1 constitutes another example of this technique, and it indicates Mark's
familiarity with ancient Jewish exegetical methods.

17. Marcus, *Mark 1–8: A New Translation with Introduction and Commentary*, AB
27 (New York: Doubleday, 2000), 222; Marcus, "Authority," 199–200.

18. Marcus, "Authority," 201–5.

19. On the Danielic background to the Markan Son of Man and how it may have
functioned polemically against Jewish revolutionaries, see Marcus, *Mark 1–8*, 528–32.

In Mark 2, a paralyzed man is brought to Jesus:

> And Jesus, after seeing their faith, said to the paralytic, "Child, your sins are forgiven." But some of the scribes were sitting there and deliberating in their hearts, "Why does this one speak in this way? He blasphemes! Who is able to forgive sins except One, that is, God [εἰ μὴ εἷς ὁ θεός]?"... [Jesus replies,] "But that you may know that the Son of Man has authority to forgive sins on the earth," he said to the paralytic, "To you I say, get up, take your mat, and go home." (Mark 2:5–7, 10–11)

In their outrage at Jesus's alleged blasphemy and his audacity in arrogating to himself the divine prerogative of forgiveness of sins, Jesus's opponents appeal to God's "oneness."[20] Marcus observes, "This reply [2:10] links Jesus with the activity of the one God, and it probably indicates that in Mark's mind it is not a violation of monotheism for Jesus to represent in the earthly sphere the heavenly God's gracious forgiveness of sins."[21] It is likely not a coincidence that Jesus's opponents invoke the Shema here; Jesus is making lofty claims about himself and performing miraculous deeds that are deeply troubling and, in fact, blasphemous, if he is not who he says he is. But by aligning Jesus with the Danielic Son of Man, just as he associates Jesus with the κύριος of the Shema and Ps 110, Mark deftly aims to refute these objections. For Mark, Jesus's unity with God does not contravene the Jewish claim that God is one. It is the one God who empowers Jesus, the Son of Man, to manifest God's royal power on earth.

In this allusion to the Shema in Mark 2, the emphasis on Jesus's unity with God seems to reflect the late first-century controversy also found in John's Gospel, where the charge of blasphemy is leveled at Jesus.[22] Both Mark and John deploy the Shema in order to defend believers in Jesus from allegations that they have broken with the core Jewish teaching that there is only one Lord: κύριος εἷς ἐστιν (יהוה אחד).[23]

---

20. Marcus argues that the use of εἷς both here and in 10:18 is somewhat awkward unless understood as an allusion to the Shema ("Authority," 197–98); cf. Luke 5:21, which uses the syntactically preferable μόνος. So also R. T. France, *The Gospel of Mark: A Commentary on the Greek Text*, NIGTC (Grand Rapids: Eerdmans, 2002), 126.

21. Marcus, *Way of the Lord*, 146.

22. Marcus, "Authority," 199.

23. See Alan F. Segal, *Two Powers in Heaven: Early Rabbinic Reports about Christianity and Gnosticism*, SJLA 25 (Leiden: Brill, 1977), passim.

## The Shema in Mark 10:18

Mark's final allusion to Deut 6:4 appears in Jesus's encounter with the rich man who asks, "Good Teacher, what should I do in order that I might inherit eternal life?" Jesus replies, "No one is good except One, that is, God [εἰ μὴ εἷς ὁ θεός]" (10:18). This last phrase is identical to the scribal challenge in 2:7, where it is used to question Jesus's authority. Here, the objection comes from Jesus himself. Initially, it might seem as if Jesus is rebuffing the young man's estimation of himself as good. This interpretation has some merit on the surface: Jesus goes on to cite some of the commandments of the Decalogue, as if to say, "God, who is certainly good, has already given commandments that lead to eternal life. Why are you asking more of me?" The young man persists; perhaps he is sincere, or perhaps he sees the crowds gathered around Jesus and, due to his social class, feels entitled to an audience with the holy man. Mark does not tell us. The young man insists, "Teacher, all these things I have done from my youth." Now he refrains from using the adjective ἀγαθός, to which Jesus had seemingly objected. The young man takes a step back, where Jesus would have him take a step forward. Mark finishes the story:

> And Jesus, after looking at him, loved him and said to him, "One thing you lack. Go, whatever you have, sell and give to the poor, and you will have treasure in heaven, and come, follow me." But being shocked at the message, he went away grieving, for he had many possessions. (Mark 10:21–22)

This meeting does not end well for the man. The story, on one level, is a critique of wealth (compare with the subsequent discussion in Mark 12:23–31). On another level, however, this encounter is about Christology. Jesus is indeed good precisely because he is one with God. If the young man had truly believed that Jesus was good, he would have recognized that Jesus's goodness is derived from God. He would have understood that following Jesus amounts to following God—that Jesus's invitation is of more value than all of the wealth he would have to leave behind.[24] Jesus's use of the phrase εἰ μὴ εἷς ὁ θεός (10:18) is not a denial of his goodness, but a

---

24. Jesus's demand coheres with a rabbinic interpretation of the Shema in which loving God בכל־מאדך (with all your strength, Deut 6:5) means with all of one's possessions; see m. Ber. 9:5. By contrast, the widow in Mark 12:42–44 stands out as a positive

challenge to see who he is on a deeper level. By using the word εἷς in connection with Jesus here and in 2:7, Mark foreshadows his christological use of the Shema in 12:29–34, culminating in its linkage with Ps 110 in 12:35–37 via the word κύριος. For Mark, Jesus is the Messiah, the Lord—the who is one with God, but who does not usurp divine authority. He is God's appointed vice-regent, the Danielic Son of Man. The Markan Shema enlightens the reader to the reality that Jesus's disciples do not yet grasp (10:26). As Marcus observes: "[Jesus's] goodness does not impugn the radicalized form of the Shema that attributes goodness only to God, because his goodness *is* God's goodness."[25] Without citing the Shema itself, John will also use the word εἷς of Jesus *and* of his disciples in order to reveal deeper christological and ecclesiological insight.

## The Shema in the Gospel of John

In his writing on the Shema in Mark, Marcus suggests that John, too, may draw upon the Shema and that John reinterprets the notion of God's oneness in order to explain the scandal of Jesus's equality with God.[26] I argue that John indeed does this and much more: even though John does not portray Jesus citing the Shema, John deploys the Shema along with key elements of its broader Deuteronomic context to claim that: (1) Jesus is equal to God; his oneness with the Father expresses his inclusion within the divine unity (Deut 6:4); (2) Jesus himself is the object of love (Deut 6:5); for John, to love God, a person must also love Jesus and keep his commandments; and (3) the unity of Jesus and the Father creates a unified people (Lev 19:18; Ezek 37:17–19; Jer 32:39); believers in Jesus constitute the eschatological people of God, the fulfillment of the prophetic hope of restoration. This restoration of Israel into one, united people was envisioned in terms of a renewed Shema. The Fourth Evangelist calls upon

---

example of someone who does, in fact, love God with all her possessions, for out of her poverty, she casts in ὅλον τὸν βίον αὐτῆς (cf. 2 Tim 2:4; 1 John 2:1; 3:17).

25. Marcus "Authority," 210.

26. See Marcus "Authority," 199, and Marcus, "Idolatry in the New Testament," *Int* 60 (2006): 161. Here, Marcus refers to C. K. Barrett, who argues that John routinely incorporates Markan Old Testament citations into his Gospel in a unique, implicit manner. C. K. Barrett, "The Old Testament in the Fourth Gospel," *JTS* 48 (1947): 161–62. Marcus's references to Barrett's thesis led me to pursue the Shema in John as my dissertation topic.

the language and imagery of the prophets in order to persuade the reader that this prophetic vision of unity is becoming realized among believers in Jesus. In what follows, I will outline the Johannine Shema in terms of these three motifs.

## 1. Jesus's Inclusion in the Divine Unity: "I and the Father are One" (10:30)

In Mark 2:7 and 10:18, the expression εἰ μὴ εἷς ὁ θεός is used to tease out christological identity. Jesus forgives sins and embodies God's goodness precisely because of his unique relationship with God. The reader understands what most of the characters in the narrative do not: Jesus is the Messiah, the Lord. By contrast, the Johannine Jesus states boldly for all to hear, ἐγὼ καὶ ὁ πατὴρ ἕν ἐσμεν (10:30). Jesus's opponents are not confused about his intentions. Unlike the scribes in Mark 2 and the rich, young man in Mark 10, Jesus's interlocutors in John 10 fully comprehend the implications of Jesus's application of the adjective εἷς to himself: they take up stones to stone him for blasphemy (10:31–33), for making himself God.[27] The accusation that Jesus had made himself equal to God is present throughout John's Gospel, and the veracity of this charge is never denied (5:18; 10:33; compare with 8:53; 19:7).[28] There is no precedent for this kind of explicit affirmation of Jesus's divinity in the Markan passages discussed above. John's Christology is higher than Mark's and more threatening to Jesus's Jewish opponents.[29]

Jesus utters the word εἷς in John 10:30, ἐγὼ καὶ ὁ πατὴρ ἕν ἐσμεν, but can this declaration be tied directly to the Shema? John's uses the adjective εἷς of Jesus earlier in the Good Shepherd discourse (John 10) supports an affirmative answer. In John 10:1–21, Jesus identifies himself as the good shepherd, who lays down his life for his sheep, in contradistinction to the

---

27. Grammatical considerations necessitate the use of the neuter ἕν in John 10:30, rather than the masculine singular εἷς, which appears in Deut 6:4 LXX. John 10:30 is probably best translated "I and the Father are one thing," a unity.

28. See Wayne A. Meeks, "Equal to God," in *The Conversation Continues: Studies in Paul and John in Honor of J. Louis Martyn*, ed. Robert T. Fortna and Beverly R. Gaventa (Nashville: Abingdon, 1990), 309–21.

29. John's high Christology is likely a reflection of late first-century struggles between some Jews who believed in Jesus and some who objected to their beliefs; see, for example, Wayne A. Meeks, "The Man from Heaven in Johannine Sectarianism," *JBL* 91 (1972): 44–72.

Jewish leaders, who do not truly care for the people.[30] It is widely accepted that this discourse draws from Ezek 34; in Ezekiel, Israel is described as a scattered flock, attacked and dispersed in foreign territory, but YHWH promises to gather them and be their shepherd: "I myself will be the shepherd of my sheep" (Ezek 34:15).[31] By identifying himself as the shepherd of Israel in John, Jesus links himself with God. The reader is invited to see Jesus in the role of YHWH, as one who would lay down his own life so that the sheep might live (10:11, 15, 17).

But the connection between John and Ezekiel runs deeper: both the Johannine Jesus and the divine shepherd of Ezek 34 are described as "one" (εἷς; MT: אחד). Jesus speaks of bringing in other sheep "who are not of this fold" who will hear his voice: καὶ γενήσονται μία ποίμνη, εἷς ποιμήν.[32] The use of εἷς to modify ποιμήν is strikingly similar to Ezekiel's description of the Messianic figure of David:

> I will raise up over them *one shepherd* [ποιμένα ἕνα/רעה אחד], and he will shepherd them—my servant David, and he shall feed them: he will shepherd them and he will be to them a shepherd. And I, YHWH, will be their God, and my servant David shall be prince among them; I, YHWH, have spoken. (Ezek 34:23–24)

---

30. Jeremiah and Zechariah contain similar condemnations of Israel's leaders as evil shepherds (Jer 23:1–2; Zech 11:3–5).

31. E.g., Raymond E. Brown, *The Gospel according to John: Introduction, Translation and Notes*, 2 vols., AB 29–29A (Garden City, NY: Doubleday, 1966–1970), 1:398; C. K. Barrett, *The Gospel according to St. John: An Introduction with Commentary and Notes on the Greek Text*, 2nd ed. (Philadelphia: Westminster, 1978), 373; C. H. Dodd, *The Interpretation of the Fourth Gospel* (London: Cambridge University Press, 1970), 358–62; Gary T. Manning Jr., *Echoes of a Prophet: The Use of Ezekiel in the Gospel of John and in Literature of the Second Temple Period*, JSNTSup 270 (London: T&T Clark, 2004), 111–35; D. Moody Smith, *John*, ANTC (Nashville: Abingdon, 1999), 205. Other Old Testament and Second Temple writers speak of YHWH as Israel's shepherd; see, e.g., Jer 23:3; Ps 23:1; 80:2; Sir 18:13; Zech 10:3; Isa 40:11; Mic 7:14; Philo, *Agr.* 50–53; *Post.* 67–68.

32. Most interpreters suggest that the gathering of other sheep refers to the inclusion of gentiles; see, e.g., Brown, *John*, 1:396; Barrett, *The Gospel according to St. John*, 376; Robert Kysar, *John*, ACNT (Minneapolis: Augsburg, 1986), 163; Barnabas Lindars, *The Gospel of John*, NCB (Grand Rapids: Eerdmans, 1972), 363; J. Louis Martyn suggests they are other Jewish Christians. J. Louis Martyn, *History and Theology in the Fourth Gospel*, 3rd ed. (Louisville: Westminster, 2003), 163–67; cf. John Painter, *The Quest for the Messiah: The History, Literature and Theology of the Johannine Community* (Edinburgh: T&T Clark, 1991), 301.

This Davidic shepherd-king also appears in Ezek 37, where he is again described as "one": "My servant David will be king over them, and there will be one shepherd for all of them" (Ezek 37:24; ποιμὴν εἷς/רועה אחד).

There is some ambiguity in these passages as to whether the shepherd in Ezekiel is God (34:15) or a Davidic servant (34:23; cf. 37:24). This ambiguity is also present in Philo. With affinities to John 1, Philo refers to the shepherd's stand-in as the Logos:

> Indeed, so good a thing is shepherding that it is justly ascribed not to kings only and wise men and perfectly cleansed souls but also to God the All-Sovereign.... For land and water and air and fire, and all plants and animals which are in these, whether mortal or divine, yea and the sky, and the circuits of sun and moon, and the revolutions and rhythmic movements of the other heavenly bodies, are like some flock under the hand of God its King and Shepherd. This hallowed flock He leads in accordance with right and law, setting over it His true Word and Firstborn Son [ὁ ὀρθὸς αὐτοῦ λόγος καὶ πρωτόγονος υἱός] Who shall take upon Him its government like some viceroy of a great king. (*Agr.* 50–51 [Colson and Whitaker]; compare *Post.* 67–68)[33]

Like the Davidic ruler of Ezekiel, the *Logos* is deputized by God to superintend God's created order or "flock." Moshe Greenberg observes that in ancient Near Eastern literature and in the prophets, "The meaning of the epithet [shepherd] vacillates between the owner of the flock (as in the case of a god) and the agent of the owner who is responsible to him."[34] The attribution of YHWH's authority, whether to a future Davidic figure, as in the Hebrew prophets, or to the *Logos*, as in Philo, thus anticipates John's portrayal of Jesus as the unique Son, who is authorized by the Father to speak God's words and perform God's works. His words and actions are not his own, and therefore his authority is not a usurpation of divine prerogatives; rather, everything that Jesus says and does is a fulfillment of the Father's will. The Son is ultimately subordinate to the Father (see 14:28: ὁ πατὴρ μείζων μού ἐστιν) and yet the author can also affirm θεὸς ἦν ὁ λόγος (1:1). John does not attempt to explain how both of these statements are

---

33. This passage is also linked to John 1 in Dodd, *Interpretation of the Fourth Gospel*, 56–57.

34. Moshe Greenberg, *Ezekiel 21–37: A New Translation with Introduction and Commentary*, AB 22A (New York: Doubleday, 1997), 708.

true; they are summed up in the declaration: ἐγὼ καὶ ὁ πατὴρ ἕν ἐσμεν. The Johannine Jesus is both λόγος and θεός (John 1:1).

While our primary focus is the linkage of Ezekiel's one shepherd with Jesus, it is also striking that three times in the Good Shepherd discourse Jesus speaks of laying down his life (ψυχή) for his sheep (10:11, 15, 17–18). The LXX employs ψυχή for נפשׁ (both terms often rendered "soul") in Deut 6:5 LXX: καὶ ἀγαπήσεις κύριον τὸν θεόν σου ἐξ ὅλης τῆς καρδίας σου καὶ ἐξ ὅλης τῆς ψυχῆς σου καὶ ἐξ ὅλης τῆς δυνάμεώς σου. Coinciding with this Johannine use of ψυχή, early rabbinic interpretation of Deut 6:5 understands the idea of loving God with all one's soul as giving one's life in the service of the kingdom of heaven. The expression "to lay down one's life/soul" is linked specifically to the martyrdom of Rabbi Akiba in rabbinic literature (y. Ber. 9:7, 14b; b. Ber. 61b; Sifre Deut. 32; compare with m. Ber. 9:5). Akiba is said to have fulfilled the command to love God with all his soul while being tortured to death by Roman soldiers in the mid-second century. Although Daniel Boyarin has argued that this story probably originated in the third century, this interpretation of the Shema may already be reflected in the foreshadowing of Jesus's death in John 10:17–18.[35] Self-sacrificial love for one's ruler certainly predates the third century: loving one's king by giving one's life in military service was known in ancient Near Eastern treaties.[36] Moreover, the author of 4 Maccabees already links the Shema with martyrdom in the first century. Speaking of the martyrdom of seven brothers, the author writes, "Each of them and all of them together looking at one another, cheerful and undaunted, said, 'Let us *with all our hearts* [ἐξ ὅλης τῆς καρδίας] consecrate ourselves to God, who gave us *our lives* [τῷ δόντι τὰς ψυχάς], and let us use our bodies as a bulwark for the law'" (4 Macc 13:13). The reference here to the whole heart and a total commitment to God, the presence of the word ψυχή, and the importance of the law together constitute a summary of the Shema in its Deuteronomic context. This raises the possibility that the rabbinic link between the Shema and martyrdom had precedents that existed prior to the codification of rabbinic literature, both within Second Temple literature and, quite possibly, within the New Testament itself. Perhaps, as Boyarin suggests, Akiba is the Polycarp of Judaism, the quintessential rabbinic

---

35. Boyarin, *Dying for God*, 102–14.

36. See, for example, Moshe Weinfeld, *Deuteronomy 1–11: A New Translation with Introduction and Commentary*, AB 5 (New York: Doubleday, 1991), 351–52; Weinfeld, "The Loyalty Oath in the Ancient Near East," *UF* 8 (1976): 383–86.

martyr; or perhaps, in light of John 10, it would also be correct to say that Akiba is the rabbinic Jesus, the quintessential Christian martyr. By laying down his life willingly, the Johannine Jesus models the Shema's command to love God with all one's soul.

2. Jesus as the Object of Love: "If You Love Me, Keep My Commandments" (14:15)

In John, Jesus's unity with the Father is expressed in terms of the Shema; Jesus and the Father are one. Central to the Shema is also the command to love God with the whole heart, soul, and strength. In Deuteronomy, God's relationship with Israel is grounded upon God's love for Israel: "The Lord loved your ancestors alone and chose you, their descendants after them, out of all the peoples, as it is today" (Deut 10:15; compare with 4:37, 7:8, 7:13, 23:5). In John, Jesus's relationship with his disciples is anchored in his love for them (John 13:1; compare with 13:34, 14:21, 15:9, 15:12): "even as the Father has loved me, so I have loved you" (15:9).

In Deuteronomy, love is also expected—commanded—in return. Love is a term in ancient political treaties that signifies absolute loyalty to a king.[37] So, too, Israel is commanded to love its divine king exclusively (Deut 6:5). This commandment reverberates throughout Deuteronomy,[38] where love for God is always linked to God's commandments and enacted by keeping them. Israel's God declares that he will show "steadfast love to the thousandth generation of those *who love me and keep my commandments*" (Deut 5:10; emphasis added). Israel's God also "maintains covenant loyalty with those *who love him and keep his commandments*, to a thousand generations" (Deut 7:9; emphasis added). The figure of Moses proclaims: "You shall love the Lord your God, therefore, and keep his charge, his decrees, his ordinances, and his commandments always" (Deut 11:1; compare with 11:13, 30:16). The Shema encapsulates the central core of Israel's covenant with God: since YHWH is Israel's one and only God, Israel's proper response is to love God wholeheartedly and keep his commandments.

In John, Jesus declares, "If you love *me*, keep *my* commandments" (14:15; emphasis added), "They who have *my* commandments and keep

---

37. William L. Moran, "The Ancient Near Eastern Background of the Love of God in Deuteronomy," *CBQ* 25 (1963): 77–87.

38. Deut 10:12; 11:1, 13, 22; 13:2; 19:9; 30:6, 16, 20.

them are those who love *me*; and those who love *me* will be loved by my Father" (14:21; emphasis added), and "Those who love me will keep my word" (John 14:23).[39] These thematic and verbal links between Deuteronomy and John's Gospel are remarkable. In Deuteronomy, the God of Israel chooses a people for himself (Deut 14:2), loves them (10:15), demands their wholehearted love and allegiance (6:4–5), and issues commandments that they must obey in order to maintain the relationship. In John, Jesus chooses a people for himself (John 15:16), loves them (15:12), and demands their love and obedience to *his* commandments. It is Jesus, who is one with God, who is the object of love.

The presence of all of these features of the Deuteronomic covenant underscores the centrality of the Shema for John. The Johannine Jesus does not speak of the Shema as the Great Commandment as Jesus does in the Synoptic Gospels. Instead, he issues his own commandment: "A new commandment I give you: that you love one another. Just as I have loved you, so also you are to love one another" (13:34). Perhaps in this way, John reinterprets the second part of the Great Commandment, the command to love one's neighbor as oneself (Lev 19:18). This command is expressed in terms of sacrificial love that believers in Jesus are to have for one another. The Johannine Jesus thus redefines the notion of loving God and neighbor, which can only be accomplished by recognizing Jesus's true identity.

But Jesus's Jewish opponents in John do not acknowledge Jesus's unity with God, nor are they portrayed as truly loving God. After the first accusation that Jesus has made himself equal to God (5:18), Jesus responds, "But I know you, that you do not have the love of God in yourselves" (5:42). If his opponents truly loved God, he says, they would believe that he was sent by God. When they profess that God is their one Father, Jesus counters, "If God were your father, you would love me! For I came forth from God and am here. I have not come on my own authority, but he sent me" (8:42). Those Jews who do not believe in Jesus do not truly love God in accordance with the Shema's command. If they believed in the one God, they would believe in him. If they loved God, they would love the one whom God sent. Jesus is not only within the divine unity; he is furthermore the proper object of love and devotion. Thus, we see in John's Gospel a thoroughly christological Shema: unless a person believes that Jesus and the Father are one, that person does not love God and is effectively excluded

---

39. Cf. the threefold word to Peter, "If you love me, feed my sheep" (21:15, 16, 17).

from the covenant, from being part of the people of God. John will go on to redefine the eschatological community in similar terms, limiting it to those who believe in Jesus.

## 3. The Eschatological Shema: That They All May Be One (17:21)

John uses the word εἷς to include Jesus in the divine unity, but he also extends this unity to believers in Jesus. In his portrayal of the unity of believers, John appropriates and redeploys an eschatological Shema that is nascent in the Hebrew prophets, where the reunification of the people of Israel in the land is described in terms of oneness. The prophets themselves reinterpret the Shema at a time in which the harsh realities of exile threaten to eclipse all hope. They envision a future restoration, where there will be a renewed covenant with a renewed Shema, in which the one God is worshiped by one people. This prophetic reimagining of the Shema often has eschatological overtones that suggest that the one God united with one people represents the end of the old age and the beginning of the new age. John embraces this vision, refracts it through his own christological lens, and through it gives hope to his community.[40]

We noted in section 1 above that the "one shepherd" in John 10 corresponds to the "one shepherd" of Ezek 34 and 37. But the Johannine Jesus also speaks of gathering his sheep, so that there will be "one flock, one shepherd" (μία ποίμνη, εἷς ποιμήν, 10:16). Ezekiel, too, envisions one people alongside the one God:

> Thus says the LORD God: I will take the people of Israel from the nations among which they have gone, and will gather [συνάξω] them from every quarter, and bring them to their own land. I will make them *one nation* [ἔθνος ἓν/גוי אחד] in the land, on the mountains of Israel; and *one king* [ἄρχων εἷς/מלך אחד] shall be king over them all…. My servant David shall be king over them; and they shall all have *one shepherd* [ποιμὴν εἷς/רועה אחד]. (Ezek 37:21–22, 24)

---

40. For more on the Shema in John and John's use of the Hebrew prophets, see Lori Baron, "The Shema in John's Gospel and Jewish Restoration Eschatology," in *John and Judaism: A Contested Relationship in Context*, ed. R. Alan Culpepper and Paul N. Anderson, RBS 87 (Atlanta: SBL Press, 2017), 165–73.

Ezekiel's "one nation" under "one king" signifies the reunification of the northern and southern kingdoms. Ezekiel performs this national reunification in a symbolic action in which he unites two sticks representing both kingdoms. God commands the prophet: "Join them together into one stick [ῥάβδον μίαν/עֵץ אֶחָד], so that they may become one [וְהָיוּ לַאֲחָדִים] in your hand" (37:17; compare with 37:19).[41] Ezekiel's word of reunification recalls the one God (Deut 6:4) who will create one people. So the promised restoration recapitulates the Shema as it anticipates a time when the one shepherd and the one nation are reunited. The evidence of John 10:16 suggests that John understands believers in Jesus as the restored nation; they are the one flock under the one shepherd, Jesus.[42]

In John 11:52, the language of reunification surfaces again when the narrator interprets the high priest's remark about the necessity of Jesus's death as a prophecy that Jesus will die for the nation and gather "into one" the dispersed children of God: τὰ τέκνα τοῦ θεοῦ τὰ διεσκορπισμένα συναγάγῃ εἰς ἕν. The verbs διασκορπίζω and συνάγω are used frequently in Zechariah, Jeremiah, and Ezekiel LXX to refer to the scattering of the people of Israel among the nations for their disobedience and God's regathering of them.[43] The presence of this language in John undergirds the idea that the Fourth Evangelist sees the regathering and restoration of Israel—expressed in terms of divine and corporate unity—as integral to his narrative about Jesus.[44]

Like Ezekiel, Jeremiah also frames the ingathering of exiles and the unification of the people in terms of oneness. At the time when Israel is restored to the land, God declares: "I will give them one heart [לֵב אֶחָד] and one way [וְדֶרֶךְ אֶחָד].... I will rejoice in doing good to them, and I will plant them in this land in faithfulness, with all my heart and all my soul [בְּכָל-לִבִּי וּבְכָל-נַפְשִׁי]" (Jer 32:39, 41). In an extraordinary move, Jeremiah inverts the terms of the Shema: it is not God who is one, but Israel, and

---

41. The LXX reads ἔσονται ἐν τῇ χειρί σου, most likely due to confusion over the breathing mark or over a double εν in a putative Ur-text (ἔσονται ἕν ἐν τῇ χειρί σου, suggested by Joel Marcus in personal correspondence).

42. So also Manning, *Echoes of a Prophet*, 127; Kysar, *John*, 163.

43. Διασκορπίζω (Zech 2:2, 4; Jer 9:15; 23:1, 2; Ezek 5:10; 12:15; 22:15); συνάγω (Zech 2:10; Jer 23:8; 38:10; Ezek 11:17; 28:25; 39:27).

44. On Jesus as prophet of eschatological restoration, relying primarily on the evidence of the actions of Jesus in the Synoptic Gospels, see E. P. Sanders, *Jesus and Judaism* (Philadelphia: Fortress, 1985).

it is God who pledges faithfulness to Israel with all God's heart and soul.[45] This reversal mirrors Israel's change of direction, first scattered due to disobedience and then regathered in divine love. This passage exemplifies the significance of the Shema in prophetic eschatology and the creativity with which the elements of the Shema could be deployed to serve a theological agenda.

Zechariah, too, expresses Israel's restoration in terms of the Shema: "And the LORD will become king over all the earth; on that day the Lord will be one and his name one [יהוה אחד ושמו אחד]" (Zech 14:9). Here, those of the nations who survive the final eschatological battle go up to Jerusalem to worship God, who is now the sole object of worship for all people. When all of the nations recognize Israel's God as king, the Lord will truly be one and Jew and gentile will worship God as one.[46]

For the Hebrew prophets, the vision of restoration contains a renewed Shema in which a united people worship the one God. For John, this prophetic eschatological restoration is now becoming a reality for followers of Jesus. In John 17, Jesus prays for the unity of his disciples:

> *That they may be one, as we are* [ἵνα ὦσιν ἓν καθὼς ἡμεῖς].... The glory that you have given me I have given them, *so that they may be one, as we are one* [ἵνα ὦσιν ἓν καθὼς ἡμεῖς ἕν], I in them and you in me, *that they may become completely one* [ἵνα ὦσιν τετελειωμένοι εἰς ἕν], so that the world may know that you have sent me and have loved them even as you have loved me. (John 17:11b, 20–23, emphasis added)

The phrase "that they may be one" echoes Ezekiel's statement concerning the reunification of Israel and Judah (ἔσονται ἕν; Ezek 37:17, 19).[47] The expression "that the world (or the nations) may know" is also common to both Ezekiel and John, where the unity of the people is to be a witness to the unity of God. In John, the goal of this unity is that the world might believe in the oneness of Father and Son and be drawn into the eschatological Shema, the mutual love that exists among Father, Son, and believers.

---

45. Noted by J. Gerald Janzen, "On the Most Important Word in the Shema (Deuteronomy VI 4–5)," *VT* 37 (1987): 288–91.

46. In Sifre Deut. 31, the authors interpret the phrase "the Lord is one" as a reference to the eschatological age when all people will acknowledge the divine unity. Admittedly, in Zech 14:9, the unity of God is more explicit than the unity of the people.

47. LXX abridged; see n. 41.

Conclusion: The Shema and the Parting of the Ways

In both Mark and John, the Shema is evoked in situations in which Jesus comes into conflict with Jewish authorities. Its use in both writings demonstrates some of the novel ways in which the Jesus movement appropriated and reinterpreted the Shema. In Mark, the affirmation of the unity of God and the injunctions to love God and neighbor comprise Jesus's teaching on the heart of the Law. Jewish authorities do not find the message itself offensive, but difficulties arise when εἷς is used in relation to Jesus, linking Jesus's power closely with God's (2:7, 10:18).

In John, the hostility between Jesus and Jewish authorities is heightened; when Jesus asserts, ἐγὼ καὶ ὁ πατὴρ ἕν ἐσμεν (10:30; compare 8:59; 11:8), he is threatened with stoning, for making himself equal to God. But the Johannine Jesus is not portrayed as a messianic pretender or a deceiver intent upon usurping divine authority; rather, John locates Jesus within the divine unity. Furthermore, John incorporates the broader context of the Shema in Deuteronomy: *Jesus* must be loved and *his* commandments must be kept.

The Johannine Jesus fulfills the Shema through his unwavering obedience to the Father and, ultimately, by laying down his life for his sheep. In so doing, he serves as an exemplar for Christian martyrdom (and perhaps for Jewish martyrdom as well; see the discussion of Akiba above). John's emphasis on the unity of Father and Son rebuts the claim that Jesus's exalted status constitutes a breach in the divine unity: believers in Jesus are the ones who truly love God. They are faithful, restored Israel, while those Jews who do not believe in Jesus are, in effect, excluded from the eschatological people of God.[48] The Johannine Shema is thus both apologetic and polemical; it explicates Jesus's unique relation to God and condemns those Jews who fail to recognize the unity of Father and Son.

Several Christian writers in the early centuries of the Church continue to look to the Shema as support for their views on Christology and the Trinity. Justin Martyr takes on John's polemical tone when he writes:

Therefore, since all righteousness is divided into two branches, namely, in so far as it regards God and men, whoever, says the Scripture, loves

---

48. For more on the idea that John's use of the Shema reverses the historical situation in which Jewish believers in Jesus are cast out of the synagogue, see Baron, *The Shema in the Gospel of John*.

the Lord God with all the heart, and all the strength, and his neighbour as himself, would be truly a righteous man. But you were never shown to be possessed of friendship or love either towards God, or towards the prophets, or towards yourselves, but, as is evident, you are ever found to be idolaters and murderers of righteous men, so that you laid hands even on Christ Himself; and to this very day you abide in your wickedness, execrating those who prove that this man who was crucified by you is the Christ. (*Dial.* 93.3)[49]

It is possible that Justin's accusation that Jews have never shown love toward God is an allusion to John 5:42: ἀλλὰ ἔγνωκα ὑμᾶς ὅτι τὴν ἀγάπην τοῦ θεοῦ οὐκ ἔχετε ἐν ἑαυτοῖς. Like John, Justin aligns the refusal to believe in Jesus with the rejection of God.

A few Christian authors cite John 10:30 alongside and in light of the Shema. For example, Athanasius writes:

"I and the Father are one"; for thus God is one, and one the faith in the Father and Son; for, though the Word be God, *the Lord our God is one Lord*; for the Son is proper to that One, and inseparable according to the propriety and peculiarity of His Essence. (*C. Ar.* 3.16 [*NPNF* 2/4:403], emphasis added)[50]

Athanasius appears to be one of the earliest Christian writers to connect John 10:30 and Deut 6:4. For him, there is no contradiction between the affirmation of the unity of God and faith in Christ as God. Hilary of Poitiers also links these two passages:

Let us see whether the confession of the apostle Thomas agrees with this teaching of the Evangelist when he says, "My Lord and my God." He is therefore his God whom he acknowledges as God. And certainly he was aware that the Lord had said, "Hear O Israel, the Lord your God is one." And how did the faith of the apostle become unmindful of the principal

---

49. Translation comes from Justin Martyr, *Dialogue with Trypho*, trans. Thomas B. Falls, FC 3 (Washington, DC: Catholic University of America Press, 2003).

50. For a discussion of patristic interpretations of John 10:30, see T. E. Pollard, "The Exegesis of John 10:30 in the Early Christian Controversies," *NTS* 3 (1957): 334–49; Pollard, *Johannine Christology and the Early Church*, SNTSMS 13 (Cambridge: Cambridge University Press, 1970); cf. Maurice F. Wiles, *The Spiritual Gospel: The Interpretation of the Fourth Gospel in the Early Church* (Cambridge: Cambridge University Press, 1960), 112–47.

commandment, so that he confessed Christ as God, since we are to live in the confession of the one God? The apostle, who perceived the faith of the entire mystery through the power of the resurrection, after he had often heard "I and the Father are one" and "All things that the Father has are mine" and "I in the Father and the Father in me," now confessed the name of the nature without endangering the faith. (*Trin.* 7.12)[51]

Hilary of Poitiers thus connects Thomas's statement "My Lord and my God" with John 10:30 and the Shema. Underlying this association is the idea that Thomas applies two words for God in the Shema—κύριος and θεός—to Jesus. For these fourth-century authors, Deut 6:4 and John 10:30 mutually interpret one another. The Shema is useful insofar as it is mediated by John 10:30 and supports Christian theological commitments. By the fourth century, Christian appropriation of the Shema appears to be firmly in place. Although the separation of Judaism and Christianity is still not complete, John's use of the Shema paved the way for later gentile Christians to redeploy it, thereby contributing to the widening of the ways.

## Bibliography

Allison, Dale C., Jr. *Resurrecting Jesus: The Earliest Christian Tradition and Its Interpreters.* London: T&T Clark, 2005.

Baron, Lori. "The Shema in John's Gospel and Jewish Restoration Eschatology." Pages 165–73 in *John and Judaism: A Contested Relationship in Context.* Edited by R. Alan Culpepper and Paul N. Anderson. RBS 87. Atlanta: SBL Press, 2017.

———. *The Shema in the Gospel of John.* WUNT 2. Tübingen: Mohr Siebeck, forthcoming.

Barrett, C. K. *The Gospel according to St. John: An Introduction with Commentary and Notes on the Greek Text.* 2nd ed. Philadelphia: Westminster, 1978.

———. "The Old Testament in the Fourth Gospel." *JTS* 48 (1947): 155–69.

Becker, Adam H., and Annette Yoshiko Reed, eds. *The Ways That Never Parted: Jews and Christians in Late Antiquity and the Early Middle Ages.* Minneapolis: Fortress, 2007.

---

51. Translation from Hilary of Poitiers, *The Trinity*, trans. Stephen McKenna, FC 25 (New York: Fathers of the Church, 1954).

Boyarin, Daniel. *Dying for God: Martyrdom and the Making of Christianity and Judaism.* Stanford, CA: Stanford University Press, 1999.

Brown, Raymond E. *The Gospel according to John: Introduction, Translation and Notes.* 2 vols. AB 29–29A. Garden City, NY: Doubleday, 1966–1970.

Conzelmann, Hans. *1 Corinthians: A Commentary on the First Epistle to the Corinthians.* Translated by J. W. Leitch. Hermeneia. Philadelphia: Fortress, 1975.

Dodd, C. H. *The Interpretation of the Fourth Gospel.* London: Cambridge University Press, 1970.

Fitzmyer, Joseph A. *First Corinthians: A New Translation with Introduction and Commentary.* AB 32. New Haven: Yale University Press, 2008.

France, R. T. *The Gospel of Mark: A Commentary on the Greek Text.* NIGTC. Grand Rapids: Eerdmans, 2002.

Gerhardsson, Birger. *The Shema in the New Testament: Deut 6:4–5 in Significant Passages.* Lund: Novapress, 1996.

Greenberg, Moshe. *Ezekiel 21–37: A New Translation with Introduction and Commentary.* AB 22A. New York: Doubleday, 1997.

Hay, David. *Glory at the Right Hand: Psalm 110 in Early Christianity.* SBLMS 18. Chico, CA: Scholars Press, 1973.

Hays, Richard B. *First Corinthians.* IBC. Louisville: John Knox Press, 1997.

Hilary of Poitiers. *The Trinity.* Translated by Stephen McKenna. FC 25. New York: Fathers of the Church, 1954.

Janzen, J. Gerald. "On the Most Important Word in the Shema (Deuteronomy VI 4–5)." *VT* 37 (1987): 280–300.

Juel, Donald. *Messianic Exegesis: Christological Interpretation of the Old Testament in Early Christianity.* Philadelphia: Fortress, 1988.

Justin Martyr, *Dialogue with Trypho.* Translated by Thomas B. Falls. FC 3. Washington, DC: Catholic University of America Press, 2003.

Keener, Craig S. *1–2 Corinthians.* Cambridge: Cambridge University Press, 2005.

Keerankeri, George. *The Love Commandment in Mark: An Exegetico-Theological Study of Mk 12,28–34.* AnBib 150. Rome: Editrice Pontificio Instituto Biblico, 2003.

Kimelman, Reuven. "The Shema Liturgy: From Covenant Ceremony to Coronation." Pages 68–80 in *Kenishta: Studies of the Synagogue World.* Edited by Joseph Tabory. Ramat-Gan: Bar-Ilan University Press, 2001.

Kysar, Robert. *John.* ACNT. Minneapolis: Augsburg, 1986.

Lindars, Barnabas. *The Gospel of John*. NCB. Grand Rapids: Eerdmans, 1972.

Manning, Gary T., Jr. *Echoes of a Prophet: The Use of Ezekiel in the Gospel of John and in Literature of the Second Temple Period*. JSNTSup Series 270. London: T&T Clark, 2004.

Marcus, Joel. "Authority to Forgive Sins upon the Earth: The *Shema* in the Gospel of Mark." Pages 196–211 in *The Gospels and the Scriptures of Israel*. Edited by Craig Evans and W. Richard Stegner. JSNTSup 104. Sheffield: Sheffield Academic, 1994.

———. "Crucifixion as Parodic Exaltation." *JBL* 125 (2006): 73-87.

———. "Idolatry in the New Testament." *Int* 60 (2006): 152–64.

———. "Mark—Interpreter of Paul." *NTS* 46 (2000): 473–87.

———. *Mark 1–8: A New Translation with Introduction and Commentary*. AB 27. New York: Doubleday, 2000.

———. *Mark 8–16: A New Translation with Introduction and Commentary*. AB 27A. New Haven: Yale University Press, 2009.

———. *The Way of the Lord: Christological Exegesis of the Old Testament in the Gospel of Mark*. Edinburgh: T&T Clark, 1992.

Martyn, J. Louis. *History and Theology in the Fourth Gospel*. 3rd ed. Louisville: Westminster, 2003.

Meeks, Wayne A. "Equal to God." Pages 309–21 in *The Conversation Continues: Studies in Paul and John in Honor of J. Louis Martyn*. Edited by Robert T. Fortna and Beverly R. Gaventa. Nashville: Abingdon, 1990.

———. "The Man from Heaven in Johannine Sectarianism." *JBL* 91 (1972): 44–72.

Meier, John P. *A Marginal Jew: Rethinking the Historical Jesus*. 5 vols. ABRL. New Haven: Yale University Press, 1991–2016.

Miller, Patrick D. "The Most Important Word: The Yoke of the Kingdom." *Iliff Review* 41 (1984): 17–29.

Moran, William L. "The Ancient Near Eastern Background of the Love of God in Deuteronomy." *CBQ* 25 (1963): 77–87.

Painter, John. *The Quest for the Messiah: The History, Literature and Theology of the Johannine Community*. Edinburgh: T&T Clark, 1991.

Philo. *On the Unchangeableness of God. On Husbandry. Concerning Noah's Work as a Planter. On Drunkenness. On Sobriety*. Translated by F. H. Colson and G. H. Whitaker. LCL. Cambridge: Harvard University Press, 1930.

Pollard, T. E. "The Exegesis of John 10:30 in the Early Christian Controversies." *NTS* 3 (1957): 334–49.

———. *Johannine Christology and the Early Church*. SNTSMS 13. Cambridge: Cambridge University Press, 1970.

Reif, Stefan C. *Problems with Prayers: Studies in the Textual History of Early Rabbinic Liturgy*. SJ 37. Berlin: de Gruyter, 2006.

Sanders, E. P. *Jesus and Judaism*. Philadelphia: Fortress, 1985.

Segal, Alan F. *Two Powers in Heaven: Early Rabbinic Reports about Christianity and Gnosticism*. SJLA 25. Leiden: Brill, 1977.

Smith, D. Moody. *John*. ANTC. Nashville: Abingdon, 1999.

———. *John among the Gospels*. 2nd ed. Columbia: University of South Carolina Press, 2001.

Weinfeld, Moshe. *Deuteronomy 1–11: A New Translation with Introduction and Commentary*. AB 5. New York: Doubleday, 1991.

———. "The Loyalty Oath in the Ancient Near East." *UF* 8 (1976): 379–414.

Wiles, Maurice F. *The Spiritual Gospel: The Interpretation of the Fourth Gospel in the Early Church*. Cambridge: Cambridge University Press, 1960.

Witherington, Ben, III. *Conflict and Community in Corinth: A Socio-rhetorical Commentary on 1 and 2 Corinthians*. Grand Rapids: Eerdmans, 1995.

Wright, N. T. *The Climax of the Covenant: Christ and Law in Pauline Theology*. Minneapolis: Fortress, 1993.

# The Johannine Community
## under Attack in Recent Scholarship

Martinus C. de Boer

## Introduction

With the publication of J. Louis Martyn's monograph *History and Theology in the Fourth Gospel* in 1968, the view that the Gospel of John originated *in* and was composed *for* a socially distinguishable group of believers in Christ—what Martyn called "the Johannine community"—has played a prominent role in Johannine scholarship.[1] A rudimentary form of Martyn's thesis about the origin and character of that community, including the relevance of the Birkat Haminim (the Benediction against the Heretics) for the Gospel's three expulsion texts (9:22; 12:42; 16:2), could already be found in the first volume of Raymond E. Brown's commentary on the Gospel of John, published in 1966.[2] Martyn and Brown,

---

An earlier version of this essay was presented as the first of two Kenneth W. Clarke Lectures given at Duke University Divinity School in Durham, North Carolina, in March 2017. I remember with much gratitude the gracious hospitality of Joel Marcus during my stay in Durham. Our friendship goes back to the late 1970s when we were both students of J. Louis Martyn (1925–2015) and Raymond E. Brown (1928–1998) at Union Theological Seminary in New York.

1. J. Louis Martyn, *History and Theology in the Fourth Gospel* (New York: Harper & Row, 1968). A second edition followed in 1979 (Nashville: Abingdon) and a third in 2003 (Louisville: Westminster John Knox). All subsequent references are to the third edition. See Martyn's retrospective discussion in J. Louis Martyn, "The Johannine Community among Jewish and Other Early Christian Communities," in *What We Have Heard from the Beginning: The Past, Present and Future of Johannine Studies*, ed. Tom Thatcher (Waco, TX: Baylor University, 2007), 183–90.

2. Raymond E. Brown, *The Gospel according to John (I–XII)*, AB 29 (Garden City, NY: Doubleday, 1966), xxxv, lxxiv–lxxv, lxxxv. See Robert Kysar, "The Whence and

who were colleagues at New York's Union Theological Seminary, together were influential in putting the Johannine community at the center of Johannine scholarship. The year 1979 saw not only the publication of the second, revised edition of Martyn's seminal book, but also a volume containing three of his Johannine essays, including "Glimpses into the History of the Johannine Community," an essay that complements his monograph.[3] That very same year, Brown published *The Community of the Beloved Disciple*.[4]

Though heavily influenced and even inspired by Martyn's work, Brown went his own way in a number of respects. Here I focus on the fact that he takes the Johannine Epistles into account, something Martyn did not do.[5] As everyone recognizes, the Gospel has numerous affinities with the Epistles in terms of vocabulary, diction, and style, indicating that they came out of the same milieu and bear some relationship to one another.[6] The traditional explanation for these affinities is the attribution of all of them to one author, usually John the son of Zebedee, though others have also

---

Whither of the Johannine Community," in *Life in Abundance: Studies of John's Gospel in Tribute to Raymond E. Brown, S.S.*, ed. John R. Donahue (Collegeville, MN: Liturgical Press, 2005), 65–81; David A. Lamb, *Text, Context and the Johannine Community: A Sociolinguistic Analysis of the Johannine Writings*, LNTS 477 (London: T&T Clark, 2014), 29–55.

3. Martyn, *History and Theology in the Fourth Gospel*; J. Louis Martyn, "Glimpses into the History of the Johannine Community: From Its Origin through the Period of Its Life in Which the Fourth Gospel Was Composed," in *The Gospel of John in Christian History: Essays for Interpreters* (New York: Paulist, 1979), 90–121. An earlier, more technical form of this essay was published two years earlier; see Martyn, "Glimpses into the History of the Johannine Community," in *L'Évangile de Jean: Sources, redaction, théologie*, ed. Marinus de Jonge, BETL 44 (Leuven: Leuven University Press, 1977), 149–75. Because it complements the monograph, "Glimpses into the History" was incorporated into the third edition of *History and Theology* as its final chapter (all subsequent references are to the latter).

4. Raymond E. Brown, *The Community of the Beloved Disciple* (New York: Paulist, 1979).

5. Note the subtitle of Martyn's "Glimpses" essay: "From Its Origin Through the Period of Its Life in Which the Fourth Gospel Was Composed." Most Johannine scholars, including Brown, think that the Johannine Epistles were written after the Gospel (with the possible exception of John 21).

6. The affinities that bind the Gospel and Epistles together also set them apart from other surviving early Christian literature. This fact has provided the basis for the view that the Johannine community to which the documents supposedly attest may have been a sect with respect to other forms of nascent Christianity. See further below.

been proposed, such as John the Elder.[7] The documents would then reflect this single author's distinctive diction and style. For Brown, a more probable explanation is that the four documents were written by a school of (two or more) writers who shared a common idiom, one also shared by the larger Johannine community for which they wrote.[8] He further worked this theory out in his commentary on the Johannine Epistles, published in 1982.[9] In Brown's analysis, the Epistles also indicate that the Johannine community consisted of several house churches, some located in the same city or town, perhaps "a large metropolitan center," and others in different towns situated nearby.[10] The word *church*—in the sense of a local congregation or house church—is used three times in 3 John, and all three epistles, according to Brown, indicate correspondence and travel between the Johannine house churches. Whatever one may say about the Gospel, the Epistles have for many provided a firm foundation for the conclusion that there was a Johannine community.

Whereas Brown and Martyn both thought that the Johannine community exhibited a sectarian profile with respect to the Judaism from which it emerged, they differed when it came to its place within nascent Christianity: Brown argued that the Johannine community was *not* a sect within early Christianity, whereas Martyn believed that to be the case.[11]

---

7. See Martin Hengel, *The Johannine Question*, trans. John Bowden (London: SCM, 1989), and Richard Bauckham, *The Testimony of the Beloved Disciple: Narrative, History, and Theology in the Gospel of John* (Grand Rapids: Baker Academic, 2007), 33–72.

8. Brown, *Gospel according to John*, xxv; Brown, *Community of the Beloved Disciple*, 101–2.

9. Raymond E. Brown, *The Epistles of John*, AB 30 (Garden City, NY: Doubleday, 1982), 94–97.

10. Brown, *Community of the Beloved Disciple*, 98–99.

11. Brown, *Community of the Beloved Disciple*, 88–91; Martyn, "Johannine Community," 125. The classic essay of Wayne A. Meeks, "The Man from Heaven in Johannine Sectarianism," *JBL* 91 (1972): 44–72, played a crucial role in their assessments. According to D. Moody Smith, it can "probably be agreed that on any reading of the Gospel and Epistles there appears a sectarian consciousness," but, as he recognizes, it is not immediately clear whether that concerns "a sense of alienation or separation from the world generally," from "the synagogue," or from "developing ecclesiastical orthodoxy." D. Moody Smith, *Johannine Christianity: Essays on Its Setting, Sources, and Theology* (Columbia: University of South Carolina Press, 1984), 3–4. All three may be involved. For the first option, see esp. Lars Kierspel, *The Jews and the World in the Fourth Gospel*, WUNT 2/220 (Tübingen: Mohr Siebeck, 2006).

Martyn referred to it as "a conventicle with its own fund of images and its own language."[12]

Numerous interpreters have come to question, from various angles and for various reasons, Martyn's and Brown's reconstructions of the origin, character, and history of this community, regarding these reconstructions as merely hypothetical with little or no basis in the text of the Gospel itself and with little or no external corroboration either.[13] In this essay, in honor of Joel Marcus, I want to focus on the work of two very influential scholars

---

12. Martyn, "Johannine Community," 190; see also 188. See Smith, *Johannine Christianity*, 22: "John's relative isolation from other streams of tradition in the New Testament seems to bear witness to a place of origin somewhat off the beaten track.... If the Johannine Gospel or tradition actually originated in a relatively remote corner of the Christian map, its distinctive character as well as its difficulty in finding acceptance in the emerging catholic church becomes more intelligible."

13. Adele Reinhartz, "The Johannine Community and Its Jewish Neighbors: A Reappraisal," in *Literary and Social Readings of the Fourth Gospel*, vol. 2 of *What Is John?*, ed. Fernando F. Segovia, SymS 7 (Atlanta: Scholars Press, 1998), 111–38; Reinhartz, "Travel, Translation, and Ethnography: Johannine Scholarship at the Turn of the Century," in Segovia, *What Is John?*, 250–56; Reinhartz, *Befriending the Beloved Disciple: A Jewish Reading of the Gospel of John* (New York: Continuum, 2001), 37–53; Reinhartz, "Response: Reading History in the Fourth Gospel," in Thatcher, *What We Have Heard from the Beginning*, 191–94; Reinhartz, "Building Skyscrapers on Toothpicks: The Literary-Critical Challenge to Historical Criticism," in *Anatomies of Narrative Criticism: The Past, Present, and Future of the Fourth Gospel as Literature*, ed. Tom Thatcher and Stephen D. Moore, RBS 55 (Atlanta: Society of Biblical Literature, 2008), 55–76; Reinhartz, "Forging a New Identity: Johannine Rhetoric and the Audience of the Fourth Gospel," in *Paul, John, and Apocalyptic Eschatology: Studies in Honour of Martinus C. de Boer*, ed. Jan Krans et al., NovTSup 149 (Leiden: Brill, 2013), 123–34; Richard J. Bauckham, "For Whom were the Gospels Written?," in *The Gospel for All Christians: Rethinking the Gospel Audiences*, ed. Richard J. Bauckham (Grand Rapids: Eerdmans, 1998), 9–48; Bauckham, *Testimony*; Robert Kysar, *Voyages with John: Charting the Fourth Gospel* (Waco, TX: Baylor University, 2005), 237–46; Kysar, "Whence and Whither of the Johannine Community"; Edward W. Klink, III, *The Sheep of the Fold: The Audience and Origin of the Gospel of John*, SNTSMS 141 (Cambridge: Cambridge University Press, 2007); Klink, "Expulsion from the Synagogue? Rethinking a Johannine Anachronism," *TynBul* 59 (2008): 9–18; Warren Carter, *John and Empire: Initial Explorations* (Harrisburg, PA: Trinity Press International, 2008); Jonathan Bernier, Aposynagōgos *and the Historical Jesus in John: Rethinking the Historicity of the Johannine Expulsion Passages*, BibInt 122 (Leiden: Brill, 2013); Stanley E. Porter, *John, His Gospel, and Jesus* (Grand Rapids: Eerdmans, 2015).

on this issue, Richard J. Bauckham and Adele Reinhartz, both of whom first went on the offensive in 1998.[14]

## Bauckham and Reinhartz: Shared Criticisms of Martyn's Work

Let me first note what they have in common in their criticism of the work of Martyn, in particular, who is their major target. Both question and reject what they refer to as Martyn's "two-level reading strategy."[15] This criticism is aimed at Martyn's claim that the Fourth Gospel, or certain sections of it, is a "two-level drama," in Martyn's own words, "one that *to some extent* told the story of the Johannine community while narrating the story of Jesus of Nazareth."[16] Martyn's two-level reading of John 9, with its reference in 9:22 to a formal decree to expel from the synagogue Jews who confessed Jesus to be the Messiah, became the lynchpin of his reconstruction of the history of the Johannine community. According to both Bauckham and Reinhartz, Martyn's reading of John on two levels turns the Gospel story into an allegory of the Johannine community,[17] which is contrary to how the Gospel actually reads, as a story about Jesus. Both emphasize this fact. Bauckham appeals to the genre of the Gospel as support: "The most obvious implication of the biographical genre is that the book is about Jesus."[18] The first readers would have read it as such, and not as the story of the Johannine community.[19] According to Reinhartz, the "two-level reading strategy presumes that the community reads the Gospel both as a story of Jesus and as its own story," but there is, says Reinhartz, an absence of "any direct references in the Gospel to the notion that the Gospel encodes the specific historical experiences of the community and should be read

---

14. See Reinhartz, "Reappraisal," and Bauckham, "For Whom?"

15. Bauckham, *Testimony*, 117; Reinhartz, "Reappraisal," 117–18 (and other essays).

16. Martyn, "Johannine Community," 186, emphasis added.

17. Bauckham, *Testimony*, 13 ("an allegorized version of their own community history"); Reinhartz, "Toothpicks," 76 ("the allegorical reading of the Fourth Gospel as a detailed account of the community's historical experiences").

18. Bauckham, *Testimony*, 21. Bauckham (*Testimony*, 17, 117) appeals in this connection to the work of Richard A. Burridge, *What Are the Gospels? A Comparison with Graeco-Roman Biography*, SNTSMS 70 (Cambridge: Cambridge University Press, 1992).

19. See Bauckham, *Testimony*, 18: "The 'two-level' reading of the Gospel of John is thus immediately suspect by this recognition of genre, as is any expectation that the Gospel is actually *about* the Johannine community."

as such."[20] The Fourth Gospel "would have been regarded by the earliest readers first and foremost as a story of Jesus," she concludes.[21]

Both Bauckham and Reinhartz also express doubts about the application and use of "the two-level reading strategy" to other parts of the Gospel. Bauckham writes that "the strategy cannot be applied to every part of the narrative, nor consistently to the parts of the narrative to which it is applied."[22] Similarly, Reinhartz claims that a two-level reading strategy of John cannot be applied elsewhere in the Gospel, analyzing 11:1–44 and 12:11 to illustrate the point: "an official Jewish policy of expulsion," she concludes, cannot explain those passages.[23]

I make the following observations in response to these shared criticisms of Martyn. First, as far as I can see, Martyn nowhere claims that the first readers were *expected* to read, or in fact did read, the Gospel narrative as a two-level drama. *Scholars do that.* As Martyn writes: "John does not in any overt way indicate to his readers a distinction between the two stages.... Only the reflective scholar intent on *analyzing* the Gospel will discover the seams which the evangelist sewed together so deftly."[24] Martyn doubts that the evangelist himself was "*analytically conscious* of ... the two-level drama, for his major concern in this regard was to bear witness to the essential *integrity* of the ... drama of Jesus' earthly life and the contemporary drama in which the Risen Lord acts through his servants."[25] A separation of the two stages is thus the result of scholarly reflection and analysis, as is the two-level reading that results.

---

20. Reinhartz, "Reappraisal," 130–31. Martyn would of course counter that the expulsion texts (9:22; 12:42; 16:2) contain "direct references" to the "historical experiences" of the Johannine community, as Reinhartz acknowledges ("Toothpicks," 58), but she denies that the expulsion texts are witnesses to historical events (see below).

21. Reinhartz, "Reappraisal," 133.

22. Bauckham, *Testimony*, 117. "Every example of the strategy" he also writes here, "in practice is riddled with arbitrariness and uncertainty."

23. Reinhartz, "Reappraisal," 121; see also Reinhartz, *Befriending*, 40–41; Reinhartz "Reading History," 193. In her view, e.g., John 12:11 indicates a voluntary departure, not a forced expulsion, from the synagogue in order to be able to join the Johannine community. She implies that Jews openly confessing their faith in Christ could have stayed in the synagogue if they had wanted to.

24. Martyn, *History and Theology*, 131.

25. Martyn, *History and Theology*, 89. The original readers would therefore have discerned that the story of Jesus as depicted in the Gospel overlapped with their own experiences.

Second, while Martyn certainly gave the material in John 10:1–16 an allegorical reading,[26] because that passage invites it, he did not read the whole Gospel, or even large portions of it, as an allegory of the Johannine community. That charge represents a caricature of his views. Martyn claimed that while telling the story of Jesus, the Gospel text "is also a *witness* [one that scholars can use to their advantage] to Jesus' powerful presence in actual events experienced by the Johannine church."[27] As D. Moody Smith astutely pointed out, "Martyn actually invoked the modern, form-critical principle that the Gospels bear testimony primarily to the life-setting in which they were produced, and only secondarily to that of the subject matter."[28] It is not often recognized that Martyn began his analysis of chapter 9 with a form-critical analysis of the miracle story (9:1–7), in the line of Bultmann. He shows how a traditional miracle story has been given a dramatic expansion (9:8–41), which provides useful clues to the Johannine *Sitz im Leben* for the scholar.[29]

Third, while Martyn tried out his two-level reading strategy (if that is what it was—I think that it would be more accurate to say that Martyn believed that he had *discovered*, through exegetical analysis, that the text could be read on two levels) on chapter 9, and then also to some extent on chapters 5 and 7, he never thought that this strategy could be mechanically applied to other passages in John or that all of John could be read in terms of expulsion from the synagogue found in chapter 9, as Reinhartz seems to think.[30] He worked from the conviction that the Gospel con-

26. Martyn, "Glimpses," 163–66.

27. Martyn, *History and Theology*, 40.

28. D. Moody Smith, "The Contribution of J. Louis Martyn to the Understanding of the Gospel of John," in *History and Theology in the Fourth Gospel*, 3rd ed. (Louisville: Westminster John Knox, 2003), 6. See also Rudolf Bultmann, *History of the Synoptic Tradition* (New York: Harper & Row, 1963), 4: "The proper understanding of form-criticism rests upon the judgment that the literature in which the life of a given community, even the primitive Christian community, has taken shape, springs out of quite definite conditions and wants of life," quoted by Kysar, "Whence and Whither," 66.

29. Martyn, *History and Theology*, 35–38. The original readers would, of course, have recognized their situation in the expansion without such a form-critical analysis.

30. See Reinhartz "Reappraisal," 117: It is "reasonable to expect" that an application of the two-level reading strategy to the whole Gospel "will paint a picture that supports, or is at least consistent with, the expulsion theory"; see also Reinhartz, *Befriending*, 41–42. See above on her analysis of 11:1–44 and 12:11. According to

tains different literary layers; he used the striking image of an archaeological tell or mound to characterize the Gospel. Each stratum of this tell
reflects different "communal interests, concerns and experiences."[31] The
first layer for Martyn was a Signs Gospel as reconstructed by his student
Robert Fortna.[32] Martyn drew from the Gospel's evident literary history
certain conclusions about its social and theological history.[33] Johannine
history thus consisted of different phases, and that means that the second
or contemporary level of the drama is not a static entity or a single experience but encompasses different and changing *Sitze im Leben* in the history
of Johannine Christianity, not just expulsion but also events leading up to
and following from that particular traumatic turn of events. A drama after
all implies a sequence of events, a series of acts.[34]

Fourth, as far as Brown is concerned, it may be noted that while he
embraced Martyn's two-level reading of the Gospel, he also writes in his
*Community of the Beloved Disciple*: "*Primarily*, the Gospels tell us how an
evangelist conceived of and presented Jesus to a Christian community in
the last third of the first century, a presentation that *indirectly* gives us an
insight into that community's life at the time when the Gospel was written."[35]
Neither Brown nor Martyn thus denies that the Fourth Gospel is primarily
a story about Jesus and would have been read as such by the first, intended

---

Martyn, John 12:11 evidently reflects a situation after the decree of expulsion has gone
into effect during which time Johannine preachers continued their missionary activity
among the Jewish population and did so with some success (*History and Theology*, 71,
93–94). Those convinced by this proclamation could then choose between (1) hiding
their faith so as to avoid expulsion (12:42) or (2) leaving the synagogue "voluntarily"
to join the Johannine community. In Martyn's view, they would have been drummed
out of the (local) synagogue if they confessed their faith openly.

31. Martyn, "Glimpses," 145.

32. Robert T. Fortna, *The Gospel of Signs: A Reconstruction of the Narrative
Source Underlying the Fourth Gospel*, SNTSMS 11 (Cambridge: Cambridge University Press, 1970).

33. Martyn, "Glimpses," 145: "We may hope to draw from the Gospel's literary
history certain conclusions about the community's social and theological history."

34. Obviously, that makes the reconstruction of this history a challenging
endeavor with many pitfalls and much uncertainty, as Bauckham rightly points out
(*Testimony*, 117), but the difficulty of the task does not vitiate the likelihood that there
was such a history, nor (contra Bauckham) does the difficulty make attempts to reconstruct that history illegitimate.

35. Brown, *Community of the Beloved Disciple*, 17, emphasis added in the
second instance.

readers. But we *scholars* seek also to read John for what it might disclose about the intended audience, its situation, identity, character, and history.[36] This can be done from a desire to understand early Christian history and the Fourth Gospel's place in it but also to increase our understanding of the Gospel's portrait of Jesus and its theology. Brown, like Martyn, sought in fact to do both.

## Bauckham's Counterproposal

In 1998, Bauckham proposed that "John, like the Synoptics, wrote his Gospel not for a specific community ... but to circulate around all the churches."[37] He subsequently suggested that the Gospel had "an even wider audience, encompassing interested nonbelievers as well as believers in general."[38] Not surprisingly, therefore, Bauckham dismisses reconstructions of the Johannine community as "largely fantasy."[39] For him, there is, after all, no Johannine community to reconstruct.

In Bauckham's view, moreover, "the Gospel is an integral whole, including both the prologue and the epilogue, and was designed as such by a single author," not by some hypothetical community or representatives thereof.[40] The aporias (narrative disjunctions or glaringly bad transitions between episodes) found throughout the Fourth Gospel (see, for example, 6:1; 14:31; and chapter 21) would speak against this view of authorship, but Bauckham remains undaunted: "The so-called aporias in the text are seen to fulfill an intelligible function in the structure and meaning of the text as we have it."[41] They are "the deliberate theological strategies of a single author."[42] According to Bauckham, the Gospel exhibits, from the prologue to the epilogue, "evidence of meticulous design" by a single "theologically creative and literarily skilled author."[43] Bauckham's rejection of a specific

---

36. The same can of course be said for the other gospels.

37. Bauckham, *Testimony*, 22, summarizing his thesis defended in "For Whom?"

38. Bauckham, *Testimony*, 22; cf. more recently, Porter, *John, His Gospel, and Jesus*, 37–62.

39. Bauckham, *Testimony*, 13, see also 28.

40. Bauckham, *Testimony*, 12.

41. Bauckham, *Testimony*, 30. The aporias provide the foundation for theories that John incorporates sources or other written traditions or that it is the product of a long and complex process of composition by one or more (Johannine) authors.

42. Bauckham, *Testimony*, 118.

43. Bauckham, *Testimony*, 12, see also 31, 115.

community as the audience seems to follow from this assumption about the author: "That someone should write one of the most sophisticated and carefully composed of early Christian literary works ... simply for members of the specific community in which he was then living, with its specific local issues determining the nature of his writing" is for Bauckham utterly "implausible."[44]

In an earlier volume on the book of Revelation, Bauckham also characterizes this work as "an astonishingly meticulous composition"[45]—so that one begins to wonder if that is not his default position for any biblical writing. Bauckham does not, I think, help his case by attributing to the meticulous author of the Fourth Gospel numerical composition techniques, discernible especially in chapter 21 with its tantalizing reference to 153 fish, but which, Bauckham claims, are also present in the remainder the Gospel.[46] In this way, one can explain even the most stubborn aporias as the product of one very creative and meticulous author. But that means that Bauckham's thesis of one meticulous author is in principle unfalsifiable; it admits no countervailing evidence.[47] One must, however, continue to point out that the last two verses of the Gospel, among other considerations, such as the aforementioned aporias, indicate that it is *unlikely* that the Gospel was written in one go or is the result of one person's meticulous design.[48]

---

44. Bauckham, *Testimony*, 115.

45. Richard Bauckham, *The Theology of the Book of Revelation* (Cambridge: Cambridge University Press, 1993), 18, see also 3, 27.

46. Bauckham, *Testimony*, 31, see also 115, 271–84.

47. According to Bauckham himself, the results of the diverse attempts to reconstruct the history of the Johannine community are "unfalsifiable" and thus to be rejected out of hand; the reason he adduces for this charge of unfalsifiability is "the complexity of possible combinations of different analyses of sources and redactions with different views of the community" (*Testimony*, 13). But the *complexity* of the matter does not mean that the results, i.e., the various proposals, are in principle unfalsifiable—whereas that *is* the case with respect to Bauckham's assumption of a meticulous author who has deliberately created aporias in the narrative presentation of Jesus. Every literary feature of the Gospel can be explained (away) with this simplistic assumption. It hides rather than explains the difficulties.

48. It was noted above that Bauckham regards reconstructions of the Johannine community "from the Gospel" as "largely fantasy" (*Testimony*, 13), but it is difficult to discern why Bauckham's theory of a single meticulous author who wrote each and every word from 1:1 to 21:25 using numerical literary techniques should not be susceptible to the same critical dismissal (see previous note). In this connection, it is

To support his claim about the wide audience of the Fourth Gospel, Bauckham focuses his criticism of a Johannine community on its supposed character as a sect within early Christianity.[49] One argument used here is that since the Gospel uses "universal language" (for example, 3:16); it "does not reflect an introverted and isolated group of Christians, uninterested in or even alienated from the rest of the Christian movement."[50] Bauckham here confuses the Gospel's theological universalism or cosmic perspective (compare with 4:42; 12:32; for example) with the scope of the intended or actual audience of the Gospel.[51] But such language may indicate only that the Johannine community, sectarian or not, made universal or cosmic claims about Christ.

One of the consequences of Bauckham's position is that it opens the door to regarding the expulsion passages and the conflict between the Johannine Jesus and the Jews as reflecting what actually happened in the ministry of Jesus (and so also as indications of eyewitness testimony[52]). The questioning of any firm or demonstrable connection between the expulsion texts and the Birkat Haminim, as argued by Martyn, has also facilitated this reading of the text, as in the work of Bauckham's student Edward Klink, and, more recently, Jonathan Bernier and Stanley Porter.[53] This interpretation of the Johannine evidence, which at first glance

---

interesting to observe that Bauckham concludes the final essay of *Testimony* with the following words: "It is essential to remember that few 'ordinary readers' of an early Christian work such as the Fourth Gospel would read it alone, with only the resources of their own knowledge to assist their comprehension, as modern readers do. Reading (which for most 'ordinary readers' was hearing) took place in community," assisted, he says, by "teachers who … may have given time and trouble to studying the text" (284). Why could that community not be a distinctively Johannine community, at least in the first instance? And why could those teachers not belong to a Johannine School whose members may not simply have studied the text but also made contributions to its final form of the Gospel and written the Johannine Epistles?

49. Bauckham, *Testimony*, 113–121; see also Klink, *Sheep of the Fold*, 64–87; Lamb, *Text*, 55.

50. Bauckham, *Testimony*, 123.

51. Also Porter, *John, His Gospel, and Jesus*, 37–62.

52. See Bauckham, *Jesus and the Eyewitnesses: The Gospels as Eyewitness Testimony*, 2nd ed. (Grand Rapids: Eerdmans, 2017), 358–471. With respect to John, there is considerable overlap with *Testimony*.

53. See Martyn, *History and Theology*, 56–66 (see further below); Klink, *Sheep of the Fold*, 140; see also Klink, "Expulsion"; Bernier, Aposynagōgos *and the Historical Jesus in John*; Porter, *John, His Gospel, and Jesus*.

seems plausible, is not convincing for at least two reasons. First, there are no convincing parallels to the expulsion texts in the other three gospels (or, for that matter, in other New Testament texts), as one might expect if such a drastic measure was taken in the time of Jesus himself. Second, the statement of "the Jews" to the blind man whom Jesus had healed that whereas "*you* are a disciple of [Jesus]," "*we* are disciples of Moses" (9:28) is, as Martyn astutely observed, "scarcely conceivable in Jesus' lifetime, since it recognizes discipleship to Jesus not only as antithetical, but also as somehow comparable to Moses. It is, on the other hand, easily understood under circumstances in which the synagogue has begun to view the Christian movement as an essential and more or less clearly distinguishable rival,"[54] that is, in the late first century CE. John Ashton, in a critical evaluation of Klink's work, uses Martyn's compelling analysis of John 9:28 to declare, equally compellingly: "There is not the slightest likelihood that the expulsion of Jesus' disciples from the synagogue began during his lifetime," whatever the link to the Birkat Haminim may or may not have been.[55] Nevertheless, it remains interesting that these scholars do not deny the historicity of the expulsion passages that formed the lynchpin of Martyn's reconstruction of the Johannine community and its history, something that cannot be said of Adele Reinhartz.

## Reinhartz's Counterproposal

Since 1998, Reinhartz has published several articles outlining and developing her position. I here rely primarily on her essay from 2008, which has the provocative title, "Building Skyscrapers on Toothpicks."[56]

---

54. Martyn, *History and Theology*, 47.

55. John Ashton, *The Gospel of John and Christian Origins* (Minneapolis: Fortress, 2014), 77. If one is convinced by Martyn's interpretation of the import of John 9:28, "one is not only justified, but also impelled to look for a historical setting and state of affairs corresponding to the nature and direction or thrust of the Gospel's tensions and conflicts" (Smith, "Contribution," 6).

56. Reinhartz, "Toothpicks." As the subtitle indicates, this article actually seeks to address the "Literary-Critical Challenge to Historical-Criticism." Reinhartz argues that literary criticism can "add depth to historical-critical work." See also Martinus C. de Boer, "Historical Criticism, Narrative Criticism, and the Gospel of John," *JSNT* 47 (1992): 35–48. The image of a skyscraper built on a toothpick is taken from Robert Kysar, "What's the Meaning of This? Reflections Upon a Life and Career," in Thatcher, *What We Have Heard from the Beginning*, 173.

In this article, Reinhartz does not reject the existence of a Johannine community, but she does emphasize that the search for a Johannine community behind *the Gospel* is a "speculative" enterprise.[57] In a 2003 article on women in the Johannine community, Reinhartz could write that the letters of John "seem to demand the existence of such a community."[58] But the case is evidently different with respect to the Gospel: "The Johannine community is entirely a scholarly construct…; we assume the existence of it from the very fact that we have a Johannine Gospel. We construct the community's contours by reading between the lines of that Gospel."[59] This assessment of the Gospel evidence allows her to attempt a plausible alternative to Martyn's proposal, though she concedes that her proposal does not in itself refute Martyn's reading.[60] At the end of the day, it is simply another *possible* reading of the textual evidence. Many things are, of course, *possible*, but when all is said and done the question is indeed whether her counterproposal is a plausible alternative to Martyn's (or Brown's). Does it present a convincing account of the available evidence (the Gospel and Epistles of John)?

Reinhartz's counterproposal takes into account what she calls the Gospel's "rhetorical dimension," what it is trying achieve with its audience.[61] The audience of the Gospel consisted not only of Jewish believers in Christ but also of Samaritan and gentile believers. She calls this audience a "community."[62] But she also insists, rejecting the approaches of Martyn and Brown, that its history cannot be reconstructed.[63] She takes the references to "your law" in John 8:17, 10:34 and to Jesus's own "sheep" in distinction from "other sheep" in 10:14–16 to "suggest that at least this community of Christ-confessors saw itself as both spiritually and organization-

---

57. Reinhartz, "Toothpicks," 70.

58. Adele Reinhartz, "Women in the Johannine Community: An Exercise in Historical Imagination," in vol. 2 of *A Feminist Companion to John*, ed. Amy-Jill Levine (London: Sheffield Academic, 2003), 17.

59. Reinhartz, "Toothpicks," 70.

60. Reinhartz, "Toothpicks," 76.

61. Reinhartz, "Toothpicks," 71.

62. Reinhartz, "Toothpicks," 72. See also Reinhartz, "Reappraisal," 134: "a post-Easter community."

63. See Reinhartz, "Forging a New Identity," 126, where she writes that the "history of this group cannot be discerned from the sources at our disposal," even though "it is reasonable to assume that at least part of their experience included the overcoming of the ethnic and other boundaries that existed in their groups of origin."

ally separate from the Jews in their geographical vicinity."[64] Her primary hypothesis is then that "the expulsion passages and other sections of the Fourth Gospel that represent Jews in a negative way constitute a *warning* against synagogue participation and that these features of the Gospel are intended to *deter* Christ-confessors—the Gospel's primary audience—for whom Judaism remains attractive."[65] The problem the Gospel thus seeks to address is possible "backsliding" into Judaism: "That 'backsliding' was a problem for early communities of Christ-confessors is," Reinhartz argues, "suggested by other New Testament texts," namely, Heb 10:29 and Paul's Letter to the Galatians, even if what is going on in Galatians is not technically "backsliding" since the Galatian believers were gentiles. Nevertheless, for Reinhartz, "These [two] examples suggest that the Fourth Gospel, even as it describes and prescribes faith in Jesus as the Christ and Son of God, may also attempt to deter those who already believe from giving up or diluting their faith by adhering to Jewish identity and community."[66]

To support this hypothesis, Reinhartz notes, first, that the Gospel seeks "to establish the superiority of faith through Jesus," and, second, that "Jesus both embodies and exceeds all of the Jewish covenantal symbols" (see John 8:31–59; compare with 14:6; 15:6; 4:13–14; 6:27, 32–34, 48–51).[67] The Jews of the Gospel, in turn, "epitomize the opposite of what readers should be striving for," for they "hate Jesus and those who follow him" (compare with 8:44; 15:20–21).[68] So the *rhetorical* point is this:

> If Judaism apart from faith in Jesus does not provide a path to the knowledge of God and salvation, and if Jews are ready to persecute and kill Jesus and his followers, why would anyone wish to be a part of the Jewish community, participate in synagogue activities, and otherwise retain a Jewish identity? Why would anyone forego the hope of eternal life and

---

64. Reinhartz, "Toothpicks," 72. "Nevertheless," she continues, "the Gospel strongly implies that movement between these two groups is possible" (72), not just from the synagogue to the Johannine church, but also in the other direction, and different believers, whether of Jews and Gentile origin, could do so "with or without relinquishing their faith in Jesus as the Messiah and Son of God" (73). The latter claim depends upon her assessment of the expulsion texts as nonhistorical (see below).

65. Reinhartz, "Toothpicks," 72, emphasis added.

66. Reinhartz, "Toothpicks," 73. In a footnote in *Befriending* (174 n. 48), Reinhartz mentions a third possible parallel: Ignatius, *Phld.* 6.

67. Reinhartz, "Toothpicks," 73–74.

68. Reinhartz, "Toothpicks," 75.

risk death in the here and now? Surely the only reasonable course is zealously to guard the believers' separation from Judaism, while at the same time systematically to reinterpret the foundational texts and symbols of Judaism in light of a new understanding of revelation and covenant.[69]

Reinhartz recognizes that the three expulsion passages in John 9:22, 12:42, and 16:2 threaten the plausibility of this scenario. She solves the problem by claiming not only that "these verses do not describe events that actually took place, or could have taken place in the life of the historical Jesus," in agreement with Martyn, but also that they, here in disagreement with Martyn, do not "refer to the actual historical experience of the Johannine community."[70] Here she follows Reuven Kimelman who designates the expulsion texts a "concoction," and Steven T. Katz who (summarizing Kimelman) labels them "fabrications."[71] For Reinhartz, again in line with Kimelman and Katz, the expulsion texts thus can only "function as *a graphic warning* to that community: just as those who confessed Christ during his lifetime were expelled from the synagogue, so will you be persecuted and excluded, both from the Jewish community and from salvation, should you seek to affiliate with the Jewish community."[72] In earlier publications, Reinhartz considers another possibility: "The background of the Gospel entails a situation in which Jews and Johannine Christians no

---

69. Reinhartz, "Toothpicks," 75. John 20:30–31, she suggests, was written in order to strengthen the faith of believers of the community in the face of the possibility of backsliding to the synagogue (75–76).

70. Reinhartz, "Toothpicks," 76.

71. Reuven Kimelman, "Birkat ha-Minim and the Lack of Evidence for an Anti-Christian Jewish Prayer in Late Antiquity," in *Aspects of Judaism in the Greco-Roman Period*, vol. 2 of *Jewish and Christian Self-Definition*, ed. E. P. Sanders, Albert I. Baumgarten, and Alan Mendelson (Philadelphia: Fortress, 1981), 234; Steven T. Katz, "Issues in the Separation of Judaism and Christianity after 70 C.E.: A Reconsideration," *JBL* 103 (1984): 66 n. 88. Reinhartz also gives another, unscientific reason for rejecting the historicity of these texts: "I am unable to imagine a first-century Jewish community, or 'synagogue,' that would expel Johannine believers from its midst.... I like to think of ancient Jews as tolerant of difference and of ancient Judaism as a more elastic category than expulsion would imply" ("Toothpicks," 71).

72. Reinhartz, "Toothpicks," 76, emphasis added. See also her discussion of Kimelman and Katz in "Reappraisal," 115–16; *Befriending*, 39. For an earlier articulation of this view, see Margaret Davies, *Rhetoric and Reference in the Fourth Gospel*, JSNTSup 69 (Sheffield: JSOT Press, 1992), 293–301.

longer saw themselves as belonging to the same community. The expulsion passages may therefore provide an etiology for this situation."[73]

In a 2013 article Reinhartz draws out the implications of this rhetorical analysis further: "In this reading the expulsion passages are not a key to the history of the Johannine community but a tribute to the rhetorical skills of the Gospel writer and the effect he was trying to produce."[74] This means that "from a rhetorical perspective, one can suggest that the Gospel's negative portraits of Jews and Judaism are not so much reflections of or responses to Jewish persecution as *tactical statements* designed to create a positive identity as Johannine believers by fostering alienation from Judaism."[75] The Gospel seeks, in other words, "to accomplish something," in fact "to create a community" of its diverse readership.[76] The Johannine community *envisaged by the evangelist* does not lie behind the text but in front of the text, as it were.[77] A preexisting Johannine community with a distinctive, traceable history thus disappears entirely, much as it does for Bauckham. Judith Lieu in a recent article has mounted a similar argument with respect to the Johannine Epistles.[78] She sketches "a picture" of the Johannine church

> that in multiple ways is diametrically opposed to that which is conventionally drawn by the approach based on "the history of the community of the Beloved Disciple," with its complex history, its sense of "tradition" and of inherited authorities or revered personalities, and, most of all, its firm anchoring in time and place. To recognize this does not mean the latter approach is wrong. It does act as an important reminder that that

---

73. Adele Reinhartz, "John and Judaism: A Response to Burton Visotzky," in *Life in Abundance: Studies of John's Gospel in Tribute to Raymond E. Brown, S.S.*, ed. John Donahue (Collegeville, MN: Liturgical Press, 2005), 113; see also "Reappraisal, 133; *Befriending*, 50.

74. Reinhartz, "Forging a New Identity," 130.

75. Reinhartz, "Forging a New Identity," 133–34, emphasis added.

76. Reinhartz, "Forging a New Identity," 134. See also Raimo Hakola, *Reconsidering Johannine Christianity: A Social Identity Approach* (New York: Routledge, 2015).

77. See Reinhartz, "Forging a New Identity, 133: "The Gospel's so-called antilanguage serves to create community solidarity." The Gospel writer has produced "a rhetorical masterpiece designed to persuade his audience to overcome their differences and live as one community" (128).

78. Judith Lieu, "The Audience of the Johannine Epistles," in *Communities in Dispute: Current Scholarship on the Johannine Epistles*, ed. R. Alan Culpepper and Paul N. Anderson, ECL 13 (Atlanta: SBL Press, 2014), 123–40.

Lieu in effect does for the Johannine Epistles what Reinhartz does for the Gospel of John. The last citadel of the Johannine community hypothesis has thereby seemingly been taken and destroyed!

Reinhartz, however, just like Lieu, leaves the door ajar for the Martyn-Brown approach of seeking to reconstruct a Johannine community with the aim of being able to say something about its origin, history, character, and setting. But Reinhartz, again like Lieu, emphasizes that any such reconstruction is the product of scholarly imagination, and thus a "construct."[80] Agreed—but the aim of such an imaginative scholarly construct or construction is normally to approximate "what actually happened" by a convincing construal of the pertinent available data.[81] R. G. Collingwood's classic book *The Idea of History* contains an illuminating chapter on the essential role of imagination in historical reconstruction. He argues that an imaginative reconstruction of the past is normally generated by a critical evaluation of the available evidence, which means that any such imaginative reconstruction can and, in fact, must be tested for plausibility against the evidence to which appeal has been made.[82] How

---

79. Lieu, "Audience," 140; see also Hakola, *Reconsidering*, 89.

80. Reinhartz, "Toothpicks," 71.

81. I use *construct* and *construction* as synonyms. Historical construction thus seeks to be historical *re*construction. What we call history is both what actually happened and *our* account of what actually happened on the basis of the evidence available. The proposed account (construction), to be convincing and morally responsible, must stand in service of approximating "what really happened" (reconstruction). Only so can historical work be distinguished from fiction.

82. R. G. Collingwood, *The Idea of History* (Oxford: Oxford University Press, 1956): "The historical imagination" has "as its special task to imagine the past.… The historian's picture of his subject, whether that subject be a sequence of events or a past state of things … appears as a web of imaginative construction stretched between certain points provided by" pieces of available evidence (242). Collingwood emphasizes that "the supposedly fixed points between which the historical imagination spins its web are not given to us ready made, they must be achieved by critical thinking" (243). That means that only critical evaluation can determine whether a piece of evidence

*plausible* then is Reinhartz's imaginative reconstruction of the Johannine situation? Does the evidence, the Gospel of John, support her proposed reconstruction?

In John 15:18–16:4a, part of the Jesus's Last Discourse to his disciples, Jesus makes predictions of persecution to come, after he is gone: "If the world hates you, know that it has hated me before it hated you.... If they persecuted me [see 5:16], they will persecute you" (15:18, 20).[83] Jesus then becomes very specific about the form this persecution will take: "They will put you out of the synagogue [ἀποσυναγώγους ποιήσουσιν ὑμᾶς]; indeed, an hour is coming when everyone who kills you will think that by doing so they are offering worship to God" (16:2). *It is extremely unlikely and implausible that such predictions would have been preserved or attributed to Jesus if they had not been fulfilled in the experience of the Johannine community after Easter.* It is even more unlikely if one takes John 16:4a into account: "I have said these things to you," Jesus continues, "so that when their hour comes you may remember that I told you of them."[84]

In her 1998 piece, and building on an article written in 1989, Reinhartz argues that "Jesus' words are treated as prophetic utterances," pointing to 18:32 and footnoting 19:34 (compare with 19:24); 6:70; 13:21 (compare with 18:3–5); and 13:38 (Peter's denial; compare with 18:17, 25, 27).[85] "Like the words of the biblical prophets," she writes, "Jesus' words are the words of God and express the divine will (14:24; cf. 8:45–47; 14:10)."[86] It is striking that Reinhartz omits any reference to 15:18–16:4a in her discussion, when that passage would be rather pertinent to the point being made. The fact is that this passage does not fit her claim that "the *aposynagōgos*

---

first, this is a mere theory, awaiting verification, which must come to it from without" (243). Like the detective, the historian "has a double task," to provide a coherent picture which is "localized in space and time" *and* "to construct a picture of things as they really were and of events as they really happened." For this reason, "the historian's picture [like the detective's] stands in a peculiar relation to something called evidence.... What we mean by asking whether an historical statement is true is whether it can be justified by an appeal to evidence" (246).

83. Unless otherwise noted, all biblical translations are mine.

84. The same can be said for 15:26: "When the Paraclete comes ... he will bear witness to me."

85. Reinhartz, "Jesus as Prophet: Predictive Prolepses in the Fourth Gospel," *JSNT* 36 (1989): 3–16.

86. Reinhartz, "Reappraisal," 132; see also *Befriending*, 49–50, for a reprise of this argument.

passages ... would have been read primarily in their context in the story of Jesus and would have been seen as having extratextual referents in the life of the historical Jesus."[87] That assertion could count for 9:22 and 12:42 but not for 16:2, which is part of the Last Discourse (and of the unit 15:18–16:4a) in which Jesus talks about the time *after Easter*. Given her own analysis of Jesus's prophetic utterances, how likely is it that Johannine authors or their audience would attribute to Jesus predictions of such *specific* forms of persecution had they not been fulfilled in actual Johannine experience? The question answers itself. The specificity of the charges could, if false, be easily disconfirmed by people right there on the ground.[88] Moreover, how plausible is it that the author, himself a Jew by birth, was maliciously mispresenting the local Jewish community and spreading despicable lies about "the Jews"?[89] It's *possible* (what isn't?), but it does not seem historically *plausible*.

## The Issue of External Verification

What then about external verification or attestation? Reinhartz's appeal to Heb 10:29 and Galatians to support her imaginative construction of the Johannine situation is reminiscent of a toothpick. These passages cannot bear the edifice she builds on them, especially since the *internal* evidence does not obviously support this construction either. The internal evidence pleads for Martyn's construction. What then about external attestation for Martyn's construction? This is an important question because it is the supposed absence of external attestation for the expulsion texts that has generated doubts about the value of the internal evidence and repeatedly validated objections to Martyn's reconstruction of Johannine Christianity.[90]

Before we seek an answer to this question, it is important to note that John 16:2 led Martyn to propose that the Johannine community at one phase of its history (what he called "the middle period") experienced *two*

---

87. Reinhartz, "Reappraisal," 133; see also *Befriending*, 50.

88. Even more so if Reinhartz's own (but dubious) argument is correct that everyone was welcome in the synagogue and that there was traffic back and forth between the Johannine community and the (local) synagogue. See further below.

89. See Martyn, "Johannine Community," 187: we would then have to attribute "a private fit of paranoia" to the Gospel writer.

90. Reinhartz, "Reappraisal," 134.

significant and distinct traumas: (1) formal expulsion[91] from the synagogue and (2) execution or martyrdom. Many Johannine scholars simply merge these two traumas (as outlined by Martyn) into one called "conflict with the synagogue" or something similar, or they see, as Reinhartz does, the second trauma as simply an aspect or an extension of the first. The basic problem, so the argument goes, is the reliability of the claims about a formal expulsion from the synagogue in 9:22, and for that reason Martyn's whole proposal stands or falls with respect to this particular issue. The collapsing of the two traumas into one has led numerous scholars, including those who are otherwise convinced by Martyn's two-level reading of the Gospel, such as Brown, Ashton, and Smith,[92] to claim that the development of a high Christology among Johannine believers in Christ provided the catalyst for the decision to formulate a decree of expulsion from the synagogue. For Martyn, however, the Gospel's high Christology was developed in the debate with the authorities of the local synagogue *after* the edict to expel believers confessing Jesus to be the expected, very human Messiah was put into effect.[93] The high Christology was thus not the cause but an effect of the expulsion. For Martyn, the high Christology caused the *second* trauma, that of execution for blasphemously confessing Jesus to be equal to God. It is precisely this second trauma, and not the first, that is reflected in the plot to arrest and kill Jesus on charges of being a blasphemer and a deceiver of the people in chapters 5, 7–8, and 10.

The issue of external attestation thus pertains to two matters, *two* distinct traumas. For the first trauma, expulsion (John 9:22; 12:42; 16:2a), Martyn famously posited a link to the Birkat Haminim, which is actually a liturgical malediction or curse of (Jewish) heretics.[94] This malediction was part of the prayer of Eighteen Benedictions or Amidah recited three times daily by pious Jews. According to rabbinic traditions (b. Ber. 28b), the Birkat Haminim was reformulated around 85 CE by the rabbinic academy

---

91. Martyn uses the word *excommunication* (as does Brown), which has ecclesiastical and institutional overtones and should perhaps be avoided.

92. Brown, *Community of the Beloved Disciple*, 34, 43, 166; John Ashton, *Understanding the Fourth Gospel*, 2nd ed. (Oxford: Oxford University Press, 2007), 23; Smith, "Contribution," 21.

93. He attributes the decision of formal expulsion of fellow Jews embracing Jesus as the expected Messiah to the dire situation of Jews after the disaster of 70 CE and the need for consolidation. See Martyn, *History and Theology*, 58; so also Brown, *Gospel According to John*, lxxiv.

94. Martyn, *History and Theology*, 56–66.

in Jamnia to curse *Jewish* heretics (*minim*), including "Nazoreans," that is, Jews embracing Jesus of Nazareth as the Messiah. The dating, original wording, precise function, and attestation of this benediction in the primary sources are all either uncertain or disputed, and for this reason Martyn's attempt to use the Birkat Haminim to corroborate the Johannine expulsion texts has come under considerable fire, especially by scholars expert in rabbinic Judaism, such as Kimelman.[95] The denial of a link to the Birkat Haminim has in turn facilitated the counterclaim that the expulsion decree was a figment of the Johannine community's (perversely paranoid?) imagination, often with the corollary that Jewish believers in Christ must have left the synagogue completely of their own volition, as a way of forging a new identity, as we see in the work of Reinhartz.[96] Other scholars, including Joel Marcus, have argued that the Birkat Haminim remains relevant for understanding the Johannine situation and rhetoric, if not directly then indirectly.[97] Still others, including Martyn himself, argue that the link is not decisive either way since the Johannine evidence (the threefold use of *aposynagōgos*) speaks for itself and is congruent with the post-70 setting of the Jewish community.[98] The objection

---

95. Kimelman, "Birkat ha-Minim"; see also Katz, "Issues"; Daniel Boyarin, *Border Lines: The Partition of Judeo-Christianity* (Philadelphia: University of Pennsylvania Press, 2004); Ruth Langer, *Cursing the Christians? A History of the Birkat HaMinim* (Oxford: Oxford University Press, 2012).

96. See Raimo Hakola, *Identity Matters: John, the Jews, and Jewishness*, NovTSup 118 (Leiden: Brill, 2005); Hakola, *Reconsidering*; Kysar, "Expulsion"; Carter, *Empire*. The rejection of any link to the Birkat Haminim has in turn allowed Bernier (*Aposynagōgos and the Historical Jesus*) to argue that the separation from the synagogue must have already occurred in the time of Jesus, as depicted in the Gospel.

97. Joel Marcus, "The Birkat ha-Minim Revisited," *NTS* 55 (2009): 523–51. See also Barnabas Lindars, "The Persecution of Christians in John 15:18–16:4a," in *Suffering and Martyrdom in the New Testament: Studies Presented to G. M. Styler*, ed. William Horbury and Brian McNeil (Cambridge: Cambridge University Press, 1981), 46–69; William Horbury, "The Benediction of the Minim and Early Christian Controversy," *JTS* 33 (1982): 19–61; W. D. Davies, "Reflections on Aspects of the Jewish Background of the Gospel of John," in *Exploring the Gospel of John: In Honor of D. Moody Smith*, ed. R. Alan Culpepper and C. Clifton Black (Louisville: Westminster John Knox, 1996), 43–64; Marius Heemstra, *The Fiscus Judaicus and the Parting of the Ways*, WUNT 2/277 (Tübingen: Mohr Siebeck, 2010).

98. Martyn, "Johannine Christianity," 187; Meeks, "Man from Heaven"; James D. G. Dunn, "Let John Be John: A Gospel for Its Time," in *Das Evangelium und die Evangelien: Vorträge vom Tübinger Symposium 1982*, ed. Peter Stuhlmacher, WUNT

that Christians were welcome in the synagogues until the fourth century (as argued by Kimelman and Pieter van der Horst[99] and appealed to by Reinhartz) is not relevant since it pertains to gentiles, whether Christian or not, sympathetic to Judaism. Such "God-fearers" (see also Acts 10:2, 22; 13:16, 26) were always welcome in the synagogues[100] and were not subject to synagogue discipline. The embrace of Jesus as the Messiah by fellow Jews would have been a different matter—and evidently *was*.[101] As Philip Alexander, another scholar of rabbinic Judaism, writes, "Rabbinic policy towards Christianity was aimed specifically at Jewish Christians. It attempted successfully to keep them marginalized and to exclude them from *Kelal Yisra'el*."[102] The Birkat Haminim played a significant role in this process, according to Alexander.[103] Kimelman's conclusion that there was no "anti-Christian Jewish prayer in antiquity," taken up in the title of his article, is often cited against Martyn, also by Reinhartz. But to support his conclusion Kimelman argues that the Birkat Haminim, which he dates to the late first century as does Martyn, "was aimed [solely] at

---

28 (Tübingen: Mohr Siebeck, 1983), 309–39; Raymond E. Brown, *An Introduction to the Gospel of John*, ed. Francis J. Moloney, ABRL (New York: Doubleday, 2003). Brown writes: "Without appealing to that blessing [the Birkat Haminim], however, one may still argue that the situation in John where many of the opponents of Jesus' ministry in the Synoptic Gospels have disappeared and only the Temple authorities and the Pharisees are specifically mentioned fits well into the 80s with the emergence of Rabbinic Judaism at Jamnia after the fall of Jerusalem" (*Introduction*, 213). Brown then appeals to Justin Martyr's, *Dialogue with Trypho the Jew*, from the middle of the second century, which in his view "represents an accumulation of the Jewish-Christian polemic that had developed throughout the second century. It often seems to stand in direct continuity with the polemic against the synagogue in John, and this offers another reason for not dating the final form of John too early in the first century" (214).

99. Kimelman, "Birkat ha-Minim," 239–40, 244; Pieter van der Horst, "The Birkat ha-Minim in Recent Research," *ExpT* 105 (1994): 363–68.

100. See Heemstra, *Fiscus Judaicus*, 186.

101. See 2 Cor 11:24; Matt 10:17; 23:24; Mark 13:9; Luke 6:22; 12:11, 21:12–13, 16b; 1 Thess 2:14.

102. Philip Alexander, " 'The Parting of the Ways' from the Perspective of Rabbinic Judaism," in *Jews and Christians: The Parting of the Ways A.D. 70–135*, ed. James D. G. Dunn, WUNT 66 (Tübingen: Mohr Siebeck, 1992), 3. See also Lawrence Schiffmann, "At the Crossroads: Tannaitic Perspectives on the Jewish-Christian Schism," in Sanders, Baumgarten, and Mendelson, 115–56; Schiffmann, *Who Was a Jew? Rabbinic and Halakhic Perspectives on the Jewish-Christian Schism* (Hoboken: Ktav, 1985).

103. Alexander, "Parting," 9.

Jewish sectarians *among whom Jewish Christians figured prominently*."[104] This conclusion is not only compatible with Martyn's thesis about a link of the expulsion texts to the Birkat Haminim.[105] It virtually confirms it.[106] On the formal decision to expel Jews confessing Jesus as the Messiah from the fellowship of the synagogue in John 9:22, Marcus comes to the notable conclusion that, "It is easy to see the self-curse of *Birkat ha-Minim* as a weapon for enforcing such an edict."[107]

For the second trauma, execution at the hand of Jewish authorities or the threat of it (John 16:2b), Martyn appealed for primary support to Justin Martyr's *Dialogue with Trypho* (16, 69, 95, 108, 110), certain rabbinic texts (y. Sanh. 25c, d; b. Sanh. 43a, 67a, 107b), and the Pseudo-Clementine literature.[108] Brown points to the reported martyrdoms of Stephen (Acts 7:58–60), James the son of Zebedee (Acts 12:2–3), and James the brother

---

104. Kimelman, "Birkat ha-Minim," 232, emphasis added.

105. Brown, in his 1966 commentary on John, used a formulation very similar to Kimelman's to *support* the hypothesis that the Birkat Haminim lies behind the expulsion texts: "The twelfth benediction, ca. 85, was a curse on the *minim* or heretics, *primarily Jewish-Christian*" (*Gospel according to John*, lxxiv, emphasis added).

106. I pointed this out already in *Johannine Perspectives on the Death of Jesus* (Kampen: Kok Pharos, 1996), 69, as did Marcus in "Birkat ha-Minim Revisited," 535 n. 52. Kysar thus misrepresents Kimelman when he writes that "Kimelman demonstrated that there was no such 'benediction' or any other formal act that would have resulted in the expulsion of *Christian Jews* from their synagogues" ("Expulsion," 239, emphasis added). The contrary is the case. Kimelman wanted to show that the Benediction was not directed at Christians generally, as was thought by Justin and Jerome, but at Christian Jews; see Martinus C. de Boer, "The Nazoreans: Living at the Boundary of Judaism and Christianity," in *Tolerance and Intolerance in Early Judaism and Christianity*, ed. Graham N. Stanton and Guy G. Stroumsa (Cambridge: Cambridge University Press, 1998), 239–62, esp. 230. On the useful distinction, not always observed in scholarly discourse, between "Christian Jews" (a messianic group within the synagogue community and at home there) and "Jewish Christians" (a community socially and religiously distinct from the synagogue), see Martyn, *History and Theology*, 70. Kimelman and Brown refer to "Jewish Christians," but they mean "Christian Jews," in Martyn's definition. Martyn's thesis is that the Birkat Haminim functioned in the Johannine setting to make "an inner-synagogue *group of Christian Jews* ... against its will" into "a separated *community of Jewish Christians*" (*History and Theology*, 70). The latter is identical with what Martyn called the Johannine community ("Glimpses," 155).

107. Marcus, "Birkat ha-Mimin Revisited," 533.

108. Martyn, *History and Theology*, 60 n. 69; 78–83; Martyn, *Gospel of John in Christian History*, 55–89.

of the Lord (Josephus, *A.J.* 20.200), all at the hands of Jewish authorities, as well as to Justin Martyr's words: "Though you have slain Christ, you do not repent; but you hate and murder us also" (*Dial.* 133.6; 95.4).[109]

We may also add here the testimony of Paul. Prior to becoming an apostle of Christ, he was a zealous Pharisee who, according to his own account in Galatians, "was violently persecuting the church of God" and "was trying to destroy it" (Gal 1:13; see also 1 Cor 15:9, Phil 3:5–6). The verb he uses in Gal 1:13 ("destroy," πορθέω) has violent, even murderous overtones, being used by Josephus for the destruction of towns and villages (*B.J.* 4.405, 534) and for the devastation of Jerusalem (*A.J.* 10.25).[110] This picture is supported by Acts, which also portrays Paul as a violent zealot, approving the death of Stephen (8:1; see further 8:2–3) and "breathing threats and murder" against Christ-confessing Jews according to Acts 9:1 (see also 22:4, "I persecuted the Way up to the point of death"; and 26:10, "I cast my vote against them when they were being condemned to death"). Paul's efforts were directed not at gentile Christians (there were not any at this time) but at Jews who had accepted Jesus as the Messiah.

These texts cannot all be taken at face value of course, as Lieu has reminded us,[111] but given the number and diversity of sources and witnesses, they do cumulatively give a considerable degree of plausibility to the historicity of the second trauma mentioned in John 16:2b. There is also the fact that, in several passages of his *Dialogue with Trypho*, Justin mentions "cursing" (a possible, and for many, a probable allusion to the Birkat Haminim which was a curse[112]) and "killing" together, such as *Dial.* 95: "You curse Him and those who believe in Him, and whenever it is in your power put them to death" (see also *Dial.* 16, 47, 96, 110). That provides for Martyn a significant parallel to the juxtaposition and sequence of expulsion and execution in John 16:2.[113]

---

109. Brown, *Community of the Beloved Disciple*, 42–43. See Acts 9:23–25 according to which "the Jews" sought to kill (ἀνελεῖν) Paul in Damascus.

110. See Martinus C. de Boer, *Galatians: A Commentary*, NTL (Louisville: Westminster John Knox, 2011), 87.

111. Judith Lieu, "Accusations of Jewish Persecution in Early Christian Sources, with Particular Reference to Justin Martyr and the *Martyrdom of Polycarp*," in Stanton and Strousma, *Tolerance and Intolerance in Early Judaism and Christianity*, 279–95.

112. See Marcus, "Birkat ha-Minim Revisited," 532–33, convincingly refuting Kimelman's objections.

113. Martyn, *History and Theology*, 60 n. 69; 71 n. 89.

Because of the tendency to collapse the two traumas posited by Martyn into one, of seeing the second merely as an effect, if an extreme one, of the first, the questioning of the historicity of the first trauma has led naturally also to an implicit questioning of the historicity of the second. If the first is shown to be unhistorical, the second must also be, and no effort needs to be made to offer a counter interpretation of the relevant texts appealed to by Martyn, or Brown for that matter. Martyn's claim that there is historical evidence corroborating the second trauma has thus generally been ignored or downplayed. Even Brown does this in his own way. He interprets the reference to execution in John 16:2 to involve denunciation of expelled Jewish-Christians to the Romans who would carry out the actual executions.[114] If the second trauma as interpreted by Martyn is historically plausible, however, it increases the probability that the first is as well, even apart from any firm or demonstrable connection to the Birkat Haminim. After all, expulsion is a much less drastic measure than execution.

As I have indicated above, the claim that both expulsion and execution were fabrications of the Johannine community is unlikely given the specificity of the charges (which, if false, could easily have been disconfirmed by the first readers of the Gospel) and the fact that, as noted earlier, they are predictions attributed to Jesus in his last discourse to his disciples *about the time after Easter*. It is unlikely that such predictions would have been preserved or attributed to Jesus if they had not been fulfilled in the experience of the Johannine community. The external evidence, such as it is, supports this reading. It is certainly stronger and more extensive than the external evidence Reinhartz summons for her counterreading of the Johannine evidence. The toothpicks supporting Martyn's edifice seem to be sturdier than the toothpicks supporting Reinhartz's.

---

114. Brown appeals to the Mart. Pol. 13.1 ("the Jews were extremely zealous, as is their custom, in assisting at this") as support. Though this work dates from a considerably later period of time (the second half of the second century), the passage reflects what may also have happened in earlier times ("as is their custom"). With respect to the wording of John 16:2, Martyn writes: "The Greek word rendered 'act of (worshipful) service' [*latreia*] refers elsewhere in the New Testament to Jewish worship, and the other experience referred to in this text, excommunication from the synagogue, points to the action of Jewish authorities." He immediately adds: "Modern relations between Jews and Christians are not helped by an anti-historical interpretation of biblical texts" (Martyn, *Gospel of John in Christian History*, 56). See next note.

## Conclusion

The Johannine community as imaginatively reconstructed by Martyn and Brown has raised numerous issues that have been the subject of intense debate, such as the entry of Samaritans and gentiles into the community, contact (if any) with other streams of early Christianity, the community's supposed sectarian profile (briefly touched on in the introduction), the community's relationship to the Roman Empire, the community and its history as a hermeneutical key to interpreting the documents and under-standing the development of Johannine theology (particularly its Christology), and, not least, the community's role in the parting of the ways, particularly as exemplified by its problematic depiction of the Jews in the Gospel narrative.[115] Martyn and Brown themselves had different views on such matters, but they did agree that there was a Johannine community and that its history can be sketched, using the expulsion texts as starting point.[116] On this essential point, their respective proposals, for all their shortcomings, uncertainties, gaps, and questionable claims,[117] represent more plausible construals of the evidence than the counterproposals of Bauckham and Reinhartz (and their respective followers and sympathizers).

---

115. This matter plays an important role in Reinhartz's scholarship on John, as she herself acknowledges ("Toothpicks," 68, 70–71; see also, e.g., "Reappraisal," 115, 137; "Travel," 253–55; *Befriending*, 75–78). As a Jew, she understandably finds the Gospel's depiction of the Jews rather "grating" (*Befriending*, 75), and Christians should too. In my view, however, Reinhartz's counterproposal arguably exacerbates what she calls "the anti-Jewish potential of the Gospel" ("Reappraisal," 112), since it turns the Gospel into a book that makes perversely malicious, despicably slanderous, and patently false claims about the Jews, demonizing them in the process. That is a deeply disturbing and problematic result for a gospel that functions as primary scripture for Christians in matters of faith and practice. I have sought to address the issue in my article "The Depiction of 'the Jews' in the Fourth Gospel: Matters of Behavior and Identity," in *Anti-Judaism in the Fourth Gospel*, ed. Reimund Bieringer, Didier Pollefeyt, and Frederique Vandecasteele-Vanneuville (Louisville: Westminster John Knox, 2001), 141–57.

116. In "Johannine History," published in 2007, Martyn indicated that he remained "thoroughly convinced on two matters: First, working chronologically back-ward and forward from the *aposynagogos* references, it is possible to sketch the history of the Johannine Community 'from its origin through the period of its life in which the Fourth Gospel was composed.' Second, so sketched, that history 'forms to no small extent a chapter in the history of *Jewish Christianity*'" (187, quoting from "Glimpses," 167). It is important to note Martyn's use of the words "sketch" and "glimpses."

117. See de Boer, *Perspectives*, 43–71.

Bibliography

Alexander, Philip. "'The Parting of the Ways' from the Perspective of Rabbinic Judaism." Pages 1–25 in *Jews and Christians: The Parting of the Ways A.D. 70–135*. Edited by James D. G. Dunn. WUNT 66. Tübingen: Mohr Siebeck, 1992.

Ashton, John. *The Gospel of John and Christian Origins*. Minneapolis: Fortress, 2014.

———. *Understanding the Fourth Gospel*. 2nd ed. Oxford: Oxford University Press, 2007.

Bauckham, Richard. "For Whom Were the Gospels Written?" Pages 9–48 in *The Gospel for All Christians: Rethinking the Gospel Audiences*. Edited by Richard J. Bauckham. Grand Rapids: Eerdmans, 1998.

———. *Jesus and the Eyewitnesses: The Gospels as Eyewitness Testimony*. 2nd ed. Grand Rapids: Eerdmans, 2017.

———. *The Testimony of the Beloved Disciple: Narrative, History, and Theology in the Gospel of John*. Grand Rapids: Baker Academic, 2007.

———. *The Theology of the Book of Revelation*. Cambridge: Cambridge University Press, 1993.

Bernier, Jonathan. Aposynagōgos *and the Historical Jesus in John: Rethinking the Historicity of the Johannine Expulsion Passages*. BibInt 122. Leiden: Brill, 2013.

Boer, Martinus C. de. "The Depiction of 'the Jews' in the Fourth Gospel: Matters of Behavior and Identity." Pages 141–57 in *Anti-Judaism in the Fourth Gospel*. Edited by Reimund Bieringer, Didier Pollefeyt, and Frederique Vandecasteele-Vanneuville. Louisville: Westminster John Knox, 2001.

———. *Galatians: A Commentary*. NTL. Louisville: Westminster John Knox, 2011.

———. "Historical Criticism, Narrative Criticism, and the Gospel of John." *JSNT* 47 (1992): 35–48.

———. *Johannine Perspectives on the Death of Jesus*. Kampen: Kok Pharos, 1996.

———. "The Nazoreans: Living at the Boundary of Judaism and Christianity." Pages 239–62 in *Tolerance and Intolerance in Early Judaism and Christianity*. Edited by Graham N. Stanton and Guy G. Stroumsa. Cambridge: Cambridge University Press, 1998.

Boyarin, Daniel. *Border Lines: The Partition of Judeo-Christianity*. Philadelphia: University of Pennsylvania Press, 2004.

Brown, Raymond E. *The Community of the Beloved Disciple*. New York: Paulist, 1979.

———. *The Epistles of John*, AB 30. Garden City, NY: Doubleday, 1982.

———. *The Gospel according to John (I–XII)*. AB 29. Garden City, NY: Doubleday, 1966.

———. *An Introduction to the Gospel of John*. Edited by Francis J. Moloney. ABRL. New York: Doubleday, 2003.

Bultmann, Rudolf. *History of the Synoptic Tradition*. New York: Harper & Row, 1963.

Burridge, Richard A. *What Are the Gospels? A Comparison with Graeco-Roman Biography*. SNTSMS 70. Cambridge: Cambridge University Press, 1992.

Carter, Warren. *John and Empire: Initial Explorations*. Harrisburg, PA: Trinity Press International, 2008.

Collingwood, R. G. *The Idea of History*. Oxford: Oxford University Press, 1956.

Davies, Margaret. *Rhetoric and Reference in the Fourth Gospel*. JSNTSup 69. Sheffield: JSOT Press, 1992.

Davies, W. D. "Reflections on Aspects of the Jewish Background of the Gospel of John." Pages 43–64 in *Exploring the Gospel of John: In Honor of D. Moody Smith*. Edited by R. Alan Culpepper and C. Clifton Black. Louisville: Westminster John Knox, 1996.

Dunn, James D. G. "Let John Be John: A Gospel for Its Time." Pages 309–39 in *Das Evangelium und die Evangelien: Vorträge vom Tübinger Symposium 1982*. Edited by Peter Stuhlmacher. WUNT 28. Tübingen: Mohr Siebeck, 1983.

Fortna, Robert T. *The Gospel of Signs: A Reconstruction of the Narrative Source Underlying the Fourth Gospel*. SNTSMS 11. Cambridge: Cambridge University Press, 1970.

Hakola, Raimo. *Identity Matters: John, the Jews, and Jewishness*. NovTSup 118. Leiden: Brill, 2005.

———. *Reconsidering Johannine Christianity: A Social Identity Approach*. New York: Routledge, 2015.

Heemstra, Marius. *The Fiscus Judaicus and the Parting of the Ways*. WUNT 2/277. Tübingen: Mohr Siebeck, 2010.

Hengel, Martin. *The Johannine Question*. Translated by John Bowden. London: SCM, 1989.

Horbury, William. "The Benediction of the Minim and Early Christian Controversy." *JTS* 33 (1982): 19–61.

Horst, Pieter van der. "The Birkat ha-Minim in Recent Research." *ExpTim* 105 (1994): 363–68.

Katz, Steven T. "Issues in the Separation of Judaism and Christianity after 70 C.E.: A Reconsideration." *JBL* 103 (1984): 43–76.

Kierspel, Lars. *The Jews and the World in the Fourth Gospel*. WUNT 2/220. Tübingen: Mohr Siebeck, 2006.

Kimelman, Reuven. "Birkat ha-Minim and the Lack of Evidence for an Anti-Christian Jewish Prayer in Late Antiquity." Pages 226–44 in *Aspects of Judaism in the Greco-Roman Period*, vol. 2 of *Jewish and Christian Self-Definition*. Edited by E. P. Sanders, Albert I. Baumgarten, and Alan Mendelson. Philadelphia: Fortress, 1981.

Klink, Edward W., III. "Expulsion from the Synagogue? Rethinking a Johannine Anachronism." *TynBul* 59 (2008): 9–18.

———. *The Sheep of the Fold: The Audience and Origin of the Gospel of John*. SNTSMS 141. Cambridge: Cambridge University Press, 2007.

Kysar, Robert. *Voyages with John: Charting the Fourth Gospel*. Waco, TX: Baylor University, 2005.

———. "What's the Meaning of This? Reflections Upon a Life and Career." Pages 163–77 in *What We Have Heard from the Beginning: The Past, Present and Future of Johannine Studies*. Edited by Tom Thatcher. Waco, TX: Baylor University Press, 2007.

———. "The Whence and Whither of the Johannine Community." Pages 65–81 in *Life in Abundance: Studies of John's Gospel in Tribute to Raymond E. Brown, S.S.* Edited by John R. Donahue. Collegeville, MN: Liturgical Press, 2005.

Lamb, David A. *Text, Context and the Johannine Community: A Sociolinguistic Analysis of the Johannine Writings*. LNTS 477. London: T&T Clark, 2014.

Langer, Ruth. *Cursing the Christians? A History of the Birkat HaMinim*. Oxford: Oxford University Press, 2012.

Lieu, Judith. "Accusations of Jewish Persecution in Early Christian Sources, with Particular Reference to Justin Martyr and the *Martyrdom of Polycarp*." Pages 279–95 in *Tolerance and Intolerance in Early Judaism and Christianity*. Edited by Graham N. Stanton and Guy G. Stroumsa. Cambridge: Cambridge University Press, 1998.

———. "The Audience of the Johannine Epistles." Pages 123–40 in *Communities in Dispute: Current Scholarship on the Johannine Epistles*. Edited by R. Alan Culpepper and Paul N. Anderson. ECL 13. Atlanta: SBL Press, 2014.

Lindars, Barnabas. "The Persecution of Christians in John 15:18–16:4a." Pages 46–69 in *Suffering and Martyrdom in the New Testament: Studies Presented to G. M. Styler*. Edited by William Horbury and Brian McNeil. Cambridge: Cambridge University Press, 1981.

Marcus, Joel. "The Birkat ha-Minim Revisited." *NTS* 55 (2009): 523–51.

Martyn, J. Louis. "Glimpses into the History of the Johannine Community: From Its Origin through the Period of Its Life in Which the Fourth Gospel Was Composed." Pages 145–67 in *History and Theology in the Fourth Gospel*. 3rd ed. Repr. from pages 90–121 in *The Gospel of John in Christian History: Essays for Interpreters*. New York: Paulist, 1979. Adapted from pages 149–75 in *L'Évangile de Jean: Sources, redaction, théologie*. Edited by Marinus de Jonge. BETL 44. Leuven: Leuven University Press, 1977.

———. *History and Theology in the Fourth Gospel*. 3rd ed. Louisville: Westminster John Knox, 2003.

———. "The Johannine Community among Jewish and Other Early Christian Communities." Pages 183–90 in *What We Have Heard from the Beginning: The Past, Present and Future of Johannine Studies*. Edited by Tom Thatcher. Waco, TX: Baylor University, 2007.

Meeks, Wayne A. "The Man from Heaven in Johannine Sectarianism." *JBL* 91 (1972): 44–72.

Porter, Stanley E. *John, His Gospel, and Jesus*. Grand Rapids: Eerdmans, 2015.

Reinhartz, Adele. *Befriending the Beloved Disciple: A Jewish Reading of the Gospel of John*. New York: Continuum, 2001.

———. "Building Skyscrapers on Toothpicks: The Literary-Critical Challenge to Historical Criticism." Pages 55–76 in *Anatomies of Narrative Criticism: The Past, Present, and Future of the Fourth Gospel as Literature*. Edited by Tom Thatcher and Stephen D. Moore. RBS 55. Atlanta: Society of Biblical Literature, 2008.

———. "Forging a New Identity: Johannine Rhetoric and the Audience of the Fourth Gospel." Pages 123–34 in *Paul, John, and Apocalyptic Eschatology: Studies in Honour of Martinus C. de Boer*. Edited by Jan Krans et al. NovTSup 149. Leiden: Brill, 2013.

———. "Jesus as Prophet: Predictive Prolepses in the Fourth Gospel." *JSNT* 36 (1989): 3–16.

———. "The Johannine Community and Its Jewish Neighbors: A Reappraisal." Pages 111–38 in *Literary and Social Readings of the Fourth*

*Gospel*, vol. 2 of *What Is John?* Edited by Fernando F. Segovia. SymS 7. Atlanta: Scholars Press, 1998.

———. "John and Judaism: A Response to Burton Visotzky." Pages 108–16 in *Life in Abundance: Studies of* John's *Gospel in Tribute to Raymond E. Brown, S. S.* Edited by John Donahue. Collegeville, MN: Liturgical Press, 2005.

———. "Response: Reading History in the Fourth Gospel." Pages 191–94 in *What We Have Heard from the Beginning: The Past, Present and Future of Johannine Studies.* Edited by Tom Thatcher. Waco, TX: Baylor University, 2007.

———. "Travel, Translation, and Ethnography: Johannine Scholarship at the Turn of the Century." Pages 250–56 in *Literary and Social Readings of the Fourth Gospel*, vol. 2 of *What is John?* Edited by Fernando F. Segovia. SymS 7. Atlanta: Scholars Press, 1998.

———. "Women in the Johannine Community: An Exercise in Historical Imagination." Pages 14–33 in vol. 2 of *A Feminist Companion to John.* Edited by Amy-Jill Levine. 2 vols. London: Sheffield Academic, 2003.

Schiffmann, Lawrence. "At the Crossroads: Tannaitic Perspectives on the Jewish-Christian Schism." Pages 115–56 in *Aspects of Judaism in the Greco-Roman Period*, vol. 2 of *Jewish and Christian Self-Definition.* Edited by E. P. Sanders, Albert I. Baumgarten, and Alan Mendelson. Philadelphia: Fortress, 1981.

———. *Who Was a Jew? Rabbinic and Halakhic Perspectives on the Jewish-Christian Schism.* Hoboken: Ktav, 1985.

Smith, D. Moody. "The Contribution of J. Louis Martyn to the Understanding of the Gospel of John." Pages 1–23 in *History and Theology in the Fourth Gospel*, by J. Louis Martyn. 3rd ed. Louisville: Westminster John Knox, 2003.

———. *Johannine Christianity: Essays on Its Setting, Sources, and Theology.* Columbia: University of South Carolina Press, 1984.

# "Among You Stands One Whom You Do Not Know" (John 1:26): The Use of the Tradition of the Hidden Messiah in John's Gospel

Susan Miller

## Introduction

Mark's Gospel presents Jesus as a mysterious figure whose identity is concealed from those around him. Scholars associate Mark's Gospel with the theory of the Messianic Secret.[1] Jesus frequently commands the demons, those he has healed, and the disciples to secrecy. He speaks in cryptic language (4:10–12; 8:14–21), and no human being fully understands Jesus's identity until the Roman centurion recognizes him as the Son of God at the crucifixion (15:39). In John's Gospel, Jesus is recognized by his disciples as the Messiah and Son of God at the beginning of the gospel (1:41, 49), and he speaks openly about his identity in a series of "I am" sayings (6:35; 8:12; 10:7, 11; 11:25; 14:6; 15:1). Jesus is "the bread of life," "the resurrection and the life," and "the true vine," and he tells his opponents "The Father and I are one" (10:30). Initially, John's Christology seems very different from that of Mark. Several features of John's Gospel, however, suggest that John also presents Jesus as a hidden Messiah.[2] Some human beings struggle to

---

1. See William Wrede, *The Messianic Secret*, trans. J. C. G. Greig (Cambridge: Clarke, 1971); Christopher Tuckett, ed., *The Messianic Secret* (London: SPCK, 1983); Joel Marcus, *The Mystery of the Kingdom of God*, SBLDS 90 (Atlanta: Scholars Press, 1986); Heikki Räisänen, *The "Messianic Secret" in Mark*, trans. Christopher Tuckett (Edinburgh: T&T Clark, 1990).

2. For a study of the portrayal of Jesus as "the elusive Christ," see Mark W. G. Stibbe, "The Elusive Christ: A New Reading of the Fourth Gospel," in *The Gospel of John as Literature: An Anthology of Twentieth-Century Perspectives*, ed. Mark W. G. Stibbe, NTTSD 17 (Leiden: Brill, 1993), 231–47.

understand Jesus's metaphorical language. Nicodemus cannot understand why he must be born "again" or "from above" (ἄνωθεν) to see the kingdom of God (3:3, 7), and the Samaritan woman is skeptical about the ability of Jesus to give her "living water" (4:11). Jesus's enemies are unable to recognize his identity as the Messiah and Son of God, and their opposition leads to his arrest and death.

Two passages within John's Gospel, moreover, are particularly associated with an apocalyptic expectation that God will conceal the identity of the Messiah for a time on earth. This belief concerning a hidden Messiah is first seen in the account of the testimony of John the Baptist (1:19–34). At the beginning of the gospel, John the Baptist tells the delegation from the religious authorities in Jerusalem, "Among you stands one whom you do not know [μέσος ὑμῶν ἔστηκεν ὃν ὑμεῖς οὐκ οἴδατε]" (1:26). John testifies that he does not know who Jesus is, and he only recognizes Jesus when he sees the Spirit descend upon him (1:33–34). In chapter 7, Jesus's opponents argue that he cannot be the Messiah because they do not expect to know the origins of the Messiah whereas they do know the origins of Jesus (see, e.g., ὁ δὲ Χριστὸς ὅταν ἔρχηται οὐδεὶς γινώσκει πόθεν ἐστίν, 7:27). Raymond Brown proposes that John alludes to a "popular theory" about the hidden Messiah.[3] Brown observes that there was an "apocalyptic strain of messianic expectation" in which the Messiah's identity would be kept hidden on earth until the appointed time for him to be revealed to his people.[4] He points out that an "echo" of this belief may be seen in Justin Martyr's *Dialogue with Trypho*. Brown notes the similarities between the Johannine passages and Justin's writing, which states, "But Christ—if He has indeed been born, and exists anywhere—he is unknown and does not even know Himself, and he has no power until Elias comes to anoint Him, and make Him manifest to all" (*Dial.* 8.4; compare with 110.1 [*ANF* 1:199]). John Ashton observes that John 7:27 "clearly depends upon the same tradition" that appears in *Dialogue with Trypho*, but he points out that John's presen-

---

3. Raymond E. Brown, *The Gospel according to John: Introduction, Translation and Notes*, 2 vols., AB 29–29A (New York: Doubleday, 1966–70), 1:53.

4. For the study of the expectations of a hidden Messiah, see Sigmund Mowinckel, *He That Cometh: The Messiah Concept in the Old Testament and Later Judaism* (Oxford: Blackwell, 1956), 304–8; Ethelbert Stauffer, "Agnostos Christos: Joh. ii 24 und die Eschatologie des vierten Evangeliums," in *The Background of the New Testament and Its Eschatology: Essays in Honour of C. H. Dodd*, ed. W. D. Davies and D. Daube (Cambridge: Cambridge University Press, 1956), 281–99.

tation differs from Justin's account of the tradition, since Jesus knows his heavenly origins and that he has been sent by God.[5] As Ashton observes, the Johannine Jesus is depicted as one who "came into the world as an outsider" and who is within the world but not "of the world."

Traditions about a hidden Messiah appear in several Jewish apocalyptic texts such as 1 Enoch, 4 Ezra, and 2 Baruch. Marinus de Jonge proposes that traditions of a hidden Messiah are associated with two different types of expectations.[6] He argues that some expectations are related to the preexistence of the Messiah who is revealed at the designated time (see 1 En. 48.6–10; 62.7; 2 Bar 29.3; 39:7; 4 Ezra 7.28; 12.32; 13.26, 32, 52) and that others focus on the concealment of the Messiah who is living in the world. De Jonge argues that John's presentation of Jesus reflects the tradition of the preexistence of the Messiah. In John's Gospel, however, Jesus also conducts a mission for a time unrecognized by many. John's use of the hidden Messiah tradition reflects the influence of apocalyptic beliefs upon the Christology of his gospel. In apocalyptic texts such as 1 Enoch and 4 Ezra, the Messiah is the one who reveals God's purposes for the world. Just as heavenly secrets are revealed at the end-time, so the identity of the Messiah is also revealed at the end of the age.

The belief in a hidden Messiah, however, does not appear to be based on particular passages within Jewish scriptures. Barnabas Lindars proposes that the source of the belief is the vision of the Son of Man who appears after the destruction of the beasts in Dan 7.[7] As Lindars points out, the concept of the hidden Son of Man was "fused" with the figure of the Messiah. In the Similitudes of Enoch, the Son of Man is described as preexistent: "For this purpose he became the Chosen One, he was concealed in the presence of the Lord of the Spirits prior to the creation of the world, and for eternity" (48.6 [trans. Isaac; *OTP* 1:35]). In 4 Ezra, the appearance of the Messiah is associated with the revelation of the secrets of the end-time. The city of Jerusalem and the land that have been kept hidden will be disclosed, and "the Messiah shall be revealed with those who are with him" (7.26–28 [trans. Metzger; *OTP* 1:537]).

5. John Ashton, *Understanding the Fourth Gospel*, 2nd ed. (Oxford: Oxford University Press, 2007), 207–11.

6. Marinus de Jonge, "Jewish Expectations about the 'Messiah' according to the Fourth Gospel," *NTS* 19 (1973): 246–70.

7. Barnabas Lindars, *The Gospel of John*, NCB (London: Marshall, Morgan & Scott, 1972), 293.

Brown and Ashton have identified a tradition of a hidden Messiah that appears in John's Gospel and in *Dialogue with Trypho*. In this essay I will assess the ways in which John employs this tradition, and I will examine the question of whether this tradition reflects themes that are evident in other passages within John's Gospel. To what extent does John's use of this tradition of a hidden Messiah contribute to a deeper understanding of John's Christology? In the first two sections of the essay, I will assess John's development of the tradition of a hidden Messiah in the account of the testimony of John the Baptist (1:19–34) and the account of Jesus's visit to Jerusalem at the Feast of Tabernacles (7:25–44). I will identify the distinctive features of John's employment of the tradition and assess the ways in which it contributes to John's Christology. In the third section of the essay, I will examine the extent to which John portrays Jesus as a hidden Messiah in the remainder of the gospel. I will then explore the ways in which the revelation of Jesus's identity takes place at the crucifixion. Finally, I will analyze the relationship between John's portrayal of Jesus as the hidden Messiah and his presentation of the disciples. Throughout John's Gospel, the religious leaders oppose Jesus because they do not believe that Jesus is the Messiah. In the Farewell Discourse, Jesus prophesies that those who confess their faith in him as the Messiah will be put out of the synagogue (16:1–4; compare with 9:22, 12:42–43). In the conclusion, I will examine the ways in which John's portrayal of Jesus as the hidden Messiah may contribute to the study of the parting of the ways.

## The Testimony of John the Baptist (1:19–34)

John's first use of the tradition of the hidden Messiah occurs in the testimony of John the Baptist. John's act of baptism in the wilderness has attracted the attention of the religious authorities in Jerusalem (1:19–28). Priests and Levites have been sent from Jerusalem to question John the Baptist about his identity and the purpose of his act of baptism. The two questions are interrelated because the act of baptism implies that John regards himself as a figure of authority. John, however, states that he is not the Messiah, Elijah, or the prophet. He does not identify himself with any one of the three expected eschatological figures, but rather he describes himself in terms of the prophecy of Isaiah: he is "one crying in the wilderness, prepare the way of the Lord" (Isa 40:3; John 1:23).

John's act of baptism is an eschatological act intended to prepare the people for the new age. The authorities, therefore, wish to know why he is baptizing people if he is not the Messiah, Elijah, or the prophet. John, however, describes his baptism as a baptism of water. He points away from himself to the greater figure who comes after him. John refers to Jesus in terms of the concept of the hidden Messiah, "Among you stands one whom you do not know [μέσος ὑμῶν ἕστηκεν ὃν ὑμεῖς οὐκ οἴδατε]" (1:26). John's testimony points to God's hidden intervention in the world. Jesus is already present in the world, but he is unrecognized. In this passage, John does not name Jesus, and there is no indication that he knows who Jesus is. John gives no clues about the identity of Jesus to the messengers from Jerusalem other than his assurance that this greater figure is coming and that he himself is not worthy to untie the thongs of this man's sandals (1:27).

The location of the tradition of the hidden Messiah at the beginning of John's Gospel emphasizes that Jesus has been sent by God into the world. John's use of the tradition points to the question of the recognition of Jesus that sits at the heart of the gospel. John the Baptist's allusion to this tradition in his testimony to the religious leaders introduces the conflict between Jesus and the religious leaders that will develop throughout Jesus's mission. The authorities set out to question John the Baptist but find themselves confronted with the prospect of a greater figure than John who already stands in their midst. The portrayal of Jesus as the hidden Messiah highlights the powerlessness of the religious authorities. They are the leaders of the people and the experts on the law, but they are unable to recognize the Messiah whom God sent into the world.

John also portrays Jesus as the hidden Messiah in the following passage in which Jesus approaches John the Baptist. John the Baptist announces that Jesus is the "lamb of God who takes away the sin of the world" (1:29). John's testimony, however, is based on his recognition of Jesus at his baptism. John states that he did not know Jesus even though he was sent to baptize in water in order to reveal Jesus to Israel (1:31). He has been told by God that the one on whom the Spirit descends and remains is the Messiah. John's Gospel does not contain a description of the baptism of Jesus. John the Baptist gives his testimony about Jesus after the baptism of Jesus has taken place. His role as a witness is emphasized since he testifies to the event that he has witnessed. He states that "he saw" the Spirit descend and remain on Jesus (1:33). In John's Gospel, the baptism of Jesus is presented as an event of revelation. John witnesses the descent of the Spirit, and he is able to interpret the significance of this event because God has told him about it before it has taken place. The Spirit descends on Jesus and remains on him, suggesting that the Spirit is the power through which Jesus will conduct his mission. The Spirit is the eschatological gift of the new age (see, for example, Joel 2:28–29; Isa 44:3, Ezek 36:26–27), and Jesus is the one who will baptize in the Holy Spirit (John 1:33).

In these passages, John employs the tradition of the hidden Messiah as a means of pointing away from the role of John the Baptist as an eschatological figure to the role of John as a witness to Jesus. John's act of baptism becomes the means by which Jesus is recognized as Son of God. It is possible that these passages are intended to counter the claims of the disciples of John the Baptist that their leader is the Messiah (compare with Ps.-Clem. Rec. 1.54, 60).[8] In John's Gospel, John the Baptist denies that he is Elijah, but in the Synoptic tradition he is identified with Elijah (Mark 9:13; Matt 11:11–14; 17:9–13). The Synoptic portrayal of John recalls the prophecies that Elijah will return before the day of the Lord (Mal 4:5; Sir 48:10), and John is depicted as a forerunner to Jesus (see Mark 9:11–13; Matt 17:10–13). Marinus de Jonge argues that John does not wish to depict John the Baptist in the role of the forerunner to Jesus.[9] He proposes that John wishes to highlight the independence of Jesus. As de Jonge points out, Jesus does not depend on John or require any human support. It is possible that John does not wish to associate John the Baptist with an eschatological figure. In John's Gospel, the expectations associated with the Messiah, Elijah, and the prophet are all to be found in Jesus.[10] Nevertheless, John the Baptist remains an important figure since he is introduced in the prologue to the gospel. He has the role of bearing witness to the light, but he is not the light (1:6–8).

John's use of the tradition of the hidden Messiah highlights the paradoxical nature of his Christology. Jesus is Messiah and Son of God. He is preexistent, and he is the Lamb of God who takes away the sin of the world. At the same time, it is not possible to differentiate Jesus from any

---

8. For an analysis of the view that John seeks to counter the claims of followers of John the Baptist, see Walter Wink, *John the Baptist in the Gospel Tradition*, SNTSMS 7 (Cambridge: Cambridge University Press, 1968), 98–105.

9. Marinus de Jonge, "John the Baptist and Elijah in the Fourth Gospel," in *The Conversation Continues: Studies in Paul and John in Honor of J. Louis Martyn*, ed. Robert T. Fortna and Beverly R. Gaventa (Nashville: Abingdon: 1990), 299–308.

10. J. Louis Martyn notes that some of Jesus's signs recall the miracles, which were performed by Moses and to a lesser extent Elijah. J. Louis Martyn, *History and Theology in the Fourth Gospel*, 2nd ed. (Nashville: Abingdon, 1979), 96–99.

other human being. In apocalyptic texts, the purposes of God are concealed until the right time has arrived. In John's Gospel, the identity of the Messiah is concealed until it is time for him to take up his role. John depicts Jesus's baptism as the time when he begins his mission. The Spirit descends on Jesus and is present within him throughout his mission. John the Baptist receives revelation from God, and he recognizes Jesus. John is portrayed as the first witness to Jesus, and he testifies to others. Human beings are unable to recognize Jesus until God reveals Jesus to them. Those who receive revelation then become witnesses to Jesus.

John employs the tradition of the hidden Messiah to introduce the conflict between Jesus and the religious authorities that lies at the heart of the gospel. The religious leaders lack the ability to recognize their Messiah who stands in their midst. John's use of the tradition indicates that the failure of the religious authorities to recognize Jesus reflects the purposes of God. The Messiah will be concealed until the time is right for him to overcome his enemies. The inability of the leaders to recognize Jesus implies that the power of Jesus is greater than their power. John, however, does not suggest that Jesus will be rejected by all his people. John the Baptist has been sent by God to bear witness to Jesus. The purpose of John's act of baptism is "to reveal God to Israel" (1:31). The conflict over the recognition of Jesus's identity will continue in the remainder of the gospel. In the next section of this essay, I will assess John's use of the tradition of the hidden Messiah in the conflict between Jesus and the religious leaders at the Feast of Tabernacles.

## Jesus at the Feast of Tabernacles (7:25–44)

John's second use of the tradition of the hidden Messiah occurs in John 7, which gives an account of the visit of Jesus to Jerusalem for the celebration of the Feast of Tabernacles. Opposition to Jesus is increasing and the religious leaders wish to arrest him. Nevertheless, Jesus continues to teach openly in the temple, and his presence leads to debates amongst the people about his identity (7:25–44). These debates concern popular messianic expectations and the means by which the Messiah may be recognized. Some people from Jerusalem ask why the authorities have not arrested Jesus, and they wonder if the leaders know that Jesus is the Messiah. Others do not believe Jesus is the Messiah since they know where he comes from. This group alludes to the tradition of the hidden Messiah (ὁ δὲ Χριστὸς ὅταν ἔρχηται οὐδεὶς γινώσκει πόθεν ἐστίν, 7:27). Some members of the crowd claim that Jesus cannot be the Messiah because they know his place of origin.

In this passage John employs the tradition of the hidden Messiah to address concerns about the birthplace of Jesus. John does not refer directly to the birthplace of Jesus, but he does associate Jesus with Galilee. In John 1, Philip described Jesus as "Jesus the son of Joseph from Nazareth" (1:45). The people know where his place of origin is, but they do not know that he has come from the heavenly realm. John's portrayal of Jesus as the hidden Messiah highlights for the reader the inability of the crowd to grasp Jesus's divine identity. As C. K. Barrett argues, John has developed the concept of Jesus as the hidden Messiah to express his theological convictions.[11] Jesus's secret heavenly origin implies that it is not possible for any human being to make judgments about the origins of the Messiah. Jesus responds to the objection to his birthplace by referring to his divine origins. He states that they may know him, but they do not know God who sent him. Jesus knows God because he has come from him (7:28–29). As Ashton points out, Jesus's nature is defined by his divine origins.[12] Jesus's heavenly origins point to his divine identity. His high christological claims lead to a division in the crowd. Some wish to arrest Jesus, but they are unable to do so because his hour has not yet come (7:30).

In this account, Jesus's speech progresses from the question of his origins to the question of his destiny. He tells his opponents that he is going to the one who sent him (ὑπάγω πρὸς τὸν πέμψαντά με, 7:33). The verb ὑπάγω ("go away, depart") is frequently used in relation to Jesus's death (8:14, 21; 13:3, 33, 36; 14:4, 28; 16:5, 10, 17). In our passage, Jesus is speaking of his death and his return to God. Jesus alludes to the time when he will again be hidden from his disciples. His opponents, however, interpret his speech as a journey to the diaspora in order to teach the Greeks (7:35). John indicates that they do not understand Jesus's metaphorical speech. Jesus has come from the heavenly realm, and he is going to return to the heavenly realm. His origins are secret, and he will remain hidden when he returns to God.

John introduces further speculation about the birthplace of Jesus on the last day of the Feast of Tabernacles (7:37–44). Some people believe him to be the prophet, and others believe that he is the Messiah. Others argue

---

11. C. K. Barrett, *The Gospel according to St John: An Introduction with Commentary and Notes on the Greek Text*, 2nd ed. (London: SPCK, 1978), 322.
12. Ashton, *Understanding*, 209–10.

that the Messiah is not expected to come from Galilee (7:41). They argue that the scriptures state that the Messiah will be a descendant of David and that he will come from Bethlehem, the town where David lived (7:42). There are many passages in Jewish scriptures that describe a future ruler who is a descendant of David (see, for example, 2 Sam 7:12–16; Isa 9:1–7; 11:1–10; Mic 5:2–4; Jer 23:5–6), and there are references to a Davidic Messiah in other Jewish writings (Pss. Sol. 17.21–22; 4 Ezra 7.28–29; 12.32; 2 Bar 29.3). The association of the Davidic Messiah with Bethlehem occurs in Mic 5:2, and this passage is cited in the birth narrative of Matthew's Gospel (2:5–6).

Mathew and Luke describe the birth of Jesus in Bethlehem, but John does not include a birth narrative.[13] Brown proposes that John expects his audience to know that Jesus was born in Bethlehem, but it is equally plausible that John does not believe that Jesus was born in Bethlehem.[14] John employs the tradition of the hidden Messiah in order to address the objection of the crowd. In this passage, we see John challenge a tradition that has a scriptural basis (Mic 5:2) with the tradition of the hidden Messiah that does not have scriptural authority. John employs the tradition to point to the origin of Jesus with God. As Barnabas Lindars notes, the earthly birthplace of Jesus is insignificant in light of the recognition of his divine origin.[15] Jesus's heavenly origin surpasses the origin of the Davidic Messiah. John lacks evidence from the scriptures to support his claim that Jesus of Nazareth is the Messiah. He develops the tradition of the hidden Messiah to support his belief concerning Jesus's divine origins.

In John 7 we see the debates among the people concerning the identity of Jesus. Some people wonder if Jesus corresponds to the traditional expectation regarding the identity of the Messiah. There is a division between the religious authorities and the crowds in Jerusalem. The crowds know that Jesus comes from Galilee, but they do not expect to

---

13. The portrayal of Jesus as the good shepherd in John 10 alludes to the portrayal of David as a shepherd in Ezek 34:23–26. It is possible that John avoids the title "Son of David" because he does not want to link Jesus with the military associations of the Davidic Messiah, which are evident in texts such as Pss. Sol. 17.

14. Brown (*Gospel according to John*, 1:330) proposes that John knows that Jesus was born in Bethlehem and that the crowd is wrong in its belief that he comes from Galilee. Brown points out that the first objection of the crowd is incorrect because Jesus is the hidden Messiah. He argues that the parallelism of the two objections suggests that they are both incorrect.

15. Lindars, *Gospel of John*, 294.

know where the Messiah comes from. John highlights the divine origins of Jesus. Jesus's birthplace in Galilee does not imply that he is not the Messiah since he has come from God. In this passage, questions about Jesus's origins lead to a conflict over Jesus's claim that he is able to reveal God because he has come from God. John's use of the tradition of the hidden Messiah points to the unique identity of Jesus and his divine origins. In this passage, the question of the origins of Jesus corresponds to the question of his destiny. They will seek Jesus and not find him (7:34). John suggests that the hidden nature of Jesus will continue in the period after his death and resurrection. I will explore this question in the final section of this essay.

## The Portrayal of Jesus as the Hidden Messiah

John's use of the tradition of the hidden Messiah in chapter 1 and chapter 7 points to the inability of human beings to recognize Jesus. The human struggle to understand Jesus, however, may be seen throughout the gospel. John's portrayal of Jesus as the hidden Messiah is related to the paradoxes of the Prologue. Jesus is identified as the Word present with God before creation who comes into being, yet is unrecognized by human beings. Jesus comes to his own, but his own people do not accept him (1:12–13). Jesus is presented as the light coming into the world that enlightens every human being. John portrays a struggle between light and darkness, but the darkness has not overcome the light (1:5). On the one hand, John depicts a cosmic struggle between darkness and light that culminates at the crucifixion of Jesus when the ruler of the world is cast out (12:31; 14:30; 16:11). On the other hand, John presents the struggle of human beings to understand Jesus. His disciples come to confess their faith in him, but the inability of his opponents to understand Jesus leads them to reject him. In the Prologue, there is hope of a positive response of human beings since those who do accept him receive the power to become children of God (1:11–12).

John illustrates the struggle to understand Jesus in a series of conversations between Jesus and human beings who move through stages of misunderstanding to confess their faith in him. The Samaritan woman wonders if Jesus could be the Messiah, and she leads the people of her town to recognize Jesus as the Savior of the World (4:42). The blind man is healed by Jesus, and he stands up to the religious authorities before finally confessing his faith in the Son of Man (9:35–38). Martha confesses her faith in Jesus as the Messiah, the Son of God, the one coming into the world (11:27).

Throughout the gospel characters ask questions about the origins of Jesus. Mark Stibbe notes that John portrays Jesus as an "elusive Christ."[16] As Stibbe points out, John frequently employs the verb "to seek" (ζητεῖν) to describe the human quest for Jesus (see 1:38; 6:24, 26; 7:11; 8:21; 11:56; 13:33; 18:7; 20:15). The first disciples ask where Jesus is staying, and they wish to remain there with him. At the wedding of Cana, the steward recognizes the high quality of the wine, but he does not know the source of the wine (οὐκ ᾔδει πόθεν ἐστίν, 2:9). The Samaritan woman asks Jesus where he will find living water (πόθεν οὖν ἔχεις τὸ ὕδωρ τὸ ζῶν, 4:11). In these passages, the gifts that Jesus offers human beings are associated with his identity as the Messiah and Son of God. Jesus's opponents, however, do not accept his divine origins. In chapter 8, Jesus tells the Pharisees that they do not know where he has come from or where he is going (οὐκ οἴδατε πόθεν ἔρχομαι ἢ ποῦ ὑπάγω, 8:14). At his trial, Pilate asks him where he has come from (πόθεν εἶ σύ, 9:9). Jesus is portrayed as the heavenly Messiah who descends to earth and then ascends to heaven through his death and resurrection.

John associates the human search for Jesus with apocalyptic thought. The quest to recognize Jesus is linked to the cosmic conflict between God and the power of evil. At the end of Jesus's mission, John speaks of the failure of Jesus's signs to convince all people (12:37–43). John alludes to Isa 6:10 to explain why Jesus has not been accepted as the Messiah by saying, "He has blinded their eyes and hardened their hearts" (Τετύφλωκεν αὐτῶν τοὺς ὀφθαλμοὺς καὶ ἐπώρωσεν αὐτῶν τὴν καρδίαν, 12:40). Isaiah 6:10 is employed frequently in the New Testament by early Christians to indicate that the rejection of Jesus by some of his own people must be interpreted within the purposes of God (see Mark 4:10–12; Luke 8:10; Acts 28:26–27).[17] John's citation of Isaiah emphasizes the role of God as the one who conceals Jesus from humanity. In Isaiah, the prophet sees God in the temple (6:1–10), but John may be influenced by the Targum on Isaiah, which states that Isaiah sees the "glory of God."[18] In John's Gospel, Jesus is identified as "the glory of God." The Prologue concludes with a statement

---

16. Stibbe, "Elusive Christ," 232–36.

17. For a study of the use of Isa 6:9–10 in the "Parable Theory" (4:10–12) of Mark's Gospel, see Marcus, *Mystery*, 73–84.

18. Brown, *Gospel according to John*, 2:486–87.

that the glory has been seen in Jesus (1:14). The signs of Jesus also reveal his glory. At the wedding at Cana, the transformation of water into wine reveals Jesus's glory leading to the faith of the disciples (2:11). The raising of Lazarus is also presented as a sign that reveals the glory of God (11:4). In our passage, John associates the responsibility of God for the "blindness" of the religious leaders with their own human responsibility for their rejection of Jesus. Some of the authorities believed in Jesus, but they are afraid to confess their faith because they prefer human glory to the "glory" of God (12:42–43).

John's allusion to Isaiah places the acceptance and the rejection of Jesus within the wider purposes of God. John, moreover, indicates that God will reveal Jesus's identity at the appointed time. In John's Gospel, the revelation of Jesus's identity is associated with the "hour" of his passion (12:23; 17:1–5). The hostility of the religious leaders increases in a series of debates with Jesus, and their opposition culminates in the "hour" of his passion when he is arrested and put to death. The opponents of Jesus believe that their purposes are prevailing at the "hour" of his arrest, but throughout the gospel, the timing of the "hour" emphasizes that events are following the will of God. The religious leaders are unable to arrest Jesus because his "hour" has not yet come (7:30; 8:20). Stibbe, moreover, rightly points out that Jesus conceals himself from the crowd.[19] After the feeding of the five thousand, he withdraws from the crowd who wish to make him their king (6:14–15). Initially, he does not wish to go up to Jerusalem to celebrate the Feast of Tabernacles on account of opposition, but later he decides to go in secret (7:1–10). Jesus hides from those who set out to stone him (8:59), and he withdraws to Ephraim with his disciples on account of a plot to put him to death (11:54). As Stibbe observes, Jesus avoids confrontation with his opponents until the hour of his passion, and at his arrest he steps forward to identify himself (18:4–5). John's portrayal of Jesus as the hidden Messiah reflects the apocalyptic influences on John's Gospel in which Jesus's identity is hidden until the "hour" has come for his glory to be revealed (13:31–32; 17:1–5).

In John's Gospel, the religious leaders do not recognize Jesus, but Jesus is not rejected by all his people since his disciples do accept him. John contrasts the hostile response of Jesus's opponents with the disciples who confess their faith in Jesus as the Messiah and Son of God. Peter

---

19. Stibbe, "Elusive Christ," 233–35.

recognizes Jesus as "the Holy One of God" (6:69), and Martha confesses her faith in Jesus as "the Messiah, the Son of God, the one coming into the world" (11:27). At times, however, the disciples do not fully understand the significance of their confessions of faith. Peter denies Jesus three times (18:15–18, 25–27), and Martha is reluctant for Jesus to open the tomb of Lazarus because she is afraid that there will be a stench (11:39). In Mark's Gospel, the disciples fail to understand the necessity of Jesus's suffering and death (see Mark 8:31–33; 9:33–37; 10:35–45). Their failures are linked to their hope for a victorious Messiah. In John's Gospel, the disciples do recognize Jesus, but they do not fully understand the implications of his words and actions.

On several occasions, John draws attention to the future understanding of the disciples. William Wrede has highlighted examples of occasions when the disciples do not understand Jesus's words or actions but will understand at a later period.[20] He points out that the disciples do not understand the action of Jesus in the temple until after the resurrection of Jesus (2:13–22). In this account, Jesus tells the people, "Destroy this temple and I will raise it up in three days" (2:19). John states that the disciples gained a deeper understanding of Jesus's saying after the resurrection (ὅτε οὖν ἠγέρθη ἐκ νεκρῶν, 2:22). Wrede also notes that the disciples do not fully understand the significance of Jesus's entry into Jerusalem (12:12–16). As Wrede points out, the disciples are unable to fully understand Jesus until after his death and resurrection. In this way, the meaning of the events in the gospel must be interpreted in relation to God's purposes in sending Jesus into the world. The portrayal of the disciples indicates that God's purposes are concealed until the Messiah has completed his mission. In John's Gospel, Jesus is the hidden Messiah until the time of his death on the cross.

John depicts the struggle of the Jewish people to recognize Jesus. At the end of Jesus's mission, John alludes to the prophecy of Isaiah to explain the lack of belief among Jesus's people. John employs this prophecy to explain the course of salvation history and to indicate that God is responsible for the inability of human beings to recognize Jesus. In the passion narrative the religious authorities persecute Jesus because they do not accept his claims. John, however, alludes to the future understanding of humanity in the period after Jesus's death and resurrection. Jesus states that "he

---

20. Wrede, *Messianic Secret*, 184.

will draw all people" to himself after his death (12:32–33). John places the opposition of the religious leaders within the inability of all human beings to recognize Jesus without the revelation of God. The disciples recognize Jesus as Messiah and Son of God, but they do not fully understand the significance of his mission. The revelation of Jesus's identity will take place on the cross. John's portrayal of Jesus as the hidden Messiah points to the role of God as the one who brings revelation. Jesus reveals God to human beings but the full understanding of his mission takes place after his death and resurrection.

## The Revelation of the Hidden Messiah

The opposition of Jesus's enemies has centered on the question of whether Jesus is the Messiah or not. In the passion narrative, Jesus is arrested and brought before Pilate and the title *Messiah* is replaced by the question of whether Jesus claims to be the king of his people. In the earlier chapters of the gospel, John has presented the opposition of the Jewish leaders, but in the trial scene, he depicts the failure of the gentile leader to recognize Jesus (18:28–38). Pilate's accusation that Jesus is a king reflects the Roman understanding of the Messiah as the king of his people. Pilate mocks Jesus by pointing out that Jesus has been handed over to him by his own people and the chief priests. The rejection of Jesus by the religious leaders convinces Pilate that Jesus cannot be a king. Pilate judges Jesus in accordance with the worldly realm of appearances. Jesus, however, responds that the source of his kingdom is not from the world (18:36). Jesus alludes to his heavenly origins. He has been sent into the world to bear witness to the truth but Pilate is unable to understand the meaning of "truth" (18:38). In the apocalyptic context of the gospel, it is not possible for human beings to understand the truth unless they receive revelation from God.

John's account of Jesus's trial before Pilate indicates that the gentile leader is also unable to recognize Jesus's identity. Throughout Jesus's trial before Pilate, John employs dramatic irony to demonstrate the gospel's claim that Jesus is king. Pilate judges Jesus, but John's narrative indicates that Pilate is the one who is being judged.[21] Pilate offers to release "the king of the Jews" to the people, but they prefer to save the brigand, Barabbas

---

21. David Rensberger, *Overcoming the World: Politics and Community in the Gospel of John* (London: SPCK, 1988), 87–106.

(18:39–40). The soldiers mock Jesus by placing a crown of thorns on his head and by dressing him in purple (19:2–3). They greet him as a king without understanding that he is truly a king. In the course of the narrative, Pilate finds no evidence that Jesus has committed a crime, and he begins to waver. The turning point occurs when Pilate asks Jesus where he has come from (πόθεν εἶ σύ, 19:9). This question recalls the earlier controversies over the origins of Jesus. John's audience has been told that Jesus is the Messiah and Son of God who has been sent into the world. John draws correspondences between the failure of Pilate to recognize Jesus and the inability of the religious leaders to accept Jesus's divine origins.

John depicts a clash between the Roman power of Pilate and the kingship of Jesus. Pilate believes that he has the power to condemn Jesus to death, but Jesus relativizes this power by telling Pilate that he only has this authority because it has been granted to him "from above" (ἄνωθεν, 19:11). John places the failure of Pilate to recognize Jesus within the purposes of God. Pilate presents Jesus to the people as "the king of the Jews," but they cry out that they have no king but Caesar. Pilate's mockery of Jesus reveals his inability to recognize Jesus's identity. John employs irony to indicate that Jesus's crucifixion is an enthronement. Jesus is crucified between two men who take the places of royal retainers. The charge against him "Jesus of Nazareth, King of the Jews" is placed above the cross.

John depicts the crucifixion as the time when Jesus's identity is revealed. Jesus casts out the ruler of the world, and he overcomes the power of evil (12:31). Jesus's own sayings present his death as a time of revelation. In chapter 3, Jesus tells Nicodemus that just as Moses raised the serpent in the wilderness, "It is necessary in this way for the Son of Man to be raised so that all may believe in him and have eternal life" (ὑψωθῆναι δεῖ τὸν υἱὸν τοῦ ἀνθρώπου, ἵνα πᾶς ὁ πιστεύων ἐν αὐτῷ ἔχῃ ζωὴν αἰώνιον, 3:14–15). Jesus has prophesied that when his opponents have "lifted him up," then they will recognize him as "I am" (ὑψώσητε, 8:28). In chapter 12 he states that when he has been "lifted up" he will draw all people to himself (ὑψωθῶ, 12:32).[22] John interprets this saying as a reference to Jesus's death (12:33). In this passage, John employs the lan-

---

22. Brown argues that these three verses may be interpreted as the Johannine equivalents to the three passion predictions found in the Gospel of Mark (8:31; 9:31; 10:33–34) (*Gospel according to John*, 1:146). In both gospels, Jesus speaks of himself as the Son of Man and emphasizes the necessity of his death. Both gospels also refer to the abundant life that comes about through his death.

guage of drawing to emphasize the initiative of God as one who leads human beings to faith. The use of the verb ὑψόω ("exalt, lift up") relates to the raising of Jesus on the cross and also to his exaltation.[23] The cross becomes a symbol of salvation that reveals God.

In the passion narrative, John portrays the death of Jesus as a victory, but we do not see Jesus's enemies being vanquished. Nevertheless, there are signs of a new beginning within the narrative. The mother of Jesus and the Beloved Disciple stand near the cross. Jesus announces to his mother that the Beloved Disciple is now her son, and he tells the Beloved Disciple that Mary is his mother (19:26–27). Jesus hands over the Spirit that descended upon him at his baptism to his mother and the Beloved Disciple, who together form the basis of the new discipleship community. At the crucifixion, a soldier pierces Jesus's side. John cites Zech 12:10, which states "They shall look on the one whom they pierced." This citation could refer to the judgment of Jesus's opponents, but it may also look forward to their future conversion. Jesus has prophesied that his opponents will recognise him when he is "lifted up" (8:28) and that he will "draw all people" to himself after his death (12:32–33). John's reference to blood and water suggests that the witnesses see the abundance that comes from the piercing of the side of Jesus. The description of water recalls Jesus's earlier prophecy in which the Spirit is described as "living water" (7:37–39). In this passage, John links the gift of the Spirit with Jesus's death.

Throughout the gospel, the religious leaders fail to recognize Jesus, and in the trial scene the gentile leader, Pilate, is also unable to understand Jesus. John contrasts the power of Caesar with the kingship of Jesus. Pilate condemns Jesus to death, but John depicts the raising of Jesus on the cross as an act that brings salvation. Jesus casts out the ruler of the world and liberates humanity from the power of evil. He reveals God's love for the world, and his identity is revealed in his act of laying down his life. Jesus has come not to judge the world but to bring salvation. The raising of Jesus on the cross is presented as an act of revelation that has the power to draw humanity to Jesus (12:32–33). The presence of the mother of Jesus and the Beloved Disciple looks forward to the new discipleship community who will continue Jesus's mission in the period after his death.

---

23. For an analysis of the relationship between Jesus's crucifixion and his exaltation, see Joel Marcus, "Crucifixion as Parodic Exaltation," *JBL* 125 (2006): 73–87.

## The Messiah Remains Hidden

The crucifixion is depicted as a turning point within the gospel in which Jesus liberates human beings and inaugurates the new creation. In chapter 1 and chapter 7, John's use of the tradition of the hidden Messiah raised the question of the origins of Jesus and the human inability to know God. The Messiah has been sent into the world and has overcome the power of evil at the crucifixion. Jesus's identity as the Messiah is revealed at the cross when he fulfils his purpose in the world. Nevertheless, there are some indications that Jesus remains a hidden Messiah. In his Farewell Discourse, Jesus prepares his disciples for his departure from the world. Jesus speaks to his disciples in terms that recall his earlier debate with his opponents in chapter 7 (ζητήσετέ με καὶ οὐχ εὑρήσετέ με, καὶ ὅπου εἰμὶ ἐγὼ ὑμεῖς οὐ δύνασθε ἐλθεῖν, 7:34). Jesus tells his disciples that he will be with them for only a short time, and then they will seek him but be unable to follow him (ζητήσετέ με ... ὅπου ἐγὼ ὑπάγω ὑμεῖς οὐ δύνασθε ἐλθεῖν, 13:33).

In the Farewell Discourse, Jesus prepares his disciples for his departure and return to God. Jesus speaks of a time of absence when he will be separated from his disciples. He tells them that he is going to prepare a place for them and that they will follow him later. They know the way because he is the way to the Father (14:6). During this period, the Paraclete, the Spirit of truth, will be given to the disciples (14:16–17). The Paraclete is closely identified with Jesus.[24] The world has not been able to accept Jesus and will not be able to accept him. In the Farewell Discourse, Jesus is hidden from the world and the world will no longer see him. The Paraclete will teach the disciples everything and interpret Jesus's teaching (14:2–6). The Paraclete will guide them into all the truth (16:13). Catrin Williams traces the influence of apocalyptic thought on the role of the Paraclete.[25] She points out that John refers to two distinctive features of the "revelatory activity" of the Paraclete. In 14:25–26, the Paraclete brings understanding of the significance of Jesus's words, and in 16:12–15 the Paraclete brings new revelation of what has been hidden. The arrival of the Paraclete is

---

24. Brown notes that the Paraclete can only come after Jesus has left the world (*Gospel according to John*, 2:1135–43).

25. Catrin H. Williams, "Unveiling Revelation: The Spirit-Paraclete and Apocalyptic Disclosure in the Gospel of John," in *John's Gospel and Intimations of Apocalyptic*, ed. Catrin H. Williams and Christopher Rowland (London: Bloomsbury, 2013), 104–27.

evidence that Jesus has conquered death and has returned to his father in heaven. Although Jesus is separated from his disciples, he is present with them through the Paraclete. Jesus is thus known to his disciples rather than to the world. The Paraclete has the role of supporting the disciples who continue Jesus's mission in the world.

In the Farewell Discourse, John examines the continuing role of Jesus in the period after his death and resurrection. Jesus exhorts his disciples to remain faithful and not to be led astray during his absence from them. He describes himself as the vine and his disciples as the branches (15:1–11). Some branches wither and are thrown into the fire but those which remain in the vine bear fruit. In Jesus's teaching about the vine, the disciples are repeatedly urged to remain in Jesus. John suggests that Jesus's presence may be experienced by the disciples who remain in his love. Those who love Jesus are drawn into the love of the Father and the Son. The relationship of love of Father and Son continues beyond death. This relationship overcomes the transitory nature of the present world. The imagery of the vine indicates that this love is demanding because it may cost the disciples their lives as it has cost Jesus his life. Nevertheless, the threat of persecution is overcome by the eternal life found by keeping Jesus's commandments.

John's portrayal of Jesus as the hidden Messiah is also reflected in his presentation of the disciples. Jesus has come from God into the world, and in the Prologue those who believe in Jesus receive power to become children of God (1:12–13). They are reborn through the power of God. Jesus is the hidden Messiah within the world since he is unrecognized by his opponents. In the Farewell Discourse, Jesus prophesies that the disciples will face persecution and they will be put out of the synagogue (16:1–4). In the Farewell Discourse, John replaces the opposition of the religious authorities with the opposition of the world. The disciples will also face opposition from gentiles as they continue Jesus's mission in the world. John suggests that the suffering of the disciples is also hidden in the world. He depicts a contrast between the disciples and the world. The world hated Jesus, and it will hate the disciples (15:18). The world persecuted Jesus and will persecute the disciples, but there is hope for the disciples since some kept the word of Jesus and some will respond to their word. The gulf between Jesus and the world is a reflection of the inability of the world to recognize Jesus. Jesus has spoken of the hour of his passion, and the disciples are warned of the hour when they will face persecution (16:1–4). The Farewell Discourse indicates that the disciples have not been abandoned since the Paraclete will come to them and guide them in the truth.

## Conclusion

John's use of the tradition of the hidden Messiah reflects the influence of apocalyptic thought upon his gospel. John develops this tradition in the account of the baptism of Jesus in John 1 and the debate between Jesus and some members of the crowd over his identity as the Messiah in John 7. Both passages connect the portrayal of Jesus as the hidden Messiah to his divine origins. John also employs this tradition to demonstrate the inability of the religious leaders to recognize the Messiah who stands in their midst. John's use of the tradition reflects his portrayal of Jesus as a hidden Messiah in the remainder of the gospel. Questions concerning Jesus's identity as the Messiah form the main point of conflict between Jesus and the religious leaders. The conflict culminates in the passion narrative when Jesus is condemned to death as a false Messiah and as "the king of the Jews."

John's portrayal of Jesus as the hidden Messiah may provide some insights into the study of the parting of the ways. John gives some indications that the conflict over Jesus's identity as Messiah continues in the later time of the Johannine Christians. In the Farewell Discourse, Jesus prophesies that his disciples will face persecution and be excluded from the synagogue (16:1–4). J. Louis Martyn notes that John refers several times to the exclusion from the synagogue of those who confess their faith that Jesus is the Messiah (9:22; 12:42–43; 16:2).[26] Martyn proposes that these references allude to the experience of the Johannine Christians who have left the synagogue in their city. The Johannine Christians may wish to explain why Jesus was unrecognized by the leaders of his own people. John emphasizes the initiative of God in bringing human beings to faith. God draws some people to Jesus but blinds others (12:37–43). Jesus's identity is concealed only for a period of time until the appointed hour of his death. The crucifixion is depicted as the time of the glorification of God and Jesus (12:23; 13:1; 17:1–5), and human beings are able to reach a new understanding of Jesus. John thus places the rejection of Jesus by some of his own people within the wider theological paradoxes of the gospel. The world was created through Jesus, but no human being is able to recognize the divinity of Jesus without revelation from God. John's presentation of the crucifixion, however, suggests that he remains hopeful that the Jewish

---

26. Martyn, *History*, 37–62.

people will come to believe in Jesus (8:28; 12:32–33). In the period after Jesus's death, the disciples will continue Jesus's mission in the world.

John's portrayal of Jesus as the hidden Messiah may resonate with the experience of the Johannine Christians. In the Farewell Discourse, Jesus prepares his disciples for his return to God, and his speech suggests that he will be hidden from his followers. Jesus, however, prophesies that the Paraclete will come to his disciples to take his place and guide them in the truth. The Johannine Christians may also identify with the experience of the hidden Messiah. Their belief in Jesus may cause them to feel like strangers in the world. Just as Jesus faced persecution, they will experience persecution (15:18–20; 16:33; 17:14–15). Their suffering is hidden in the world, but they believe that they have not been forgotten by God. John's portrayal of Jesus as the hidden Messiah may therefore bring comfort and encouragement to the Johannine Christians because it indicates that events are following the purposes of God.

## Bibliography

Ashton, John. *Understanding the Fourth Gospel*. 2nd ed. Oxford: Oxford University Press, 2007.

Barrett, C. K. *The Gospel according to St John: An Introduction with Commentary and Notes on the Greek Text*. 2nd ed. London: SPCK, 1978.

Brown, Raymond E. *The Gospel according to John: Introduction, Translation and Notes*. 2 vols. AB 29–29A. New York: Doubleday, 1966–1970.

Jonge, Marinus de. "Jewish Expectations about the 'Messiah' according to the Fourth Gospel." *NTS* 19 (1973): 246–70.

———. "John the Baptist and Elijah in the Fourth Gospel." Pages 299–308 in *The Conversation Continues: Studies in Paul and John in Honor of J. Louis Martyn*. Edited by Robert T. Fortna and Beverly R. Gaventa. Nashville: Abingdon: 1990.

Lindars, Barnabas. *The Gospel of John*. NCB. London: Marshall, Morgan & Scott, 1972.

Marcus, Joel. "Crucifixion as Parodic Exaltation." *JBL* 125 (2006): 73–87.

———. *The Mystery of the Kingdom of God*. SBLDS 90. Atlanta: Scholars Press, 1986.

Martyn, J. Louis. *History and Theology in the Fourth Gospel*. 2nd ed. Nashville: Abingdon, 1979.

Mowinckel, Sigmund. *He That Cometh: The Messiah Concept in the Old Testament and Later Judaism*. Oxford: Blackwell, 1956.

Räisänen, Heikki. *The "Messianic Secret" in Mark*. Translated by Christopher Tuckett. Edinburgh: T&T Clark, 1990.

Rensberger, David. *Overcoming the World: Politics and Community in the Gospel of John*. London: SPCK, 1988.

Stauffer, Ethelbert. "Agnostos Christos: Joh. ii 24 und die Eschatologie des vierten Evangeliums." Pages 281–99 in *The Background of the New Testament and Its Eschatology: Essays in Honour of C. H. Dodd*. Edited by W. D. Davies and D. Daube. Cambridge: Cambridge University Press, 1956.

Stibbe, Mark W. G. "The Elusive Christ: A New Reading of the Fourth Gospel." Pages 231–47 in *The Gospel of John as Literature: An Anthology of Twentieth-Century Perspectives*. Edited by Mark W. G. Stibbe. NTTSD 17. Leiden: Brill, 1993.

Tuckett, Christopher, ed. *The Messianic Secret*. London: SPCK, 1983.

Williams, Catrin H. "Unveiling Revelation: The Spirit-Paraclete and Apocalyptic Disclosure in the Gospel of John." Pages 104–27 in *John's Gospel and Intimations of Apocalyptic*. Edited by Catrin H. Williams and Christopher Rowland. London: Bloomsbury, 2013.

Wink, Walter. *John the Baptist in the Gospel Tradition*. SNTSMS 7. Cambridge: Cambridge University Press, 1968.

Wrede, William. *The Messianic Secret*. Translated by J. C. G. Greig. Cambridge: Clarke, 1971.

# John Makes a Way:
# A Narrative-Critical Reading of Psalm 69 in John 2:17

## Jill Hicks-Keeton

The parting of the ways was not a singular event. The disentangling of an entity called Christianity from a different entity called Judaism happened in fits and starts over time, and it involved both new hermeneutics and changing sociological contexts. The question of how to describe such partings is fundamentally a historical one, inasmuch as we attempt to piece together how, when, and why a movement that began as a Jewish group centered around a Jewish figure eventually became something identifiably not-Jewish or "Christian." The project is made complicated, even maddening, by the nature of some of the earliest literary evidence internal to this movement: the gospels, likely written in the last third of the first century CE or beginning of the second century CE. Examining the gospels for evidence for how the ways parted demands careful literary analysis, given that they are confessional stories written about Jesus that not only depict disputes happening between (Jewish) believers in Jesus and (Jewish) non-believers in the time of their narrative settings (the time of Jesus) but also encode into their stories dynamics and theologies from their own, later time periods.[1] That is, they both imagine earlier partings and participate in contemporary way-making.

---

I offer this essay in honor of Joel Marcus, under whose guidance I first navigated historical questions about the so-called parting of the ways.

1. J. Louis Martyn, *History and Theology in the Fourth Gospel*, 3rd ed. (Louisville: Westminster, 2003); see also Adele Reinhartz, "'Common Judaism,' 'The Parting of the Ways,' and 'The Johannine Community,'" in *Orthodoxy, Liberalism, and Adaptation: Essays on Ways of Worldmaking in Times of Change from Biblical, Historical and Systematic Perspectives*, ed. Bob Becker, Studies in Theology and Religion 15 (Leiden: Brill, 2011), 69–88.

In this essay I foreground literary analysis as a means of examining one gospel writer's new hermeneutic in light of one sociological change in antiquity that impacted how Jews, including Jesus followers, thought about themselves and their God in the world: the destruction of the Jerusalem temple in 70 CE. I focus in particular on the temple incident narrated in John 2. Here, the story takes a puzzling turn. In a dramatic series of events, the Johannine Jesus makes a whip, overturns the temple tables, and evicts the merchants. The disciples, for their part, stand back and quote scripture to themselves.[2] The reader is told that the disciples, upon observing Jesus's outburst, "remembered that it was written, 'Zeal for your house will consume me'" (NRSV). The quotation of Ps 69:9 here is both arresting and perplexing, which has led interpreters to posit explanations for it that are not readily apparent in the narrative.[3] The overwhelming scholarly consensus is that this quotation is a proleptic reference to Jesus's impending death.[4] While I am persuaded that it functions

---

2. Here and throughout, I use the term *scripture* (as John's author uses it) to refer to Israel's scriptures (LXX/OG). On John's use of scripture in general, see Maarten J. J. Menken, "Old Testament Quotations in the Gospel of John," in *New Testament Writers and the Old Testament: An Introduction*, ed. John M. Court (London: SPCK, 2002), 29–45.

3. I follow the NRSV numbering. This verse is Ps 69:10a in the MT and Ps 68:9 in the OG.

4. The most forceful case has come from Maarten Menken, who explains the tense shift of the verb from the Septuagint's aorist κατέφαγέν ("consumed") to the Gospel's future καταφάγεταί ("will consume") by arguing that the citation foreshadows Jesus's impending violent death, thereby confirming for the reader that Jesus's crucifixion accorded with God's plan because it had already been proclaimed in scripture. Maarten J. J. Menken, *Old Testament Quotations in the Fourth Gospel: Studies in Textual Form*, CBET 15 (Kampen: Kok Pharos, 1996), 37–45. Menken was not the first to suggest such an interpretation but rather presents, in my judgment, the most thorough and persuasive case for it. Menken is also by no means alone in this judgment. Writing of the temple narrative, Christopher Bryan concludes: "So the final thrust of the passage is that (for the first time in the Gospel) our attention is drawn clearly to the cross, and its significance." Christopher Bryan, "Shall We Sing Hallel in the Days of the Messiah? A Glance at John 2:1–3:21," *SLJT* 29 (1985): 26. Bruce Schuchard likewise claims that "John's citation represents to those who view it from a post-resurrection perspective a prophecy concerning Jesus' crucifixion." Bruce Schuchard, *Scripture within Scripture: The Interrelationship of Form and Function in the Explicit Old Testament Citations in the Gospel of John*, SBLDS 133 (Atlanta: Scholars Press, 1992), 32. Mary Coloe also interprets this citation as a passion prediction: "The remembering of the disciples at verse 17 points ahead to the death of Jesus." Mary Coloe, *God Dwells with Us: Temple*

to foreshadow Jesus's passion, I am not satisfied that this interpretation exhausts the quotation's reference. Some commentators have suspected that the quotation might also foreshadow Jesus's resurrection because Ps 69 contains imagery of God's rebuilding.[5] Yet is there any literary evidence to support such a reading? Are there methodological grounds on which one may understand this Psalm citation as a proleptic reference to Jesus's resurrection? Is there anything in the Gospel itself that invites, or demands, such an interpretation?

I think so. Below I present a narrative-critical reading of John's temple incident and find that the pedagogy of the text compels the reader to interpret Ps 69:9 as a reference to Jesus's resurrection (in addition to his death). I contend that this reading follows more closely the overall method of scripture interpretation that the Gospel of John itself promotes and, more importantly, teaches its reader to practice: remembering in light of Jesus's resurrection. After a preliminary methodological note about the Gospel's "reader," I present evidence for a Johannine hermeneutic of postresurrectional remembering, demonstrating that the Gospel invites its reader into this interpretive practice. I then offer a close reading of the temple narrative in order to reveal the way in which it both employs this method of interpretation and attempts to engage the reader in its practice. I intend to show that, when read with the interpretive method and hermeneutical lens with which the temple narrative itself equips its reader, the quotation must be read as a reference not only to Jesus's crucifixion, but also to his resurrection.

---

*Symbolism in the Fourth Gospel* (Collegeville, MN: Liturgical Press, 2001), 75. Alan Kerr writes similarly, "At the level of discourse, it's a prophecy that came to fulfillment with Jesus' *crucifixion*." Alan Kerr, *The Temple of Jesus' Body: The Temple Theme in the Gospel of John*, JSNTSup 220 (London: Sheffield Academic, 2002), 83.

5. In fact, Menken himself reveals a suspicion that there is more at stake here: he posits, almost in passing, that the Psalm citation may refer also to Jesus's resurrection (*Old Testament Quotations*, 45). Richard Hays's work on this intertextual link includes a similar suggestion. He states that "it is perhaps not sheerly coincidental that the psalm's final verses speak of God's saving Zion and *(re)building* the cities of Judah—an image that echoes suggestively in counterpoint with Jesus' prophecy that he will raise up the destroyed temple of his body." Richard B. Hays "Reading Scripture in Light of the Resurrection," in *The Art of Reading Scripture*, ed. Ellen F. Davis and Richard B. Hays (Grand Rapids: Eerdmans, 2003), 223, emphasis original. Neither Menken nor Hays offers an accompanying argument based on the logic of the Johannine text itself.

John's use of Ps 69 in chapter 2 thus interrupts the story to anticipate the *whole* story—a story that captures one moment of parting in the writer's own day, since here Jesus is offered as a replacement for the Jewish temple as the locus of God's dealings with Israel. The Gospel of John thus reads Israel's scriptures through "resurrection-goggles"[6] as the narrative accounts for the destruction of the Jerusalem temple in 70 CE. This reading mode and nascent replacement theology were developed in a historical context in which radical distinctions were not made between Jews and Christians—but rather (Jewish) followers of Jesus and *some* unbelieving Jews.[7] Yet as this local argument went global, it would come to have drastic repercussions in future generations as gentile Christians defined themselves over against, and in place of, Jews.

### Who Is John's Reader? Methodological Concerns

The question of the identity of the reader of this text is an important one.[8] Many studies of the Gospel of John have focused on the historical identity of the intended readers, asking sociological questions about a potential Johannine community or a historicized theology.[9] Drawing on categories articulated by Murray Krieger, R. Alan Culpepper notes that John has often been used "as a 'window' through which the critic can catch 'glimpses' of

---

6. I have here adapted Warren Carter's useful term "Jesus-glasses" (*Seven Events That Shaped the New Testament World* [Grand Rapids: Baker Academic, 2012], 35).

7. Martyn, *History and Theology in the Fourth Gospel*.

8. There has been a great deal of debate in scholarship on the compositional and redactional history of John. On this, see, for example, Raymond E. Brown, *The Gospel according to John I–XII*, AB 29 (Garden City, NY: Doubleday, 1966), xxiv–xl; Helmut Koester, *Introduction to the New Testament*, 2nd ed., 2 vols. (New York: de Gruyter, 2000), 2:182–99. This essay does not engage in these debates but rather presents arguments based on the form of John presented in NA[28].

9. In the introduction to his narrative-critical work on John, R. Alan Culpepper points to Robert Kysar's *The Fourth Evangelist and His Gospel: An Examination of Contemporary Scholarship* (Minneapolis: Augsburg, 1975) as evidence of the extent to which Johannine scholarship was dominated by such concerns at that time. See R. Alan Culpepper, *Anatomy of the Fourth Gospel: A Study in Literary Design* (Philadelphia: Fortress, 1983), and Mark W. G. Stibbe, *John as Storyteller: Narrative Criticism and the Fourth Gospel*, SNTSMS 73 (Cambridge: Cambridge University Press, 1992). Such historical questions are certainly important, and I see my project in this essay as in service to them, though I do not prioritize them here.

the history of the Johannine community."[10] Culpepper's narrative-critical study of John represented an important shift in focus from deriving
meaning by looking through a Johannine window to deriving meaning by
approaching the text as a mirror: "This model assumes that the meaning of
a text lies on this side of it, between mirror and observer, text and reader.
Meaning is produced in the experience of reading the text as a whole and
making the mental moves the text calls for its reader to make."[11] With this
methodology, the text derives meaning from the engagement of the reader
with the rhetorical moves that the text lays out for its reader.[12]

Rather than positing actual historical readers, a narrative-critical
methodology focuses on the "implied reader" or the "ideal reader"—
a reader that the text itself constructs. Literary theorist Wolfgang Iser's
study of readers and reading is particularly helpful here. In *The Act of
Reading: A Theory of Aesthetic Response*, Iser explains that the implied
reader "embodies all those predispositions necessary for a literary work to
exercise its effect—predispositions laid down, not by an empirical outside
reality, but by the text itself.... Thus the concept of the implied reader designates a network of response inviting structures, which impel the reader
to grasp the text."[13] The text constructs its own internal reader—one that
responds to the "network" that the text constructs. Taking into account
the implied reader's relationship to the rhetorical moves of the text, Jack
Dean Kingsbury describes it as "the imaginary person in whom the inten-

---

10. Culpepper, *Anatomy of the Fourth Gospel*, 3. He cites Murray Krieger, *A
Window to Criticism: Shakespeare's Sonnets and Modern Poetics* (Princeton: Princeton
University Press, 1964).

11. Culpepper, *Anatomy of the Fourth Gospel*, 4. For a critical reading of Culpepper's use of the imagery of window and mirror for reading John, see Stephen D.
Moore, *Poststructuralism and the New Testament: Derrida and Foucault at the Foot of
the Cross* (Minneapolis: Fortress, 1994), 78–81.

12. This narrative-critical methodology differs from the biblical studies category
of rhetorical criticism, since it seeks to interpret the text from the point of view of the
implied reader rather than looking outside the text at the original, historical, actual
reader who is subject to commonly-attested rhetorical forms. On this, see in particular Mark Alan Powell, *What Is Narrative Criticism?* (Minneapolis: Fortress, 1990), 15.
This methodology also diverges from the biblical studies category of reader-response
criticism because the implied reader is an imaginary reader—ultimately, a rhetorical
device.

13. Wolfgang Iser, *The Act of Reading: A Theory of Aesthetic Response* (Baltimore:
Johns Hopkins University Press, 1978), 34.

tion of the text is to be thought of as always reaching its fulfillment."[14] The text constructs its own imaginary, ideal reader that responds fully to its rhetorical goals.

Narrative criticism, then, asks the interpreter to derive meaning from the text in the first instance by identifying (what I will call) its narrative pattern—the complex of rhetorical moves it exercises upon its implied reader. In order to locate the implied reader, one must ask questions about the rhetorical strategies and effects of the text: What does the text require of the reader? How does the text *work* on the reader as a means of fulfilling its rhetorical goals? By identifying the text's rhetorical strategies—as well as the way in which the text envisions its reader responding to these strategies—we may derive conclusions about the text's meaning as it emerges from the implied reader's movement through the text's narrative pattern. By reading as the implied reader, we may intuit ways in which the text attempts to direct its own interpretation.

It is important to note that I am not making historical claims with these observations. I do not mean to suggest that the ancient audience of the Gospel of John read it individually and in concert with the text's rhetorical goals. As we know, historically the Gospel would have been read aloud and likely in community. When making historical claims, then, it is perhaps more accurate to speak of auditors than of readers. Yet, the aim of this study is to trace the narrative's rhetorical effects by marking how the text works upon the audience that it imagines as fully receptive to its designs. Thus, for ease of reference, I will use the term *reader* as shorthand for the rhetorical device *implied reader*, which should not be confused with a historical reader or intended audience. It is my hope that such narrative-critical observations, which hold historical inquiry at bay for the time being, may enhance historical work on the Gospel of John by serving as a precursor. That is, what I offer here is meant to be a *first step* in historical study of John by its description of what the text says on the text's own terms.[15] I return briefly to this issue at the conclusion. With this methodological caveat in mind, I turn first to examine the Gospel as a whole and then to the immediate passage at hand.

---

14. Jack Dean Kingsbury, *Matthew as Story* (Philadelphia: Fortress, 1986), 38.

15. Such a methodological stance is very much in concert with that of Martinus C. de Boer in his "Narrative Criticism, Historical Criticism, and the Gospel of John," *JSNT* 47 (1992): 35–48.

## Retrospection and Scripture in John

One of the most salient literary features of John's Gospel is its casting the story of Jesus as the fulfillment of scripture, thereby connecting Jesus's life, death, and resurrection with God's promises to Israel. The narrative itself is a post-Easter reflection on Jesus in conversation with the scriptures of Israel. The Gospel of John offers such retrospective interpretation as normative in three ways. First, by portraying the disciples as those who understand (versus those who misunderstand—a common trope in John), the narrative endorses the disciples' retrospection in 2:17, 22, and in 12:16. In fact, Jesus's disciples are portrayed as only understanding *fully* after the resurrection. Here, rightly understanding Jesus and his relationship to scripture means interpreting his words and actions in light of a postresurrectional reading—or remembering—of scripture. Second, the text inserts narratival cues that conspicuously invoke or presume practices of postresurrectional interpretation. Relating "the other disciple's" discovery of the empty tomb in 20:8b–9, the text states that he "saw and believed; for as yet they [Peter and "the other disciple"] did not understand the scripture, *that he must rise from the dead*" (NRSV, emphasis added). We learn here, significantly, that for this narrative, Israel's scriptures culminate in Jesus's resurrection, to which scripture points when read properly. For John, Jesus's *resurrection* emerges as the focal point of fulfilled scripture.

The third means by which the narrative endorses postresurrectional remembering is the most subtle but also perhaps the most effective. It draws the reader into its practice. From a rhetorical standpoint, the narrative is constructed in such a way that the reader is required to—at least temporarily—employ postresurrectional reflection. By virtue of the fact that the written Gospel itself is recollection shaped by faith, the reader participates in the faithful recollecting by the very act of reading it. Thus, when the narrator practices postresurrectional reflection, the reader practices it along with the narrator, whether or not the reader is consciously aware of it. The use of the first-person plural pronoun "we" in the prologue (1:14, 16) and epilogue (21:24) points toward such a technique. As a grammatical choice, the we-statements set the narrative in a context of believing confession. As a rhetorical device, the we-statements compel the reader into the confession. When the reader reads "we" in these verses, the reader participates in the confession of having seen the Word's glory (1:14), having received "grace upon grace" (1:16), and acknowledging the purported truth of the writer's testimony (21:24). As captive audience, the reader joins in the text's postresurrectional recollection that the text has prescribed as normative.

## Retrospection and Scripture in John 2:13–23

John's temple story is a signal example of the way in which the narrative engages the reader in such reflection and, more specifically, in resurrection-focused scripture interpretation. In what follows, I argue that the narrator cleverly—cunningly?—compels the reader to interpret this citation of Ps 69:9 as a proleptic reference not only to Jesus's death, as many commentators have suggested, but also to Jesus's resurrection. I suggest that this (more characteristically Johannine) interpretive option emerges when one considers the way in which the temple passage engages the reader through its narrative pattern. Since it is the narrator who informs the reader of the remembered scripture in 2:17, we must pay attention to both *what* the narrator tells (and does not tell) and *how* the narrator tells (including the order in which information is told).

In this passage, the narration that mentions Passover and Jerusalem in verses 13 and 23 marks off a literary unit. Within the unit, the narrative relates two rounds of Jesus's action/dialogue and the response of the disciples and "the Jews."[16] While the narrative does not address the reader directly in the first round, it interrupts the second round to offer an interpretive comment. A visual representation of this pattern appears here with its explanation below:

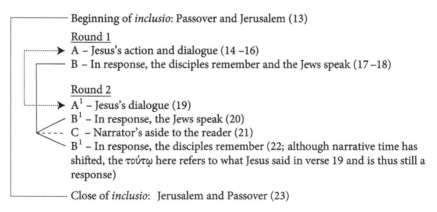

Beginning of *inclusio*: Passover and Jerusalem (13)

Round 1
A – Jesus's action and dialogue (14–16)
B – In response, the disciples remember and the Jews speak (17–18)

Round 2
A¹ – Jesus's dialogue (19)
B¹ – In response, the Jews speak (20)
C – Narrator's aside to the reader (21)
B¹ – In response, the disciples remember (22; although narrative time has shifted, the τούτῳ here refers to what Jesus said in verse 19 and is thus still a response)

Close of *inclusio*: Jerusalem and Passover (23)

16. After this I do not use quotation marks around *the Jews*, since in John's Gospel they are literary characters, just as the Johannine Jesus and disciples are characters.

In A/A¹, Jesus acts and/or speaks. In B/B¹, the disciples (via the omniscient narrator) and the Jews respond. A clear distinction emerges, as elsewhere in the narrative, between the insider disciples who understand (though only after the resurrection) and the outsiders who do not understand. In C, which occurs only in Round 2, the narrator conspicuously interrupts the pattern. The narrative here explicitly interprets Jesus's action for the reader before reporting the disciples' response (the rest of B¹). There are three significant rhetorical moves here:

1. The passage normalizes remembering as an interpretive method, while leaving ambiguous *how* it is effective.
2. The passage invites the reader into the insider group, compelling the reader to practice this interpretive method along with the narrator.
3. The passage makes explicit that the resurrection is the hermeneutical key by which remembering takes place.

The sequence of these moves is particularly important. First, the text normalizes remembering as an interpretive method by reporting that the disciples, having seen Jesus's action in the temple, remember a specific scripture citation (2:17). A circumstance that occurs throughout John's Gospel emerges here as instructive: the disciples are portrayed as those who understand in contrast to the Jews who do not. The narrator thus endorses the disciples' technique of interpreting Jesus's action. Yet the narrator does not make explicit *how* this quotation interprets Jesus's action. While the method of remembering is authorized, the meaning of the citation in relation to Jesus's activity in the temple is left ambiguous.

Acknowledging such an ambiguity, Bruce Schuchard has written that the reader is to overlook it:

> John offers no answers to these questions [of how the disciples understand Ps 69:9 in reference to Jesus's action in the temple]. Because he proceeds quickly to other issues, the reader probably should do so as well, noting at least that in seeing Jesus' zeal and "remembering" the disciples understand little and probably think only of the immediate present.[17]

Yet the narrator gives no indication that the disciples are confused here. Moreover, as we continue to read, we discover that narrative time has shifted: the repetition of ἐμνήσθησαν οἱ μαθηταὶ αὐτοῦ in verses 17 and 22

---

17. Schuchard, *Scripture within Scripture*, 31.

(in which it is explicit that they remember after the resurrection) supports the notion that both instances are subsequent to the resurrection. Most importantly, however, Schuchard's suggestion ignores the fact that the reader experiences the narrative in a different way than the disciples as characters are shown to experience the event within the narrative. His claim thus neglects the level of discourse. While the level of *story* comprises the characters' experience of the narrative's events (that is, what the characters see and hear), the level of *discourse* comprises the readers' experience of the narrative (that is, what the narrator tells and the way in which the narrator tells).[18] Treating the ambiguity as a legitimate rhetorical device rather than overlooking it acknowledges this dual-level feature of narrative. The rhetorical effect of the ambiguous relationship between the disciples' quotation and Jesus's activity is significant for the reader's engagement with the passage.

Investigating the potential rhetorical effects of narratorial silence, Culpepper explains that "*how much* exposition is given has a determinative effect upon the kind of response a narrative evokes from its readers. A narrator may tell the reader all the vital information, or the reader may be required to figure things out as the story progresses."[19] Where Culpepper's analysis of the Johannine narrator falls short, however, is his contention that it "is neither unreliable nor deliberately suppressive," a description that circumscribes the narrator to an unnecessarily static role and that does not allow for rhetorical artistry.[20] In 2:16–17, the narrator withholds information that is necessary for the reader to join in the disciples' understanding by leaving ambiguous the meaning of Ps 69:9 in relation to Jesus's action.

The passage thereby sets up textual circumstances in which the reader must participate in the construction of textual meaning—what Iser has called "gaps of indeterminacy." The text leaves a gap that the reader must fill. John Miles Foley, following Iser, describes "gap of indeterminacies" as "those uncharted areas in the textual map where the reader is invited and indeed required to contribute an imaginative solution."[21] He goes on to claim that these gaps "must be filled in accordance with the explicit read-

---

18. See "Story and Discourse" in Powell, *What Is Narrative Criticism?*, 23–34.
19. Culpepper, *Anatomy of the Fourth Gospel*, 19.
20. Culpepper, *Anatomy of the Fourth Gospel*, 19.
21. John Miles Foley, *Immanent Art: From Structure to Meaning in Traditional Oral Epic* (Bloomington: Indiana University Press, 1991), 42.

ing signals that make up the text."[22] John's reader is not left to an independent imagination to fill in the narratorial silence here. The reader must fill the gap in a way that coheres with the pedagogy of the literary piece as a whole. And, as I have already discussed, the Gospel of John provides *Jesus's resurrection* in conversation with Israel's scriptures as the perspective from which the reader must fill the gap.[23]

Indeed, the present pericope begins to equip the reader with these necessary tools in its next rhetorical move, though the first-time reader is likely not yet able to apprehend them fully. After reporting Jesus's response to the Jews and their retort (vv. 19–20), the narrator offers an aside that compels the reader to practice *along with the narrator* postresurrectional interpretation of Jesus's words. Speaking directly to the reader, the narrator explains: "But he was speaking about the temple of his body" (v. 21). The narrator can only know that Jesus was speaking of "the temple of his body" after—and because of—the resurrection (as is revealed in v. 22). Though the narrator's retrospection only becomes evident as the reader continues reading the Gospel—in 2:22, 7:39, 12:16, and 20:9—the rhetorical strategy of 2:21 nevertheless compels the reader to practice postresurrectional interpretation by virtue of reading the narrator's postresurrectional reflection, whether or not the reader recognizes it as such.

The third rhetorical move is that the narrator makes the postresurrection method of interpretation explicit. The resurrection is the hermeneutical lens through which one may understand that both the scripture (τῇ γραφῇ) and Jesus's word (τῷ λόγῳ ὅν εἶπεν ὁ Ἰησοῦς) are to be interpreted and understood from the perspective of the resurrection backwards. By withholding the precise interpretive methodology that the narrative advocates until the end of the pericope, the narrator creates an opportunity for the reader to use this new information retrospectively. That is, the text performs the very thing it instructs. Now that the reader knows the key—resurrection—the reader may retrospectively interpret the significance of the disciples' remembered quotation (that is, what the narrator left ambiguous). The ambiguity discussed above thus becomes rhetorically powerful: the text provides an opportunity for the reader to *practice* the hermeneutic that the Gospel of John offers as normative without the immediate help of the narrator. The rhetorical effect of the pericope, then,

---

22. Foley, *Immanent Art*, 42.

23. Moore uses the Derridean concept of an "aporia" to argue for the importance of gaps in the Johannine narrative (*Poststructuralism and the New Testament*, 66–74).

is that it asks the reader to supply the meaning of the Ps 69 quotation in John 2:17 through postresurrectional interpretation.

Thus far I have argued (1) that the Gospel of John offers Jesus's resurrection as a hermeneutical key that enables what it conceives to be the proper understanding of scriptures, and (2) that the temple narrative offers John's reader the opportunity to practice such interpretation by seeing in Ps 69:9 a reference not only to Jesus's death but also to his resurrection. In my judgment, there are two further pieces of evidence that support this interpretation of John 2:17: (1) the Gospel's use of the whole of Ps 69 as an interpretive lens, and (2) the contribution that such a rhetorical strategy makes to the Gospel's stated purpose (20:31).

First, Ps 69 shows up in two other places in John's Gospel and specifically in the passion narrative: John 15:25 alludes to Ps 69:4 and John 19:28 alludes to Ps 69:21. A detailed study of these allusions is outside the scope of this essay, but their very presence in the text is important to my argument for this reason: the cumulative effect of three references to this Psalm—in three textual moments where scholars agree that Jesus's passion is in view—is that Ps 69 becomes a *lens* through which Jesus's passion is understood. I suggest that the reference in John 2:17 therefore functions metaleptically; it invokes the entire psalm, not just the piece explicitly stated. Drawing upon the work of literary theorist John Hollander, Richard Hays describes the phenomenon of metalepsis in this way: "Allusive echo functions to suggest to the reader that text B should be understood in light of a broad interplay with text A, encompassing aspects of A beyond those explicitly echoed."[24] A reader familiar with the whole of Ps 69 knows that being "consumed with zeal" is not the end of its story.[25] The conclusion (69:35–36) is one of hope, as it expresses expectation for salvation and rebuilding: "For God will save Zion and rebuild the cities of Judah; and his servants shall live there and possess it; the chil-

---

24. Richard B. Hays, *Echoes of Scripture in the Letters of Paul* (New Haven: Yale University Press, 1989), 20. Hays cites John Hollander, *The Figure of Echo: A Mode of Allusion in Milton and After* (Berkeley: University of California Press, 1981). The presence of an echo does not in itself justify a metaleptic reading. Rather, there must be further evidence that the whole of text A matters to text B. Here, I am suggesting that a metaleptic reading is supported by the following evidence: (1) the Gospel's triple use of this psalm and (2) the thematic overlap between the psalm's temple-building and John's temple-building (in Jesus's body).

25. This point is important to stress, since my reading is contingent on the implied reader of John having a familiarity with Ps 69 as a whole.

dren of his servants shall inherit it, and those who love his name shall live in it" (NRSV). The psalm ends with hopeful images of rebuilding.

Further evidence for the appropriateness of a metaleptic reading is the thematic overlap between the Johannine temple narrative and Ps 69, namely, (re)building. A close reading of the pericope demonstrates that the rebuilding is most significant part of the pattern. In response to Jesus's statement in verse 19 ("Destroy this temple, and in three days I will raise it up"), the Jews focus their attention on the *rebuilding* rather than the destruction of the temple: "This temple has been under construction for forty-six years, and will you raise it up in three days?" (2:20, NRSV). Although destruction is here assumed, the spotlight is on the temple-building and temple-rebuilding (ἐγερεῖς). By narrating this rebuilding-focused dialogue, the narrator draws the reader's attention not to the destruction—Jesus's death—but to the rebuilding/raising—Jesus's resurrection. Just as destruction is not the end of the psalm-speaker's story, so death is not the end of Jesus's story in John. Jesus, as the temple rebuilt, is raised from the dead in resurrection.

Without the benefit of a postresurrection perspective and resurrection-centered hermeneutic, the disciples' remembering part of this psalm is grim indeed; it points toward Jesus's death at the hands of outsider enemies (καταφάγεταί με). Yet for the reader who responds to the exhortation and education offered in John 2:13–23, the Ps 69 citation functions metaleptically to point not only toward Jesus's suffering and death but also toward hope for salvation and rebuilding—decisive acts of which God is the subject (ὁ θεὸς σώσει ... καὶ οἰκοδομηθήσονται). As the reader interprets Jesus's story in conversation with Ps 69, the psalm's unstated conclusion, with its emphasis on God's saving and rebuilding, points toward the resurrection.

A second piece of evidence that supports this reading of John 2:17 is its coherence with the Gospel's explicit assertion of its rhetorical goal in 20:31: "But these are written so that you may come to believe that Jesus is the Messiah, the Son of God, and that through believing you may have life in his name" (20:31, NRSV). The author/editor/redactor constructs a narrative about Jesus's life, death, and resurrection that is purposed to incite or to prolong in its reader belief in Jesus.[26] Reading the Gospel of John is

---

26. There is a textual variant in this verse: the aorist subjunctive πιστεύσητε (usually translated "come to believe") versus the present subjunctive πιστεύητε (usually translated "continue to believe"). This variant has been given extended attention in

not, then, a passive experience that one may undertake without engagement; rather, reading the Gospel of John is an exercise intended to teach its actively-participating reader. This text means to persuade.

Likewise, postresurrectional remembering is not, for the Gospel of John, an aloof, cerebral activity that one may practice merely intellectually. Rather, the narrative conceives it as a practice with agency: it enables believing. At the end of the temple pericope, verse 22 connects the disciples' remembering to their belief (καὶ ἐπίστευσαν ["and they believed"]). Postresurrectional remembering leads to belief. The narrator's comment in 20:8b–9 is again important: "the other disciple" "saw and believed; for as yet they [Peter and "the other disciple"] did not understand the scripture, that he must rise from the dead" (20:8b–9, NRSV). Explicit here is the conviction that scripture points to the resurrection of Jesus, as we have already seen; *implicit* here is the notion that if one recognizes the scriptures' pointing to Jesus's resurrection, one will believe.

Since, in 2:13–23, the narrative not only teaches its reader this belief-enabling postresurrectional remembering but also invites the reader to practice it, the stakes of reading this passage are high. Functioning as a rhetorical microcosm of the Gospel as a whole, this pericope seeks to persuade its reader toward (perhaps continued) believing. That is, through its well-crafted narratorial silence—its "gap of indeterminacy"—the pericope compels its reader to remember rightly and, in the process, it attempts to enable belief. Once the reader learns how to interpret scripture postresurrectionally, as the Gospel desires, he or she may continue reading (or perhaps the second time through) as an insider disciple—one who has been shown the hermeneutical key to understand the scripture (here, Ps 69:9) as pointing to Jesus's resurrection. Thus, rather than "seeing and believing"—as "the other disciple" did (20:8)—the reader is

---

print by D. A. Carson ("The Purpose of the Fourth Gospel: John 20:31 Reconsidered," *JBL* 106 [1987]: 639–51; and "Syntactical and Text-Critical Observations on John 20:30–31: One More Round on the Purpose of the Fourth Gospel," *JBL* 124 [2005]: 693–714). Carson argues that the Gospel's purpose is to *incite* belief. Against Carson, Gordon Fee has argued that the present subjunctive is here preferable and the Gospel was written to a believing community in order that they may continue in belief. He points to the antiquity of this reading's external attestation and its status as the *lectio difficilior*. Gordon Fee, "On the Text and Meaning of John 20,30–31," in *The Four Gospels: Festschrift Frans Neirynck*, 3 vols., ed. Frans van Segbroeck et al., BETL 100 (Leuven: Leuven University Press, 1992), 3:2193–2205. In my judgment, the decision about this verb does not affect my main point here.

now equipped to *remember* and believe, thereby realizing the narrative's explicit rhetorical goal.

## Conclusions: From Literary Analysis to Historical Reconstruction

The ambiguous relationship between Jesus's temple action/dialogue and Ps 69:9 should be resolved by employing a postresurrectional hermeneutic—the interpretive method that the narrative attempts to teach and persuade the reader toward by providing the opportunity for the reader to practice it. What I have done in this essay is to supply the methodological grounds on which we can affirm that the citation in 2:17 is indeed (at the level of discourse) a prefiguration of the resurrection as well as Jesus's death. In fact, my analysis has shown that the Johannine pericope demands such a reading. Interpreting the psalm citation as a reference only to Jesus's death falls short of the Gospel's rhetorical goal.

Thus far I have focused on narrative-critical concerns. By way of conclusion, I offer one implication of these findings for the historical project (though there are, of course, more possibilities) and for the larger question of the parting of the ways that motivates this volume. Situating the Gospel of John in its historical context—after the destruction of the Jerusalem temple in 70 CE—allows us to contextualize the Gospel's literary moves within its theology that understands Jesus as the new temple. The Gospel's post-70 CE casting of Jesus's resurrection as the temple rebuilt indicates the evangelist's judgment that God has not left Israel without a temple, despite the Roman destruction. The temple, as the primary locus of Israel's relations to God, is now, for John, located in the resurrected Christ. Jesus thus replaces the temple.[27] This claim is consistent with Alan Kerr's proposal that John's Gospel is in part a response to the destruction of the second temple: "With the demise of the Temple and its associated rituals John presents Jesus as the replacement and fulfillment of the Jewish Temple complex. In effect Jesus is John's answer to the urgent question following the fall of the temple in 70 CE, What now?"[28] By presenting Jesus

---

27. For examinations of the other temple references in the Gospel of John as confirming the notion of Jesus as the new temple, see especially Kerr, *Temple of Jesus' Body*; and Coloe, *God Dwells with Us*.

28. Kerr, *Temple of Jesus' Body*, 25–26.

as the raised temple, the Gospel of John envisions Jesus as the hope amidst potential hopelessness at the loss of the Jewish temple.[29]

After observing that the Gospel of John invokes Ps 69 and other psalms of the Righteous Sufferer, Menken notes that "throughout his gospel, John identifies Jesus with the Old Testament figure of the righteous sufferer who will be vindicated by God."[30] Yet Ps 69—significantly—ends with hopeful images of *communal* restoration. While the concluding images of Ps 69 certainly include the vindication of the suffering speaker, the focus is on saving *Zion* and rebuilding the *cities of Judah*. It is not the salvation of the righteous sufferer that is most explicit but the salvation and rebuilding of his community. For John, then, Jesus's resurrection is not only a rebuilding of the temple (of his body), but it is the redemption and rebuilding of the community of Israel. When we read according to the logic of the Johannine text, the resurrection emerges as a paramount moment in Israel's relationship to God. Jesus's triumph is Israel's victory as well.

The Gospel of John thereby provided one theological solution to a perceived historical problem. In so doing, the writer adopted a Jesus-centered reading practice of Israel's scriptures and participated in a broader conversation in which various groups affiliated with the God of Israel wrestled over who should be the proper inheritors of the traditions of ancient Israel and Judah—that is, whose way was the right way (compare with John 14:6). This widespread discursive project represents one thread, tangled rather than linear, that helps us as modern readers and historians to observe how our ancient literary texts forged small, local partings that provided templates for bigger, later partings. When we read the Gospel of John, we watch in action the development of the raw materials by which later gentile followers of Jesus would adopt the mantle of inheritance for themselves. And yet our own position as modern observers sets us up well to contextualize John's supersessionism as but one way in which ancient Jews interpreted their scriptures and but one way in which ancient Jews dealt with the loss of their temple. In such wrestling, ancient identities—ways—were made, remade, and eventually parted.

---

29. Such an observation does not discount—but rather exists in tandem with and in tension alongside—the famous (potentially) anti-Judaic elements in John's Gospel.

30. Menken, *Old Testament Quotations*, 42.

# Bibliography

Boer, Martinus C de. "Narrative Criticism, Historical Criticism, and the Gospel of John." *JSNT* 47 (1992): 35–48.

Brown, Raymond E. *The Gospel according to John I–XII.* AB 29. Garden City, NY: Doubleday, 1966.

Bryan, Christopher. "Shall We Sing Hallel in the Days of the Messiah? A Glance at John 2:1–3:21." *SLTJ* 29 (1985): 25–36.

Carson. D. A. "The Purpose of the Fourth Gospel: John 20:31 Reconsidered." *JBL* 106 (1987): 639–51.

———. "Syntactical and Text-Critical Observations on John 20:30–31: One More Round on the Purpose of the Fourth Gospel." *JBL* 124 (2005): 693–714.

Carter, Warren. *Seven Events That Shaped the New Testament World.* Grand Rapids: Baker Academic, 2012.

Coloe, Mary. *God Dwells with Us: Temple Symbolism in the Fourth Gospel.* Collegeville, MN: Liturgical Press, 2001.

Culpepper, R. Alan. *Anatomy of the Fourth Gospel: A Study in Literary Design.* Philadelphia: Fortress, 1983.

Fee, Gordon. "On the Text and Meaning of John 20,30–31." Pages 2193–2205 in vol. 3 of *The Four Gospels: Festschrift Frans Neirynck.* 3 vols. Edited by Frans van Segbroeck et al. BETL 100. Leuven: Leuven University Press, 1992.

Foley, John Miles. *Immanent Art: From Structure to Meaning in Traditional Oral Epic.* Bloomington: Indiana University Press, 1991.

Hays, Richard B. *Echoes of Scripture in the Letters of Paul.* New Haven: Yale University Press, 1989.

———. "Reading Scripture in Light of the Resurrection." Pages 216–38 in *The Art of Reading Scripture.* Edited by Ellen F. Davis and Richard B. Hays. Grand Rapids: Eerdmans, 2003.

Hollander, John. *The Figure of Echo: A Mode of Allusion in Milton and After.* Berkeley: University of California Press, 1981.

Iser, Wolfgang. *The Act of Reading: A Theory of Aesthetic Response.* Baltimore: Johns Hopkins University Press, 1978.

Kerr, Alan. *The Temple of Jesus' Body: The Temple Theme in the Gospel of John.* JSNTSup 220. London: Sheffield Academic, 2002.

Kingsbury, Jack Dean. *Matthew as Story.* Philadelphia: Fortress, 1986.

Koester, Helmut. *Introduction to the New Testament.* 2nd ed. 2 vols. New York: de Gruyter, 2000.

Krieger, Murray. *A Window to Criticism: Shakespeare's Sonnets and Modern Poetics*. Princeton: Princeton University Press, 1964.

Kysar, Robert. *The Fourth Evangelist and His Gospel: An Examination of Contemporary Scholarship*. Minneapolis: Augsburg, 1975.

Martyn, J. Louis. *History and Theology in the Fourth Gospel*. 3rd ed. Louisville: Westminster, 2003.

Menken, Maarten J. J. *Old Testament Quotations in the Fourth Gospel: Studies in Textual Form*. CBET 15. Kampen: Kok Pharos, 1996.

———. "Old Testament Quotations in the Gospel of John." Pages 29–45 in *New Testament Writers and the Old Testament: An Introduction*. Edited by John M. Court. London: SPCK, 2002.

Moore, Stephen D. *Poststructuralism and the New Testament: Derrida and Foucault at the Foot of the Cross*. Minneapolis: Fortress, 1994.

Powell, Mark Alan. *What Is Narrative Criticism?* Minneapolis: Fortress, 1990.

Reinhartz, Adele. " 'Common Judaism,' 'The Parting of the Ways,' and 'The Johannine Community.' " Pages 69–88 in *Orthodoxy, Liberalism, and Adaptation: Essays on Ways of Worldmaking in Times of Change from Biblical, Historical and Systematic Perspectives*. Edited by Bob Becker. Studies in Theology and Religion 15. Leiden: Brill, 2011.

Schuchard, Bruce. *Scripture within Scripture: The Interrelationship of Form and Function in the Explicit Old Testament Citations in the Gospel of John*. SBLDS 133. Atlanta: Scholars, 1992.

Stibbe, Mark W. G. *John as Storyteller: Narrative Criticism and the Fourth Gospel*. SNTSMS 73. Cambridge: Cambridge University Press, 1992.

# Christian Persecutions and the Parting of the Ways

## Bart D. Ehrman

It has become clear that the debate over the parting(s) of the ways has, in no small measure, devolved into a disagreement over terms: What is a Jew? What is a Christian? What constitutes a parting?[1] On one side are scholars who think in essentialized categories. A Jew is this. A Christian is that. A parting occurs when this is no longer that. Such a parting occurred in the year 70, or 96, or 135, or ... name your date.[2] On the other side are those who recognize fluidity and flux, for whom any relatively extensive interaction between adherents of one religious tradition and another indicates basic continuity. Contact, debate, or influence demonstrates that the religions are not so different and have not really parted company.

This scholarly contretemps will never be resolved to the satisfaction of all parties involved, in part because both positions tend toward the

---

It is with real pleasure that I write this article in honor of my long-time friend and colleague Joel Marcus, with whom I have worked, played, eaten, drunk, debated, and even agreed for well over thirty years now. Solid support from a trusted friend is an all-too rare commodity, and I have been privileged to enjoy it from Joel, over all this time. My thanks to my University of North Carolina colleague Hugo Mendez, my student Luke Drake, and my colleague Candida Moss for their bibliographical suggestions for this essay.

1. The two extremes are most obviously represented by James D. G. Dunn, *The Partings of the Ways: Between Christianity and Judaism and Their Significance for the Character of Christianity*, 2nd ed. (London: SCM, 2006), including the new preface, xi–xxx, which only partially mitigates the problem, and Adam H. Becker and Annette Yoshiko Reed, eds., *The Ways That Never Parted: Jews and Christians in Late Antiquity and the Early Middle Ages*, TSAJ 95 (Tübingen: Mohr Siebeck, 2003), whose essays, in the main, belie the provocative title.

2. A recent attempt to set *the* date is Marius Heemstra, *The Fiscus Judaicus and the Parting of the Ways*, WUNT 2/227 (Tübingen: Mohr Siebeck, 2010), who argues vigorously for 96 CE.

absolutist, in their own, different, ways. But the converse is true as well: both contain an important element of truth. Rather than enter into the debate by urging one of the sides or by joining forces with those who prefer some kind of tertium quid, this essay will examine the issue from a different perspective, not considering the (true?) essence of ancient Judaism (Judaisms) and of Christianity (Christianities) to see how they are either different or alike at one moment of antiquity or another, but looking at the matter from (ancient) outsiders' eyes, those of pagans who comment on Judaism and Christianity.

Broadly conceived, that topic would be the subject of a large book, not a short essay. So, for the purposes of this brief study, I will restrict myself to outside observers of the early Christian movement and focus, in particular, on how Christians were considered and construed by pagan antagonists. Just that matter alone could constitute a full monograph; and so what I will do is much simpler: I will look at the most historically significant moments of imperial opposition to the burgeoning Christian movement up to the early fourth century to see what they can tell us about the relationship of Christians to Jews, in the eyes of a wider world at large.

I will not be addressing this issue from the perspective of the Christian persecuted; as is well known, there was a long-standing tradition for Christians to blame Jews for the persecutions inflicted by the Romans—most notably in the Martyrdom of Pionius, and its model, the Martyrdom of Polycarp, and its own models the New Testament gospels (with respect to Jesus)—all the way back to the apostle Paul.[3] These are polemical treatments of considerable value for ascertaining Christian views. Their authors clearly saw a difference between themselves and the Jews. But they are not of similar help in knowing the views of the Roman persecutors.

My concern will instead be with the historical record of Roman imperial opposition. By that I mean not general acts of polemic, threat, social ostracizing, familial turmoil, and the like, but actual administrative actions against Christians that are connected in one way or another with Roman emperors, from Claudius to Diocletian. What can be shown—as has been noted before, though perhaps not sufficiently appreciated in the ongoing debates—is that in virtually this entire period (with the one

---

3. On Pionius and Polycarp, see E. Leigh Gibson, "Jewish Antagonism or Christian Polemic: The Case of the *Martyrdom of Pionius*," *JECS* 9 (2001): 339–58, and Gibson, "The Jews and Christians in the Martyrdom of Polycarp," in Becker and Reed, *The Ways That Never Parted*, 145–58. On Paul, see 1 Thess 2:14–16, which I take to be authentic.

question involving Claudius, to whom I will devote special attention), emperors knew, or thought they knew, the difference between Christians and Jews.[4] My thesis is that what was true of rulers was probably true, for the most part, of the people they ruled. Most pagans in the empire, most of the time for the first three centuries of Christianity, had no difficulty recognizing that it meant something different to be a Jew and to be a Christian.

That would seem to provide ammunition to the essentializing element in the debate over the parting of the ways, but that would be a misreading, for two reasons. The first is that I will not be arguing that Christianity actually was distinct from Judaism, only that it appeared that way to most outsiders most of the time throughout the period. The second is that, in one interesting respect, the Roman opposition to Christianity drove Christian thinkers and writers—and presumably the people who listened to them and were influenced by their views—to embrace one of the truly key elements of the Jewish religion, taking it over for themselves for purposes of their own. The Christians adopted for themselves—co-opted, one might say—the Jewish scriptures. That historical fact itself has interesting implications because the adherence to Jewish scriptures could make Christians appear in some ways to be like Jews. But since in adhering to these scriptures Christian apologists denied their Jewish counterparts the right also to appeal to them, they were very much at odds with Jews.

I will be arguing that the Christian attempt to secure the Jewish scriptures for themselves was itself again related to the outside perception of and pagan assault on this "new" religion, in a world prejudiced against novelty. In large part, it was a rear-guard apologetic move by Christians, who embraced the Old Testament—attempting to wrest it from the Jews— because it provided their religion with a claim to antiquity.

## Roman Persecutions and Perceptions

As one would expect, official persecution of Christians becomes better documented the later we move into the religion's first three centuries,

---

4. Among others who have made the point, see Shaye J. D. Cohen, *From the Maccabees to the Mishnah*, 3rd ed. (Louisville: Westminster John Knox, 2014), 234–36; James Carleton Paget, review of *The Fiscus Judaicus and the Parting of the Ways*, by Marius Heemstra, *JEH* 4 (2011): 354; and, much earlier, E. A. Judge, "Judaism and the Rise of Christianity: A Roman Perspective," *TynBul* 45 (1994): 355–68.

when opposition became more widespread and determined.[5] So it may be most convenient to start at the end of the period with the decade-long "Great Persecution" under Diocletian, driven principally by his caesars in the East. We have adequate documentation concerning the main contours of this final confrontation of Christianity and empire in part because Christian intellectuals who lived through it, chiefly Eusebius and Lactantius, give us the essential details.[6]

The persecution was spottily enforced—scarcely at all in the West, under Constantius—but in places it was severe. It involved the well-known four edicts, which show clearly that the persecutors' intention was to wipe out the Christian church. Under the first edict, churches were closed and scriptures confiscated; under the second, Christian leaders were arrested; under the third, they were required to perform sacrifices to pagan gods in order to be released; and under the fourth, all citizens of the empire (except Jews) were (where the edict was enforced) required to sacrifice. The edicts themselves show clearly how imperial officers—at least Diocletian and Galerius, and then Maximin—perceived the Christians and the threat they posed. The Christians could not survive without their meetings, their scriptures, and their church officials; in particular, Christians refused to sacrifice to the gods. This refusal, as we will see, drove all the persecutions from Trajan onward.

By the time of Diocletian's persecution, the presence of Christians—cells of nonconformists who refused to worship the Roman gods—was an increasing problem. It is usually estimated that, by now, Christians numbered some five to seven million in an empire of sixty million.[7] That estimate, which goes back to Harnack, is probably too large, but even if it is halved, it remains that a significant portion of the empire had, at this point, abandoned the worship of the traditional gods. The fact that Christian leaders, and then all the millions of Christian laity, could escape punishment by performing ritual sacrifice reveals the underlying threat

---

5. The literature on early Christian martyrdom is massive. For a recent full study, see Candida Moss, *Ancient Christian Martyrdom: Diverse Practices, Theologies, and Traditions*, ABRL (New Haven: Yale University Press, 2012), and the literature she cites there.

6. See Eusebius, *Hist. eccl.* 8; Lactantius, *Death of the Christian Persecutors*.

7. See my discussion of Christian numbers in Bart D. Ehrman, *The Triumph of Christianity* (New York: Simon & Schuster, 2018), appendix. The book itself is for a general audience, but the appendix is also geared toward specialists.

posed by the Christians. This was a world in which our own concepts of religion and politics were inextricably intertwined (on both the practical and linguistic level: as often noted, there are no Greek or Latin words that neatly designate and differentiate between the two concepts). It was still widely believed that since the gods provided all that was important to live and survive—individually and collectively—and that all they required was due attention through established modes of worship (prayer and sacrifice), anyone who failed in their cultic duties, and any community that housed such persons, could be subject to divine wrath, which could take any one of many unpleasant forms.

From a century earlier, Tertullian famously summarized the religious sentiment and fear that applied for our entire period:

> They think the Christians the cause of every public disaster, of every affliction with which the people are visited. If the Tiber rises as high as the city walls, if the Nile does not send its waters up over the fields, if the heavens give no rain, if there is an earthquake, if there is famine or pestilence, straightway the cry is, "Away with the Christians to the lion!" (*Apol.* 40 [Glover])

But why the Christians in particular? Jews also were (in)famous for not reverencing the traditional gods. But, as is well known, they were always seen as the exception to the rule—originally, possibly, for political reasons going back to Jewish support for the winning sides at the end of the Republic. But throughout our period, they were excused because they followed their own very ancient customs (even if they were considered bizarre), and so they posed no real threat.[8]

My point here is a simple one: the Great Persecution was not directed against everyone in the empire who refused to worship the traditional gods; it was directed only against Christians. Jews were exempt. No one in the imperial apparatus appears to have had any difficulty distinguishing one group from the other.

---

8. So, from the beginning of our period, see Claudius's letter to the Alexandrians from the beginning of his reign, where he directs them to "show themselves forbearing and kindly towards the Jews ... and dishonor none of the rites observed by them in the worship of their god, but allow them to observe their customs as in the time of the Deified Augustus, which customs I also ... have sanctioned" (edict of Nov. 10, 41 CE; translation of John Granger Cook, *Roman Attitudes toward the Christians: From Claudius to Hadrian*, WUNT 261 [Tübingen: Mohr Siebeck, 2010], 12).

From here we can move backward to earlier persecutions, but we will need to restrict ourselves only to some of the key moments involving Decius, Trajan, Nerva, Nero, and, possibly, Claudius.[9]

In the fall or early winter of 249 CE, the emperor Decius issued a decree requiring all inhabitants of the empire to perform an animal sacrifice to the gods (any god they chose), taste the meat, swear they had always sacrificed, and receive a certificate from a local official who had observed their actions.[10] Almost always, this is taken to be the first empire-wide persecution of Christians, but Roman historian James Rives has shown that this is probably a misreading of the situation.[11] Christians were not the explicit target of the decree, even if they were the ones who most frequently paid the price for noncompliance.

The decree came right in the middle of the "crisis of the third century," a truly awful period of economic crises, barbarian invasions, break-away states, and imperial assassinations, one after the other. Decius appears to have wanted to return the empire to its religious roots in the face of turmoil and upheaval, believing, in the words of Rives, that "people were neglecting the proper worship of the gods to such an extent that radical steps were needed to reassert the importance of traditional cult acts."[12] Not only Christians, but also some philosophers, their followers, and other newer cults refused sacrifice. A return to ancestral religion was a move to restore the world from chaos.

Yet here again there was an exception clause. Jews were almost certainly not required to participate.[13] Christians, on the other hand—or at least those who did not take measures to escape notice—from leaders such as Cyprian on down, were persecuted. As was true a half century later, under Diocletian, in 249–251 CE imperial authorities on all levels from the emperor to local magistrates appear to have had no difficulty recognizing who were Jews and who Christians.

---

9. The other known imperial interventions—Valerian, Marcus Aurelius (sanctioning the persecution of Lyons and Vienne), Hadrian (the rescript given by Justin)—would simply confirm, not complicate, the results.

10. We have four contemporary sources of information: letters of Cyprian, letters of Dionysius of Alexandria quoted by Eusebius, the Passion of Pionius, and, most notably, forty-five of the actual libelli. See James B. Rives, "The Decree of Decius and the Religion of Empire," *JRS* 39 (1999): 135–54.

11. Rives, "Decree of Decius."

12. Rives, "Decree of Decius," 151.

13. Rives, "Decree of Decius," 138 n.16, with reasons.

We might call the grounds just surveyed for Christian persecution in the third and fourth centuries the "sacrifice rule": licit religious practices involve sacrifices to the traditional gods, and anyone refusing sacrifice adhered to an illicit, and punishable, cult. The same applies to earlier times as well, going back at least to Trajan and, given Pliny's comments about his confrontations with Christians in his province of Bithynia, almost certainly earlier still (Pliny, *Ep.* 10.96).[14] If local magistrates or provincial governors sensed a problem with Christians, there was one way to deal with them: force them to sacrifice to the traditional gods. If they complied, they obviously were not Christians. If they refused, they were to be punished. It scarcely needs to be pointed out that this modus operandi is attested abundantly in Christian sources as well, particularly the martyrologies, some of which appear to be based on actual *Acta*, official accounts of the trial proceedings.[15]

The problem Christians posed in official imperial eyes was not that they were guilty of the infamous *flagitia* (e.g., socially disruptive and murderous orgies, infanticide, cannibalism), although these may well have been the widespread suspicion of the pagan masses and possibly their motivation for appealing to imperial intervention. In a sense, Christians were never charged with any standard crimes. A crime is normally punishable after having been committed. When Christians were put on trial, they were not tortured to make them confess to a crime, so they could receive their due justice. They were tortured to force them to stop being Christian. The crime was *being* a Christian, not *having been* a Christian. Once someone apostasized, they were released, with no penalty. That is unlike any other crime: a murderer cannot be released from punishment by declaring that even though he had once committed murder, he is doing so no longer. Christians, though, were released on just those grounds.

---

14. Pliny coyly indicates that he has never been at earlier trials and does not know from their precedent how to proceed; but the fact that he has very clear ideas about the matter suggests that his comments were a rear-guard action in case the current emperor had other ideas about how to deal with the situation.

15. The best source continues to be Herbert Musurillo, *Acts of the Christian Martyrs* (Oxford: Oxford University Press, 1972); on some of the accounts going back to *Acta*, see Gary Bisbee, *The Pre-Decian Acts of Martyrs and Comentarii* (Philadelphia: Fortress, 1988).

The requirement was sacrifice. This is the much-remarked test used by Pliny, in the best-documented and most widely-discussed case.[16] The crime Christians were committing was being a Christian. They were punished "for the name." But the reason the name was a problem was not because Pliny or (he suggests) his predecessors did not like the name per se. It was a problem because of what the name meant: anyone who claimed the name worshiped only one God and refused to honor the traditional gods, through sacrifice. That made it very easy to detect who was at fault and who was not. Anyone who denied being a Christian simply had to prove it by performing a sacrifice to an image of the emperor and the gods.

Once again, Jews were almost certainly exempt. It is significant that now we are no longer in the early fourth or mid-third century, but in the very early second. Pliny and Trajan appear to have had no difficulty distinguishing Christians from Jews, already in 112 CE. Why was that?

Recent studies have shown that it may well have been because of what happened less than twenty years earlier, under Nerva. At issue is the *fiscus Judaicus*, as it was altered in 96 CE in a way so as to shift the definition of what it meant to be a Jew—in the eyes of Roman imperial authorities—away from a question of ethnic origins to a question of religious practices.[17] In the eyes of Roman authorities, Christians, whatever their ethnic origin, did not do the religious things that Jews did. They were therefore not Jews and therefore not granted exceptional legal status. (Again, I am not arguing that no Christians did practice Judaism; I am indicating that the typical Christian was seen by outsiders as something other than a Jew.)

The *fiscus Judaicus* is well known and much discussed, including a fairly recent monograph devoted entirely to it by Marius Heemstra.[18] There is much both to agree and disagree with in Heemstra's work, but for our purposes the broad historical outlines of the course of the *fiscus* are secure.[19] When Jerusalem fell in 70 CE, the emperor Vespasian shifted the annual temple tax paid by Jews, not just in Judea but throughout the

---

16. See the very full recent discussion (of every aspect of the account) in Cook, *Roman Attitudes*, 138–251.

17. See n. 18. Among older works, fundamental and highly instructive still (despite his later changes of opinions) is Martin Goodman, "Nerva, the Fiscus Judaicus, and Jewish Identity," *JRS* 79 (1989): 40–44.

18. Heemstra, *Fiscus Judaicus*.

19. Probably the most controversial claim is that the date of the "Parting of the Ways" can now be set at 96 CE.

world, to a kind of Jewish tax, to be paid by all Jews, male and female, into the Roman treasury. Initially the money was used to fund the rebuilding of the recently destroyed temple of Jupiter Capitolinus, but the tax continued long after the temple was completed. The *fiscus* was the administrative mechanism for collecting the tax. The tax itself was, in a sense, a cost of being a Jew.

But who counted as a Jew? It appears that the enforcement of the *fiscus* under Vespasian was somewhat lax, but his son and successor Domitian tightened the screws. In the words of Suetonius, in his *Life of Domitian*:

> Besides other taxes, that on the Jews was levied with the utmost rigor [*acerbissime*] and those were prosecuted who without publicly acknowledging that faith yet lived as Jews, as well as those who concealed their origin and did not pay the tribute levied upon their people. (12.2)[20]

It thus appears that under Vespasian there were both secret Jews, who practiced Judaism without acknowledging it publicly, and (to no great surprise) Jewish tax evaders. For officials involved with detecting members of the latter group, there were some relatively simple, if occasionally humiliating, modes of detection. Suetonius recounts an event he had personally observed as a young man: a suspected elderly Jew, who had not been paying the tax, was brought into court and forcibly disrobed, to see if he was circumcised (*Dom.* 12). He was. He had to pay the tax.

For our purposes, more important than Domitian's enhanced enforcement policies is what happened after his assassination. When his successor Nerva ascended to the throne, he wanted to curry favor with various groups of his subjects and so reversed a number of Domitian's harsher policies, including those connected with the *fiscus Judaicus*. Among the coins Nerva issued are those that announce: *Fisci Iudaici calumnia sublata*, which Martin Goodman translates as: "The malicious accusation with regard to the Jewish tax has been removed."[21]

It is not that Nerva brought the *fiscus Judaicus* to a grinding halt. He simply backed off the overly-rigorous collection policies of his predecessor. Now, if a person was born to a Jewish family, she or he was not necessarily taxed. The tax applied only to those who were actively and regularly

---

20. Translation of Heemstra, *Fiscus Judaicus*, 24.

21. Martin Goodman, "Diaspora Reactions to the Destruction of the Temple," in Becker and Reed, *The Ways That Never Parted*, 33.

engaged in established Jewish practice. As Dio Cassius tells us later, these were Jews who continued to observe their "ancestral customs" (*Hist. rom.* 66.7.2). That meant that Jews who apostasized and abandoned their traditions would no longer pay the tax. In the eyes of the state, they were no longer Jews.

For that reason, being a Jew (in the view of the imperial administration) no longer involved ethnic origins but religious practices.[22] These practices almost certainly entailed those aspects of Judaism widely recognized in the culture at large as making Jews strange and distinct: circumcision, Sabbath observance, kosher food laws, Jewish festivals, and so on.[23]

Obviously the lines could be blurred, even for imperial eyes. But the larger point is that being a Jew meant something religiously. We have no record of any Christians being subject to the *fiscus Judaicus*. The reason is clear: Christians were not considered to be Jews. As Cohen has expressed it: "Christianity was now seen by the Romans as non-Judaism.... One consequence of this fateful step is that Christians lost the legal protections that Jews had enjoyed for decades under Roman rule."[24]

My main objection to Cohen's phrasing is that it presupposes that Christians previously *had* enjoyed those protections, and that, I think, is difficult to prove. It does seem to be true that, as Goodman has pointed out, "a clear distinction between Jews and Christians begins regularly to appear in pagan Roman texts after A.D. 96."[25] On the other hand, one need scarcely point out that there simply are no pagan Roman texts that mention Christianity *prior* to 96 CE or, for that matter, nearly fifteen years afterward (Pliny, *Ep.* 10.96, is the first). So it may not be the case that Nerva's relaxation of the *fiscus Judaicus* is the absolute turning point in the parting of the ways, as Heemstra and others have tried to argue.

Moreover, Heemstra is almost certainly not right to claim that "it was in the interest of Domitian's successor Nerva and the Roman authorities in general to be able to make a clear distinction between Judaism and Christianity."[26] Such claims are far too Christian-centric and assume that

---

22. As Cohen has succinctly put it (*Maccabees to the Mishnah*, 236) the reform of the *fiscus* involved redefining "Judaism as a religion."

23. See, for example, Judith Lieu, "The Parting of the Ways: Theological Construct or Historical Reality?," *JSNT* 56 (1994): 110.

24. Cohen, *Maccabees to the Mishnah*, 236.

25. Goodman, "Diaspora Reactions," 33.

26. Heemstra, *Fiscus Judaicus*, 199.

Christianity was a far, far bigger nightmare for the Romans than in fact it was at the end of the first century. Part of the problem is that scholars have no realistic conception of the number of Christians at the time. There are compelling reasons for thinking that out of an empire of some sixty million, no more than eight to ten thousand at most were Christian at the time.[27] Despite the exorbitant claims of later Christian authors—such as Tertullian, who maintained there were more Christians than pagans in the empire of his day! (*Apol.* 37)—the massive importance of Christianity in later times simply cannot be retrojected onto this earlier period. At the end of the first century, most people in the empire had never heard of Christians, let alone felt threatened by them.

Even so, once imperial authorities had heard of Christians, they appear to have no difficulty differentiating Christians and Jews. The finding is confirmed yet earlier in the familiar account in book 15 of the *Annales* of Tacitus of the persecution of the Christians in Rome under Nero (Tacitus, *Ann.* 15.44.2–5).[28] It would be a mistake to think that Tacitus himself is differentiating between Christians and Jews because he is living after the tax reform of Nerva. He is recounting an event that happened three decades before the reform, and there is no reason to suspect that he has altered its essential character in light of what was to transpire later.[29]

I do not need to recount the familiar details of the episode at any length here. The main point is that this was not a persecution against the Christians for their refusal to worship state gods or for engaging in whatever religious practices they did engage in. There were two batches of arrests. The first involved persons suspected of setting Rome on fire. Tacitus appears to have thought that Nero himself may have been responsible for the fire, but whether true or not, he chose the Christians as his scapegoats. They were not, in any event, charged with engaging in illegal religious activities but for arson. There would not need to be many Christians considered responsible—even in the popular imagination, a handful could have started the fires. But from what was learned from these people, a

---

27. Ehrman, *Triumph*, appendix; see the discussion of Christians in the time of Claudius below.

28. Discussed in detail, with full apparatus, in Cook, *Roman Attitudes*, 29–111.

29. The recent claim by Brent Shaw that the Neronian Persecution never occurred ("The Myth of the Neronian Persecution," *JRS* 105 [2015]: 73–100) has now been answered by Christopher P. Jones, "The Historicity of the Neronian Persecution: A Response to Brent Shaw," *NTS* 63 (2017): 146–52.

second group of Christians was rounded up, because of their *odio humani generis*. Almost always this is taken to mean that the Christians "hated the human race," although it could equally mean that "the human race hated them." In either case, the problem is not explicitly religious but social; it is not that they refuse to sacrifice but that they were a distinct and detested social group.[30]

Again, it is clear that this is a group understood to be completely distinct from the large Jewish community in Rome. That does not necessarily mean that there were no Jews who worshiped as Christians or Christians who worshiped as Jews. But it does mean that in imperial eyes, it was the Christians who were the problem, not Jews. The communities were distinct. As Judith Lieu has put it "Nero's actions suggest that Christians were already being viewed as a self-standing group open to the suspicion of disloyalty."[31]

Did those suspicions originate in Rome at the time, in the days of Nero? I am afraid that it is impossible to say. The only other incident that is commonly claimed to involve Christians in Rome is highly fraught, for reasons almost never considered. This is the episode referred to so enigmatically by Suetonius in his *Life of Claudius*, when the emperor expelled the Jews from Rome "at the instigation of Chrestus [*impulsere Chresto*]" (*Claud.* 25.4).[32]

That something happened early in Claudius's reign involving Jews in the capital city is independently attested in Acts 18:2, which states that Aquila and Priscilla had come to Corinth because "Claudius had commanded all the Jews to leave Rome." Often this elusive reference is taken, whether wittingly or not, as a hermeneutical key to Suetonius's comment. In the interpretation common among New Testament scholars and historians of earliest Christianity, Suetonius has made a simple, but common, spelling mistake. Even though he knows about and comments on Christians elsewhere, spelling their designation correctly, in this passage he was not referring to someone named Chrestus (a common name, especially among slaves and freedmen) but to Christ.[33]

---

30. In ancient eyes, these two things would have been related.
31. Lieu, "Parting of the Ways," 111.
32. Full discussion, with conclusions that I will be rejecting, in Cook, *Roman Attitudes*, 11–28.
33. Recently and at length, Cook, *Roman Attitudes*, 15–22.

Obviously, the reasoning goes, Suetonius could not mean that Christ himself created some kind of disturbance in Rome in the days of Claudius. He had been executed nearly twenty years earlier and had certainly never made a visit to Rome. So the "instigation of Chrestus" must refer to a social disturbance—riots in the streets?—between the Jewish followers of Christ and their non-Christian Jewish counterparts. Possibly there were massive disturbances in the synagogues around the city as Christians took the opportunity of Sabbath worship to proclaim their newfound faith. Possibly other Jews found such proclamation highly disturbing. Possibly they came to blows. Possibly there were uprisings. Possibly…. Well, historians can use their imaginations, and they often have.

It may be useful to take a more sober approach to the issue and ask a question of basic demographics. How many Jews were in Rome at the time, and how many Christians?

One of the most recent assessments, by Heemstra, concludes that the event under Claudius took place in 41 CE.[34] We do not have reliable figures for the Jewish population of Rome at the time (or for Rome itself, for that matter), but John Barclay's impressive study of Jews in the diaspora notes that common estimates range between twenty thousand and sixty thousand.[35] So let us simply suppose that it is somewhere in the middle, possibly thirty to fifty thousand Jews.

How many Christians? This is the point that almost no one appears to think about. We are talking about followers of Jesus in Rome itself, roughly a decade after the crucifixion. In relatively recent times, the one scholar who has made a sustained effort at estimating Christian population figures was not an expert on antiquity but a sociologist of religion, Rodney Stark. His popular study, *The Rise of Christianity*, is problematic on many grounds, as reviewers expert in the field have vigorously noted.[36] But one thing a sociologist can do is crunch numbers, and what Stark argues is that

---

34. Heemstra, *Fiscus Judaicus*, 25, based on the arguments of Rainer Riesner, *Die Frühzeit des Apostels Paulus: Studien zur Chronologie, Missionsstrategie und Theologie*, WUNT 71 (Tübingen: Mohr Siebeck, 1994).

35. John M. G. Barclay, *Jews in the Mediterranean Diaspora: From Alexander to Trajan (323 BCE–117 CE)* (Berkeley: University of California Press, 1996), 295 n. 32. My thanks to John for this reference.

36. Rodney Stark, *The Rise of Christianity: How the Obscure, Marginal Jesus Movement Became the Dominant Religious Force in the Western World in a Few Centuries* (San Francisco: HarperSanFrancisco, 1996). For response, see the articles published together in volume six of the *Journal of Early Christian Studies*, especially Elizabeth A.

in order to grow from a tiny group at the start of the Christian movement to become about 7 to 10 percent of the Roman population at the beginning of the fourth century, the church would need to grow only at a rate of 40 percent per decade. That is not an unreasonable rate, and it would not require either massive evangelistic rallies or miracles. It is only 3.4 percent a year. If you have a hundred Christians this year, you need only three or four more next year.

There are real and tangible problems with Stark's numbers, but the general concept and the basic progressions are not implausible.[37] What is implausible is his starting number. He assumes that in 40 CE there were a thousand Christians in the world. For this number, he is influenced by the manifest exaggerations of the book of Acts, which is enthusiastic, to say the least, in its estimate of early church growth (with well over eight thousand Christians in Jerusalem just a couple of months after Jesus's death; see Acts 2:41, 47; 4:4). But looked at just on Starks's own term, there is a huge problem with his opening number. Suppose the New Testament is correct (and when it comes to this particular datum, it is hard to see how it could not be) that the earliest believers in Jesus's death and resurrection—say, right away after the resurrection happened—comprised something like a dozen men and a handful of women. That would mean there were some twenty believers in the year 30 CE. To get to a thousand people a decade later would entail a growth rate of 4,900 percent. Are we to think that for three centuries the church grew at a rate of 40 percent, except for its first decade, when it grew at a rate of 4,900 percent?

Perhaps we should try to be more realistic. Suppose the early enthusiasm of the church was indeed such that the earliest believers really did make lots of converts right away—say, among people who had been impressed by Jesus's preaching while he was alive. Let us also say that rather than 40 percent that first decade (or 25 percent or 60 percent—pick a reasonable number for the following years), the growth rate was a whopping 1000 percent. That would mean that by the accession of Claudius there would be something like 200–250 Christians in the world. In the entire world. Most of them would be located in or near the homeland of Jesus and the disciples themselves: Jerusalem, elsewhere in Judea, up in Galilee, off in Antioch, away in Damascus, possibly in Nabatea. Naturally

---

Castelli, "Gender, Theory, and the Rise of Christianity: A Response to Rodney Stark," *JECS* 6 (1998): 227–57.

37. See my full discussion in *Triumph*, appendix.

some few others would be scattered elsewhere, and if you had to choose one other likely place of residence outside the environs of Palestine, Rome would be an obvious choice.

But how many Christians would there be there: ten? twenty? thirty? Assume, as is probably safe, that all of these are Jews who continue worshiping in the synagogues. How many synagogues are involved: one? two? three?

Now think about the implications of these figures for the comments of Suetonius. Is it likely that a few followers of Jesus in one, two, or three synagogues (several followers in each one?) created such havoc "at the instigation of Chrestus" that Claudius expelled, say, forty or fifty thousand Jews from Rome? I do not see how it is at all plausible.

Possibly one could argue that Suetonius did not mean that Claudius expelled *all* the Jews from Rome (despite Acts 18:2), but only those who were rioting over Chrestus. But if the numbers are as small as they seem to be (and I think a 1,000 percent growth is a wildly enthusiastic estimate[38]), then we are talking about handfuls of people. Surely this would not be something that would come to the attention of the emperor, on one hand, or more importantly, to his biographer seventy years later, on the other. Suetonius is talking about a major disruption in Jewish life in Rome in 41 CE.

For these reasons, I think it simply is not plausible to think that Suetonius was recording an incident involving uprisings caused by the followers of Christ, misspelled as Chrestus (itself, as I said, a common name). What is the alternative? That there were problems caused by someone named Chrestus. This does not at all seem to be to be a "recourse of despair" charged by Cook;[39] it seems the only sensible solution. Thus, I agree with Barclay's terse comment on the view that Chrestus refers to Christ: "It is possible that this discovery of a Christian dimension is a mirage."[40]

What about Aquila and Priscilla, then? If in fact Acts is right that they were expelled from Rome, then it was not because they were Christians but because they were Jews. In other words, they were still active in a synagogue and were practicing Jews, even as they were followers of Jesus. But does this not indicate that Roman imperial officials in 41 CE did not clearly differentiate between Christians and Jews? In one sense,

---

38. See my discussion in *Triumph*, appendix.
39. Cook, *Roman Attitudes*, 28.
40. Barclay, *Jews in the Mediterranean Diaspora*, 304.

yes, it probably does mean that, but not for the reason one might think. Claudius probably did not differentiate between the two groups because he had never heard of the Christians. There were problems among (some of) the Jewish population, and so he expelled them.

Twenty-three years later, in the days of Nero, the Christians were known to exist as troublesome social groups in the city. Strikingly, as we have seen, they were known not to be Jews. Why were they not Jews (if early Priscilla and Aquila were)? In my judgment, it is because most Christians by that point—in Rome or elsewhere—in fact were not Jews and never had been Jews.

This view, too, cuts against the grain of a good deal of scholarship,[41] but I think it has support from the New Testament itself. It is certainly the case that the earliest communities of which we have any definite knowledge are made up of followers of Jesus from pagan extraction. These, of course, are the churches established by Paul, and what was explicitly true of the former idol-worshipers in Thessalonica and Corinth (1 Thess 1:9–10; 1 Cor 12:2) was almost certainly true of his other churches as well.

I would maintain it was also true of the great majority of the churches whose existence we can infer from the New Testament. If we begin by returning to the city of Rome, we have hard evidence. Paul not only had not founded the church, but he had never visited it. These were not his own pagan converts. Even so, as is well known, in the final chapter of his letter to the church, he greets twenty-six people by name. Six, and only six, of these he identifies as "of his own race," that is, as fellow Jews (Rom 16:7, 11, 21). Since this is his way of distinguishing these from all the others, we can be assured that the rest were originally pagans. Rome may have had a mixed Christian community, but it was not equally mixed. It was predominantly gentile.

So too is the case for most of the other communities implied by the authors of the New Testament. The data are too well known to require any full explication here. Mark presupposes that his readers do not know about Jewish customs—and he himself is ill informed about them (Mark 7:3). He was a gentile. They were gentiles. Luke's stress on the gentile mission, among other things, clearly suggests both he and his readers are not

---

41. See the rather astounding claim of Philip S. Alexander that in the mid-first century, Christianity was *entirely* within the realm of Judaism. "'The Parting of the Ways' from the Perspective of Rabbinic Judaism," in *Jews and Christians: The Parting of the Ways A.D. 70 to 135*, ed. James D. G. Dunn (Grand Rapids: Eerdmans, 1999), 2.

from Jewish extraction. One could debate about the Fourth Gospel (and many have), but it is reasonable to think that John's indiscriminate labeling of the Jews as the enemies of Jesus, his references to "your law," and his scattered but vehement anti-Jewish polemic all suggest that, even if his community originated as a group of Jews alienated from the synagogue, by the time the Gospel was published the community had no ongoing connection with non-Christians and probably was made up itself of non-Jewish converts. Among the gospels that leaves only Matthew, the "most Jewish" of the gospels—but one that is famously anti-Jewish as well. It is striking and often noted that in Jesus's insistence that his followers "keep the law" better than the scribes and Pharisees, he never refers to those features of Jewish practice that were recognized in the wider environment as intrinsic and distinctive to Jewish people (circumcision, Sabbath, kosher foods, festivals, and so forth). He instead urges his followers to adhere to social behaviors (involving such things as anger, lust, reactions to violence, and so on) more stringently than required by scripture. Would outsiders see such excessively moral people necessarily as Jews?

For other books of the New Testament, the matter is even more clear. Hebrews, for example, is written to a community that had to be instructed in the essential features of traditional Judaism when they converted (6:1–2); 1 Peter is written to former idol worshipers (1:18); the Johannine epistles show no interest in or knowledge of the practices of Judaism, but the recipients have to be warned about idols (1 John 5:21).

It would be profligate to insist that every author of the New Testament (except for Paul) was originally gentile or that there were absolutely no Jews worshiping in their Christian communities. But it is equally profligate, and simply wrong, to claim that most of the converts to the Christian faith in the first century were from Jewish extraction or that most early Christians practiced Judaism. They were not and did not.

At the same time, Christians—whether Jewish or gentile—did adhere to several features of traditional Judaism, including, most obviously, monolatry and certain ethical principles that are distinctively, although not uniquely, Jewish. But why these principles? In no small measure because they were taught in scripture. That takes us to the second topic I want to address in this essay, which I can cover in much shorter order. Even though Christians were easily distinguished from Jews by imperial authorities from Nero to Domitian, Christians embraced aspects of Judaism that made them, in some specific ways, *like* Jews. No aspect is more striking or historically significant than the Christian adoption—or cooption—of the

Jewish scriptures. This decision to have an Old Testament is part and parcel of numerous questions involving Christian-Jewish relations. What is not as widely recognized is a very important obverse, that it is intimately connected with Christian-Roman relations as well.

### Romans, Christians, and Jewish Scriptures

Why do Christians have an Old Testament? There are numerous reasons that can be and have been given over the years. Jesus himself was a Jew, as were his followers, and for all of them the Hebrew Bible were *the* scriptures. The Christian church started out as a group of Jewish followers who not only adhered to Jewish scripture but taught their followers to do so as well.

Over time, though, more and more gentiles converted to the faith. Many of these may well have been introduced for the first time to scripture at that point—unless they had already been connected with synagogues—and saw in it a revelation of God.[42] Eventually, theological controversies arose that challenged the centrality of the Jewish scriptures for the Christian faith, driving Christian intellectuals to debate the utility of maintaining a patently Jewish book for what was becoming in some circles a notably anti-Jewish religion.

In proto-orthodox communities of the second century, an adherence to the Old Testament proved invaluable in the battle with various heretical movements. Against Marcion and his declaration that there were two gods, that the God of the Jews was not the God of Jesus, heresiologists such as Irenaeus and Tertullian insisted that there was continuity between the God revealed in the Old Testament and the God they worshiped. Against Sethians, Valentinians, and other Gnostic groups, these same proto-orthodox defenders of the faith insisted on the oneness of God and on the inherent goodness of the created order, both revealed emphatically in the Old Testament.

Such authors had to explain to outsiders (and to their own readers) why they claimed for themselves a set of scriptures whose laws they chose not

---

42. It is often claimed that the majority of early converts came out of the ranks of the God-fearers. I think that is difficult to prove, and precisely the features that show the implied audiences of the letters of Paul, Mark, Luke, Hebrews, 1 Peter, 1 John, etc.—mentioned above—speak against it. A number of—most?—converts in the mid-first century onward had been idol-worshipers.

to follow. It seems from the distance of centuries that they could well have jettisoned the Jewish Bible and still found ways to affirm the oneness of God and the goodness of his creation. But there was one compelling reason they could not do so. Embracing and affirming the Old Testament as their own—claiming that it attested and supported their own religious claims and theological beliefs—provided the proto-orthodox with an unassailable (in their view) anchor to the past. It gave their religion antiquity.

These second- and third-century Christians lived in a world where philosophical and religious claims required an ancient lineage. What was new, recent, and novel could not be true. In antiquity, nothing was respected so much as antiquity. Without the ancient credentials provided by a set of ancient writings, the Christian truth claims would have been puffs of smoke.[43]

So much becomes clear on page after page of the early Christian apologists who were defending their faith in the face of pagan opposition. This particular opposition did not principally come in the form of official engagement and actual persecution. It was a war of words. But these were words that were to determine the course and fate of the Christian tradition. Pagans leveled social, ethical, and religious charges against the Christians, and the (very few) intelligentsia among the Christians responded, as early, apparently, as Quadratus and moving up to such surviving authors as Justin, Tatian, Athenagoras, Theophilus, Tertullian, Origen, and others.

Most of the social and ethical charges could simply be denied. How, asked the Christian defenders of the faith, can you accuse us of incestuous ritual orgies? We teach that it is wrong even to commit lust in the heart. You say that we perform infanticide? We do not even allow abortions. You charge us with eating babies? We do not even expose them. On and on, page after page of the apologists.

But how could the equally serious religious charge of novelty be warded off? In one way only: by claiming ancient roots. Therein lay the problem. The religion in fact was not ancient; Jesus died at the hands of Pontius Pilate, recently, during the reign of Tiberius. So Christians had

---

43. A standard and still valuable treatment is Arthur Droge, *Homer or Moses: Early Christian Interpretations of the History of Culture*, HUT 26 (Tübingen: Mohr Siebeck, 1989). A more recent and concise statement can be found in Wayne C. Kannaday, *Apologetic Discourse and the Scribal Tradition: Evidence of the Influence of Apologetic Interests on the Text of the Canonical Gospels*, TCS 5 (Atlanta: Scholars Press, 2004), 1–57.

to appeal to another source of antiquity. They did so by affirming the Old Testament and claiming that its authors—starting all the way back with Moses—were the actual founders of their ancient faith.

Such claims presumably did not sit well with Jews who knew of them. So it is no surprise that some of the same Christian authors who engaged in apologetic discourse to ward off charges of pagans also produced polemical tractates attacking Jews.[44] Sometimes the appeals to scripture itself carried anti-Jewish sentiments. Often these were expressed with vitriol, as in Melito's *Paschal Homily*; other times they appear (on the surface) to be reasoned and even-handed (for example, Justin's *Dialogue with Trypho*). In every case, it is clear that the Christian authors needed to latch on to the Jewish scriptures and deprive them from Jews to defend against the pagan charge of novelty.

The charge can be seen with particular clarity in the apology of the late-second century Theophilus, where he addresses his supposed pagan reader ("supposed" because almost certainly Theophilus, like the other apologists, is actually addressing Christians): you "are still of the opinion that the word of truth is an idle tale, and suppose that our writings are recent and modern" (*Ad Autolycum* 3.1 [trans. Dods, *ANF* 2:111]). Or there is the charge against the Christians leveled by Celsus, as quoted by Origen: "In fact they worship to an extravagant degree this man who appeared recently" (*Cels.* 8.12).[45]

Similar charges lie at the heart of almost all the Christian apologies, and the response is reiterated time and again: Christianity is as old as Moses, who wrote long before any of the pagan authors. Justin states the case succinctly: in the ancient prophets Christ was "foretold in truth, before He actually appeared, first five thousand years before, then three thousand, then two thousand, then one thousand and finally eight hundred. For in succeeding generations new prophets rose time and again" (*1 Apol.* 31).[46] Justin proceeds to point to prophecy after prophecy in scripture to the birth, life, death, and resurrection of Jesus. What is more, Justin charges that Plato and others "plagiarized from our teachers" in his

---

44. One naturally thinks immediately of Justin and Tertullian.

45. Translation from Origen, *Contra Celsum*, ed. and trans. Henry Chadwick (Cambridge: Cambridge University Press, 1953).

46. All Justin quotations are taken from the edition of Thomas Falls, *Saint Justin Martyr*, FC 6 (Washington, DC: Catholic University of America Press, 1948).

writings (*1 Apol.* 59). Christianity is not only prior to the best of pagan thought; it is its source.

Justin's pupil Tatian takes the claim a step further: "Our history is not only earlier than Greek culture but even than the invention of writing" (*Or. Graec.* 31).[47] The oldest important pagan religious texts from antiquity were Homer's *Iliad* and *Odyssey*, written necessarily, Tatian points out, no earlier than the Trojan war. Moses, on the other hand, lived even before the founding of Troy, by many years. More than that, "Moses is not only older than Homer but is older even than the writers before him, Linus ... Thamyris ... Orpheus, Musaeus, ..." and so on (*Or. Graec.* 41).

Some decades later, Tertullian works to be yet more precise: "By nearly four hundred years—only seven less—[Moses] precedes Danaus, your most ancient name; while he antedates by a millennium the death of Priam. I might affirm, too, that he is five hundred years earlier than Homer" (*Apol.* 19 [trans. Thewell, *ANF* 3:33]). Even more than that, for Tertullian all of pagan religion—all its gods, temples, oracles, and rites— "are less ancient than the work of a single prophet [Moses], in whom you have the thesaurus of the entire Jewish religion, and therefore too of ours" (*Apol.* 19).

This last phrase of Tertullian shows why appealing to the antiquity of Moses assists the Christian apologetic cause. Moses has been taken over by the Christians. That, at least in part, is because he has been either misread or abandoned by the Jews. Some of the apologists are explicit on the point. As Origen argues, "For Christians the introduction to the faith is based on the religion of Moses and the prophetic writings.... The Jews, on the other hand, have not looked deeply into them but read them superficially and only as stories" (*Cels.* 2.4). Much earlier Justin had made the claim yet more explicit: "There were certain men among the Jews who were prophets of God, through whom the prophetic Spirit predicted events that were to happen, before they actually took place." These books "are in the possession of every Jew, wherever he be. But these Jews, though they read the books, fail to grasp their meaning and they consider us as their enemies and adversaries, killing and punishing us, just as you do, whenever they are able to do so" (*1 Apol.* 31).

---

47. Translation from Tatian, *Oratio ad Graecos and Fragments*, ed. and trans. Molly Whittaker (Oxford: Clarendon, 1982).

This debate over the rightful heirs of Moses and the prophets involves the question of the very legitimacy of Christianity as a religion that wants to stake its claim to antiquity through the religion of the Jews, a religion these Christians reject. At stake is the question: who are the true people of God? For the Christian apologist, there is no ambiguity. Justin is the first on record to point out that the prophet Jeremiah had predicted a "new covenant" was to be given to those who are (alone) faithful to the God of Israel. So, "We [Christians] have been led to God through this crucified Christ, and we are the true spiritual Israel, and the descendants of Judah, Jacob, Isaac, and Abraham, who, though uncircumcised, was approved and blessed by God because of his father and was called the father of many nations" (*Dial.* 11). It is the uncircumcised gentiles who believe in Christ who are the true heirs not only of the prophets and Moses but also of the Jewish patriarchs, from the beginning, starting with Abraham.

In short, pagan opposition to Christians led Christian intellectuals to embrace the Jewish scriptures; this, in no small measure, is why the Christian canon contains an Old Testament.

## Conclusions

The question of the parting of the ways is entangled and complex, and no one approach to the problem will untie all the knots. As I stated at the outset, the extremes in the discussion are represented, on one hand, by essentialists who claim that Judaism is one thing, Christianity is something else, and there was a definite point in time (or even a prolonged period) at which they separated. On the other hand, the somewhat more theoretically sophisticated opponents of this view—at the other extreme—claim, in one nuanced way or another, but equally problematically, that the ways never parted.

This disagreement will probably never subside. But one helpful approach to the question involves a consideration of pagan opposition to the Christian movement. Facets of this opposition reveal why both sides in the debate are in some sense right. Imperial opposition to the Christians, from its first recorded instance under Nero to its denouement under Diocletian and his successors, shows that Roman authorities and those who served under them had no difficulty differentiating between Christians and Jews. It would be perverse to argue that these authorities were exceptions to the rule in the empire, that their views were distinctive to themselves. Surely most people, most of the time, throughout the first three centuries, thought that Jews were not Christians and Christians were not Jews, even if there were individuals and groups here and there who insisted for themselves that they were both things at once.

At the same time, pagan opposition to the Christian movement elicited a response that helps show how Christianity could be seen as joined at the hip, usually not happily, with the Judaism out of which the religion originally emerged. In part for apologetic reasons, proto-orthodox Christians felt compelled to latch on to the Jewish scriptures and claim them as their own. This did not create common cause and produce good feelings between Christians and Jews. On the contrary, from the Christian side at least, it led to heightened animosity, not just over the interpretation of one supposed messianic prophecy or another, but over the very question of the legitimacy of one entire religion instead of (rather than alongside of) another.

In short, Christians may have wanted to claim to be the true Israel—and in fact did make that claim—but in the eyes of the Roman state, and probably the world at large, they were not Jews.

## Bibliography

Alexander, Philip S. "'The Parting of the Ways' from the Perspective of Rabbinic Judaism." Pages 1–25 in *Jews and Christians: The Parting of the Ways A.D. 70 to 135*. Edited by James D. G. Dunn. Grand Rapids: Eerdmans, 1999.

Barclay, John M. G. *Jews in the Mediterranean Diaspora: From Alexander to Trajan (323 BCE–117 CE)*. Berkeley: University of California Press, 1996.

Becker, Adam H., and Annette Yoshiko Reed, eds. *The Ways That Never Parted: Jews and Christians in Late Antiquity and the Early Middle Ages*. TSAJ 95. Tübingen: Mohr Siebeck, 2003.

Bisbee, Gary. *The Pre-Decian Acts of Martyrs and Comentarii*. Philadelphia: Fortress, 1988.

Castelli, Elizabeth A. "Gender, Theory, and the Rise of Christianity: A Response to Rodney Stark." *JECS* 6 (1998): 227–57.

Cohen, Shaye J. D. *From the Maccabees to the Mishnah*. 3rd ed. Louisville: Westminster John Knox, 2014.

Cook, John Granger. *Roman Attitudes toward the Christians: From Claudius to Hadrian*. WUNT 261. Tübingen: Mohr Siebeck, 2010.

Droge, Arthur. *Homer or Moses: Early Christian Interpretations of the History of Culture*. HUT 26. Tübingen: Mohr Siebeck, 1989.

Dunn, James D. G. *The Partings of the Ways: Between Christianity and Judaism and Their Significance for the Character of Christianity*. 2nd ed. London: SCM, 2006.

Ehrman, Bart D. *The Triumph of Christianity*. New York: Simon & Schuster, 2018.

Falls, Thomas. *Saint Justin Martyr*. FC 6. Washington, DC: Catholic University of America Press, 1948.

Gibson, E. Leigh. "Jewish Antagonism or Christian Polemic: The Case of the *Martyrdom of Pionius*." JECS 9 (2001): 339–58.

——. "The Jews and Christians in the Martyrdom of Polycarp." Pages 145–58 in *The Ways That Never Parted: Jews and Christians in Late Antiquity and the Early Middle Ages*. Edited by Adam H. Becker and Annette Yoshiko Reed. TSAJ 95. Tübingen: Mohr Siebeck, 2003.

Goodman, Martin. "Diaspora Reactions to the Destruction of the Temple." Pages 27–38 in *The Ways That Never Parted: Jews and Christians in Late Antiquity and the Early Middle Ages*. Edited by Adam H. Becker and Annette Yoshiko Reed. TSAJ 95. Tübingen: Mohr Siebeck, 2003.

——. "Nerva, the Fiscus Judaicus, and Jewish Identity." JRS 79 (1989): 40–44.

Heemstra, Marius. *The Fiscus Judaicus and the Parting of the Ways*. WUNT 2/227. Tübingen: Mohr Siebeck, 2010.

Jones, Christopher P. "The Historicity of the Neronian Persecution: A Response to Brent Shaw." NTS 63 (2017): 146–52.

Judge, E. A. "Judaism and the Rise of Christianity: A Roman Perspective." TynBul 45 (1994): 355–68.

Kannaday, Wayne C. *Apologetic Discourse and the Scribal Tradition: Evidence of the Influence of Apologetic Interests on the Text of the Canonical Gospels*. TCS 5. Atlanta: Scholars Press, 2004.

Lieu, Judith. "The Parting of the Ways: Theological Construct or Historical Reality?" JSNT 56 (1994): 101–19.

Moss, Candida. *Ancient Christian Martyrdom: Diverse Practices, Theologies, and Traditions*. ABRL. New Haven: Yale University Press, 2012.

Musurillo, Herbert. *Acts of the Christian Martyrs*. Oxford: Oxford University Press, 1972.

Origen. *Contra Celsum*. Edited and translated by Henry Chadwick. Cambridge: Cambridge University Press, 1953.

Paget, James Carleton. Review of *The Fiscus Judaicus and the Parting of the Ways*, by Marius Heemstra. *JEH* 4 (2011): 354.

Riesner, Rainer. *Die Frühzeit des Apostels Paulus: Studien zur Chronologie, Missionsstrategie und Theologie.* WUNT 71. Tübingen: Mohr Siebeck, 1994.

Rives, James B. "The Decree of Decius and the Religion of Empire." *JRS* 39 (1999): 135–54.

Shaw, Brent. "The Myth of the Neronian Persecution." *JRS* 105 (2015): 73–100.

Stark, Rodney. *The Rise of Christianity: How the Obscure, Marginal Jesus Movement Became the Dominant Religious Force in the Western World in a Few Centuries.* San Francisco: HarperSanFrancisco, 1996.

Tatian. *Oratio ad Graecos and Fragments.* Edited and translated by Molly Whittaker. OECT. Oxford: Clarendon, 1982.

Tertullian. "Apology." Translated by S. Thewell. *ANF* 3:17–55.

———. *Apology; De Spectaculis.* Translated by T. R. Glover. LCL 250. Cambridge: Harvard University Press, 1931.

Theophilus. "To Autolycus." Translated by Marcus Dods. *ANF* 2.89–121.

# Why Ignatius Invented Judaism

## Daniel Boyarin

It is an honor for me to contribute to this volume celebrating the work of an old friend, colleague, and occasional disputant a piece on one of the moments, to wit, the letters of Ignatius of Antioch, in which a difference between *Ioudaismos* and *Christianismos* was being made. This is surely a matter of interest to the honoree of this volume, and I begin, moreover, with a brief consideration of the apostle Paul, always at the center of his scholarly *oeuvre*.

When the apostle declares in Galatians that formerly he was very advanced in *Ioudaismos*, he is surely not referring to an abstract category or an institution but the practice of Jewish ways of loyalty to the traditional doings of Jews, described by his contemporary Josephus as "the ancestral [traditions] of the *Ioudaioi*" (τὰ πάτρια τῶν Ἰουδαίων, *A.J.* 20.41 and passim). Now, one might be tempted simply to gloss this as the Jewish religion were it not for the fact that this is exactly the usage that we find in Thucydides describing the Plataeans Medizing, namely, that they are accused of "forsaking *their* ancestral traditions" (παραβαίνοντες τὰ πάτρια, Thucydides, *P.W.* 3.61.2).[1]

Other attestations of *Ioudaismos* seem also to bear out the interpretation of *Ioudaismos* as a verbal noun, a practice and not an institution. Paradoxically Paul's usage in Galatians has typically been taken as evidencing the exact opposite. The most important passage is Gal 1:13–14, where we read (words to be discussed below are left untranslated): "For you have

---

1. Steve Mason, "Jews, Judaeans, Judaizing, Judaism: Problems of Categorization in Ancient History," *JSJ* 38 (2007): 463. See also Matthew V. Novenson, "Paul's Former Occupation in *Ioudaismos*," in *Galatians and Christian Theology: Justification, the Gospel, and Ethics in Paul's Letter*, ed. Mark W. Elliott et al. (Grand Rapids: Baker Academic, 2014), 24–39.

heard of my *anastrophe* then in *Ioudaismos*, how I persecuted the congregation of God and tried to destroy it. And I had advanced in *Ioudaismos* beyond many of my own age among my people, so extravagantly zealous was I for the traditions of my ancestors."[2] Let us begin with the word *anastrophe* usually translated as "life," as in "former life." Mason has argued that the "accompanying noun ἀναστροφή is stronger than '[my former] life,' as often translated (e.g., NRSV, ASV). It should indicate some sort of 'bent, inclination' or 'turning toward' something, 'a going back' to it, or a 'preoccupation' with it (cf. LSJ *s. v.*). The *zeal* mentioned in 1:14 confirms this sense."[3] Mason is right, in my opinion, that "former life" rather prejudices the case and does not correspond to the most frequent usages of this word in Greek. I think, however, we need not go quite as far as he does, and I would prefer to translate "conduct," as we find it, for instance in Tob 4:14: πρόσεχε σεαυτῷ, παιδίον, ἐν πᾶσι τοῖς ἔργοις σου καὶ ἴσθι πεπαιδευμένος ἐν πάσῃ ἀναστροφῇ σου, where the last phrase translates well as "be well instructed in all of your conduct," paralleling the first clause which would read "be careful in all of your works." Paul, then, would be referring to his former conduct in Judaizing, namely, his persecution of the *ekklēsia* of God. The use of *Ioudaismos* in the second verse makes this point even stronger. One does not advance in an institution, for instance, an alleged "religion" (except, perhaps, by being promoted within it, obviously inapplicable here), but in a practice, the practice of Judaizing in which Paul was more advanced because he was more learned and zealous than the others. Finally, Paul's usage of the verbal noun *Ioudaismos* must be interpreted with reference to his use of the verb as well. In Gal 2:14, Paul inveighs:

> But when I saw that they were not straightforward about the truth of the gospel, I said to Cephas before them all, "If you, though a *Ioudaios*, live like a gentile and not like a *Ioudaios*, how do you force the gentiles to *Ioudaizein*?"[4]

The phrase clearly means to live according to Judean ways as the opposite of living in the gentile manner. *Ioudaismos*, the noun derived from this

---

2. Unless otherwise indicated, all translations of ancient sources are my own.

3. Mason, "Jews," 469 n. 21.

4. ἀλλ' ὅτε εἶδον ὅτι οὐκ ὀρθοποδοῦσιν πρὸς τὴν ἀλήθειαν τοῦ εὐαγγελίου, εἶπον τῷ Κηφᾷ ἔμπροσθεν πάντων Εἰ σὺ Ἰουδαῖος ὑπάρχων ἐθνικῶς καὶ οὐκ Ἰουδαϊκῶς ζῇς, πῶς τὰ ἔθνη ἀναγκάζεις ἰουδαΐζειν.

verb, clearly means as well, then, Judaizing, living according to Judean/Jewish ways and not being a member of an institution called Judaism. That this is the case is shown by Mason's observation that "Paul denounces Peter because, though Peter allegedly lives as a foreigner [literally, ethnically] and not as a Judaean [that is, Judaically] (ἐθνικῶς καὶ οὐχὶ Ἰουδαϊκῶς), 'you compel the foreigners to Judaize' (τὰ ἔθνη ἀναγκάζεις ἰουδαΐζειν; Gal 2:14)—a cultural movement that Paul connects tightly with circumcision and observance of Judaean law (2:12, 21)."[5] Since ethnicizing is surely not observing a religion, neither is Judaizing here and hence certainly also not the noun derived quite regularly from this verb, Ioudaismos.

A final argument that Ioudaismos, in Paul, is not the name for the Jewish religion is the following: Paul never considered himself anything other than a Jew. Were Ioudaismos to mean the entirety of Judaic practice and belief, or the religion of the Jews, this verse would constitute a reading of himself out of it. It follows that Ioudaismos, if Paul is out of it, simply cannot be read as the alleged Jewish religion or even as a name for all that Jews do! It must mean, in his work, therefore, the practice of the commandments of the torah, which he rejects. Once again, I arrive at results very similar—if not identical—to those of Mason but by slightly different routes of interpretation. Ioudaismos, "Judaizing," seems in all of these cases to mean hanging on (zealously) to the customs (traditions of the ancestors) of the Judeans. Any other interpretation (and there are some that seem possible within the context alone) involves importing the later sense of -ism words, as the names of institutions or, at least, movements, and applying them anachronistically to Ioudaismos. Nonetheless, Paul's intervention had highly significant historical implications, indeed.

It is Ignatius of Antioch who has been generally held to be the first Christian writer to contrast Christianismos to Ioudaismos. Lately, however, several scholars have identified a lost text of Marcion, his Antitheses, as our first source for this terminology.[6] This is doubly interesting since that quite extreme figure preached that there is absolutely no continuity between the

---

5. Mason, "Jews," 464.

6. The case is dependent on taking certain terminology found in Tertullian's writings about Marcion as being drawn from that author, as claimed explicitly by Judith Lieu, *Image and Reality: The Jews in the World of the Christians in the Second Century* (Edinburgh: T&T Clark, 1996), 344. See the more extensive discussion in Markus Vinzent, *Tertullian's Preface to Marcion's Gospel*, Studia Patristica Supplements 5 (Leuven: Peeters, 2016), 342–47.

Hebrew Bible and its God and the Father of the Christ, rendering necessary an absolute break between following *Christianismos* (following the
doings of the Christ) and *Ioudaismos* (following the ways of the Judean
god). Ignatius, who is the earliest directly and well-attested writer to use
this terminology is no gnostic but also is mightily striving to produce a
distance between what he calls *Christianismos* and what he terms *Ioudaismos* (whether he learned the term from Marcion, which seems to me
unlikely, or borrowed it from Paul who, as we have seen above, however,
uses it quite differently). The bishop and future-martyred saint inveighed
mightily against those who blurred the boundaries between Jew and
Christian. His very criticisms, however, are indicative of the ideological
work that he is performing. For Ignatius, it seems, one can be a follower
of Jesus and (heretically in his eyes) nonetheless engage in *Ioudaismos*:
"It is perverse to talk of Jesus Christ and to Judaize [ἄτοπόν ἐστιν Ἰησοῦν
Χριστὸν λαλεῖν καὶ ἰουδαΐζειν]" (*Magn.* 10.3),[7] he proclaims, thus making
both points at once, the drive of the nascent orthodoxy—understood as a
particular social location and as a particular form of self-fashioning and
identity making—to normative separation and the actual lack of such clear
separations "on the ground." There is, however, an important, even crucial, further wrinkle in this verse. The Ignatian verse goes on to say: "For
*Christianismos* did not believe on *Ioudaismos* but *Ioudaismos* believed on
*Christianismos*" (ὁ γὰρ Χριστιανισμὸς οὐκ εἰς Ἰουδαϊσμὸν ἐπίστευσεν, ἀλλ'
Ἰουδαϊσμὸς εἰς Χριστιανισμόν). This sentence is rather puzzling: Does it
mean that Judaism has been founded on and derived from a putatively
earlier Christianity? Will the Greek suffer such a construal? Letting that
be as it may, it would seem fair to conclude in any case that *Ioudaismos*
for Ignatius is some kind of abstract noun that can serve as the subject
of a sentence. Whatever it means for Ignatius, this formal shift is in itself
highly significant; we will not see its like among Jews until the end of the

---

7. William R. Schoedel, *Ignatius of Antioch: A Commentary on the Letters of Ignatius of Antioch*, Hermeneia (Philadelphia: Fortress, 1985), 126. See Lieu, *Image*, 28 and
passim, for an exploration of the anxieties to which this fuzzy border gave rise. This
position is partially *pace* Keith Hopkins, "Christian Number and Its Implications,"
*JECS* 6 (1998): 187, who seems to regard such fuzziness (or "porosity" in his language)
as particularly characteristic of Christianity. Hopkins's paper is very important and
will have to be reckoned with seriously in any future accounts of Judaeo-Christian
origins and genealogies. See also on this passage Shaye J. D. Cohen, "Judaism without Circumcision and 'Judaism' without 'Circumcision' in Ignatius," *HTR* 95 (2002):
398–99.

nineteenth century! It will, however, have a long history within Christian discourse.[8]

The question of names and naming—naming Christian, naming Jew, naming *Christianimos*, naming *Ioudaismos*—is central to the Ignatian enterprise. Near the very beginning of his letter to the Ephesians, in a passage the significance of which has been only partly realized in my view, Ignatius writes,

> Having received in God your much loved name, which you possess by a just nature according to faith and love in Christ Jesus, our Savior—being imitators of God, enkindled by the blood of God, you accomplished perfectly the task suited to you. (*Eph.* 1.1)[9]

Although this interpretation has been spurned by most commentators and scholars of Ignatius,[10] I would make a cornerstone of my construction to read this as a reference to the name *Christians*.[11] It was, after all, in Ignatius's Antioch that the people were first called by that name (Acts 11:26). Ignatius is complimenting the church in Ephesus as being worthy, indeed, to be called by the name of Christ owing to their merits.[12] Indeed, as William R. Schoedel does not fail to point out, in *Magn.* 10.1, Ignatius writes, "Therefore let us become his disciples and learn to live according to the Christianizing. For one who is called by any name other than this, is not of God."[13] Even more to the point, however, is Ignatius, *Magn.* 4.1: "It is

---

8. For extensive documentation and discussion of this claim, see Daniel Boyarin, *Judaism: The Genealogy of a Modern Notion*, Key Words for Jewish Studies (New Brunswick, NJ: Rutgers University Press, 2018), from which this section of the current paper is extracted and redacted for this context. See also earlier, Boyarin, "Apartheid Comparative Religion in the Second Century: Some Theory and a Case Study," *JMEMS* 36 (2006): 3–34; repr. in *Defining Judaism: A Reader*, ed. Aaron W. Hughes (London: Routledge, 2014), 89–116.

9. Text and translation from Schoedel, *Ignatius of Antioch*, 40; Ἀποδεξάμενος ἐν θεῷ τὸ πολυαγάπητόν σου ὄνομα, ὃ κέκτησθε φύσει δικαίᾳ κατὰ πίστιν καὶ ἀγάπην ἐν Χριστῷ Ἰησοῦ τῷ σωτῆρι ἡμῶν· μιμηταὶ ὄντες θεοῦ, ἀναζωπυρήσαντες ἐν αἵματι θεοῦ τὸ συγγενικὸν ἔργον τελείως ἀπηρτίσατε.

10. Schoedel, *Ignatius of Antioch*, 41.

11. Henning Paulsen, *Die Briefe des Ignatius von Antiochia und der Brief Des Polykarp von Smyrna*, HNT 18 (Tübingen: Mohr Siebeck, 1985), 25.

12. Other interpretations, seeing this as a reference to the name Ephesus, seem to me quite far-fetched.

13. Schoedel, *Ignatius of Antioch*, 126: μαθηταὶ αὐτοῦ γενόμενοι, μάθωμεν κατὰ

right, then, not only to be called Christians but also to be."[14] Ignatius tells the Ephesians, then, that they are not just called Christians but are Christians, by nature (φύσει), as it were.[15] Ignatius goes on in verse 2 to write, "For hearing that I was put in bonds from Syria for the common name and hope, hoping by your prayer to attain to fighting with beasts in Rome, that by attaining I may be able to be a disciple, you hastened to see me."[16] Once again, the interpretative tradition seems to have missed an attractively specific interpretation of name here that links it to the name in the previous verse. It is not, I opine, the name of Christ that is referred to here[17] but the name of Christian, which equals disciple (compare again with Acts 11:26: "And the *disciples* were called Christians first in Antioch"). The "common hope" is Jesus Christ (see also Ignatius, *Eph.* 21.1; Ignatius, *Trall.* 2.2),[18] but the common name is Christian.

I would suggest that Ignatius represents here the theme of the centrality of martyrdom in establishing the name "Christian" as the legitimate and true name of the disciple; this, in accord with the practice whereby "*Christianos eimi*" were the last words of the martyr, the name for which she died.[19] Similarly, in *Eph.* 3.1 Ignatius explicitly connects martyrdom with the name: "I do not command you as being someone; for even though I have been bound in the name, I have not yet been perfected in Jesus Christ." The name in which Ignatius has been bound (that is, imprisoned and sent to Rome for martyrdom) is the name *Christianos.*[20] The

---

Χριστιανισμὸν ζῆν. ὃς γὰρ ἄλλῳ ὀνόματι καλεῖται πλέον τούτου, οὐκ ἔστιν τοῦ θεοῦ. I shall have more to say about this passage anon.

14. Πρέπον οὖν ἐστὶν μὴ μόνον καλεῖσθαι Χριστιανούς, ἀλλὰ καὶ εἶναι. See also Ignatius, *Rom.* 3.2.

15. For φύσει in this sense, cf. Ignatius, *Trall.* 1.1 and discussion in Schoedel, *Ignatius of Antioch*,138.

16. Schoedel, *Ignatius of Antioch*, 40.

17. *Pace* Schoedel, *Ignatius of Antioch*, 43.

18. Schoedel, *Ignatius of Antioch*, 95, 140.

19. Judith Lieu, "'I Am a Christian': Martyrdom and the Beginning of 'Christian' Identity," in *Neither Jew Nor Greek? Constructing Christian Identity* (Edinburgh: T&T Clark, 2003), 211–31. See too, Carlin A. Barton, "The 'Moment of Truth' in Ancient Rome: Honor and Embodiment in a Contest Culture," *Stanford Humanities Review* 6 (1998): 16–30.

20. Similarly, it seems to me that in 7.1 of that letter in which Ignatius writes, "For some are accustomed with evil deceit to carry about the name, at the same time doing things unworthy of God" (translation of Schoedel, *Ignatius of Antioch*, 59), it is *not* the name "Christ" that these folks are carrying about (*pace* Schoedel: "that is, they move

nexus between having the right to that name and martyrdom or between martyrdom and identity, and the nexus between them and heresiology, separation from *Judaizing* is also clear.[21] In opening his letters with this declaration, I think, Ignatius is declaring one of his major themes for the entire corpus: the establishment of a new "orthodox" (by his lights) Christian identity, distinguished and distinguishable from *Ioudaismos*, which is manifestly not Judaism but a form of what we would call Christianity to which Ignatius denies legitimacy. Neither *Christianismos* nor *Ioudaismos* signify Christianity or Judaism. If this is seen as a highly marked moment in his texts, then one can follow this as a dominant theme throughout his letters, and the protoheresiology of Ignatius is profoundly related to this theme, as well.[22]

This issue is most directly articulated in Ignatius's *To the Magnesians*. He exhorts: "Be not deceived by *heterodoxiai* nor by old fables, which are useless. For if we continue to live until now according to *Ioudaismos*, we confess that we have not received grace" (*Magn.* 8.1).[23]

Ignatius here defines *Ioudaismos* as "heterodoxies and old myths," but what precisely does he mean? Let us go back to the beginning of the letter. Once more, Ignatius makes a reference to the name: "For having been

---

from place to place looking for converts to their version of Christianity") but the name *Christian*. Cf. Justin's remark, "For I made it clear to you that those who are Christians in name, but in reality are godless and impious heretics, teach in all respects what is blasphemous and godless and foolish" (*Dial.* 80.3–4; translation of A. Lukyn Williams, ed. and trans., *Justin Martyr: The Dialogue with Trypho*, Translations of Christian Literature [London: SPCK, 1930], 169–71; cf. Justin, *Dialogus cum Tryphone*, ed. Miroslav Marcovich, PTS 47 [Berlin: de Gruyter, 1997], 208–9.

21. As Lieu remarks, "The claiming of this identity involves the denial of other alternatives" ("I Am," 215). Hence the importance of the name, martyrdom, and *Ioudaismos* in Ignatius. If one can be a Jew and a Christian, then Ignatius's martyrdom would, indeed, be in vain.

22. Schoedel, *Ignatius of Antioch*, 12, who sees "heresy" and "heterodox" as quasi-technical terms in Ignatius. But cf. Schoedel, *Ignatius of Antioch*, 147: "But we should note first that in referring to the 'strange plant' as 'heresy' Ignatius is mainly concerned about the false teachers themselves rather than their teaching. 'Heresy,' then, is still basically a matter of people who disrupt unity and create 'faction.'"

23. Schoedel, *Ignatius of Antioch*, 28; Μη πλανασθε ταις ετεροδοξιαις μηδε μυθευμασιν τοις παλαιοις ανωφελεσιν ουσιν· ει γαρ μεχρι νυν κατα Ιουδαισμον ζωμεν, ομολογουμεν χαριν μη ειληφεναι. See also C. K. Barrett, "Jews and Judaizers in the Epistles of Ignatius," in *Jews, Greeks and Christians: Essays in Honor of William David Davies*, ed. Robin Scroggs, SJLA 21 (Leiden: Brill, 1976), 220–44.

deemed worthy of a most godly name, in the bonds which I bear I sing the churches" (1.1).[24] Here, as Schoedel recognizes, it is almost certain that only the name Christian will fit the context. This thought about the name is continued explicitly in Ignatius's famous, "It is right, then, not only to be called Christians but to be Christians" (4.1).[25] On my reading, it is the establishment of that name, giving it definition, "defining, … policing, the boundaries that separate the name of one entity [*Christianismos*] from the name of another [*Ioudaismos*]"[26] that provides one of the two thematic foci for the letter (and the letters) as a whole, the other—and related— one, being, of course, the establishment of the bishop as sole authority in a given church. But what are these two entities *Ioudaismos* and *Christianismos* for Ignatius?

*Ioudaismos*, so far, for Ignatius does not seem to be what it means in other writers of and before his time, namely, the "false views and misguided practice," or "insisting especially on the ritual requirements of that system."[27] Ignatius troubles to let us know that this is not the case, as we learn from the aforementioned famous and powerful rhetorical paradox in his *To the Philadelphians*:

> But if anyone *expounds Ioudaismos* to you, do not listen to him; for it is better to hear *Christianismos* from a man who is circumcised than *Ioudaismos* from a man uncircumcised; both of them, if they do not speak of Jesus Christ, are to me tombstones and graves of the dead on which nothing but the names of men is written. (*Phld.* 6.1)[28]

After *considering* various options that have been offered for the interpretation of this surprising passage,[29] Schoedel arrives at what seems to me the

---

24. Schoedel, *Ignatius of Antioch*, 104.

25. Schoedel, *Ignatius of Antioch*, 108.

26. Paul de Man, "The Epistemology of Metaphor," in *On Metaphor*, ed. Sheldon Sacks (Chicago: University of Chicago Press, 1979), 17.

27. *Pace* Schoedel who considers Ignatius's usage the same as that of 2 Maccabees, Paul, and the Pastoral Epistles (*Ignatius of Antioch*, 118).

28. Schoedel, *Ignatius of Antioch*, 200 (emphasis added); Ἐὰν δέ τις Ἰουδαϊσμὸν ἑρμηνεύῃ ὑμῖν, μὴ ἀκούετε αὐτοῦ. ἄμεινον γάρ ἐστιν παρὰ ἀνδρὸς περιτομὴν ἔχοντος Χριστιανισμὸν ἀκούειν ἢ παρὰ ἀκροβύστου Ἰουδαϊσμόν. ἐὰν δὲ ἀμφότεροι περὶ Ἰησοῦ Χριστοῦ μὴ λαλῶσιν, οὗτοι ἐμοὶ στῆλαί εἰσιν καὶ τάφοι νεκρῶν, ἐφ' οἷς γέγραπται μόνον ὀνόματα ἀνθρώπων.

29. Schoedel, *Ignatius of Antioch*, 202–3.

most compelling interpretation, "perhaps it was the 'expounding' (exegetical expertise) that was the problem and not the 'Judaism' (observance)."[30] I would go further than Schoedel by making one more seemingly logical exegetical step, namely, to assume that for Ignatius, *Ioudaismos* is the expounding. In Ignatius, I suggest, *Ioudaismos* no longer means observance of the Judean way of life, the torah, as it had in Paul.[31] In other words, for Ignatius, but not for Paul, *Christianismos* and *Ioudaismos* are two *doxas*, two theological positions, a wrong one (ἑτεροδοξία, 8.1)[32] and a right one, a wrong interpretation of the legacy of the prophets and a right one. The right one is that which is taught by the prophets "inspired by his grace" and called *Christianismos* as it is that which is "revealed through Jesus Christ his Son, who is his Word" (8.1). The words quoted certainly seem to mean that *Christianismos* consists of "speaking of Jesus Christ," gospel—still oral—[33]while *Ioudaismos* is devoting oneself to the study of scripture. Although, to be sure in Ignatius, *Magn.* 9, Ignatius mentions one aspect of practice, namely, the abandonment of the Sabbath for "the Lord's Day," assuming that the plausible translation "Lord's Day" for κυριακή is

---

30. Schoedel, *Ignatius of Antioch*, 203. See too Cohen, "Judaism without Circumcision," 403–4.

31. I slightly disagree with David Nirenberg in his formulation to the effect that "in the tradition of Saint Paul Judaizing had always been a Christian vice, not a Jewish one," a statement hard to sustain given that for Paul there were not yet any Christians. On the other hand, I totally affirm the next sentence that "It [Judaizing, Judaism] had also always been understood as a linguistic error, a basic miscomprehension of how words work to relate humans to each other, their God, and their world." This is certain, it would seem, from Ignatius on. David Nirenberg, *Anti-Judaism: The Western Tradition* (New York: Norton, 2013), 229.

32. In contrast to Schoedel (*Ignatius of Antioch*, 118), I do not see here a near-technical term for heresy, preferring the view of Adelbert Davids, "Irrtum und Häresie: 1 Clem—Ignatius von Antioch—Justinus," *Kairós* 15 (1973): 165–87.

33. Schoedel, *Ignatius of Antioch*, 201. There is a great deal of controversy regarding the question of Ignatius's knowledge of and use of written gospel texts. I am convinced from my reading of his works that for him gospel is the good news of Christ's death and resurrection, just as he says here, suggesting strongly that he does not have written gospels. For this judgment, Helmut Koester remains definitive. Helmut Koester, *Synoptische Überlieferung bei den apostolischen Vätern* (Berlin: Akademie, 1957). More recently, Koester has continued to maintain this view. Koester, *Ancient Christian Gospels: Their History and Development* (Harrisburg, PA: Trinity Press International, 1990), 7.

correct,[34] but the issue there, too, as we can see, is not *nomos* versus grace but an insufficient Christocentrism; by keeping the scriptural Sabbath and not the Lord's day, these Christians belie that they are true "disciples of Jesus Christ, our only teacher."[35] Ignatius explicitly links those who maintain the Sabbath and not the Lord's Day alone as those who deny Christ's death as well (9.1), a point that will take on greater significance below.

I would emphasize again that this has nothing to do with anything that we would call Judaism, since for Ignatius *Christianismos* and *Ioudaismos* both are species of what we would call Christianity. The argument that for him *Ioudaismos* and *Christianismos* are both versions of what we would call Christianity comes from his clear statement that his opponents are those who say, "unless in the archives I find (it), in the gospel I do not believe (it)" (Ignatius, *Phld.* 8.2).[36] Ignatius's antagonists, real or imagined, are clearly folks for whom the gospel is richly significant, but Christians, even uncircumcised ones, who preach some "heterodox" attachment to Christ—on Ignatius's view—or even merely an insistence that everything in the gospel be anchored in scriptural (the only scripture they had, the "Old Testament") exegesis.[37] They do not put Christ first, and therefore they are preaching *Ioudaismos*, and they are "tombstones."

---

34. Schoedel, *Ignatius of Antioch*, 123 n. 3.

35. Schoedel, *Ignatius of Antioch*, 123–24: "But Ignatius makes a characteristic move when he links the resurrection with the mystery of Christ's death and emphasizes the latter as that through which faith comes. For it is Christ's death that stands out as a 'mystery' in Ignatius' mind (*Eph.* 19.1). One purpose of Ignatius here is to present the passion and resurrection (not Scripture as misinterpreted by the Jews and Judaizers) as that which determines the shape of Christian existence (and makes sense of Scripture)."

36. Cohen, "Judaism without Circumcision," 397; Schoedel, *Ignatius of Antioch*, 207. See discussion immediately here below.

37. For further discussion of this difficult passage, see Schoedel, *Ignatius of Antioch*, 207–9, and especially William R. Schoedel, "Ignatius and the Archives," *HTR* 71 (1978): 97–106. For another recent discussion of these passages, see Birger Pearson, *The Emergence of the Christian Religion: Essays on Early Christianity* (Harrisburg, PA: Trinity Press International, 1997), 11–14. For the interpretation that I have suggested here, see also Einar Molland, "The Heretics Combatted by Ignatius of Antioch," *JEH* 5 (1954): 1–6. Arguing that Ignatius indicates that he has heard this preaching, Barrett writes: "Presumably in some kind of church meeting (like that in which Ignatius prophesied [7.1]—an important point, for it must mean that the persons in question were Christian, even if (in Ignatius' eyes) unsatisfactory Christians. Ignatius is unlikely

What is this *Ioudaismos*, and how does it define *Christianismos*? A closer reading of the passage will help answer this question:

> I exhort you to do nothing from partisanship but in accordance with Christ's teaching. For I heard some say, "unless in the archives I find (it), in the gospel I do not believe (it),"[38] and when I said, "It is written," they answered me, "That is just the question." But for me the archives are Jesus Christ, the inviolable archives are his cross and death and his resurrection and faith through him—in which, through your prayers, I want to be justified. (*Phld.* 8.2)[39]

Once we concede that it is not written, fixed gospel texts that are being referred to here, it makes perfect sense that some would say that, if they cannot ground it in the scripture, they do not believe it is in the gospel. These Christian adherents of what Ignatius called *Ioudaismos* simply deny as part of the gospel itself anything of the story of Jesus that contradicts scripture or is not grounded in scripture. The group in Philadelphia to which the future martyr is objecting so strongly would be, on this reading, Christians who insist that the gospel can only contain scriptural truth, and this was acceptable to the Philadelphian congregation with whom they were in communion. For Ignatius there is, in contrast, only one source of truth, that is, the gospel, the narrative of Jesus's actual death and resurrection. That must be the correct interpretation—whether or not Ignatius had some sort of written texts about Jesus—for otherwise the statement that the "archives are Jesus Christ, his cross and death" makes no sense.

Gospel, I suggest, for Ignatius functions semantically very much as it does in Paul, except—and this is critical—for Paul the opposition is gospel/

---

to have made his way into the synagogue" ("Ignatius," 233). Finally, cf. Paulsen, *Briefe des Ignatius*, 85–86.

38. For this correct translation, see Charles E. Hill, "Ignatius, 'the Gospel,' and the Gospels," in *Trajectories through the New Testament and the Apostolic Fathers*, ed. Andrew F. Gregory and Christopher M. Tuckett (Oxford: Oxford University Press, 2005), 272. I confess to remaining unpersuaded by Hill's overall argument but this is not the venue for detailed examination.

39. From Schoedel, *Ignatius of Antioch*, 207: Παρακαλῶ δὲ ὑμᾶς μηδὲν κατ᾽ ἐρίθειαν πράσσειν, ἀλλὰ κατὰ χριστομαθίαν. ἐπεὶ ἤκουσά τινων λεγόντων ὅτι Ἐὰν μὴ ἐν τοῖς ἀρχείοις εὕρω, ἐν τῷ εὐαγγελίῳ οὐ πιστεύω· καὶ λέγοντός μου αὐτοῖς ὅτι Γέγραπται, ἀπεκρίθησάν μοι ὅτι Πρόκειται. ἐμοὶ δὲ ἀρχεῖά ἐστιν Ἰησοῦς Χριστός, τὰ ἄθικτα ἀρχεῖα ὁ σταυρὸς αὐτοῦ καὶ ὁ θάνατος καὶ ἡ ἀνάστασις αὐτοῦ καὶ ἡ πίστις ἡ δι᾽ αὐτοῦ· ἐν οἷς θέλω ἐν τῇ προσευχῇ ὑμῶν δικαιωθῆναι.

*nomos*, while for Ignatius the opposition is gospel/scripture, accepting the good news of Jesus's actual physical death and resurrection versus exegeting scripture.[40] The somewhat confounding moment, however, is Ignatius's statement that "it is written," which seems to counteract this view. There are two possible interpretations that I would suggest: the one is that Ignatius first simply declares that whatever he claims as being in the gospel is/must be already written in the archives, and when they retort by saying that is the question, he resorts to his claim that the gospel *is* the archives, the only archives that matter. A second possibility would be that when Ignatius says "It is written," he already means it is written, as it were, in the only archives that matter to him, Jesus Christ, his death and resurrection

---

40. I partly disagree with Schoedel's remark that, "We may observe in this connection that Ignatius speaks of Judaism where Paul would more naturally have spoken of the law. Thus Ignatius' contrast is between grace and Judaism and not, as in Paul, between grace and law" (*Ignatius of Antioch*, 119). For Schoedel's "grace" here, I would put "gospel," so the contrast is between gospel and *Ioudaismos*, or better between gospel and scripture with the reliance on the latter defined as *Ioudaismos*. To be sure, this makes Ignatius a distant ancestor to Marcion, only in this, his rejection of scripture. I think that Ignatius simply does not operate with an opposition between grace and law at all, as we can see from Ignatius, *Magn.* 2: "because he is subject to the bishop as to the grace of God and to the presbytery as to the law of Jesus Christ." Indeed, Schoedel's remark is somewhat puzzling, since he himself argues that "Ignatius uses 'grace' and 'law' as parallel expressions" (*Ignatius of Antioch*, 239). Ignatius's Judaizers are apparently *uncircumcised*, making them very different from Paul's opponents indeed (cf. Ignatius, *Phld.* 6.1; see discussion in Josep Rius-Camps (*The Four Authentic Letters of Ignatius, the Martyr: A Critical Study Based on the Anomalies Contained in the Textus Receptus*, Christianismos 2 [Rome: Pontificium Institutum Orientalium Studiorum, 1979], 41), who nonetheless insists that the Judaizers and the Gnostic-docetics must be two "irreducibly" different groups. This flows from Rius-Camps's misapprehension that Ignatius's Judaizers are the representatives of "*Judaizing* tendencies similar to those that sprang up in the Pauline communities," notwithstanding the fact that virtually the entire content of the Pauline opposition was their insistence on Jewish law especially circumcision, while Ignatius's Judaizing opponents' error is christological and not connected with any insistence on Jewish practice, notwithstanding their maintenance of the Sabbath. Lightfoot's arguments all stand up to Rius-Camps's attempt at withering critique of them (see Rius-Camps, *Four Authentic Letters*, 40–51). Rius-Camps seems to believe that by defining Judaizing as a form of Christianity which "inculcates Jewish observances and practices" (Rius-Camps, *Ignatius*, 42), he has then proven that if Ignatius refers to those who expound *Ioudaismos*, they must too be inculcating such observances and practices, in spite of the fact that Ignatius himself refers to them as "uncircumcised"!

in the flesh. They misunderstand, retorting that it is not written, which he then clarifies with his Jesus as the archive. That is exactly the question that they put to Ignatius: "They answered me, 'That is just the question,'" to wit: indeed Ignatius, whether or not the physical death of the Son of Man is written in the archives is precisely the question. For Ignatius, however, for whom the nonscriptural kerygma is central and, who sees, as he insists over and over, such reliance on scripture is itself, *Ioudaismos*, the following of Jewish scriptures, and not *Christianismos*, the following of Christ's birth, actual death, and resurrection in the flesh alone. Whether or not Ignatius had access to any written gospels or pregospel literature, his claim is absolutely clear and unambiguous: the archives are Jesus Christ, *not what is written in scripture*. For what seems to be the first time, the tension between holding the sacredness of scripture for Christians and their rejection in favor of a new dispensation will be, if not solved, reduced by the expedient of naming that tension Judaism. As David Nirenberg points out, "'Judaism,' [was projected] as a form of interpretation, an attitude toward word and world."[41] Having very little to do with "real Jews," this would nonetheless have consequences for Jews going forward.[42] This opposition between Ignatius and these other Christians, referred to as practitioners of *Ioudaismos*, has been symbolized by him already as an opposition between those who keep the Sabbath and those who only observe the Lord's Day.

Here Ignatius draws it out further via an epistemological contrast between that which is known from scripture (= *Ioudaismos*) and that which is known from the very facts of the Lord's death and resurrection (= χριστομαθία). As we have seen above, for Ignatius those who observe the Sabbath are implicated as ones who deny the Lord's death as well (Ignatius, *Magn.* 9.1). These ostensible Christians who, according to Ignatius, Judaize might very well have held a Christology that was too high for Ignatius's taste. I have argued elsewhere that Jews who held a version of Logos theology, and perhaps might even have seen in Christ the manifestation of the Logos, might yet have balked at an incarnational Christology,[43] adopting a way-too-high, docetic Christology, rather than the low Christology

---

41. Nirenberg, *Anti-Judaism*, 238.

42. See, just for one example, the remarks of Nirenberg: "The Middle Ages created for the Jews a political and legal status analogous to their hermeneutic one" (*Anti-Judaism*, 193).

43. Daniel Boyarin, "The Gospel of the *Memra*: Jewish Binitarianism and the Prologue to John," *HTR* 94 (2001): 243–84.

of which so-called Jewish-Christians are usually accused. These Christians might have insisted on a docetism that denied that the Logos ever took on flesh, and Ignatius's *Ioudaismos* might then be a *doxa* that the Christians of Philadelphia had inherited from such a tendency. That which is not found in the archives, then, is precisely the notion that the Logos could die! That is exactly that which Ignatius himself claims as the something that the gospel has that is distinctive over-against the Old Testament: "the coming of the Savior, our Lord Jesus Christ, his passion and resurrection" (Ignatius, *Magn.* 9.2). This suggests strongly that, if not precisely the same people—if, indeed, there were such people altogether—it is the same complex of Christian-Jewish ideas, accepting Jesus, accepting the Logos, denying actual physical death and resurrection, which Ignatius names as engaging in *Ioudaismos*, Judaizing, the product of over-valuing of scripture against the claims of the gospel, which alone must be first and foremost for those who would have the name Christian, that name for which Ignatius would die.

Schoedel has surely advanced our understanding by showing that "it was Ignatius and not they [the "heretics"] who polarized the situation."[44] Ignatius produced his *Ioudaismos* in order to more fully define and articulate the new identity for the disciples as true bearers of the new name, *Christianoi*. Ignatius has, in some important sense, taken the first step in the invention of Judaism as a defining other to Christianity. In a pattern to be repeated throughout history *ad nauseam*, the Judaism that he creates has very little to do, it seems, with Jews, not even in his imagining. Similarly, an early modern writer, the "Bachelor Marcus of Toledo," indicts Christians who "bind themselves like livestock to the letter" and "have always given and still give false meaning to divine and human scripture," are "in confederation with the synagogue." As Nirenberg emphasizes, "the targets of his [the bachelor's] accusations of Judaism, were not 'real' Jews." Indeed, they included even the pope in Rome in their beastly congregation.[45] "Real Jews," however, as argued throughout my forthcoming book, have no such names for themselves or their doings, calling it all just torah.

This Judaism is, therefore, a Christian device.

---

44. Schoedel, *Ignatius of Antioch*, 234. To be sure, Schoedel in accord with his view would see this as only applicable in the case of the "Gnostic docetics," while I would extend the point, either by seeing all the opponents as essentially one, particularly so if they are being polarized by Ignatius himself, or as applicable to both of the cases if the two heresy view holds.

45. For the text and analysis, see Nirenberg, *Anti-Judaism*, 212–13.

## Bibliography

Barrett, C. K. "Jews and Judaizers in the Epistles of Ignatius." Pages 220–44 in *Jews, Greeks and Christians: Essays in Honor of William David Davies*. Edited by Robin Scroggs. SJLA 21. Leiden: Brill, 1976.

Barton, Carlin A. "The 'Moment of Truth' in Ancient Rome: Honor and Embodiment in a Contest Culture." *Stanford Humanities Review* 6 (1998): 16–30.

Boyarin, Daniel. "Apartheid Comparative Religion in the Second Century: Some Theory and a Case Study." *JMEMS* 36 (2006): 3–34; repr. pages 89–116 in *Defining Judaism: A Reader*. Edited by Aaron W. Hughes. London: Routledge, 2014.

———. "The Gospel of the *Memra*: Jewish Binitarianism and the Prologue to John." *HTR* 94 (2001): 243–84.

———. *Judaism: The Genealogy of a Modern Notion*. Key Words for Jewish Studies. New Brunswick, NJ: Rutgers University Press, 2018.

Cohen, Shaye J. D. "Judaism without Circumcision and 'Judaism' without 'Circumcision' in Ignatius." *HTR* 95 (2002): 395–415.

Davids, Adelbert. "Irrtum und Häresie: 1 Clem—Ignatius von Antioch—Justinus." *Kairós* 15 (1973): 165–87.

Hill, Charles E. "Ignatius, 'the Gospel', and the Gospels." Pages 267–85 in *Trajectories through the New Testament and the Apostolic Fathers*. Edited by Andrew F. Gregory and Christopher M. Tuckett. Oxford: Oxford University Press, 2005.

Hopkins, Keith. "Christian Number and Its Implications." *JECS* 6 (1998): 185–226.

Justin. *Dialogus cum Tryphone*. Edited by Miroslav Marcovich. PTS 47. Berlin: de Gruyter, 1997.

Koester, Helmut. *Ancient Christian Gospels: Their History and Development*. Harrisburg, PA: Trinity Press International, 1990.

———. *Synoptische Überlieferung bei den apostolischen Vätern*. Berlin: Akademie, 1957.

Lieu, Judith. "'I Am a Christian': Martyrdom and the Beginning of 'Christian' Identity." Pages 211–31 in *Neither Jew Nor Greek? Constructing Christian Identity*. Edinburgh: T&T Clark, 2003.

———. *Image and Reality: The Jews in the World of the Christians in the Second Century*. Edinburgh: T&T Clark, 1996.

Man, Paul de. "The Epistemology of Metaphor." Pages 11–28 in *On Metaphor*. Edited by Sheldon Sacks. Chicago: University of Chicago Press, 1979.

Mason, Steve. "Jews, Judaeans, Judaizing, Judaism: Problems of Categorization in Ancient History." *JSJ* 38 (2007): 457–512.

Molland, Einar. "The Heretics Combatted by Ignatius of Antioch." *JEH* 5 (1954): 1–6.

Nirenberg, David. *Anti-Judaism: The Western Tradition*. New York: Norton, 2013.

Novenson, Matthew V. "Paul's Former Occupation in *Ioudaismos*." Pages 24–39 in *Galatians and Christian Theology: Justification, the Gospel, and Ethics in Paul's Letter*. Edited by Mark W. Elliott et al. Grand Rapids: Baker Academic, 2014.

Paulsen, Henning. *Die Briefe des Ignatius von Antiochia und der Brief Des Polykarp von Smyrna*. HNT 18. Tübingen: Mohr Siebeck, 1985.

Pearson, Birger. *The Emergence of the Christian Religion: Essays on Early Christianity*. Harrisburg, PA: Trinity Press International, 1997.

Rius-Camps, Josep. *The Four Authentic Letters of Ignatius, the Martyr: A Critical Study Based on the Anomalies Contained in the Textus Receptus*. Christianismos 2. Rome: Pontificium Institutum Orientalium Studiorum, 1979.

Schoedel, William R. "Ignatius and the Archives." *HTR* 71 (1978): 97–106.

———. *Ignatius of Antioch: A Commentary on the Letters of Ignatius of Antioch*. Hermeneia. Philadelphia: Fortress, 1985.

Vinzent, Markus. *Tertullian's Preface to Marcion's Gospel*. Studia Patristica Supplements 5. Leuven: Peeters, 2016.

Williams, A. Lukyn, ed. and trans. *Justin Martyr: The Dialogue with Trypho*. Translations of Christian Literature. London: SPCK, 1930.

# The Paraleipomena Jeremiou and Anti-Judaism

Dale C. Allison Jr.

## Introduction

The Paraleipomena Jeremiou, also known as 4 Baruch, is in large measure a collection of haggadic legends. It opens by recounting Jerusalem's destruction in the time of Jeremiah (chs. 1–4), and it concludes with the joyful return of the exiles from Babylon (ch. 9). In between is the tale of Abimelech who, as a reward for his righteousness, sleeps through the entirety of the exile (ch. 5). Most scholars who have looked into the issue have decided that the book goes back to a Jewish original composed between the first and second Jewish revolts.[1] In its present form, however, 4 Baruch is decidedly and stridently Christian. As the book nears its end, Jeremiah has a vision, after which he utters these words in public:

> Glorify God with one voice, all (of you) glorify God and the Son of God who awakens us, Jesus Christ the light of all the ages, the unquenchable light, the life of faith. And it will happen after these times that there will be another 477 years, and he will come to earth. And the tree of life, which is planted in the middle of paradise, will make all the unfruitful

I am delighted to offer this essay, inadequate as it is for the purpose, as a sign of my admiration for, and of my great debt to, my good friend Joel Marcus. We first met in Glasgow in January of 1996, and he has allowed me to fulfil the imperative of Jehoshua ben Perahjah: "Get for yourself a *ḥābēr*."

1. Representative statements include Jens Herzer, *Die Paralipomena Jeremiae: Studien zu Tradition und Redaktion einer Haggada des frühen Judentums*, TSAJ 43 (Tübingen: Mohr Siebeck, 1994), passim; Berndt Schaller, *Historische und legendarische Erzählungen: Paralipomena Jeremiou*, JSHRZ 1/8 (Gütersloh: Gütersloher Verlagshaus, 1998), 677–78; Christian Wolff, "Die Paralipomena Jeremiae und das Neue Testament," *NTS* 51 (2005): 126–36.

trees bear fruit, and grow, and send forth shoots. And it will make the
trees that had (earlier) sprouted and grown great and said, "We have
sent our top to the sky," together with their high branches, to shrivel
up; and that firmly rooted tree will cause them to be condemned. And
it will make that which is scarlet to become white as wool. The snow
will be turned black, the sweet waters will become salty, and the salty
will become sweet in the great light of the joy of God. And he will bless
the islands so that they produce fruit by the word from the mouth of
his Christ. For he will come, and he will go out, and he will choose for
himself twelve apostles, so that they might preach the good news among
the nations. He whom I have seen has been adorned by his Father, and
he is coming into the world upon the Mount of Olives; and he will fill the
hungry souls. (4 Bar 9:13–18)[2]

Immediately following this speech, and because of it, the people of Jerusalem decide to do away with the prophet: "While Jeremiah was saying these
things concerning the Son of God, that he is coming into the world, the
people became furious and said, 'These are once again the words spoken
by Isaiah the son of Amos when he said, "I saw God and the Son of God."
Come then, and let us not kill him by the death (with which we killed) that
one, but let us stone him with stones'" (9:19–21). In the event, they carry
out what they propose, and so the book ends.

On its face, 4 Bar 9 contains unalloyed polemic against Jews and Judaism. Nonetheless, J. Rendel Harris, in his ground-breaking edition of 4
Baruch, thought otherwise. His verdict was that 4 Baruch—a Christian
text from the beginning to his mind—was written immediately after the
Bar Kokhba revolt, when Hadrian had banned Jews from Jerusalem. It was
intended to function as "the Church's Eirenicon to the Synagogue." If only
Jews would submit to Christian baptism—Harris found this imperative in
the enigmatic 6:23 ("You [Jeremiah] will test them [the returning Jewish
exiles] by the water of the Jordan. The one not heeding will become manifest. This is the sign of the great seal")—they could still have access to the
holy city: "The meaning of it all is that the Christians, who are evidently
not affected by the imperial edict … have suggested to Jews that by becoming Christian by way of baptism they can evade the force of the edict, and
no longer be strangers to Jerusalem."[3]

---

2. The translations of 4 Baruch herein are from my forthcoming commentary, Dale
C. Allison Jr., *Paraleipomena Jeremiou (4 Baruch)*, CEJL (Berlin: de Gruyter, 2018).

3. J. Rendel Harris, *The Rest of the Words of Baruch: A Christian Apocalypse of*

That 4 Baruch is not unconditionally hostile to Jews and Judaism is also the judgment of Jens Herzer, who has contributed more in recent times to the study of the book than anyone else. On his view, "The Christian redaction [of the Jewish original][4] is not anti-Jewish but rather the redactor's attempt to develop a positive view of Jewish history in light of the failed rebellion" of Bar Kokhba. In fact, "a missionary element can be found, as the very act of developing a Jewish writing suggests: the Jewish people should learn from their past and listen to the voices that the writer of 4 Baruch let speak loudly, which in the view of the Christian redactor ultimately point to the coming of Christ."[5] Pablo Torijano, in his recent compact commentary, sees things the same way: the Christian edition of 4 Baruch is "a missionary work addressed to the Jewish people."[6]

In my judgment, Torijano, Herzer, and Harris have, regarding 4 Baruch and Judaism, gone astray. The main Christian redactor did not hope for Jewish readers who might have a change of mind and heart. The book is rather, and regrettably, testimony to a perception that Judaism belongs wholly to the past, so that its faithful adherents are without a future. Fouth Baruch is in fact a specimen of gentile Christian triumphalism and, in its present form, belongs with the so-called *Adversus Judaeos* literature. It is in no way conciliatory. On the contrary, its theological relatives, when it comes to Jews and Judaism, are Melito of Sardis's *On the Passover* and Tertullian's *Answer to the Jews*. If any real Jews ever heard or read 4 Baruch in its Christian form, they would not have found it irenic but would rather have taken offense. Ironically, although (against Harris) a Jew wrote the original 4 Baruch, the Christian redaction turned it into an anti-Jewish work without any good word for non-Christian Jews. The book sadly stands as testimony to a perceived parting of the ways in some part of the Christian world in the second half of the second century or

---

the Year 136 A.D.; The Text Revised with an Introduction (London: Clay & Sons; Cambridge: Cambridge University Press, 1889), 14, emphasis omitted.

4. Herzer, unlike Harris, thinks of 4 Baruch as a Jewish text to which a Christian added the story of the prophet's martyrdom in ch. 9.

5. Jens Herzer, *4 Baruch (Paraleipomena Jeremiou)*, WGRW 22 (Leiden: Brill, 2005), xxxv, emphasis omitted.

6. Pablo Torijano, "4 Baruch," in *Outside the Bible: Ancient Jewish Writings related to Scripture*, ed. Louis H. Feldman, James L. Kugel, and Lawrence H. Schiffman, 3 vols. (Philadelphia: Jewish Publication Society, 2013), 3:2661.

soon thereafter. It represents a Christianity that had gone its own non-Jewish way.

In order to support this conclusion, I shall, in what follows, argue that, although 4 Baruch was initially a Jewish text, the Christian elements are more extensive than widely thought, and, further, that the Christian version of 4 Baruch sees no future for Jews or Judaism. After making those points, I shall offer some suggestions as to the possible circumstances in which the Jewish 4 Baruch became the Christian 4 Baruch.

## A Jewish Original?

The martyrdom of Jeremiah in 4 Bar 9, introduced above, is manifestly Christian, and the book survives because Christians copied it, so some have thought that the whole work was Christian from the outset. In addition to Harris, Marc Philonenko proposed that the author of 4 Baruch belonged to a syncretistic Jewish-Christian baptist sect.[7] More recently, Pierluigi Piovanelli has argued that the Paraleipomena is a Christian rewriting, after the second revolt, of the Jewish text behind the Coptic Jeremiah Apocryphon.[8] Rivka Nir also identifies 4 Baruch as a Christian writing: the text comes from "an ascetic community" akin to the "Syriac-speaking churches of the second and third centuries," a community "that demanded of those joining it abstention from marriage, that is, bachelor-hood, as a necessary condition of baptism."[9]

While I am, for reasons to be given below, of another opinion, namely, that the first edition of 4 Baruch was Jewish, I concur that the Christian elements are not, as so often claimed,[10] confined to the concluding chapter and

---

7. Marc Philonenko, "Simples Observations sur les Paralipomènes de Jérémie," *RHPR* 76 (1996): 157–77.

8. Pierluigi Piovanelli, "Les Paralipomènes de Jérémie dépendent-ils de l'Histoire de la captivité babylonienne?," *Bulletin de l'AELAC* 7 (1997): 10–14; Piovanelli, "Paralipomeni di Geremia," in *Apocrifi dell'Antico Testamento*, ed. Paolo Sacchi, 5 vols. (Brescia: Paideia, 1999), 3:265–73; Piovanelli, "In Praise of 'The Default Position,' or Reassessing the Christian Reception of the Jewish Pseudepigraphic Heritage," *NedTT* 61 (2007): 233–50. For the Coptic Jeremiah Apocryphon, which merits far more attention than it has received, see K. H. Kuhn, "A Coptic Jeremiah Apocryphon," *Mus* 83 (1970): 95–135, 291–350.

9. Rivka Nir, *The Destruction of Jerusalem and the Idea of Redemption in the Syriac Apocalypse of Baruch*, EJL 20 (Atlanta: Society of Biblical Literature, 2002), 237.

10. See esp. Gerhard Delling, *Jüdische Lehre und Frömmigkeit in den Paralipom-*

its tale of Jeremiah's vision and martyrdom. On purely linguistic grounds, a number of phrases from earlier portions likely stem from a Christian hand. Here are six examples:

(1) After learning of God's intention to destroy Jerusalem, Jeremiah says, in 1.6, "May it not be, Lord! But if it is your will [ἀλλ᾽ εἰ θέλημά σού ἐστιν], let it be destroyed by your own hands." The conditional phrase in parenthesis has precise parallels in several texts of Egyptian monasticism and, to my knowledge, only in such texts.[11]

(2) In 5.21, Baruch explains to Abimelech, who has been asleep during the entirety of the exile: "For Jeremiah is in Babylon with the people. For they were taken captive by Nebuchadnezzar the king, and with them is Jeremiah, who brings good news to them and instructs them in the word." The Greek behind the last clause is: καὶ μετ᾽ αὐτῶν ἐστιν Ἰερεμίας εὐαγγελίσασθαι αὐτοῖς καὶ κατηχῆσαι αὐτοὺς τὸν λόγον. The phrase sounds Christian. It is true that εὐαγγελίζω by itself could be Jewish, as it is twenty times in the LXX. Yet in 9.18, where the twelve apostles announce good news, the verb is indisputably Christian, and the addition of κατηχέω plus the unqualified τὸν λόγον more than suggests the same judgment here. For although κατηχέω occurs in both non-Jewish and Jewish sources, its combination with the unqualified, definite, singular λόγον—which here means something like "the divine word" or even "the word of the gospel"[12]—appears to be uniquely Christian. Parallels include Gal 6:6 (κατηχούμενος τὸν λόγον); Pseudo-Clem. Hom. 1.13.3 (τοῦ ἀληθοῦς λόγου ... κατηχήσας με); Apos. Con. 7.39 (κατηχεῖσθαι τὸν λόγον); Basil of Caesarea, Spir. 29.25 (τὸν λόγον κατηχουμένων); Cyril of Alexandria, Comm. John (ed. Pusey 2:484) (κατηχείτω λόγον).[13] The

---

ena Jeremiae, BZNW 100 (Berlin: Töpelmann, 1967), whose work has greatly influenced German scholarship; also Herzer, Paralipomena, 171–76, and Wolff, "Die Paralipomena Jeremiae und das Neue Testament."

11. Apophth. Patr. 25 (alphabetical collection, PG 65.193); Apophth. Patr. 15.33 (systematic collection, ed. Guy SC 474); Paphnutius, Onuphrio 1; Vit. Pach. Φ 146; Vit. Pach. 3 (ed. Halkin, p. 402).

12. Cf. Mark 4:15; 16:20; Luke 1:2; Acts 4:4; 1 Pet 2:8; 1 John 2:7.

13. Peter Stuhlmacher, Das paulinische evangelium I: Vorgeschichte, FRLANT 95 (Göttingen: Vandenhoeck & Ruprecht, 1968), 178 n. 2, argues, to the contrary, that the language of 4 Baruch has a parallel in the targumic אלף + אורייתא or פתגם אורייתא; cf. Tg. Neof. 1 and Tg. Pseudo-J. Gen 49:10; Tg. Neof. 1 Deut 32:29; Tg. Isa. 2:3, 30:10, 32:6. He cites, however, no examples of אלף + unqualified פתגם; and אורייתא, which

coordinated use of εὐαγγελίζω and κατηχέω is also characteristically Christian.[14]

(3) After Baruch learns the truth about Abimelech, he delivers a speech that includes these peculiar words: "Be cheered in your tent, my virginal faith, and believe that you will live" (6.4). The qualification of "faith" by "virginal"—presumably the sense is "pure" or "unadulterated faith"—betrays a Christian hand. While there are no Jewish parallels, there are close Christian parallels in Origen, *Hom. Lev.* 12:5 (*fidei uirginalis et simplicis cultum*) and in the Greek translation of a fifth-century Armenian historian, Agathangelos and his *Hist. Armen.* 63 (τὸν μαργαρίτην τῆς παρθενικῆς ἡμῶν πίστεως).[15]

(4) Baruch's prayer in 6.9 contains the elaborate phrase "I implore and entreat your goodness [παρακαλῶ καὶ δέομαί σου τῆς ἀγαθότητός]." Παρακαλῶ καὶ δέομαί is characteristic of Christian texts (albeit in exhortations to Christians instead of in petitions to God[16]), and the same holds for "your goodness," which occurs in prayers.[17] Further, παρακαλοῦμεν τὴν σὴν ἀγαθότητα became Christian liturgical language.[18]

(5) When Jeremiah, in chapter 9, celebrates the return of the people and, as the great high priest, offers sacrifice, he composes a prayer with this introduction: "Holy, holy, holy, the incense of the living trees, the true

---

means "law," "instruction," or "lesson" (Jastrow, s.v.), is an imperfect parallel to λόγος. If the meaning were "to teach the law," would we not expect νόμος?

14. Note, e.g., Socrates Scholasticus, *Hist. eccl.* 7.4; Pseudo-Basil of Seleucia, *Vit. Thecl.* 1.28; Cosmas Indicopleustes, *Top.* 10.11.

15. Delling, *Jüdische Lehre*, 9 n.22, and Jan Riaud, *Les Paralipomènes du prophète Jérémie: Présentation, texte original, traduction et commentaires*, Cahiers du Centre Interdisciplinaire de Recherches en Histoire, Lettres et Langues 14 (Angers: Université Catholique de l'Ouest, 1994), 189, who suppose the expression comes from a Jewish hand, can cite for comparison only Rev 14:4. This refers only to the virgins who follow the lamb and says nothing about faith, and it is in any case Christian.

16. John Chrysostom, *Hom. Gen.* 18 (PG 53:158); Theodore the Studite, *Magn. Cat.* 2, 17.

17. Cf. Didymus of Alexandria, *Fr. Ps.* 741a (παρακαλῶ μὴ ἀπορριφῆναι ἀλλὰ συνεργεῖσθαι ὑπὸ τῆς ἀγαθότητός σου); Acts Phil. 144 (ὁ Φίλιππος ηὔξατο ... Κύριε ... ἐχαρίσω δὲ ἡμῖν τὴν βουλὴν τῆς ἀγαθότητός σου); Theodoret of Cyrrhus, *Comm. Ps.* (PG 80:1681) (δεηθῆναί σου τῆς ἀγαθότητος); Agathangelus, *Hist. Armen.* 42 (οἰκτείρησον οὖν ἐν τῇ χάριτι τῆς σῆς ἀγαθότητος); Theodore the Studite, *Ep.* 21 (δεόμεθά σου τῆς ἀγαθότητος).

18. See the Liturgy of Saint Basil (PG 31:1648). Schaller, *Paralipomena*, 732, cites the Introit to the Liturgy of James (ed. Mercier, PO 26:164). The phrase occurs also in Gregory Nazianzen, *Ep.* 219.3; Maximus the Confessor, *Ascet.* 37.

light that enlightens me [τὸ φῶς τὸ ἀληθινὸν τὸ φωτίζον με] until I am taken up to you" (9.3). In addition to the obvious borrowing from the famous Isa 6:3, the phrase, "the true light that enlightens me," almost certainly derives from John 1:9: ἦν τὸ φῶς τὸ ἀληθινὸν ὃ φωτίζει πάντα ἄνθρωπον.[19] Apart from 4 Baruch, τὸ φῶς τὸ ἀληθινόν plus φωτίζω appears only in John and Christian texts familiar with John,[20] and "the collocation of words [in 4 Baruch] is so peculiar, that it is almost impossible to refer the language to any other than St John."[21] The clause appears to be from the same hand as 9.13, where Jesus Christ is the light of all ages ("Glorify God with one voice, all [of you] glorify God and the Son of God who awakens us, Jesus Christ the light of all the ages, the unquenchable light, the life of faith"). It is, moreover, suggestive that the undisputedly Christian conclusion to 4 Baruch shares another phrase with John 1:9. If the latter speaks of "the word," the true light, "coming into the world [ἔρχεται εἰς τὸν κόσμον]," in the former, Jeremiah speaks of the Son of God, that "he is coming into the world [ἔρχεται εἰς τὸν κόσμον]" (9.19).[22]

All this is a problem for those who argue that 4 Bar 9.3 is not Christian. Delling, citing Ps 43:3; Sir 45:17; 1QS II, 3; 1QH XII, 5, and 27, argues that the idea of God enlightening the righteous is "thoroughly possible" in a Jewish context.[23] This is true, yet none of the texts he cites is very close to 4 Bar 9.4, and none features τὸ φῶς τὸ ἀληθινόν plus φωτίζω plus human object. As for Wolff's objection that the christological statement in John 1:9 is unlikely to have become, in 4 Bar 9.3, a theological statement,[24] it comes up against (a) the possibility that the prayer in 9.3 is addressed to Jesus, as is the prayer in 9.25 ("Light of the ages, transform this stone into my likeness until

---

19. Cf. 1 John 2:8 (τὸ φῶς τὸ ἀληθινὸν ἤδη φαίνε) and note esp. the use of τὸ φῶς τὸ ἀληθινὸν τὸ φωτίζον—not ὃ φωτίζει—in patristic texts that adapt John 1:9: Pseudo-Justin, *Expositio rectae fidei* (ed. Morel, p. 390); Eusebius, *Comm. Ps.* (PG 23:501); Pseudo-Gregory of Nyssa, *In annuntiationem* (ed. Montagna, line 10); Hesychius of Jerusalem, *Hom.* 5.2.24.

20. Clement of Alexandria, *Strom.* 2.5.21.2; Eusebius, *Comm. Isa.* 2:50; Epiphanius, *Anc.* 3.9; etc. Note, however, that τὸ ἀληθῶς φῶς occurs in Plato, *Phaed.* 109e, and ἀληθῶς φῶς in Philo, *Leg.* 1.17.

21. So Harris, *Baruch*, 26. Cf. the Christian addition in MS C at 5.33: τὸ φῶς τὸ ἀληθινόν, ἡ ἀληθινὴ ἀνταπόδοσις, ὁ ὤν, μέγας θαυμαστὸς εἰς τοὺς αἰῶνας, ἀμήν.

22. The relevant Greek phrase appears to be attested first in John and otherwise only in subsequent Christian literature.

23. Delling, *Jüdische Lehre*, 35.

24. Wolff, "Neue Testament," 133–34.

I have fully divulged to Baruch and Abimelech all that I saw"), and (b) the probability that the Christian redactor, who interpreted Israel's vision of "the Lord" (Isa 6:1) as a vision of God's Son (9.20), was a binitarian or trinitarian.

(6) In 9.6, Jeremiah addresses God as ὁ ἀγέννητος καὶ ἀπερινόητος, as "the unbegotten and incomprehensible." While ἀγέννητος occurs in secular sources, it is characteristic of Christian texts.[25] As for the rarer ἀπερινόητος, it too, although attested in non-Christian sources, is characteristic of ecclesial texts, where it refers both to God and to the Son of God.[26] The combination of the two words, which appear together in lists of divine attributes in Hippolytus, *Haer.* 6.29, and Pseudo-Cyril of Alexandria, *Trin.* (PG 77:1120), is likely from a Christian hand.[27]

Taken together, the preceding observations are weighty, and given that most of 4 Baruch's final chapter is indisputably Christian, and given further that Christian scribes preserved the whole work, why resist the natural implication of the linguistic facts? Even if there is cause to believe that 4 Baruch goes back to a Jewish original, Christian hands have tampered with more than the ending. It accords with this that certain words and expressions in 9.10–32 appear before that passage and so could reflect a common hand.[28]

Despite the observations just made, I believe, with R. H. Charles and others, that 4 Baruch seems "to be a Jewish work recast."[29] The main reason

---

25. Lampe, s.v. "ἀγέννητος." In Ignatius, *Eph.* 7.2; Acts Phil. 141, and Basil of Seleucia, *Or.* 25.4, it refers to Jesus (despite John 1:18: μονογενὴς Θεός). Other texts, however, dissociate the term from the Son: Pseudo-Athanasius, *Trin.* 1.18; etc. The word occurs as a v.l. in Josephus, *C. Ap.* 2.167. By contrast, the similar ἀγένητος is well-attested in Philo and Josephus; see Delling, *Jüdische Lehre*, 37. Schaller, *Paralipomena*, 750, suggests that the Jewish original had ἀγένητος and that a later Christian hand turned this into ἀγέννητος. Cf. Delling, *Jüdische Lehre*, 37.

26. Of God: Theophilus, *Autol.* 1.3.1; Clement of Alexandria, *Ecl.* 21; Chrysostom, *Hom. Matt.* 26.39. Of the Son: Diogn. 7.2; Acts John 77; Chrysostom, *Hom. Matt.* 2.2.

27. Cf. also Tri. Trac. 59.32–33. Torijano, "4 Baruch," 3:2677, citing Justin, *1 Apol.* 14.1–2; *Dial.* 5.1, 4–6; and Clement of Alexandria, *Strom.* 2.5.4, observes that "these adjectives describing God are unusual in Jewish writings" and sensibly offers that "they could be a Christian interpolation."

28. A few examples: imperative of ἑτοιμάζω + reflexive pronoun occurs in 6.3 and 9.10; ἀκούω + τῆς φωνῆς in 3.8; 6.10, 22; and 9.12; σκήνωμα (of the human body) in 6.3–4 and 9.12; γλυκύς in 9.3 and 9.16; εὐαγγελίζω in 3.11, 5.21, and 9.18; ῥῆμα in 1.9; 2.9; 3.3, 4; 8.4; and 9.20; πάντα ὅσα in 7.22 and 9.23, 25; νομίζω + ὅτι in 5.26 and 9.27, 30; and (οἱ) υἱοὶ Ἰσραήλ in 1.1; 6.13.

29. R. H. Charles, *The Apocalypse of Baruch translated from the Syriac* (London: Black, 1896), xviii.

for so thinking is the number of crucial elements that are characteristic of Jewish texts as opposed to Christian texts or which are far more common in Jewish sources than in Christian sources. The most obvious are these:

(1) The call to separate from foreign spouses is a significant plot element from chapter 6 on, and it signifies "a specifically Jewish interest."[30] Such an imperative, which conflicts with the gentile triumphalism of 9.14–18, is not what one would expect from most Christians, especially given that Paul explicitly opposed separating from nonbelieving pagans (1 Cor 7:12–13; compare with 1 Pet 3:1).

(2) A major motif in chapters 1–5 is lamentation over the destruction of Jerusalem. Repeatedly, we read that Jeremiah and Baruch wept (2.1–10, 3.14, 4.5–11). Furthermore, throughout the book, life without the temple is liminal: Abimelech sleeps (5.1) while Baruch sits in a tomb and mourns (4.6–11, 6.1), and Jeremiah and the exiles pass their time in misery (7.23–29). All this reflects a post-70 Jewish ethos, one likewise manifest in 4 Ezra and 2 Baruch but not in Christian books from the same period or later.[31] Instead of mourning the fall of Jerusalem, most Christians, including Jewish Christians such as the author of Matthew, discerned in the event the vindication of Jesus—who purportedly predicted it—and of their own cause.[32] Indeed, "virtually nowhere in the literature of early Christianity or Jewish Christianity do we find evidence of regret over Jerusalem's loss…. The available testimony points overwhelmingly toward an attitude of rejection and condemnation."[33]

(3) Chapter 8 offers an unflattering etiology of the Samaritans: they descend from exiles who married foreign women and, in disobedience to God's prophet, refused to separate from them. This legend is of a piece

---

30. So E. Kautzsch, *Die Apokryphen und Pseudepigraphen des Alten Testaments*, 2 vols. (Tübingen: Mohr Siebeck, 1900), 2:403.

31. That many Jews mourned the events of 70 is the only point here, not that the date necessarily marks a transformation of Judaism or a division between Jewish eras.

32. See G. W. H. Lampe, "A.D. 70 in Christian Reflection," in *Jesus and the Politics of His Day*, ed. Ernst Bammel and C. F. D. Moule (Cambridge: Cambridge University Press, 1984), 153–71; and Adele Reinhartz, "The Destruction of Jerusalem as a Trauma for Nascent Christianity," in *Trauma and Traumatization in Individual and Collective Dimensions: Insights from Biblical Studies and Beyond*, ed. Eve-Marie Becker, Jan Dochhorn, and Else K. Holt, Studia Aarhusiana Neotestamentica 2 (Göttingen: Vandenhoeck & Ruprecht, 2014), 274–88.

33. So Daniel C. Harlow, *The Greek Apocalypse of Baruch (3 Baruch) in Hellenistic Judaism and Early Christianity*, SVTP 12 (Leiden: Brill, 1996), 108.

with negative portrayals of the Samaritans in several Jewish writings.[34] By contrast, and beginning with Acts and the Gospel of John, early Christian sources reflect a much more positive view of these people.[35] In addition, and on the whole, Jews had, it is fair to say, more interest in Samaritan origins than did Christians.

(4) Fourth Baruch exhibits not only a keen interest in Jerusalem and the temple but also in the latter's keys and instruments (3.7–8, 14; 4.3). It further presumes the validity of temple sacrifices and associates them with rejoicing (9.1). If 4 Baruch is Jewish, all this is unsurprising. If, however, 4 Baruch is Christian, we have an anomaly. Most Christians rejected the ritual laws of Judaism,[36] and original Christian compositions otherwise show little or no interest in what happened to the temple's keys and vessels.

(5) The notion that Baruch was sinless (6.3: οὐ γὰρ γέγονέ σοι) is foreign to conventional Christian theology, which came to venerate Jesus as the only perfect individual. This presumably explains why the Ethiopic drops the characterization of Baruch as sinless from 6.3. Jewish texts, by contrast, speak of any number of individuals as perfect, blameless, or sinless.[37]

One could, in responding to these points, protest that the argument is too simple, that it wrongly posits a clean antithesis between Judaism and Christianity and fails to take into account the complexity and diversity

---

34. On the different Jewish opinions from second temple and rabbinic times, see Gedalyahu Alon, *Jews, Judaism and the Classical World: Studies in Jewish History in the Time of the Second Temple and the Talmud* (Jerusalem: Magnes, 1977), 354–73. For overviews of the problem of the Samaritans in rabbinic literature, see Moshe Lavee, "The Samaritans May Be Included—Another Look at the Samaritan in Talmudic Literature," in *Samaritans: Past and Present; Current Studies*, ed. Menachem Mor and Friedrich V. Reiterer, SJ 53 (Berlin: de Gruyter, 2010), 147–73.

35. Note, e.g., Luke 10:25–37; 17:11–19; John 4:4–42; Acts 1:8, 8:4–25.

36. See L. V. Rutgers, *The Hidden Heritage of Diaspora Judaism*, 2nd ed., CBET 20 (Leuven: Peeters, 1998), 235–84.

37. Note, e.g., Pr. Man. 8 ("Abraham, Isaac, and Jacob did not sin"); T. Mos. 9.4 ("Never did [our] fathers nor their ancestors [the patriarchs presumably] tempt God by transgressing his commandments"); T. Abr. RecLng. 10.13–14 ("Abraham has not sinned"); T. Iss. 7.1–7: ("I [Issachar] am 122 years old, and I am not aware of having committed a sin unto death.... There was no deceit in my heart; no lie passed through my lips.... I acted in piety and truth all my days"); T. Reub. 4.4 ("from that time to this I [Reuben] have kept a careful watch and have not sinned"); 2 Bar 9.1 ("Jeremiah, whose heart was found to be pure from sins"); 61.7 (the generation of Solomon "did not sin"); Deut. Rab. 11:10 ("I [Moses] have not sinned from my youth").

within both.[38] Why not infer that 4 Baruch was composed by an anti-Pauline Jewish Christian author who rejected marrying gentiles and who cared deeply about the temple and everything associated with it?[39] This, however, would be at odds with the gentile triumphalism of 9.14–17, where, as we shall see, Israel exits salvation-history and the twelve apostles preach the good news to the nations.[40]

Literary-critical considerations support the judgment that 4 Baruch is fundamentally not Christian but Jewish. The undisputedly Christian ending—which contains a large number of words found nowhere else in 4 Baruch[41]—strikes one as secondary. The disjunction between 9.9, where the people mourn the prophet's apparent death, and 9.19–32, where they angrily stone him, is jarring, and nothing in the preceding narrative prepares readers for Jeremiah's violent execution.[42] The people who, in one chapter, and unlike the Samaritans, prove themselves to be obedient and faithful, all of sudden, in the very next chapter, murder God's representative. There is also a startling mismatch between the antigentile attitude of

---

38. Relevant here are James R. Davila, *The Provenance of the Pseudepigrapha: Jewish, Christian, or Other?*, JSJSup 105 (Leiden: Brill, 2005), 15–63, and Richard J. Bauckham, "The Continuing Quest for the Provenance of Old Testament Pseudepigrapha," in *The Pseudepigrapha and Christian Origins: Essays from the Studiorum Novi Testamenti Societas*, ed. Gerbern S. Oegema and James H. Charlesworth (New York: T&T Clark, 2008), 9–29.

39. One should note, however, that the anti-Pauline Ebionites, or at least some of them, evidently opposed the sacrificial cult. Cf. frag. 6 of the Gospel of the Ebionites *apud* Epiphanius, *Pan.* 30.16.4–5: "I am come to do away with sacrifices, and if you do not cease from sacrificing, the wrath of God will not cease from you." The same hostility appears in Ps.-Clem. Hom. 1.37.2–4; 39.2; 48.5–6; 54.1; and 64.1–2, which likely preserve Ebionite teaching. See further Simon J. Joseph, "'I Have Come to Abolish Sacrifices' (Epiphanius, Pan. 30.16.5): Re-examining a Jewish Christian Text and Tradition," *NTS* 63 (2017): 92–110.

40. Torleif Elgvin, "Jewish Christian Editing of the Old Testament Pseudepigrapha," in *Jewish Believers in Jesus: The Early Centuries*, ed. Oskar Skarsaune and Reidar Hvalvik (Peabody, MA: Hendrickson, 2007), 278–304, can attribute the main redaction of 4 Baruch to a Jewish Christian only by urging that 9.16–20 is a gentile Christian interpolation.

41. By my count, there are, if one begins the count at 9.10, sixty-three such words.

42. See Emil Schürer, review of *The Rest of the Words of Baruch: A Christian Apocalypse of the Year 136 A.D.; The Text Revised with an Introduction*, by J. Rendel Harris, *TLZ* 15 (1890): 83: the martyrdom of Jeremiah is, in its larger context, "completely unmotivated and leaves the impression of being a clumsy Christian addition."

chapters 6–8, with their denunciation of "the defilements of the gentiles of Babylon," and the glowing picture of gentile conversion in 9.14–18. Additionally, and with regard to the linguistic elements before chapter 9 that are likely to be Christian (see above), not one is integral to the book. They are all readily attributed to later scribal revision.

A Jewish original is consistent with yet three more facts. First, the books that, in terms of content, overlap most with 4 Baruch—namely, 2 Baruch, the Coptic Jeremiah Apocryphon, and Pesiqta Rabbati 26[43]— are Jewish compositions.[44] Second, 4 Baruch is full of stories, themes, and additional elements that otherwise appear in Jewish sources,[45] and sometimes—as with the episode of the keys of the temple being hidden (4.3–4)—appear exclusively there. Third, it is perhaps worth noting that, although the popular legend of the seven sleepers of Ephesus reflects the influence of 4 Baruch,[46] most of the church fathers seemingly did not know our book or at least found no use for it, for traces of it in their writings are very hard to find.

## Further Notes on the Christian Redaction

Fourth Baruch, then, appears to be a Christian edition of an older Jewish work. How extensive was the Christian revision? There can be no definitive answer, in part because there were, as well as additions, probably subtractions, and those we cannot uncover. One especially wonders how the book originally ended. Did Jeremiah die of old age? Did 4 Baruch conclude— much like the Coptic Jeremiah Apocryphon—with Jeremiah offering sacrifice and the people celebrating a feast in Jerusalem, with no notice being taken of Jeremiah's death? Or did the book end with an apocalyptic vision of the future, which a Christian turned into prophecy of Jesus? Whatever the truth, this writer believes that de Jonge's judgment—"there is a case to

---

43. For an overview of the parallels, see Herzer, *4 Baruch*, xvi–xxvi.

44. The view that 2 Baruch is Christian—so Nir, *Destruction*—remains marginal. On the Jewish character of the Jeremiah Apocryphon, see A. Marmorstein, "Die Quellen des neuen Jeremia-Apocryphons," *ZNW* 27 (1928): 327–37; Kuhn, "Apocryphon," 102–4; Piovanelli, "Default Position."

45. Here the work of Delling, *Jüdische Lehre*, retains its value.

46. See Bernard Heller, "Éléments, parallèles et origine de la légende des sept dormants," *REJ* 49 (1904): 213–14, and Pieter W. van der Horst, "Pious Long-Sleepers in Pagan, Jewish and Christian Antiquity," in *Studies in Ancient Judaism and Early Christianity* (Leiden: Brill, 2014), 265.

be made for a much more thoroughgoing Christian redaction of the Paralipomena than is commonly accepted"[47]—likely claims too much. While
the Christian contribution is not, as we have seen, confined to 9.10–32,
the document nonetheless, and for the most part, leaves the impression of
being a Jewish composition, with a Christian ending and Christian revisions and insertions here and there.[48] In this connection, however, a few
additional subjects require exploration.

(1) The first has to do with a text-critical issue. In 7.25, Harris's Greek
edition has the exiles in Babylon praying, Ἐλέησον ἡμᾶς, ὁ θεὸς Ζάρ, that
is, "Have mercy upon us, O God Zar." This is the larger context: "For often
when I [Jeremiah] left [the city], I found some of the people who had been
hung up by Nebuchadnezzar the king weeping and saying, 'Have mercy
upon us, O God Zar.' When I heard these things, I would grieve and cry a
double lamentation, not only because they were hung up, but because they
called upon a foreign God, saying, 'Have mercy upon us.'"

Ὁ θεὸς Ζάρ is not, however, the reading of any Greek text. It is rather
Harris's conjecture. The two Greek witnesses for this verse (MSS C and L)
have ὁ θεὸς σαβαώθ. Harris, urging that Ζάρ transliterates the Hebrew זר
("strange" or "foreign"), so that the exiles are worshipping a foreign God,[49]
based his proposed reading upon the Ethiopic. His subjoined note offers
this documentation: "*mss. aeth* Zar, Sorot, Sarot."

Although the later critical editions of Kraft-Purintun and Herzer
follow Harris here, Piovanelli has observed that Harris not only employed
Dillmann's woefully incomplete apparatus, but that Ethiopic MS a actually reads *Sor*, not *Zar*.[50] Piovanelli is, in addition, persuasive when he
contends that the Ethiopic *Sor* is an abbreviated form of *Sorot*, and that
the latter is a variant of *Sarot*, which appears in the best Ethiopic wit-

---

47. Marinus de Jonge, *Pseudepigrapha of the Old Testament as Part of Christian
Literature: The Case of the Testaments of the Twelve Patriarchs and the Greek Life of
Adam and Eve*, SVTP 18 (Leiden: Brill, 2003), 55–56.

48. While most or all of 9.10–32 seems to come from a single hand, the earlier
additions may come from other hands.

49. Cf. 7.26, which refers to θεὸν ἀλλότριον.

50. August Dillmann, *Chrestomathia Aethiopica: Edita et glossario explanata*
(Leipzig: Weigel, 1866), 11; Robert A. Kraft and Ann-Elizabeth Purintun, *Paraleipomena Jeremiou*, SBLTT 1, Pseudepigrapha Series 1 (Missoula, MT: Scholars Press,
1972), 38; Herzer, *4 Baruch*, 28. For the reading of Ethiopic MS a and what follows, see
Piovanelli, "Paralimpomeni," 268; Piovanelli, "Ricerche sugli apocrifi veterotestamentari etiopici" (MA thesis, University of Florence, 1986), 146–47, 196.

nesses. *Sarot* in turn is readily explained, as the Greek witnesses strongly suggest, as a corruption of σαβαώθ: ΣΑΒΑΩΘ became ΣΑΡΑΩΘ and then ΣΑΡΩΘ.[51] What all this means is that there is no good cause to reject the reading of the only extant Greek manuscripts for 7.25: ὁ θεὸς σαβαώθ. In other words, the best and earliest-attested text has Jeremiah mourn when the people call upon the foreign god they address as ὁ θεὸς σαβαώθ. This text-critical decision is consistent with 9.3, where the ἅγιος, ἅγιος, ἅγιος of Isa 6:3 appears without Isaiah's following Κύριος σαβαώθ. This makes sense on the supposition that "Lord Sabaoth" is, in 4 Baruch, a rejected title.

If all this is so, it is indeed very hard to imagine that a Jew penned 7.25. Here, then, is one more sign of a Christian hand. What, however, might a Christian have intended to say here? Piovanelli raises the possibility that 4 Baruch stems from a Christian who, like some so-called gnostics, distinguished between the false God Sabaoth and the true God of Abraham, Isaac, and Jacob.[52] He further proposes that 4 Baruch may polemicize against Jews, especially Christian Jews, who engaged in what the author took to be obsolete Jewish practices.[53]

Piovanelli could be correct. I should like to suggest, however, that the explanation for the rejection of the God Sabaoth lies in magical texts, for the verse could polemicize against people perceived as syncretistic, Jewish or not. Although early Christian literature, like the Pseudepigrapha, generally shies away from σαβαώθ, it and the Hebrew it transliterates are common in magical texts,[54] and Origen wrote that "Sabaoth"

---

51. So also now Bernhard Heininger, "Der Brief Jeremias an Baruch (ParJer 7,23–30): Ein Beitrag zur Textkritik apokrypher Schriften," *SNTU* 34 (2009): 72–76.

52. For sources in which Sabaoth is not the highest God, see Francis T. Fallon, *The Enthronement of Sabaoth: Jewish Elements in Gnostic Creation Myths*, NHS 10 (Leiden: Brill, 1978). See also the Manichaean statement in Hegemonius, *Acta Archelai* 11.4: "this name Sabaoth, which in your eyes is great and distinguished, he [Mani] says is the nature of man and the father of lust."

53. See Pierluigi Piovanelli, "Le sommeil séculaire d'Abimélech dans l'Histoire de la captivité babylonienne et les Paralipomènes de Jérémie: Texte—intertextes—contextes," in *Intertextualités: La Bible en échos*, ed. Daniel Marguerat and Adrian Curtis, MdB 40 (Paris: Labor et Fides, 2000), 82–83; Piovanelli, "Default Position," 246–49.

54. Philo and Josephus also avoid the expression. It occurs in the Pseudepigrapha and early Christian literature in Sib. Or. 1.304, 316; Jas 5:4; Rom 9:29 (a citation of LXX Isa 1:9); 1 Clem. 34.6 (a quotation of LXX Isa 6:3); Sib. Or. 2.239 (part of a Christian interpolation). For the usage in magical texts, see CIJ 673, 674, 717; T. Sol. 1.6, 7; 5.9;

was "frequently employed in incantations" (*Cels.* 5.45). Moreover, some of these texts, such as the Magical Papyri, are highly syncretistic and, among other things, employ both Babylonian names (for example, the underground goddess Ereschigal) and Jewish names, including Sabaoth. One could take the assimilating Jews in 4 Bar 7 to be comparable. Beyond this, while the LXX prefers Κύριος Θεὸς σαβαώθ or (much more often) Κύριος σαβαώθ,[55] several magical texts have the precise form in our text, ὁ θεὸς σαβαώθ.[56]

Unfortunately, we have no way of determining exactly what theological *Sitz im Leben* might have led to 4 Bar 7.25, which means we cannot know whether Piovanelli's conjecture or mine or some other is correct. Yet, whatever the precise explanation one has for ὁ θεὸς σαβαώθ in 7.25, one fact is evident. Rejection of the God Sabaoth is less likely to come from a Jew than from a gentile Christian. It thus adds to the case for Christian redaction and an un-Jewish outlook extending beyond the second half of the last chapter.

(2) Another issue concerning the Christian redaction of 4 Baruch that I should like to touch upon has to do with the book's eschatology. In its current form, 4 Baruch promotes hope within history by narrating how God remembered the covenant and saved the exiles. At the same time, the book teaches that, at death, the faithful enter "the upper city, Jerusalem" (5.34; 6.3; 9.3, 5), and further that, at history's end, the dead will be raised to life (6.4–7; compare with 7.17–18). Boyeon Birana Lee, however, has urged that at least 5.34, 6.3, and 9.3 are secondary. He thereby raises the possiblity that the original 4 Baruch—which he takes to have been Jewish—may have implied nothing about postmortem existence or an

---

18.16; *PGM* II.15; III.76; IV.981, 1377, 1485; David Noy, *Jewish Inscriptions of Western Europe*, 2 vols. (Cambridge: Cambridge University Press, 1993–1995), 1:212 (no. 159); Walter Ameling, *Inscriptiones Judaicae Orientis II: Kleinasien*, TSAJ 99 (Tübingen: Mohr Siebeck, 2004), 533 (Magica 4); etc. For צבאות and variants on magical amulets and bowls, see Josephu Naveh and Shaul Shaked, *Amulets and Magic Bowls: Aramaic Incantations of Late Antiquity* (Jerusalem: Magnes; Leiden: Brill, 1985), 40, 56, 94, 96, 102, 164, 180; Charles D. Isbell, *Corpus of the Aramaic Incantation Bowls*, SBLDS 17 (Missoula, MT: Scholars Press, 1975), 52.

55. Only LXX Isa 44:6 has the simple Θεὸς σαβαώθ.

56. Suppl. Mag. Pap. 27:2 (ed. Daniel and Maltomini); P. Paris Suppl. gr. 574; T. Sol. 11.6 (MS P); 24.2 (MS Q); 10.53 (MS C).

other-worldly Jerusalem.[57] The same possibility has occurred to Marinus de Jonge.[58]

Although it is beyond the scope of this essay to explore Lee's proposal in any detail, I should like to observe that it gains some support from Piovanelli's work (which Lee does not cite). Piovanelli has argued that a late first- or early second-century version of the Coptic Jeremiah Apocryphon lies behind 4 Baruch.[59] Although I prefer to think of something closely related to the Coptic Jeremiah Apocryphon rather than of the Apocryphon itself, what matters is that the Apocryphon, which is in many ways so close to 4 Baruch, is wholly this-worldly. It tells the tale of exile and return without raising the subject of what happens at death. Furthermore, although it, like 4 Baruch, recounts the fable of a man sleeping through the entirety of the exile, it fails, unlike 4 Baruch, to tie the incredible yarn to the doctrine of the resurrection of the body. If, then, Piovenelli is near the truth, 4 Baruch's use of Abimelech's awakening as a parable or prophecy of resurrection was not originally part of the Jewish tale that found its way into that book. One understands why Piovanelli ascribes to a Christian hand the allegorizing of Abimelech's sleep as a symbol of eschatological revivification.[60] Unfortunately, however, as with so many issues having to do with 4 Baruch, the data do not allow us here to pass beyond the possible to the probable.

(3) The third matter concerning the main Christian redaction has to do with its date. Several points are germane. One is that it must postdate the Jewish edition, which is typically, and for good reason, assigned to the first third of the second century.[61] Another is that it must predate the

---

57. Boyeon Birana Lee, "The Development of the Jeremiah Figure in *2 Baruch* and *4 Baruch*: A Response to Jens Herzer," in *Jeremiah's Scriptures: Production, Reception, Interaction, and Transformation*, ed. Hindy Najman and Konrad Schmid, JSJSup 173 (Leiden: Brill, 2017), 398–416.

58. Marinus de Jonge, "Remarks in the Margin of the Paper 'The Figure of Jeremiah in the *Paralipomena Jeremiae*,' by J. Riaud," *JSP* 22 (2000): 45–49. Whereas Lee thinks of both editions as Jewish, de Jonge thinks of the second, and perhaps also the first, as Christian.

59. See Piovanelli, "L'Histoire de la captivité babylonienne"; also his commentary, "Paralipomeni di Geremia."

60. That the related stories about Honi the circle drawer in y. Ta'an. 66d (3:9) and b. Ta'an. 23a say nothing about eschatological resurrection is also pertinent.

61. See esp. Herzer, *Paralipomena*, 177–92; Herzer, *4 Baruch*, xxx–xxxiv. Thorsten Klein, *Bewährung in Anfechtung: Der Jakobusbrief und der Erste Petrusbrief als christ-*

legend of the seven sleepers of Ephesus, which depends upon it (see note 46 above). The earliest Greek version of this—Symeon the Metaphrast's *Menologion* (see PG 115:427–48)—preserves a story that, in its essentials, goes back to the fifth century.[62] In accord with this, the Ethiopic manuscripts of 4 Baruch descend from a translation of the Greek made between the fourth and seventh centuries,[63] so dating the text to any time after the fourth century would be hazardous.

There is, moreover, a possible allusion to 4 Baruch from a much earlier time. According to Pseudo-Cyprian, *Adv. Jud.* 25 (64), "they [the Jews] stoned Jeremiah as he was prophesying Christ [*Hieremiam lapidabant Christum uaticinantem*]." This text likely comes from late second-century Rome.[64] It is tempting to suppose that the close association of Jeremiah's stoning with his prophesying of Christ reflects knowledge of 4 Baruch in its Christian form.[65] Lamentably, we can do no more than suppose.

Nonetheless, a date in the second century remains the best educated guess.[66] The theme of the gentiles replacing Israel is prominent in 5 Ezra and other second- and third-century texts, such as Tertullian's *Adversus Judaeos*. Also relevant is 8.9, which holds forth hope for the Samaritans: "And Jeremiah sent (a message) to them [the Samaritans], saying: 'Repent. For the righteous angel comes, and he will lead you to your exalted place.'" If this is a Christian addition,[67] it more likely stems from an early period

---

*liche Diaspora-Briefe*, NET 18 (Tübingen: Francke, 2011), 150 n. 483, rightly observes that, regarding 4 Baruch's date, there is "ein relativer Forschungskonsens."

62. See Ernest Honigmann, "Stephen of Ephesus (April 15, 448–Oct. 29, 451) and the Seven Sleepers," in *Patristic Studies*, StT 173 (Vatican City: Biblioteca apostolica vaticana, 1953), 125–68.

63. So Albert-Marie Denis, *Introduction à la littérature religieuse judéo-hellénistique: Pseudépigraphes de l'Ancien Testament* (Turnhout: Brepols, 2000), 700. The Ethiopic represents the early period of Geʿez. See further Ignazio Guidi, *Storia della Letteratura Etiopica* (Rome: Istituto per l'Oriente, 1932), 11–21.

64. So Dirk Van Damme, *Pseudo-Cyprian Adversus Iudaeos gegen die Judenchristen: Die älteste lateinische Predigt* (Fribourg: Universitätsverlag, 1969), 74–91.

65. See Christian Wolff, *Jeremia im Frühjudentum und Urchristentum*, TUGAL 118 (Berlin: Akademie, 1976), 91.

66. See Riaud, *Paralipomènes*, 131; Elgvin, "Editing," 295, 298; Torijano, "4 Baruch," 3:2663.

67. So S. E. Robinson, "4 Baruch," in *The Old Testament Pseudepigrapha*, ed. James H. Charlesworth, 2 vols., ABRL (New York: Doubleday, 1983–1985), 2:423 n.8b ("The Christian redactor has changed the original Jewish polemic against the Samaritans into a promise of exaltation"), and Lee, "Development." I agree: (1) The call in v. 9

in church history, for whereas the Gospel of Luke and the Gospel of John reflect positive attitudes toward the Samaritans, "little sympathy is wasted upon them by such early Christian writers as Hegesippus in the 2nd century, by Origen, by Hippolitus of Rome (in his Philosophuemena) and by the Pseudeo-Clementine (in his homilies) of the 2nd/3rd century, and by Eusebius and Philaster of Brescia, of the 4th century. Epiphanius, who served in the 370's as bishop in Cyprus, strikes in his Panarion a distinctly anti Samaritan note."[68] Taking everything in account, then, it seems that the Christian version of 4 Baruch appeared, as Herzer has urged, not too long after the Jewish version.[69]

## Judaism in 4 Baruch

We come now to the subject of how 4 Baruch, in its current form, construes Judaism. Harris and others, as noted earlier, have deemed the work to possess, in part, a missionary orientation. This ill comports with 9.14–18. These verses declare that the tree of life planted in the midst of paradise—presumably the cross on Golgotha[70]—"will make all the unfruitful

---

stands in tension with what has come before and, if the chapter ended at v. 8, nothing would be amiss. (2) A Christian informed by New Testament texts that speak positively of Samaritans (see n. 35) could have envisaged the Samaritans repenting and becoming Christian. (3) The structure of the final words is the same as that of a well-known line in Matthew:

Matt 3:2: μετανοεῖτε ... ἤγγικεν γὰρ ἡ βασιλεία τῶν οὐρανων
Matt 4:17: μετανοεῖτε ... ἤγγικεν γὰρ ἡ βασιλεία τῶν οὐρανων
4 Bar 8.9: μετανοήσατε ... ἔρχεται γὰρ ἄγγελος τῆς δικαιοσύνης

All three lines have an imperatival form of μετανοέω + verb with the sense of "arrive" or "come" + explanatory γάρ + nominative noun + genitive article + descriptive genitive. (4) Two words in 8.9 (μετανοέω and ὑψηλός) are hapax legomena for 4 Baruch.

68. So Nathan Schur, History of the Samaritans, BEATAJ 18 (Frankfurt am Main: Lang, 1989), 81–82.

69. As for the local origin of the primary Christian redaction, the data do not allow an informed decision. The Jewish original was probably composed in Israel.

70. See Justin, Dial. 86.1 (the tree of life is a σύμβολον of the crucifixion); Clement of Alexandria, Strom. 5.2.72.2 ("our life was hung upon it [the tree of life] in order that we might believe"); Tertullian, Adv. Jud. 13 ("'and the tree,' he says, 'has brought forth his fruit'—not that tree in paradise that yielded death to the protoplasts but the tree of the passion of Christ"; "in order that what had formerly perished through the tree in Adam should be restored through the tree in Christ"); Cave of Treasures 48.9 ("Christ climbed the cross, the tree of life"); Encomium of Mary Magdalene 17 ("God planted

trees bear fruit, and grow, and send forth shoots. And it will make the trees that had (earlier) sprouted and grown great and said, 'We have sent our top to the sky,' together with their high branches, to shrivel up; and that firmly rooted tree will cause them to be condemned." The unfruitful trees are the gentiles, as is clear from the later line which declares that, when he comes, Jesus Christ will "choose for himself twelve apostles, so that they might preach the good news among the nations." So our text envisages a successful gentile mission. What of Israel? It is depicted as a group of trees that, once great, high, and firmly rooted, have boasted and are now shriveled up and condemned (κριθῆναι).[71] Does this not, in the words of J. Edward Wright, involve "an anti-Jewish inversion of Paul's censure of gentile boasting in his extended metaphor of the olive tree (Rom 11:17–24)"?[72]

The accompanying series of dramatic contrasts encourages an affirmative response: the scarlet will become white as wool, the snow will be turned black, the sweet waters will become salty, and the salty will become sweet. These improbable transformations capture the role reversal that, for the author, the Son of God's advent wrought. That which is scarlet becoming white as snow refers to gentiles coming to faith, as does the image of salty waters becoming sweet. The snow becoming black and the sweet waters becoming salty refer to Israel losing its privileged place.

It says much that Chrysostom, in his infamous sermons on the Jews, offers something similar. In *Jud. gent.* 1.2, he takes up Rom 11:17–14,

---

the tree of life in the middle of paradise, namely, the cross of our salvation"); Michael Choniates, *Orat.* 6 (ed. Lampros, 1:128) ("in the middle of these things the tree of life, the cross, stands"). For full discussion of this motif see Stephen Jerome Reno, *The Sacred Tree as an Early Christian Literary Symbol: A Phenomenological Study*, FARG 4 (Saarbrücken: Homo et Religio, 1978), 124–86.

71. A few commentators—Riaud, *Les Paralipomènes du prophète Jérémie*, 200; Luis Vegas Montaner, "Paralipomenos de Jeremías," in *Apócrifos del Antiguo Testamento*, ed. Alejandro Díez Macho, 5 vols. (Madrid: Ediciones Cristiandad, 1982–1987), 2:353–83 (382); and Schaller, *Paralipomena*, 753—imagine that the firmly-rooted tree is the Roman empire. Yet neither Rome nor its prototype, Babylon, has anything to do with 4 Bar. 9. All the focus is instead upon Jeremiah and the "foolish children of Israel" (9.30). Beyond that, the contrast is between "the nations" (which is unlikely to exclude Rome) and some other group; and the assertion that "the sweet waters will become salty" is not plausibly a characterization of the Roman empire, as though it went from good to bad.

72. J. Edward Wright, *Baruch ben Neriah: From Biblical Scribe to Apocalyptic Seer* (Columbia: University of South Carolina Press, 2003), 201–2.

omits Paul's hope for Israel, and then, like 4 Baruch, mentions fruit—"we were not part of that root, yet we have produced the fruits of piety." He follows this with paradoxical contrasts between Jew and gentile: "The sun of righteousness rose on them first, but they turned their back on its beams and sat in darkness. But we, who were nurtured in darkness, welcomed the light…. They read the prophets from ancient times, yet they crucified the one spoken of by the prophets. We had not heard the holy scriptures, yet we now worship the one about whom the prophets speak." Israel is past tense.

Chrysostom was elaborating a traditional arboreal topos. According to Irenaeus, in *Haer.* 4.36.8, the parable of the fig tree in Luke 13:6–9 teaches that, when the Messiah came, he searched for "the fruit of righteousness" from Israel and did not find it, so that the tree was hewn down, in accord with the lamentation in Luke 13:34 and Matt 23:37: "O Jerusalem, Jerusalem, you that kill the prophets, and stone those that are sent unto you…. Behold, your house shall be left unto you desolate." Thus, although gentiles have believed the preaching of the apostles, "the children of the kingdom shall go into outer darkness," where there will be "weeping and gnashing of teeth" (Matt 8:11–12). Aphraates, *Dem.* 5.22, finds something comparable in Luke 20:9–19: because the vineyard (= Israel) produced bad fruit, "its Lord uprooted it and cast it in to the fire, and he planted good fruit-bearing vines in the vineyard, such as gladden the husbandman…. Vineyard was formed in place of vineyard." The third-century Legend of Aphroditianus holds more of the same: "For those whom a flame threatens, the dew has come…. Judea has bloomed, but now it is withering. To gentiles and foreigners salvation has come, to the miserable there is more than enough refreshment" (5.3–4). According to this text, the Christ annulled the Jewish law and the Jewish synagogue (8.3).

These texts, like 4 Baruch, are very different than Rom 11:17–24. Paul insists that the gentile branches should not boast, for they do not support the root but the root supports them. The apostle also declares that "even the others [non-Christian Jews], if they do not persist in their unbelief, will be grafted in, for God has the power to graft them in again. For if you have been cut from what is by nature a wild olive tree, and grafted, contrary to nature, into a cultivated olive tree, how much more will these natural branches be grafted back into their own olive tree" (vv. 23–24). Indeed, Israel's hardening is temporary, and will last only "until the full number of the gentiles come in" (v. 25). Then, in the end, "all Israel will be saved" (v. 26).

Fourth Baruch has nothing like this, nor does the book even hint at such a prospect. On the contrary, it says nothing except that "the trees that had (earlier) sprouted and grown great" will "shrivel up" and be "condemned." There is no parallel to Apoc. Pet. 2, where, although Luke 13:6–9 stands as a warning, there is hope that the house of Israel will burst into flower at the end,[73] nor anything like Did. apost. 21.5.19, which calls for prayers for the Jewish people, "that the Lord hold not their guilt for the betrayal with which they betrayed our Lord against them until the end, but grant them room for repentance, conversion and forgiveness for their wickedness" (21.5.19).

One fails to see how 4 Baruch's unqualified contrast of condemned Jews over against believing gentiles can have missionary potential. Not only is Judaism characterized as judged or condemned (9.15: κριθῆναι) without qualification, but no attempt is made to lay out common ground between Jews and Christians.[74] Beyond that, there is no call for Israel to repent—quite a striking fact given that Jeremiah issues just such a call to the disobedient Samaritans (8.9).

Against Herzer, 4 Baruch does not have "a positive view of Jewish history," and one fails to see why "a missionary element can be found" in "the very act of developing a Jewish writing."[75] What would non-Christian Jews have found persuasive in the crude transformation of the Jewish prophet Jeremiah into a publicly-professing Christian? What would those who knew the pre-Christian 4 Baruch have made of the new, artificial edition, with its contrived ending that out of the blue introduces Jesus Christ the Son of God? Would they not have found the product something other than new and improved? And might they not have rightly thought that the book had been tendentiously rewritten, just as Christians sometimes accused Jews of tendentiously altering texts (see Justin, *Dial.* 72–73)?

---

73. "Then shall the boughs of the fig-tree, that is, the house of Israel, sprout, and there shall be many martyrs" by the hand of the false Christ.

74. Although Herzer takes κριθῆναι to be metaphorical (*4 Baruch*, 37), κρίνω is not an agricultural term, and I prefer to give the verb its natural sense, "judge." Indeed, given the negative outcome, "condemn" likely catches the sense; for this meaning see BDAG, s.v. "κρίνω 5." On identifying common ground as a common missionary strategy of Christians in antiquity, see Dale C. Allison Jr., *A Critical and Exegetical Commentary on the Epistle of James*, ICC (New York: Bloosmbury, 2013), 39–41.

75. Herzer, *4 Baruch*, xxxv.

## The Transition from Jewish to Christian

How, to draw matters to a close, did the Jewish 4 Baruch become the Christian 4 Baruch? We can envisage at least three different scenarios. One is that a gentile Christian obtained a copy of the Jewish text from a book-shop and then introduced it to a gentile Christian church, after which it came to be revised. Another and more likely option is that a Jew who knew 4 Baruch in a purely Jewish setting became a Christian and, in his new religious context, recited the book to followers of Jesus; and then, once the story had entered the ecclesial tradition, a gentile Christian thought he could improve upon it. It is also possible to envision the same scenario with a so-called God-fearer, that is, a gentile who, at one time, heard not just scripture but other religious works, including 4 Baruch, in a syna-gogue or other Jewish religious setting.

How long 4 Baruch, once introduced to gentile Christians, retained its Jewish form and ending is beyond our knowledge. It may have been a few years or a few decades. Whatever the truth on that score, at some point a follower of Jesus thought a new edition of the book prudent. Why that indi-vidual felt the freedom to rewrite 4 Baruch is unclear. Christians appear to have passed on Jubilees, 1 Enoch, the Psalms of Solomon, Pseudo-Philo, and 2 Baruch without introducing significant alterations. Other books, to the contrary—books such as the Sibylline Oracles, the Testaments of the Twelve Patriarchs, the Testament of Abraham, and 3 Baruch—suffered substantial change. Fourth Baruch belongs with the latter group, with the Jewish books that some Christians considered ripe for revision.

The revision of 4 Baruch fundamentally altered the nature of the work, so that a Jewish tale with a Jewish purpose became a Christian tale with a Christian purpose. The original aimed at entertaining, edifying, and giving hope to Jews in the aftermath of the debacle of 70. In the Christian revi-sion, by contrast, Israel becomes chiefly a foil for Christian apologetics. What Israel used to be, the church is now, and Jeremiah, who prophesied Jesus by name and was martyred for it, has become a Christian.[76] The book dispossesses Israel of its religious heritage and abolishes 4 Baruch's origi-nal message of God's faithfulness to Israel despite its failings. For Christian readers, the sins of Israel[77] would no longer be the occasion for an effective

---

76. See the Martyrdom and Ascension of Isaiah (a book known by the Christian redactor of 4 Baruch): this effectively turns Isaiah into a Christian.

77. See esp. 1.1, 7; 2.2–5; 6.13–14, 21–22; 7.22, 28, 32.

repentance but would rather explain why Israel has lost its place to the church of the gentiles.

The point of view is no longer that of a distressed group seeking hope in its past history but that of a confident upstart with an uncharitable take on the Jewish Other. Whether 4 Baruch implies heartfelt contempt or a bland, taken-for-granted dismissal, gentile Christianity has displaced Judaism as the authentically ancient and so true religion. Fourth Baruch is supersessionistic, and in it the parting of the ways is complete.

## Bibliography

Allison, Dale C., Jr. *A Critical and Exegetical Commentary on the Epistle of James*. ICC. New York: Bloosmbury, 2013.

———. *Paraleipomena Jeremiou (4 Baruch)*. CEJL. Berlin: de Gruyter, 2018.

Alon, Gedalyahu. *Jews, Judaism and the Classical World: Studies in Jewish History in the Time of the Second Temple and the Talmud*. Jerusalem: Magnes, 1977.

Ameling, Walter. *Inscriptiones Judaicae Orientis II: Kleinasien*. TSAJ 99. Tübingen: Mohr Siebeck, 2004.

Bauckham, Richard J. "The Continuing Quest for the Provenance of Old Testament Pseudepigrapha." Pages 9–29 in *The Pseudepigrapha and Christian Origins: Essays from the Studiorum Novi Testamenti Societas*. Edited by Gerbern S. Oegema and James H. Charlesworth. New York: T&T Clark, 2008.

Charles, R. H. *The Apocalypse of Baruch Translated from the Syriac*. London: Black, 1896.

Daniel, Robert W., and Franco Maltomini. *Supplementum Magicum*. 2 vols. Köln: Westdeutsher Verlag, 1990–1992.

Davila, James R. *The Provenance of the Pseudepigrapha: Jewish, Christian, or Other?* JSJSup 105. Leiden: Brill, 2005.

Delling, Gerhard. *Jüdische Lehre und Frömmigkeit in den Paralipomena Jeremiae*. BZNW 100. Berlin: Töpelmann, 1967.

Denis, Albert-Marie. *Introduction à la littérature religieuse judéo-hellénistique: Pseudépigraphes de l'Ancien Testament*. Turnhout: Brepols, 2000.

Dillmann, August. *Chrestomathia Aethiopica: Edita et glossario explanate*. Leipzig: Weigel, 1866.

Elgvin, Torleif. "Jewish Christian Editing of the Old Testament Pseudepigrapha." Pages 278–304 in *Jewish Believers in Jesus: The Early Centuries*.

Edited by Oskar Skarsaune and Reidar Hvalvik. Peabody, MA: Hendrickson, 2007.

Fallon, Francis T. *The Enthronement of Sabaoth: Jewish Elements in Gnostic Creation Myths.* NHS 10. Leiden: Brill, 1978.

Guidi, Ignazio. *Storia della Letteratura Etiopica.* Rome: Istituto per l'Oriente, 1932.

Halkin, François. *Le corpus athénien de Saint Pachome.* Geneva: Cramer, 1982.

Harlow, Daniel C. *The Greek Apocalypse of Baruch (3 Baruch) in Hellenistic Judaism and Early Christianity.* SVTP 12. Leiden: Brill, 1996.

Harris, J. Rendel. *The Rest of the Words of Baruch: A Christian Apocalypse of the Year 136 A.D.; The Text Revised with an Introduction.* London: Clay & Sons; Cambridge: Cambridge University Press, 1889.

Heininger, Bernhard. "Der Brief Jeremias an Baruch (ParJer 7,23–30): Ein Beitrag zur Textkritik apokrypher Schriften." *SNTU* 34 (2009): 72–76.

Heller, Bernard. "Éléments, parallèles et origine de la légende des sept dormants." *REJ* 49 (1904): 213–14.

Herzer, Jens. *4 Baruch (Paraleipomena Jeremiou).* WGRWSup 22. Leiden: Brill, 2005.

———. *Die Paralipomena Jeremiae: Studien zu Tradition und Redaktion einer Haggada des frühen Judentums.* TSAJ 43. Tübingen: Mohr Siebeck, 1994.

Honigmann, Ernest. "Stephen of Ephesus (April 15, 448–Oct. 29, 451) and the Seven Sleepers." Pages 125–68 in *Patristic Studies.* StT 173. Vatican City: Biblioteca apostolica vaticana, 1953.

Horst, Pieter W. van der. "Pious Long-Sleepers in Pagan, Jewish and Christian Antiquity." Pages 248–66 in *Studies in Ancient Judaism and Early Christianity.* Leiden: Brill, 2014.

Isbell, Charles D. *Corpus of the Aramaic Incantation Bowls.* SBLDS 17. Missoula, MT: Scholars Press, 1975.

Jonge, Marinus de. *Pseudepigrapha of the Old Testament as Part of Christian Literature: The Case of the Testaments of the Twelve Patriarchs and the Greek Life of Adam and Eve.* SVTP 18. Leiden: Brill, 2003.

———. "Remarks in the Margin of the Paper 'The Figure of Jeremiah in the *Paralipomena Jeremiae*,' by J. Riaud." *JSP* 22 (2000): 45–49.

Joseph, Simon J. "'I Have Come to Abolish Sacrifices' (Epiphanius, Pan. 30.16.5): Re-examining a Jewish Christian Text and Tradition." *NTS* 63 (2017): 92–110.

Kautzsch, E. *Die Apokryphen und Pseudepigraphen des Alten Testaments*. 2 vols. Tübingen: Mohr Siebeck, 1900.

Klein, Thorsten. *Bewährung in Anfechtung: Der Jakobusbrief und der Erste Petrusbrief als christliche Diaspora-Briefe*. NET 18. Tübingen; Basel: Francke, 2011.

Kraft, Robert A., and Ann-Elizabeth Purintun. *Paraleipomena Jeremiou*. SBLTT 1, Pseudepigrapha Series 1. Missoula, MT: Scholars Press, 1972.

Kuhn, K. H. "A Coptic Jeremiah Apocryphon." *Mus* 83 (1970): 95–135, 291–350.

Lampe, G. W. H. "A.D. 70 in Christian Reflection." Pages 153–71 in *Jesus and the Politics of His Day*. Edited by Ernst Bammel and C. F. D. Moule. Cambridge: Cambridge University Press, 1984.

Lampros, Spyridōn. Μιχαὴλ Ἀκομινάτου τοῦ Χωνιάτου: Τὰ σωζόμενα. 2 vols. Athens: Parnassos, 1879–1890.

Lavee, Moshe. "The Samaritans May be Included—Another Look at the Samaritan in Talmudic Literature." Pages 147–73 in *Samaritans: Past and Present; Current Studies*. Edited by Menachem Mor and Friedrich V. Reiterer. SJ 53. Berlin: de Gruyter, 2010.

Lee, Boyeon Birana. "The Development of the Jeremiah Figure in *2 Baruch* and *4 Baruch*: A Response to Jens Herzer." Pages 398–416 in *Jeremiah's Scriptures: Production, Reception, Interaction, and Transformation*. Edited by Hindy Najman and Konrad Schmid. JSJSup 173. Leiden: Brill, 2017.

Marmorstein, A. "Die Quellen des neuen Jeremia-Apocryphons." *ZNW* 27 (1928): 327–37.

Montagna, Davide M. "La lode alla theotokos nei testi greci dei secoli iv–vii." *Marianum* 24 (1962): 536–39.

Montaner, Luis Vegas. "Paralípomenos de Jeremías." Pages 353–83 in vol. 2 of *Apócrifos del Antiguo Testamento*. Edited by Alejandro Díez Macho. 5 vols. Madrid: Ediciones Cristiandad, 1982–1987.

Morel, Charles. *Sancti patris nostri Iustini philosophi et martyris Opera*. 1636.

Naveh, Joseph, and Shaul Shaked. *Amulets and Magic Bowls: Aramaic Incantations of Late Antiquity*. Jerusalem: Magnes; Leiden: Brill, 1985.

Nir, Rivka. *The Destruction of Jerusalem and the Idea of Redemption in the Syriac Apocalypse of Baruch*. EJL 20. Atlanta: Society of Biblical Literature, 2002.

Noy, David. *Jewish Inscriptions of Western Europe*. 2 vols. Cambridge: Cambridge University Press, 1993–1995.

Philonenko, Marc. "Simples Observations sur les Paralipomènes de Jérémie." *RHPR* 76 (1996): 157–77.

Piovanelli, Pierluigi. "In Praise of 'The Default Position,' or Reassessing the Christian Reception of the Jewish Pseudepigraphic Heritage." *NedTT* 61 (2007): 233–50.

———. "Les Paralipomènes de Jérémie dépendent-ils de l'Histoire de la captivité babylonienne?" *Bulletin de l'AELAC* 7 (1997): 10–14.

———. "Paralipomeni di Geremia." Pages 265–73 in vol. 3 of *Apocrifi dell'Antico Testamento*. Edited by Paolo Sacchi. 5 vols. Brescia: Paideia, 1999.

———. "Ricerche sugli apocrifi veterotestamentari etiopici." MA thesis, University of Florence, 1986.

———. "Le sommeil séculaire d'Abimélech dans l'Histoire de la captivité babylonienne et les Paralipomènes de Jérémie: Texte—intertextes—contexts." Pages 73–96 in *Intertextualités: La Bible en échos*. Edited by Daniel Marguerat and Adrian Curtis. MdB 40. Paris: Labor et Fides, 2000.

Reinhartz, Adele. "The Destruction of Jerusalem as a Trauma for Nascent Christianity." Pages 274–88 in *Trauma and Traumatization in Individual and Collective Dimensions: Insights from Biblical Studies and Beyond*. Edited by Eve-Marie Becker, Jan Dochhorn, and Else K. Holt. Studia Aarhusiana Neotestamentica 2. Göttingen: Vandenhoeck & Ruprecht, 2014.

Reno, Stephen Jerome. *The Sacred Tree as an Early Christian Literary Symbol: A Phenomenological Study*. FARG 4. Saarbrücken: Homo et Religio, 1978.

Riaud, Jan. *Les Paralipomènes du prophète Jérémie: Présentation, texte original, traduction et commentaires*. Cahiers du Centre Interdisciplinaire de Recherches en Histoire, Lettres et Langues 14. Angèrs: Université Catholique de l'Ouest, 1994.

Robinson, S. E. "4 Baruch." Pages 413–25 in vol. 2 of *The Old Testament Pseudepigrapha*. Edited by James H. Charlesworth. 2 vols. ABRL. New York: Doubleday, 1983–1985.

Rutgers, L. V. *The Hidden Heritage of Diaspora Judaism*. 2nd ed. CBET 20. Leuven: Peeters, 1998.

Schaller, Berndt. *Historische und legendarische Erzählungen: Paralipomena Jeremiou*. JSHRZ 1/8. Gütersloh: Gütersloher Verlagshaus, 1998.

Schur, Nathan. *History of the Samaritans.* BEATAJ 18. Frankfurt am Main: Lang, 1989.

Schürer, Emil. Review of *The Rest of the Words of Baruch: A Christian Apocalypse of the Year 136 A.D.; The Text Revised with an Introduction,* by J. Rendel Harris. *TLZ* 15 (1890): 83.

Stuhlmacher, Peter. *Das paulinische evangelium I: Vorgeschichte.* FRLANT 95. Göttingen: Vandenhoeck & Ruprecht, 1968.

Torijano, Pablo. "4 Baruch." Pages 2662–80 in vol. 3 of *Outside the Bible: Ancient Jewish Writings related to Scripture.* Edited by Louis H. Feldman, James L. Kugel, and Lawrence H. Schiffman. 3 vols. Philadelphia: Jewish Publication Society, 2013.

Van Damme, Dirk. *Pseudo-Cyprian Adversus Iudaeos gegen die Judenchristen: Die älteste lateinische Predigt.* Fribourg: Universitätsverlag, 1969.

Wolff, Christian. "Die Paralipomena Jeremiae und das Neue Testament." *NTS* 51 (2005): 126–36.

———. *Jeremia im Frühjudentum und Urchristentum.* TUGAL 118. Berlin: Akademie, 1976.

Wright, J. Edward. *Baruch ben Neriah: From Biblical Scribe to Apocalyptic Seer.* Columbia: University of South Carolina Press, 2003.

# "The Blessed Land and the Inheritance of Israel": The Old Testament and Judaism in a Fourth-Century Refutation of Marcion

Lucas Van Rompay

Following the publication of his enlightening overview essay on "Jewish Christianity" in 2006, Joel Marcus turned his attention to the Syriac/ Syrian world[1] as a possible haven for "trace elements" of Jewish Christianity as well as, more generally, for Christian attitudes less antagonistic toward Judaism or Jews than is often found in mainstream Greek or Latin Christianity. After the demise of Jewish Christianity—in the late second or the third century—"the church became more and more Gentile in complexion, and the question arose as to how to deal with the increasingly marginalised Jewish Christian minority."[2] Even though the existence of Torah-observant Christians and their place within the larger Christian community largely remain elusive, a small number of our sources attest to an ongoing awareness of continuity and proximity between Judaism and Christianity.[3] In the Pseudo-Clementine literature, for instance, and in

---

1. In the present essay, I use *Syriac* for anything expressed in, or related to, the Syriac language, *Syrian* as referring to the wider geographical area of Syria, extending from the coastland around Antioch well into Mesopotamia. Syria was largely bilingual, in particular in those parts that belonged to the Roman Empire. Texts often circulated in either Greek or Syriac, without it always being clear which version came first. The Syriac Didascalia, e.g., is believed to have moved from a Greek-speaking Syrian into a Syriac orbit.

2. Joel Marcus, "Jewish Christianity," in *Origins to Constantine*, ed. Margaret M. Mitchell and Frances M. Young, CHC 1 (Cambridge: Cambridge University Press, 2006), 101.

3. Even though not entirely unrelated, this is different from the search for Jewish traditions in Syriac sources, for some of our Syriac authors are heavily indebted to Jewish traditions while at the same time exhibiting (some degree of) antagonism, or

certain sections of the Syriac Didascalia, the Jewish background of some Christians or Judaism *tout court* is positively valued. In addition to these well-known sources, Marcus in recent years has pointed to passages in the Testament of the Twelve Patriarchs and in the works of Hippolytus that show a more inclusive approach toward Judaism or Jews.[4]

In the following pages, I will use Marcus's careful and balanced analysis of these texts as a model for my own reading of a source that has received very little scholarly attention so far and that—if my reading is correct— shares with the documents mentioned above a more positive evaluation of Christianity's heritage within a nascent and increasingly distinct Judaism. The text first needs some introduction.

## Pseudo-Ephrem, *An Exposition of the Gospel*

The text I want to focus on exists in Armenian only and is accessible in a 1968 edition and English translation by George A. Egan.[5] The title in Egan's edition is *An Exposition of the Gospel* (henceforth *Exposition*), which reflects the title in the lead manuscript (*T'argmanut'iwn Awetarani*). Subsequent to the text's first publication in the Mekhitarist edition of 1836, scholarship started appearing in the beginning of the twentieth century.[6] A number of largely unsolved questions, however, still remain today. First, while the text exists only in Armenian, the general assumption is that it was translated from Syriac. Second, scholars of Syriac Christianity have largely dismissed the claim, solely espoused by Egan, that the *Exposition*

---

even hostility, toward Judaism. For the broader question of traces of Jewish traditions in Syriac Christianity, see, e.g., Sebastian Brock, "Jewish Traditions in Syriac Sources," *JJS* 30 (1979): 212–32; and Gerard Rouwhorst, "Jewish Liturgical Traditions in Early Syriac Christianity," *VC* 51 (1997): 72–93.

4. Joel Marcus, "The *Testaments of the Twelve Patriarchs* and the *Didascalia Apostolorum*: A Common Jewish-Christian Milieu?," *JTS* 61 (2010): 596–626; Marcus, "Israel and the Church in the Exegetical Writings of Hippolytus," *JBL* 131 (2012): 385–406.

5. George A. Egan, *Saint Ephrem: An Exposition of the Gospel*, CSCO 291–292/ Arm. 5–6 (Leuven: Secrétariat du CorpusSCO, 1968).

6. This text was included in the second volume (261–345) of the four-volume edition of the Armenian works attributed to Ephrem the Syrian (Venice, 1836). For details, see Kees den Biesen, *Annotated Bibliography of Ephrem the Syrian* (self-pub., 2011), 474–78. The text of the *Exposition* in the Mekhitarist edition was based on one manuscript only, MS San Lazzaro, no. 452.

is a genuine work of Ephrem, the preeminent representative of fourth-century Syriac Christianity. Third, even though a fourth-century date seems plausible, it is very hard to contextualize this text in either Syriac or Armenian Christianity.[7]

Egan's critical edition is based on two twelfth-century Armenian manuscripts, both kept in the library of the Mekhitarist Convent of San Lazzaro, Venice, numbers 452 (henceforth MS A) and 312 (henceforth MS B) respectively.[8] Both manuscripts were written in the same year, 1195 CE, but it is unlikely that one was copied from the other or even that both were copied from the same model, as the scriptoria in which they were written—these are specifically mentioned in the colophons—were more than 800 kilometers apart. One was in the Monastery of Hałbat, near the border with Georgia;[9] the other was in Cilician Armenia, in Tarsus, the city of the Apostle Paul. In addition to their physical distance, in the late twelfth century ecclesial and political strife arose between these two places. The Hałbat monks were known for their resistance to the attempts at unification between the Armenian-Orthodox Church and the Greek and Latin Churches. These attempts were initiated in Cilicia, and the scribe of MS B, Nersēs Lambronacʻi, who was the Armenian archbishop of Tarsus from 1176 to 1198, was one of their strongest promoters.[10]

---

7. George A. Egan, *An Analysis of the Biblical Quotations of Ephrem in "An Exposition of the Gospel" (Armenian version)*, CSCO 443, Subsidia 66 (Leuven: Peeters, 1983) studies the biblical quotations of the text in some detail. While his general conclusion that many quotations point to Syriac sources is convincing, for several of the passages further study would be needed, taking the present state of scholarship into account.

8. Bernard Outtier points out the existence of a third manuscript, MS Madrid, Escorial. Ψ II.9, dated 1564/1565. Bernard Outtier, "Une explication de l'Evangile attribuée à Saint Ephrem: A propos d'une édition récente," *ParOr* 1 (1970): 405–7. This manuscript, which contains a collection of texts attributed to Ephrem (without, however, the *Commentary on the Diatessaron*), has the *Exposition* in its entirety (folios 4r–47r), in a form close to MS Venice 452. As far as I know, this manuscript has not yet been used in scholarship.

9. On the important Monastery of Hałbat (and its sister Monastery of Sanahin), see Jean Mécérian, *Histoire et institutions de l'Église arménienne* (Beirut: Imprimerie catholique, 1965), 272–76.

10. For an overview of this period as well as the translation and study of a number of documents (in which the Monastery of Hałbat is regularly mentioned), see Isabelle Augé, *Églises en dialogue: Arméniens et Byzantins dans la seconde moitié*

In contrast to the well-known Bishop Nersēs Lambronac'i, the scribe of MS A is known by name only, the monk Xač'atur (while a second monk, Ananias, is mentioned as well),[11] but we do not have any further information on either Xač'atur's or Ananias's life or work. As a scribe, however, Xač'atur appears to have copied his model faithfully, whereas Bishop Nersēs—as was his habit when he transcribed ancient texts—updated the text both linguistically and stylistically, changing the syntax, replacing words with synonyms, adding explanatory notes, and bringing the biblical quotations more in line with the Armenian Vulgate.[12] This makes the Hałbat manuscript (MS A) the obvious starting point for any textual study, even though the Tarsus manuscript (MS B), amidst its reworked text, may occasionally preserve an original reading.[13]

Despite the scribes' different approaches to their work, the two manuscripts have a great deal in common. Most significantly, both manuscripts feature the *Exposition* alongside the *Commentary on the Diatessaron*, explicitly attributed to Ephrem the Syrian: "Explanation of the concordant Gospel, which is composed by Lord Ephrem, the Syrian teacher" (*Meknut'iwn Awetarani hamabarbaṙ zor arareal ē Teaṙn Ep'remi xorin Asorwoy*).[14] Some time before 1195, therefore, possibly long before that

---

*du XIIe siècle*, CSCO 633, Subsidia 124 (Leuven: Peeters, 2011); on Nersēs's positions, see esp. 39–43.

11. Basing himself on the work of the Mekhitarist scholars, Louis Leloir wonders whether this Ananias might have been the translator or the one who inspired the assembling of the collection. Louis Leloir, *Saint Éphrem: Commentaire de l'Évangile concordant*, 2 vols., CSCO 137 and 145, Arm. 1–2 (Leuven: Secrétariat du CorpusSCO, 1953–1964), 1:iii. The question of the date of the translation, from Syriac into Armenian, of either the *Exposition* or the *Commentary on the Diatessaron* has not yet been settled definitely.

12. See Egan, *Saint Ephrem: An Exposition of the Gospel*, iv–vii; Outtier, "Une explication de l'Evangile," 404–5.

13. In our quotations of the text, we will follow MS A, mostly ignoring Nersēs's revisions, which only very rarely affect the content.

14. This text was first published in the second volume (pp. 3–260) of the 1836 Mekhitarist edition of Ephrem's work (see n. 6). For a more recent edition, with Latin translation, see Leloir, *Saint Éphrem: Commentaire de l'Évangile concordant*. For a description of the two manuscripts, see 1:ii–viii. For the somewhat problematic term *xor*, which is often attached to Ephrem's name in Armenian, see Edward G. Mathews, "A First Glance at the Armenian Prayers Attributed to Surb Ep'rem Xorin Asorwoy," in *Worship Traditions in Armenian and the Neighboring Christian East*, ed. Roberta R. Ervine (Crestwood, NY: Saint Vladimir's Seminary Press, 2006), 171 n. 1.

date, the *Exposition* and the *Diatessaron Commentary* were joined together and started being transmitted in tandem. The entire content of the manuscript was probably seen as Ephrem's work, translated from Syriac into Armenian. For the *Diatessaron Commentary*, we now have proof that it is indeed based on a Syriac original, thanks to the discovery in the second half of the twentieth century of large portions of the Syriac original in a manuscript from Deir al-Surian in Egypt (now in Dublin's Chester Beatty Library), datable to the fifth century.[15] For its sister piece, the *Exposition*, such a discovery has not, or not yet, been made.

## Scholarship on the *Exposition*

In spite of its inclusion in the Mekhitarist edition of 1836, it was only in the beginning of the twentieth century that the *Exposition* became more widely known among scholars of early Christianity. Francis C. Burkitt briefly mentioned the *Exposition* in his classical work on the Old Syriac gospels (1904), and Erwin Preuschen devoted a preliminary study to it in 1911.[16] The first substantial investigation was a 1915 doctoral dissertation in Breslau by Joseph Schäfers, an expanded version of which posthumously appeared in 1917 (following Schäfers's premature death

---

15. See the edition and Latin translation in Louis Leloir, *Saint Éphrem: Commentaire de l'Évangile concordant; Texte syriaque (Manuscrit Chester Beatty 709)*, CBM 8 (Dublin: Hodges Figgis, 1963), and Leloir, *Saint Éphrem: Commentaire de l'Évangile concordant; Texte syriaque (Manuscrit Chester Beatty 709): Folios additionnels*, CBM 8 (Leuven: Peeters, 1990). For a recent assessment of the text and the question of authorship, see Christian Lange, *The Portrayal of Christ in the Syriac Commentary on the Diatessaron*, CSCO 616, Subsidia 118 (Leuven: Peeters, 2005); the same author also published a richly annotated German translation: Christian Lange, *Ephraem der Syrer: Kommentar zum Diatessaron*, Fontes Christiani 54.1–2 (Turnhout: Brepols, 2008).

16. Francis C. Burkitt, *Evangelion Da-Mepharreshe: The Curetonian Version of the Four Gospels, with the Readings of the Sinai Palimpsest*, 2 vols. (Cambridge: Cambridge University Press, 1904), 2:188–89. Burkitt recognized that the work was translated from Syriac. He further dated it to the late fourth century and rejected Ephrem's authorship. Erwin Preuschen ("Eine altkirchliche antimarcionitische Schrift unter dem Namen Ephräms," *ZNW* 12 [1911]: 243–69) also saw the work as a translation from Syriac but thought that the Syriac, in its turn, was a translation from Greek (and he presented several sections in a back translation in Greek). He suggested a late second-century date and a Palestinian or Antiochene origin. The theory of a Greek original has not been espoused by later scholars.

in Mosul in 1916).[17] Primarily a New Testament scholar, Schäfers provided a thorough study of the New Testament quotations, in addition to
a full and annotated German translation along with a broader study of
the text, its possible origin and historical context, and its transmission.

Schäfers's first merit was that he identified the *Exposition* as an anti-
Marcionite work, thus allowing it to be used as an important source for
scholarship on Marcion and the Marcionites. Additionally, Schäfers made
a strong case that the *Exposition* should not be seen as one homogeneous
work but that it in fact consists of three clearly distinct essays, which,
Schäfers argued, should be regarded as the remains of three different
works by three different authors,[18] even though all three were translated
from Syriac into Armenian, possibly by the same Armenian translator. Schäfers argued that the three parts differ strikingly in content. The
first and by far the longest part (part A) deals with a number of gospel
parables and their Old Testament antecedents, apparently in response to
Marcion's claim that everything in the gospel is entirely new; the second
(part B) is a short ascetic treatise; and the third (part C) is a sermon on
the end time. While the first treatise is clearly anti-Marcionite and the
second as well has an explicit anti-Marcionite comment, the third part
does not have any reference to Marcion or the Marcionites. According
to Schäfers, Ephrem cannot possibly have been the author of any of the
three different parts.

The biblical quotations of the *Exposition* are an important focus of
Schäfers's study. When we limit ourselves to the New Testament quotations, the picture is very complex. While the quotations in the A text often
reflect the Old Syriac gospels (known in the *Codex Curetonianus* and the
*Codex Sinaiticus*), Schäfers also assumes that the author knew and used
the Syriac *Diatessaron*. In addition, the A author was familiar—as he himself points out to his readers—with the Marcionite scriptures, that is, the
gospel (mainly Luke), the Apostolicon (ten expurgated Pauline Epistles),

---

17. Joseph Schäfers, *Eine altsyrische antimarkionitische Erklärung von Parabeln
des Herrn und zwei andere altsyrische Abhandlungen zu Texten des Evangeliums: Mit
Beiträgen zu Tatians Diatessaron und Markions Neuem Testament*, NTAbh 6.1–2
(Münster: Aschendorff, 1917).

18. Schäfers, *Eine altsyrische antimarkionitische Erklärung*, 199: "Es sind drei deu-
tlich verschiedene Abhandlungen unter einem Titel vereinigt, und wenn die Überlieferung des Textes eine einheitliche ist, auch drei verschiedene Verfasser anzunehmen."

and probably with Marcion's *Antitheses* as well.[19] Author B as well knew the Old Syriac. Whether, in addition, he knew the *Diatessaron* remained for Schäfers an open question. He does not share Author A's focus on, and engagement with, the Marcionite scriptures. Finally, Author C is the only one who not only betrays familiarity with an Old Syriac type of text but also explicitly quotes the four evangelists by their name. The introduction of one passage with the words "as Mark has written in the four-headed Gospel" (*i č'orek'glxean awetarani*; §98) seems to specifically point to the separate gospels in contrast to the *Diatessaron*.[20]

Schäfers's study was written well before the publication of Harnack's classic monograph, *Marcion: Das Evangelium vom fremden Gott* (1921) as well as before Charles W. Mitchell's edition and translation of Ephrem's Syriac *Prose Refutations* (1912–1921),[21] which contain several treatises against Marcion that unquestionably belong to Ephrem. While Harnack used our Armenian text in his work[22] and paid due attention to its quotations from Marcionite writings, the *Exposition* is absent from most subse-

---

19. The author (§1) points to a work by Marcion for which he quotes the title as *Peronewengelion* (*sic* in MSS A and B), which "translated into our language is called: before the Gospel [*yaṙaj k'an zawetaran*]." Harnack identified this work as the *Antitheses*; see Adolf Harnack, *Marcion: Das Evangelium vom fremden Gott; Eine Monographie zur Geschichte der Grundlegung der katholischen Kirche*, 2nd improved and exp. ed. (Leipzig: Hinrichs, 1924), 74–75, 87 (where this quotation is described as "der einzige längere Satz den wir aus M.s Feder wörtlich besitzen"), and 256*. Harnack's study was originally published in 1921; references in this essay are to the second edition, published in 1924. Outtier, however, wonders whether this may be a reference to the preface of Marcion's edition of the Gospel of Luke ("Une explication de l'Evangile," 390), a suggestion which was made already by James Rendel Harris, "Tatian: Perfection according to the Saviour," *BJRL* 8 (1924): 17. On this quotation, see also Judith M. Lieu, *Marcion and the Making of a Heretic: God and Scripture in the Second Century* (Cambridge: Cambridge University Press, 2015), 271–72.

20. See A. Strobel, "Das Begriff des 'vierkapiteligen Evangeliums' in Pseudo-Ephrem C," *ZKG* 70 (1959): 112–20.

21. Harnack, *Marcion*; C. W. Mitchell, *S. Ephraim's Prose Refutations of Mani, Marcion, and Bardaisan*, 2 vols. (London: Williams & Norgate, 1912–1921).

22. Harnack, *Marcion*, 354*–56*. Harnack misrepresents Schäfers when he writes, "Die Schrift besteht, wie Schäfers gezeigt hat, aus drei selbständigen Abhandlungen eines Verfassers" (345*). Schäfers assumes that there were three authors involved; see Schäfers, *Eine altsyrische antimarkionitische Erklärung*, 199 and 206 ("für jeden Teil einen eigenen Verfasser"). It was Harris who suggested that the three different treatises might have been written by one author; see "Tatian," 15–51.

quent studies on Marcion and Marcionites, general studies as well as studies focusing on Syria.[23] It receives very few references in Judith M. Lieu's
recent monograph on Marcion.[24]

When Egan published a new edition and translation of the text (1968),
followed by a companion volume on the biblical quotations (1983), he saw
his work primarily as "an important tool for the textual criticism of the New
Testament."[25] Unfortunately, he made no further effort to interrogate the
text for its possible evidence on early Syriac or early Armenian Christianity. In spite of this rather narrow scope, he cast a critical light on several
of Schäfers's conclusions regarding the origin and transmission of the text.
Considering parallels and similarities among the three sections (A, B, and
C), Egan rejected Schäfers's tripartite division. According to Egan, all the
three treatises "make reference to the authority of the Sayings of Jesus, the
Prophets and the Apostles" and "quote the Diatessaron and the Old Syriac
Gospels." The evidence taken together is considered "sufficient to declare
the unity of this treatise."[26] Directly contradicting Burkitt's and Schäfers's
negative assessment of the possibility of Ephrem's authorship of the *Exposition*, Egan argues that "only Ephrem Syrus fits the facts of the situation," considering the scholarly consensus on a fourth-century date.[27] Thereby, Egan
affirms the authenticity of the *Exposition* as a genuine work by Ephrem.[28]

-----

23. The *Exposition* is not mentioned or referred to in Gerhard May, Katharina
Greschat, and Martin Meiser, eds., *Marcion und seine kirchengeschichtliche Wirkung:
Vorträge der Internationalen Fachkonferenz zu Marcion, gehalten vom 15–18. August
2001 in Main = Marcion and his Impact on Church History*, TUGAL 150 (Berlin: de
Gruyter, 2002). It is also not taken into account in H. J. W. Drijvers, "Marcionism
in Syria: Principles, Problems, Polemics," *SecCent* 6 (1987–1988): 153–72. David
Bundy, however, duly considers the *Exposition* in "Marcion and the Marcionites in
Early Syriac Apologetics," *Mus* 101 (1988): 21–32 (esp. 26–28), and in his follow-up
paper, "The Anti-Marcionite Commentary on the Lukan Parables (Pseudo-Ephrem
A): Images in Tension," *Mus* 103 (1990): 111–23.

24. Lieu, *Marcion and the Making of a Heretic*, esp. 151 n. 32; 269 n. 112; 271–72;
and 285. Lieu does not engage in any serious discussion of the text; on 151 n. 32 she
misrepresents the view of Egan.

25. Egan, *Saint Ephrem*; Egan, *Analysis of the Biblical Quotations of Ephrem*. For
the quotation, see the preface in Egan, *Saint Ephrem*.

26. Egan, *Saint Ephrem*, xvi.

27. Egan, *Saint Ephrem*, xviii.

28. See also George A. Egan, "A Re-consideration of the Authenticity of Ephrem's
'An Exposition of the Gospel,'" in *Kyriakon: Festschrift Johannes Quasten*, ed. Patrick
Granfteld and Josef A. Jungman (Münster: Aschendorff, 1970), 128–34.

Since Egan showed very little interest in the content of the text, failed to study any of the text's theological, literary, or stylistic aspects, and did not give much consideration to any of Ephrem's undoubtedly authentic writings, it is rather surprising that he made his statements on the origin of the text and its authorship with so much confidence. In subsequent scholarship, however, no one among those more familiar with Ephrem has accepted Egan's conclusions.[29] In an extensive review, which appeared in 1970, Bernard Outtier points out the weaknesses of Egan's thesis and the lack of evidence for an attribution to Ephrem.[30] As for the tripartite division, Outtier rehearses Schäfers's arguments and adds some of his own, suggesting that the amalgamation of the three once-separate works may have resulted from an accident in the manuscript transmission. Following Outtier, David Bundy, first in his overview essay of anti-Marcionite polemics in Syriac (1988) and then in his more detailed study of Pseudo-Ephrem A (1990), was critical of Egan and adopted the views proposed by Schäfers and Outtier.[31]

In the following pages, my remarks on the text will be limited to the first part, as defined by Schäfers (= Pseudo-Ephrem A), as no evidence of equal significance seems to be present in either of the other parts.[32] I will not go into any further discussion of the question of the unity of the text, which may need more research before a final conclusion can be reached. As for the text's authorship, I side with all Syriac scholars and regard the text as the work of one or more of the many Pseudo-Ephrems.

## Anti-Marcionite Polemics

As is well-known, by disconnecting the Hebrew Bible/Old Testament from the Christian faith, Marcion proposed a drastic change in Christianity's relationship to Judaism, not necessarily delegitimizing it but declaring it

---

29. See, e.g., Robert Murray, *Symbols of Church and Kingdom: A Study in Early Syriac Tradition* (Cambridge: Cambridge University Press, 1975), 32.

30. Outtier, "Une explication de l'Evangile."

31. Bundy, "Marcion and the Marcionites," 26–28; Bundy, "The Anti-Marcionite Commentary."

32. With regard to the second part (B), Outtier remarks: "L'ambiance de cette partie est donc très irénique, plutôt favorable aux Juifs" and in the third part (C) as well he sees the "traits judéo-chrétiens" as "assez abondants" ("Une explication de l'Evangile," 395–97). I find these general characterizations rather unhelpful.

irrelevant. In their response, Christians had to walk a fine line, arguing for the significance of Jewish tradition, on the one hand, and for Christianity's uniqueness and independence from it, on the other.[33]

Our text opens with a polemical statement:[34]

> Whatever writings are written from the human mind without taking into account the Law and the Prophets are books, products, and inventions of rebellious minds. And if one starts to examine their meaning, one finds them to be erring and wavering because they are not based upon the true foundation of the Holy Scriptures. (§1; Schäfers, 3)

The author then goes on with a quotation from "Marcion's book" *Pro-ewengelyon*, the title of which he translates as "prior to the Gospel," and which he then derides, since according to Marcion, God's appearance— "new and strange"—began with the gospel and there could not be anything before it.[35] Marcion's quotation is said to be from the very beginning of his work:

> Oh greatness of greatnesses, folly, power,[36] and wonder, that one cannot say anything about it [that is, the Gospel] or think about it or compare it [to anything]![37] (§1; Schäfers, 4–5)

---

33. See Stephen G. Wilson, "Marcion and the Jews," in *Anti-Judaism in Early Christianity*, ed. Stephen G. Wilson, 2 vols., SJC 2 (Waterloo, ON: Wilfrid Laurier University Press, 1986), 2:45–58; W. A. Bienert, "Marcion und der Antijudaismus," in *Marcion und seine kirchengeschichtliche Wirkung*, ed. Gerhard May, Katharina Greschat, and Martin Meiser, TUGAL 150 (Berlin: de Gruyter, 2002), 191–205. Compare Lieu, *Marcion and the Making of a Heretic*, 413: "There is little to suggest that the question of the role of the Jews was a compelling issue for Marcion himself."

34. In all references to the text and translation, I adopt the division in paragraphs (§) and their numbering that were introduced by Egan (following the unnumbered paragraph division in the 1836 Mekhitarist edition); Schäfers's translation is referred to with page numbers.

35. For the identification of this work, see n. 19. For the accusation of newness leveled against Marcion, see Lieu, *Marcion and the Making of a Heretic*, 406–8.

36. Instead of "folly, power" (*yimarut'iwn zawrut'iwn*), MS B reads: "wisdom of power" (*imastut'iwn zawrut'ean*). Egan prefers the B reading and is followed by Lieu, *Marcion and the Making of a Heretic*, 272.

37. Compare the rendering in Harnack, *Marcion*, 256* (based on Schäfers's translation): "O Wunder über Wunder, Verzückung, Macht und Staunen ist, daß man gar nichts über das Evangelium sagen, noch über dasselbe denken, noch es mit irgend etwas vergleichen kann."

Herewith the stage is set for the entire work. The author goes on to refute Marcion's statement by pointing out that our Lord himself "in his Gospel" compared his faith (or: "the instruction of his teaching") to many different things, such as a building, wine, a garment, fire, seeds, a kingdom, silver, a talent, a plant, a grain of mustard-seed, and leaven. The author of the *Exposition* then embarks on an extended discussion of these comparisons and adds a few more.[38] He seems to have a twofold purpose. First, the possibility of the comparison itself disproves Marcion's initial claim. Second, each of these comparisons is shown to have its precedent or its parallel in the Old Testament. The Old Testament parallel texts, mostly from the books of Isaiah, Jeremiah, Ezekiel, and Psalms, are quoted at length, whereby the New Testament passages are often described in terms of "fulfillment." The author's anti-Marcionite focus is strengthened by the fact that his New Testament quotations are mostly taken from the Gospel of Luke and, less frequently, from the letters of Paul; that is, he refers to those writings that were part of the Marcionite canon. Twice he starts from a non-Lukan Gospel passage (in §§44 and 64) and shows awareness that the relevant passage is not in the text that "the strange ones" (*awtark'*), that is, the Marcionites, read, but in both cases he provides additional evidence in Luke or in Paul, which should convince the Marcionites of the validity of his text choice.

Following two introductory paragraphs (§§1–2), in which Marcion is named five times and directly addressed twice ("you, Marcion"!), the following sections can be distinguished, each centered around a parable or a cluster of parables:

| § | Topic | Gospel or New Testament Reference | Fulfills or Parallels |
| --- | --- | --- | --- |
| 3–8 | building | Luke 9:22; 6:47–48 | Isa 49:14–16; Ps 118:22–23 |
| 9–14 | wine | Luke 5:37–38 | Ps 104:14–15 |
| 15–18 | garments | Luke 5:36 | Lev 10:4–6 |
| 19–21 | fire | Luke 12:49 | Jer 5:14; 20:9 |

38. The list of comparisons discussed in the actual text is somewhat different from the list given in the introduction (§2). In particular, the two final sections, on the sheep and on the bride and groom, are not included in the initial list. This should not be seen, however, as an indication that these sections are an afterthought in the mind of the author or a later addition, for they are the most developed and serve as a climax and conclusion. Moreover, they exhibit the same structure and similar terminology.

| §     | Topic                 | Gospel or New Testament Reference              | Fulfills or Parallels                          |
|-------|-----------------------|-----------------------------------------------|------------------------------------------------|
| 22–27 | seeds                 | Luke 8:5–8, 12–15                             | Jer 4:3–4[39]                                  |
| 28–31 | mustard seed/leaven   | Luke 13:18–19, 20–21                          |                                                |
| 32–42 | silver/talents        | Luke 19:12–13                                 | (Jer 33:20–21); Prov 25:11–12                  |
| 43    | city/cities           |                                               |                                                |
| 44–51 | plants/vine-yard      | Mark 12:1; John 15:5; Rom 6:5; 1 Cor 3:6      | Isa 5:1–7; 7:23–25; Ezek 17:22–24              |
| 52–63 | sheep                 | Luke 15:4; 12:32; 10:3                        | Ezek 34:1–23                                   |
| 64–76 | bride and groom       | John 3:29; Luke 5:34; Eph 5:28–32; 2 Cor 11:2; Col 2:10 | Isa 62:5; Ps 19:5–6; Jer 2:35–3:3; 3:20; Ezek 16:1–24 |

Unfortunately, the author does not provide much evidence to help us understand his own social and historical location. His main opponents are Marcion and his followers, who are explicitly mentioned a number of times. In §39, he castigates "sects of heretics," without telling us, however, who these are. His own community—in his view the true representative of legitimate Christianity—is described on a few occasions as having a pagan, gentile past.[40] There is no reference to any empire. But in an interesting explanation of the parable of the master who gave talents to his servants before traveling abroad (§40), the author sees the ten talents as standing for ten cities, and further on he interprets them as a reference to all the peoples of the world, which he starts listing as: the Greeks, the

----

39. The quotation of these two verses (in §§23 and 25) does not agree with any of the other versions. The rendering of v. 3b (MT: נִירוּ לָכֶם נִיר ["Break up the untilled ground"]) as "Choose for yourselves a good and fertile land" is vaguely similar to LXX (νεώσατε ἑαυτοῖς νεώματα), but it is entirely different from Peshitta (which, in the form as we know it, copies here part of Hos 10:12). In v. 4a, the Armenian text ("be purified before the Lord and remove the evil from your hearts") does not preserve the circumcision language that is found here in MT ("circumcise yourselves for the Lord and remove the foreskins of your heart") as well as in LXX and Peshitta. The closest parallel to the Armenian quotation may be found in Targum Jonathan: "Return to the worship of the Lord and remove the evil of your heart" (comp. Robert Hayward, *The Targum of Jeremiah*, ArBib 12 [Wilmington, DE: Glazier, 1987], 58–59).

40. See §13: "we came from paganism" (*i het'anosut'enē*); §59: "we were born out of paganism (*i het'anosut'enē*); §74: "our people are from the pagans" (*i het'anosac'*).

Romans, the Syrians (*Asorikʻ*), the Parthians, and so on (without, unfortunately, continuing his list). Here he seems to give us an inkling of his own Syrian background, as the Syrians are mentioned after the powerful Greeks and Romans, while the Parthians (listed after the Syrians!) are the main power in the East, even though politically they had been replaced by the Sassanians in the early third century.[41] The twelfth-century bishop Nersēs Lambronacʻi, the scribe of MS B, inserted "the Armenians" (*Haykʻ*) before "the Syrians," an emendation not only revelatory of Nersēs's conviction of who took, or should take, precedence, but also indicative of the original author's self-referential invocation.

## Israel and the Jews

In addition to highlighting his own community as well as that of Marcion and his followers, the author includes a number of references to Israel of the Old Testament and to its continuation in the New Testament and contemporary Judaism. Considering his own community's gentile past, these references to Judaism are of particular interest. Echoing some initial comments of Outtier, David Bundy already noted the absence of any anti-Judaism in the text, which, he suggested, may indicate that the author's Christian community "still retained close ties to the Jewish community" or that "a significant number of the target audience were Jewish."[42] No specific passages were studied by either Outtier or Bundy (or by any of the other scholars). I have selected a few passages for closer investigation.

The emphasis on Christianity's connection with the Old Testament has the risk of deemphasizing Christian uniqueness. The author tries to keep the balance by going back and forth between the Old and the New Testament, taking elements of his interpretation from the Old into the New Testament and from the New into the Old. Moreover, the language of fulfillment helps maintain the centrality of the New Testament.[43] With regard to

---

41. With the Parthians, the author may also refer to Edessa, often described as "the daughter of the Parthians."

42. The former suggestion is found in Bundy, "Marcion and the Marcionites," 28, the latter in Bundy, "The Anti-Marcionite Commentary," 122.

43. One might think of a parallel with Aphrahat who is particularly interested in viewing New Testament events as a continuation of the Old Testament, whereby the New Testament outweighs the Old. See Robert Murray, "Some Rhetorical Patterns in Early Syriac Literature," in *A Tribute to Arthur Vööbus: Studies in Early Christian*

the Old Testament, the term "Israel" and "Israelite" is always used. In the New Testament context the Armenian equivalent of "Jew, Jewish," *Hrēay*, is used.

The concept of fulfillment does not explain the whole story. In the author's view, fulfillment does not necessarily lead to replacement of Judaism by Christianity. Our text does contain some interesting passages pointing to a more nuanced approach.

### Christ Preached Circumcision and Uncircumcision

The comparison between faith and a building contains a section (§6) that begins with a quotation of Ps 118:22: "The stone that the builders despised became the chief corner (stone) of the building." The author goes on:

> Again David says: "The stone that the builders despised became the chief corner (stone) of the building" (Ps 118:22). This happened in the Lord. And Paul takes this from the Prophet and from the Gospel, (and) says: "Christ is the chief corner (stone) of the building, through whom the entire building is joined and fitted" (Eph 2:20–21).
>
> And (Paul) makes clear that we, the believing ones, are the building and Christ the chief corner (stone) of the building. And David did not become the (corner) stone, for one wall of the building was built in him, circumcision only. But since Christ preached circumcision [*t'lp'atut'iwn*] and uncircumcision [*ant'lp'atut'iwn*], two walls were built from him, and he became the chief (corner stone). (§6; Schäfers, 8–9)

As Schäfers points out, the image of the two walls—the one standing for the Jews, the other for the gentiles—is not without parallels in early Christian literature (see, for example, Augustine, *Civ.* 18.28).[44] In our text, the centrality of Christ, the corner stone (over against David) accommodates,

---

*Literature and Its Environment, Primarily in the Syrian East*, ed. R. H. Fischer (Chicago: The Lutheran School of Theology, 1977), 109–31. Peter Bruns, *Das Christusbild Aphrahats des Persischen Weisen*, Hereditas 4 (Bonn: Borengässer, 1990), 121, notes: "Bei aller Analogie liegen jedoch alttestamentliches Symbol und neutestamentliche Wahrheit nicht auf derselben heilsgeschichtlichen Ebene. Gegenüber dem alttestamentlichen Vorbild enthält die neutestamentliche Realität ein Mehr an Heil, was sich in der Universalisierung und Spiritualisierung des alttestamentlichen Stoffes niederschlägt." Outtier already noted that the exegesis of the Armenian text "est plus proche d'Aphraate que de la manière d'Ephrem" ("Une explication de l'Evangile," 401 n. 22).

44. Schäfers, *Eine altsyrische antimarkionitische Erklärung*, 9.

rather than neutralizes, the distinction between, and the coexistence of, Jewish and gentile Christians.[45] Echoing perhaps Gal 2:7 ("I was entrusted with the gospel of uncircumcision just as Peter with [the gospel] of circumcision"), the author claims that the coexistence of Jewish and gentile Christianity can be attributed to Christ himself.

## "The Blessed Land and the Inheritance of Israel"

In the comparison between faith and sheep, the author mentions both Jacob and Joseph as types of Christ. Let us first focus on Jacob:

> Jacob, the patriarch of the fathers, was a shepherd for Isaac his father and he was persecuted by his brother who was older than he. And subsequently he received a Syrian [*asori*] flock. Likewise Christ as well became a teacher of the Jews [*Hrēicʿ*], the first flock. And when he was persecuted by Herod the monarch, he became a shepherd of Syrian pagans [*hetʿanosacʿ asorocʿ*].
>
> In the time when Jacob became shepherd of the flock of Laban, Laban took (and) separated a select flock for Jacob [in such a way] that every lamb that would be dappled and speckled would be Jacob's, and the sheep that would be entirely of one color would be Laban's. Jacob painted the rods according to the word of the Lord and cast [them] in front of the sheep. And the offspring of the sheep resembled the color as it appeared on the painted rods. And the flock followed the righteous shepherd to the blessed land of the Israelites, which they had not seen. The mothers that had one color [as] usual, which gave birth to multicolored lambs, had been reared in the impure land.
>
> In the same way we also were born from paganism [*i hetʿanosutʿenē*], [yet] we are spotted and speckled as a result of the whitened marks, in the likeness of the cross—according to the marks of the rods. And we do not resemble our impious parents from whom we were born. And in the likeness of Jacob's flock, we follow the righteous shepherd to the blessed land and to the inheritance of Israel.
>
> And our parents who have begotten us amidst paganism [*i hetʿanosutʿean*] and on whom the marks of the rods are not found remain in the impure land. And in the same way as Jacob in his persecution brought foreign [*awtar*] sheep back to the land of Israel, so also Christ,

---

45. For this terminology, see Joel Marcus, "The Circumcision and the Uncircumcision in Rome," *NTS* 35 (1989): 67–81 (esp. 73–81). In our text, the terms are used without any polemical overtone.

when he was persecuted by the Jews [*i Hrēic‘*], brought pagan humans
[*zhet‘anos mardik*] to his devotion and into the first inheritance of Israel
[*i žaṙangut‘iwn Israyēli yaṙaǰinn*]. (§59; Schäfers, 53–55)

In the initial paragraph of this section, the comparison between Jacob
and Christ—presented as "patriarch" (*nahapet*) and "teacher" (*varda-
pet*) respectively—is briefly summarized. Both Jacob and Christ in the
end became shepherds of a Syrian flock. Whereas the characterization of
Jacob's flock as "Syrian" (*asori*) initially derives from the ethnic identity of
"Laban the Aramean" (Gen 31:20—ὁ Σύρος in the Septuagint), the term
"Syrian" assumes an additional meaning of non-Israelite (or "pagan"),
based on the secondary meaning of *ārāmāyā* in Syriac, which renders
"Hellene" (Ἕλλην) in the Peshitta New Testament in the sense of "non-
Jewish" or "gentile, pagan" (see, for example, Acts 21:28, Rom 1:16, and
in John 7:35, where the Old Syriac has *ārāmāyē* [pl.] as opposed to *‘ammē*
"nations" or "gentiles" in the Peshitta).[46]

Using this subtle play of shifting meanings, the author is able to set
up an extended comparison between the way in which Jacob and Christ
acquired their flock. His focus is on the story of Jacob's trick with the
painted rods, as narrated in Gen 30. Jacob was persecuted by his brother
Esau; Jesus is first said to have been persecuted by King Herod, but later
the Jews are mentioned as persecutors.

Following divine instruction, Jacob succeeds in gaining a flock out of
Laban's non-Israelite sheep. In the same way, Christ opens up his teaching
to a non-Jewish following. Neither for Jacob nor for Christ is this a definitive departure from Israelite tradition but rather an emergency measure,
made necessary by the persecution. Once separated from their non-Israelite and non-Jewish parents, the new flocks have to follow "the righteous
shepherd" (Jacob and Jesus, respectively), who brings them home "to the
blessed land and to the inheritance of Israel," which had been their final
destination all along.

---

46. See George Kiraz, *Comparative Edition of the Syriac Gospels*, 2nd ed., 4 vols.
(Piscataway, NJ: Gorgias, 2002). The distinction between *ārāmāyā* ("Aramean") and
*ārmāyā* ("pagan") belongs to a later period. See Schäfers, *Eine altsyrische antimarkio-
nitische Erklärung*, 53 n. 7, and Sebastian P. Brock and J. F. Coakley, "Arameans," in
*Gorgias Encyclopedic Dictionary of the Syriac Heritage*, ed. Sebastian P. Brock et al.
(Piscataway, NJ: Gorgias, 2011), 30–31.

Jacob's manipulation of Laban's flock thus becomes an allegory for the formation of a new flock out of pagan parents, an allegory for the vocation of the gentiles. The newly established flock, however, first and foremost has to follow its shepherd and to embark on a journey "to the blessed land of the Israelites, which they had not seen" and "to the first inheritance of Israel"—as if Christianity can thrive only when it is connected with its roots in Israel.

Interestingly, the same biblical episode is also used in Hippolytus's *Commentary on the Song of Songs*, which was studied by Marcus.[47] For Hippolytus, however, it is the replacement of one flock with the other that is prefigured.[48] At the same time, Hippolytus hopes for the reunion of the separated flocks and expects that when Israel will repent and acknowledge Christ, she will regain her former glory.[49] In contrast with Hippolytus, our author in this passage does not want to place the burden on Israel and to wait for her repentance and conversion but rather enjoins his community to go out in search of Israel, in order to become whole again.

## Joseph and His Brothers

The theme of persecution also plays an important role in the comparison that the author draws between Joseph and Christ. After having been persecuted and sold by his brothers, the monarch of Egypt entrusts Joseph with nourishing the people in the time of famine. When Joseph's brothers come to Egypt and bow down before him, he feeds them. Like other early Christian authors, the *Exposition* portrays Joseph's brothers as prefigurements of the Jews. But, interestingly, in contrast to most other authors, the author does not focus on the brothers' betrayal of Joseph and their plan to kill or to sell him but rather foregrounds the moment when they recognize Joseph, he feeds them, and all the brothers reunite.

---

47. Marcus, "Israel and the Church."

48. A Latin translation of the relevant Georgian text is found in Gérard Garitte, *Traités d'Hippolyte sur David et Goliath, sur le Cantique des cantiques et sur l'Antéchrist*, CSCO 264, Iberici 16 (Leuven: CorpusSCO, 1965), 32–33.

49. For this painful awareness of incompleteness and expectation, Gertrud Chappuzeau uses the expression "heilsgeschichtliche Traurigkeit" ("Die Auslegung des Hoheliedes durch Hippolyt von Rom," *JAC* 19 [1976]: 79 n. 279])"—which is quoted approvingly in Marcus, "Israel and the Church," 394.

The same is true of Christ. His brothers were older shepherds. God his Father sent him to see the shepherds and their flock. And his brothers the Israelites contemplated death for him, because they envied him. And according to the word of Judah he was sold and killed....

And after he was sold, the Monarch of Eternity made him lord of the life of the living. And whoever puts his trust in him, he nourishes him with food. And in the same way as the brothers of Joseph, when they bowed down before him, were nourished more than anyone else, so also the Israelites who are his killers, sellers, and persecutors, when they come and submit to Christ, obtain from him life and become honored. (§60; Schäfers, 55–56)

In spite of their nefarious machinations, Joseph's brothers and the later Israelites (that is, the Jews of Christ's day), when they recognize their brother, receive nourishment and life—from Joseph and Christ, respectively—"more than anyone else." Extending this comparison a bit further, the author posits that Joseph's brothers at first did not believe that Joseph could still be alive and needed time before recognizing him. In the same way, the "killers, persecutors, and sellers" of Christ will need more time before recognizing him!

The fraternal theme emerges one more time, in the discussion of Abel, the shepherd, and Cain (§57). Cain stands here for the Israelites "who do not acknowledge Christ," who "persist in the mindset of Herod [*kan mnan i mitsn Herodiay*]," and who follow "the murderous Pharisees." This is the strongest anti-Jewish statement to be found in the text. At the same time, the evil of "the Israelites who do not acknowledge Christ" is tied to Herod and to "the murderous Pharisees." Throughout the text, the blame for killing Christ is put on Herod and (more rarely) on the Pharisees, perhaps in an attempt to tone down the Israelites' direct responsibility. In §61, Herod "the wicked king" is juxtaposed to the wicked king Saul wanting to kill David.[50]

---

50. Our text shares the very negative image of Herod that is found in early Syriac literature, even though the phrase "paltry fox" (*ṭaʿlā šiṭā*), attested in Ephrem, is absent. Compare Manolis Papoutsakis, *Vicarious Kingship: A Theme in Syriac Political Theology in Late Antiquity*, Studien und Texte zu Antike und Christentum 100 (Tübingen: Mohr Siebeck, 2017), 120–24.

## Return to the Land

As is clear from several of the passages that have been quoted, the theme of return plays a crucial role in the author's view of the relationship between Christianity, on the one hand, and Israel, the Old Testament, and Judaism, on the other. Faithful to his initial anti-Marcionite statement, he insists time and again that—quite the opposite of what Marcion claims!—the Christian faith is *not* new and that it realizes its full integrity only when it honors its Israelite roots.

Let us briefly consider the author's lengthy explanation of the betrothal of Rebecca to Isaac (§73–76). This is part of the long section on "bride and groom," in which the author considers the role of bridal mediators or matchmakers.

The story begins with Abraham who dwells in the land of Canaan and asks his senior servant, with an oath, not to take a wife for his son Isaac from the daughters of the Canaanites but rather to go to Abraham's own land (*yašxarh*) and inheritance (*žaṙanguťiwn*) and find for him a wife there (Gen 24:1–4). In the land of Canaan, the Presence (*hangist*)[51] of God dwelled, yet the inhabitants of the land were evil and unjust. An important stipulation for the servant's mission is that the woman has to follow the servant back to Canaan; on no account could Isaac be brought there (Gen 24:5–6). If in the end the woman would not consent to come to Canaan, the servant would be absolved of his oath (Gen 24:8). The whole plan would then come to naught.

In the author's retelling of this story, the land of Canaan stands for the house of Israel, where the Presence of God dwelled, yet the inhabitants "were not worthy to be united to Christ [that is, Isaac in the original story] because of their wickedness." The apostles, as matchmakers, were sent out to find a wife for Christ in gentile land. This wife is the gentile Christian community, which was "called to go to inherit the inheritance which they had never seen" (§74) and was "carried to the great and honorable inheritance" (§76). The response alone to the apostles' preaching would be ineffective; the gentile community cannot stand on its own. Just as in Rachel's

---

51. Egan translates "peace" *Saint Ephrem* (§73); Schäfers "Ruhe" (*Eine altsyrische antimarkionitische Erklärung*, 69, with n. 7). Perhaps we are dealing here with an Armenian rendering of *Shekhinah*, which in its Aramaic form, *Shekhintā*, is not uncommon in early Syriac theology and literature. See Papoutsakis, *Vicarious Kingship*, 164–65, with nn. 75 and 76 (and further references).

case, the gentile community has to travel to "the land and the inheritance of Israel." Without this return, their wedding agreement with Christ would be void.[52]

## Concluding Remarks

In light of the author's repeated assertion that his Christian community is of pagan descent, that is, that the Christian faith is new to them, it is all the more significant that he insists on several occasions that his community should maintain a direct connection with the first inheritance of Israel.

Not much can be said about the author's or his community's Christian profile. In addition to their commitment to the scriptures of the Old Testament (often referred to as "the Law and the Prophets") and the New Testament (mainly "the gospel" and "the apostle"), the faithful are encouraged to embrace an ascetic lifestyle. Christ is said to be true man, for "he clothed himself with humanity" (§38), and truly God (§§30 and 54). Whether the absence of anti-Judaism and the positive view of Christianity's Jewish legacy are related to the author's (or his community's) familiarity or proximity with (any type of) torah-observant Christians or with non-Christian Jews, we do not know. It may go too far to suggest, as Bundy does, that the author's community "still retained close ties to the Jewish community" or that "a significant number of the target audience were Jewish."[53]

It also remains unknown whether, and to what extent, the author's emphasis on the connection with the Old Testament and with the "first inheritance" of Israel has a specific role within his polemical exchange with Marcion and the Marcionites. Regardless of its specific situation and environment, a Christian community in fourth-century Syria or Armenia may have—in addition to the fundamentals of the Christian faith and the striving for an ascetic lifestyle—developed a world view in which the Old Testament and Israelite component of salvation history continued to be

---

52. It should be noted that in a different context the author once uses the language of "grafting," reminiscent of Rom 11. In §47, the text reads as follows (Schäfer, *Eine altsyrische antimarkionitische Erklärung*, 42): "from the first people he takes a plant (*tunk*), (and) engrafts (*patuastē*) onto them Jesus Christ so that he (or: 'it,' i.e., the plant) would be taken from the nation of the house of Judah." This is followed by a long quotation of Ezek 17:22–24.

53. See note 42.

taken very seriously and in which there was room "for a continuing divine embrace of the Jews as well."[54]

This sustained reflection on the proximity and interdependence between Judaism and Christianity, as found in the present text and in the texts studied by Marcus, may serve as a corrective to the paradigm of separation and exclusion that has gained dominance all too often.[55] That many centuries later the text was faithfully copied by Xač'atur of Hałbat and slightly updated by Bishop Nersēs of Tarsus may indicate that the message of this text still resonated in twelfth-century Armenia, as it does with some of us today.[56]

## Bibliography

Augé, Isabelle. *Églises en dialogue: Arméniens et Byzantins dans la seconde moitié du XIIe siècle*. CSCO 633, Subsidia 124. Leuven: Peeters, 2011.

Bienert, W. A. "Marcion und der Antijudaismus." Pages 191–205 in *Marcion und seine kirchengeschichtliche Wirkung*. Edited by Gerhard May, Katharina Greschat, and Martin Meiser. TUGAL 150. Berlin: de Gruyter, 2002.

Biesen, Kees den. *Annotated Bibliography of Ephrem the Syrian*. Self-published, 2011.

Brock, Sebastian. "Jewish Traditions in Syriac Sources." *JJS* 30 (1979): 212–32.

Brock, Sebastian P., and J. F. Coakley. "Arameans." Pages 30–31 in *Gorgias Encyclopedic Dictionary of the Syriac Heritage*. Edited by Sebastian P. Brock et al. Piscataway, NJ: Gorgias, 2011.

Bruns, Peter. *Das Christusbild Aphrahats des Persischen Weisen*. Hereditas 4. Bonn: Borengässer, 1990.

---

54. Marcus, "The *Testaments of the Twelve Patriarchs*," 603.

55. See n. 4. For Syriac Christian attitudes toward Judaism, a more nuanced picture may be needed than the one recently provided in Dominique Cerbelaud, "Les Pères syriens et les juifs," in *L'antijudaïsme des Pères: Mythe et/ou réalité?*, ed. Jean-Marie Auwers, Régis Burnet, and Didier Luciani, Théologie historique 125 (Paris: Beauchesne, 2017), 183–95.

56. Sincere thanks are due to Erin Galgay Walsh (Duke University) and to Theo van Lint (Oxford University), whose assistance in the final stage of the preparation of this paper was crucial.

Bundy, David. "The Anti-Marcionite Commentary on the Lukan Parables (Pseudo-Ephrem A): Images in Tension." *Mus* 103 (1990): 111–23.

———. "Marcion and the Marcionites in Early Syriac Apologetics." *Mus* 101 (1988): 21–32.

Burkitt, Francis C. *Evangelion Da-Mepharreshe: The Curetonian Version of the Four Gospels, with the Readings of the Sinai Palimpsest.* 2 vols. Cambridge: Cambridge University Press, 1904.

Cerbelaud, Dominique. "Les Pères syriens et les juifs." Pages 183–95 in *L'antijudaïsme des Pères: Mythe et/ou réalité?* Edited by Jean-Marie Auwers, Régis Burnet, and Didier Luciani. Théologie historique 125. Paris: Beauchesne, 2017.

Chappuzeau, Gertrud. "Die Auslegung des Hoheliedes durch Hippolyt von Rom." *JAC* 19 (1976): 45–81.

Drijvers, H. J. W. "Marcionism in Syria: Principles, Problems, Polemics." *SecCent* 6 (1987–1988): 153–72.

Egan, George A. *An Analysis of the Biblical Quotations of Ephrem in "An Exposition of the Gospel" (Armenian version).* CSCO 443, Subsidia 66. Leuven: Peeters, 1983.

———. "A Re-consideration of the Authenticity of Ephrem's 'An Exposition of the Gospel.'" Pages 128–34 in *Kyriakon: Festschrift Johannes Quasten.* Edited by Patrick Granfteld and Josef A. Jungman. Münster: Aschendorff, 1970.

———. *Saint Ephrem: An Exposition of the Gospel.* CSCO 291–292, Arm. 5–6. Leuven: Secrétariat du CorpusSCO, 1968.

Garitte, Gérard. *Traités d'Hippolyte sur David et Goliath, sur le Cantique des cantiques et sur l'Antéchrist.* CSCO 264, Iberici 16. Leuven: CorpusSCO, 1965.

Harnack, Adolf. *Marcion: Das Evangelium vom fremden Gott; Eine Monographie zur Geschichte der Grundlegung der katholischen Kirche.* 2nd. improved and exp. ed. Leipzig: Hinrichs, 1924.

Harris, James Rendel. "Tatian: Perfection according to the Saviour." *BJRL* 8 (1924): 15–51.

Hayward, Robert. *The Targum of Jeremiah.* ArBib 12. Wilmington, DE: Glazier, 1987.

Kiraz, George. *Comparative Edition of the Syriac Gospels.* 2nd ed. 4 vols. Piscataway, NJ: Gorgias, 2002.

Lange, Christian. *Ephraem der Syrer: Kommentar zum Diatessaron.* Fontes Christiani 54.1–2. Turnhout: Brepols, 2008.

———. *The Portrayal of Christ in the Syriac Commentary on the Diatessaron*. CSCO 616, Subsidia 118. Leuven: Peeters, 2005.

Leloir, Louis. *Saint Éphrem: Commentaire de l'Évangile concordant; Texte syriaque (Manuscrit Chester Beatty 709)*. CBM 8. Dublin: Hodges Figgis, 1963.

———. *Saint Éphrem: Commentaire de l'Évangile concordant; Texte syriaque (Manuscrit Chester Beatty 709); Folios additionnels*. Chester Beatty Monographs 8. Leuven: Peeters, 1990.

———. *Saint Éphrem: Commentaire de l'Évangile concordant; Version arménienne*. 2 vols. CSCO 137 and 145, Arm. 1–2. Leuven: Secrétariat du CorpusSCO, 1953–1964.

Lieu, Judith M. *Marcion and the Making of a Heretic: God and Scripture in the Second Century*. Cambridge: Cambridge University Press, 2015.

Marcus, Joel. "The Circumcision and the Uncircumcision in Rome." *NTS* 35 (1989): 67–81.

———. "Israel and the Church in the Exegetical Writings of Hippolytus." *JBL* 131 (2012): 385–406.

———. "Jewish Christianity." Pages 87–102 in *Origins to Constantine*. Vol. 1 of *The Cambridge History of Christianity*. Edited by Margaret Mitchell and Frances Young. Cambridge: Cambridge University Press, 2006.

———. "The *Testaments of the Twelve Patriarchs* and the *Didascalia Apostolorum*: A Common Jewish-Christian Milieu?" *JTS* 61 (2010): 596–626.

Mathews, Edward G. "A First Glance at the Armenian Prayers Attributed to Surb Epʿrem Xorin Asorwoy." Pages 161–74 in *Worship Traditions in Armenian and the Neighboring Christian East*. Edited by Roberta R. Ervine. Crestwood, NY: Saint Vladimir's Seminary Press, 2006.

May, Gerhard, Katharina Greschat, and Martin Meiser, eds. *Marcion und seine kirchengeschichtliche Wirkung: Vorträge der Internationalen Fachkonferenz zu Marcion, gehalten vom 15–18. August 2001 in Main = Marcion and his Impact on Church History*. TUGAL 150. Berlin: de Gruyter, 2002.

Mécérian, Jean. *Histoire et institutions de l'Église arménienne*. Beirut: Imprimerie catholique, 1965.

Mitchell, C. W. S. *Ephraim's Prose Refutations of Mani, Marcion, and Bardaisan*. 2 vols. London: Williams & Norgate, 1912–1921.

Murray, Robert. "Some Rhetorical Patterns in Early Syriac Literature." Pages 109–31 in *A Tribute to Arthur Vööbus: Studies in Early Christian*

*Literature and Its Environment, Primarily in the Syrian East.* Edited by R. H. Fischer. Chicago: The Lutheran School of Theology, 1977.

——. *Symbols of Church and Kingdom: A Study in Early Syriac Tradition.* Cambridge: Cambridge University Press, 1975.

Outtier, Bernard. "Une explication de l'Evangile attribuée à Saint Ephrem: A propos d'une édition récente." *ParOr* 1 (1970): 385–407.

Papoutsakis, Manolis. *Vicarious Kingship: A Theme in Syriac Political Theology in Late Antiquity.* Studien und Texte zu Antike und Christentum 100. Tübingen: Mohr Siebeck, 2017.

Preuschen, Erwin. "Eine altkirchliche antimarcionitische Schrift unter dem Namen Ephräms." *ZNW* 12 (1911): 243–69.

Rouwhorst, Gerard. "Jewish Liturgical Traditions in Early Syriac Christianity." *VC* 51 (1997): 72–93.

Schäfers, Joseph. *Eine altsyrische antimarkionitische Erklärung von Parabeln des Herrn und zwei andere altsyrische Abhandlungen zu Texten des Evangeliums: Mit Beiträgen zu Tatians Diatessaron und Markions Neuem Testament.* NTAbh 6.1–2. Münster: Aschendorff, 1917.

Strobel, A. "Das Begriff des 'vierkapiteligen Evangeliums' in Pseudo-Ephrem C." *ZKG* 70 (1959): 112–20.

Wilson, Stephen G. "Marcion and the Jews." Pages 45–58 in vol. 2 of *Anti-Judaism in Early Christianity.* Edited by Stephen G. Wilson. 2 vols. SJC 2. Waterloo, ON: Wilfrid Laurier University Press, 1986.

# Narrative and Counternarrative:
## The Jewish Antigospel (The *Toledot Yeshu*) and the Christian Gospels

Philip S. Alexander

### The Jewish Antigospel: The *Textus Receptus*

Christians have long been aware that an antigospel, contradicting and even mocking the Christian gospels, has been in circulation among Jews. The best-known version of this antigospel today is the one printed in Hebrew with a Latin translation by the German Christian Hebraist, Johann Christoph Wagenseil (1633–1705) in his collection of Jewish anti-Christian tracts called *Tela Ignea Satanae* ("The Fiery Darts of Satan"), published in Altdorf in 1681, during his tenure of the chair of Oriental Languages at the university in that city.[1] Wagenseil's version carried the title *Toledot Yeshu*, literally, "The Generations of Jesus," or "The History of Jesus," taking *toledot* in its broader sense. The title ultimately alludes to the opening of the Gospel of Matthew, Βίβλος γενέσεως Ἰησοῦ Χριστοῦ, which is rendered by Shem Tov ben Shaprut in his anti-Christian polemical treatise the *'Even Boḥan* ("The Touchstone") (c. 1400) as *Elleh toledot Yeshu*.[2] The title *Toledot Yeshu* is indeed found in some manuscripts, but there are other titles as well, a more common one being *Ma'aseh Yeshu ha-Notzri* ("The Story of Jesus the Nazarene"). Many versions of the *Toledot*

---

1. Johann Christoff Wagenseil, *Tela Ignea Satanae* (Altdorf: Johann Heinrich Schönnerstaedt, 1681).

2. George Howard, *The Hebrew Gospel of Matthew* (Macon, GA: Mercer University Press, 1995), 1. Franz Delitzsch, *Sifrei ha-Berit ha-Hadashah* (Leipzig: Ackermann & Glaser, 1877), and Isaac Salkinson, *Ha-Berit ha-Hadashah* (ed. C. D. Ginsburg [Vienna: Fromme, 1885]), both translate in the same way, though with Yeshua' for Yeshu. It is the obvious translation.

do have an account of the birth and infancy of Jesus, and the title *Toledot* is particularly apt for them. It is less obviously appropriate, however, for those that lack this element.

The version of the *Toledot Yeshu* found in the Wagenseil text falls into three large sections. The first is an account of the birth and childhood of Jesus. It is a kind of Jewish anti–Infancy Gospel.[3] Here the main thrust of the story is that Jesus was born of rape, his mother Miriam, a pious Jewish girl, having been tricked into intercourse by a villain named Joseph Pandera, who lived nearby. Her betrothed Yoḥanan, a studious Yeshivah Bocher, when it became clear that Miriam was pregnant but not by him, went off in shame to Babylonia and never returned. The story of the virgin birth was concocted to hush up the shameful fact of Jesus's birth. Jesus proved to be a precocious boy, and Miriam employed a sage to teach him. Jesus honored his own teacher, but he was pointedly disrespectful to the other sages. The sages, shocked at this, inquired into the circumstances of his birth, and, discovering he was a bastard and the son of a menstruant as well, excommunicated him.

The second section is concerned primarily with the trial, death, and burial of Jesus, and it constitutes an anti–Passion Gospel.[4] But it opens with an account of Jesus's ministry to explain how he came to be tried and put to death. Jesus learns the pronunciation of the Tetragrammaton and, using this, begins to do miracles and to lead people to believe that he is the Son of God. The sages decide something has to be done about him, so they bring him for trial before Queen Helena the wife of King Yannai (in whose reign, nearly a hundred years before the birth of Jesus, the events are bizarrely set), but the queen dismisses the case when Jesus does miracles in her presence. The sages are then aided by one of their number, Judas, who infiltrates the company of Jesus's disciples and finally manages to bring him to book. Jesus is apprehended by the authorities, tried, stoned, and hung. The sages bury him near where he was executed,

---

3. See further Philip S. Alexander, "Jesus and his Mother in the Jewish Anti-Gospel (the *Toledot Yeshu*)," in *Infancy Gospels: Stories and Identities*, ed. Claire Clivaz et al., WUNT 281 (Tübingen: Mohr Siebeck, 2011), 588–616; Peter Schäfer, "Jesus' Origin, Birth and Childhood according to the *Toledot Yeshu* and the Talmud," in *Judaea-Palaestina, Babylon and Rome: Jews in Antiquity*, ed. Benjamin Isaac and Yuval Shahar, TSAJ 147 (Tübingen: Mohr Siebeck, 2012), 139–64.

4. See further Hillel I. Newman, "The Death of Jesus in the *Toledot Yeshu* Literature," *JTS* 50 (1999): 59–79.

but, unknown to them, Judas removes the body and buries it in his garden, so that Jesus's disciples should not steal it away. The disciples come and, finding the tomb empty, proclaim the resurrection, but after three days, Judas, having learned what has happened, produces the body, which is publicly exposed.

The third section covers the period immediately following the death of Jesus and constitutes a sort of anti-Acts.[5] The main point here is that the parting of the ways between Christianity and Judaism was engineered by Peter, who, like Judas, serves clandestinely as an agent of the sages. Through doing the same sort of miracles as Jesus, he convinces the Christians that he speaks in Jesus's name. He persuades them that, since Jesus hated the Jews and the Jewish scriptures, they should do the same and separate themselves from Israel. After his death, someone called Elijah comes along and almost undoes Peter's work, but before he can persuade the Christians to return to Jewish practices, God intervenes and strikes him dead. So the two communities—Christians and Jews—remain apart.

## The Jewish Antigospel: Variant Traditions

The Wagenseil version is only one of a large number of versions of the *Toledot* that have been preserved. The tradition is one of the most complex in Jewish literature, and its transmission history and literary profile pose formidable problems of description and analysis. The analysis has been hugely facilitated by the recent important new edition of the work by Michael Meerson and Peter Schäfer, *The Toledot Yeshu: The Life Story of Jesus*,[6] which gives the texts of the major manuscripts, in Hebrew and Aramaic, with variant readings, English translations, and detailed introductions. Of the 112 manuscripts on which Meerson and Schäfer base their

---

5. See further John Gager, "Simon Peter, Founder of Christianity or Saviour of Israel," in *Toledot Yeshu ("The Life Story of Jesus") Revisited: A Princeton Conference*, ed. Peter Schäfer, Michael Meerson, and Yaacov Deutsch, TSAJ 143 (Tübingen: Mohr Siebeck, 2011), 220–45; W. J. van Bekkum, " 'The Rock on Which the Church Is Founded': Simon Peter in Jewish Folktale," in *Saints and Role Models in Judaism and Christianity*, ed. Marcel Poorthuis and Joshua Schwarz, Jewish and Christian Perspectives 7 (Leiden: Brill, 2004), 289–310.

6. Michael Meerson and Peter Schäfer, *The Toledot Yeshu: The Life Story of Jesus; Two Volumes and a Database*, 2 vols., TSAJ 159 (Tübingen: Mohr Siebeck, 2014). This replaces Samuel Krauss's pioneering edition, *Das Leben Jesu nach jüdischen Quellen* (Berlin: S. Calvary, 1902).

edition, 6 are in Aramaic and 106 are in Hebrew. This is a work of immense erudition and industry, a turning point in the study of this important text, but rich though it is, it is still not exhaustive.

It does not include the translations of the *Toledot* into Jewish languages. Meerson and Schäfer list eighteen Yiddish versions, twenty-one Judeo-Arabic, two Ladino, and one Judeo-Persian. The Judeo-Arabic manuscripts are particularly important because some of them are early.[7] Translations are crucial for the history of the *Toledot Yeshu*, since not only was the Hebrew rendered into other Jewish languages, a circumstance that helped to spread and popularize the work, but also the translations were sometimes, it seems, subsequently retroverted back into Hebrew.[8] This can result in the confusing situation where two manuscripts contain essentially the same storyline, as to plot, episodes, and *dramatis personae* (and so look like the same recension), but they differ as to precise wording. Translations are also important for establishing the provenance or at least the circulation of a particular recension of the work.

The major printed editions are referenced by Meerson and Schäfer but their full texts, understandably, are not given. A systematic bibliography of them remains a desideratum. They are more numerous than is sometimes supposed. The most important are the *Toledot* in Raymundus Martini's *Pugio Fidei* (composed around 1270 but not printed till 1651), the Wagenseil print of 1681 already mentioned, the Huldreich print of 1705, and the *Tam u-Muʿad* version. Copies of the *Tam u-Muʿad* are rare and its publication history confused, but a useful edition of it was published by Günter Schlichting in 1982.[9] The printed versions are important because some of the manuscripts were copied from them and not from other manuscripts.

---

7. See Miriam Goldstein, "Judeo-Arabic Versions of *Toledot Yeshu*," *Ginzei Qedem* 6 (2010): 9–42.

8. For the Yiddish translations, see Erich Bischoff, *Ein jüdisch-deutsches Leben Jesu* (Leipzig: Friedrich, 1895). Bischoff fired the opening shots in the modern study of the *Toledot*. He seems to have inspired Krauss to undertake his much more extensive and important research.

9. Wagenseil's text of the *Toledot* (n. 1) has been reprinted a number of times. Raymundus Martini, *Pugio Fidei ... adversus Mauros et Hebraeos ... cum observationibus Iosephi de Voisin* (Paris: Henault & Henault, 1651), better known in the reprint, with an introduction by Benedict Carpzov, published by Friedrich Lanckisch (Leipzig, 1687); Johann Jacob Huldreich, *Sefer Toledot Yeshuaʿ ha-Notzri/Historia Jeschuae Nazareni* (Severinum: Johannes du Vivie, 1705); Günter Schlichting, *Ein jüdisches Leben Jesu: Die verschollene Toledot-Jeschu-Fassung Tam ū-mūʿād; Einleitung, Text,*

There were several reasons for this. Some of the manuscripts were written in regions where Hebrew printing was not well developed, and so printed texts from outside the region got circulated in handwritten copies. The Yemen is a case in point: hand-copying of printed books continued there down to the twentieth century. Another factor was the fear that printing such a virulently anti-Christian work might rouse the ire of the Christian authorities. It would never get past the censor, where censorship was in operation. The *Toledot Yeshu* was underground, subversive literature. Ironically it was Christians, like Wagenseil and Huldreich, who gave it the oxygen of publicity and provided *Jews* with printed texts that they could circulate further among themselves in handwritten copies. The Christian attitude to the *Toledot* was complex. There were Christians who commissioned manuscript copies of it from Jewish scribes. If they referred to it, or published it, it was with noisy outrage and horror. But they were clearly fascinated by it, representing as it did something transgressive and forbidden. Similar attitudes to Jesus are not unknown in the Jewish tradition—repulsion linked with guilty fascination.[10]

Building on earlier work by Erich Bischoff, Samuel Krauss, William Horbury, and Riccardo Di Segni,[11] Meerson and Schäfer offer a preliminary classification of the various manuscripts. I have presented a modified version of this in the appended table. This classification is immensely useful, but it needs some further refinement. Its terminology, "group," "sub-group," "recension," "version," are not clearly defined. It relies heavily on provenance—Oriental, Yemenite, Byzantine, Ashkenazi, Italian,

---

*Übersetzung, Kommentar, Motivsynopse, Bibliographie*, WUNT 24 (Tübingen: Mohr Siebeck, 1982).

10. To complete the picture of the *Toledot* we should also, ideally, record its *testimonia*, i.e., the quotations and allusions to it in other texts, both Jewish and Christian, and trace its reception history. Christians have known the *Toledot* since at least the ninth century (it features in the writings of Agobard, Archbishop of Lyon, and of his disciple and successor Amulo). References to it in Christian authors since the Reformation are also common (see, e.g., Luther's *Vom Schem Hamphoras und Geschlecht Christi*, 1543). They sometimes turn up in the most unexpected places. And it was extensively exploited by rationalists like Voltaire to attack established Christianity. See Daniel Barbu, "Voltaire and the *Toledoth Yeshu*," in Clivaz et al., *Infancy Gospels*, 618–27.

11. Bischoff, *Das Leben Jesu*; Krauss, *Das Leben Jesu*; William Horbury, "A Critical Examination of the Toledoth Yeshu" (PhD diss., Cambridge University, 1970); Riccardo Di Segni, *Il Vangelo del Ghetto* (Rome: Newton Compton, 1985).

Sefardi, Slavic. But this criterion is not universally applied: chronology also plays some part—early versus late. And what are we to do with the categories Wagenseil and Huldreich, which classify manuscripts according to their literary affinities to two printed texts? Both these printed versions clearly circulated in the Ashkenazi cultural domain, so why not classify them as Ashkenazi?

Moreover, how is *provenance* to be determined? The script in which the manuscripts are written plays a part. This is reasonable but only up to a point, because one cannot assume that the region in which a version circulated is the region where it originated. Thus, Meerson and Schäfer admit that their Ashkenazi A version almost certainly originated in Spain, but is it not then, arguably, a *Sefardi* recension? And script purely on its own is a problematic taxonomic criterion, because it could divide two similar versions that are written in two different regional scripts. To be meaningful, differences in script have to coincide with differences in *substance*. But what differences of substance should we allow as criteria for the purposes of classification? We could classify according to language, but that runs into the problem that we have substantially the *same* versions in *different* languages. We could classify according to precise wording, exact or more or less exact verbal overlaps (the standard criterion for constructing *stemma codicum* in classical text criticism). That is of some value and would at least identify versions that were in whole or in part very close to one another, but we have, as already mentioned, the curious case of versions close to one another as to storyline, plot, and motifs, which differ as to precise wording.

We could classify as to storyline, plot, and motif. This is a serviceable approach for this kind of tradition, but it has to be theorized with care. The smallest building block has to be the motif, used in the folklore sense as employed by Stith Thompson in his *Motif-Index of Folk Literature*.[12] A series of motifs create a storyline and a plot. Versions could be classified according to whether or not they reproduce the same motifs in the same order and generate the same, or similar, storylines and plots. The most extensive analysis of the motifs of the *Toledot Yeshu* tradition has been done by Schlichting.[13] Meerson and Schäfer work with bigger units—narratives, anecdotes, or episodes—though they do not use these terms. We need, in fact, both

---

12. Stith Thompson, *Motif-Index of Folk-Literature*, 6 vols. (Bloomington: Indiana University Press, 1955–1958).

13. Schlichting, *Ein jüdisches Leben Jesu*, 229–66.

approaches. Meerson and Schäfer have done scholarship a great service in clarifying the textual tradition of the *Toledot Yeshu*. We now need to build on this by moving on to a comprehensive literary analysis. This has to be pursued at three levels: (1) the identification of the discrete *motifs* of which the tradition *grosso modo* is made up; (2) the identification of the discrete *pericopes*, created by combining motifs into mini-narratives; (3) literary analysis of the storyline, plot, characterization, and general coherence of the longer texts created by aggregating discrete pericopes into larger, more complex literary structures.

The *Toledot Yeshu* tradition is so complex that one might be forgiven for wondering if it is possible to trace its transmission history. Indeed, is it meaningful to talk as if there is a *unified* tradition? Is the *Toledot Yeshu* not simply a modern construct, created by scholars by lumping together a whole series of *different* Jewish antigospels? There is force in this view, if we look simply at the synchronic level, but at the diachronic level, we are clearly dealing with something that *can* be profiled as *a single evolving tradition*. There is too much in common between the various versions to suppose that they originated in isolation, and in some cases lines of literary dependency can be traced beyond reasonable doubt.

## A Tentative Profile of the Tradition as a Whole

I would broadly profile the tradition as follows:[14]

(1) Taken at its maximal recorded extent, the *Toledot Yeshu* falls, as I have already indicated, into three main blocks of material: (a) stories relating to Jesus's birth and childhood (the anti–Infancy Gospel); (b) stories relating to his public ministry from its beginning down to his death and resurrection (the anti–Passion Gospel); and (c) stories relating to the early post-Easter church, covering the period of the Acts but in some cases coming all the way down to the time of Constantine (the Anti-Acts). Of these three blocks, the second, the anti–Passion Gospel, forms the core of the tradition as we now have it. The anti–Infancy Gospel and the Anti-Acts were added later to this core.

---

14. For a masterly historical overview of the tradition, see Peter Schäfer, *Jüdische Polemik gegen Jesus und das Christentum: Die Enstehung eines jüdischen Gegenevangeliums* (Munich: Carl Friedrich von Siemens Stiftung, 2017). Further: Schäfer, Meerson, and Deutsch, *Toledot Yeshu*.

(2) We should not conclude from this, however, that the traditions contained in both the anti–Infancy Gospel and the Anti-Acts are late. Some of them are demonstrably very old—as old as the second century CE, evidenced by the fact that Celsus knew a version of the Joseph Pandera tradition.[15] The *Toledot Yeshu* marks the *literary* crystallization of individual anecdotes about Jesus that were circulating among Jews. It strings together a series of these into a continuous narrative, which has a storyline, characters, and a plot, but it originated as discrete mini-stories. The discrete stories were prior to and continued to be transmitted alongside the literary texts. We have evidence from the Talmud of Jewish anti-Jesus stories that were transmitted for centuries alongside the *Toledot* and were only incorporated into it, if at all, at a very late date.[16] It is possible the anti–Infancy Gospel had developed some way (on the basis of individual anecdotes) into a literary construct before it was attached to the anti–Passion Gospel. The same may be true of elements of the anti-Acts such as the so-called Peter Legend.

(3) I cannot stress enough the importance of modelling the *Toledot Yeshu* as fundamentally a *literary* construct or series of constructs drawn off from a broader stream of Jesus anecdotes that circulated among Jews. The Jesus tradition in Christianity is analogous. The canonical gospels clearly build on discrete Jesus anecdotes that were circulating among the early Christians. These discrete anecdotes are still in many cases recognizable in our gospel texts, though in the infancy and passion narratives they have been fused into larger literary constructions involving continuous narrative, strong characterization, and plot. The canonization of the Four Evangelists did little to stop the creation of new stories about Jesus, nor the crystallization of these into new apocryphal gospels. Nor should we forget the Islamic Jesus traditions, both in the form of stories (some of them clearly adapting Christian stories, apocryphal as well as canonical) and in the form of Jesus sayings.[17] These three great traditions about Jesus

---

15. Origen, *Cels.* 1.28, 32, 39. See Loveday Alexander, "The Four among Pagans," in *The Written Gospel*, ed. Markus Bockmuehl and Donald Hagner (Cambridge: Cambridge University Press, 2005), 222–37; Maren Niehoff, "Jewish Critique of Christianity from Second-Century Alexandria," *JECS* 21 (2013): 151–75.

16. Peter Schäfer, *Jesus in the Talmud* (Princeton: Princeton University Press, 2007); Thierry Murcia, *Jésus dans le Talmud et la littérature rabbinique ancienne* (Turnhout: Brepols, 2014).

17. These Jesus stories and sayings are found in both Qur'an and Hadith. For a

taken at their widest extent—the Christian, the Jewish, and the Muslim—interacted dynamically over the centuries and should not be studied in isolation. The *Toledot Yeshu* is only a part of this much larger reception history of the figure of Jesus.

(4) This stress on discrete Jesus anecdotes as playing an important role in the *Toledot Yeshu* raises the question of the interaction between orality and literacy within the tradition. There can be little doubt that the tradition as we have it, in the Wagenseil and other versions, is *literary* in character. The storyline is too long and convoluted, the plot too carefully managed, the characterization too strong for us to think in terms other than *literary* composition. But as I have suggested, this literary construct drew on discrete anecdotes that must have circulated orally, and even after the creation of our present written, literary texts, even after these were printed, orality continued to play a part. The literary texts were, in turn, broken down into anecdotes and passed on as *discrete* stories by word of mouth—right down to modern times. The oral tradition—the folkloristic form consisting of short anecdotes passed on by word of mouth—was never systematically collected, and it is probably too late to do so now.[18] The tradition was constantly oscillating between oral and written modes of transmission. This goes some way towards explaining its fluidity. Even when copying a written text, scribes clearly felt free to change it—to improve it stylistically, to make the story sharper, more coherent, more effective—because the *Toledot Yeshu* was an "open book." Every copying, every retelling, could be treated as a *re-creation* of the text to suit the needs of the occasion. What tended to remain constant were the basic motifs, characters, episodes, and plots, but these could be delivered in a variety of ways.

(5) The life settings in which the *Toledot Yeshu*, in the form of both extended literary texts and discrete anecdotes, was passed on are not entirely clear. The basic purpose of the tradition was polemical: to refute

---

collection, see Tarif Khalidi, *The Muslim Jesus: Sayings and Stories in Islamic Literature* (Cambridge: Harvard University Press: 2003). Further Philip S. Alexander, "The Toledot Yeshu in the Context of Jewish-Muslim Debate," in Schäfer, Meerson, and Yaacov, *Toledot Yeshu ("The Life Story of Jesus") Revisited*, 137–58. The curious Gospel of Barnabas may be a very late attempt to produce some sort of Muslim Gospel.

18. For a rich and important analysis of the *Toledot Yeshu* from a folklore perspective see Eli Yassif, "Toledot Yeshu: Folk-Narrative as Polemics and Self Criticism," in Schäfer, Meerson, and Yaacov, *Toledot Yeshu ("The Life Story of Jesus") Revisited*, 101–35.

the Christian claims about Jesus. Many of our surviving manuscripts are clearly *scholarly* copies, which in some cases have *scholarly* annotations. Several versions of the *Toledot* have sometimes been copied together, along with other Jewish anti-Christian treatises such as the Ḥizzuq Emunah of Isaac Troki. The *Sitz im Leben* here is surely the scholar's study, or the Beit Midrash, and the aim was to provide the scholar with weapons with which to defend his faith and refute Christian claims.

(6) We should never underestimate the theological pressure under which Jews lived in Christian lands. At the times in the Christian liturgical year when that pressure became intense, the *Toledot Yeshu* or stories from it may have served as reassurance, their performance an intracommunal act of defiance. The *Toledot*'s version of the Passion of Christ could obviously serve such a function in Holy Week—as a kind of Jewish response to the Passion Plays with their deeply negative portrayal of Jews. Jews were certainly accused, for example, in the Canons of the Fourth Lateran Council,[19] of mocking Christ and Christian solemnities in Holy Week. The anti–Infancy Gospel in the *Toledot* could have served a similar purpose at Christmas. The *Toledot* could also have played a role at Purim when in some Purim *Spielen* Christ was mocked under the guise of Haman, who, of course, like Jesus, came to a bad end on the gallows.[20] *Toledot Yeshu* was literature of subversion in which an oppressed minority expressed its defiance of its oppressors.

(7) The separate anecdotes about Jesus, passed on by word of mouth, should be seen as fundamentally belonging to folklore. They are part of the hugely rich tradition of Jewish folktale, and they would have been told

---

19. Canons of the Fourth Lateran Council 68: "Moreover, during the Days of Lamentation and of the Passion of our Lord, they [the Jews] shall not show themselves in public at all, for the reason that, on those very days (as we have heard), some of them are not ashamed to go about more splendidly attired than usual, and are not afraid to mock the Christians who, in preserving the memory of the most holy Passion, display the signs of mourning. Moreover, we most strictly forbid that anyone should so far presume as to break forth into insults against the Redeemer. And, since we ought not to ignore any insult offered to Him who blotted out our transgressions, we command that secular princes should restrain such impudent persons by imposing on them fitting punishment, lest they should so far presume as to blaspheme Him who was crucified for us" (my translation).

20. See Sarit Kattan Gribetz, "Hanged and Crucified: The Book of Esther and *Toledot Yeshu*," in Schäfer, Meerson, and Yaacov, *Toledot Yeshu ("The Life Story of Jesus") Revisited*, 159–80.

in all the settings in which folktales were told. At this level, women may have played a part in the transmission of Jesus-anecdotes, just as they did in the case of other folktales—sitting as they worked together round the fire, amusing one another or the children. Records of the Spanish Inquisition attest just such a setting for the transmission of the *Toledot Yeshu*, and it rings true.[21] Transmission by women might account for the interest in Mary in some versions of the *Toledot*, and in the surprisingly sympathetic treatment she receives. In the oral setting, a basic polemical function may still be discerned (folktales are important bearers of the worldview and values of the group), but one can surely detect an additional element of entertainment. There are also huge doses of comedy and burlesque in the *Toledot*. It *parodies* the gospels. This comes through strongly in the literary forms of the tradition as well. The humor is coarse but nonetheless effective as a polemical ploy. It is reminiscent in places of Rabelais, or the *Letters of Obscure Men*, or parts of the *Bovo Buch* of Elias Levita. Such coarseness was typical of the inter-religious polemics of the late middle ages and early modern times. Martin Luther was one of its masters.[22]

---

21. See Paola Tartakoff, "The Toledot Yeshu and Jewish-Christian Conflict in the Medieval Crown of Aragon," in Schäfer, Meerson, and Yaacov, *Toledot Yeshu ("The Life Story of Jesus") Revisited*, 297–309. The situation described so vividly by Tartakoff on the basis of inquisitorial records in the archive of Barcelona Cathedral (Codex 126) does not conform precisely to the scenario I envisage above. It was a man (Jucef) who quoted stories from the *Toledot*, and the purpose was clearly polemical, to persuade an old Jewish friend, Altazar, to come back to Judaism, but I find it very suggestive. Three women were present, and the setting was the kitchen of a Jewish home, sitting round the fire.

22. See Alexander, "Jesus and his Mother," 597–59. Further, Holger M. Zellentin, *Rabbinic Parodies of Jewish and Christian Literature*, TSAJ 139 (Tübingen: Mohr Siebeck, 2010), though he does not discuss the *Toledot Yeshu*; David Stern, "The Alphabet of Ben Sira and the Early History of Parody in Jewish Literature," in *The Idea of Biblical Interpretation: Essays in Honor of James L. Kugel*, ed. Hindy Najman and Judith H. Newman, JSJSup 83 (Leiden: Brill, 2004), 423–48. It is worth noting here the development in the modern period of *Jewish* parodies of such venerable items of Jewish liturgy as the *Yigdal* and the *'Adon 'Olam* to poke fun of Jesus. This phenomenon seems doubly disrespectful—of Judaism as well as Christianity! Some of these parodies clearly echo the *Toledot Yeshu*, and they should be seen as part of its reception history. See Israel Davidson, "Parody in Jewish Literature" (PhD diss., Columbia University, 1907); Alexander Marx, "A List of Poems on the Articles of the Creed," *JQR* 9 (1918–1919): 305–36; Marx, "The Polemical Manuscripts in the Library of the Jewish Theological Seminary in America," in *Studies in Jewish Bibliography and Related Sub-*

(8) The *Toledot Yeshu* has been a dynamic, evolving tradition for at least 1,500 years. The earliest evidence for a text comes from Aramaic fragments from the Cairo Genizah. The version represented by these is generally agreed to be pre-Islamic, but just when and where it arose is debated. I am inclined to agree with Willem Smelik that, although there is evidence of the influence of Babylonian Jewish Aramaic on the texts as we have them, the text was originally composed in Galilean Aramaic probably in the fourth century.[23] I cannot stress enough, however, that this should be seen only as the beginning of the *literary tradition* of the *Toledot Yeshu* as we know it today. The Aramaic work got translated into Hebrew and Arabic and was then passed down and spread throughout the Jewish world, evolving and changing as it went in response to ongoing Jewish interaction with Christianity. But this was not the beginning of Jewish anti-Jesus stories. There is clear and indisputable evidence that these had been circulating among Jews all the way back to the second century, and, as we shall see in a moment, possibly even to the first.

### Three Case Studies of Counternarrative

The rest of this paper will be devoted to one literary device that helps to explain, at least in part, the nature and evolution of the *Toledot Yeshu* tradition. It is the literary mechanism that I will call counternarrative. Counternarrative is used in literary theory to denote a variety of phenomena. I use it in the sense of a narrative constructed for polemical purposes to counter a prior narrative, as a way of negating the prior narrative's key claims.[24] The counternarrative typically narrates what is recognizably the same story, so it will share basic facts with the prior narrative, but it will spin the prior narrative at key points so as to stand it on its head and subvert it. A counternarrative, though it can serve as an instrument of

---

*jects, in Memory of Abraham Solomon Freidus* (New York: Alexander Kohut Memorial Foundation, 1929), 247–78.

23. Willem F. Smelik, "The Aramaic Dialect(s) of the *Toledot Yeshu* Fragments," *AS* 7 (2009): 39–73; Michael Sokoloff, "The Date and Provenance of the Aramaic *Toledot Yeshu* on the Basis of Aramaic Dialectology," in Schäfer, Meerson, and Yaacov, *Toledot Yeshu ("The Life Story of Jesus") Revisited*, 13–26. Smelik's view that the text originated in the Galilee accords with a widespread pattern in the transmission of Jewish texts in late antiquity: until the early Middle Ages, the predominant movement was from west to east.

24. I develop here ideas adumbrated in "Jesus and his Mother," esp. 593–97.

repression (for example, in the hands of colonial powers, necessitating subsequent postcolonial deconstruction), tends to be used as a defense mechanism by which an oppressed minority resists the discourse of a dominant, oppressing power. It typically functions both internally, within the oppressed minority, to minister comfort and reassurance, and, insofar as it envisages an external audience, to weaken and subvert the social and political status quo.

## The Resurrection

I begin with *Toledot Yeshu*'s counternarration of the story of the resurrection (Mark 15:42–16:8; Matt 27:62–28:15; Luke 23:50–24:12; John 19:31–20:18). All the *Toledot* versions of the burial of Jesus agree that after his burial, the body could not, for a time, be found, and on the basis of its disappearance the Christians proclaimed that he had risen from the dead, and that this miracle proved he was the Son of God. The body was, however, finally produced, and the Christian claim decisively refuted. But the versions differ in detail, and they correlate with the prior-narrative in the gospels in slightly different ways. I analyze the story told in the Wagenseil version I summarized above.

A number of points stand out. (1) According to the *Toledot Yeshu*, Jesus was buried on the eve of Sabbath, so as not to desecrate the Sabbath. "And it was in the evening that the sages said, 'It is not correct to nullify (even) one letter from Scripture on account of this bastard, even though he led men astray. Let us do for him according to the requirements of Scripture"—a reference to Deut 21:23, "His corpse must not remain on the tree," the text of which is actually quoted in some manuscripts. In all the gospels as well, Jesus is crucified on Sabbath eve, but it is only in John that we find the motif that the Jewish authorities were concerned that the corpse should not be left exposed during the holy day, with implicit reference to Deut 21:23: "Since it was the day of Preparation, the Jews did not want the bodies left on the cross during the Sabbath, especially because that Sabbath was a day of great solemnity" (John 19:31)

(2) Jesus was buried in a garden. According to the *Toledot Yeshu*, Jesus was buried on the orders of the sages in the place where he was executed, but his body was removed by Judas and buried in his garden. In this version, the reason for Judas's action is only hinted at. He removes the body because he sees the disciples loitering around the tomb. The implication

is that he wants to *hide* the body. Other versions of the *Toledot* give as his reason his concern that the disciples will steal the body and then proclaim that Jesus has risen from the dead. Compare Matt 27:62–66:

> The next day, that is, after the day of Preparation, the chief priests and the Pharisees gathered before Pilate and said, "Sir, we remember what that imposter said while he was still alive, After three days I will rise again. Therefore, command that the tomb be made secure until the third day; otherwise his disciples may go and steal him away, and tell the people, He has been raised from the dead, and the last deception would be worse than the first." Pilate said to them: "You have a guard of soldiers; go make it as secure as you can." So they went with the guard and made the tomb secure by sealing the stone. (ESV)

In the gospels, Jesus is buried by Joseph of Arimathea, not the sages, but Mark and Luke both state that Joseph was "a respected member of the council" (Mark 15:42), who "had not agreed to their plan and action" (Luke 23:50), so he was one of "the sages." This lends credence to the claim that the garden belonged to one of the sages, though the owner was Judas, says the *Toledot Yeshu*, not Joseph of Arimathea. John locates this garden "in the place where Jesus was crucified" (John 19:41). The motif of the garden comes up again in John 20:14–16: Mary "turned round and saw Jesus standing there, but she did not know that it was Jesus. Jesus said to her, 'Woman why are you weeping? For whom are you looking?' Supposing him to be the gardener, she said to him, 'Sir, if you have carried him away, tell me where you have laid him, and I will take him away.' Jesus said to her, 'Mary!'"

(3) Both the *Toledot Yeshu* and the gospels agree that it was after three days that the disciples of Jesus discovered that his body was not in the tomb in which he had been buried and proclaimed that he had risen from the dead. The *Toledot Yeshu* claims, however, that the tomb was empty because the body had been moved, a possibility, which, as we have seen, is alluded to in John in the story of Mary's encounter with the supposed gardener, and it is implicit in the High Priests' and Pharisees' request to have the tomb closely watched, though there the fear is that the *disciples* will remove the body and claim Jesus had risen, whereas in the *Toledot* it is an agent of the sages (Judas) who removes it precisely to forestall such an outcome.

The counternarratival character of the *Toledot Yeshu*'s version of the burial of Jesus should now be clear. It runs parallel to the gospel account and coincides with it at significant points, but it spins the story in such a way as to present an alternative explanation of events that denies the central gospel claim that Jesus rose from the dead on the third day. According to the *Toledot*, yes, Jesus was buried on the eve of Sabbath, and three days later his disciples found his tomb empty, but this was because an agent of the sages (acting to be sure without their knowledge, which initially caused confusion) removed the body and hid it in his garden, so that his disciples could not steal it, proclaim he was risen from the dead, and so prove him to be the Son of God. When Judas discovered that, contrary to his intention, he had unwittingly given the disciples grounds for such a claim, he rapidly produced the body and publicly exposed it, thus decisively refuting them.

So far so good, but the situation may be more complicated than we might at first suppose. The fact is that the gospel account of the burial and resurrection of Jesus is *already* in itself a counternarrative to a Jewish narrative of events. This is particularly obvious in the Gospel of Matthew. Is it possible that the *Toledot Yeshu* contains some distant memory of that first-century Jewish narrative that the gospels are countering? On the face of it, this would seem unlikely, given that the Wagenseil version of the *Toledot*, which I have analyzed, was composed fifteen hundred years after the canonical gospels. The possibility is rendered even more unlikely by the fact that the narrative the gospel story is countering is significantly different from the one in the Wagenseil *Toledot*. The Jewish narrative that the Gospel of Matthew counters is rather clear. It accepts that on the third day the body of Jesus was not in the tomb in which he was buried, but it explains this by saying the disciples stole it away, precisely to be able to claim that Jesus had risen from the dead. This explains Matthew's insistence that the tomb was heavily guarded and so the disciples' removing of the body was impossible, and his assertion that the guards were bribed by the Jewish authorities to say that Jesus's disciples came by night and stole him away while they were asleep. This story, says Matthew, "is still told among the Jews to this day" (Matt 28:15). The story in the *Toledot* flatly contradicts this. It was not the disciples who removed the body but an agent of the sages, and far from accepting that the body was never found, it was produced and publicly exposed.

It is puzzling that the *Toledot* counternarrates in this way and does not accept the underlying Jewish narrative that Matthew counternarrates, despite the fact that Matthew presents it "on a plate," so to speak. It is possible that the *Toledot* simply did not want to accept that the body was never found. That would have conceded too much. It would have left too much doubt. The *Toledot* wanted bluntly and categorically to state that the body *was* found and publicly displayed. But it is equally possible that the *Toledot* did not know the canonical story directly or all that well. It may have known just the outlines, at second hand. This lack of detailed knowledge of the gospels, leading to some quite bizarre and totally incredible claims (for example, that Jesus lived in the time of King Yannai!) is a general feature of the *Toledot*, though one can see attempts in some versions to correct more egregious errors and pull the story more into line with gospel "facts." Counternarrative as a polemical strategy would seem to work best when the counternarrative closely shadows the prior narrative but then at a crucial point or points introduces a plausible twist that subverts it. This failure of the *Toledot* to shadow the gospels more closely may be significant. Some Jews had direct access to the text of the gospels at least since the tenth century.[25] I have already alluded in passing to the Hebrew translation of Matthew in the fourteenth century *'Even Bohan* by Shem Tov ben Shaprut.[26] Certainly the scribe of Leipzig BH 27, who copied the Wagenseil version of the *Toledot* in the seventeenth century, must have known that his version was questionable as to key facts. He copies it along with Troki's *Hizzuq Emunah*, which has numerous accurate quotations from the gospels. This suggests to me that the shape of this story was established quite early (at least by the early Middle Ages, if not earlier), at a time when Jewish knowledge of the gospels was very derivative. It was difficult subsequently to change it very much, without throwing into question its authenticity.

The Beelzebub Pericope

There is another case of the *Toledot Yeshu* not picking up on the Jewish narrative that a gospel story is explicitly counternarrating. It is in the Beelzebub pericope in Mark 3:19–30, Matt 12:22–32, and Luke 11:14–22. Here the prior Jewish narrative that is being countered is again clear: Jesus was able to perform his miracles of healing because he is in league with Beelze-

---

25. This was certainly true in the Arab-speaking world. See Sagit Butbul and Philip Alexander, "Rylands Gaster Heb. Ms. 1623/3 and the *Qiṣṣat Mujādalat al-Usquf*," in *From Cairo to Manchester: Studies in the Rylands Genizah Fragments*, ed. Renate Smithuis and Philip S. Alexander (Oxford: Oxford University Press, 2013), 249–89.

26. See n. 2 above.

bub, the prince of demons. The *Toledot*, however, claims that he performed his miracles because he had stolen the secret of how to pronounce the Explicit Name of God (the *Shem ha-Meforash*). The Talmud recognizes the possibility of producing real effects by using demonic powers,[27] so the Jewish line of argument alluded to in the canonical gospels would, on the face of it, have been open to the *Toledot*. This makes it all the more curious why it did not accept yet again the narrative that the gospels themselves handed it on a plate. The use of the Divine Name alters the argument. It does not make Jesus a magician (though the *Toledot* uses the terms "magician" and "sorcerer" of him from time to time). Nor does it deny that his miracles were genuine deeds of power. In other words, it eschews the argument that it was all done by conjuring and trickery (again a concept well understood in rabbinic literature).[28] Use of the Divine Name might open Jesus to the charge of blasphemy (by actually pronouncing the Ineffable Name of God), but again, curiously, this is not the charge that the *Toledot* brings. Rather the charge is that he employed the power of the divine name *to lead Israel astray*. He used it to create genuine miracles to bolster his false claim that he was the Son of God.

## The Virgin Birth

In the case, then, of the story of the resurrection and the Beelzebub pericope, the *Toledot Yeshu* does not appear to connect directly with the Jewish narrative that the gospels are counternarrating. In the case of the story of the virgin birth, however, the possibilities are, I think, a little more open. It has long been argued that, historically speaking, there was something unclear about Jesus's parentage on his father's side. There was a Jewish story circulating that he was conceived either out of wedlock or through rape, and the story of the virgin birth (a miraculous birth, it was alleged, foretold in scripture) was an attempt to counter this.[29] It is noteworthy that

---

27. See Alexander, "The Talmudic Concept of Conjuring ('Ahizat 'Einayim) and the Problem of the Definition of Magic (*Kishuf*)," in *Creation and Re-creation in Jewish Thought: Festschrift in Honor of Joseph Dan on the Occasion of His Seventieth Birthday*, ed. Rachel Elior and Peter Schäfer (Tübingen: Mohr Siebeck, 2005), 7–20.

28. See Alexander, "The Talmudic Concept of Conjuring."

29. It is hard, all things considered, not to see in John 8:41 (εἶπαν αὐτῷ· Ἡμεῖς ἐκ πορνείας οὐ γεγεννήμεθα) an allusion to rumors that Jesus was illegitimate. So, e.g., C. K. Barrett, *The Gospel according to St John*, 2nd ed. (London: SPCK, 1978), 348, quot-

the virgin birth occurs in only two of the gospels, suggesting it emerges somewhat late in the evolution of the Jesus tradition. The antiquity of the Jewish account of Jesus's birth is proved by the fact that Celsus in the second century learned a version of it from a Jewish informant, though some details of Celsus's story differ from the *Toledot* versions.[30]

## The *Toledot Yeshu*'s Place in the Study of the Gospels

The *Toledot Yeshu* will not help us get back to the historical Jesus. That is not my claim. Nevertheless, I argue that students of the gospels should not ignore it, because it helps us, in a way that few other texts do, to understand an important but neglected dynamic in the evolution of the Jesus-tradition, namely, narrative and counternarrative—a dynamic that goes all the way back to the time of Jesus himself. Biblical scholarship is increasingly recognizing the importance of reception history not just for the *afterlife* of the New Testament writings but also for how we understand them *in their historical context*.[31] Interest in the apocryphal gospels is growing, and there is an increasing recognition that the distinction between canonical and noncanonical texts is, from a tradition-historical perspective, artificial. It is time, I would suggest, to count *Toledot Yeshu* among the apocryphal gospels,[32] to compare and contrast its evolution with the evolution of the gospel tradition, seen from its widest perspective. To be sure, it has not been totally ignored. It is already discussed, not surprisingly, by Joseph Klausner in *Jesus of Nazareth* (1922), and it provides some grist for Morton Smith's mill in *Jesus the Magician* (1978).[33] More recently it has been noticed in Jane Schaberg's *The Illegitimacy of Jesus* (1987), in Andrew

---

ing m. Yevam. 4:13: "R. Simeon b. Azzai said: I found a family register in Jerusalem and in it was written, 'Such-a-one is a bastard through [a transgression of the law of] thy neighbour's wife'" (trans. Danby; the Hebrew is: אמר רבי שמעון בן עזאי, מצאתי מגלת יוחסין בירושלים וכתוב בה, איש פלוני ממזר מאשת איש). But the Mishnaic context is not clear. See Johann Maier, *Jesus von Nazareth in der talmudischen Überlieferung* (Darmstadt: Wissenschaftliche Buchgesellschaft, 1978), 49–50.

30. See above n. 15.

31. For an important analysis of the theory of reception history, see Robert Evans, *Reception History, Tradition and Biblical Interpretation: Gadamer and Jauss in Current Practice*, LNTS 510 (London: Bloomsbury, 2014).

32. So Hans-Josef Klauck, *Apocryphal Gospels: An Introduction* (London: T&T Clark, 2004), 211–20.

33. Joseph Klausner, *Jesus of Nazareth: His Life, Times and Teaching*, trans. Her-

Lincoln's *Born of a Virgin?* (2013), and in Stephen Davis's *Christ Child: Cultural Memories of a Young Jesus* (2014),[34] but these treatments, while welcome, are brief, and not abreast of the most recent work on the Jewish text. Hopefully they are harbingers of greater involvement by New Testament scholars with the *Toledot Yeshu.* There is much more to be said on its relationship to the gospels, both canonical and noncanonical.[35]

---

bert Danby (London: Allen & Unwin, 1925); Morton Smith, *Jesus the Magician* (San Francisco: Harper, 1978).

34. Jane Schaberg, *The Illegitimacy of Jesus: A Feminist Theological Perspective on the Infancy Narrative*, exp. ed. (Sheffield: Sheffield Phoenix, 2006); Andrew Lincoln, *Born of a Virgin? Reconceiving Jesus in the Bible, Tradition, and Theology* (Grand Rapids: Eerdmans, 2013); Stephen J. Davis, *Christ Child: Cultural Memories of the Young Jesus* (New Haven: Yale University Press, 2014).

35. There is also scope for bringing the anti-Acts material in the *Toledot Yeshu* into dialogue with early Christian sources, including the apocryphal Acts. There has been much debate recently about the figure of Simon Peter in early Christian tradition, with some arguing that he is treated with hostility in certain early texts. See, for example, Robert H. Gundry, *Peter: False Disciple and Apostate according to Saint Matthew* (Grand Rapids: Eerdmans, 2015). Might the Peter Legend in the *Toledot Yeshu* suggest that Jews had caught a whiff of this negativity in some Christian circles? It would certainly give an edge to the claim that the Prince of the Apostles and the first Pope was an imposter and actually working for them—a claim even more sharp, if it originated among the Jews of Rome. For recent discussion of the figure of Peter, see Markus Bockmuehl, *The Remembered Peter in Ancient Reception and Modern Debate*, WUNT 262 (Tübingen: Mohr Siebeck, 2010); Bockmuehl, *Simon Peter in Scripture and Memory: The New Testament Apostle in the Early Church* (Grand Rapids: Baker Academic, 2012); Helen K. Bond and Larry W. Hurtado, eds., *Peter in Early Christianity* (Grand Rapids: Eerdmans, 2015), especially the chapter by Paul Foster, "Peter in Noncanonical Traditions," 222–62.

A Taxonomy of the Hebrew and Aramaic Manuscripts of the *Toledot Yeshu* (after Meerson and Schäfer)

| Level 1 | Level 2 | Level 3 | Level 4 | Level 5 |
|---|---|---|---|---|
| Group 1 | | | | |
| | Early Oriental | Early Oriental A (five MSS) | | |
| | | Early Oriental B (three MSS) | | |
| | | Early Oriental C (one MS) | | |
| | Early Yemenite (two MSS) | | | |
| | Byzantine (one MS) | | | |
| Group 2 | Ashkenazi | Ashkenazi A (three MSS) | | |
| | | Ashkenazi B (two MSS) | | |
| | Late Yemenite | Late Yemenite A (nine MSS) | | |
| | | Late Yemenite B (five MSS) | | |
| | Late Oriental (three MSS) | | | |
| | Italian | Italian A | Italian A 1 | Italian A 1a (two MSS) |
| | | | | Italian A 1b (five MSS) |
| | | | Italian A 2 (two MSS) | |
| | | | Italian A 3 (one MS) | |
| | | | Italian A 4 (one MS) | |
| | | Italian B | Italian B 1 (one MS) | |

| Level 1 | Level 2 | Level 3 | Level 4 | Level 5 |
|---|---|---|---|---|
| *Group 2 (cont.)* | | | Italian B 2 | Italian B 2a (two MSS) |
| | | | | Italian B 2b (six MSS) |
| | Sefardi (two MSS) | | Italian B 3 (two MSS) | |
| | | | Slavic B 1 (one MS) | |
| | Slavic | Slavic B | Slavic B 2 (fifteen MSS) | |
| Group 3 | Wagenseil | Wagenseil A (eight MSS) | | |
| | | Wagenseil B (five MSS) | | |
| | | [Wagenseil C (five MSS)] | | |
| | Huldreich | Huldreich A (seven MSS) | | |
| | | Huldreich B (one MS) | | |
| | Slavic | Slavic A | Slavic A 1 | Slavic A 1.1 (two MSS) |
| | | | | Slavic A 1.2 (two MSS) |
| | | | | Slavic A 1.3 (one MS) |
| | | | Slavic A 2 (three MSS) | |
| | | | Slavic A 3 (one MS) | |
| | | | Slavic A 4 (one MS) | |
| Group 4 | Slavic | Slavic C (one MS) | | |

# Bibliography

Alexander, Loveday. "The Four among Pagans." Pages 222–37 in *The Written Gospel*. Edited by Markus Bockmuehl and Donald Hagner. Cambridge: Cambridge University Press, 2005.

Alexander, Philip S. "Jesus and His Mother in the Jewish Anti-Gospel (the *Toledot Yeshu*)." Pages 588–616 in *Infancy Gospels: Stories and Identities*. Edited by Claire Clivaz, Andreas Dettwiler, Luc Devillers, and Enrico Norelli. WUNT 281. Tübingen: Mohr Siebeck, 2011.

———. "The Talmudic Concept of Conjuring (*'Ahizat 'Einayim*) and the Problem of the Definition of Magic (*Kishuf*)." Pages 7–20 in *Creation and Re-creation in Jewish Thought: Festschrift in Honor of Joseph Dan on the Occasion of His Seventieth Birthday*. Edited by Rachel Elior and Peter Schäfer. Tübingen: Mohr Siebeck, 2005.

———. "The Toledot Yeshu in the Context of Jewish-Muslim Debate." Pages 137–58 in *Toledot Yeshu ("The Life Story of Jesus") Revisited: A Princeton Conference*. Edited by Peter Schäfer, Michael Meerson, and Yaacov Deutsch. TSAJ 143. Tübingen: Mohr Siebeck, 2011.

Barbu, Daniel. "Voltaire and the *Toledoth Yeshu*." Pages 618–27 in *Infancy Gospels: Stories and Identities*. Edited by Claire Clivaz, Andreas Dettwiler, Luc Devillers, and Enrico Norelli. WUNT 281. Tübingen: Mohr Siebeck, 2011.

Barrett, C. K. *The Gospel according to St John*. 2nd ed. London: SPCK, 1978.

Bekkum, W. J. van. "'The Rock on Which the Church Is Founded': Simon Peter in Jewish Folktale." Pages 289–310 in *Saints and Role Models in Judaism and Christianity*. Edited by Marcel Poorthuis and Joshua Schwarz. Jewish and Christian Perspectives 7. Leiden: Brill, 2004.

Bischoff, Erich. *Ein jüdisch-deutsches Leben Jesu*. Leipzig: Friedrich, 1895.

Bockmuehl, Markus. *The Remembered Peter in Ancient Reception and Modern Debate*. WUNT 262. Tübingen: Mohr Siebeck, 2010.

———. *Simon Peter in Scripture and Memory: The New Testament Apostle in the Early Church*. Grand Rapids: Baker Academic, 2012.

Bond, Helen K., and Larry W. Hurtado, eds. *Peter in Early Christianity*. Grand Rapids: Eerdmans, 2015.

Butbul, Sagit, and Philip Alexander. "Rylands Gaster Heb. Ms. 1623/3 and the *Qiṣṣat Mujādalat al-Usquf*." Pages 249–89 in *From Cairo to Manchester: Studies in the Rylands Genizah Fragments*. Edited by Renate Smithuis and Philip S. Alexander. Oxford: Oxford University Press, 2013.

Davidson, Israel. "Parody in Jewish Literature." PhD diss., Columbia University, 1907.

Davis, Stephen J. *Christ Child: Cultural Memories of the Young Jesus*. New Haven: Yale University Press, 2014.

Delitzsch, Franz. *Sifrei ha-Berit ha-Hadashah*. Leipzig: Ackermann & Glaser, 1877.

Di Segni, Riccardo. *Il Vangelo del Ghetto*. Rome: Newton Compton, 1985.

Evans, Robert. *Reception History, Tradition and Biblical Interpretation: Gadamer and Jauss in Current Practice*. LNTS 510. London: Bloomsbury, 2014.

Foster, Paul. "Peter in Noncanonical Traditions." Pages 222–62 in *Peter in Early Christianity*. Edited by Helen K. Bond and Larry W. Hurtado. Grand Rapids: Eerdmans, 2015.

Gager, John. "Simon Peter, Founder of Christianity or Saviour of Israel." Pages 220–45 in *Toledot Yeshu ("The Life Story of Jesus") Revisited: A Princeton Conference*. Edited by Peter Schäfer, Michael Meerson, and Yaacov Deutsch. TSAJ 143. Tübingen: Mohr Siebeck, 2011.

Goldstein, Miriam. "Judeo-Arabic Versions of *Toledot Yeshu*." *Ginzei Qedem* 6 (2010): 9–42.

Gribetz, Sarit Kattan. "Hanged and Crucified: The Book of Esther and *Toledot Yeshu*." Pages 159–80 in *Toledot Yeshu ("The Life Story of Jesus") Revisited: A Princeton Conference*. Edited by Peter Schäfer, Michael Meerson, and Yaacov Deutsch. TSAJ 143. Tübingen: Mohr Siebeck, 2011.

Gundry, Robert H. *Peter: False Disciple and Apostate according to Saint Matthew*. Grand Rapids: Eerdmans, 2015.

Horbury, William. "A Critical Examination of the Toledoth Yeshu." PhD diss., Cambridge University, 1970.

Howard, George. *The Hebrew Gospel of Matthew*. Macon, GA: Mercer University Press, 1995.

Huldreich, Johann Jacob. *Sefer Toledot Yeshua' ha-Notzri/Historia Jeschuae Nazareni*. Severinum: Johannes du Vivie, 1705.

Khalidi, Tarif. *The Muslim Jesus: Sayings and Stories in Islamic Literature*. Cambridge: Harvard University Press: 2003.

Klauck, Hans-Josef. *Apocryphal Gospels: An Introduction*. London: T&T Clark, 2004.

Klausner, Joseph. *Jesus of Nazareth: His Life, Times and Teaching*. Translated by Herbert Danby. London: Allen & Unwin, 1925.

Krauss, Samuel. *Das Leben Jesu nach jüdischen Quellen*. Berlin: Calvary, 1902.

Lincoln, Andrew. *Born of a Virgin? Reconceiving Jesus in the Bible, Tradition, and Theology*. Grand Rapids: Eerdmans, 2013.

Maier, Johann. *Jesus von Nazareth in der talmudischen Überlieferung*. Darmstadt: Wissenschaftliche Buchgesellschaft, 1978.

Martini, Raymundus. *Pugio Fidei … adversus Mauros et Hebraeos … cum observationibus Iosephi de Voisin*. Paris: Henault & Henault, 1651.

Marx, Alexander. "A List of Poems on the Articles of the Creed." *JQR* 9 (1918–1919): 305–36.

———. "The Polemical Manuscripts in the Library of the Jewish Theological Seminary in America." Pages 247–78 in *Studies in Jewish Bibliography and Related Subjects, in Memory of Abraham Solomon Freidus*. New York: Alexander Kohut Memorial Foundation, 1929.

Meerson, Michael, and Peter Schäfer. *The Toledot Yeshu: The Life Story of Jesus; Two Volumes and a Database*. 2 vols. TSAJ 159. Tübingen: Mohr Siebeck, 2014.

Murcia, Thierry. *Jésus dans le Talmud et la littérature rabbinique ancienne*. Turnhout: Brepols, 2014.

Newman, Hillel I. "The Death of Jesus in the *Toledot Yeshu* Literature." *JTS* 50 (1999): 59–79.

Niehoff, Maren. "Jewish Critique of Christianity from Second-Century Alexandria." *JECS* 21 (2013): 151–75.

Salkinson, *Ha-Berit ha-Hadashah*. Edited by C. D. Ginsburg. Vienna: Fromme, 1885.

Schaberg, Jane. *The Illegitimacy of Jesus: A Feminist Theological Perspective on the Infancy Narrative*. Exp. ed. Sheffield: Sheffield Phoenix, 2006.

Schäfer, Peter. *Jesus in the Talmud*. Princeton: Princeton University Press, 2007.

———. "Jesus' Origin, Birth and Childhood according to the *Toledot Yeshu* and the Talmud." Pages 139–64 in *Judaea-Palaestina, Babylon and Rome: Jews in Antiquity*. Edited by Benjamin Isaac and Yuval Shahar. TSAJ 147. Tübingen: Mohr Siebeck, 2012.

———. *Jüdische Polemik gegen Jesus und das Christentum: Die Enstehung eines jüdischen Gegenevangeliums*. Munich: Carl Friedrich von Siemens Stiftung, 2017.

Schlichting, Günter. *Ein jüdisches Leben Jesu: Die verschollene Toledot-Jeschu-Fassung Tam ū-mūʿād; Einleitung, Text, Übersetzung, Kommen-*

*tar, Motivsynopse, Bibliographie.* WUNT 24. Tübingen: Mohr Siebeck, 1982.

Smelik, Willem F. "The Aramaic Dialect(s) of the *Toledot Yeshu* Fragments." *AS* 7 (2009): 39–73.

Smith, Morton. *Jesus the Magician.* San Francisco: Harper, 1978.

Sokoloff, Michael. "The Date and Provenance of the Aramaic *Toledot Yeshu* on the Basis of Aramaic Dialectology." Pages 13–26 in *Toledot Yeshu ("The Life Story of Jesus") Revisited: A Princeton Conference.* Edited by Peter Schäfer, Michael Meerson, and Yaacov Deutsch. TSAJ 143. Tübingen: Mohr Siebeck, 2011.

Stern, David. "The Alphabet of Ben Sira and the Early History of Parody in Jewish Literature." Pages 423–48 in *The Idea of Biblical Interpretation: Essays in Honor of James L. Kugel.* Edited by Hindy Najman and Judith H. Newman. JSJSup 83. Leiden: Brill, 2004.

Tartakoff, Paola. "The Toledot Yeshu and Jewish-Christian Conflict in the Medieval Crown of Aragon." Pages 297–309 in *Toledot Yeshu ("The Life Story of Jesus") Revisited: A Princeton Conference.* Edited by Peter Schäfer, Michael Meerson, and Yaacov Deutsch. TSAJ 143. Tübingen: Mohr Siebeck, 2011.

Thompson, Stith. *Motif-Index of Folk-Literature.* 6 vols. Bloomington: Indiana University Press, 1955–1958.

Wagenseil, Johann Christoff. *Tela Ignea Satanae.* Altdorf: Johann Heinrich Schönnerstaedt, 1681.

Yassif, Eli. "Toledot Yeshu: Folk-Narrative as Polemics and Self Criticism." Pages 101–35 in *Toledot Yeshu ("The Life Story of Jesus") Revisited: A Princeton Conference.* Edited by Peter Schäfer, Michael Meerson, and Yaacov Deutsch. TSAJ 143. Tübingen: Mohr Siebeck, 2011.

Zellentin, Holger M. *Rabbinic Parodies of Jewish and Christian Literature.* TSAJ 139. Tübingen: Mohr Siebeck, 2010.

# Contributors

**Philip S. Alexander** is Emeritus Professor of Postbiblical Jewish Literature at the University of Manchester.

**Dale C. Allison Jr.** is the Richard J. Dearborn Professor of New Testament at Princeton Theological Seminary.

**John M. G. Barclay** is the Lightfoot Professor of Divinity in the Department of Theology and Religion at Durham University.

**Lori Baron** is a Postdoctoral Fellow in the Department of Theological Studies at Saint Louis University.

**Albert I. Baumgarten** is Professor Emeritus in the Department of Jewish History at Bar Ilan University.

**Martinus C. de Boer** is Emeritus Professor of New Testament at Vrije Universiteit Amsterdam.

**Daniel Boyarin** is the Hermann P. and Sophia Taubman Professor of Talmudic Culture in the Departments of Near Eastern Studies and Rhetoric at University of California at Berkeley.

**Susan Grove Eastman** is Associate Research Professor of New Testament at Duke Divinity School.

**Bart D. Ehrman** is the James A. Gray Distinguished Professor in the Department of Religious Studies at the University of North Carolina at Chapel Hill.

**Suzanne Watts Henderson** is Professor of Religion at Queens University of Charlotte.

**Jill Hicks-Keeton** is Assistant Professor of Religious Studies at the University of Oklahoma.

**Susan Miller** is Theology and Religious Studies Tutor for the Centre for Open Studies at the University of Glasgow.

**Claudia Setzer** is Professor of Religious Studies at Manhattan College.

**Matthew Thiessen** is Associate Professor of Religious Studies at McMaster University.

**Lucas Van Rompay** is Professor Emeritus of Religious Studies at Duke University.

**Timothy Wardle** is Associate Professor of Religion at Furman University.

**Michael Winger** is an independent scholar and a retired attorney in New York City. He holds a PhD in Religion from Columbia University.

# Ancient Sources Index

# Modern Authors Index

CPSIA information can be obtained
at www.ICGtesting.com
Printed in the USA
BVHW07s0156241018
530941BV00001B/1/P

9 781628 372168